Published by **Hero Collector Books**, a division of Eaglemoss Ltd. 2021
Eaglemoss Ltd., Premier Place, 2 & A Half Devonshire Square, EC2M 4UJ, LONDON, UK
Eaglemoss France, 144 Avenue Charles de Gaulle, 92200 NEUILLY-SUR-SEINE

General Editor: **Ben Robinson**
Project Manager: **Jo Bourne**
Designers: **Stephen Scanlan and Katy Everett**

Most of the contents of this book were originally published as part of *STAR TREK – The Official Starships Collection* and *STAR TREK DISCOVERY – The Official Starships Collection* by Eaglemoss Ltd. 2013-2021

To order back issues: Order online at
www.shop.eaglemoss.com

ISBN 978-1-85875-999-9

Printed in China

10 9 8 7 6 5 4 3 2 1

www.herocollector.com

PR7EN011BK

STAR TREK
STARFLEET SHIPS
2294–THE FUTURE
— UPDATED AND EXPANDED —

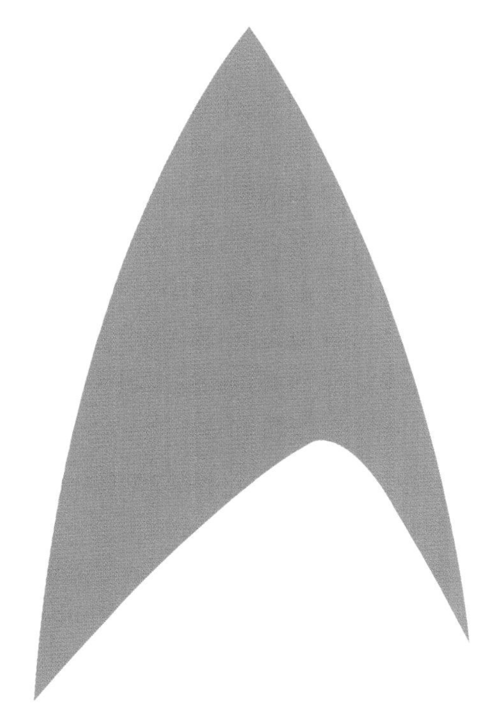

THE ENCYCLOPEDIA OF STAR TREK SHIPS

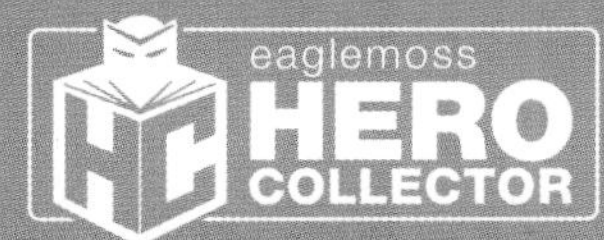

CONTENTS

ACKNOWLEDGMENTS

We'd like to thank Jason Zimmerman, who oversees the visual effects on the current shows, and Shawn Ewashko, who makes sure we have all the new CG models as they are produced. Special thanks are also due to William Budge in the *STAR TREK* art department, who has kept track of ship sizes, names, and appearances for everyone.

In particular, we'd like to acknowledge the work of all the VFX companies – Pixomondo, Foundation Imaging, Digital Muse, Eden FX, and Blue Sky/VIFX – who created many of the CG models that fill the pages of this book. Before that, Greg Jein, Bill George, Adam Buckner, and Tony Meininger's Brazil Fabrications were responsible for many of the physical models, which were recreated by our own talented CG modelers Fabio Passaro and Ed Giddings. We'd also like to thank Rob Bonchune and Adam 'Mojo' Lebowitz, who not only introduced us to Ed and Fabio, but also created many of the renders you will find inside this book.

We'd especially like to acknowledge the work of the modelers at the CG companies. Sadly, we don't always know the names of everyone involved, but we know that particular thanks are due to Pierre Drolet, Brandon MacDougall, and Koji Kuramura. The ships wouldn't exist without the talented artists who designed them, including Andrew Probert, Rick Sternbach, John Eaves, Doug Drexler, Scott Schneider, William Budge, and Ryan Dening. We'd like to add all the VFX supervisors and producers whose role in creating the final ships is often overlooked.

Mike Okuda and Doug Drexler have always been there to help us and we could not wish for better friends, and Alex Jaeger provided us with the reference that allowed us to recreate the ships he designed for *STAR TREK: FIRST CONTACT*. We'd also like to thank Jörg Hillebrand and the website Ex Astris Scientia, who have passionately cataloged *STAR TREK* ships for many years and have been incredibly generous and helpful to us.

We'd like to thank our friends at CBS Consumer Products: Risa Kessler, Marian Cordry, and John Van Citters. And of course, the greatest thanks are due to Gene Roddenberry and Matt Jefferies for starting it all in the first place.

FOREWORD

This is an updated version of the most popular entry in our multivolume series of Shipyards books, which is building into a comprehensive reference work that covers all the ships that have appeared in *STAR TREK*. This new, expanded edition contains an incredible 17 ships from the first season of *STAR TREK: PICARD* and the third season of *STAR TREK: DISCOVERY*, the latter season bringing the *Discovery* crew to the 32nd century and into this volume. They join the ships from the *STAR TREK: NEXT GENERATION* era and the handful of Starfleet ships that we know about from the early years of the 24th century.

We know that people will be desperate to find out as much as possible about these new ships, and we wish we could tell you more, but remember that, as we write, many of these ships have barely appeared on-screen. Much more remains to be revealed about them and they may well take center stage in future stories. It's too early to tie the hands of the people who write those episodes, but for now we can show you the ships in unprecedented detail from every angle, using brand new CG renders taken from the original VFX models that appeared on-screen.

Our job is to provide official canon information about the ships, so wherever possible you will find detailed, in-universe profiles of the ships along with plan views. Some people may be surprised to discover that the list of canon ships includes three that have only appeared in *STAR TREK: LOWER DECKS*. Despite being from an animated series, they are an official part of *STAR TREK* history, and it is right that they take their place here. You will also find a classic ship that was omitted from the original edition of this book: the *Akira* class. We are delighted to restore it to its proper place.

A note on housekeeping: all the ships in this book are from the Prime timeline and don't take account of the vessels that can be found in the movies made since 2009, or in some of the parallel realities that we have seen on the show. This is not the place for ships that have only appeared in books, games, calendars, or the original animated *STAR TREK* series. For now at least, there won't be any ships that have only been referred to in dialogue or seen as graphics on a computer display.

This volume does include all the Starfleet ships from *STAR TREK: THE NEXT GENERATION*, *STAR TREK: DEEP SPACE NINE*, and *STAR TREK: VOYAGER*, and provides an extraordinary vision of future technology. Other volumes in the series cover earlier Earth and Starfleet vessels, the Klingon fleet, the ships of the Delta Quadrant, and before long, we will add volumes that cover the Alpha and Beta Quadrants and the Dominion. We are proud to say that together they build into an encyclopedia of every ship that has appeared in *STAR TREK*.

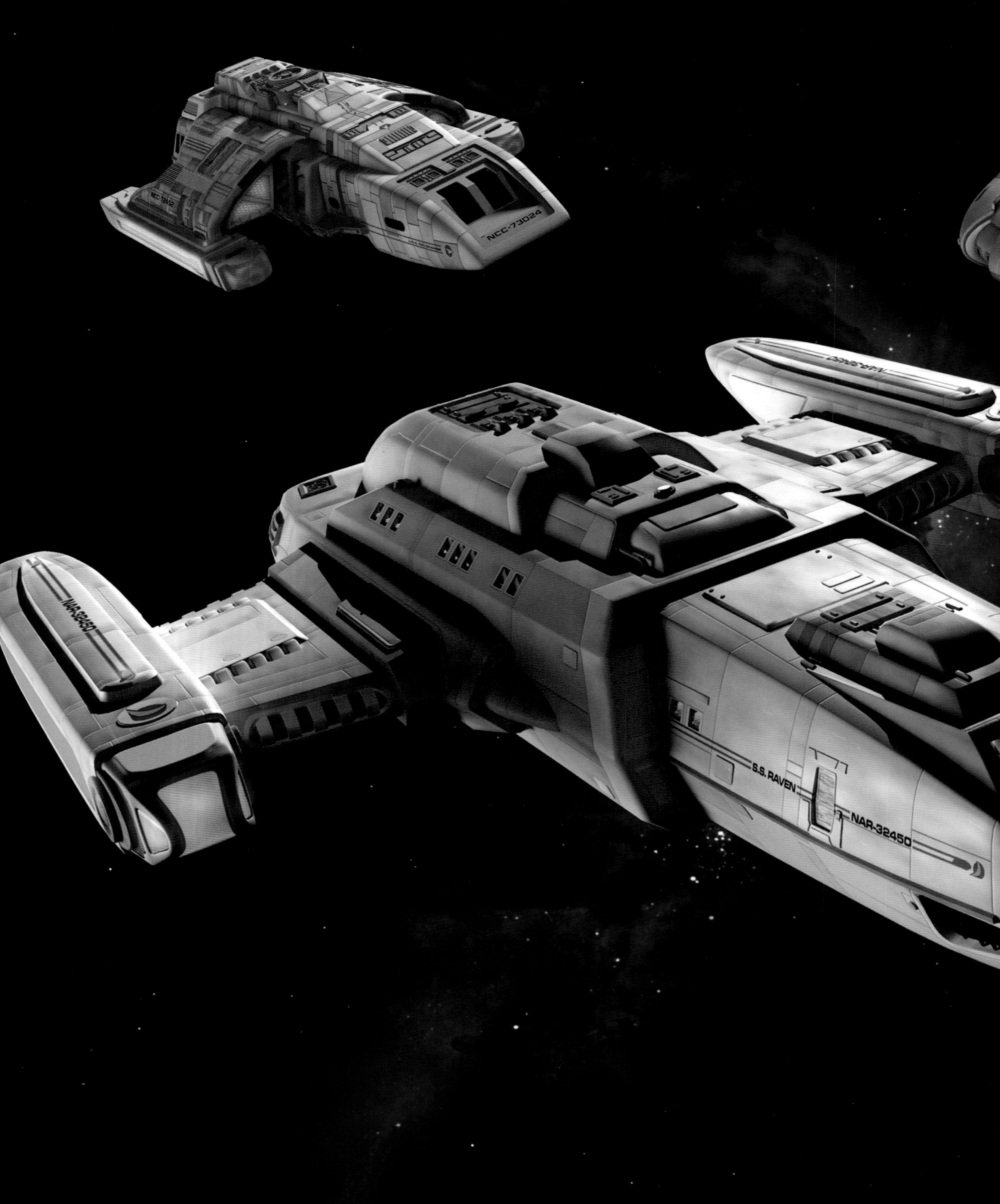
NCC-73024
NAR-32450
S.S. RAVEN
NAR-32450

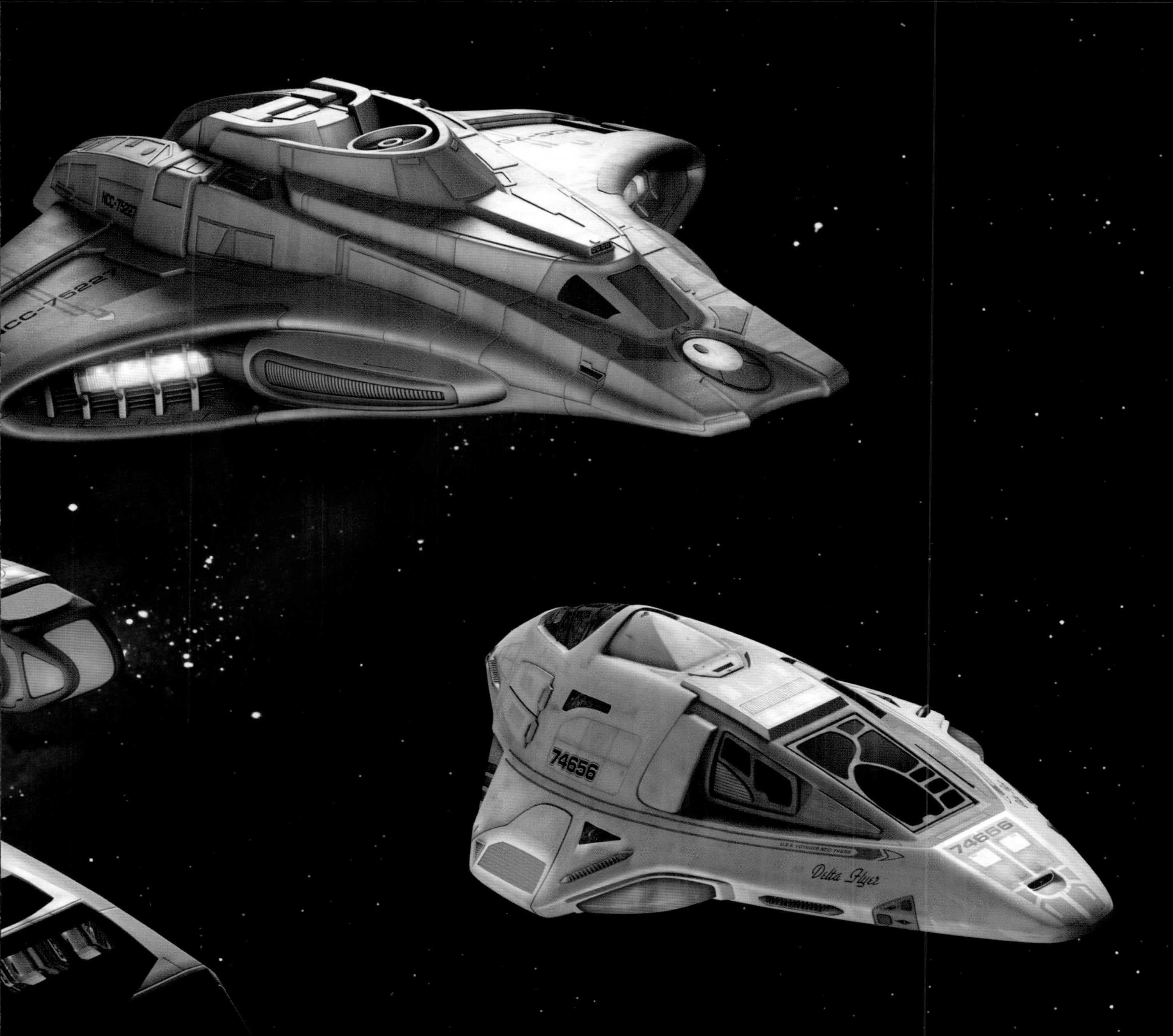

CHAPTER 1
SMALL TRANSPORTS

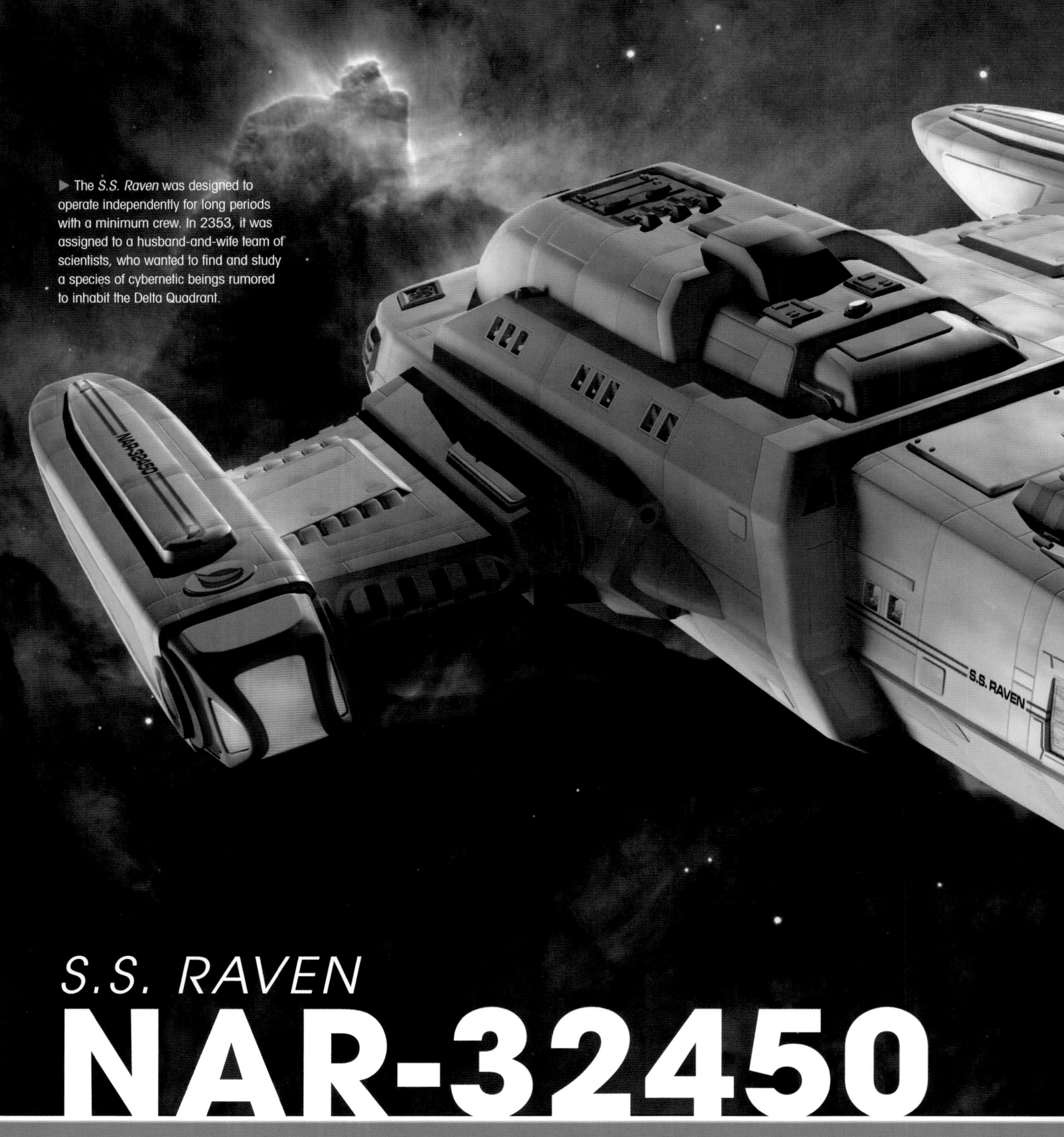

▶ The *S.S. Raven* was designed to operate independently for long periods with a minimum crew. In 2353, it was assigned to a husband-and-wife team of scientists, who wanted to find and study a species of cybernetic beings rumored to inhabit the Delta Quadrant.

S.S. RAVEN
NAR-32450

The exploratory Federation vessel was modified by the Hansen research team for a unique journey to study the Borg.

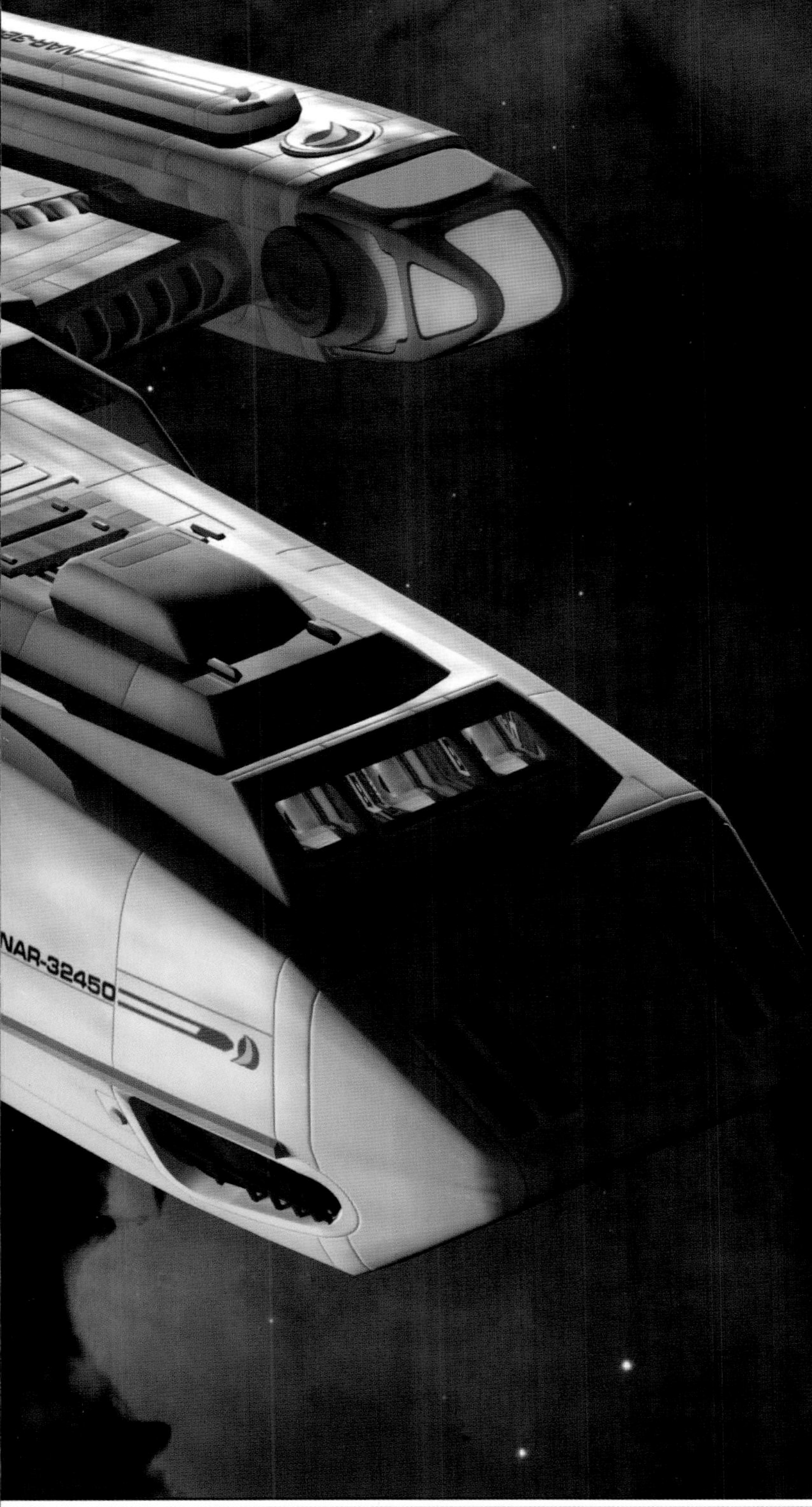

The long-range Federation vessel, *S.S. Raven* NAR-32450, was similar in style to a *Danube*-class runabout. It measured about 90 meters in length and was used mainly for exploratory and scientific purposes. In 2353, the *Raven* was assigned to Federation exobiologists Magnus and Erin Hansen. They successfully petitioned the Federation research council to grant them the resources to pursue and study a rumored cybernetic species that was eventually revealed to be the Borg.

The *Raven* had four decks and was capable of functioning independently for extended periods of time. Of course, the dilithium supply for the warp engines was limited, but the Hansens could gather new supplies from planets without having to return to a starbase. This was important since their mission ended up taking them far from Federation space.

MOBILE HOME

The extended nature of the *Raven*'s mission meant that it served as the Hansens' only home for nearly three years. The family, which also included their daughter Annika, who was just four years old when they left, principally occupied just a single deck. The other decks contained cargo bays and equipment necessary for their protracted journey.

The basic design of the *Raven* comprised three components: the rectangular main section; the slimmer forward module that included the bridge;

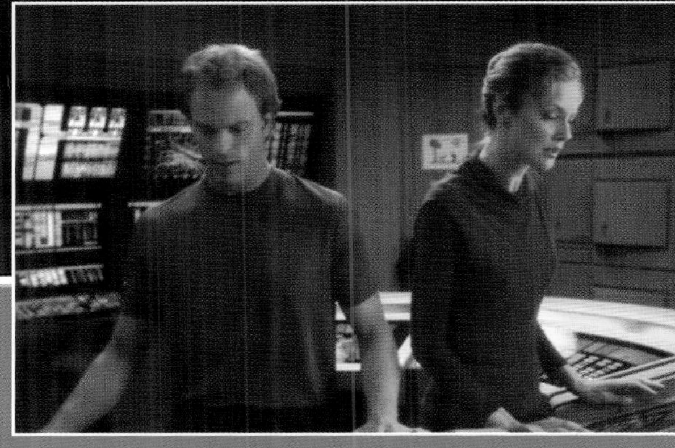

▲ The Hansens were maverick exobiologists, and many considered them unorthodox. They took the brave, some might say foolhardy, decision to try and track the Borg. They had little time for Starfleet or the Federation, preferring instead to follow their own agenda.

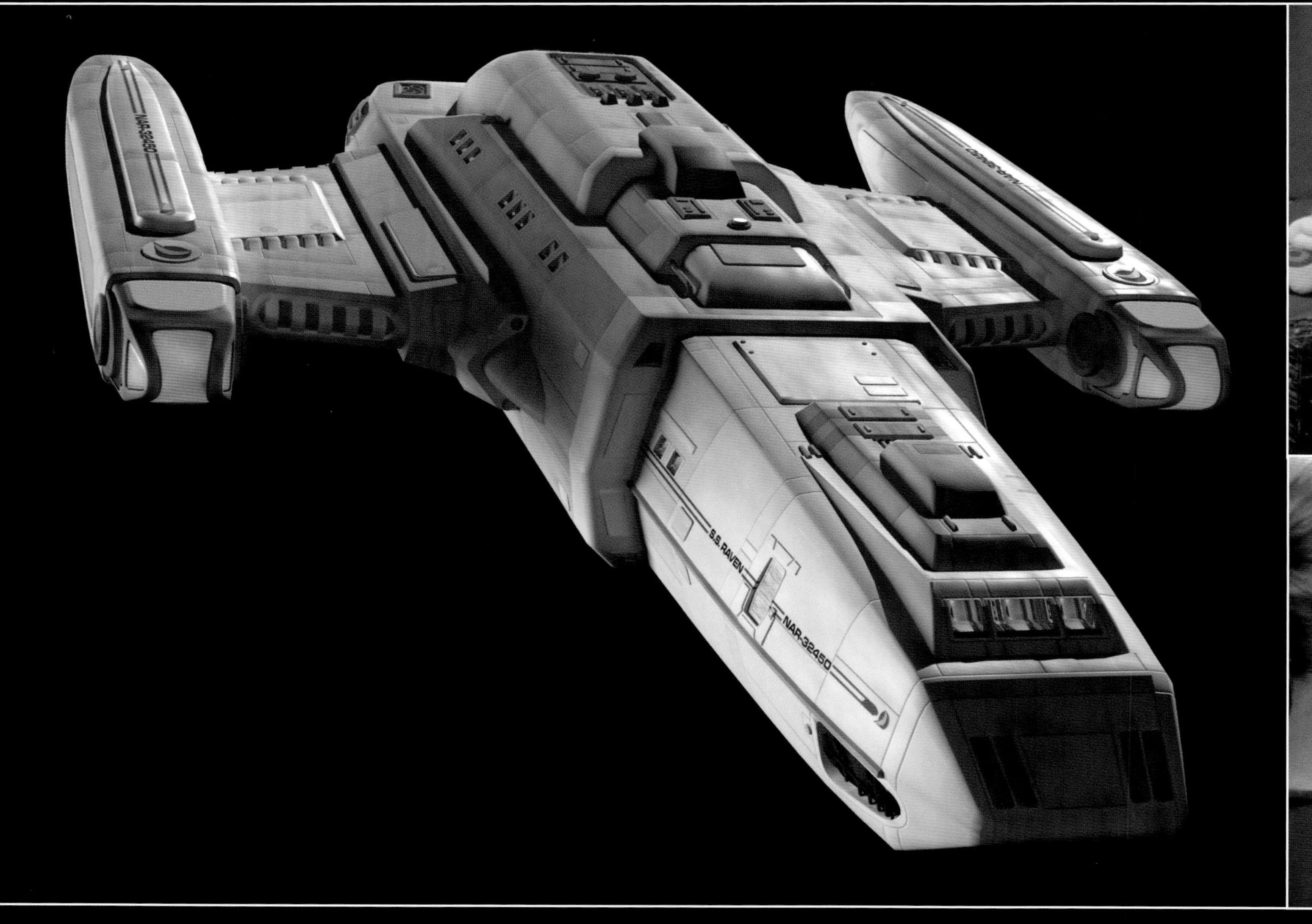

▲ At approximately 90 meters in length and with four decks, the *Raven*'s design was somewhere between a runabout and a small, fully fledged starship. With its suite of sophisticated sensors, it was perfect for extended scientific missions – but it was never intended to operate independently for nearly three years, especially not on the other side of the Galaxy in the Delta Quadrant.

and the warp nacelles. Like a runabout, the *Raven* also had landing gear, warp engines, and sophisticated sensors.

In 2352, the Hansens set off in the *Raven* to see if the Borg were more than the "rumor and sensor echoes" some people claimed. Many of their colleagues, who had held them in high regard, believed that they were wasting their time.

The last recorded sighting of the *Raven* was at the remote Drexler outpost in the Omega sector. Thereafter, they deviated from their flight plan, crossed the Neutral Zone separating Federation and Romulan space, and even disobeyed a direct order to return. In pressing on, Magnus and Erin realized they were burning their bridges with the Federation and could not rely on their help.

The Hansens tracked potential Borg readings for eight months without success, before finally stumbling upon a Borg cube. While monitoring the massive ship, the *Raven* became caught in a transwarp conduit, and emerged on the other side of the Galaxy in the Delta Quadrant. Instead of panicking, the Hansens decided to begin their study of the Borg in earnest.

PIONEERING TECHNOLOGY

During this time, they invented a number of technologies to help them. Principal among these was multiadaptive shielding, which kept the *Raven* invisible to Borg sensors. They also invented a device called a biodampener, which created a field around the body that simulated the physiometric conditions within a Borg vessel. Each biodampener was tailored to its user's physiology, allowing them to transport to a Borg cube and observe drones in action without being detected.

Using the device, Magnus was able to transmit visual and audio data from the cube back to Erin

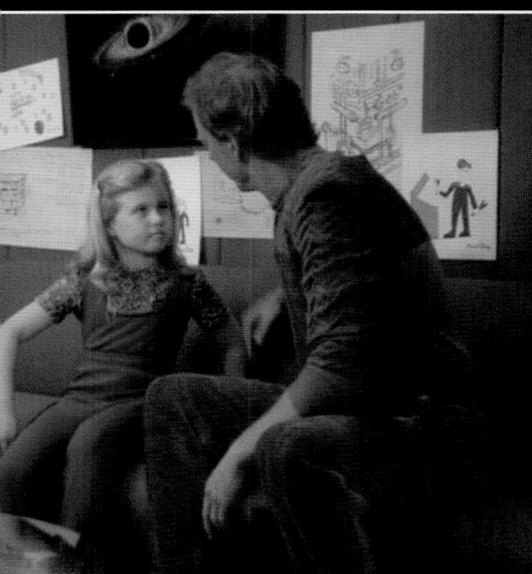

◀ The *Raven* became home to the Hansens for nearly three years. They did their best to turn the main living area into a more domestic setting by putting Annika's paintings on the wall.

▶ The Hansens equipped the *Raven* with multi-adaptive shielding that hid their ship from Borg sensors. It enabled them to study a Borg cube and its drones up close without being detected.

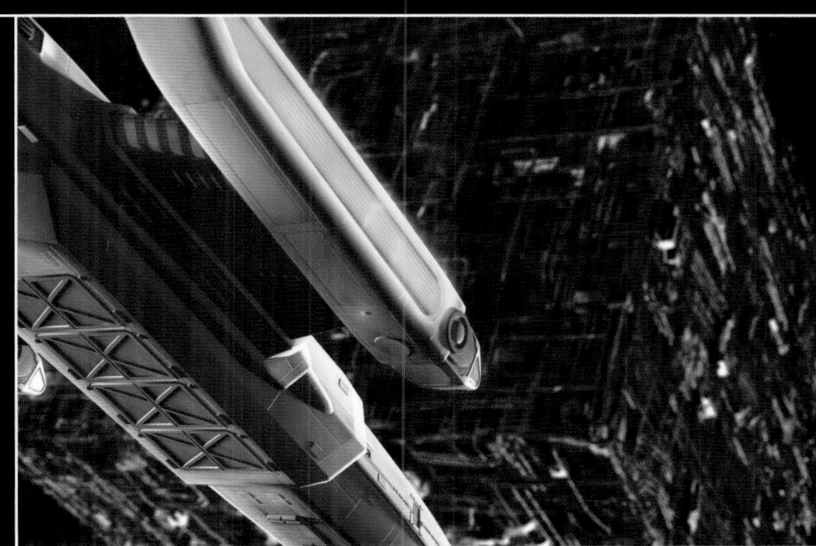

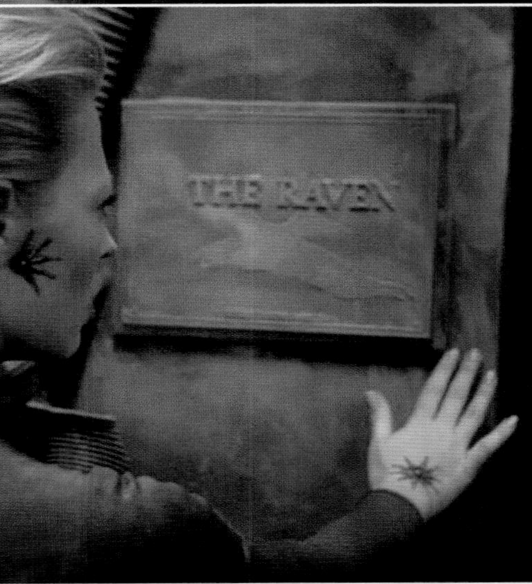

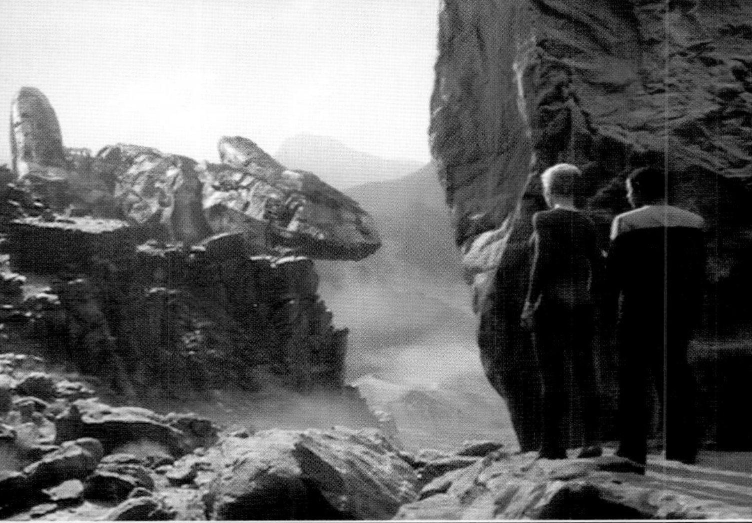

◀ After the multiadaptive shielding briefly failed, the *Raven* was finally detected by the Borg. Several drones beamed over to the ship and assimilated the Hansens. The *Raven* ended its days in a crumpled heap after crash-landing on a desolate moon in B'omar space. The craft continued to emit a Borg resonance frequency, which eventually drew Seven to its location.

▲ Seven could not remember being assimilated until she reached the crash site of the *Raven*. When she uncovered the ship's plaque, her memories come flooding back.

on the *Raven*. The couple learned a great deal about the Borg in a short period, such as the fact that drones from different sub-units interacted, and that the Collective must logically have a queen. They even developed pet names for the drones, such as Junior, Bill, and Needle Fingers.

The Hansens even beamed drones back to their ship during regeneration cycles to make more detailed physiological examinations. Magnus scanned the body while Erin worked on the cranium, and they tagged drones they wished to keep observing with a subdermal probe.

In 2356, during their third year of study, the Hansens' luck finally ran out. The *Raven*'s multiadaptive shielding failed for just 13.2 seconds during an ion storm. It was enough time for the Borg to detect them. The Hansens tried masking their warp trail, but it was too late, and they were caught and assimilated.

Nearly two decades later, the wreck of the *Raven* was discovered by *U.S.S. Voyager* NCC-74656 crew members Lieutenant Commander Tuvok and Seven of Nine – formerly Annika Hansen. The ship had been partially assimilated by the Borg and was still emitting a Borg homing signal. Shortly after this, the remains of the *Raven* were obliterated by a highly territorial species known as the B'omar.

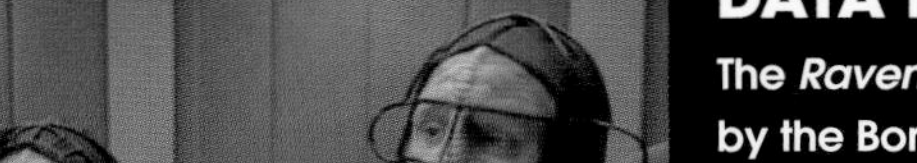

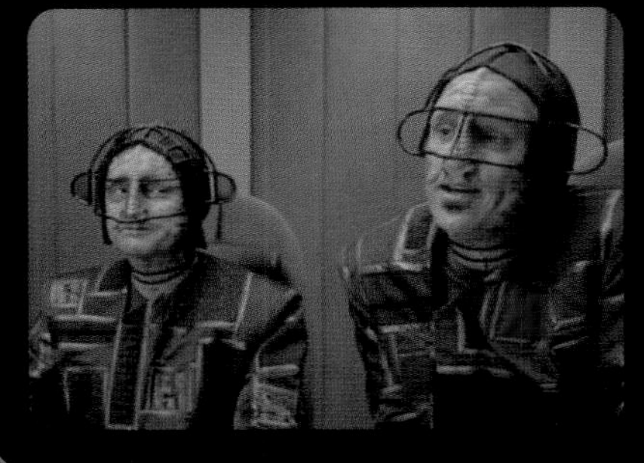

DATA FEED

The *Raven* was partially assimilated by the Borg and crashed into an M-class moon in B'omar territory. The wreck remained there until 2374, when it was destroyed by the B'omar. They reacted violently after Seven of Nine made an unauthorized journey into their space looking for the ship.

COMPREHENSIVE STUDY

Magnus and Erin Hansen were the first humans to study the Borg. Like all good scientists, they kept extensive field notes, detailed journals, and biokinetic analyses. They made more than 9,000 log entries, comprising 10 million terraquads of data. As time went on, the Hansens became bolder in their investigation of the Borg, despite occasional close calls. On one occasion, Magnus had to spend the night in a maturation chamber aboard a Borg cube when the *Raven*'s transporter went offline.

Even after this scare, the Hansens did not abandon their study, and in fact went further by transporting regenerating drones back to the *Raven*. They were so engrossed in their study that they did not appear to recognize the danger they were in, or just how vulnerable they were in the Delta Quadrant.

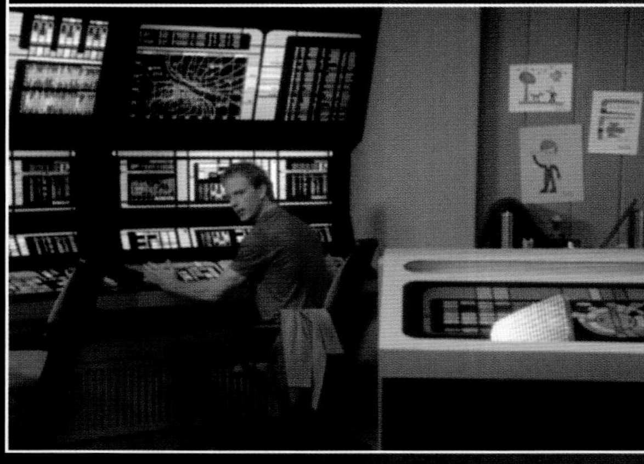

▲ The *Raven* acted as a mobile research facility for Magnus and Erin Hansen as they obsessively compiled copious notes on the Borg.

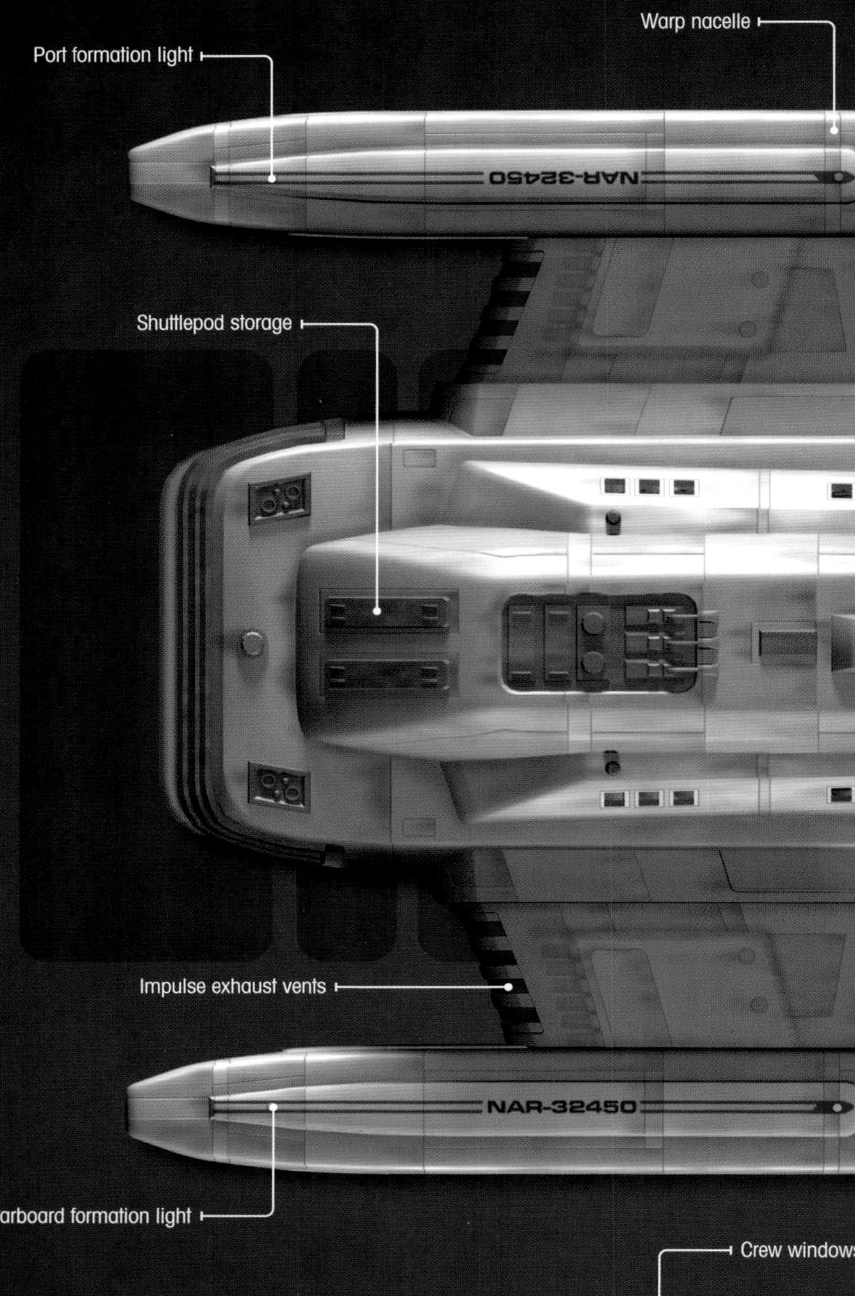

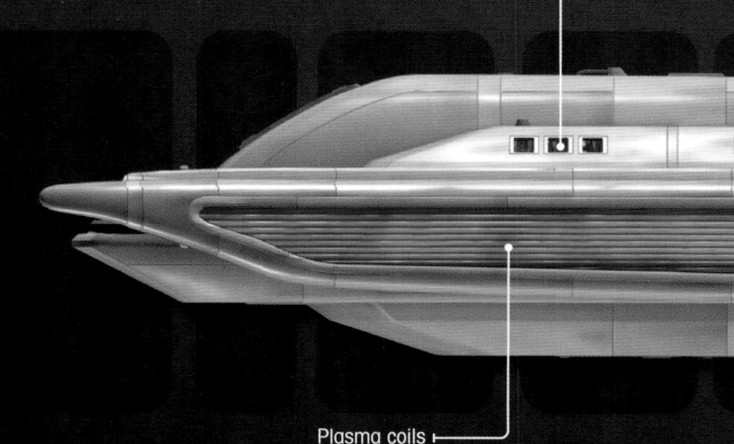

DATA FEED

In 2375, the crew of the *U.S.S. Voyager* incorporated the same multiadaptive shielding that had been used on the *Raven* into the systems of the *Delta Flyer*. This shuttlecraft was then used to facilitate a rescue mission of Seven of Nine, who was being held captive by the Borg Queen in the Unicomplex.

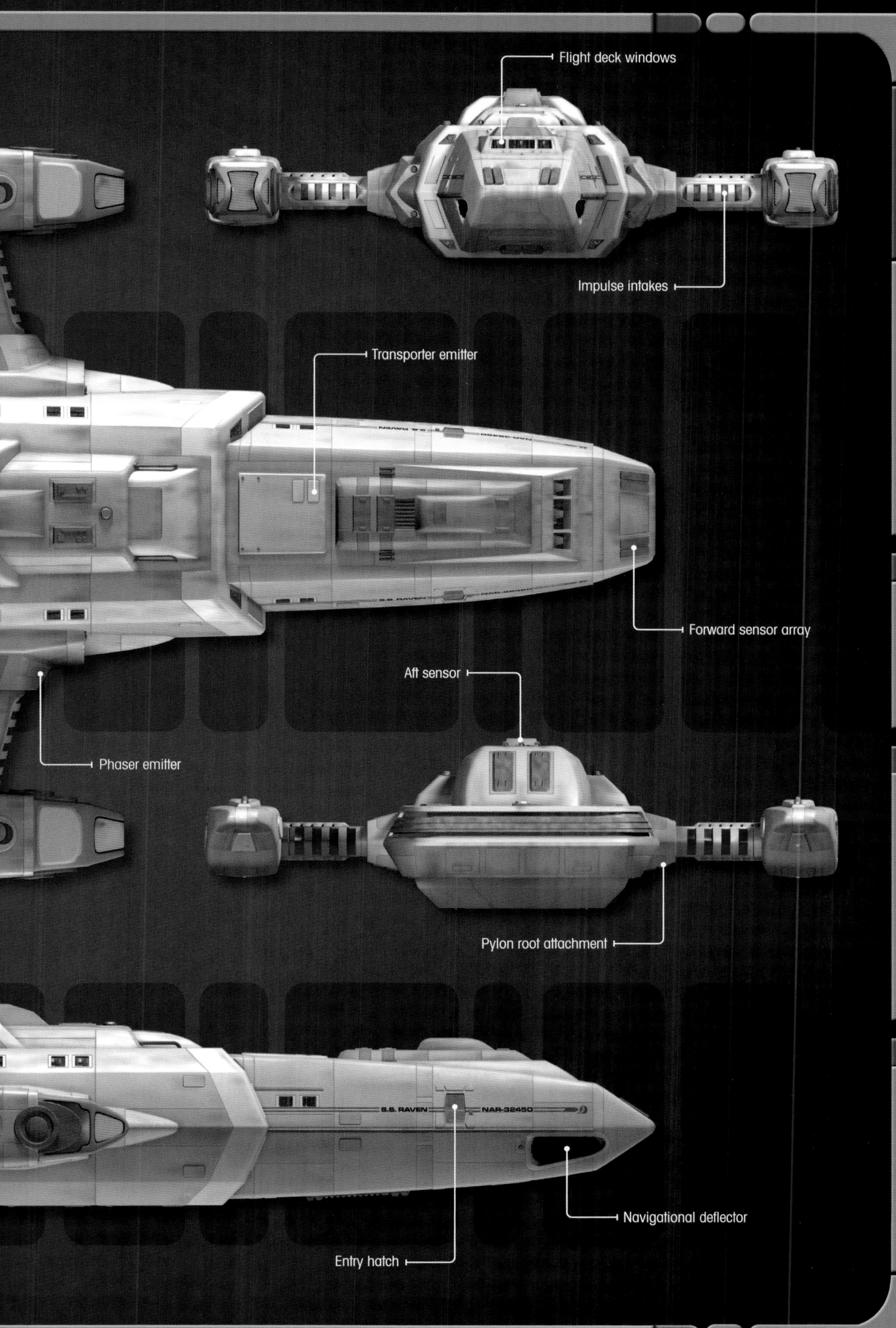

AUXILIARY CRAFT

According to the large, wall-mounted master systems display seen on the bridge of the *Raven,* the ship had a small shuttlepod stored in the aft section.

IRREGULAR PREFIX

The *Raven* had a non-Starfleet registry of NAR-32450, indicating it was a civilian ship. Official Starfleet records identified it with the prefix *S.S.* rather than the *U.S.S.* of most Starfleet vessels. This may have signified its primary function as a survey ship.

DILITHIUM SUPPLY

Eight months after setting out, Magnus Hansen observed that the *Raven* could travel for another 20 light years before needing to refuel, if they took the replicators offline and ran environmental systems at half power.

STARFLEET RUNABOUT

Resembling an enlarged shuttlecraft, runabouts were multipurpose ships often assigned to space stations.

Runabout was the generic name for small, warp-capable, *Danube*-class Starfleet ships that were in operation in the latter half of the 24th century. At 23.1 meters in length, they were larger than standard shuttlecraft but smaller than fully fledged starships. This meant they were capable of more protracted missions and carrying more cargo than shuttles, while not wasting the resources and personnel that a full-size starship would require.

Runabouts were designed to carry out a number of roles, such as scientific expeditions, personnel and cargo transportation, and covert tactical missions – and even act as mobile defense platforms.

ADAPTABLE VESSEL

The prototype runabout was called the *U.S.S. Danube* NX-72003, and in keeping with Starfleet tradition, this type of vessel became known as the *Danube* class. Typically, runabouts were operated from the cockpit by a crew of two to four, while a habitat module with rudimentary sleeping quarters was located at the rear of the vessel. The midsection contained a detachable module that could be changed for different mission profiles. This meant it could carry science, medical, defense, or cargo payloads, depending on the assignment it was undertaking.

The runabout's most ground-breaking – and useful – feature was its compact warp reactor core. This ingenious piece of engineering was located in the middle of the spine that ran along the top of the vessel, and worked in conjunction with the nacelles. Despite being much smaller than the warp cores found on full-size starships, it was still capable of propelling the ship to speeds as high as warp 5.

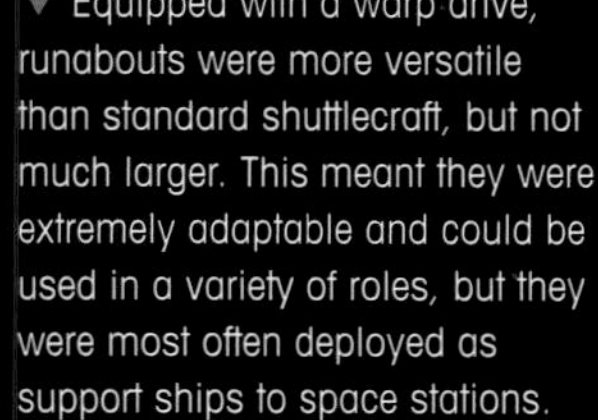

▼ Equipped with a warp drive, runabouts were more versatile than standard shuttlecraft, but not much larger. This meant they were extremely adaptable and could be used in a variety of roles, but they were most often deployed as support ships to space stations.

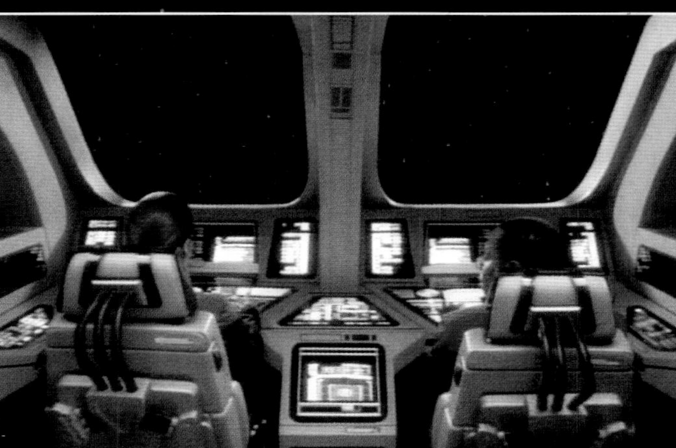

◀ The cockpit of a runabout was similar to that found on shuttlecraft, but was slightly larger. The primary flight controls were duplicated at the two forward stations, but the normal configuration was to have the port station set as the mission commander's controls, and the starboard station set as the pilot's controls.

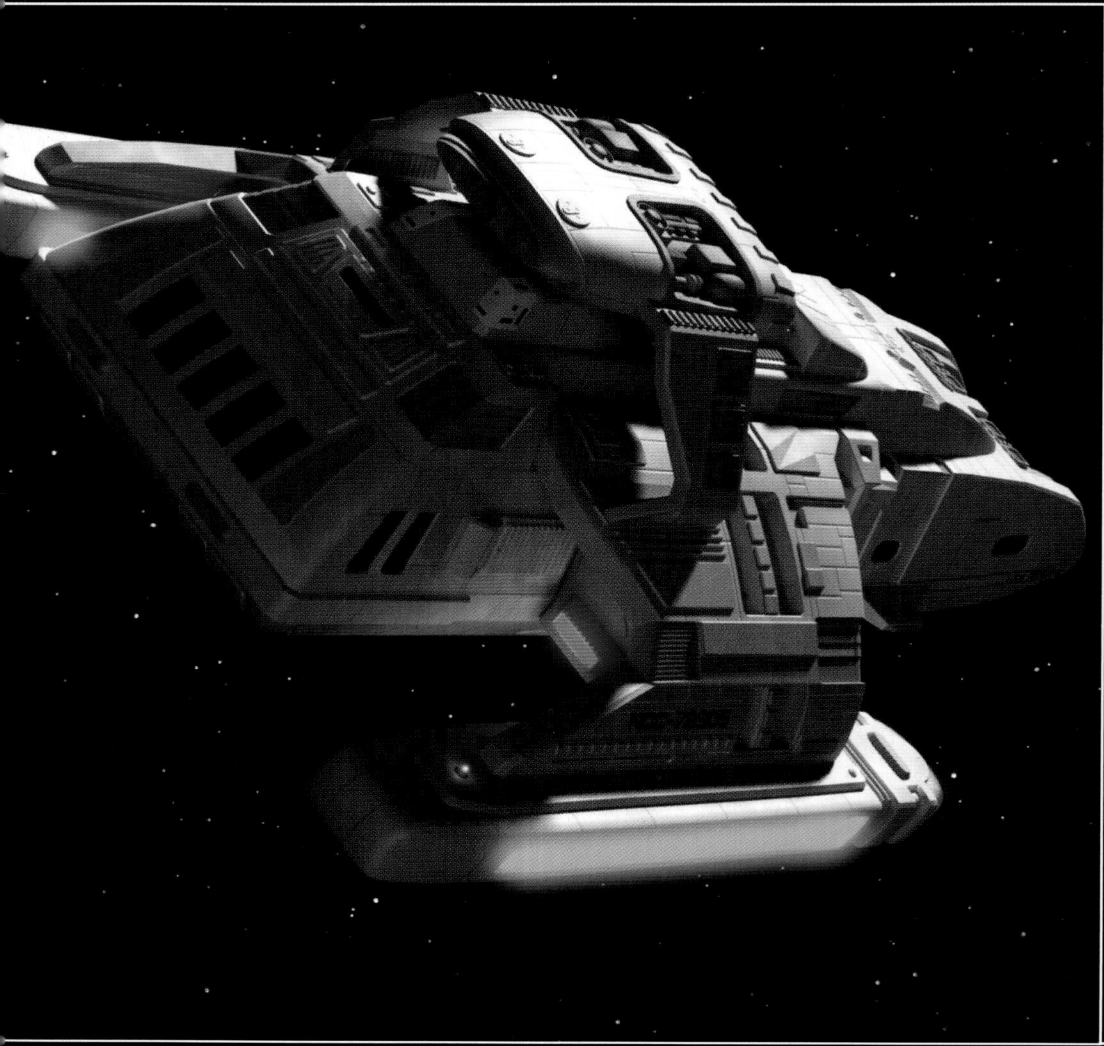

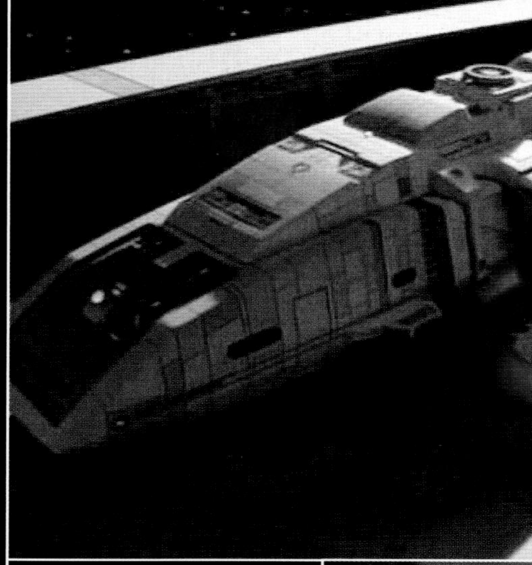

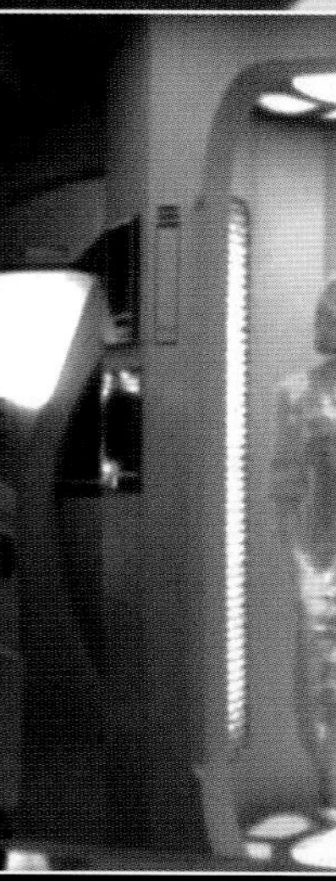

▶ Runabouts featured a two-person transporter that, in the original design, was located at the rear of the cockpit. Personnel could beam down to a planetary surface, leaving the runabout unmanned in standard orbit.

▲ The runabout was designed to enable a small crew to undertake longer interstellar missions than was possible with a standard shuttle. This was mainly due to its small, flattened warp core that, in conjunction with its warp nacelles, was capable of powering it to speeds as high as warp 5. It was also fitted with thrusters that allowed it to make planetary landings.

Their ability to travel at relatively high warp speeds meant that runabouts were able to travel between planetary systems to carry out missions, unlike impulse-only shuttlecraft. They could also land and take off from planetary surfaces, since they were fitted with vertical lift vents under the winglets.

For defense, the runabout was armed with six phaser strips and a microtorpedo launcher that was located at the front of the vessel, under the cockpit. These armaments, together with its defensive shields, meant the runabout was able to engage much larger vessels in combat.

Additional sensors could be added to runabouts in the form of a roll bar module that was fitted over the top of the ships. These removable bars could be added for specific types of mission and extended the ship's sensor capabilities.

Other features of the runabout included a two-person transporter and a food replicator that were initially located immediately behind the cockpit stations. Later these facilities were moved further back in the ship and a secondary tactical console was positioned in the cockpit. The exterior of the vessel featured an aft tractor beam emitter that was powerful enough to tow a ship at least as large as a Cardassian *Galor*-class warship.

SPACE STATION SUPPORT

Deep Space 9 initially took delivery of three runabouts in 2369, and they were housed in dedicated launch bays situated around the habitat ring. These vessels were called the *U.S.S. Ganges*, the *U.S.S. Yangtzee Kiang*, and the *U.S.S. Rio Grande* – all additional runabouts supplied to Deep Space 9 over the following years were also named after Earth rivers.

These runabouts provided the primary method of transport for people living on Deep Space 9, in

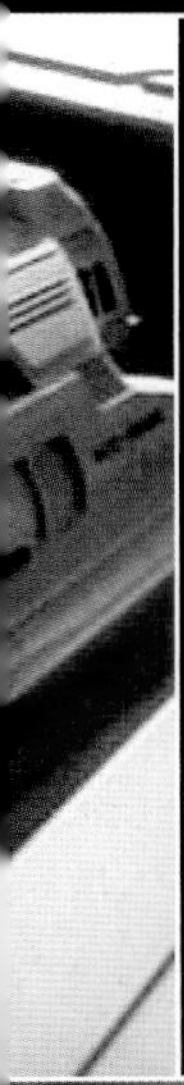

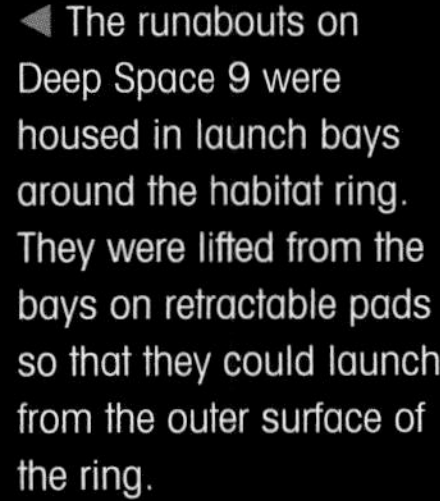

◀ The runabouts on Deep Space 9 were housed in launch bays around the habitat ring. They were lifted from the bays on retractable pads so that they could launch from the outer surface of the ring.

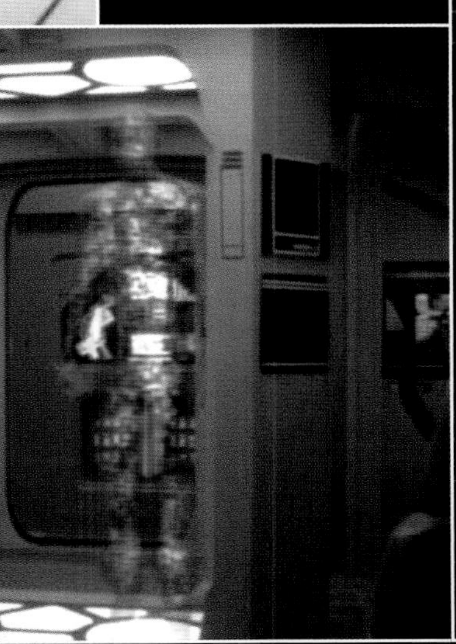

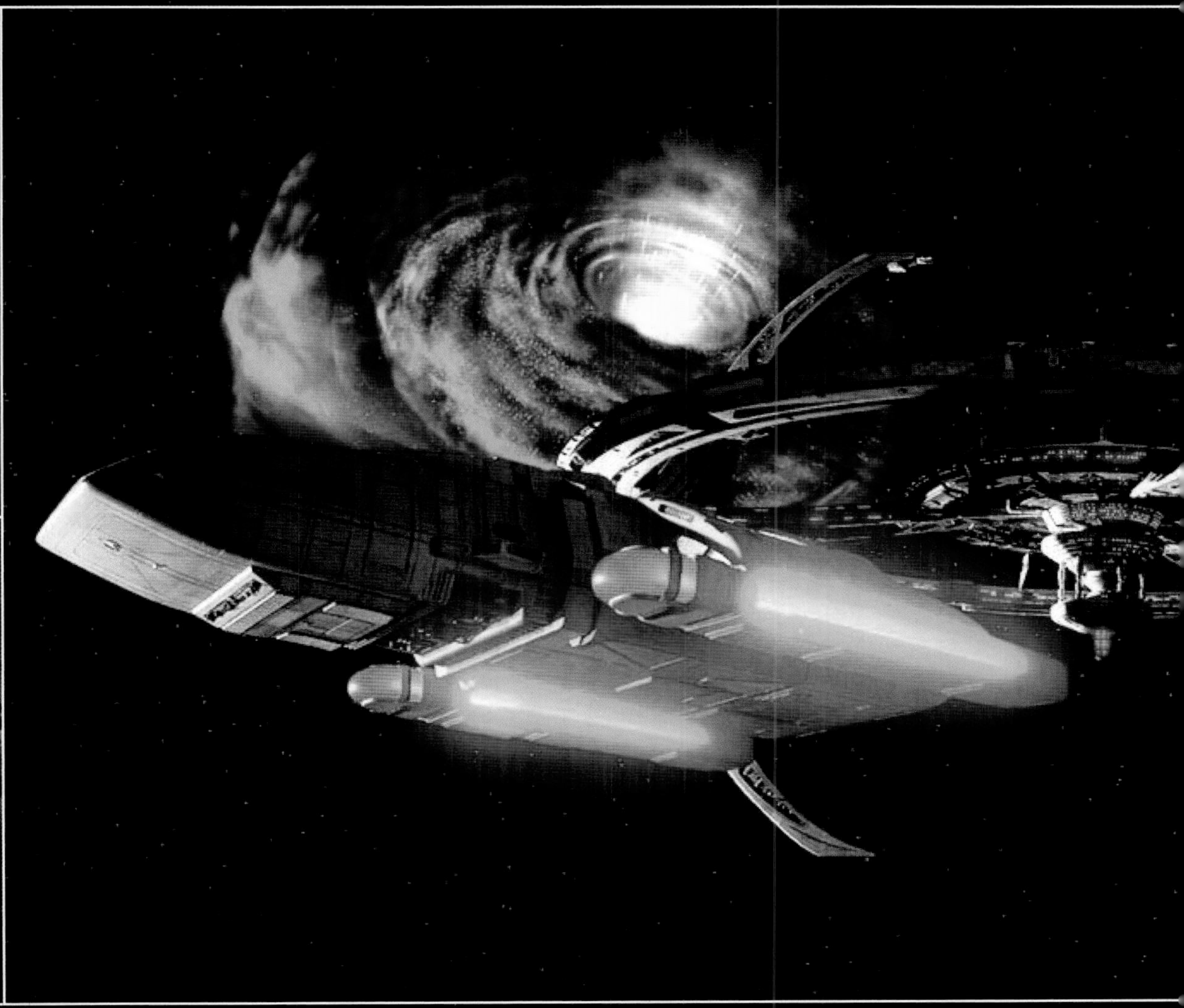

addition to providing defensive support. During their first few of years of service, the runabouts proved particularly useful in helping to evacuate the inhabitants during violent plasma storms in 2370, and when the Circle, a separatist group, tried to seize control of the station. They were also used extensively in the Badlands to track down members of the renegade Maquis organization. Runabouts were ideal for exploration and were instrumental in discovering many new worlds in the Gamma Quadrant, as well as the Bajoran wormhole itself.

As the threat from the Dominion rose, it became clear that the runabouts did not provide sufficient protective cover for Deep Space 9, so in 2371, the *U.S.S. Defiant* NX-74205 was brought in to bolster the space station's defenses. Nevertheless, runabouts still operated widely in a number of capacities. For example, in 2373, a runabout took part in a covert mission to rescue Enabran Tain and Dr. Bashir from a Dominion prison, Internment Camp 371. Runabouts continued to play an important role throughout the Dominion War and were deployed in exercises with the Ninth Fleet in 2374. At the climax of the war, Colonel Kira Nerys traveled to Cardassia Prime in a runabout to help with Damar's resistance movement.

▲ Three runabouts were initially assigned to Deep Space 9 in 2369. They provided a means of transportation off the station and remained its primary defensive support until the arrival of the *U.S.S. Defiant*.

DATA FEED

Runabouts could be equipped with a roll bar-mounted pod over the spine of the vessel. These pods were easily removed and normally contained sensor equipment.

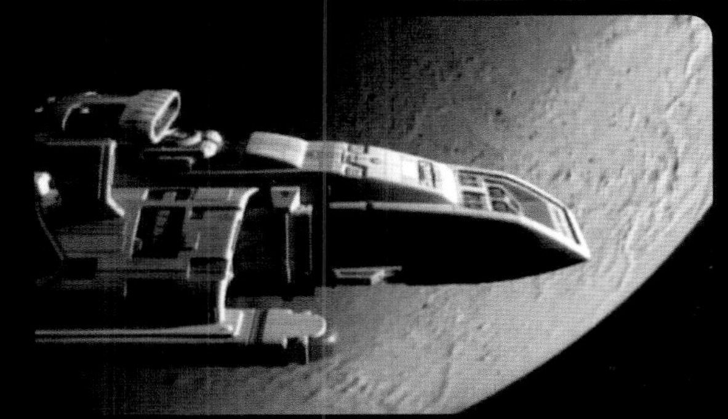

CREATURE COMFORTS

The habitat module at the rear of the runabout provided everything the crew needed to keep them comfortable on extended missions. The main feature of the compartment was a large meeting/dining table where the crew could discuss their mission objectives, relax, and eat. A replicator provided food and drink, but if it failed there were backup supplies in the form of emergency rations. Small bunk beds for the crew to use were located on each side of the exit leading to the middle section. There was also a computer console with a chair on one side of the compartment, where the crew could access a comprehensive library for research purposes, record the activities of their mission, and control some of the ship's primary systems. This section housed medical kits, four emergency EVA pressure suits, and a selection of hand phasers.

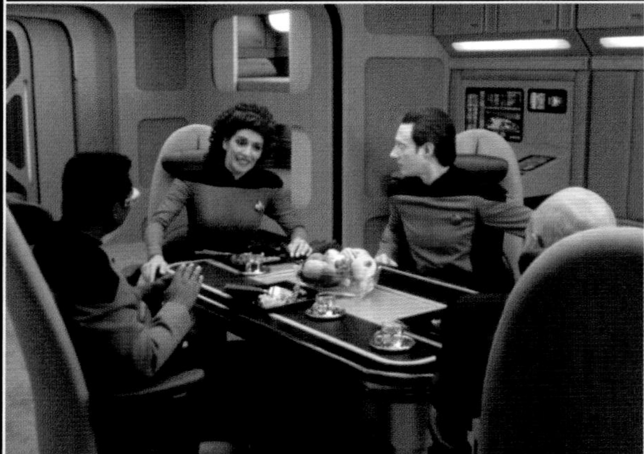

▲ Captain Picard and his colleagues enjoyed a meal together in the habitat module of a runabout on their way back to the *U.S.S. Enterprise* NCC-1701-D, after attending a psychology conference.

DATA FEED

Defensive payloads, special laboratories, emergency habitats, and additional living quarters were just some of the different modules that could be fitted to the swappable central section of a runabout, between the cockpit and the habitat area.

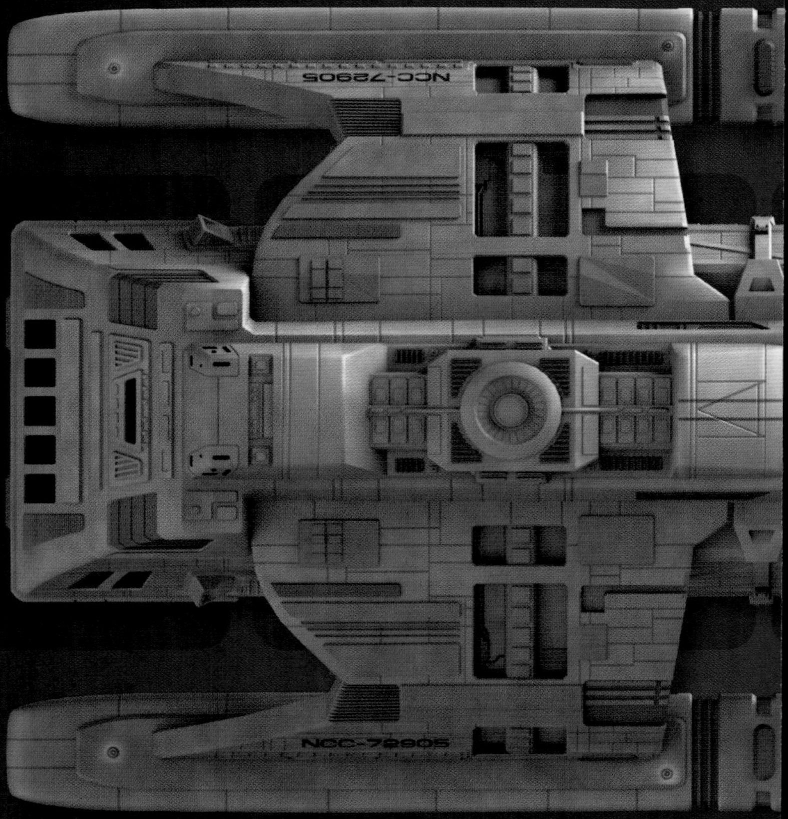

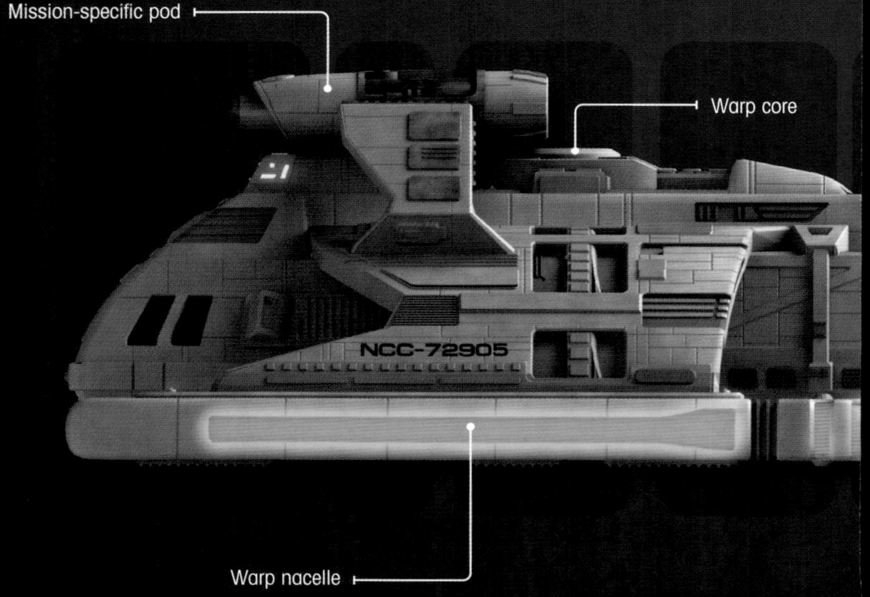

NCC-72905
Mission-specific pod
Warp core
Warp nacelle

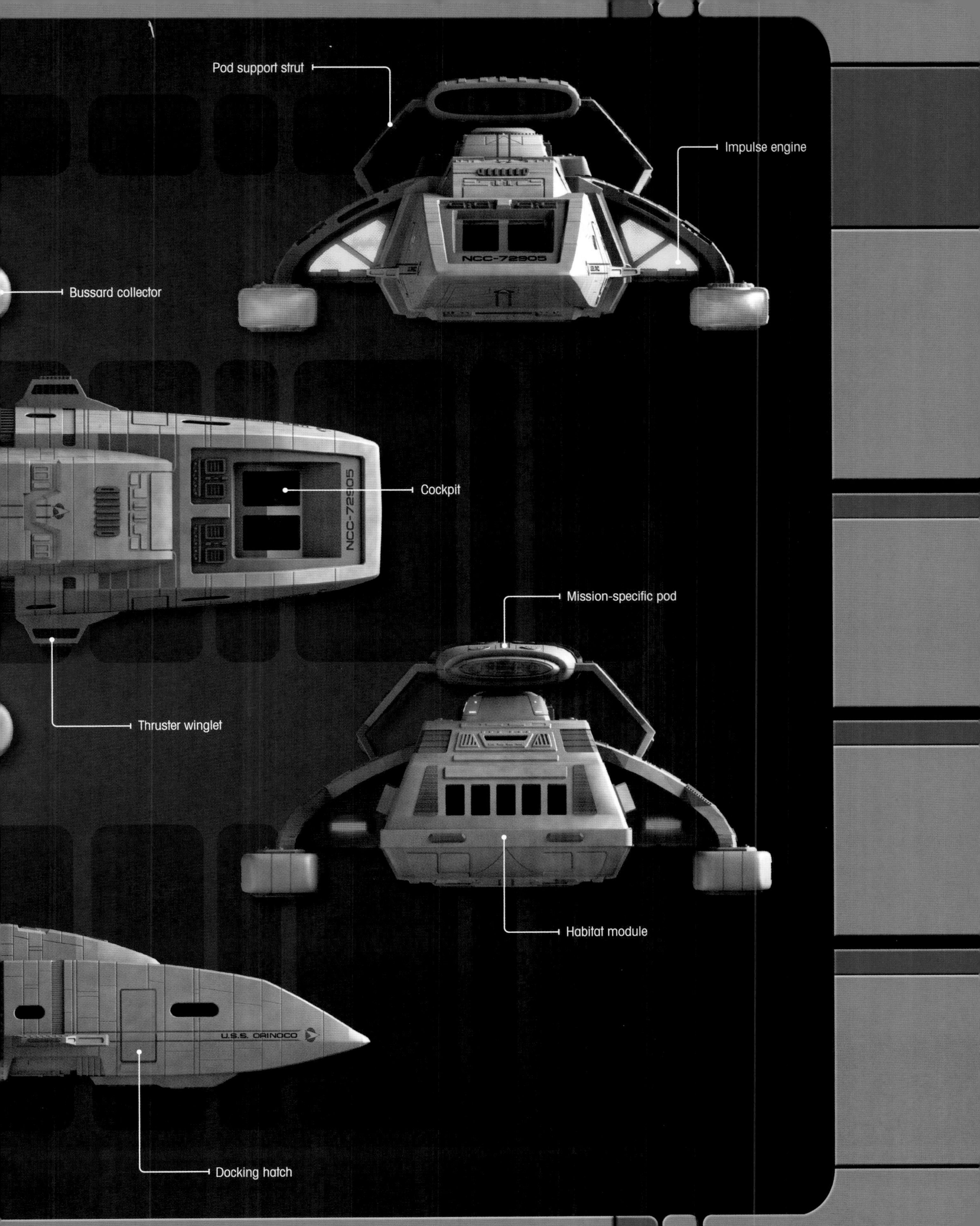

Pod support strut
Impulse engine
NCC-72905
Bussard collector
NCC-72905
Cockpit
Mission-specific pod
Thruster winglet
Habitat module
U.S.S. ORINOCO
Docking hatch

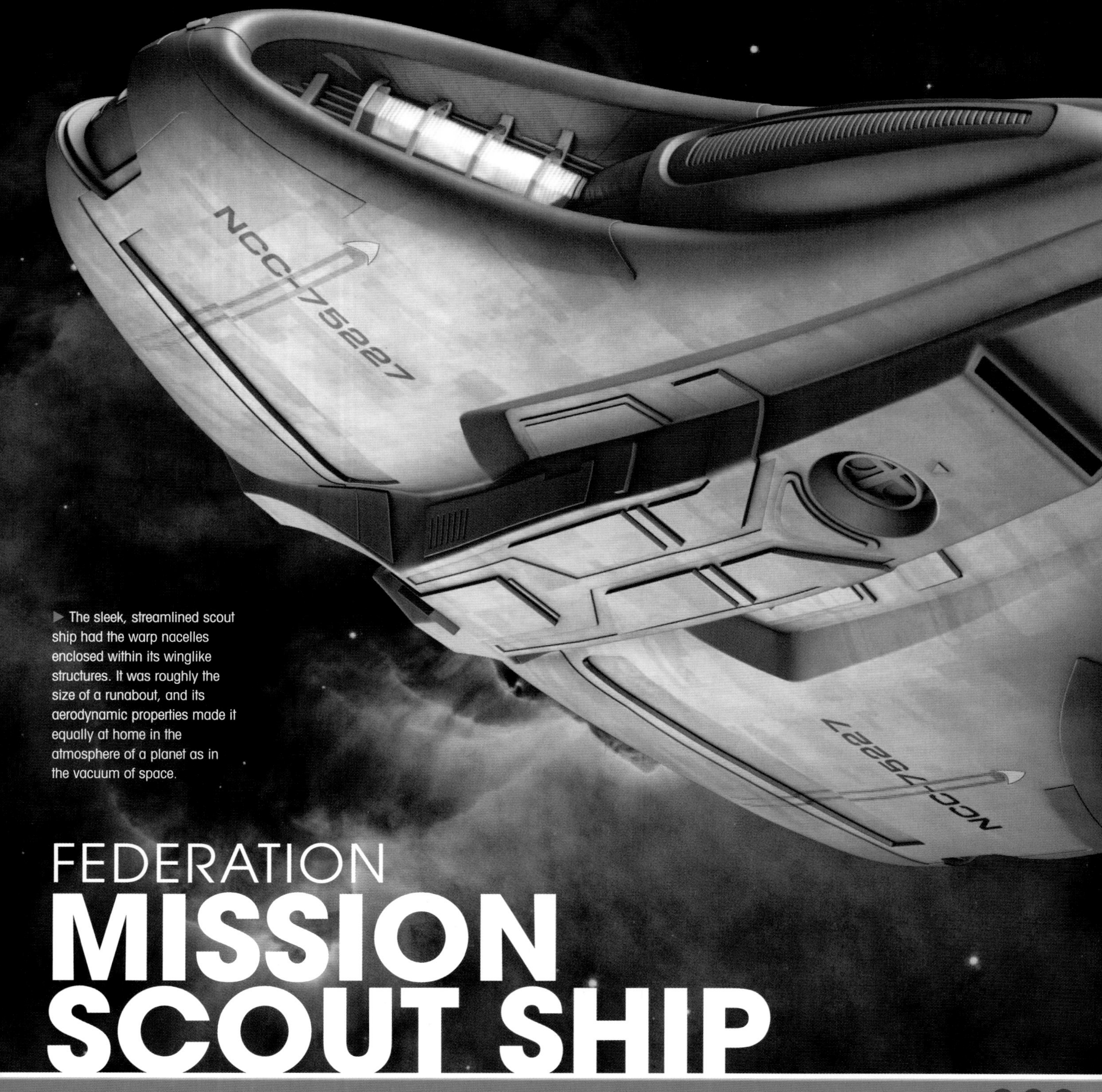

▶ The sleek, streamlined scout ship had the warp nacelles enclosed within its winglike structures. It was roughly the size of a runabout, and its aerodynamic properties made it equally at home in the atmosphere of a planet as in the vacuum of space.

FEDERATION MISSION SCOUT SHIP

The scout ship was a support vessel mainly used to help survey teams study planets and star systems.

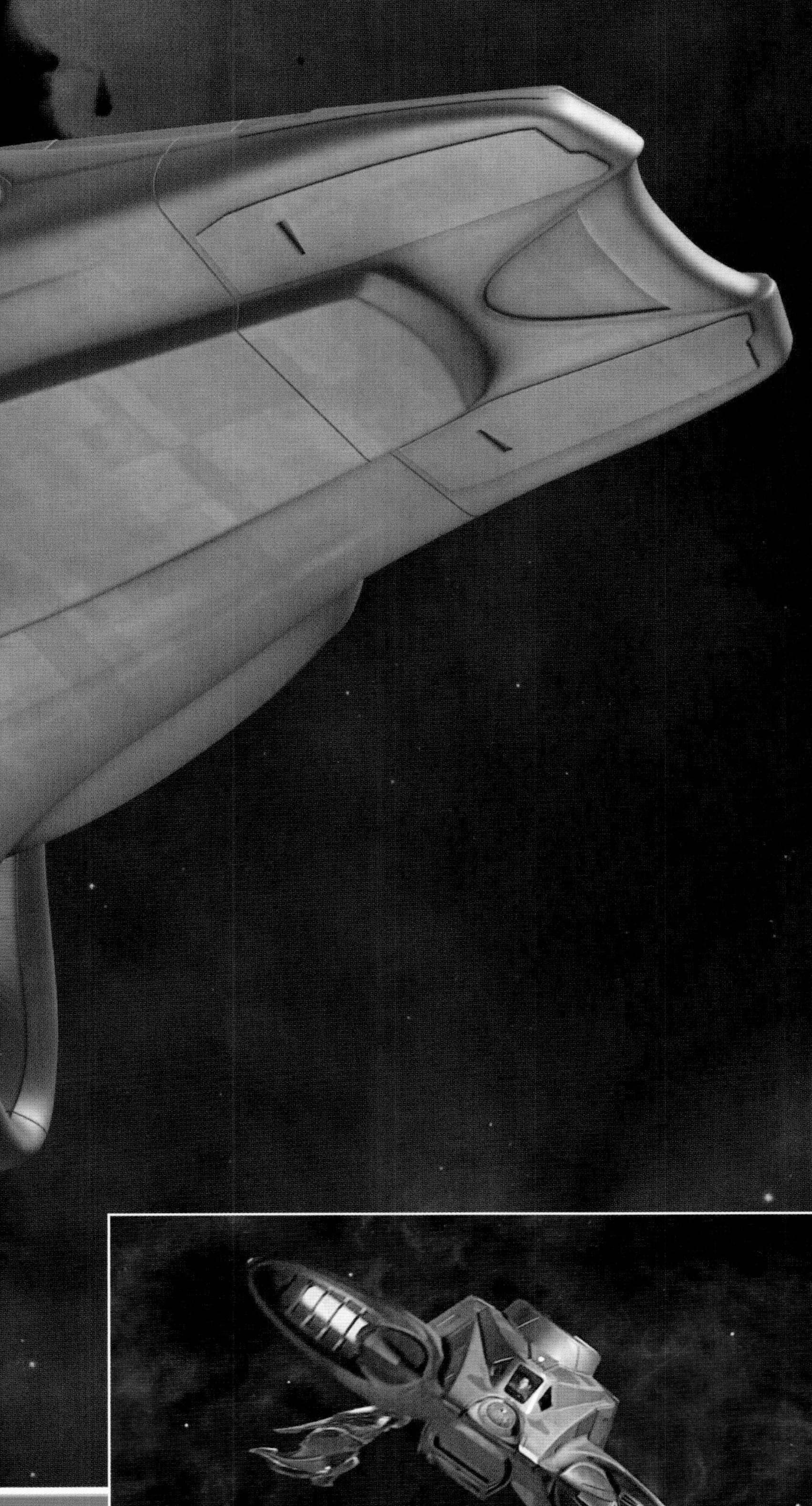

The 24th-century Federation scout ship was primarily used in research missions to gather scientific data and aid in planetary and cultural surveys. These vessels were ideal in scenarios where a larger, fully fledged starship would have been a drain on resources.

At approximately 24 meters in length, the scout ship was roughly six meters longer than a Type-11 shuttlecraft, but was still small enough to be carried aboard a standard Starfleet vessel's shuttlebay. The scout ship only required one pilot, who sat in a cockpit similar to that of a Type-9 shuttlecraft. The one major difference was a set of panoramic windows at the front that gave the pilot an excellent view ahead, to the sides, and above. Inside the craft, the space at the rear included a number of science stations and provided enough room for five to ten passengers.

RUGGED AND NIMBLE

In many ways the scout ship resembled a runabout, although it was more agile and robust. The warp nacelles were encased within its "wings" for better protection, and it was capable of reaching a top speed of warp 5 for limited periods. Impulse engines were located within two spurs that projected from the back of the main body.

The design of the scout ship was more svelte and streamlined than that of a runabout or shuttlecraft, and its aerodynamic properties really paid off when it was flying within a planetary atmosphere. Thanks to its RCS thrusters, it was capable of performing high-speed, intricate

◀ The scout ship had a sophisticated array of sensor equipment, making it ideally suited for research duties, but it was also well armed with phasers and torpedoes. The Son'a found this out when Data attacked Ru'afo's flagship and caused significant damage to its outer hull, before retreating quickly back to the safety of the Ba'ku planet.

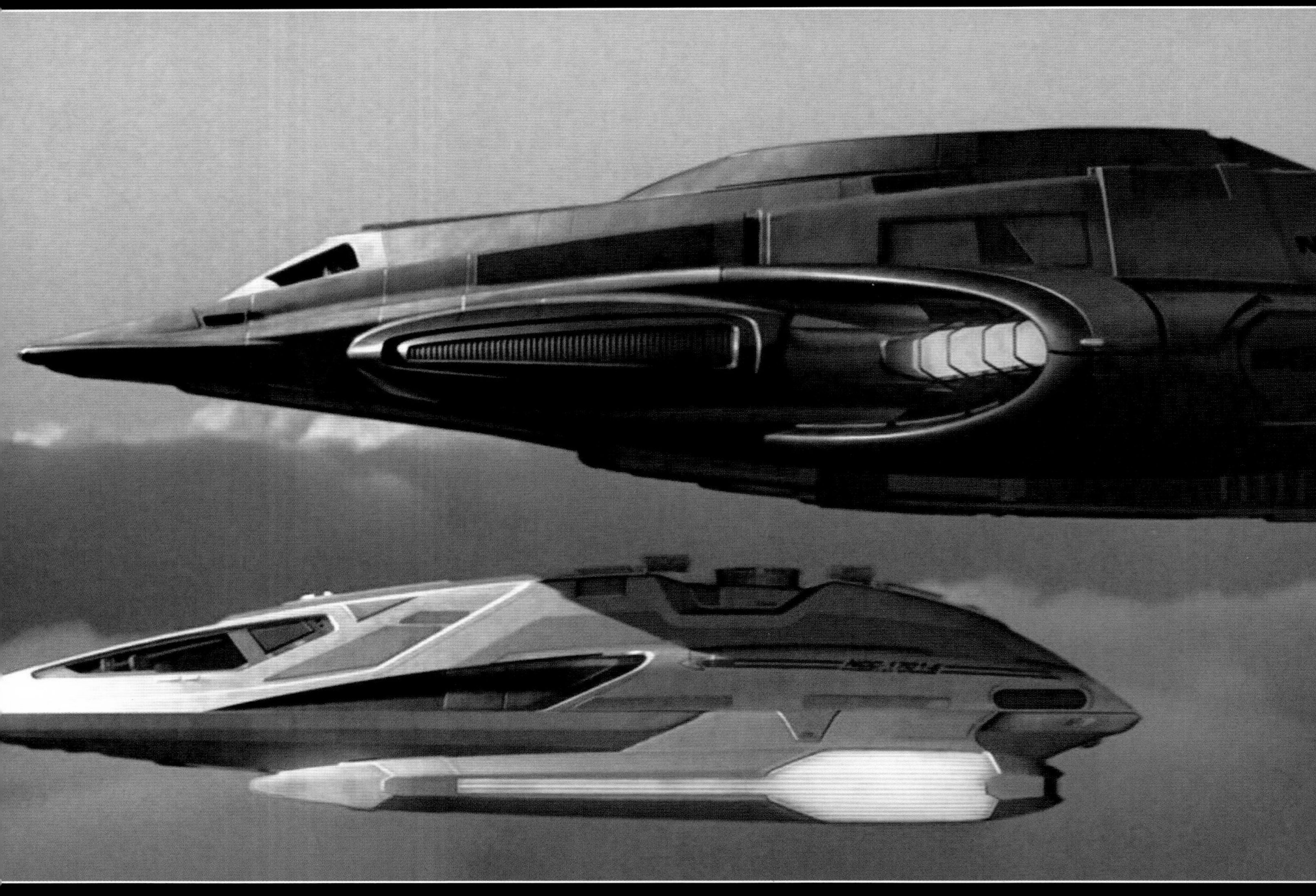

▲ The scout ship was noticeably larger than a Type-11 shuttlecraft, as was seen when Captain Picard flew his craft directly below Data's ship. Picard wanted to stop Data by extending the emergency hatch on top of his vessel and docking it with the hatch on the bottom of the scout ship. He hoped Worf could then climb between the two ships and neutralize Data.

maneuvers and extreme swoops and spins, much like an old-style jet fighter.

While the scout ship primarily acted as a support vessel by collecting sensor readings for planetside research stations, it could also be used for military reconnaissance, providing aerial intelligence on enemy troop movements. In this role, it could carry out the reconnaissance of entire star systems, collating information on the attack capabilities of an enemy force. This could obviously be a dangerous undertaking, so the scout ship was armed with dual-mounted phaser banks and torpedo launchers to defend itself.

In 2375, a Federation scout ship with the suffix NCC-75227 was employed by a joint Federation-Son'a surveillance team, who were covertly observing a Ba'ku settlement on a planet in the Briar Patch. It was hijacked by an apparently malfunctioning Lieutenant Commander Data, who used it to ambush the Son'a flagship that was in high orbit of the planet. Data made a surprise attack, emerging from a low-density gas cloud before blasting away with phasers and multiple photon torpedoes. Data then retreated to the surface of the Ba'ku planet in the scout ship, without any explanation for his actions.

SECURING DATA

Once Captain Picard was informed of Data's bizarre behavior, he elected to take the *U.S.S. Enterprise* NCC-1701-E to the planet's location to try and safely capture Data.

Picard and Lieutenant Commander Worf then headed toward the planet in a Type-11 shuttlecraft, transmitting a wide-band covariant signal to attract Data's attention. As they were flying over the planet, Data suddenly appeared in the scout ship, firing a phaser blast that hit the

▶ The scout ship had a tough, robust look to it, not unlike the *U.S.S. Defiant*. It was certainly able to carry out swift attacks, as Data proved when he launched an assault on the Son'a.

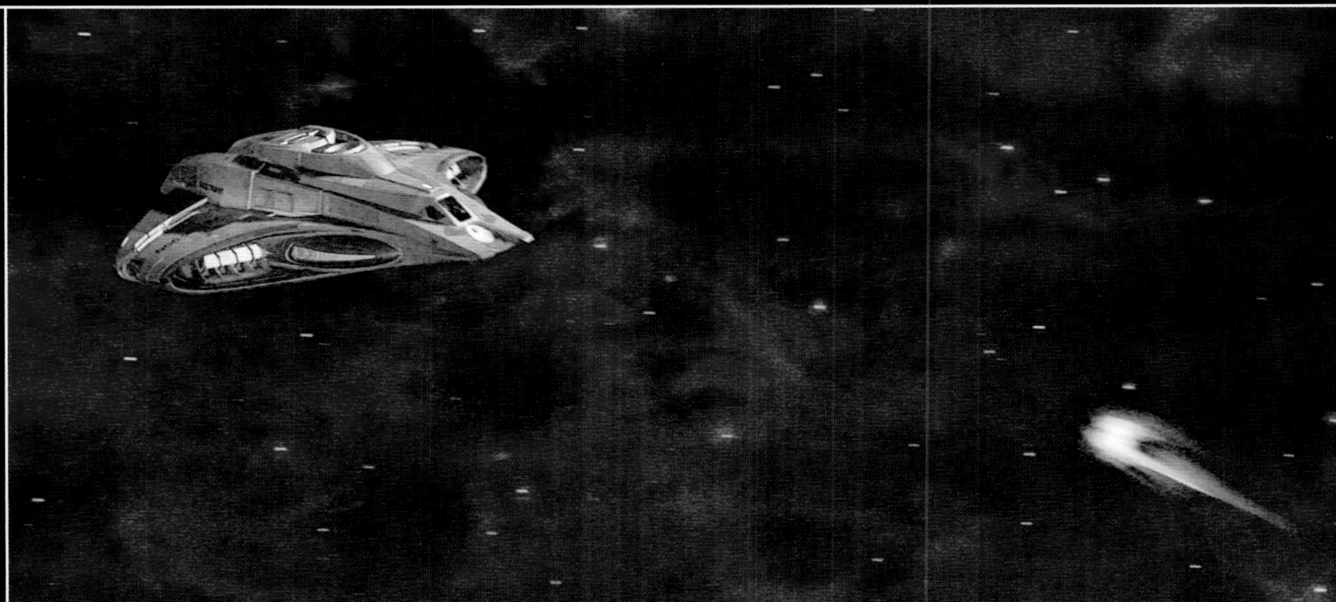

▼ The tactical ability of the scout ship was superior to the Type-11 shuttlecraft's, but Picard managed to gain an advantage by distracting Data, then flying inches below his ship so Data could not see him.

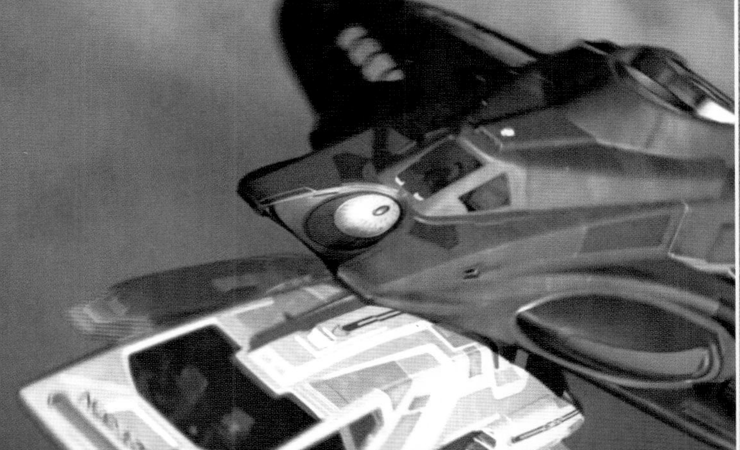

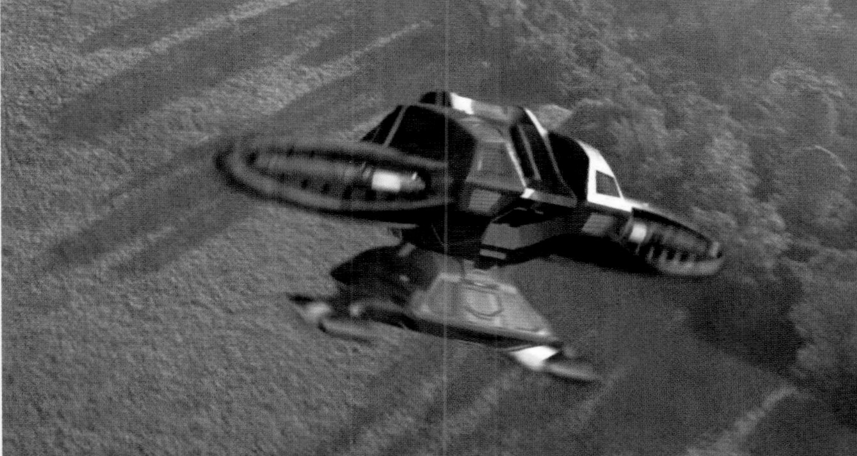

shuttle. As Picard performed extreme evasive maneuvers to avoid more phaser blasts, he tried to open communications with Data – who refused to acknowledge them and continued his attack.

Attempts to beam Data off the scout ship failed, because he had anticipated their plan and activated a transporter inhibitor. As the battle continued into the atmosphere of the planet, Picard managed to maneuver his vessel below the scout ship. He then forcibly locked the two ships together by means of the docking hatches. This caused them to spiral out of control, and as they plunged toward the ground, the inertial coupling on the shuttlecraft soon exceeded tolerance. Picard refused to let go, however, and rerouted emergency power to the inertial dampers. This allowed him to pull the ships out of the dive and into a stable flight path.

Worf climbed through the hatch and into the scout ship. He then aimed a modified tricorder at Data and pushed a button. When nothing happened, Worf frantically pushed the button over and over again as Data lunged at him. It finally worked and Data shut down, collapsing motionless just a few inches from Worf. Having achieved their aim, Picard and Worf returned Data safely to the *Enterprise*, while both ships remained largely intact.

▲ After their emergency hatches were forcibly docked, both ships were locked together and out of control. Picard only just managed to avoid a catastrophic crash by rerouting power to the inertial dampers.

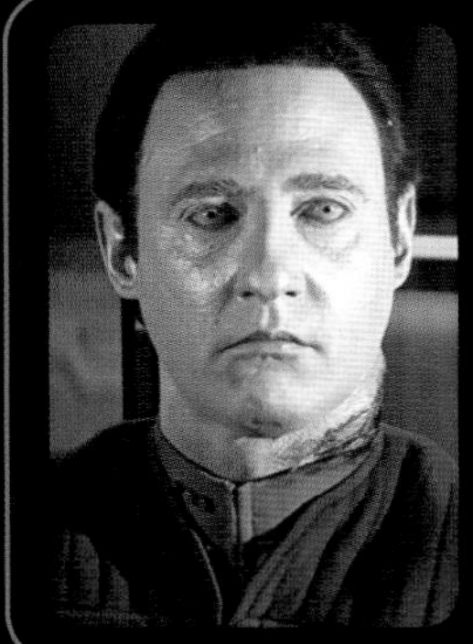

DATA FEED

Data was assigned to help the joint Federation-Son'a survey team study the Ba'ku, when he discovered a plot to coerce them into relocating. As Data was about to report his findings, he was shot by a Son'a weapon. This caused him to lose his memory, but he entered a self-protection mode in which all he knew was right from wrong. He tried to protect the Ba'ku by exposing the survey team and using the scout ship to attack the Son'a flagship orbiting the planet.

AIR-TO-AIR COMBAT

The scout ship piloted by Data attacked the shuttlecraft operated by Captain Picard and Lieutenant Commander Worf in orbit of the Ba'ku planet. To shake off Data's pursuit, Picard entered the planet's atmosphere in the hope that the turbulence from the ionospheric boundary would thwart him. Despite the massive turbulence, however, the scout ship remained on their tail and Data fired more shots.

As Picard worked hard to stabilize his ship, he came up with a new plan: to distract Data with a burst of song from a Gilbert and Sullivan opera. Data had been rehearsing a part in *H.M.S. Pinafore* before he left for the Ba'ku mission, and somewhere inside his damaged positronic brain he remembered this and began to sing along. He was so preoccupied with the song that he did not notice Picard's shuttlecraft sliding under his scout ship.

The ships flew closer and closer together until the hatch on top of Picard's shuttlecraft locked onto an emergency hatch on the scout ship with a magnetic docking clamp. Data rocked the scout ship back and forth to try and shake it loose, but this caused both vessels to tumble through the sky, seemingly out of control. Just a split second before the ships smashed into the ground, Picard regained control and stabilized their flight, with both ships still locked together. Worf was then able to board the scout ship and use a modified tricorder to neutralize Data, before taking him safely into custody.

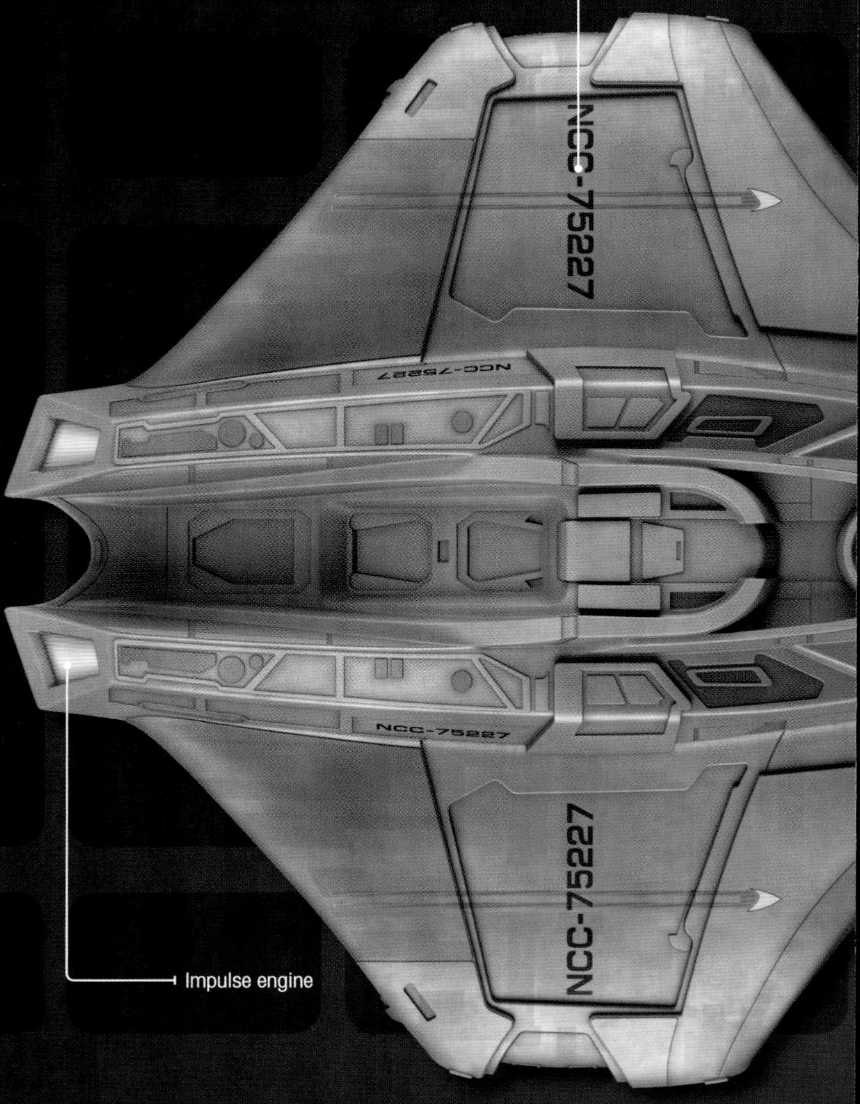

Nacelle housing

NCC-75227

NCC-75227

NCC-75227

NCC-75227

Impulse engine

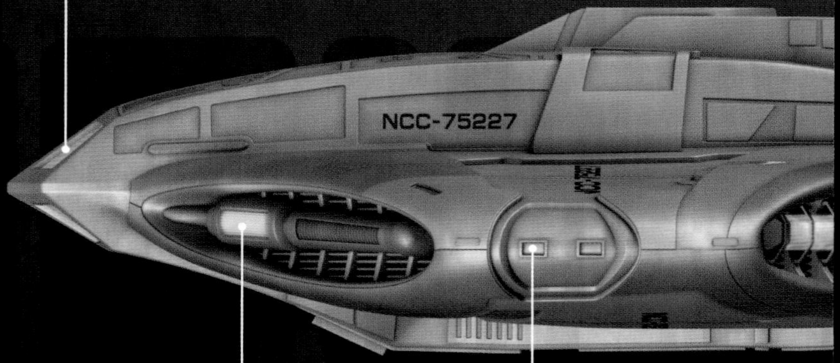

Impulse exhaust nozzles

NCC-75227

RCS thrusters

Passenger entry door

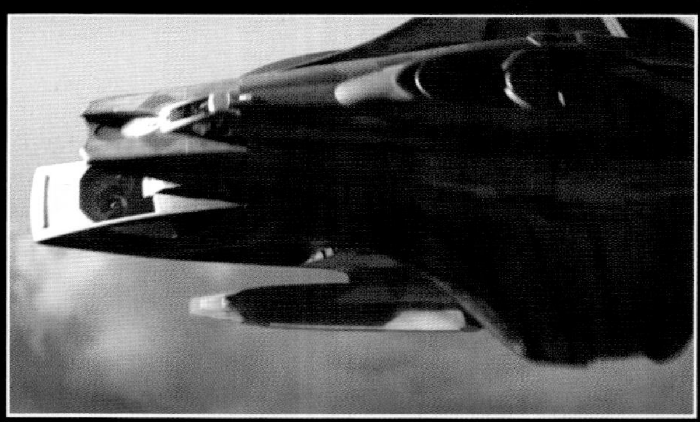

The plan to lock the vessels together so Worf could board the scout ship almost ended in disaster. But rerouting power to the shuttle's inertial dampers pulled both ships out of their terminal dive.

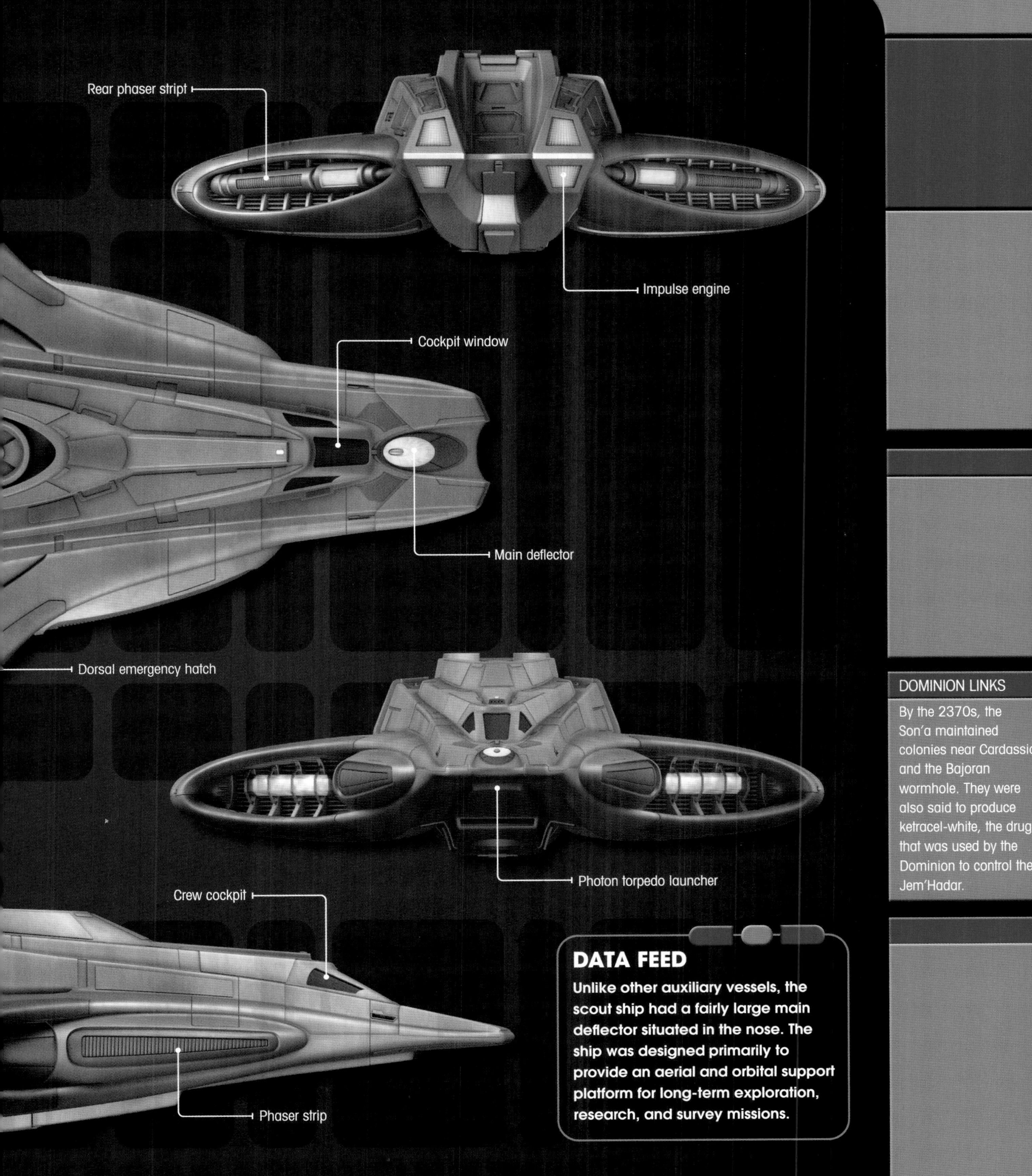

DOMINION LINKS

By the 2370s, the Son'a maintained colonies near Cardassia and the Bajoran wormhole. They were also said to produce ketracel-white, the drug that was used by the Dominion to control the Jem'Hadar.

DATA FEED

Unlike other auxiliary vessels, the scout ship had a fairly large main deflector situated in the nose. The ship was designed primarily to provide an aerial and orbital support platform for long-term exploration, research, and survey missions.

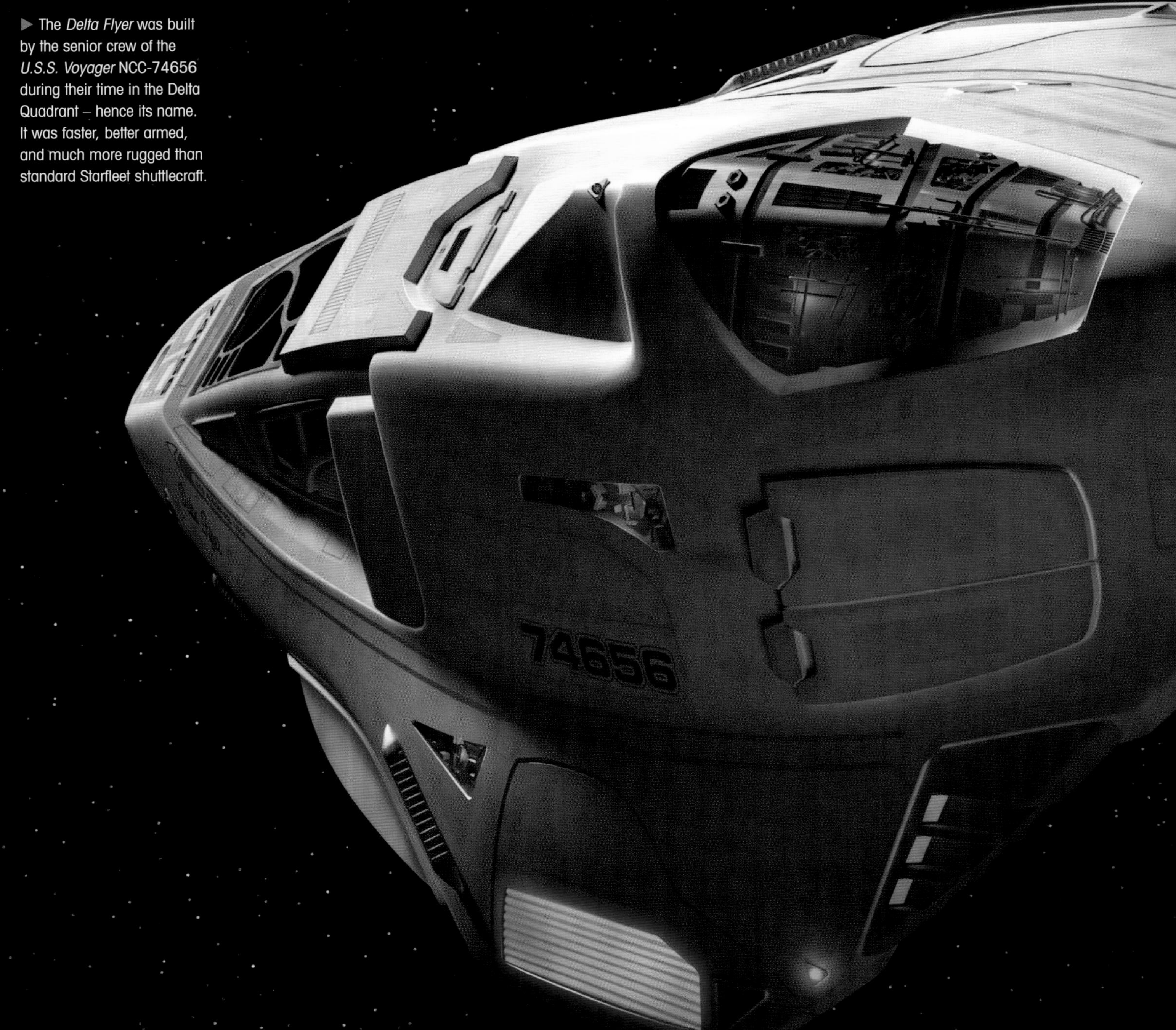

▶ The *Delta Flyer* was built by the senior crew of the *U.S.S. Voyager* NCC-74656 during their time in the Delta Quadrant – hence its name. It was faster, better armed, and much more rugged than standard Starfleet shuttlecraft.

DELTA FLYER

This unique shuttlecraft was designed to withstand the extreme rigors of life in the hostile Delta Quadrant.

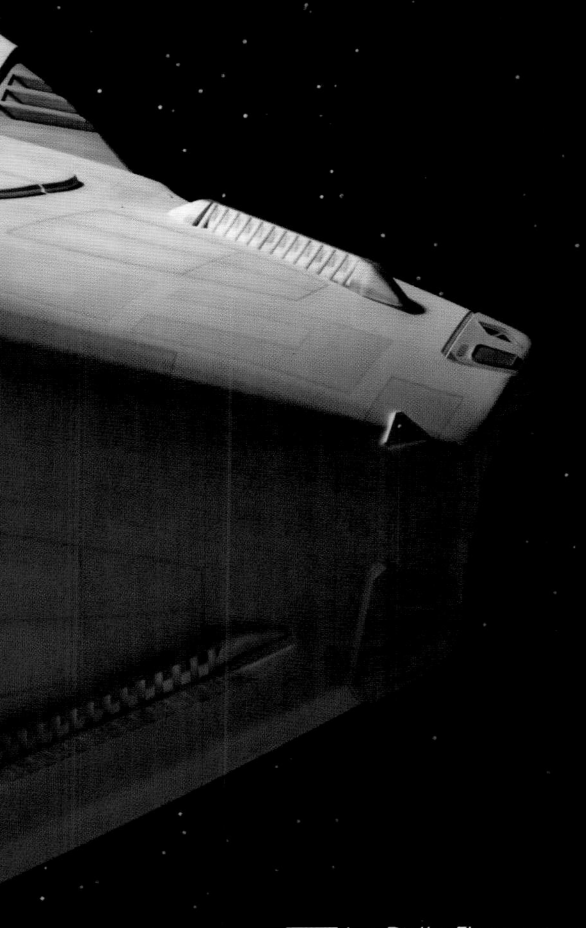

DATA FEED

The initial idea for the *Delta Flyer* came from Seven of Nine during a mission to survey a proto-nebula aboard a Class-2 shuttle. She heard B'Elanna Torres and Tom Paris complaining of having "Class-2 claustrophobia," a term used by Starfleet cadets when they were packed into shuttles for weeks at a time as part their training. Seven then suggested that they design a larger, more efficient shuttle.

The *Delta Flyer* was a larger, more resilient type of shuttlecraft that was developed by the crew of the *U.S.S. Voyager* NCC-74656 after they were stranded in the Delta Quadrant. It combined traditional Starfleet design principles with Borg technology and unimatrix shielding designed by Commander Tuvok. At 21 meters in length, it was larger than a Starfleet Class-2 shuttle, but smaller than a *Danube*-class runabout.

The main proponent for the creation of the *Delta Flyer* was *Voyager*'s helmsman Tom Paris, who repeatedly championed the idea of building a specialized shuttlecraft (in his words, a "hot rod") that was more suited to the crew's needs than normal shuttles. At first, Captain Janeway and Commander Chakotay rejected his suggestion because they felt that the crew did not have the time to design and build a ship from scratch, so Paris began work on the design in his spare time.

BORN OF NECESSITY

In 2375, the argument swung decisively in his favor, when the crew had to retrieve a multiphasic probe from the atmosphere of a Class-6 gas giant to prevent it falling into the Malon's hands. Since no alternative was available, Captain Janeway gave the go-ahead to build the *Delta Flyer*. The entire senior staff contributed to the project, adapting and improving Paris's initial design.

The most serious design problems were related to the *Flyer*'s structural integrity system, since retrieving the probe from the gas giant's atmosphere would push the small craft to its limits. B'Elanna Torres suggested using titanium alloys for the hull, but on Seven of Nine's recommendation the crew instead chose tetraburnium because of its higher structural integrity. Even so, the pressures

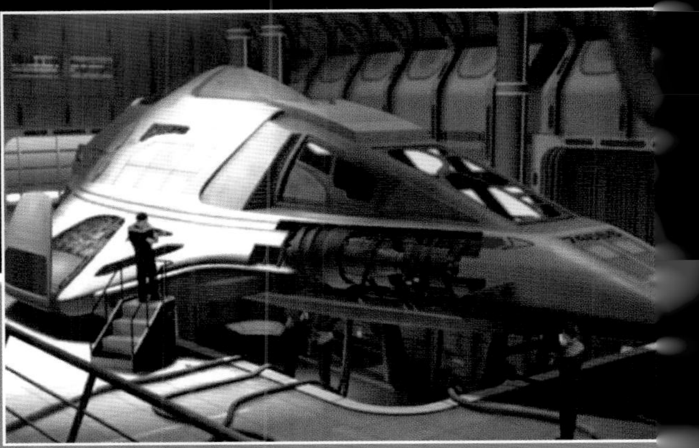

▶ With the team working around the clock, the *Delta Flyer* was built in just a few days. Alloys and new design components were replicated, while spare parts from storage were also used in its construction. It featured retractable warp nacelles, unimatrix shielding, and Borg-inspired weapons. Tom Paris called it an "ultra-responsive hot rod."

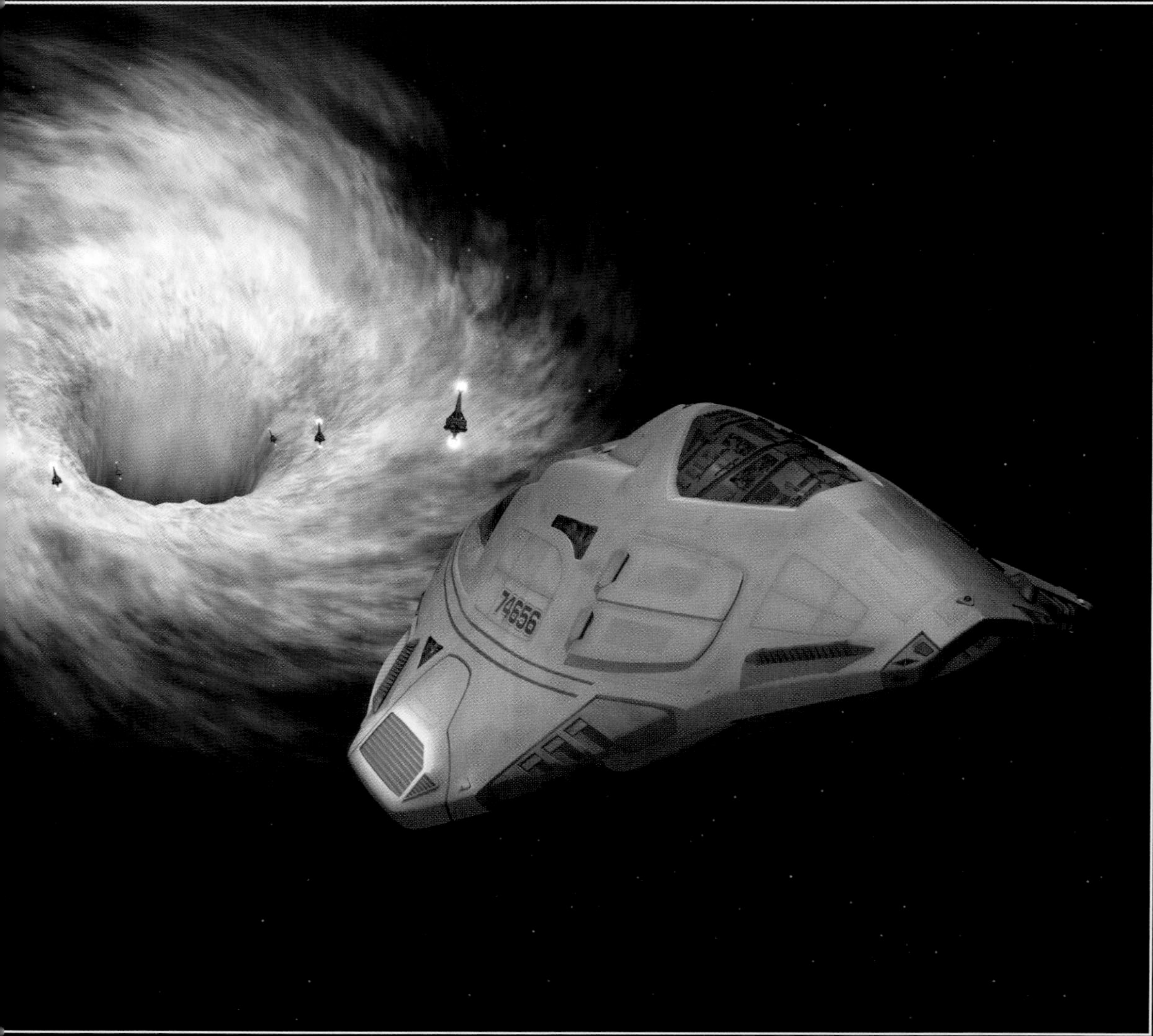

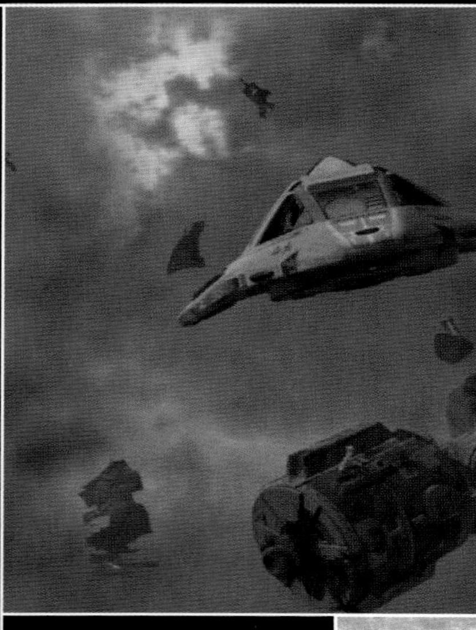

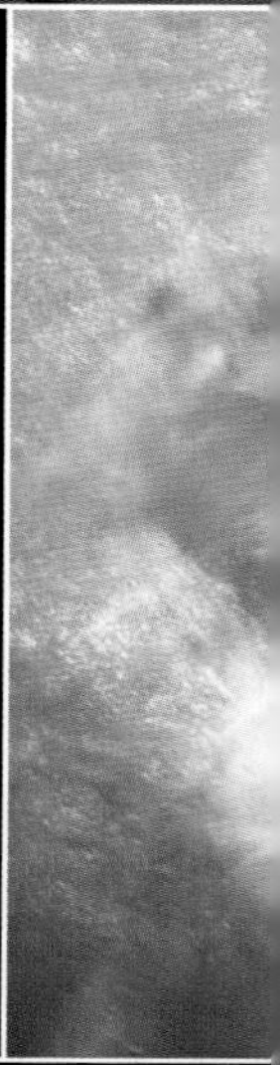

▶ With the addition of immersion shielding, the *Delta Flyer* had the necessary structural integrity to dive to a depth of nearly 600 km on the Monean ocean world.

▲ The *Delta Flyer II* could achieve even faster sublight speeds than its predecessor, thanks to its pop-out impulse thrusters. These proved especially useful when navigating the course near a Möbius Inversion during the Antarian Trans-Stellar Rally.

involved were so great that the ship was only able to maintain a structural integrity field for a few minutes before microfractures began to form in the parametallic hull. The problems were never entirely solved, but the ship successfully retrieved the probe.

ADVANCED SYSTEMS

The *Delta Flyer* was equipped with warp and impulse engines, a tractor beam emitter, and a narrow beam transporter; it used a tuned, circumferential warp reaction chamber and extendable warp nacelles. When fitted with a Borg transwarp coil, it was more than capable of traveling at transwarp velocities. The ship was also capable of atmospheric flight and landing on the surface of a planet.

Power distribution was maximized by the use of isomagnetic EPS conduits in the plasma manifold, and many of its systems incorporated Borg enhancements suggested by Seven. In particular, the *Flyer*'s weapons systems were inspired by Borg technology; it had fore and aft phaser strips, and a nose-mounted microtorpedo launcher that could fire photonic missiles.

The ship's design proved extremely adaptable. Shortly after the crew completed its construction, they modified its thrusters and added immersion shielding so that it could operate deep within the Monean ocean planet. On another occasion, the ship was modified so that it could generate multiadaptive shielding that rendered it invisible to the Borg's sensors. This enabled the crew to steal a transwarp coil from a damaged Borg sphere.

The *Delta Flyer*'s resilience was tested time after time, and it even survived a crash-landing that left it buried three kilometers beneath the surface of a Class-M planetoid. It also withstood the extreme

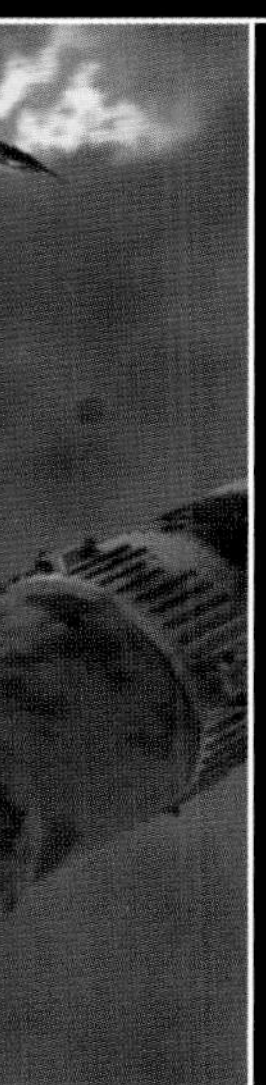

◀ Shield enhancements enabled the *Delta Flyer* to withstand huge gravimetric distortions and safely enter a graviton ellipse. Here it found Ares IV, an early Mars mission command module that had gone missing in 2032.

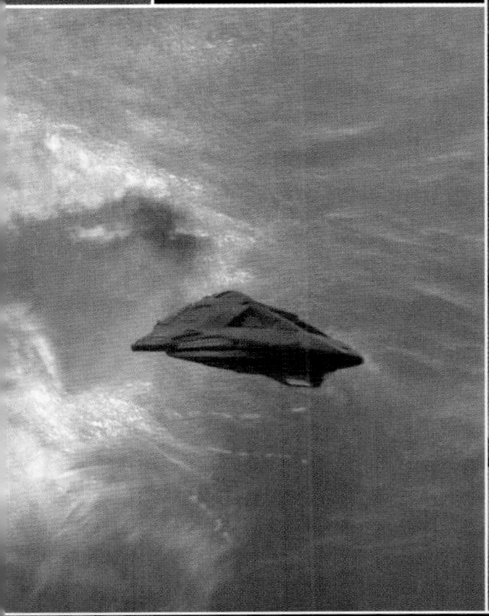

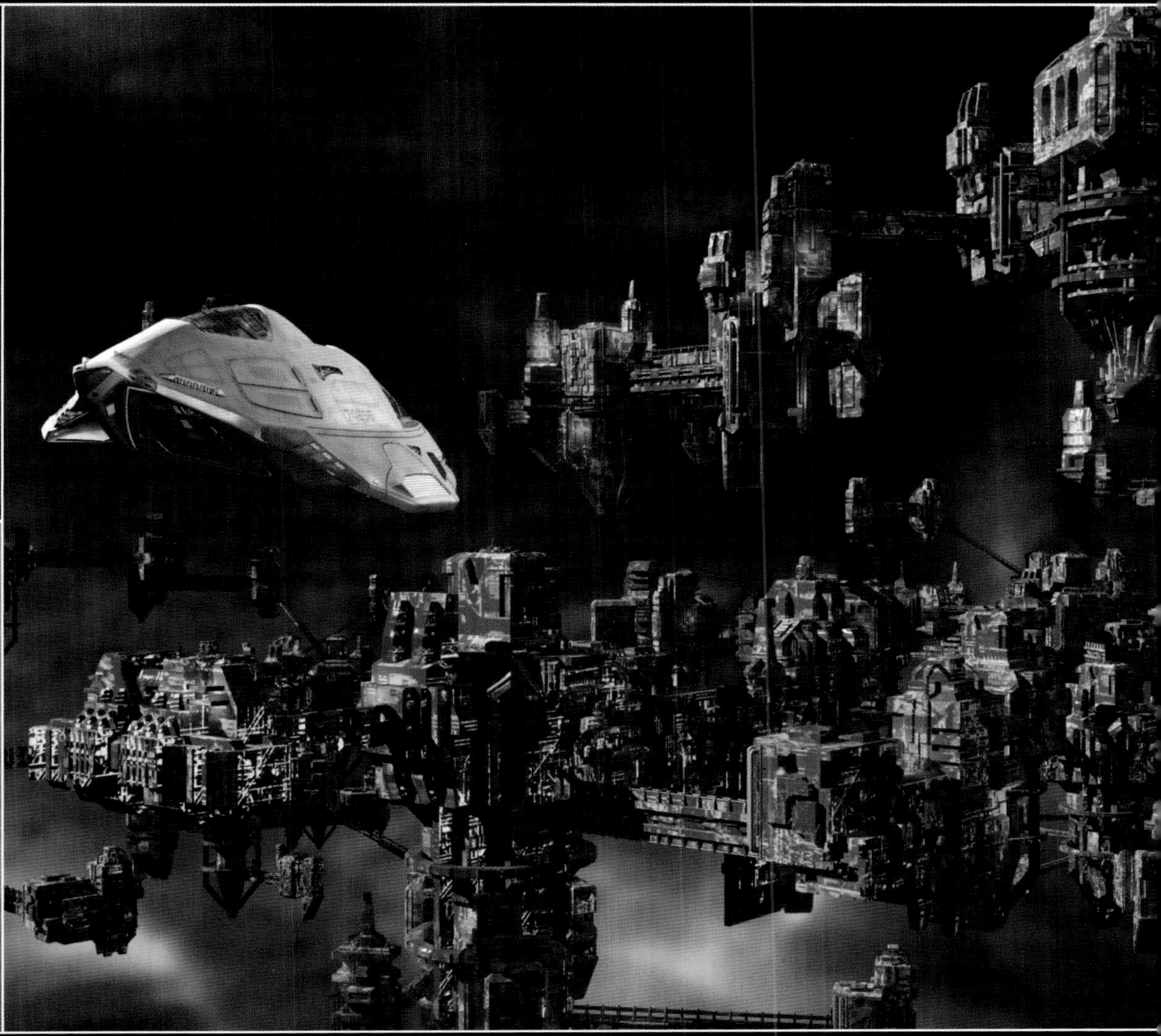

subspace distortions inside a graviton ellipse while attempting to retrieve Ares IV, an early Mars mission spacecraft from 2032.

TAKING ON THE BORG

The *Delta Flyer* ultimately met its demise in early 2377, when it was used in a daring raid on a Borg tactical cube as part of a mission to help the drones of Unimatrix Zero. The Borg Queen targeted the *Flyer* and destroyed it, but not before the occupants had beamed onto the cube.

The *Delta Flyer* had proved so useful that the *Voyager* crew decided to build another one. The *Delta Flyer II* featured a number of improvements on its earlier incarnation. These included pop-out impulse thrusters that provided faster sublight speeds. The interior was redesigned for greater comfort and its arsenal was supplemented with a pulse-phased weapon system.

The *Delta Flyer II* was soon put through its paces when it took part in the Antarian Trans-Stellar Rally. This 2.3 billion-kilometer sublight race was the ultimate test of a ship's design and the pilot's skills, since obstacles included dwarf star clusters, K-class anomalies, and subspace distortions. The *Flyer II* was winning the race when it was discovered that it had been rigged to explode at the finish line. Its destruction was averted at the last second after its warp core was ejected into a Class-J nebula.

As with its predecessor, the *Delta Flyer II* went on to play a vital role in routine scientific and diplomatic missions, as well as being used to scout for supplies, such as dilithium. It also proved pivotal on several occasions in helping to save *Voyager* and its crew, most notably in 2377. This mission involved rescuing most of the ship's personnel after they had been abducted and brainwashed by a group of aliens called the Quarren.

▲ After a mission on which the *Voyager* crew stole a Borg transwarp coil, Seven of Nine was captured by the Collective. The coil was installed on the *Delta Flyer,* which was then used to travel to the vast Borg Unicomplex to rescue Seven.

INTERIOR LAYOUT

The interior of the *Delta Flyer* comprised a cockpit, a small midsection, and an aft compartment that featured wall-mounted work stations, a replicator, a retractable biobed, and a caged locker containing spacesuits and handheld weapons.

The cockpit featured distinct workstations for tactical, operations, and engineering personnel. A ramp led down to the pilot's seat, located on its own in the nose of the cockpit. In the original *Delta Flyer,* Tom Paris designed several retro control panels that he claimed allowed him to "feel" how the ship was responding. In the *Delta Flyer II,* the flight controls were updated with two identical joysticks for the pilot to change course and speed, providing an extremely responsive method of control.

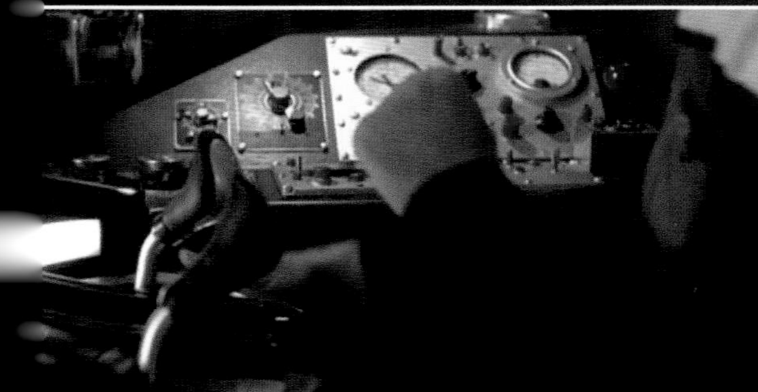

▲ Instead of a standard Starfleet LCARS interface, the pilot's station eatured analog-style dials and toggle switches and levers, while the *Delta Flyer II* also featured two manual steering columns.

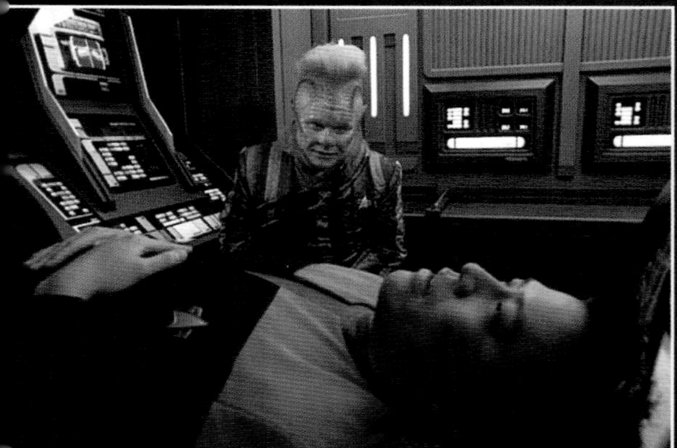

▲ The large aft compartment on the *Delta Flyer* provided the ccupants with space to work, relax, or sleep. It even featured retractable biobed in case of a medical emergency.

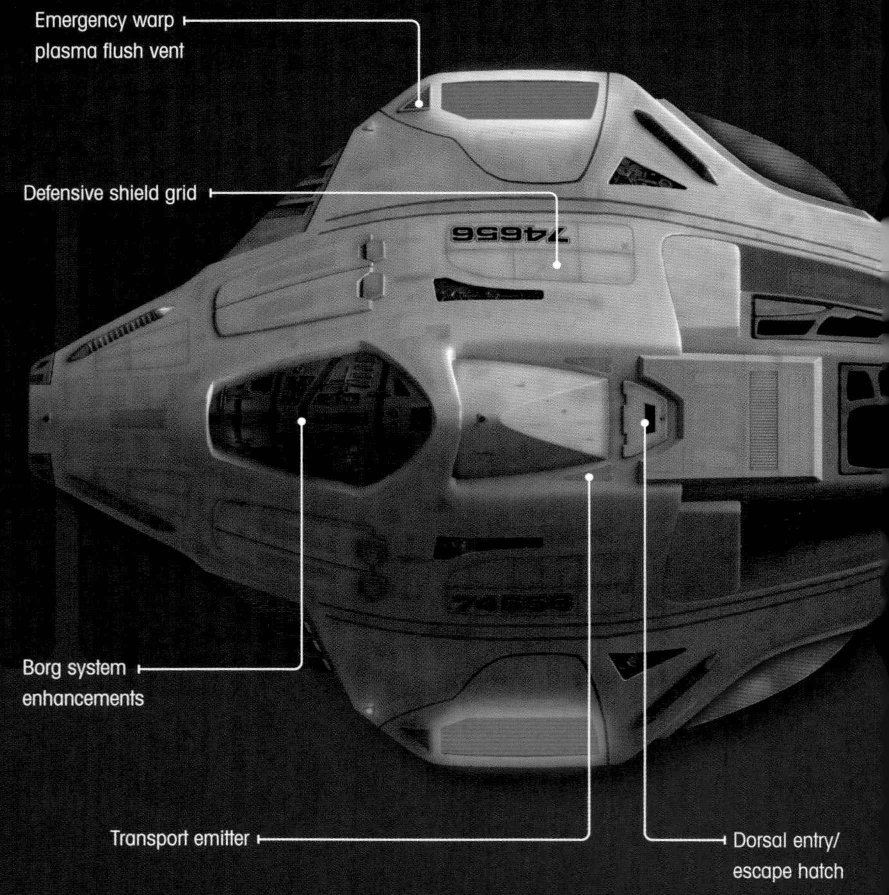

Emergency warp plasma flush vent

Defensive shield grid

Borg system enhancements

Transport emitter

Dorsal entry/ escape hatch

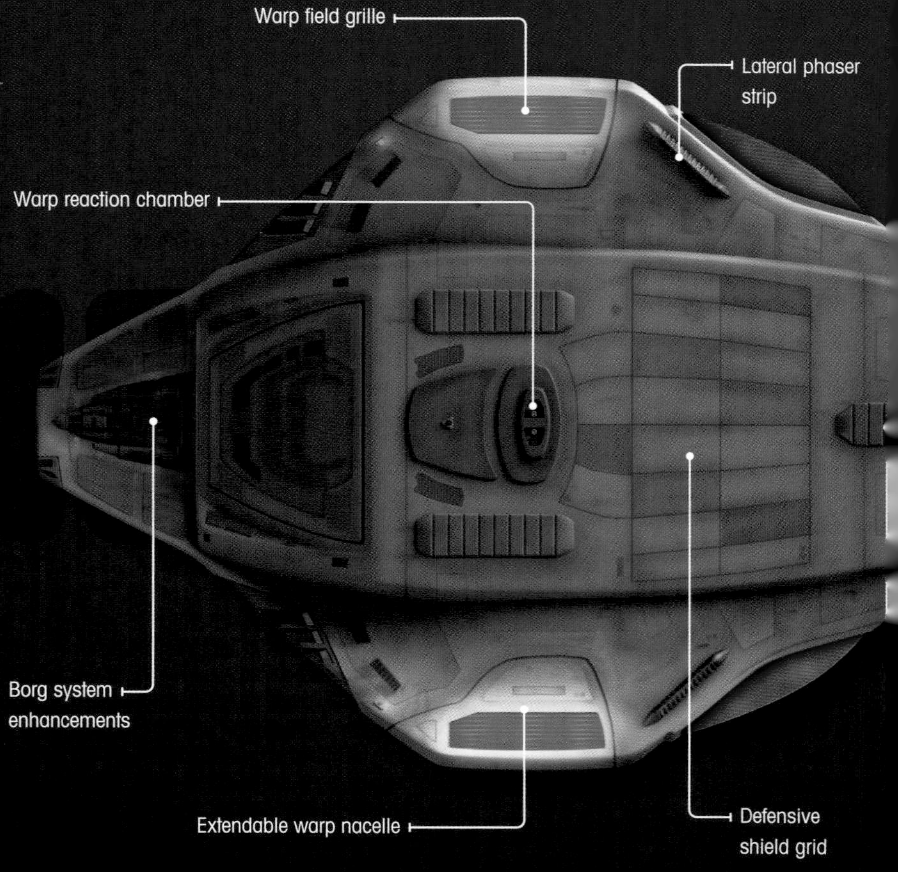

Warp field grille

Lateral phaser strip

Warp reaction chamber

Borg system enhancements

Extendable warp nacelle

Defensive shield grid

DATA FEED

The first version of the *Delta Flyer* featured two torpedo launchers on either side of the vessel facing forward, while the *Delta Flyer II* was equipped with a single launcher on the ventral surface.

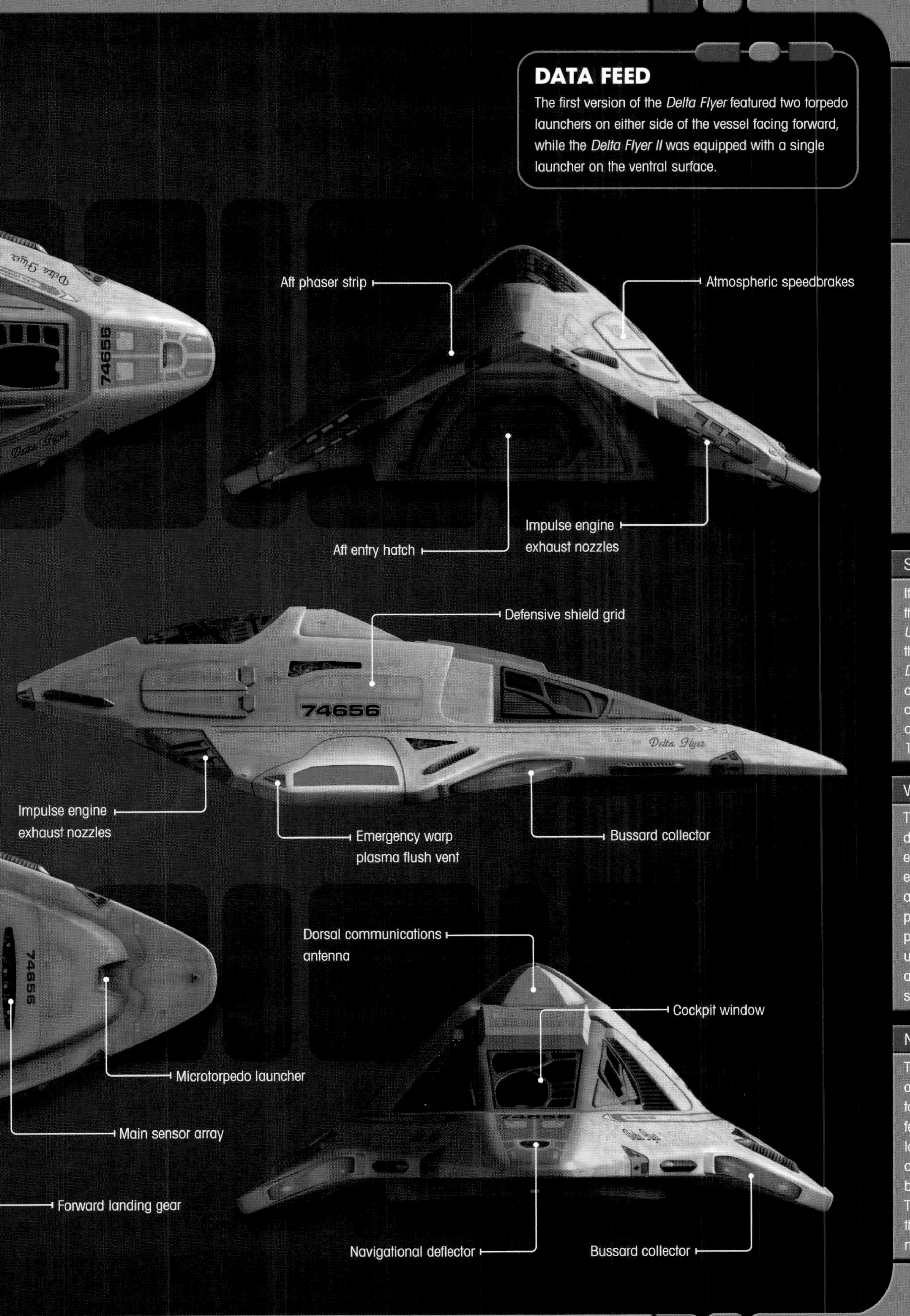

SHUTTLECRAFT LOSS

It was not surprising that the crew of the *U.S.S. Voyager* felt the need to create the *Delta Flyer*. By the end of 2375, they had crashed, destroyed, or otherwise lost a total of 18 shuttlecraft.

WELL SHIELDED

The *Delta Flyer* was designed to survive extremely hostile environments. In addition to its parametallic hull plating, it featured unimatrix, immersion, and multiadaptive shielding.

NO EMBELLISHMENTS

Tom Paris wanted to add dynametric tail fins to the *Delta Flyer,* as he felt they would help it look "mean" and make other ships think twice before taking it on. But Tuvok told him to take them off as they served no practical purpose.

SMALL TRANSPORTS

SIZE CHART

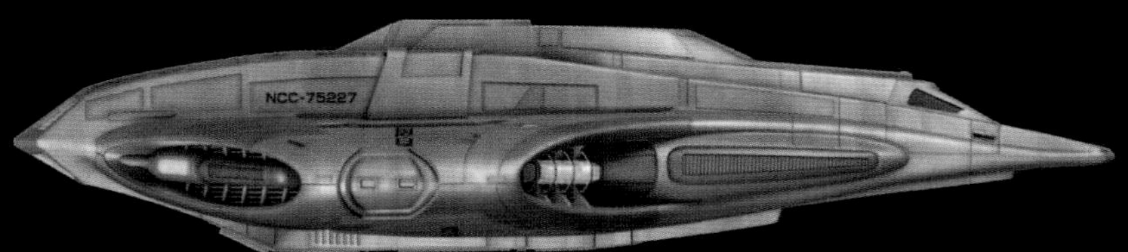

FEDERATION MISSION SCOUT SHIP

24m

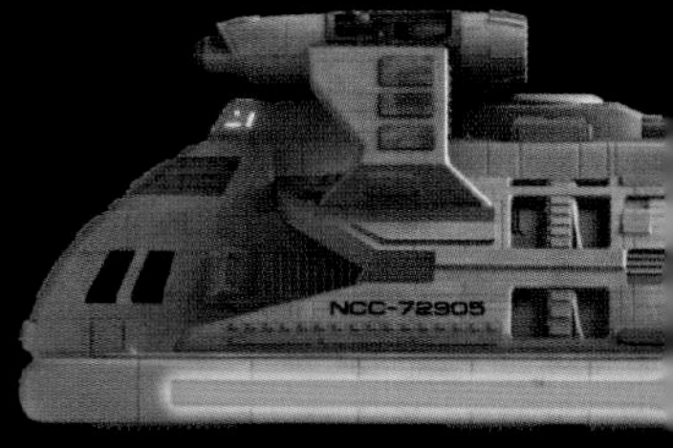

STARFLEET RUNABOUT

23.1m

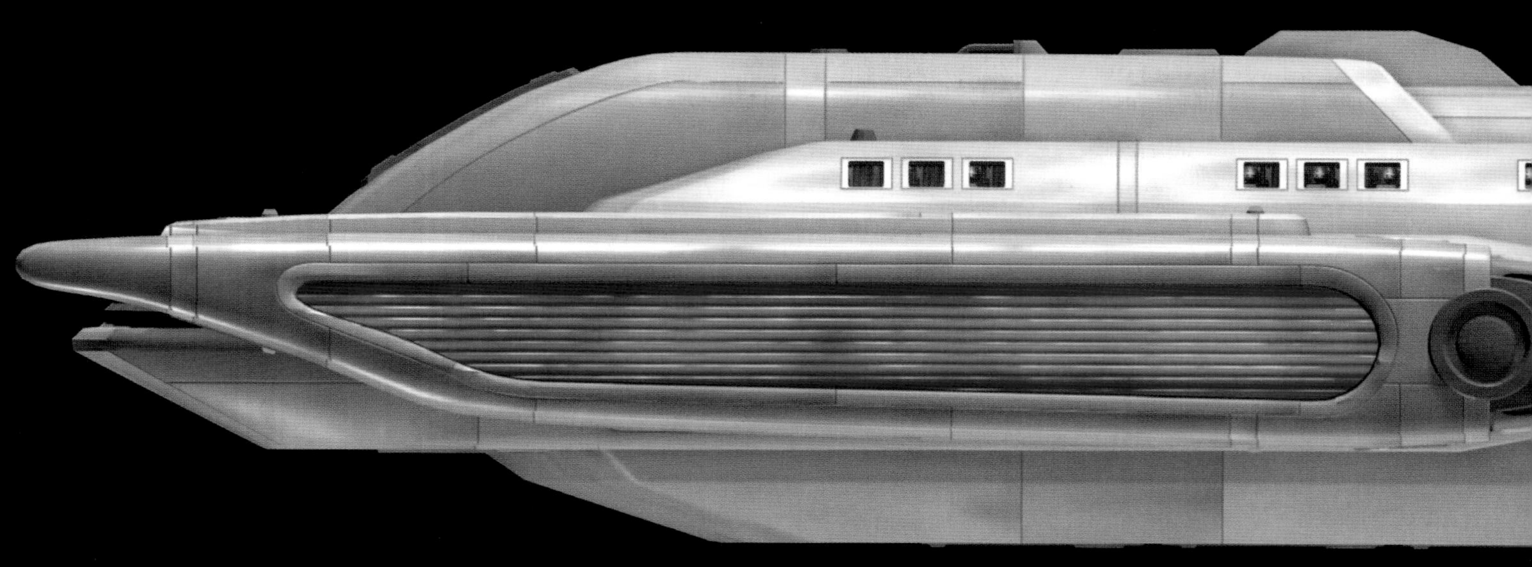

S.S. RAVEN NAR-32450

90m

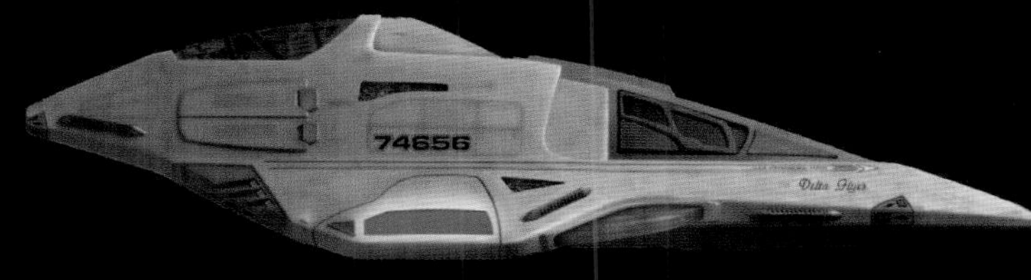

DELTA FLYER

21m

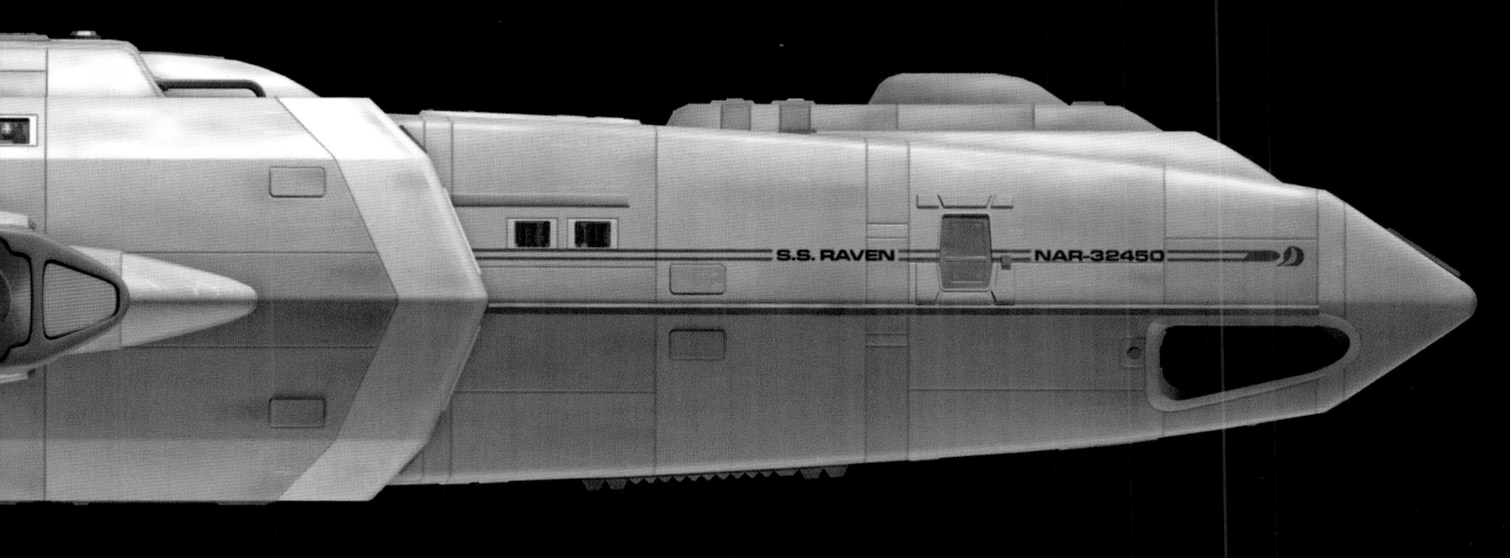

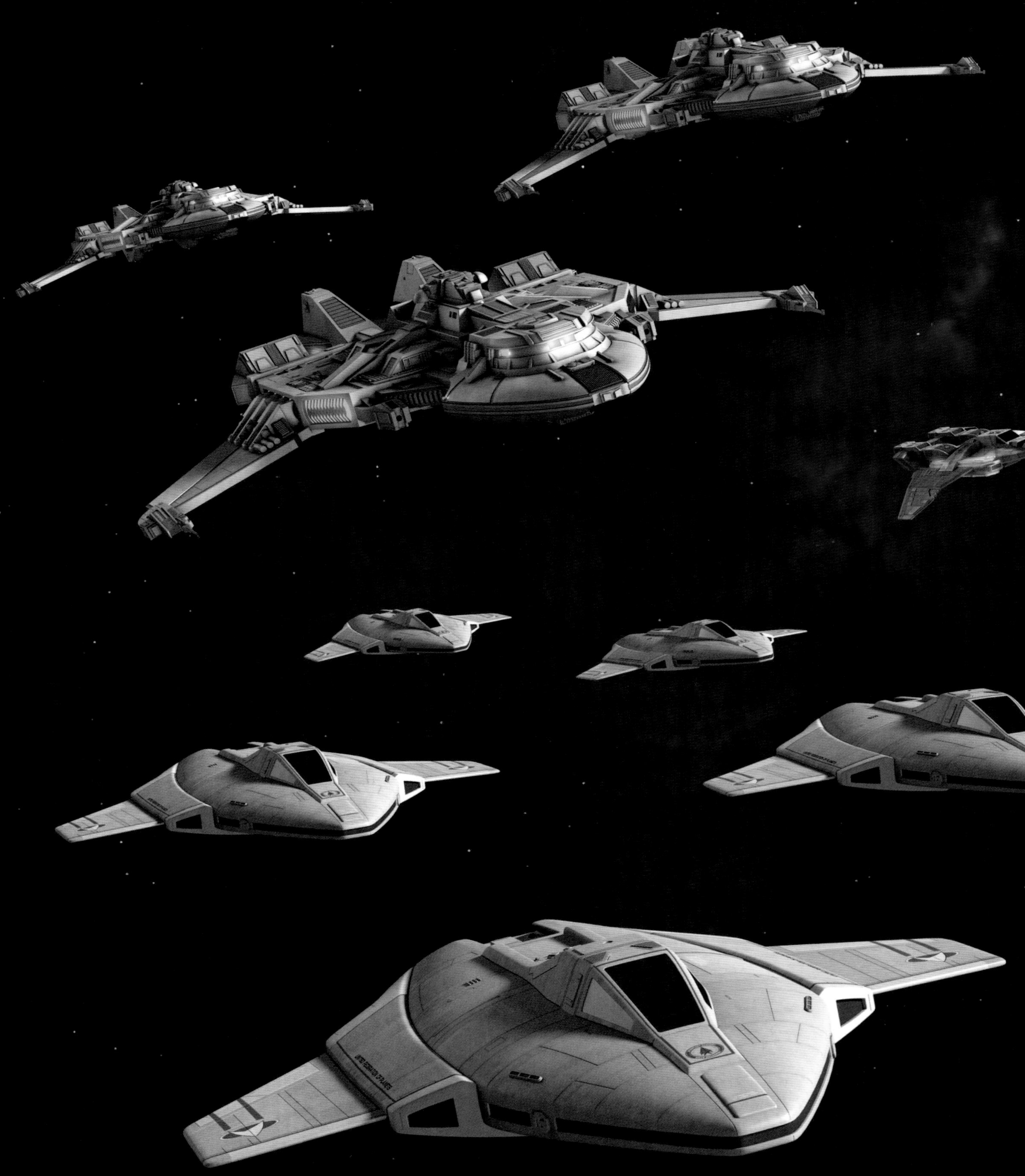

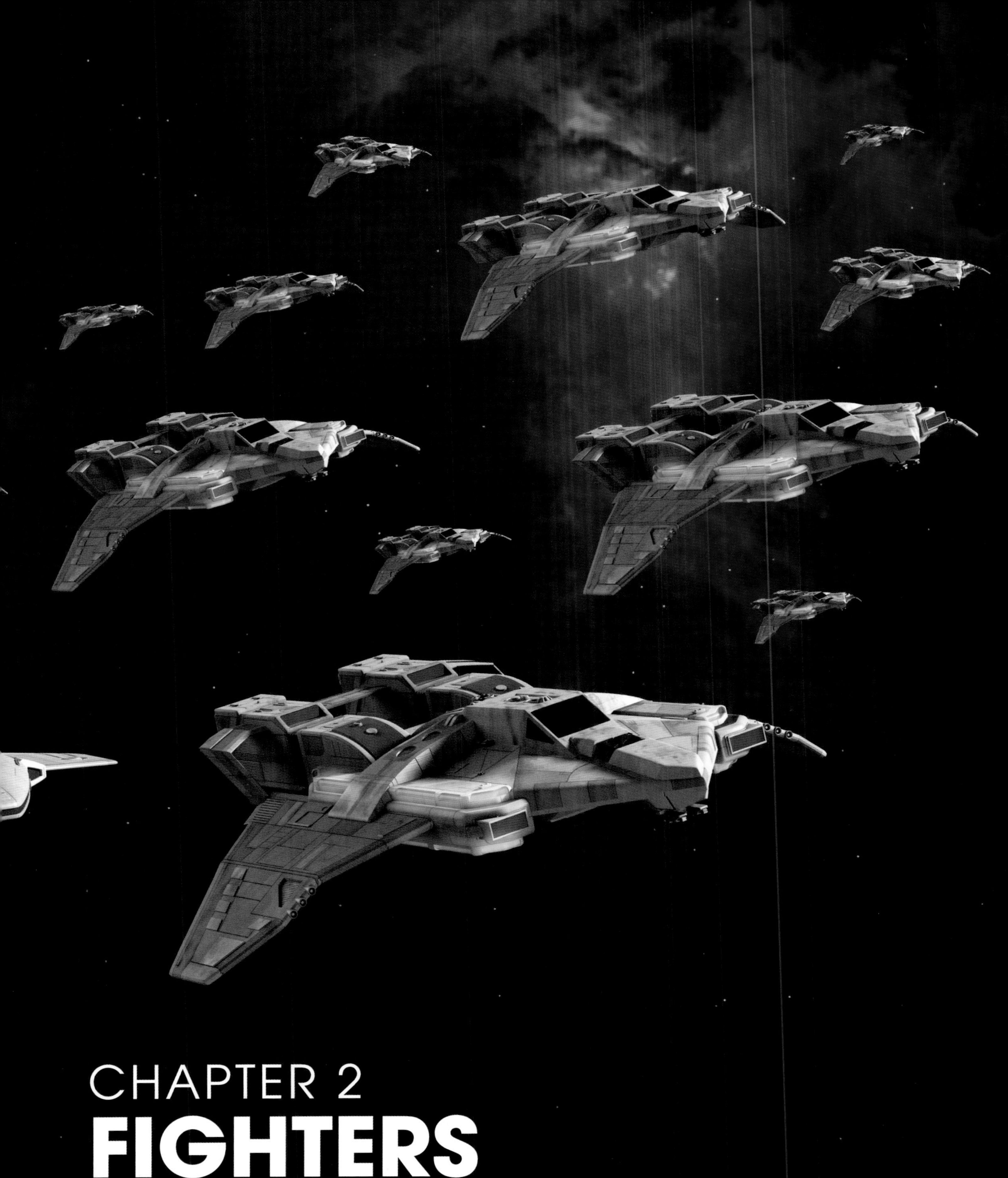

CHAPTER 2
FIGHTERS

The Maquis raider *Val Jean*, under the command of Chakotay, was fitted with a 39-year-old rebuilt engine. This would indicate that by 2371 the raiders were well over 40 years old. Despite their age, they proved highly effective in surprise attacks against the Cardassians.

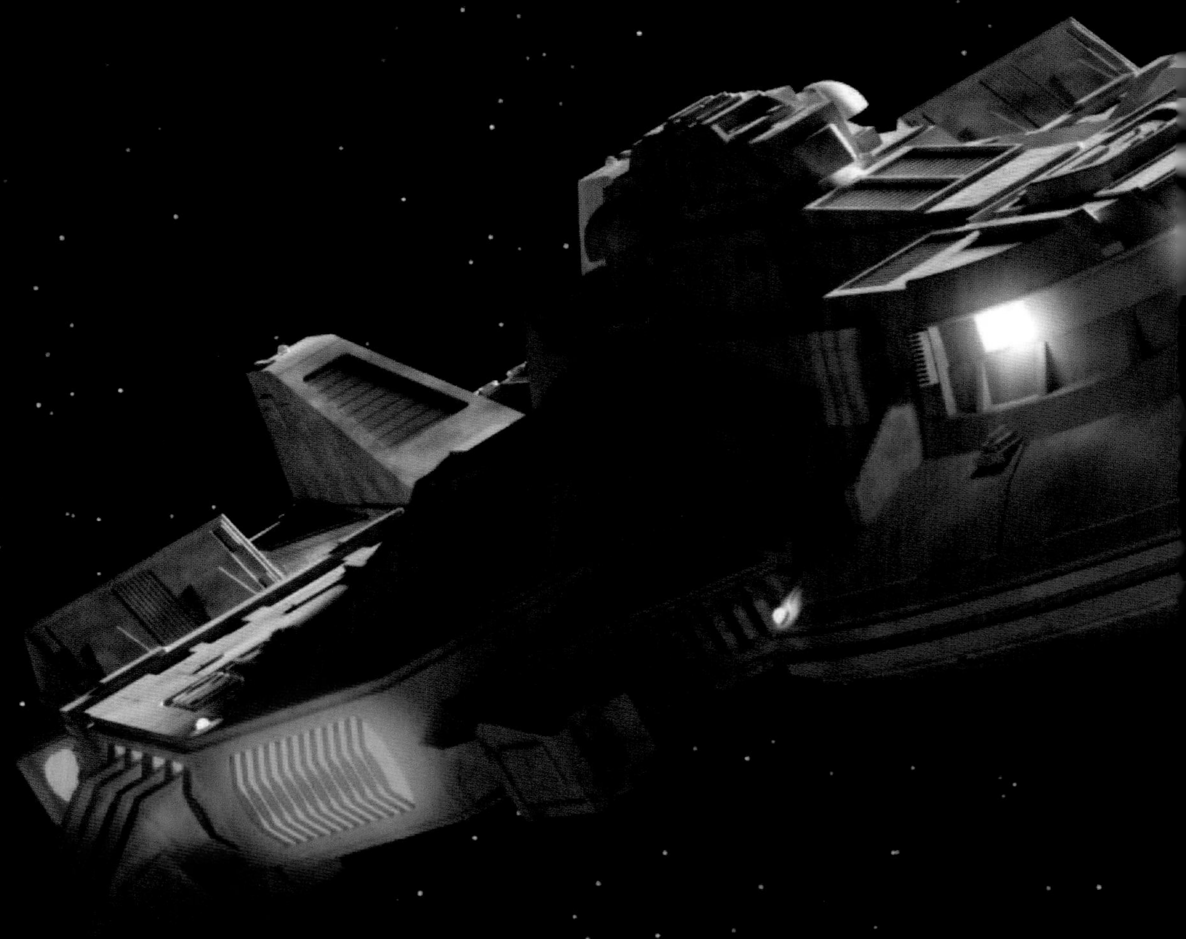

MAQUIS RAIDER

This type of upgraded Federation transport ship served in covert attacks on the Cardassians by Maquis rebels.

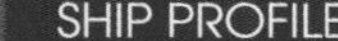

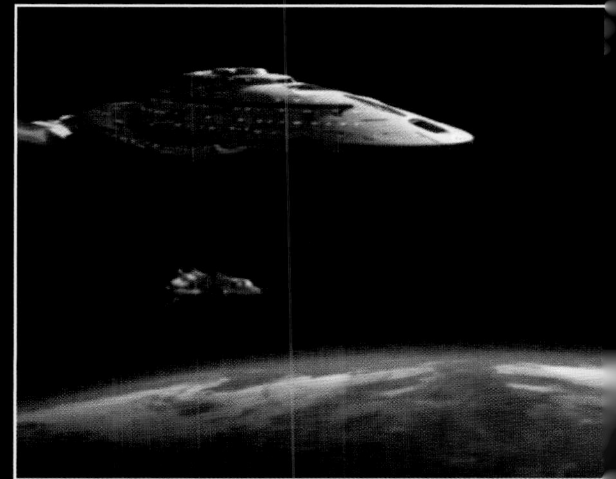

▲ At 68.5 meters long, the Maquis raider was roughly 20 percent the length of the *U.S.S. Voyager* NCC-74656. Unlike the smaller Maquis fighter, the raider had a more pronounced cockpit structure, while the main body was similar to the secondary hull found on *Yeager*-class ships and could accommodate around 30 personnel.

The raiders operated by the Maquis guerrilla network started life as small Federation transport vessels from the early 24th century. In the 2370s, they were heavily modified with enhanced engines and weaponry and used by the Maquis to conduct raids on other starships or bases during their conflict with the Cardassians.

These ships were 68.5 meters long, with a runabout-style bridge at the front and a rear hull similar in appearance to a *Yeager*-class ship. They also featured two small warp nacelles attached to the ends of wing structures on either side of the main body. They were capable of high warp speeds and flight within a planetary atmosphere.

Before these vessels were utilized by the Maquis, they were mostly deployed as cargo or personnel transport. The rear section could hold at least 30 people or a sizable load of cargo, such as medical supplies. They had originally been used by Federation colonists to transfer shipments between worlds and bring supplies to new settlements.

WEAPON UPGRADES

By 2370, these simple Federation transport ships had been appropriated by the Maquis and transformed into raiders. Their engines were rebuilt and extra armaments, including photon torpedo launchers and wingtip phaser cannons, were fitted. They then played a crucial part in the Maquis fight against the Cardassian occupation of the former Federation colonies in the Demilitarized Zone.

Maquis raiders were no match for Cardassian *Galor*-class warships in a straight fight, but they were used for swift, effective strikes on Cardassian freighters and on small Cardassian colonies in order to steal their supplies.

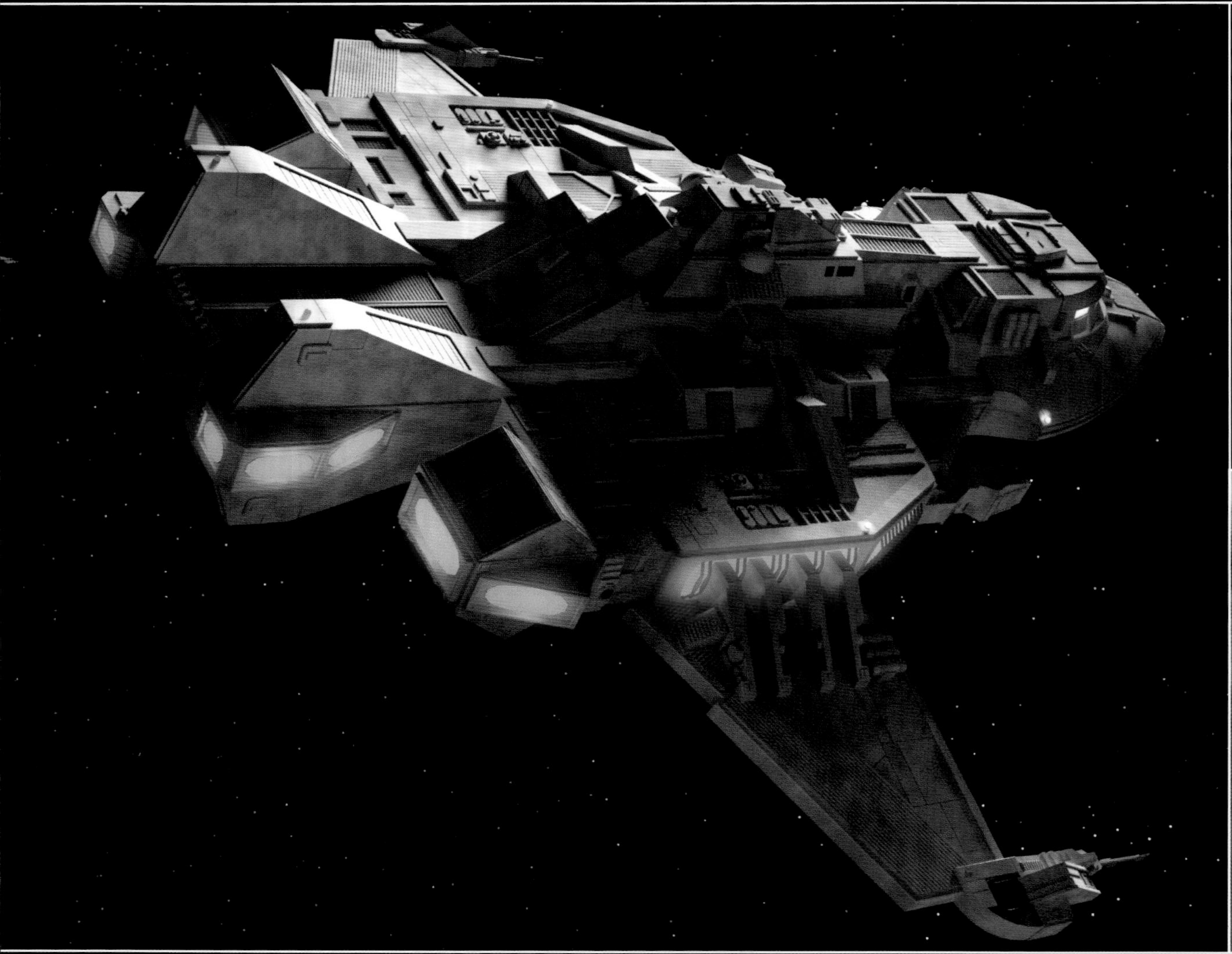

▶ The Maquis outfitted their raiders with wing-mounted phasers, plus fore and aft torpedo launchers. Despite this weaponry, a single raider could barely dent the shields of a Cardassian *Galor*-class warship.

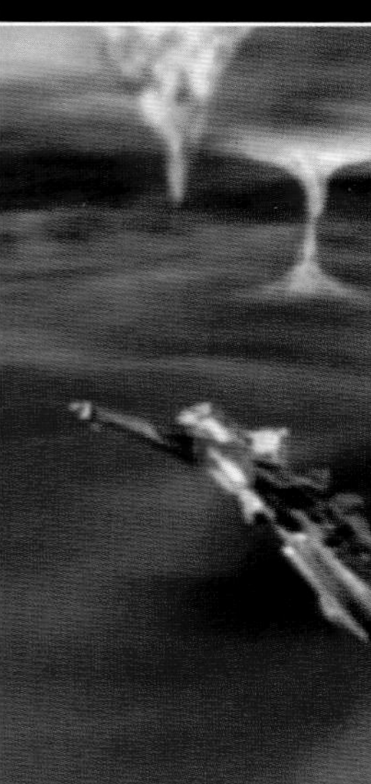

▲ Despite being modified transport vessels, Maquis raiders proved highly effective in conducting precision strikes on starships and bases. They were also used to smuggle vital supplies to Maquis colonies and obtain weaponry through backdoor channels.

One of the reasons why Maquis raiders were so successful was that they were able to take advantage of the Badlands. This region of space between the borders of the Federation and the Cardassian Union was filled with intense plasma storms and gravitational anomalies that severely limited sensor ranges. This meant that the raiders could hide here from Cardassian patrols, especially because the larger Cardassian ships did not have the maneuverability to avoid the unpredictable spatial disturbances in the area.

In 2371, a Maquis cell operating under the command of former Starfleet officer Chakotay was aboard a Maquis raider called the *Val Jean*, when it was pursued into the Badlands by the *Vetar*, a Cardassian *Galor*-class warship. The *Val Jean*'s weapons could make no impression on the *Vetar*'s shields, but the raider was able to evade the plasma streamers inside the Badlands, while the Cardassian ship was hit on the port blade. It seemed the *Val Jean* was about to successfully outrun the *Vetar*, when it was suddenly hit by a massive displacement wave and thrown into the Delta Quadrant.

SHIP SACRIFICE

The *Val Jean* was later destroyed when Chakotay set it on a collision course with a Kazon vessel that was attacking the *U.S.S. Voyager* NCC-74656. Chakotay's actions saved *Voyager*, but it meant his Maquis crew no longer had a ship, so they had little choice but to join *Voyager*'s crew.

While *Voyager* was making its long journey home from the Delta Quadrant, the Maquis in the Alpha Quadrant continued to fight the Cardassian occupation of their homes. In 2373, a number of raiders under the command of former Starfleet officer Michael Eddington launched biogenic

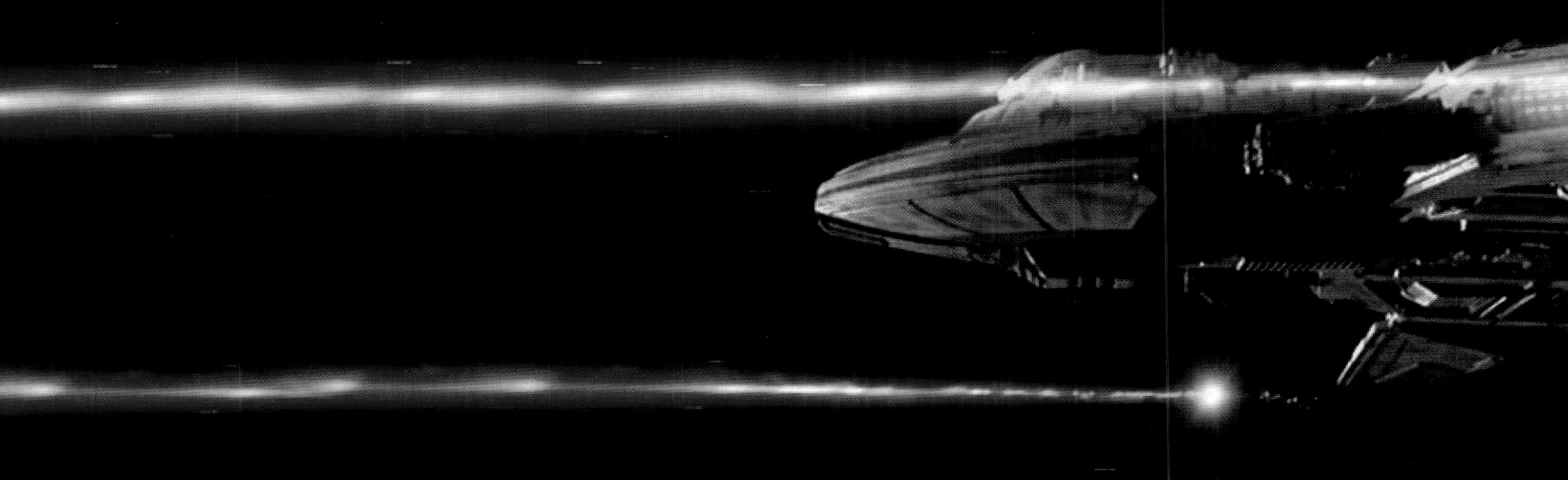

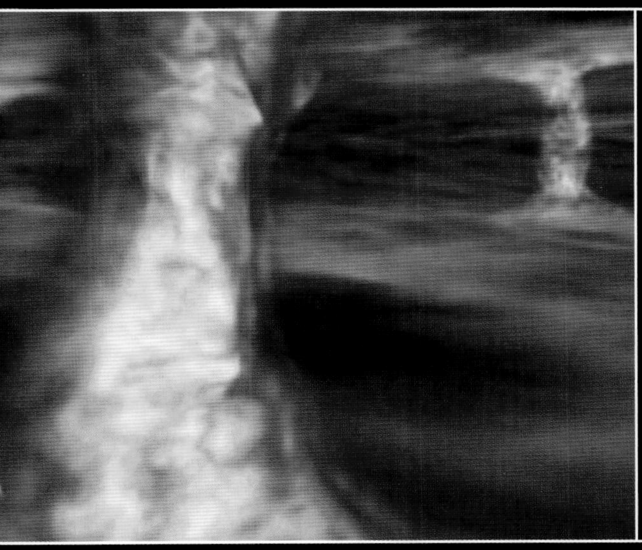

◀ Maquis raiders were highly maneuverable and able to weave between the dangerous gravitational anomalies and plasma streamers that filled the Badlands.

▶ The cockpit of the *Val Jean* had a similar configuration to a *Danube*-class runabout's, with stations for up to four crewmembers. Chakotay's crew was a mixture of former Starfleet officers, colonists, and criminals.

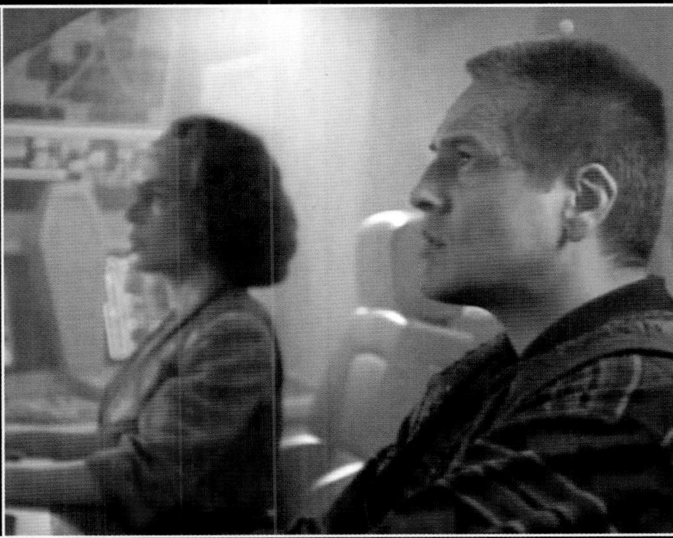

weapon attacks on two Cardassian colonies.

Eddington looked set to drive more Cardassians from their homes until Captain Benjamin Sisko used his own tactics against him. In the atmosphere of a Maquis colony on Solosos III, Sisko detonated a trilithium resin toxin that was lethal to humans but harmless to Cardassians. He then threatened to perform the same action on every Maquis colony in the Demilitarized Zone, unless Eddington turned over his biogenic weapons and surrendered himself to Starfleet.

Despite the setback of Eddington's capture, the Maquis were winning their struggle, mainly because the Klingons had launched a major assault against the Cardassians. The Klingons had also supplied the Maquis with 30 class-4 cloaking devices to mount on their ships.

It appeared to be just a matter of time before the Maquis emerged victorious, when Gul Dukat announced that the Cardassian Union had become a part of the Dominion. Backed by the might of the huge Jem'Hadar fleet, the Cardassians were able to go on the offensive. The ragtag Maquis fleet, comprising mostly raiders and other small fighters, stood little chance, and it was not long before every Maquis colony was wiped out, leaving the rebel group defeated.

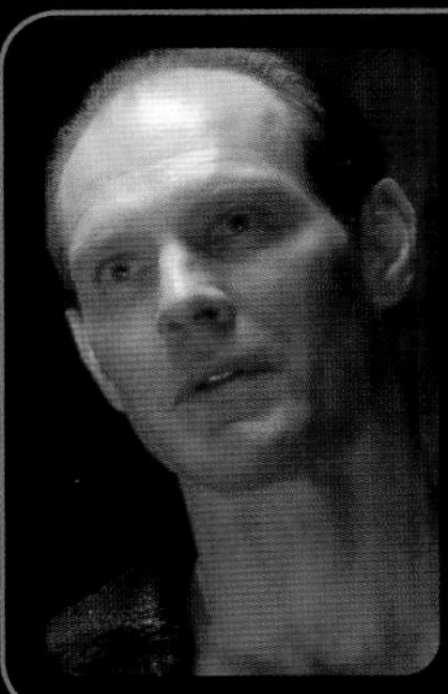

DATA FEED

Michael Eddington, the former chief of Starfleet security aboard Deep Space 9, defected to the Maquis in 2372 and became one of their most important leaders. Captain Benjamin Sisko took his betrayal personally and became obsessed with bringing him to justice. Eddington proved particularly elusive, however, and used a Maquis raider on more than one occasion to evade capture. He later orchestrated biogenic attacks by Maquis raiders on Cardassian colonies.

SUPPLY AND ATTACK

Maquis raiders were often used to smuggle essential goods to former Federation colonists living in the Demilitarized Zone. In 2372, Captain Kasidy Yates' freighter, the *Xhosa*, met with a Maquis raider inside the Badlands to deliver emergency supplies.

Maquis raiders were particularly effective in covert missions, but they could also take on much more powerful vessels by adopting clever tactics. In 2373, the Maquis raider carrying Michael Eddington was able to trigger a cascade computer virus on the *U.S.S. Defiant* NX-74205 that was in pursuit, thus completely disabling it. The raider then strafed the *Defiant* with phaser fire to add to the damage, before escaping into the Badlands.

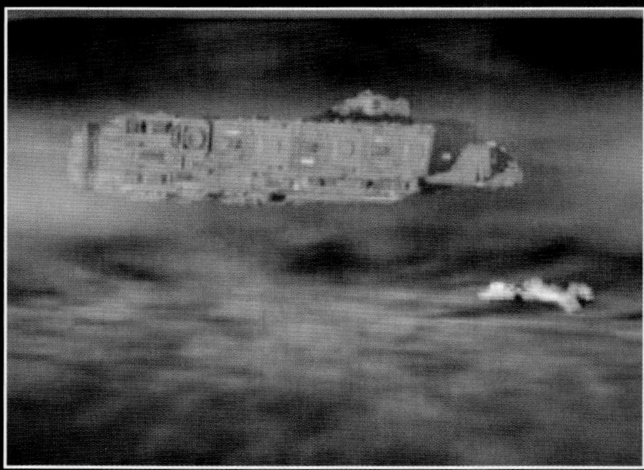

▲ The *Xhosa* rendezvoused with a Maquis raider under the cover of the Badlands, where it handed over food and medical supplies that had been smuggled out of Deep Space 9.

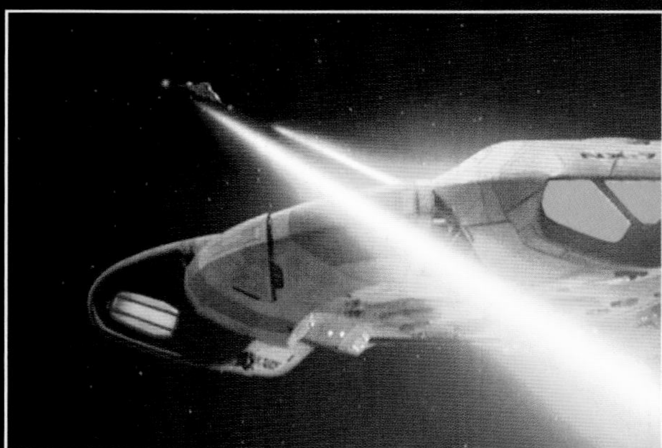

▲ A Maquis raider commanded by Michael Eddington fired on the *U.S.S. Defiant* after he had sent a signal that released a computer virus onboard the Starfleet ship, rendering it completely helpless.

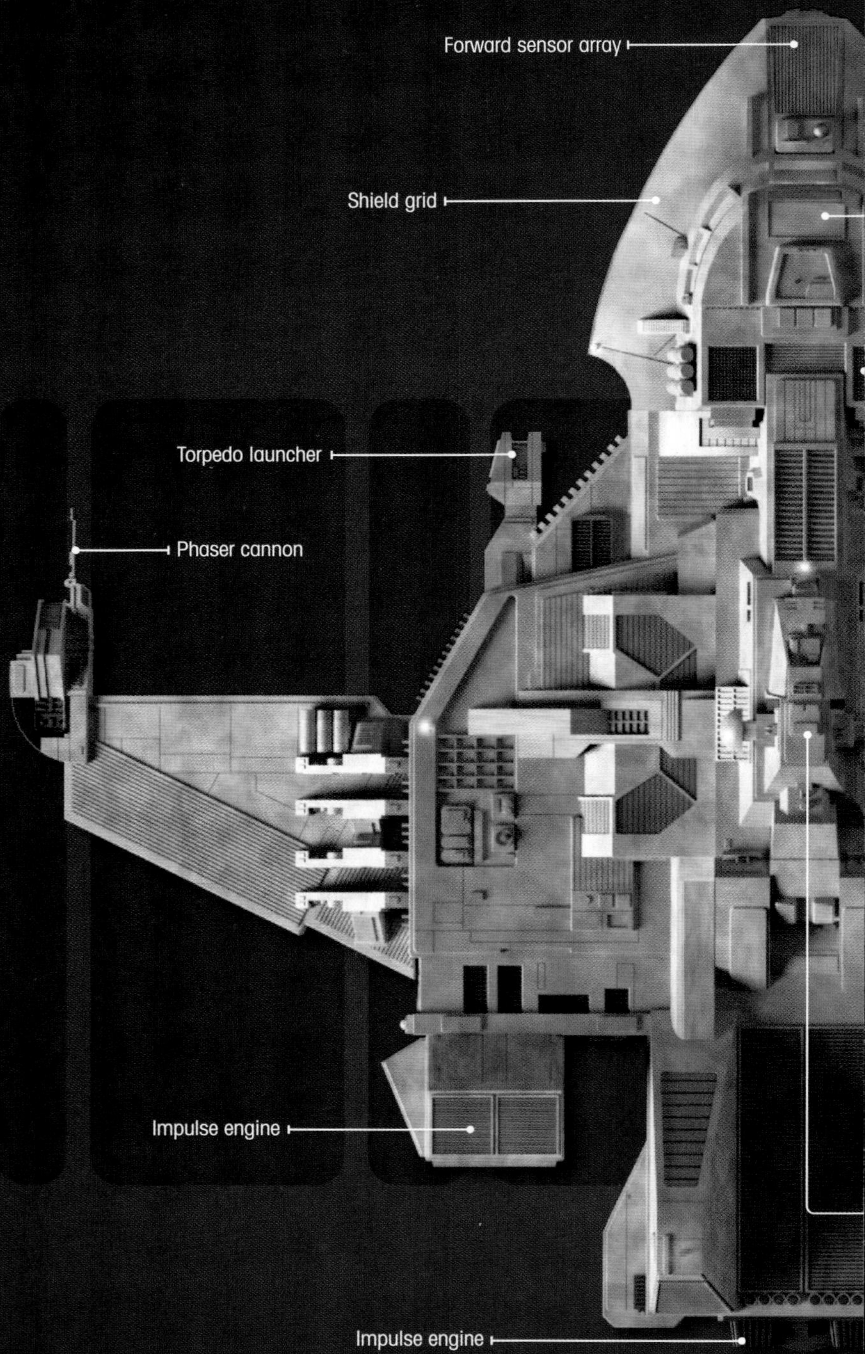

Forward sensor array

Shield grid

Torpedo launcher

Phaser cannon

Impulse engine

Impulse engine

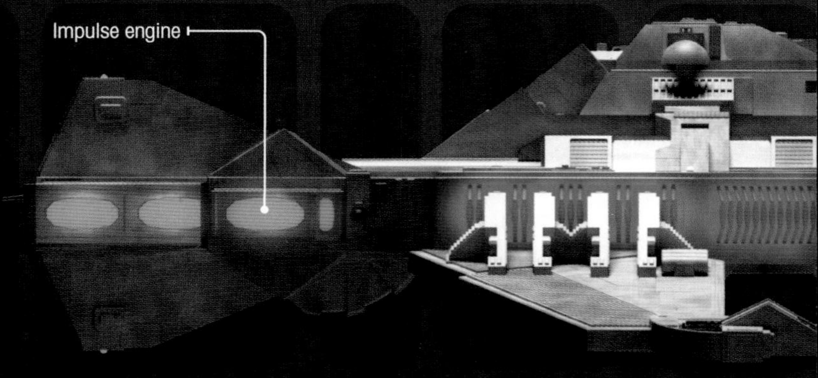

Impulse engine

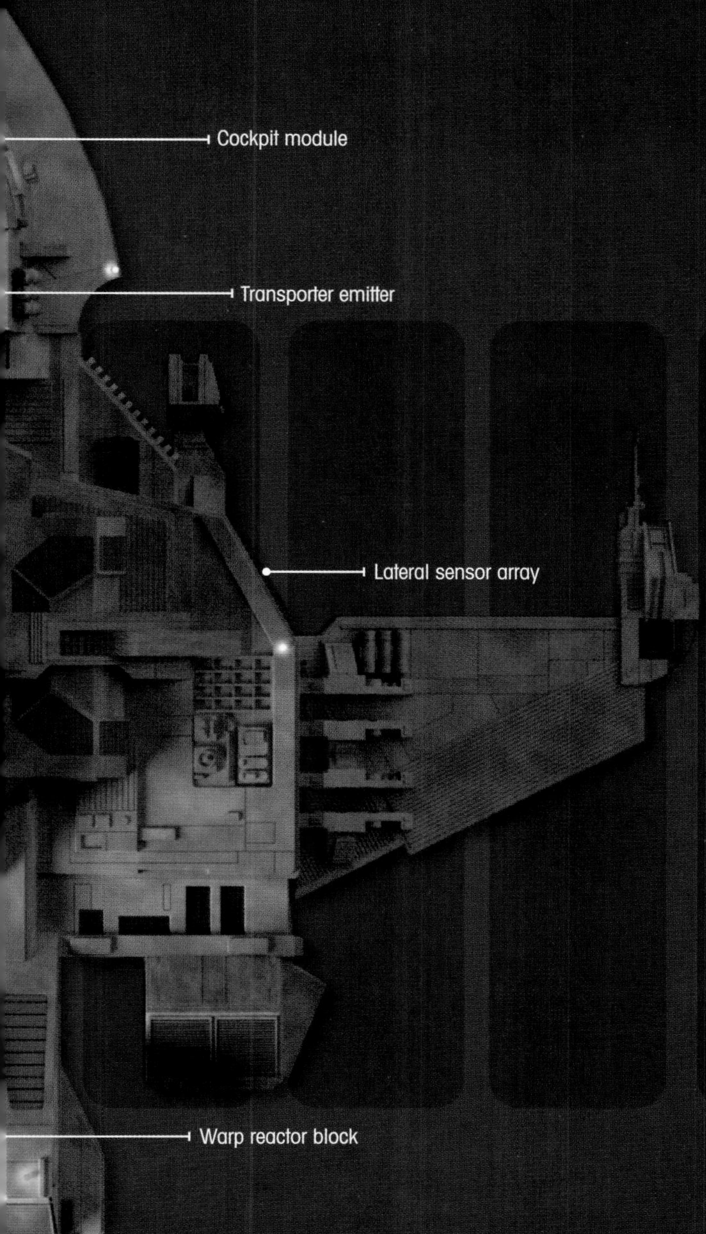

Cockpit module

Transporter emitter

Lateral sensor array

Warp reactor block

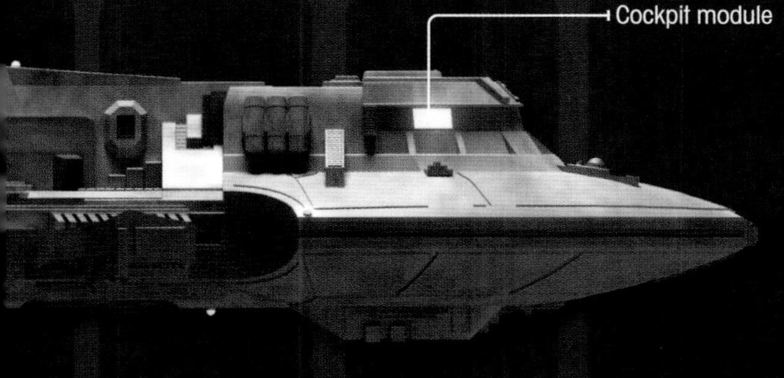

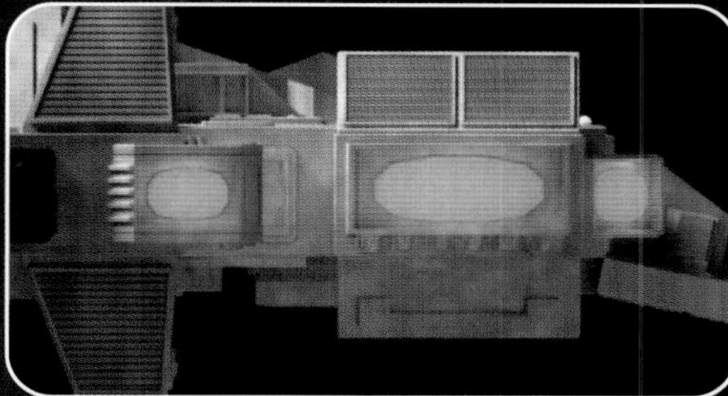

Impulse engines

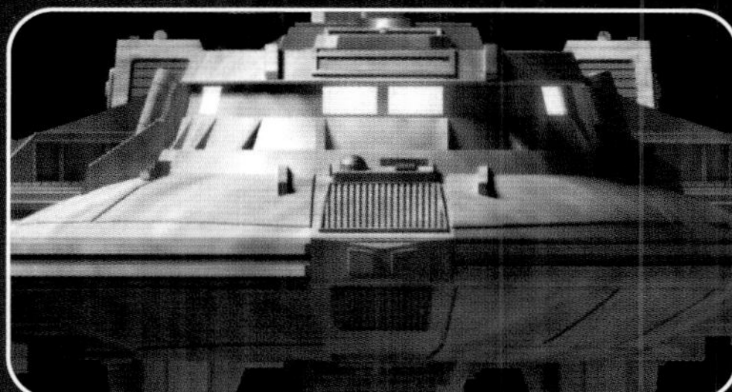

Cockpit module

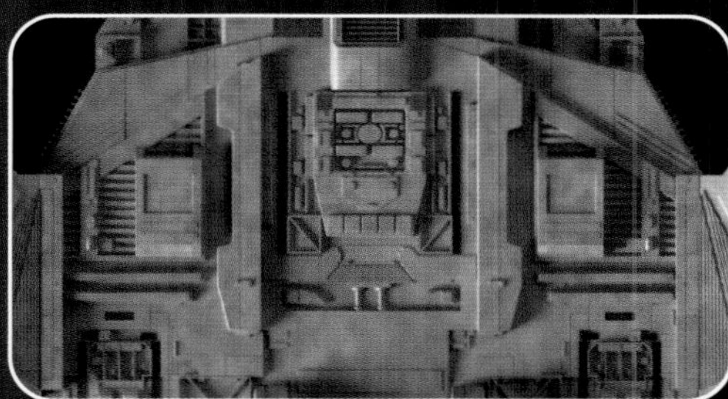

Warp reactor block

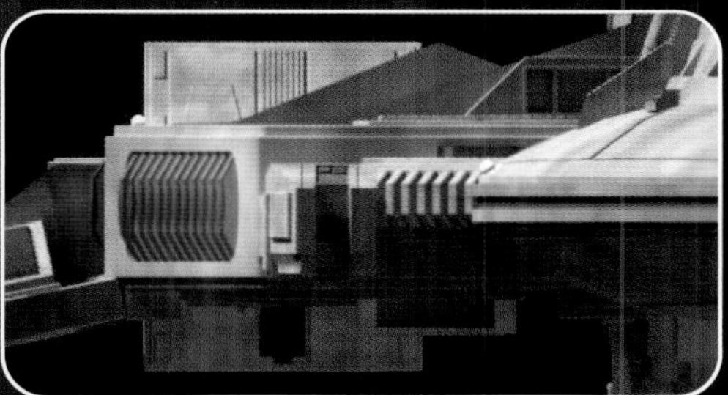

Sensor array

Cockpit module

Phaser cannon

DATA FEED

It was extremely difficult to locate a Maquis raider once it had entered the Badlands, because the spatial disturbances severely limited sensor ranges. It was not impossible, however, since raiders left behind residual neutrino levels that could be tracked.

MAQUIS FLEET

Other vessels that made up the Maquis fleet included Bajoran raiders and interceptors, Federation attack fighters, *Peregrine*-class ships, and Maquis fighters.

CREW NUMBERS

It is not known how many Maquis were aboard the *Val Jean* when it was taken by the Nacene entity, the Caretaker. However, 22 Maquis crewmembers were referred to by name during the *U.S.S. Voyager*'s journey.

ILLEGAL ARMS

The Maquis generally had to arm their ships with whatever weapons they could steal or procure on the black market. These included photon torpedoes, pulse cannons, high-energy disruptors, and particle accelerators.

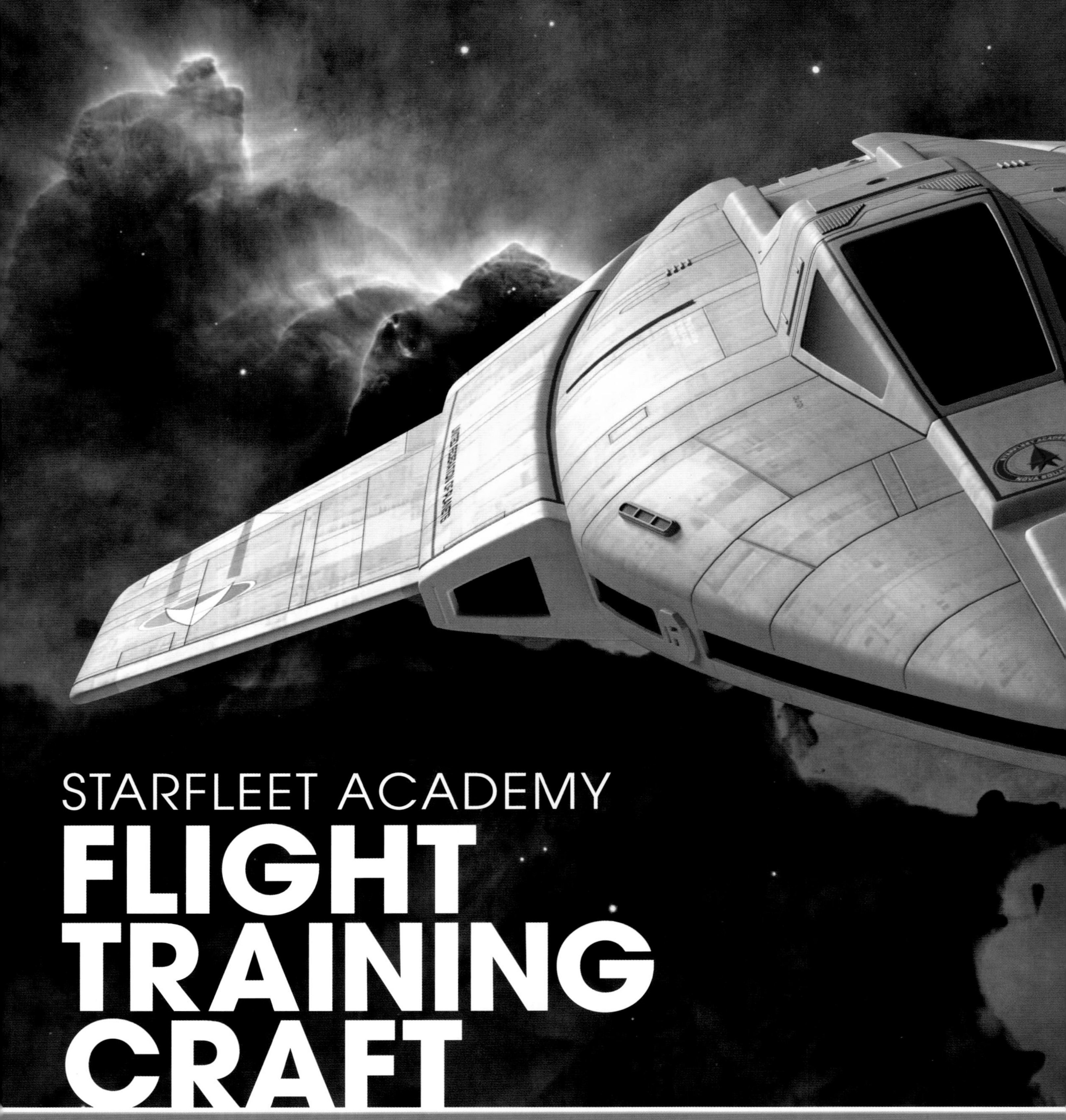

STARFLEET ACADEMY FLIGHT TRAINING CRAFT

During the 24th century, Starfleet cadets learned flying skills and battle maneuvers at the controls of nimble training craft.

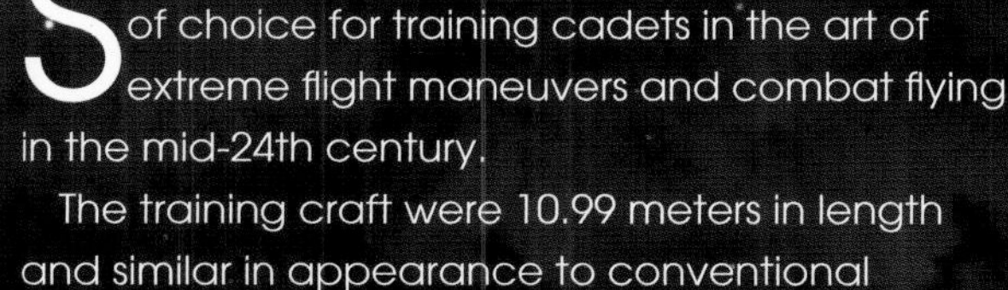

◀ The Academy training craft were sleek and aerodynamic, since they had to operate in the atmosphere of a planet as well as in space. Cadets often practiced flying the ships on the Academy flight range near Saturn, where they learned more complex maneuvers.

Small, sublight ships were Starfleet's vessels of choice for training cadets in the art of extreme flight maneuvers and combat flying in the mid-24th century.

The training craft were 10.99 meters in length and similar in appearance to conventional atmospheric aircraft. They featured short, forward-swept, stubby wings, a pointed nose, and a glass canopy surrounding the pilot's position.

They were designed for both atmospheric and space flight and were extremely agile. Equipped only with impulse engines and thrusters, these ships were not able to achieve warp flight and normally flew at speeds of around 80,000 kph. They were also equipped with landing struts for touchdown on planetary surfaces, and with proximity alarms and emergency transporters.

COCKPIT LAYOUT

The training craft were normally operated by just one pilot, but could accommodate a second person or an instructor if necessary. Instrumentation included various computer readouts showing speed, course, g-forces, and sensor information.

These craft gave cadets a practical education in the art of aerobatics, while also teaching them the fundamentals of starship operations. Students had to learn such disciplines as astrophysics and navigation, subjects that they would need once they had completed their training and were assigned to a starship.

Cadets who excelled during flight exercises were picked to join an elite flight team at Starfleet

◀ Former ensign of the *U.S.S. Enterprise* NCC-1701-D Wesley Crusher was accepted to Starfleet Academy in 2367. He excelled at flight training and soon became a member of the elite Nova Squadron. During a flight display to mark their graduation ceremony, an accident occurred which cost a cadet his life, and Wesley broke his arm.

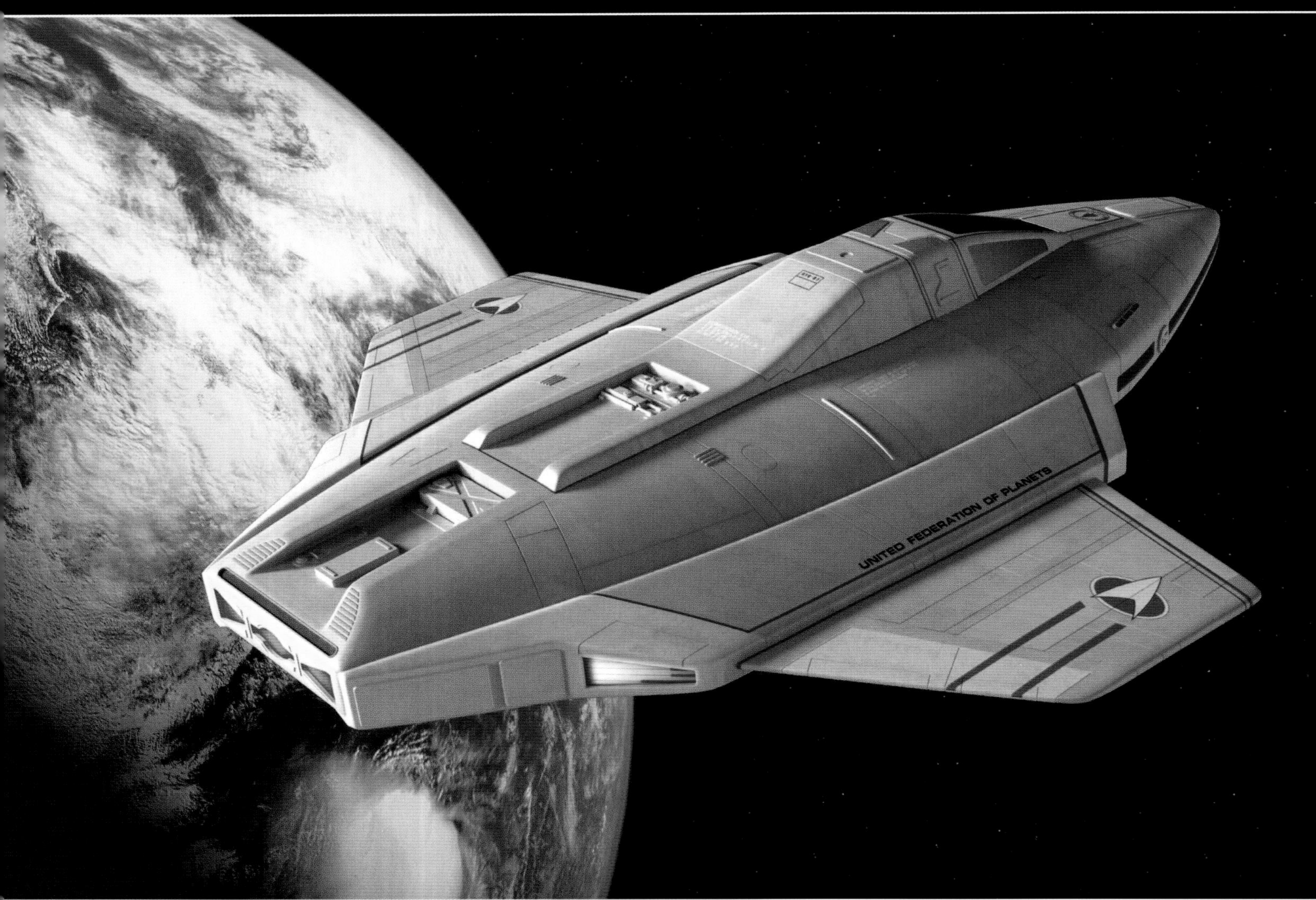

▲ The training craft had a fairly flat cross-section and short wings. They were designed for performing complex aerobatic maneuvers at speeds of at least 80,000 kph. These craft taught cadets not only the rudiments of flying, but also what was possible when they were pushed to extremes.

Academy. This was an extremely prestigious position, much like making the football team at a traditional college, and only the most gifted and accomplished cadets were chosen.

These cadets went on to learn and perform various complex formations and maneuvers as a demonstration of their flight prowess. Other students looked up to these cadets, and cheered them on when they competed against other flight schools in competitions such as the Rigel Cup.

In 2368, Wesley Crusher, a former ensign aboard the *U.S.S. Enterprise* NCC-1701-D, was part of Nova Squadron, one of the elite flying teams at Starfleet Academy. This five-person team also included Nicholas Locarno, Jean Hajar, Joshua Albert, and Sito Jaxa, a Bajoran. Together they had achieved almost legendary status at the Academy by winning the Rigel Cup, which resulted in celebrations that, according to groundskeeper Mr. Boothby, made the parrises squares champion celebrations of 2324 look like a dinner party.

Driven by the ambition of their leader Locarno, Nova Squadron planned to put on a flight show – scheduled to be transmitted at the graduation ceremony of 2368 – that no one would forget. That was exactly what they achieved, but unfortunately for all the wrong reasons.

TRAGIC OUTCOME

During practice for the flight demonstration, there was an accident that cost the life of one of the pilots: Joshua Albert. The other members of Nova Squadron managed to transport to safety and survived, although Wesley suffered second-degree burns and multiple fractures of his arm.

At first, all the surviving Nova Squadron pilots said they could not understand how the accident had happened. They were flying in close formation

▶ Nova Squadron practiced on the Academy flight range, which was located near Saturn. They were in close formation here when a collision occurred that destroyed all five ships.

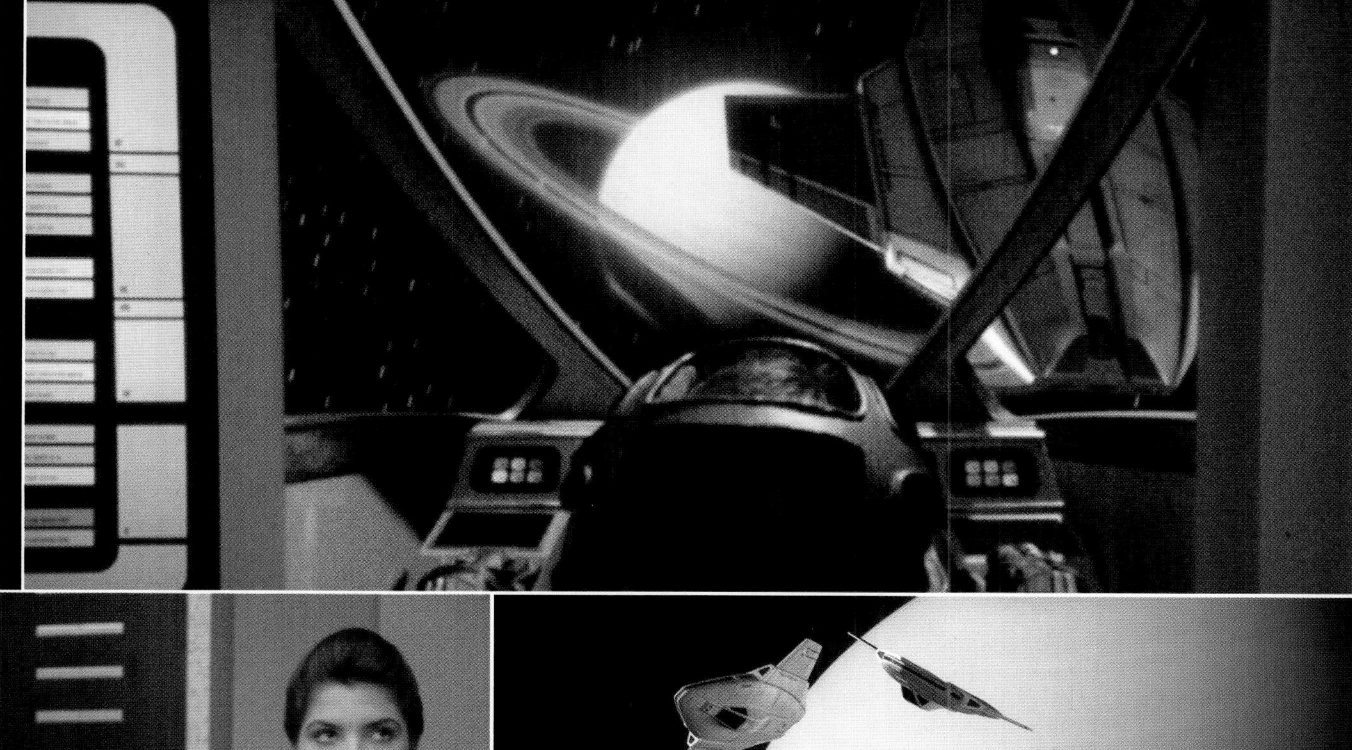

▼ Sito Jaxa and Jean Hajar were also part of Nova Squadron. Like Wesley, they looked up to their team leader, Nicholas Locarno, and were prepared to do anything he told them to keep their team together.

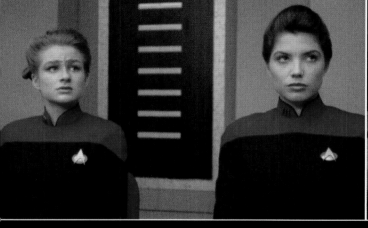

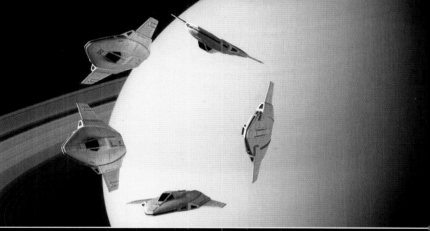

on the Academy flight range near Saturn when the collision occurred.

Only one of the ships' data recorders was recovered, but this did not reveal what had happened at the moment of the crash. Locarno claimed that they were preparing for a maneuver known as the Yeager loop when Albert's ship collided with Hajar's. They had less than two seconds to perform an emergency beam out to the evac station on Mimas, one of Saturn's moons, but Albert did not make it.

It was only when Captain Picard looked into the matter that the truth emerged. He deduced that the squadron were trying to perform a maneuver known as the Kolvoord Starburst. This stunt required great precision and was very dangerous. In fact, it had not been performed for more than a century, because the last time it had been attempted, all five participating cadets had died.

In the end, Wesley's guilty conscience led him to tell the truth at the inquest. Locarno was expelled from the Academy, but in an impassioned plea he stated that he alone had convinced the others to try the Kolvoord maneuver, and that it was his idea to cover up the truth. He sacrificed himself to save the rest of the squadron, and Wesley and the others were allowed to remain at the Academy.

▲ To prove their piloting prowess, cadets performed aerobatic maneuvers in close formation. While these looked impressive, the exercises were not about showing off, but prepared cadets for combat flying.

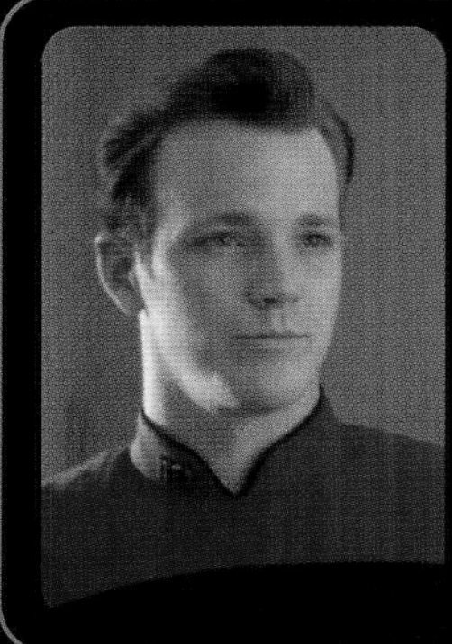

DATA FEED

Cadet First Class Nicholas Locarno headed up Nova Squadron. Confident, charismatic, and seemingly a born leader, he inspired complete trust and loyalty in his fellow cadets. But he was hugely ambitious. He persuaded his squadron to perform the prohibited Kolvoord Starburst maneuver, so they would become legends at the Academy. When it led to a death, Locarno tried to persuade his copilots to cover up what had really happened.

KOLVOORD STARBURST

The Kolvoord Starburst was the name given to a spectacular but highly dangerous aerobatic space maneuver.

Five training craft were needed to execute the display. They began by arranging themselves in a circular formation, flying extremely close together. They then burst out simultaneously in different directions, igniting their plasma trails in their wake. This produced a spectacular "starburst" effect, for which the maneuver was named.

The display was certainly impressive, but a decision had been taken to ban it after five cadets had died in attemping the stunt. Despite knowing this, Nova Squadron leader Nicholas Locarno was determined to repeat the attempt and persuaded his team to take part, even though they were not given official authorization.

The squadron found out firsthand just how dangerous it was when their training craft collided during the maneuver, and all five ships were destroyed. Four team members managed to use their emergency transporters just in time and beam to safety, but Joshua Albert died in the accident.

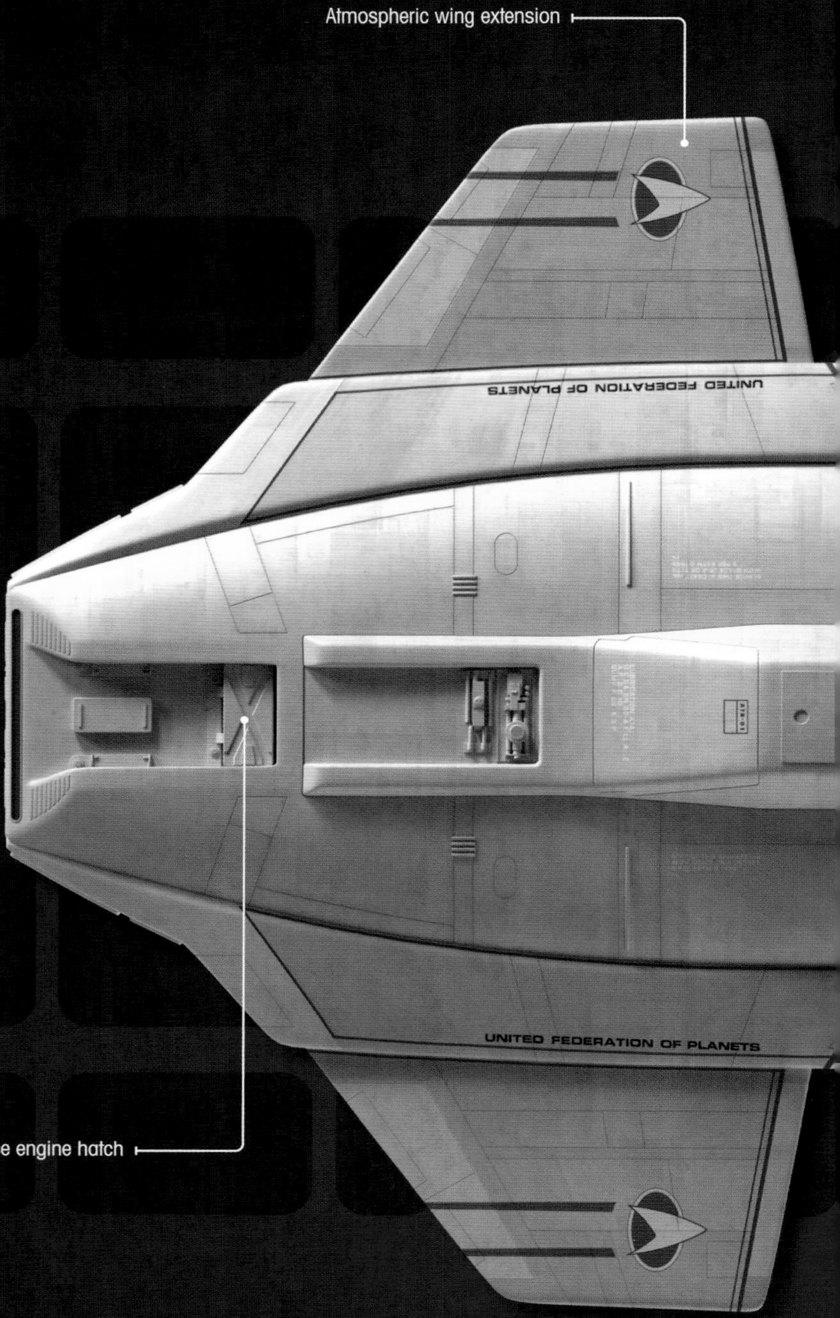

Atmospheric wing extension

UNITED FEDERATION OF PLANETS

UNITED FEDERATION OF PLANETS

Impulse engine hatch

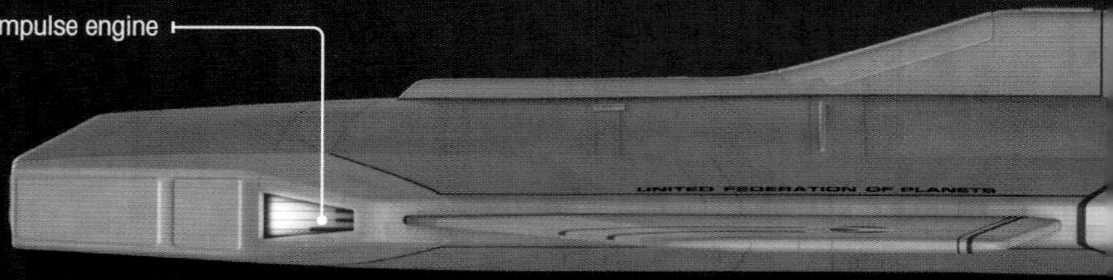

Impulse engine

UNITED FEDERATION OF PLANETS

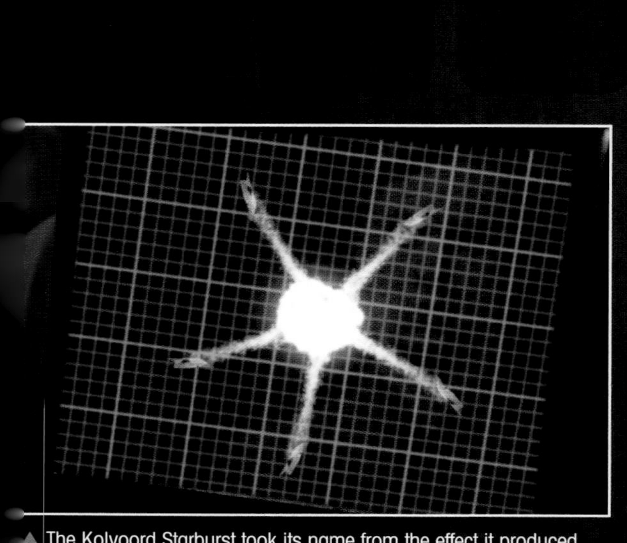

▲ The Kolvoord Starburst took its name from the effect it produced when five ships came together before flying apart with their plasma trails ignited, creating a dazzling, neon-white star shape in space.

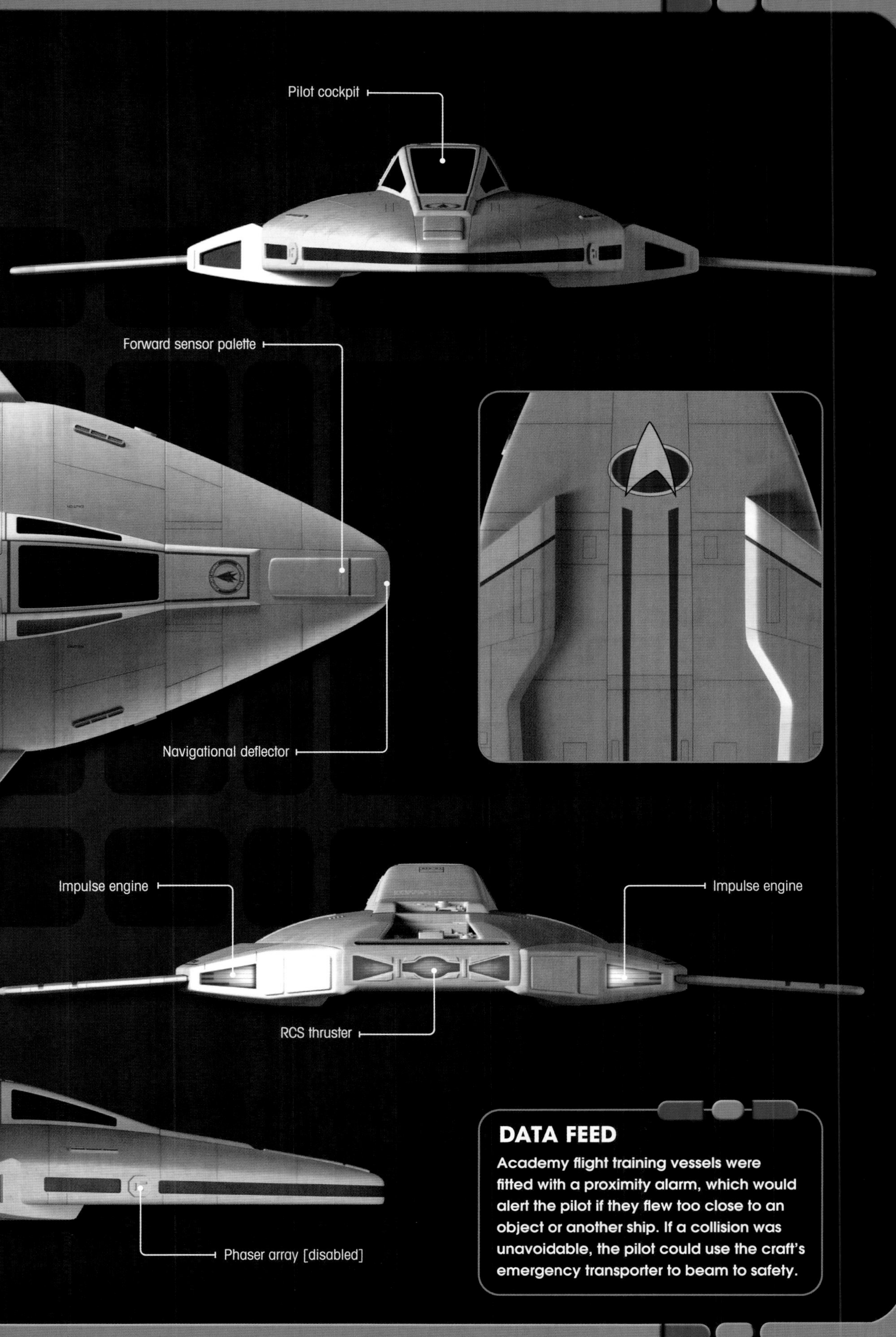

DATA FEED

Academy flight training vessels were fitted with a proximity alarm, which would alert the pilot if they flew too close to an object or another ship. If a collision was unavoidable, the pilot could use the craft's emergency transporter to beam to safety.

LATIN GRAMMAR

The Starfleet Academy logo featured the Latin phrase *Ex Astra, Scientia*. This was grammatically incorrect and was later updated to *Ex Astris, Scientia,* meaning 'From the stars, knowledge.'

SECOND CHANCE

Sito Jaxa, the Bajoran member of Nova Squadron, was later assigned to the *U.S.S. Enterprise* NCC-1701-D at the request of Captain Picard, because he wanted to make sure she had a fair chance to redeem herself.

SQUAD TROUBLE

In addition to Nova Squadron, Starfleet Academy operated an elite group of cadets known as Red Squad. In 2372, some Red Squad cadets unwittingly aided Admiral Leyton's coup attempt on Earth's government, by disabling the global power grid in Lisbon.

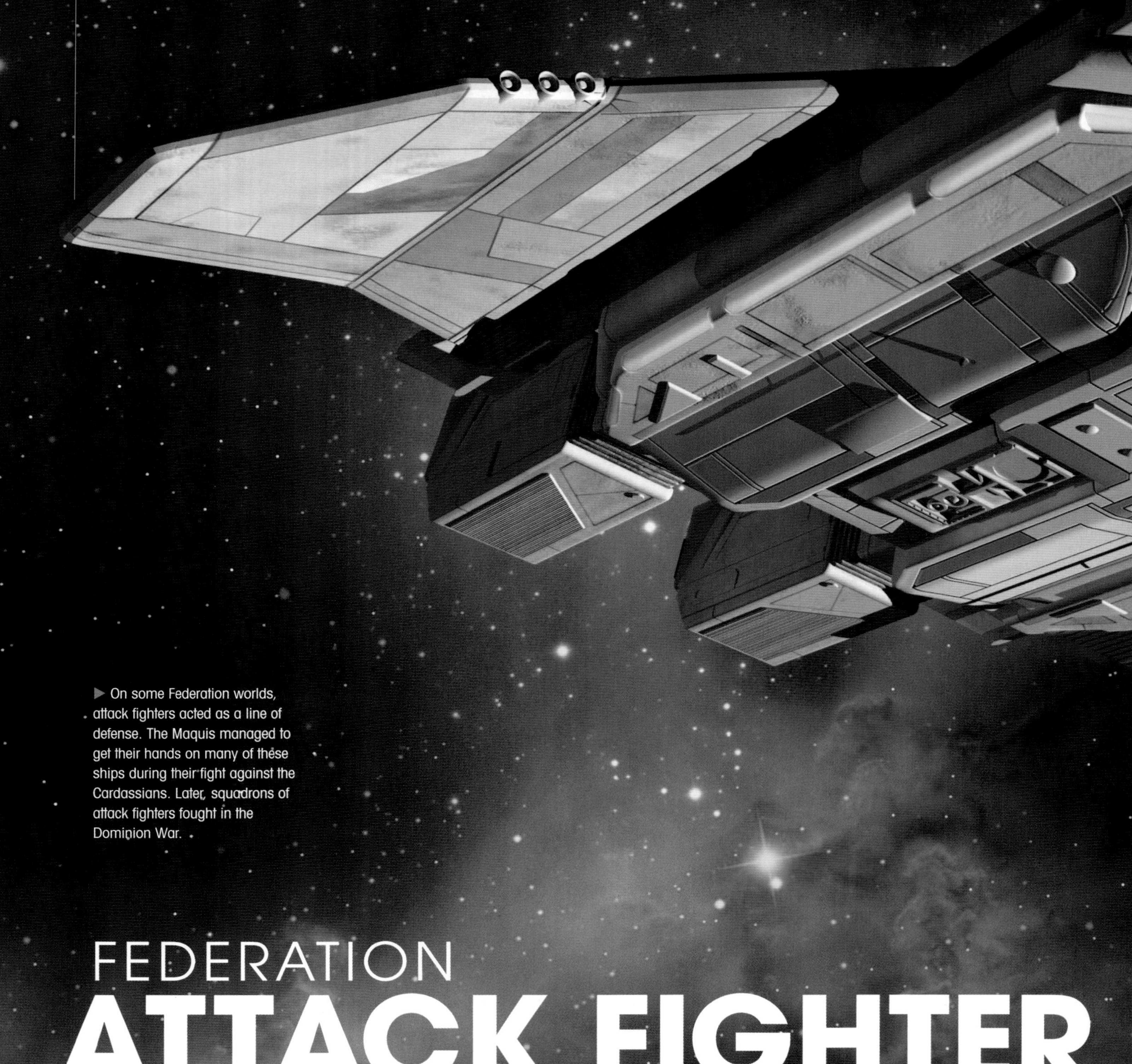

▶ On some Federation worlds, attack fighters acted as a line of defense. The Maquis managed to get their hands on many of these ships during their fight against the Cardassians. Later, squadrons of attack fighters fought in the Dominion War.

FEDERATION ATTACK FIGHTER

These versatile combat craft could be configured to fire a wide range of weaponry and were key to recapturing Deep Space 9.

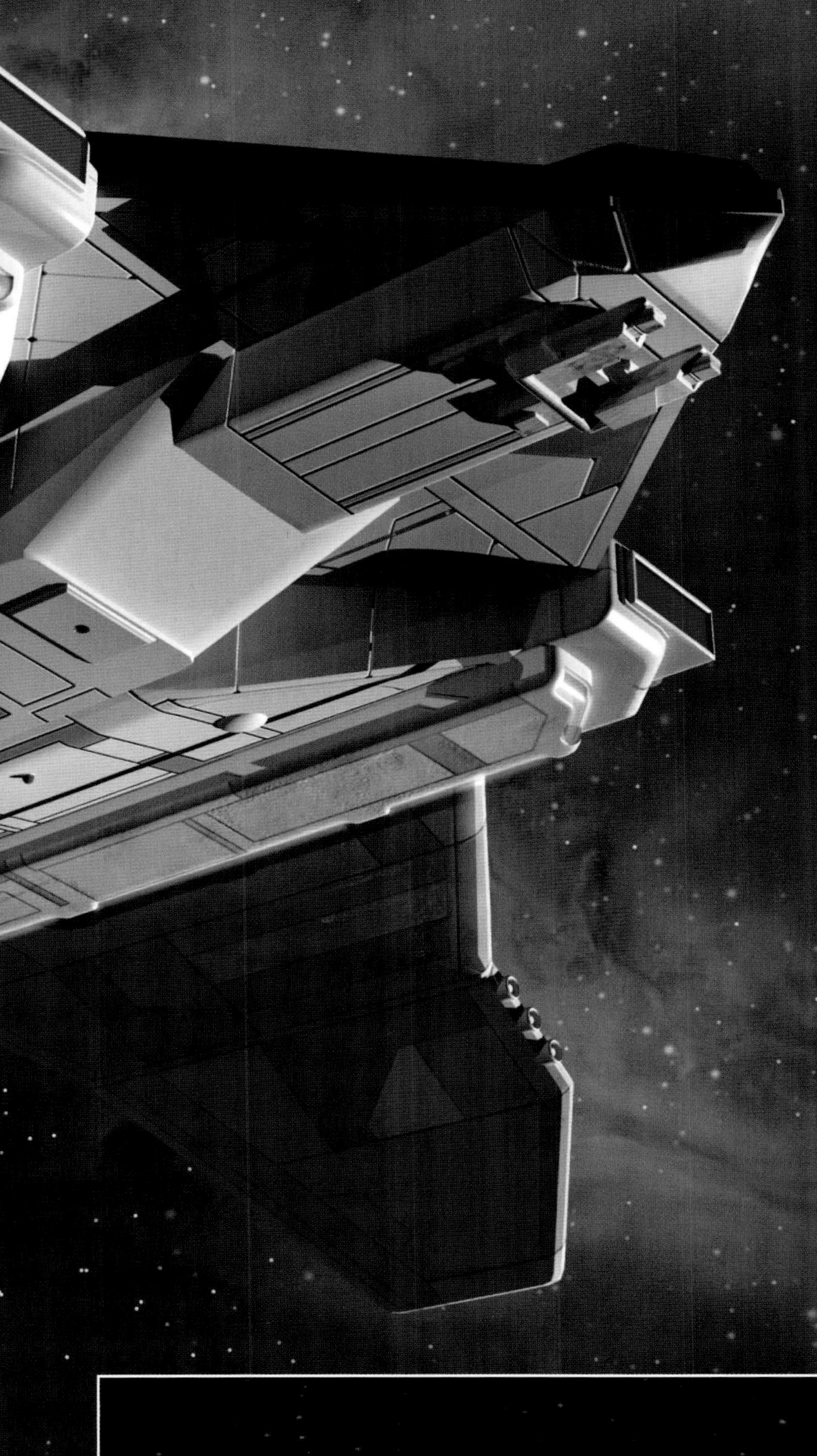

This small, highly maneuverable starship packed a powerful punch for its size. It was warp capable and performed a defensive role on Federation worlds in the mid- to late 24th century. Many were later appropriated by the Maquis for their insurrection against the Cardassians, and in the mid-2370s, Starfleet employed these vessels in squadrons in the fight against the Dominion and their allies.

In appearance, the Federation attack fighter was much more like a suborbital aircraft. It featured downward-swept gull wings and two impulse engines fixed to a spar at the rear. These fixtures indicated that the vessels were designed for both atmospheric and space flight. Certainly they were capable of extreme aerobatic-style maneuvers, making them difficult to hit while carrying out attacks.

PROTECTED PROPULSION

The fighters possessed warp engines, while inboard warp nacelles were located between the main body of the ship and the wings. As the nacelles were protected, it was more difficult for enemy craft to target their propulsion units.

Despite being approximately 25 meters in length, attack fighters could be armed with a formidable array of weaponry. This included pulse cannons in the wings, energy disruptors, particle accelerators, and photon torpedoes. These weapons, together with the ships' deflector shields, meant attack fighters posed a considerable threat, especially

◀ Federation attack fighters featured an impressive arsenal, which included pulse cannons, phaser emitters, and torpedo launchers. They could also be retrofitted to fire third-party weapons. For example, in 2370, the Maquis engineered them to fire weapons provided by the Pygorians, including particle accelerators and high-energy disruptors.

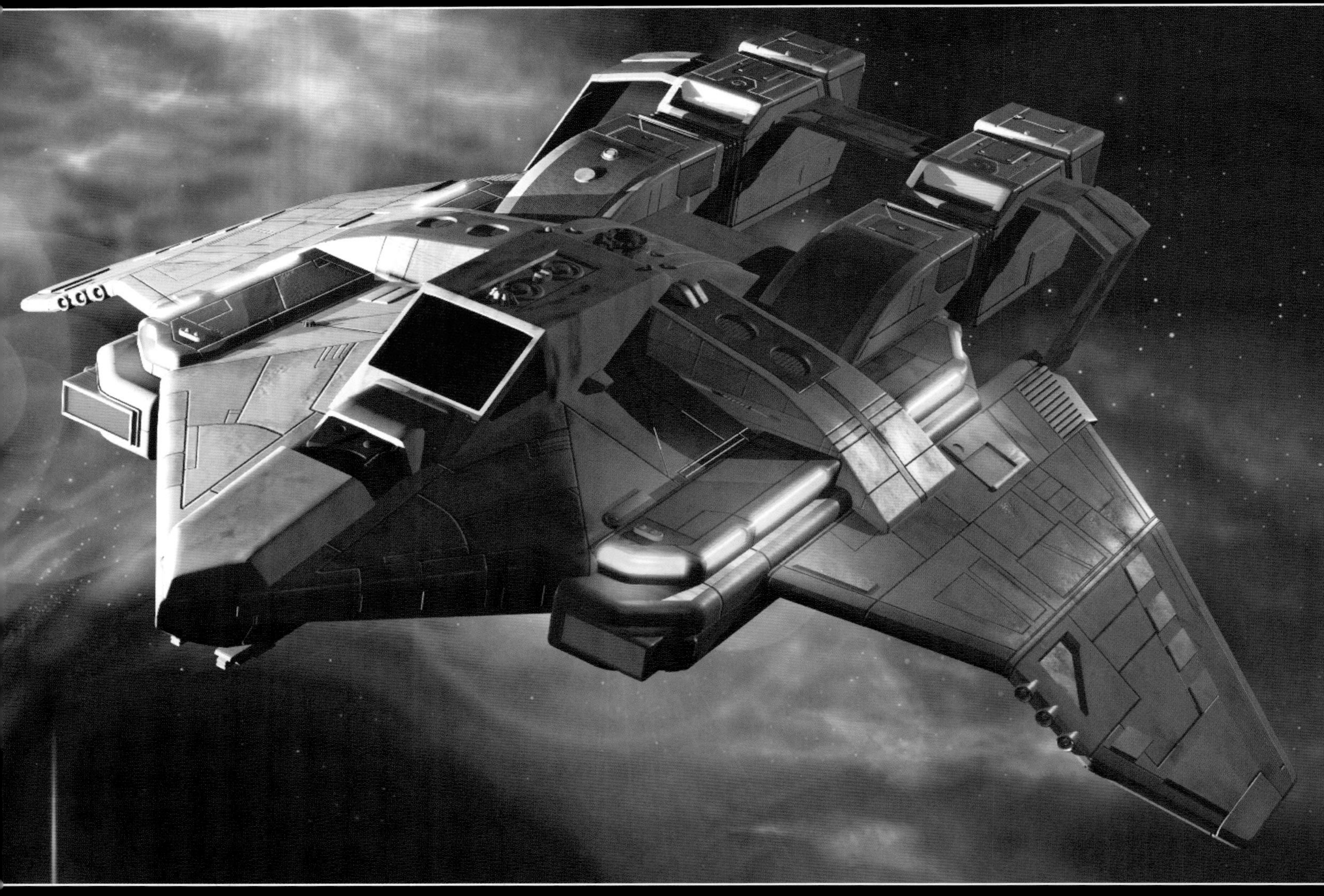

▲ The overall design of the attack fighter resembled an atmospheric aircraft more than a spaceship. The wings provided added stability for extreme flight maneuvers, making it hard to target in combat situations. Its warp nacelles were enclosed within the main body, in much the same way as they were on the *Defiant* class, helping to keep them protected.

when they launched a coordinated assault in numbers. By attacking in formation, the ships were capable of disabling or destroying much larger opponents.

The cockpit of an attack fighter was very similar to the layout on Starfleet shuttles, and normally contained just two seats for the pilot and copilot. At the rear of the cramped space was a single transporter pad.

By 2370, a number of Federation attack fighters had been stolen by the Maquis to assist in their fight against the Cardassians. The Maquis resistance had to use any means at their disposal to arm the attack ships, and with Quark as a go-between, they obtained weapons from the Pygorians. These black market goods included deflector shields, navigation arrays, pulse cannons, and energy disruptors, which could all be modified to work on the attack fighters.

Calvin Hudson, a former Starfleet officer turned Maquis leader, planned to use two attack fighters to carry out a strike against the Bryma colony, a world that the Maquis believed was being used as a weapons depot by the Cardassians. Commander Benjamin Sisko learned of this imminent attack and managed to put a stop to it using three runabouts, but Hudson and his colleagues got away.

TARGETING THE CARDASSIANS

Later in 2370, Gul Evek's *Galor*-class vessel came under assault from several Federation fighters deployed by the Maquis. According to Evek, these attack ships were armed with photon torpedoes and type-8 phasers. The Cardassian ship would surely have been destroyed, had not the *U.S.S. Enterprise* NCC-1701-D come to its rescue and driven off the fighters.

▶ The Maquis managed to acquire several attack fighters to aid their uprising against the Cardassians. They used two closely related designs; Lieutenant Ro's version featured a larger central cockpit.

▼ The interior of an attack fighter was small, with room for only two occupants. It had space at the rear for a single transporter pad, which Ro used to beam medical supplies aboard.

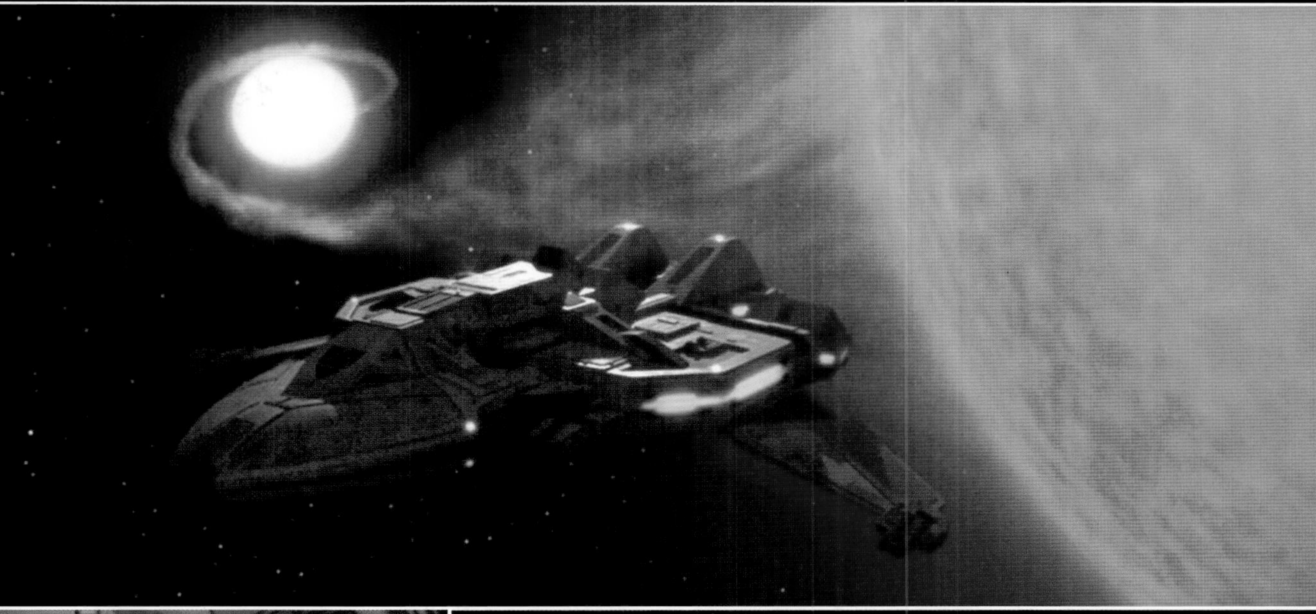

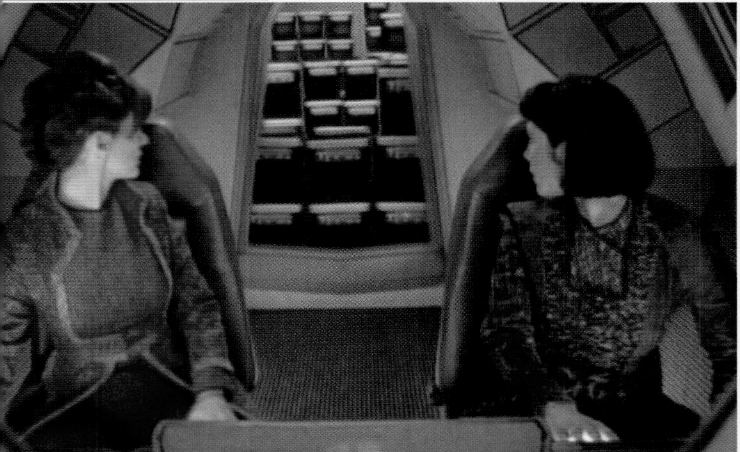

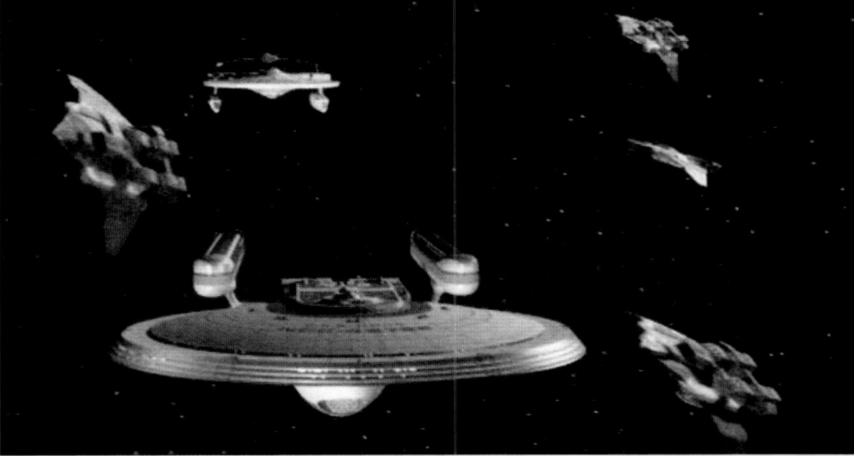

At around the same time, it was decided that more had to be done to stop the Maquis, and Lieutenant Ro Laren was tasked with infiltrating one of their resistance cells. To gain the trust of the Maquis, Ro staged a raid by an attack fighter on the *Enterprise* and stole medical supplies.

Later, Ro was supposed to lure a Maquis cell into a trap set by Starfleet. She was to lead several attack fighters in a raid against a Cardassian convoy presumed to be carrying components for a biogenic weapon. The plan was that a Starfleet force would ambush them as the attack began, but in the end Ro's sympathies lay with the Maquis. She exposed the Starfleet vessels that were lying in wait, and the attack fighters turned back at the last minute, so the Maquis could live to fight another day, with Ro by their side.

By 2374, Federation attack fighters were being deployed by Starfleet against the Dominion and its allies. During "Operation Return," squadrons of fighters gathered in a concerted effort to take back control of Deep Space 9. Eight successive waves of fighters were unleashed to attack Cardassian ships. The aim was to provoke them into breaking formation, thereby creating an opening through which larger Starfleet ships could advance toward Deep Space 9.

▲ In the battle to regain Deep Space 9 from the Dominion, Starfleet used several squadrons of attack fighters, alongside larger ships, to try and force a break in the lines of enemy vessels.

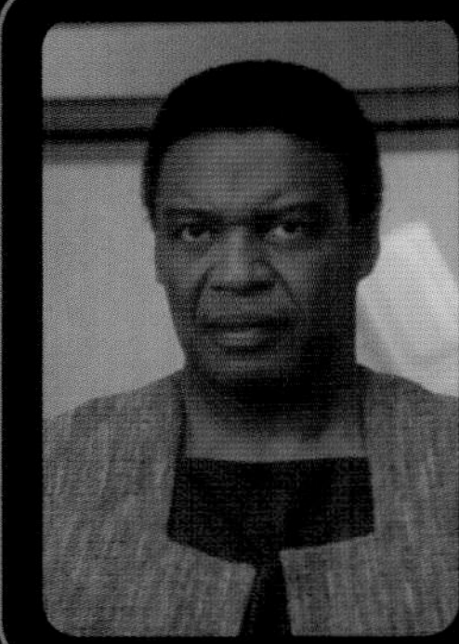

DATA FEED

Calvin Hudson was Starfleet's attaché to the Federation colonies in the Demilitarized Zone. After years of witnessing the brutal treatment of colonists at the hands of Cardassians, he secretly joined the Maquis. Hudson led two attack fighters in a raid against the Bryma colony that was believed to be storing weapons for the Cardassians. In the end, the mission was stopped by his old friend Benjamin Sisko, but Hudson escaped to continue the Maquis' fight.

OPERATION RETURN

Federation attack fighters played a pivotal role in the battle to retake Deep Space 9 in 2374. Captain Sisko devised a plan in which attack ships would swarm Cardassian vessels before retreating, in the hope that the Cardassians would follow them. The idea was that this would create a weakness in their defenses, which larger Starfleet ships could then push through.

After the eighth wave of attack fighters flew in, Gul Dukat appeared to take the bait. But he was merely laying a trap, because he left several *Galor*-class destroyers in reserve. Sisko recognized that it was an ambush, but still pressed ahead as he felt they might not get a better chance. Only the *Defiant* managed to get through enemy lines, but as it closed in on Deep Space 9, the minefield that was preventing Dominion forces coming through the wormhole was brought down.

With hundreds of Dominion reinforcements ready to emerge in the Alpha Quadrant, Sisko ordered the *Defiant* to engage them in the wormhole. Just as it was about to meet the Dominion forces, the Bajoran Prophets intervened. They mysteriously made the Dominion reinforcements disappear, much to the bafflement of everyone. By this time, Starfleet forces had been joined by the Klingons and 200 allied ships had broken through Dominion lines. The Dominion and Cardassian occupation force had to abandon Deep Space 9, while the rest of their fleet had already broken off the fight and were in full retreat.

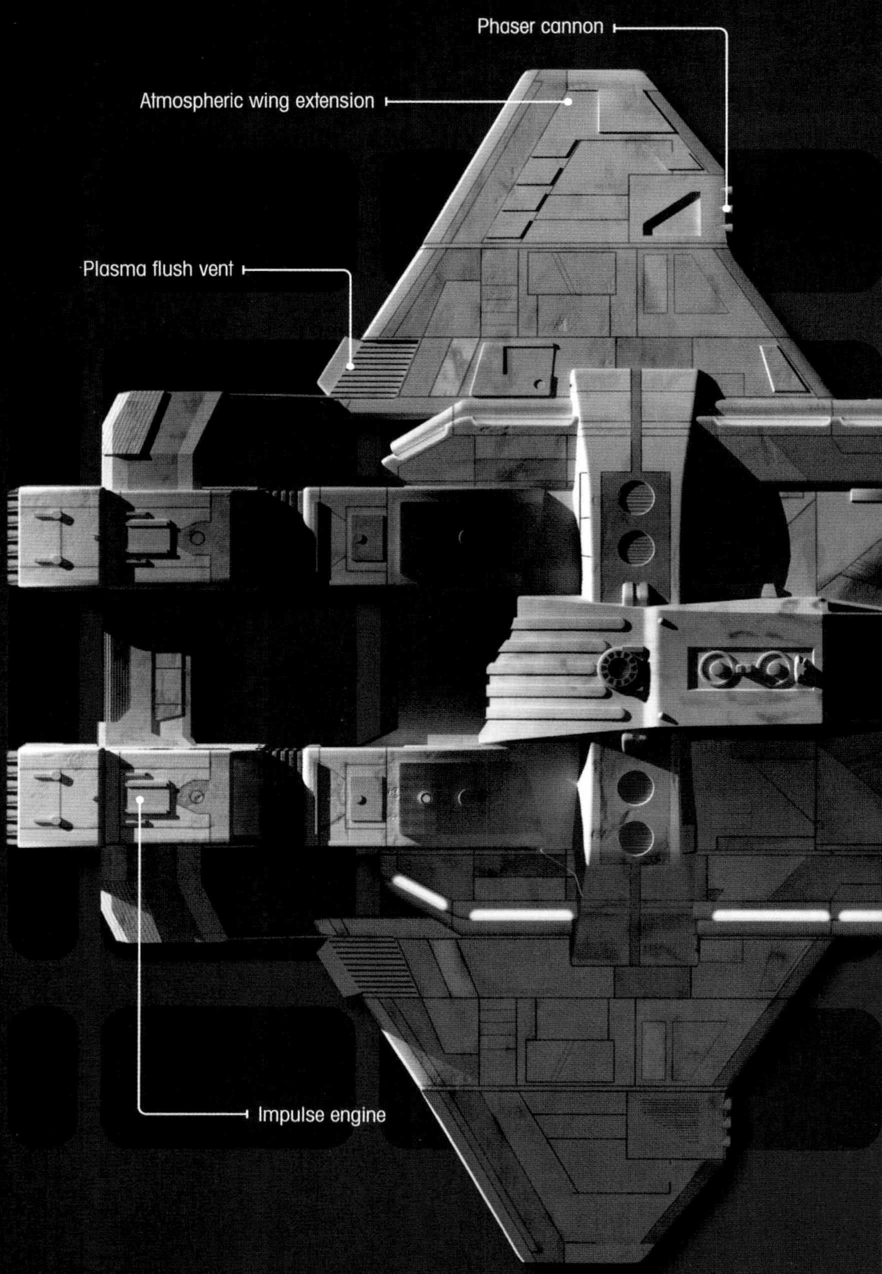

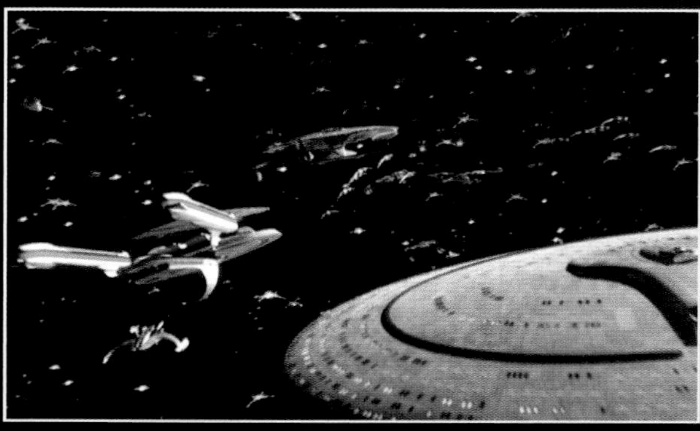

▲ Starfleet destroyer units provided cover as squadrons of attack fighters swooped in on Cardassian vessels, hoping that they would be followed and a gap in the Dominion's defenses opened up.

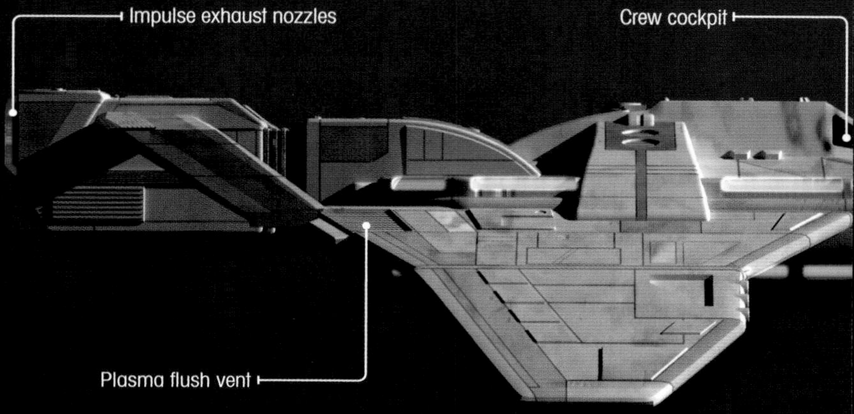

Phaser cannon
Atmospheric wing extension
Plasma flush vent
Impulse engine

Impulse exhaust nozzles
Crew cockpit
Plasma flush vent

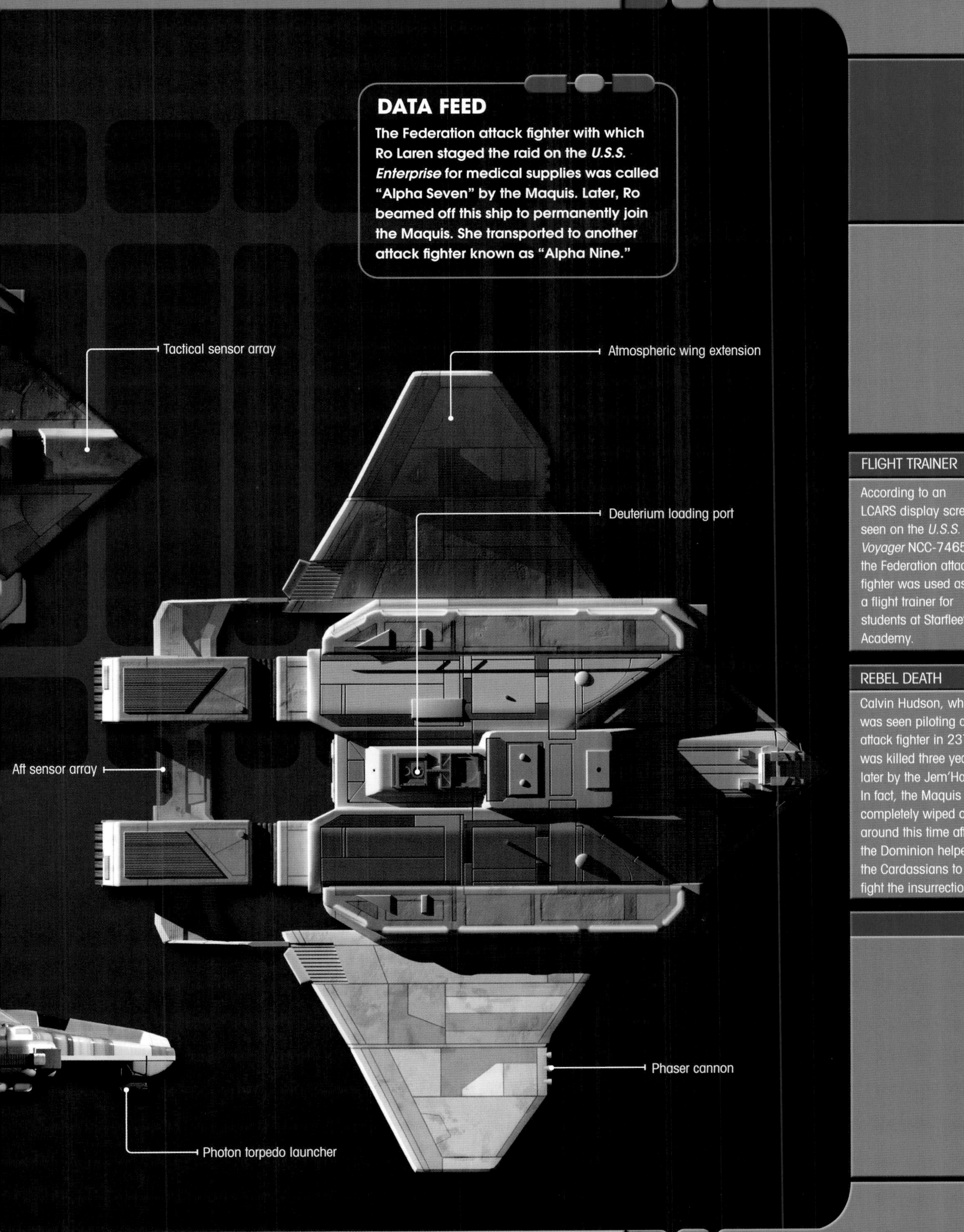

DATA FEED

The Federation attack fighter with which Ro Laren staged the raid on the *U.S.S. Enterprise* for medical supplies was called "Alpha Seven" by the Maquis. Later, Ro beamed off this ship to permanently join the Maquis. She transported to another attack fighter known as "Alpha Nine."

FLIGHT TRAINER

According to an LCARS display screen seen on the *U.S.S. Voyager* NCC-74656, the Federation attack fighter was used as a flight trainer for students at Starfleet Academy.

REBEL DEATH

Calvin Hudson, who was seen piloting an attack fighter in 2370, was killed three years later by the Jem'Hadar. In fact, the Maquis were completely wiped out around this time after the Dominion helped the Cardassians to fight the insurrection.

FIGHTERS
SIZE CHART

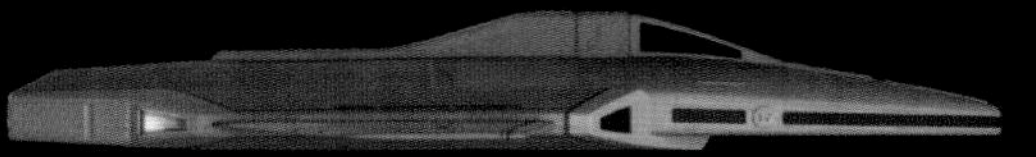

FLIGHT TRAINING CRAFT

10.99m

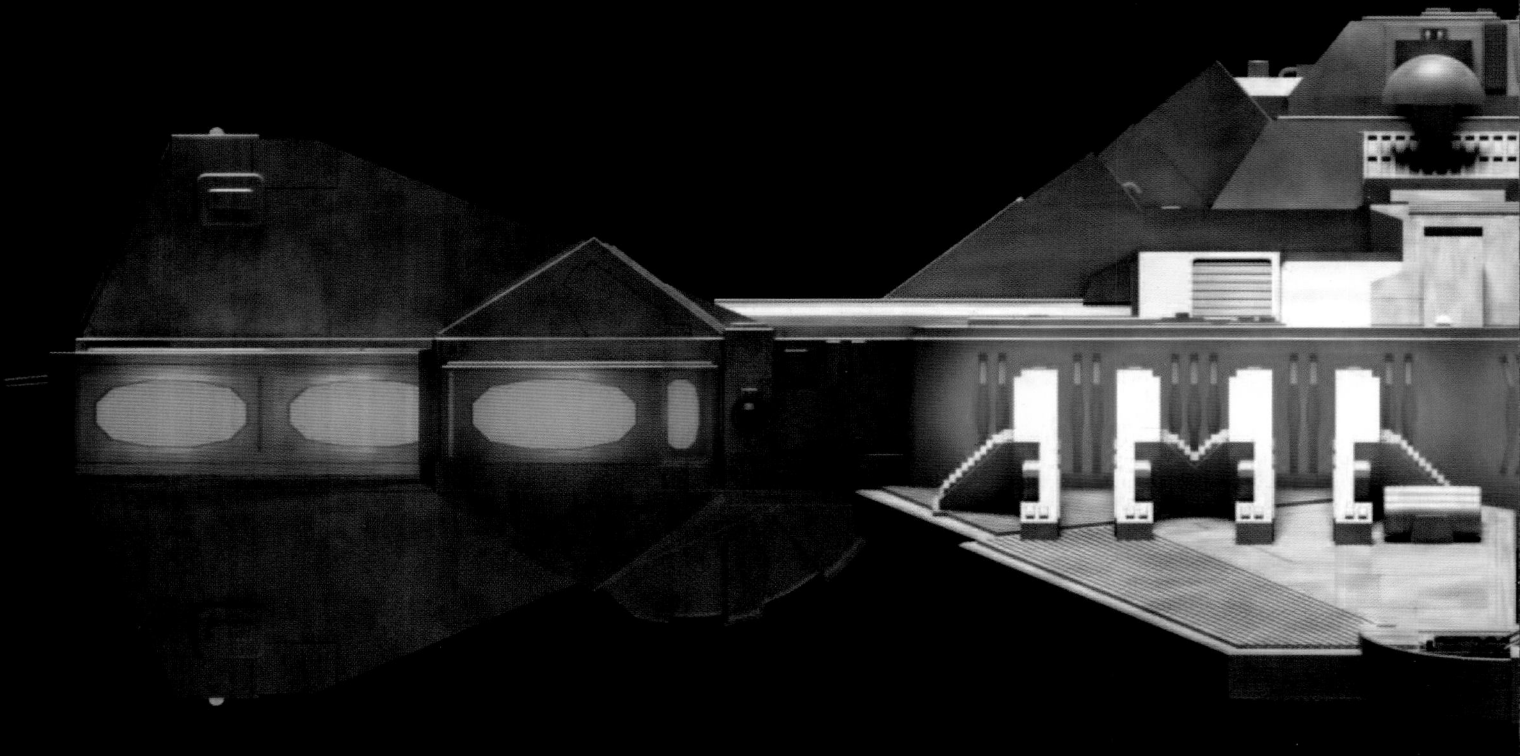

MAQUIS RAIDER

68.5m

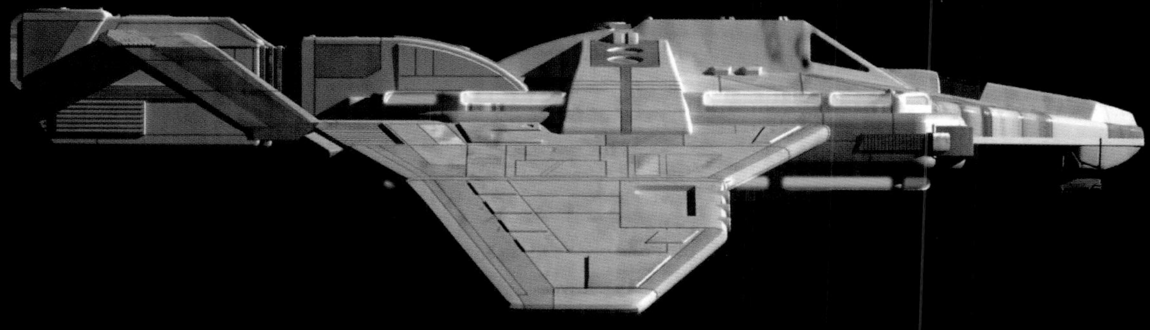

FEDERATION ATTACK FIGHTER

25m

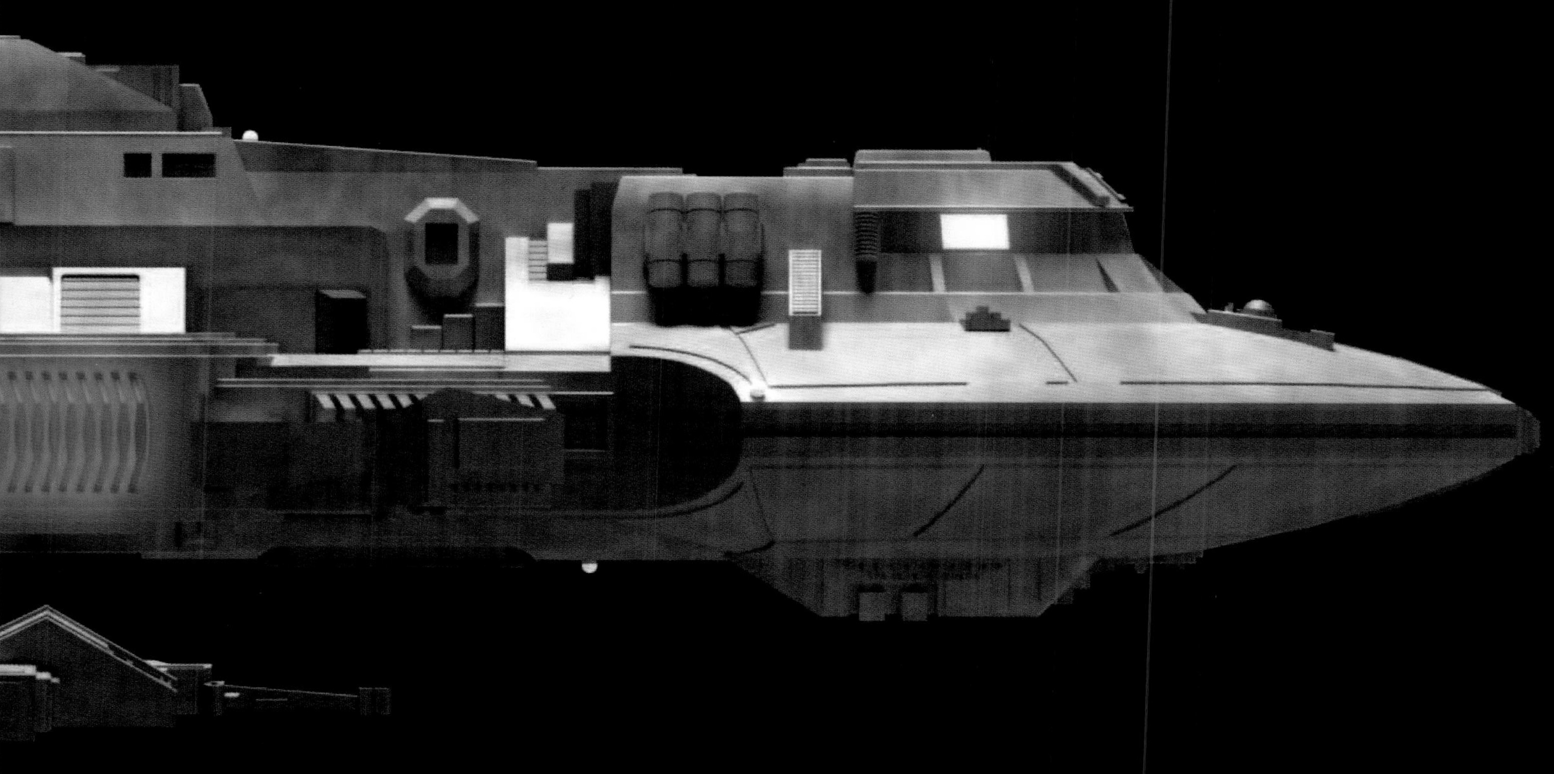

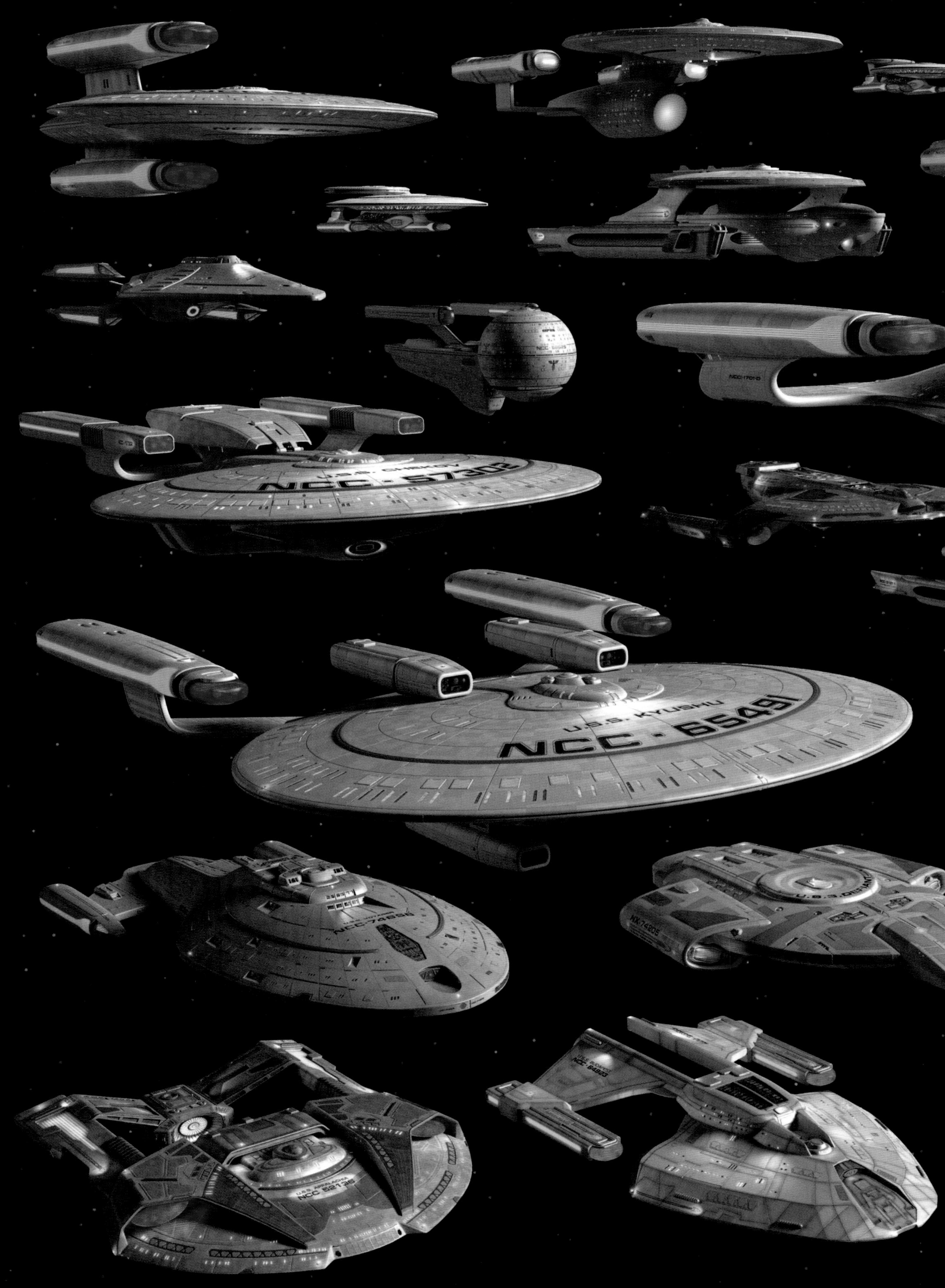
NCC - 57302
U.S.S. KYUSHU
NCC - 65491

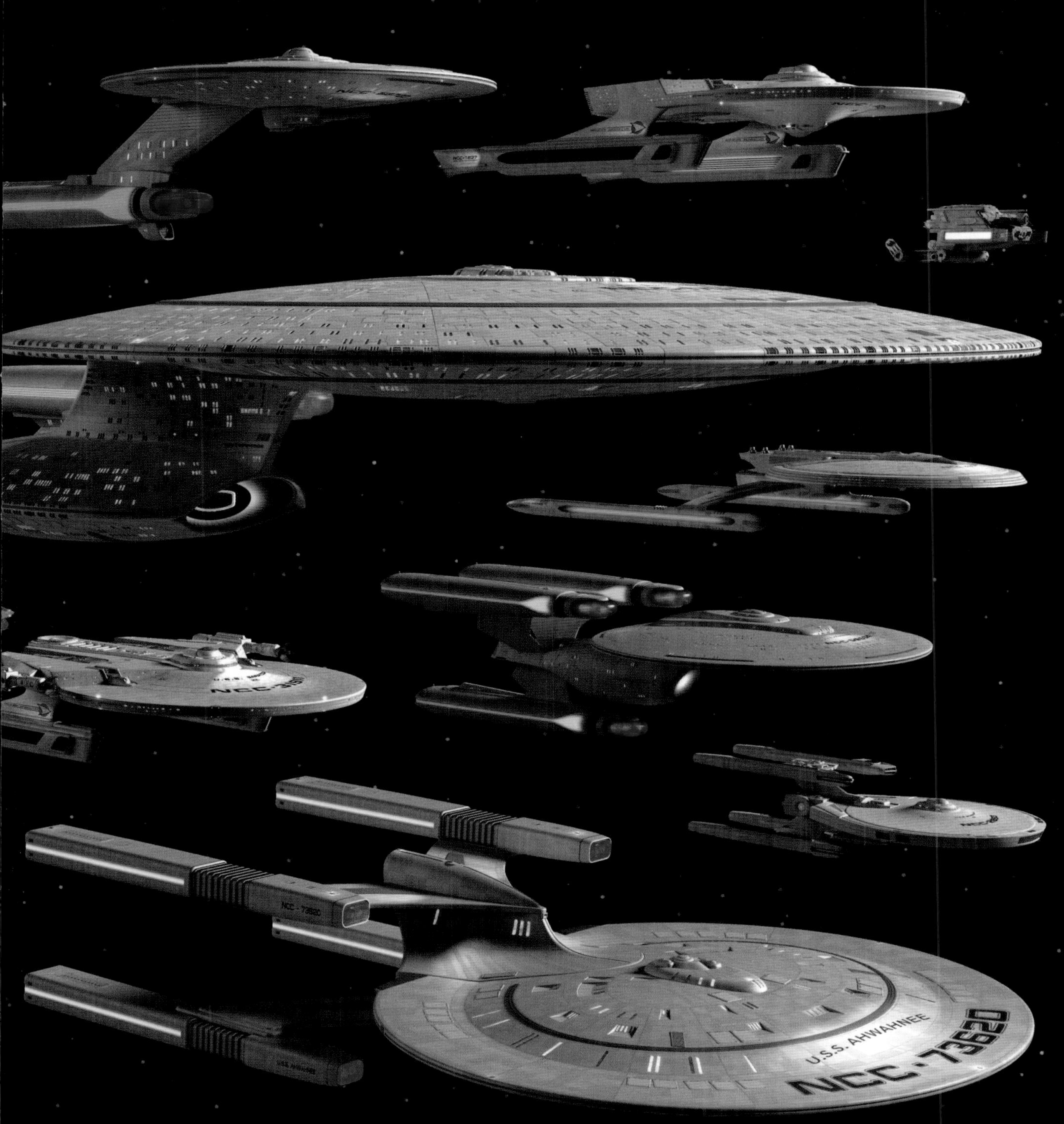

CHAPTER 3

MULTI-MISSION EXPLORERS

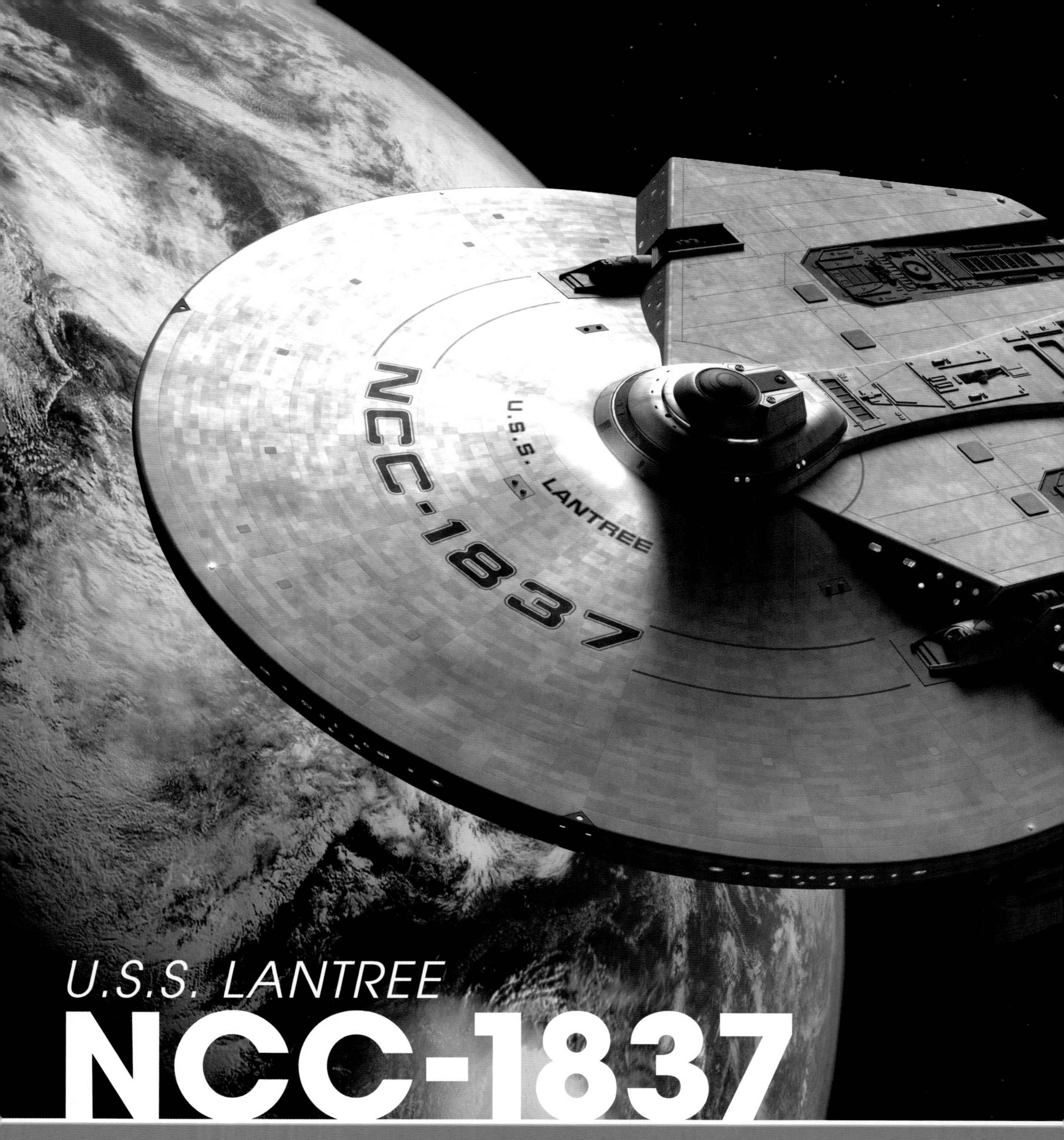

U.S.S. LANTREE

NCC-1837

An inexplicable event in 2365 transformed the *Lantree* from an unremarkable supply vessel into a harbinger of death.

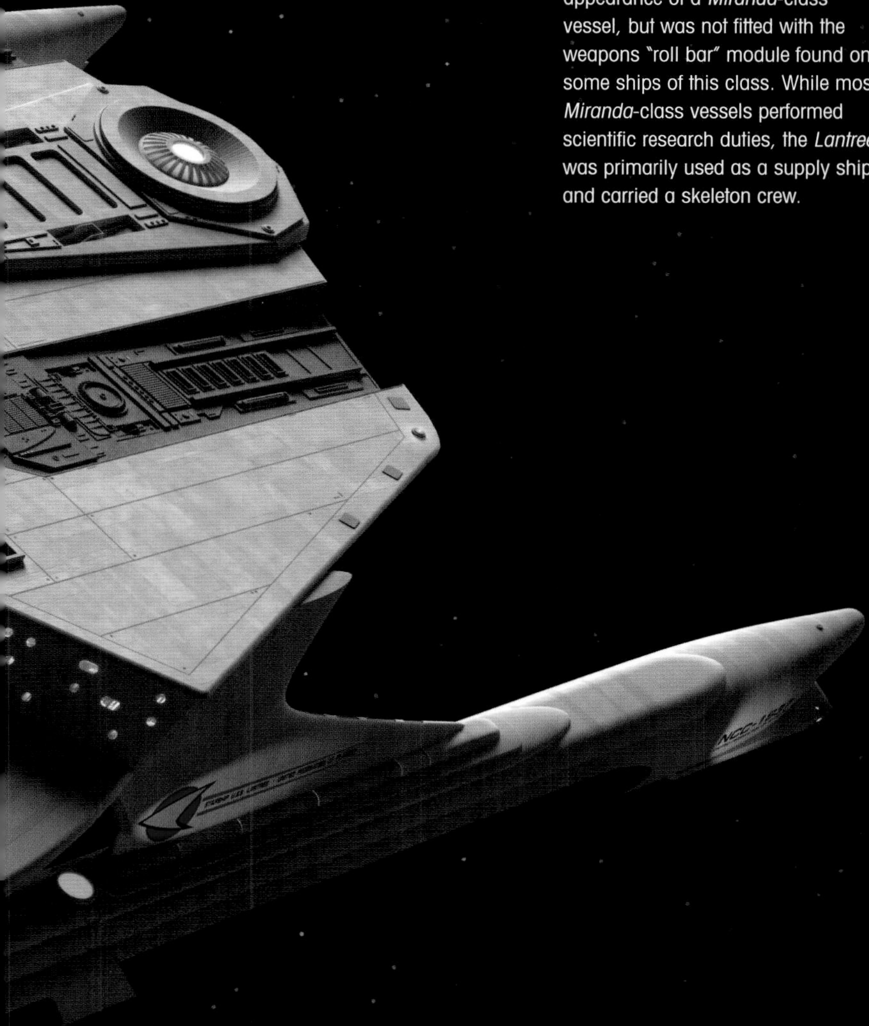

◀ The *Lantree* had the typical appearance of a *Miranda*-class vessel, but was not fitted with the weapons "roll bar" module found on some ships of this class. While most *Miranda*-class vessels performed scientific research duties, the *Lantree* was primarily used as a supply ship and carried a skeleton crew.

Operating from at least the 2290s through to 2365, the *U.S.S. Lantree* NCC-1837 was a *Miranda*-class starship commanded by Captain L. Isao Telaka.

Miranda-class vessels were normally assigned to scientific missions or patrol duties, but by the mid-24th century their aging design meant that many had been removed from frontline services and transferred to less demanding tasks. The *Lantree*, for example, had become a class-6 supply ship, transporting cargo, spare parts, and materials to colonies, space stations, and other ships. In 2365, it was known that the *Lantree* operated mainly in Gamma 7 Sector, and had a crew complement of just 26, whereas earlier vessels of this class normally operated with around 200 personnel.

STANDARD CONFIGURATION

The outward appearance of the *Lantree* was very similar to that of other *Miranda*-class ships in that it was 243 meters in length, and did not feature a separate engineering hull. Instead, it comprised an elongated saucer section, with two warp nacelles mounted on pylons below. The rear half of the saucer section was occupied by cargo holds, with the impulse engines at the very rear and two shuttlebays on either side of the engines. The *Lantree* had a top speed of warp 9.2, which it could sustain for 12 hours.

Some *Miranda*-class ships featured a weapons roll bar attached over the saucer section, but the *Lantree* was not equipped with this accessory. In fact, it was relatively poorly armed, being fitted only with class-3 defensive armaments. These included six type-7 phaser emitters on the saucer section and two aft phaser emitters positioned below the impulse engines, as well as a photon torpedo launcher.

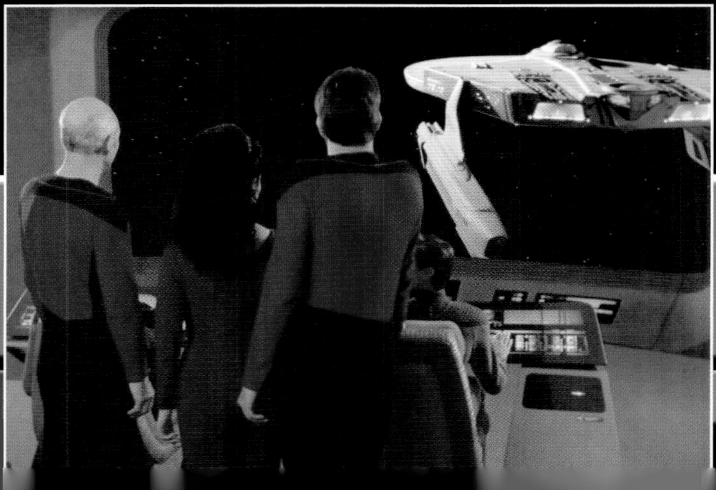

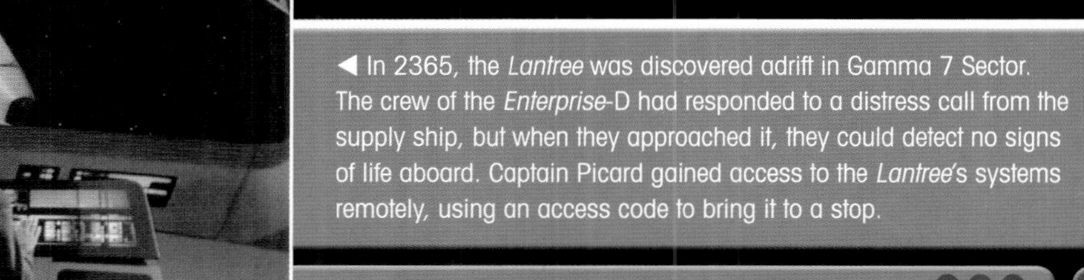

◀ In 2365, the *Lantree* was discovered adrift in Gamma 7 Sector. The crew of the *Enterprise*-D had responded to a distress call from the supply ship, but when they approached it, they could detect no signs of life aboard. Captain Picard gained access to the *Lantree*'s systems remotely, using an access code to bring it to a stop.

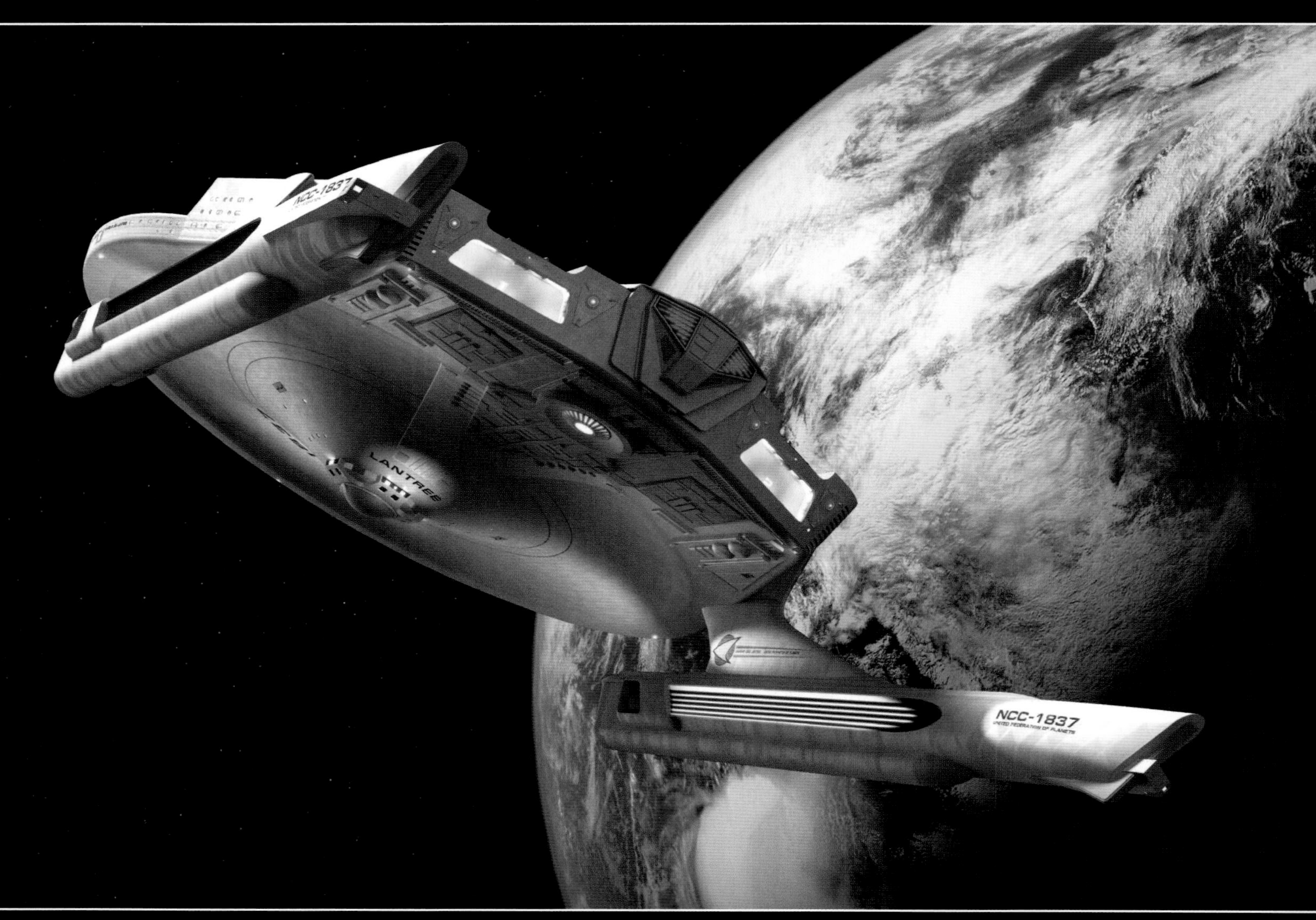

▲ The *Lantree*, like all *Miranda*-class ships, did not have a separate engineering hull. Instead, an enlarged squared-off section was fitted to the rear of the saucer. This area contained the ship's warp core and impulse engines, as well as large cargo holds and two shuttlebay doors.

In 2365, the *Lantree* broadcast a distress signal on an open subspace frequency, which was picked up by the *U.S.S. Enterprise* NCC-1701-D. It was an audio-only transmission in which a desperate voice said, "Can't hold out any more. People dying. Too many to help."

When the *Enterprise*-D reached the *Lantree*'s location, the crew found the ship adrift, though there were no indications of battle damage and all its systems appeared functional and in good order. But with no life signs onboard, it was to all intents and purposes a ghost ship. Captain Picard was able to take control of the *Lantree* remotely from the *Enterprise*-D and shut down its engines. He then activated its viewscreen to take a look at the bridge.

The sight that greeted him was extremely unsettling. The *Lantree*'s Captain Telaka, who was 32 years old, was slumped in his chair and looked extraordinarily aged and withered. The rest of the bridge crew had clearly been similarly afflicted, demonstrating a wizened appearance way in advance of the real-life age of any crewmember. The *Enterprise*'s Dr. Pulaski surmised that they had all died of extreme old age.

LOOKING FOR ANSWERS

The *Lantree*'s ship log was downloaded to see if it offered any clues as to what had led to this mystery. They discovered that the crew had undergone a complete medical examination eight weeks earlier, which had found them in perfect health. After that, there was just one recent medical entry noting that five days earlier the first officer had been treated for Thelusian flu. This was a harmless rhinovirus, similar to Earth's common cold, and could not possibly have caused the extreme aging.

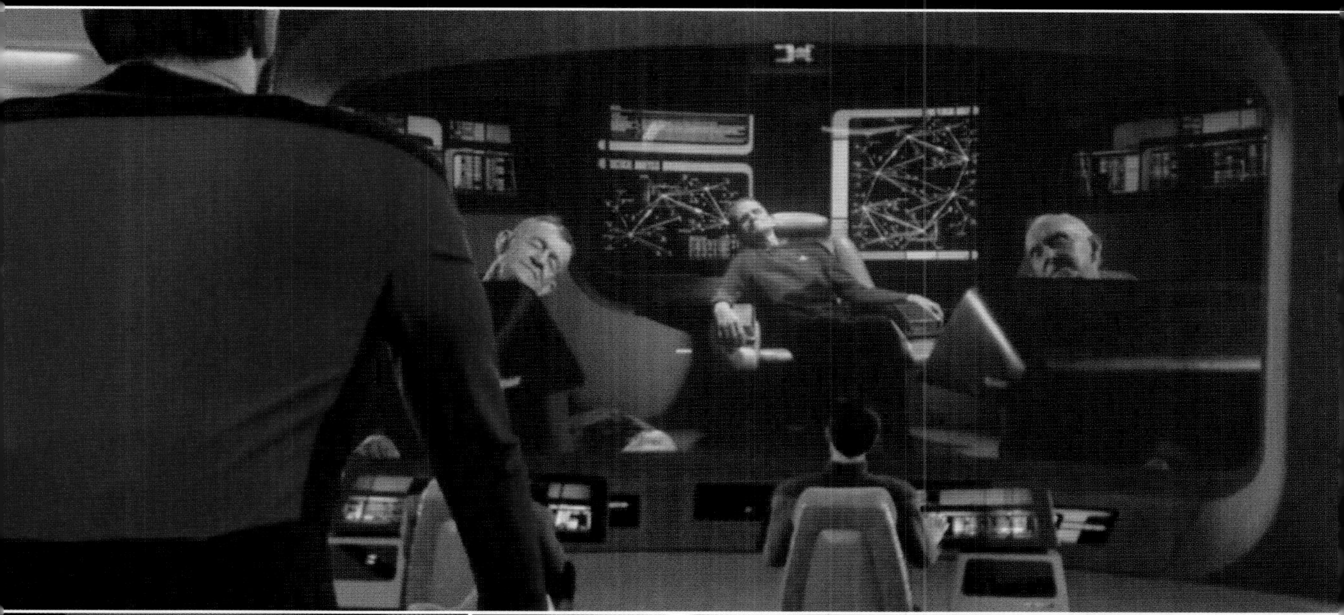

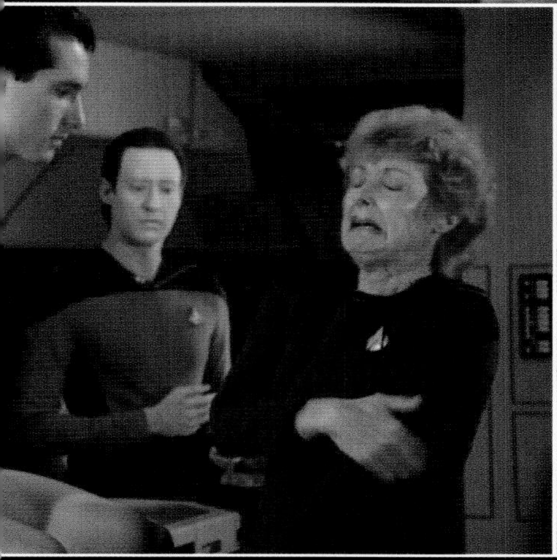

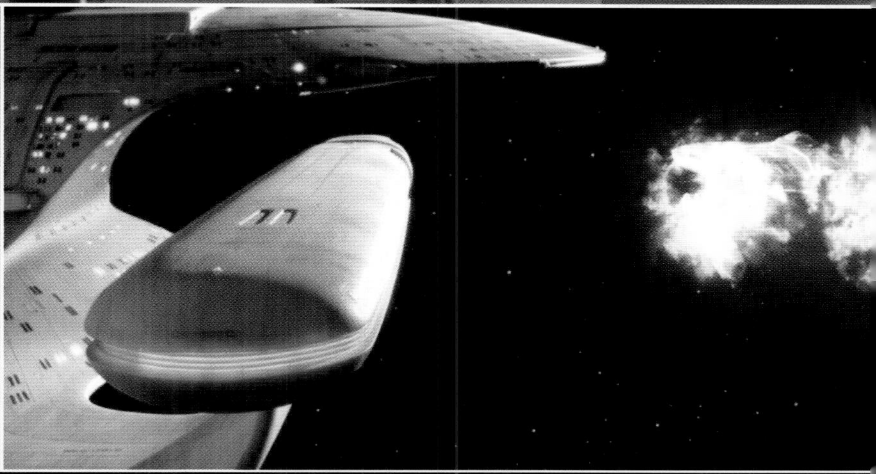

…recorded that its last port of … Genetic Research Station on …ski reasoned that whatever …he crew could have originated …ery least they should warn …potential fatal virus. Captain … before they left, he ordered …antine transmitters and marker …vated to warn off other ships. …tion, the *Enterprise*-D crew … head physician, Dr. Sara … leading a genetic-engineering … children with an immune …y sought out disease. When the … contact with the *Lantree*'s first …n Thelusian flu, their airborne …d the virus. Unfortunately, they … of altering the DNA of healthy …yper-accelerated aging.

The station personnel, and later Dr. Pulaski, also contracted the disease. Fortunately, a cure was found, which involved using the transporter to rid the disease from those infected.

The *Enterprise*-D returned to the *Lantree*'s position, where a single photon torpedo fired at a range of 40 kilometers destroyed it, ensuring that no one else would be at risk of contracting the disease.

▲ It was felt that the only way to be absolutely sure of wiping out the cause of the aging disease was to destroy the *Lantree*. With the shields down and fired from close proximity, one photon torpedo blew the ship to smithereens.

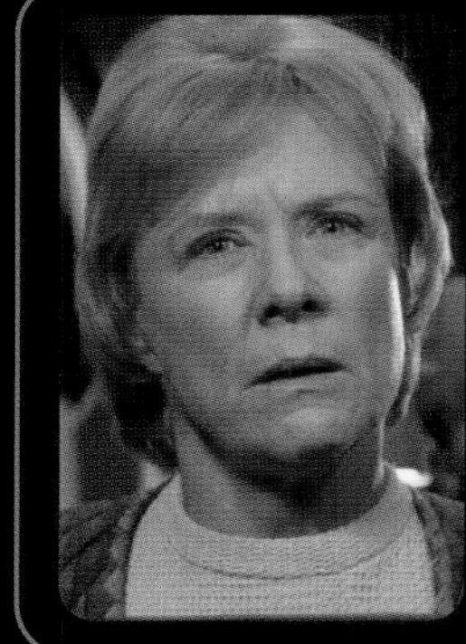

DATA FEED

Dr. Sara Kingsley led the research project on the Darwin Station to develop Humans with enhanced powers through genetic modification. Her work led to telepathic children who were extremely healthy. Unfortunately, their immune systems were too advanced and attacked diseases before they entered the Human body. Their antibodies also inadvertently mutated DNA, which caused rapid aging in normal Humans.

DEADLY SCIENCE

The deaths of all 26 members of the *U.S.S. Lantree*'s crew were caused by the unexpected consequences of a cutting-edge medical research project. It almost claimed the lives of Dr. Kingsley and her staff at the Darwin Genetic Research Center, too – the very people who had unwittingly caused the infection in the first place.

Dr. Kingsley was leading a genetic-engineering project to develop children with an immune system capable of protecting them from nearly all forms of disease. Their antibodies were so aggressive that they fought pathogens not only in their own bodies, but also in the surrounding environment. When the children came into contact with the Thelusian flu virus affecting *Lantree*'s first officer, their immune systems created airborne antibodies to attack it. However, these antigens also altered Human DNA and precipitated hyper-accelerated aging.

By this point, Dr. Pulaski had also succumbed to the abnormal process, but the *Enterprise*-D crew found a way to return an infected person's DNA to normal by means of the transporter. Using a transporter bio-pattern of a person before they contracted the disease, the crew were able to remove the offending antibodies and rematerialize the patient back to health. The station's staff were all cured in this way, but the bio-engineered children could not live among them until a means of controlling their immune systems had been found.

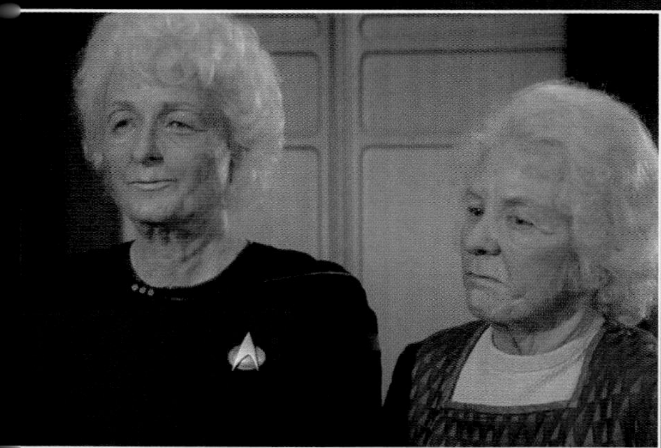

▲ Dr. Pulaski and Dr. Kingsley were both infected by a mutation that caused them to age decades in a matter of hours. It was the same infection that had killed the crew of the *Lantree*.

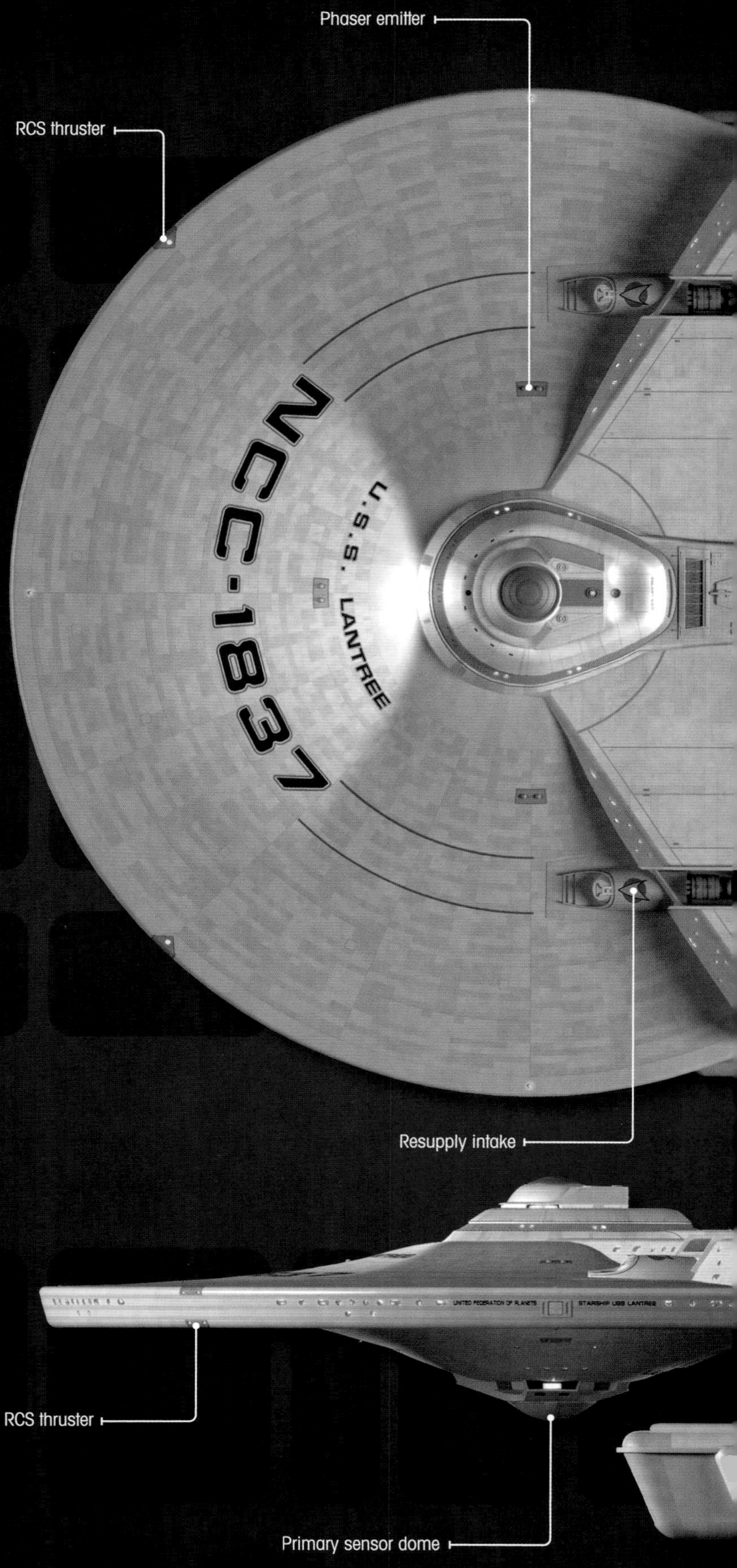

Phaser emitter

RCS thruster

NCC-1837

U.S.S. LANTREE

Resupply intake

RCS thruster

Primary sensor dome

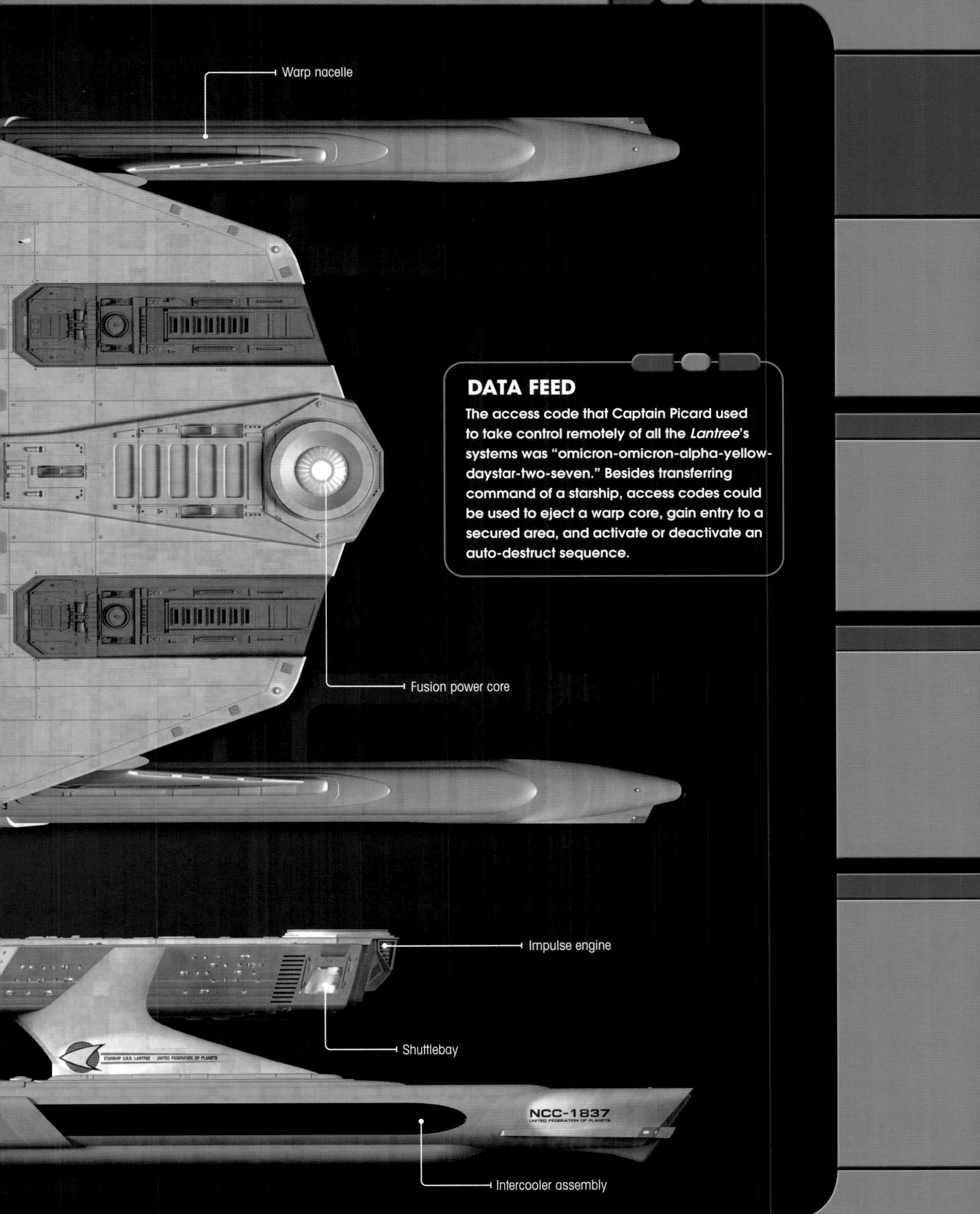

DATA FEED

The access code that Captain Picard used to take control remotely of all the *Lantree*'s systems was "omicron-omicron-alpha-yellow-daystar-two-seven." Besides transferring command of a starship, access codes could be used to eject a warp core, gain entry to a secured area, and activate or deactivate an auto-destruct sequence.

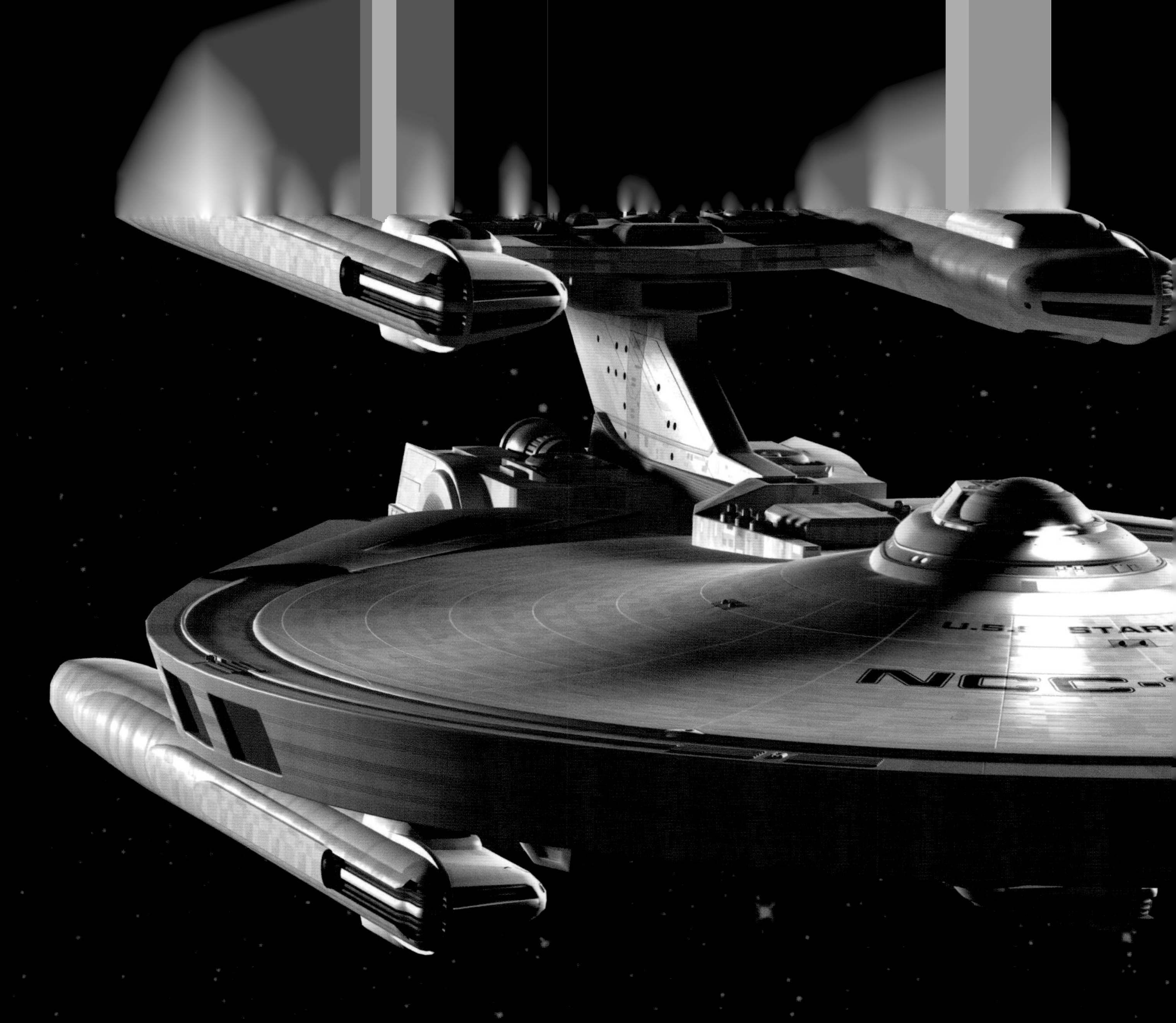

U.S.S. STARGAZER

NCC-2893

The *Constellation*-class *Stargazer* was captained for much of its service in deep space by Jean-Luc Picard.

Built at the San Francisco Fleet Yards on Earth, the *U.S.S. Stargazer* was designed primarily for deep space exploration and defensive patrol duty. It was in service from the early to mid-24th century.

The *Stargazer* was slightly shorter than a *Constitution*-class vessel and its appearance resembled that of *Miranda*-class ships in lacking a secondary or engineering hull. Instead, its warp nacelles were attached to a spar at the rear of the saucer section.

Unusually for Starfleet vessels, those of the *Constellation* class were equipped with four warp nacelles; two were mounted on a pylon above the command saucer and two hung below.

COLORFUL HISTORY

The warp engine was installed vertically and could power the ship to warp 9. The *Stargazer* was also fitted with fusion reactors and avidyne impulse engines that were constructed at the Yoyodyne facility at the Copernicus Ship Yards on Luna.

The ship carried standard Starfleet weaponry, including phasers and photon torpedoes. It was capable of firing six photon torpedoes in a single spread, and was protected by powerful defensive shields.

▲ The *Stargazer* was unusual for a Starfleet vessel in having four rather than two warp nacelles.

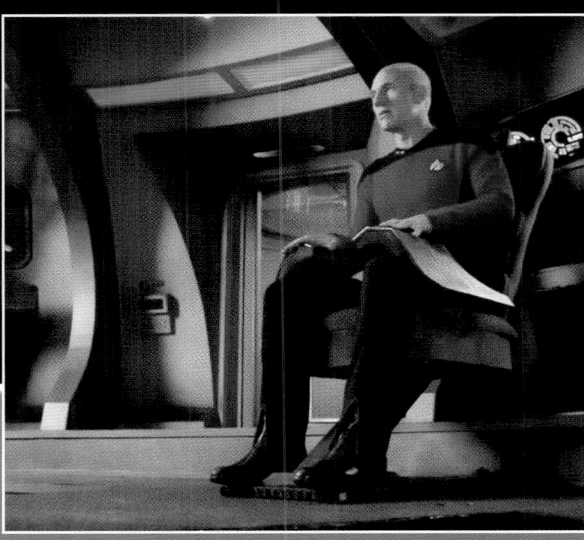

▶ In 2333, Lieutenant Commander Jean-Luc Picard was serving as a bridge officer on the *U.S.S. Stargazer* when the ship's captain was killed and the first officer injured. Picard took control of the situation and saved the ship. His initiative so impressed Starfleet Command that they made him the ship's new captain.

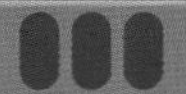

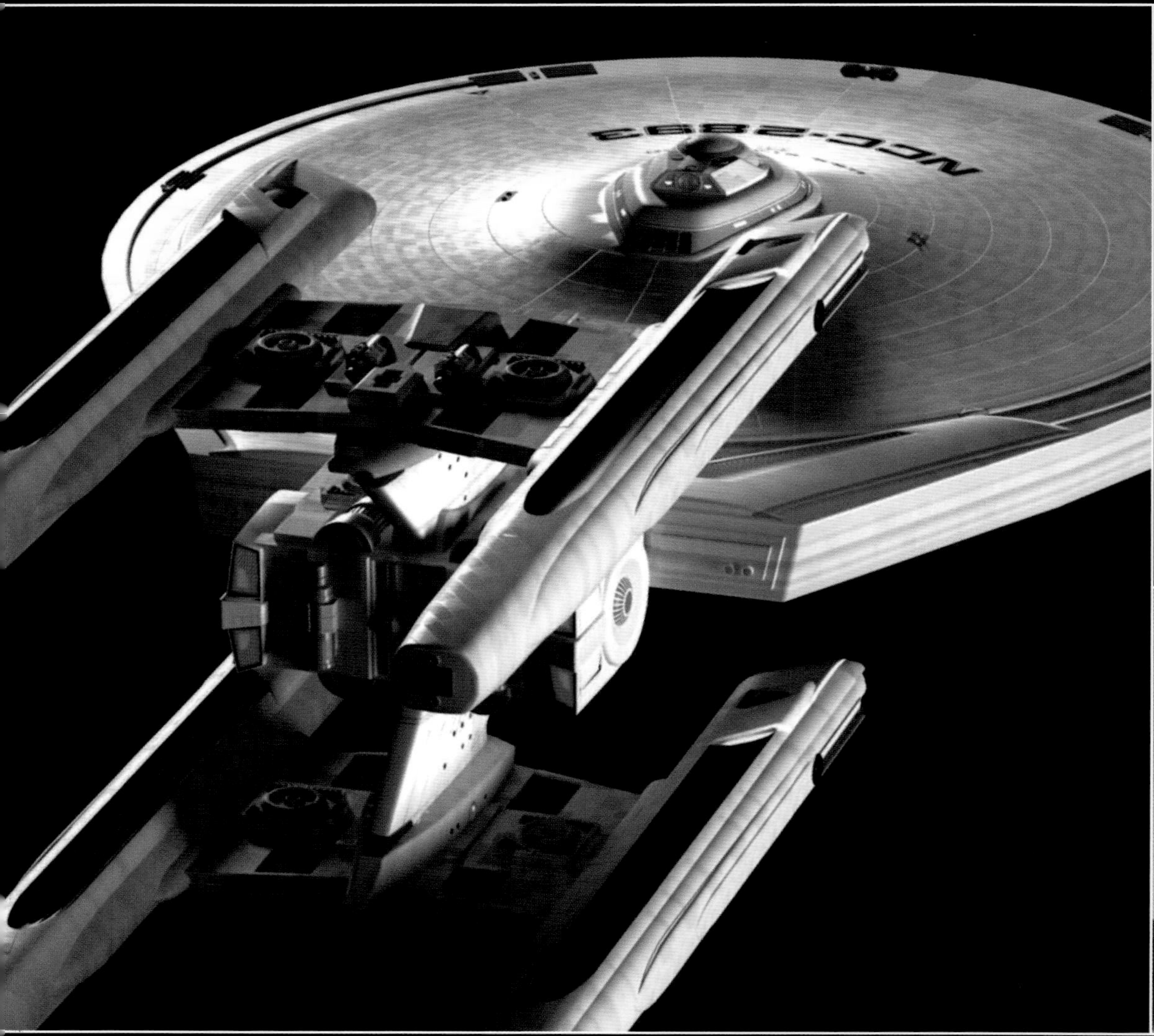

◀ The *Stargazer* was designed as a fast science vessel and was fitted with a substantial hangar bay and a large number of sensor arrays. It was tasked with exploring the edges of Federation space and was responsible for making first contact with more than one species. Unlike the *Galaxy*-class *Enterprise*-D, it did not carry families. By the 2360s, the *Constellation* class was considered redundant and the ships were retired.

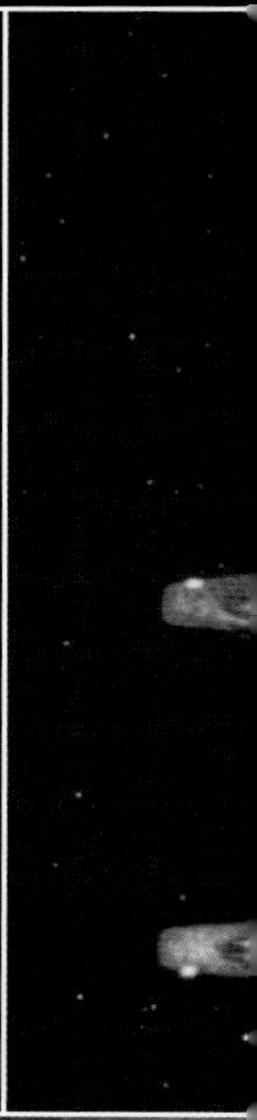

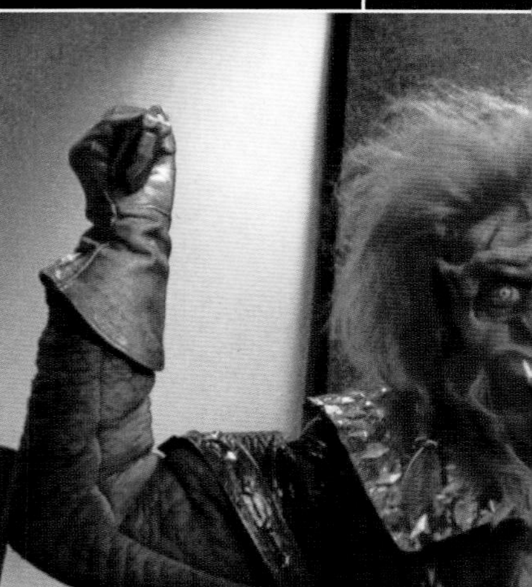

In 2333, Jean-Luc Picard, then Lieutenant Commander, took charge of the *Stargazer* after the captain was killed, and, in recognition of the leadership qualities he displayed, he was offered permanent command of the ship. He was then just 28 years old, making him the youngest captain in the fleet. The *Stargazer* remained under Picard's command for the next 22 years.

OPERATIONAL HISTORY

Stargazer's history consisted mainly of exploration and establishing contact with other species. In 2354, the ship encountered a lawless society known as the Chalnoth. It also saw action in the Cardassian Wars. During the exploration of Sector 21503, *Stargazer* made contact with a Cardassian warship and lowered its shields as a gesture of good will. The Cardassians opened fire anyway and *Stargazer* only just managed to get away without being destroyed.

Its service came to an abrupt end in 2355 ,when it was traveling at warp 2 through the Maxia Zeta system. An unidentified ship, later revealed as Ferengi, rose from a deep moon crater and fired twice from close range. With the *Stargazer's* shields failing, Picard improvised, employing what has since come to be known as the "Picard Maneuver." Using the warp drive with pinpoint accuracy, he achieved an effect whereby the *Stargazer* appeared to be in two places at once. This tactic allowed the Starfleet ship to use six photon torpedoes to destroy the attacker – but at a high cost to itself. The *Stargazer* was badly damaged and Picard ordered all hands to abandon ship. The crew, in Picard's own words, had to "limp through space in shuttlecraft for weeks" before they reached safety.

In the standard procedure following the loss of

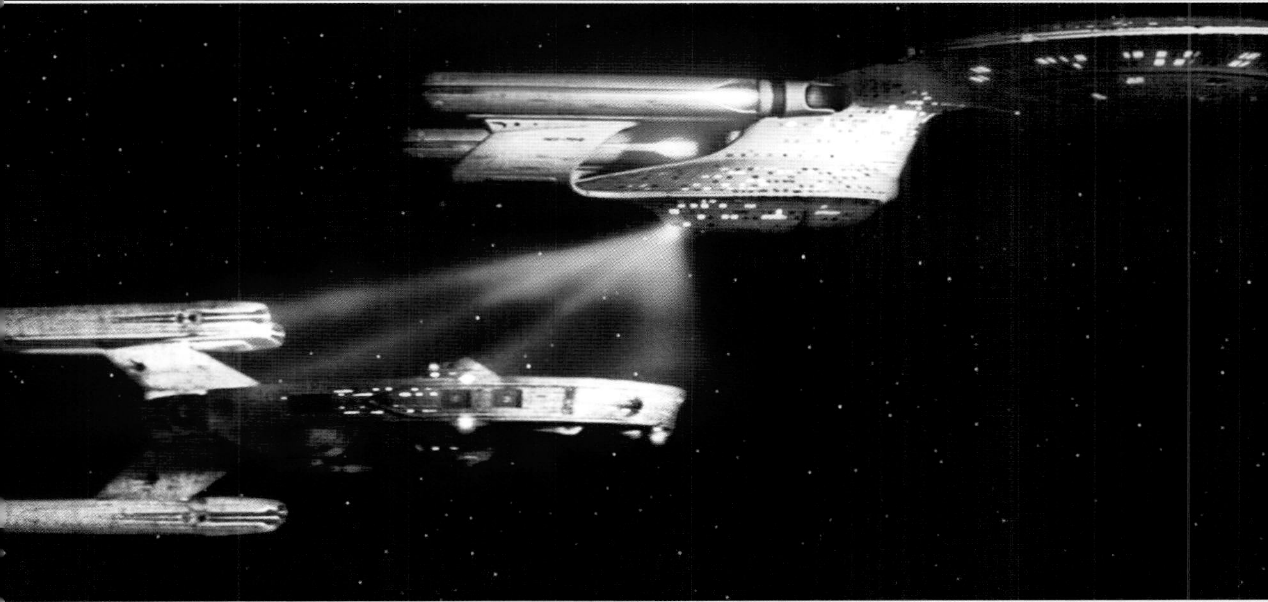

◀ Starfleet believed that the *Stargazer* was destroyed during its encounter with the Ferengi vessel. It was certainly incapable of supporting life when Picard gave the order to abandon ship. But DaiMon Bok became obsessed with Picard and recovered the damaged ship. After Bok's attempted frame-up was exposed, the *U.S.S. Enterprise*-D towed *Stargazer* away and it was eventually taken to Xendi Starbase 9.

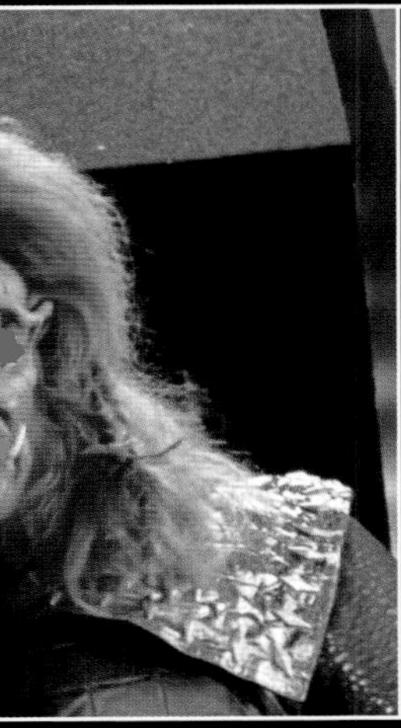

◀ During the *Stargazer*'s operational history, the crew made first contact with the Chalnoth, a warlike species from the planet Chalna. Their society rejected the rule of law and even the concept of government in favor of a system where the strong prospered. As a result, their species existed in a state of permanent anarchy.

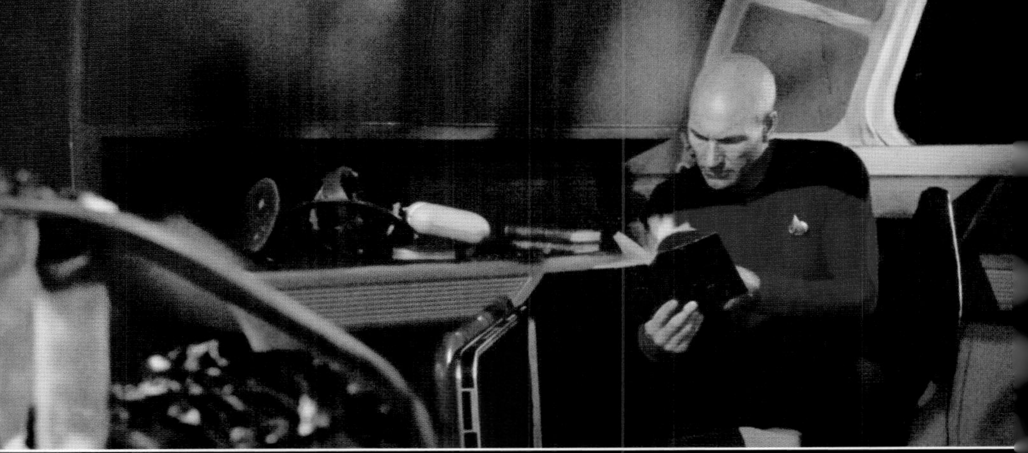

▲ Picard's return to the *Stargazer* prompted him to sift through the debris and reminisce about the 22 years he spent as its commander.

a starship, Picard was court-martialed. The trial did not end in a conviction, however, and Picard was cleared of any wrongdoing.

THE FINAL TWIST

This was not, as might be expected, the end of the story. Nine years after the incident that had become known as the Battle of Maxia, Ferengi commander DaiMon Bok met Picard in the Xendi Sabu system and presented him with the hulk of the *Stargazer*. Bok claimed to have found it adrift in space on the far side of the star system.

Commander Data found a *Stargazer* log entry that seemed to suggest that the ship Picard had fired upon did not attack first, but was under a flag of truce, and that the fire on the *Stargazer*'s bridge had been supposedly caused by an accident in engineering. Though Picard knew the log was false, it still led him to question whether he had done the right thing. Using their technical expertise, Data and conn officer Geordi La Forge proved the log was a fake. It had been created by DaiMon Bok in an act of revenge, because the commander of the destroyed Ferengi vessel was his only son. Responding to Picard's request, a Starfleet tug met with the *Enterprise* and towed *Stargazer* to Xendi Starbase 9.

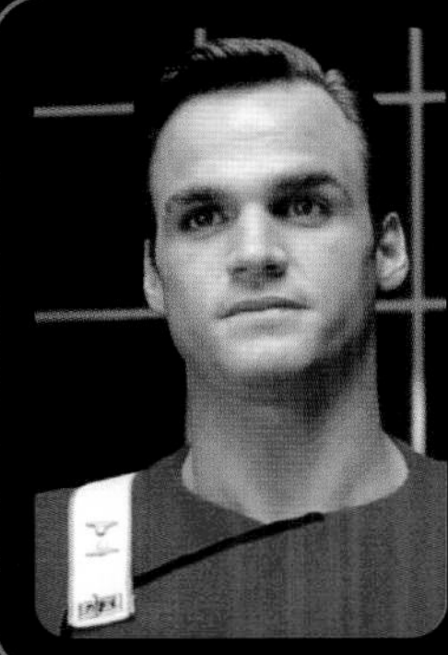

DATA FEED

Lieutenant Commander Jack Crusher served under Captain Picard on the *U.S.S. Stargazer*. The pair were good friends, but in 2354 Crusher was killed during an away mission. Picard found himself in an impossible situation when he saved the life of another team member at the expense of his friend's. Picard returned Jack's body to his wife Beverly and son Wesley. Both went on to serve with Picard onboard the *U.S.S. Enterprise* NCC-1701-D.

STANDARD BRIDGE

Over their years of service, different *Constellation*-class vessels were fitted with various designs of bridge, but the *Stargazer*'s had the usual Starfleet configuration, with the captain's chair in the center. Two duty stations were combined into a single console in front of the captain; navigation was front right of the captain's position and helm to the left. While on duty, personnel stood at stations around the perimeter bulkhead, which was supported by dark, heavy buttresses. One unusual feature of the bridge was that all duty stations were clearly named in large white letters.

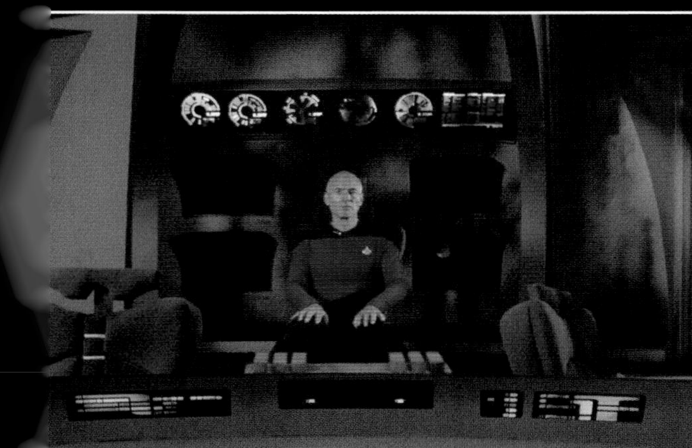

▲ Described as a "cramped little bridge" by Captain Picard, the *Stargazer*'s command center was very similar to the bridges found on the refit *Constitution*-class vessels of the late 23rd century.

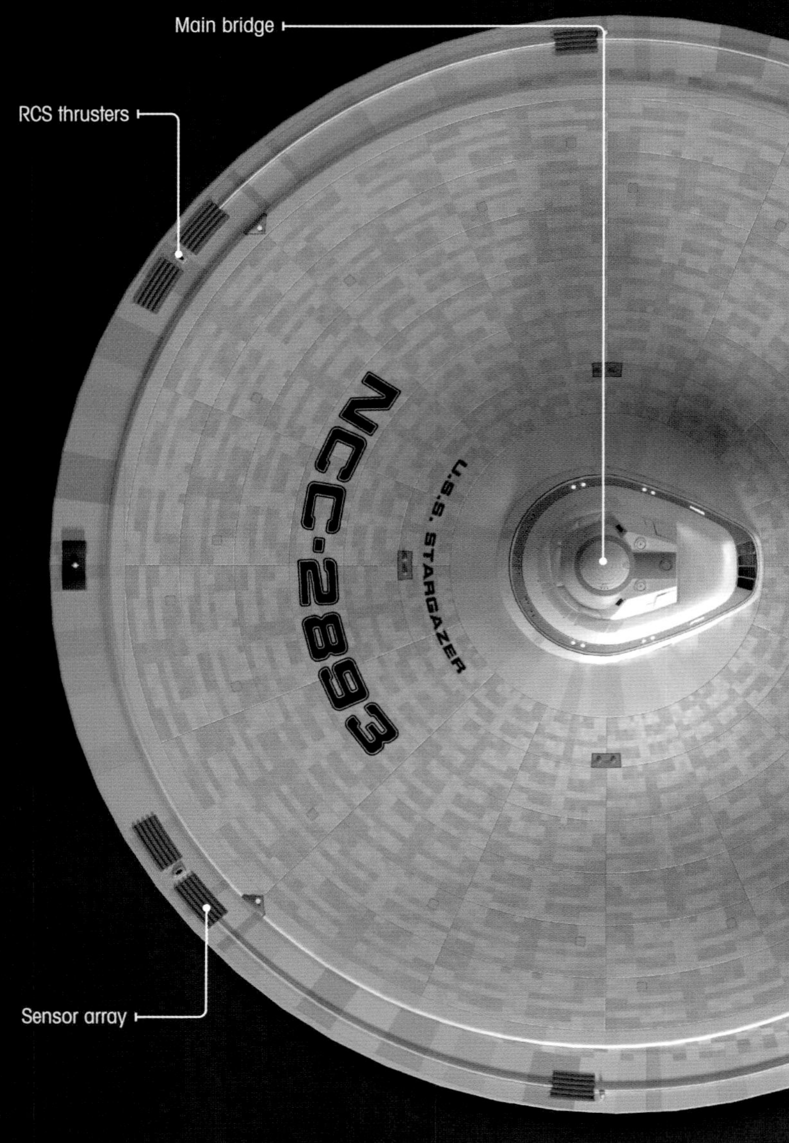

DATA FEED

Other classes of Starfleet ships featuring four nacelles included the *Cheyenne* and *Prometheus* classes, and some variants of the *Nebula* class.

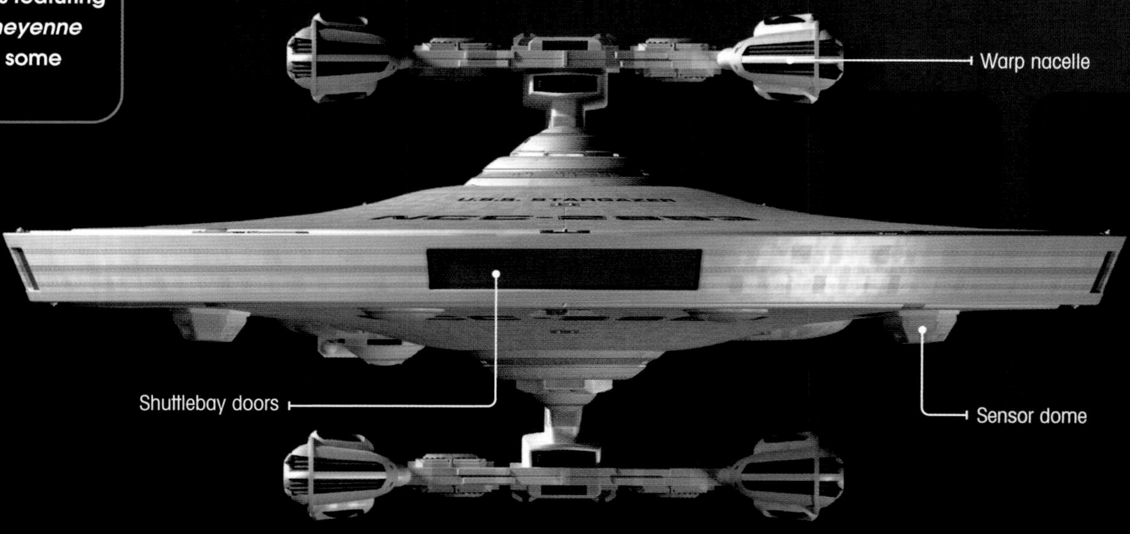

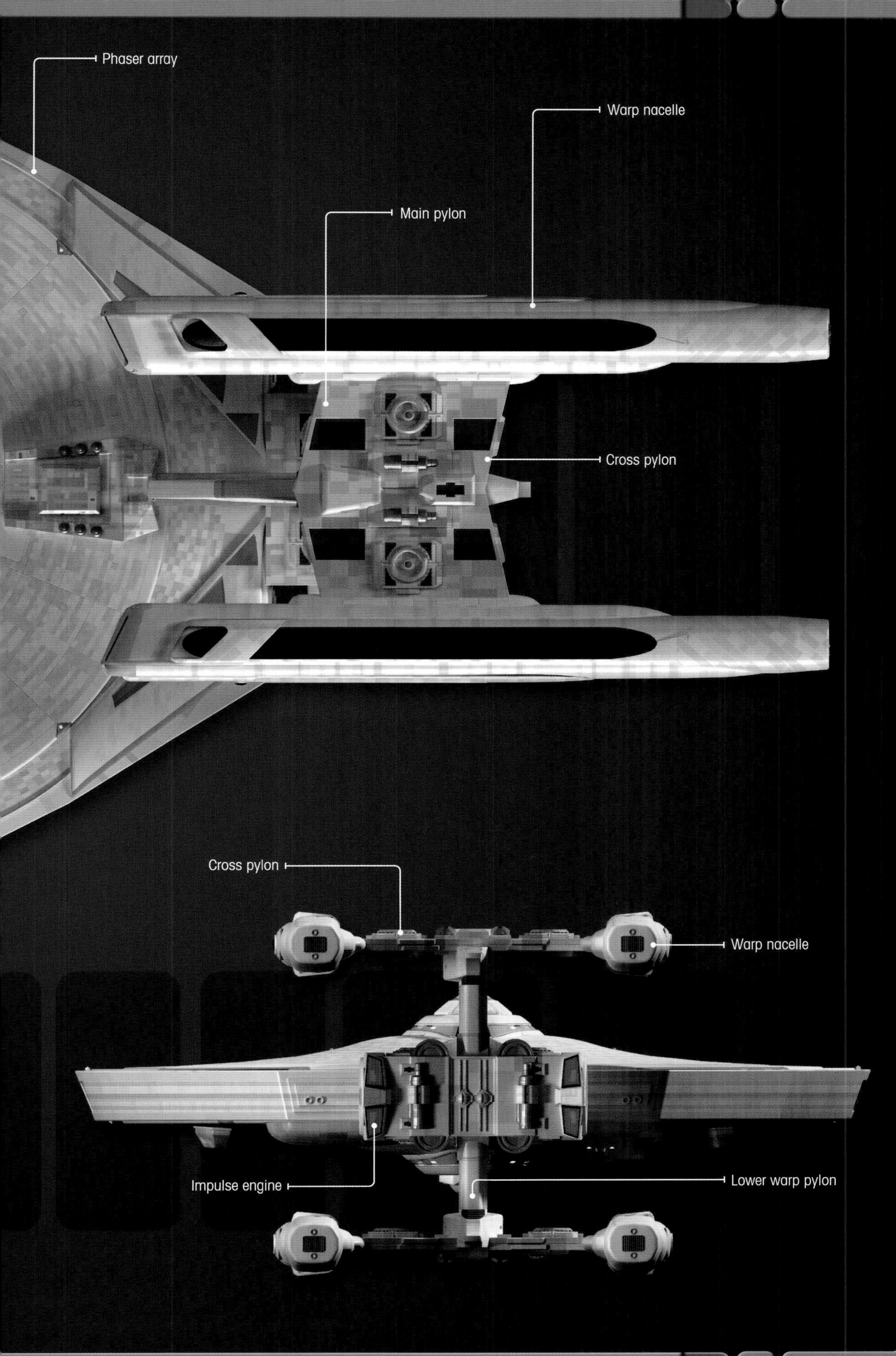

DEDICATION PLAQUE

The dedication plaque on the bridge of the *Stargazer* bore the motto: "To bring light into the darkness." This was a quote taken from the novel *Flowers for Algernon* by Daniel Keyes.

CONSTELLATION CLASS

Other *Constellation*-class vessels included the *U.S.S. Constellation* NX-1974, the *U.S.S. Hathaway* NCC-2593, the *U.S.S. Victory* NCC-9754, and the *U.S.S. Gettysburg* NCC-3890.

WORKHORSE

When talking to Captain Montgomery Scott, Captain Picard described the *U.S.S. Stargazer* as being an "overworked, underpowered vessel that was always on the verge of flying apart at the seams."

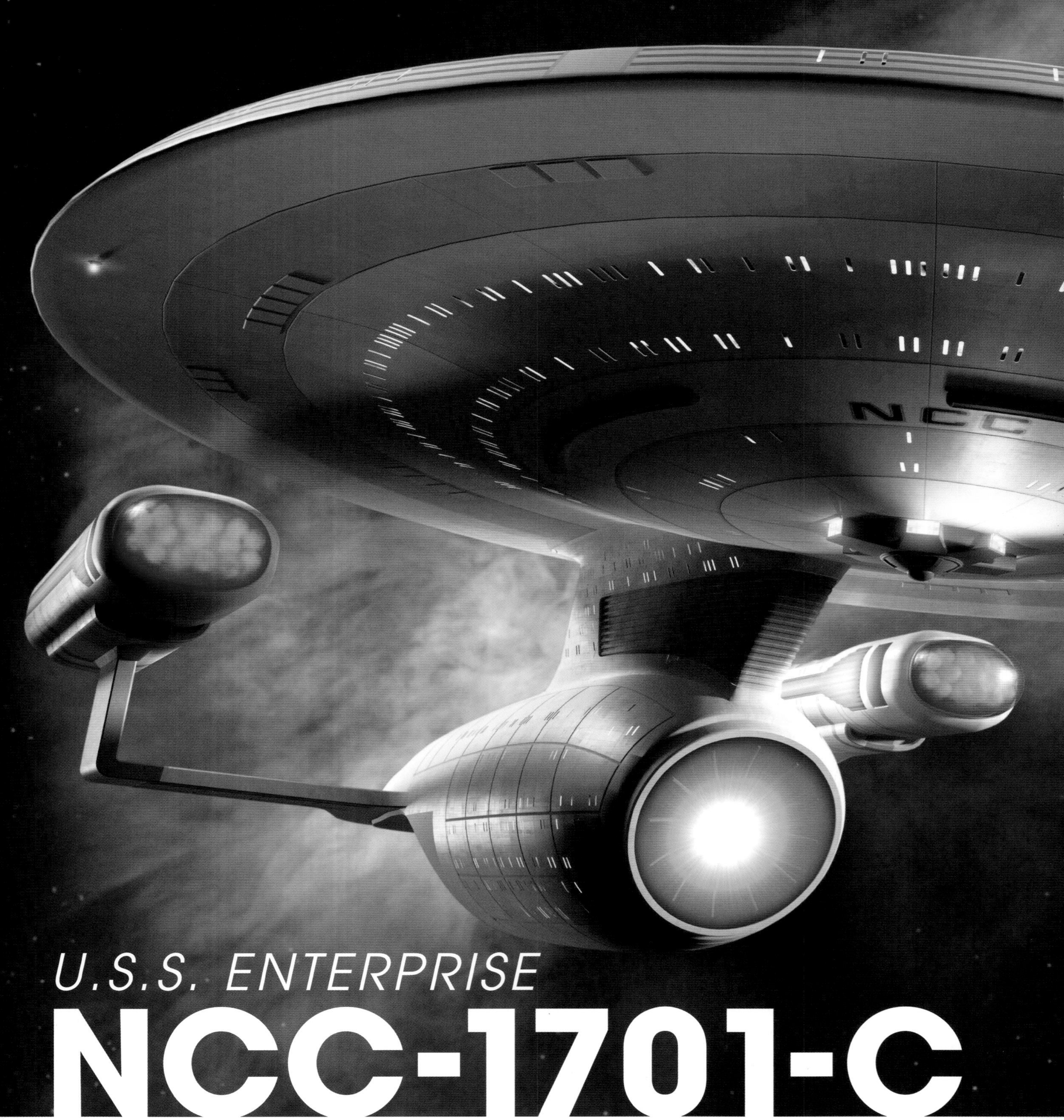

U.S.S. ENTERPRISE

NCC-1701-C

A ship of deep space discovery, the *Enterprise*-C earned a surprise place in history for gallantry in battle.

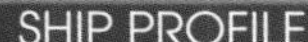

◀ The *Enterprise*-C was designed for exploration and spent much of its operational life charting stellar phenomena.

This *Ambassador*-class *Enterprise*-C was operational in the early part of the 24th century, but in 2344 achieved unexpected fame after it was lost with all hands. This occurred while it was defending the Klingon outpost on Narendra III from a Romulan attack. This act of heroism impressed the Klingon Empire and was instrumental in leading to a treaty between the Klingons and the Federation.

The *Enterprise*-C was constructed at Earth Station McKinley during the 2320s and commissioned in 2332. It was given the name *Enterprise* after the *Enterprise*-B was declared lost in 2329, so becoming the fourth Federation starship to bear the name. Six months before its launch, the ship was placed under the command of 33-year-old Captain Rachel Garrett, who had previously served as the first officer on the *U.S.S. Hood*. Garrett was the *Enterprise*-C's first and only commanding officer.

The *Enterprise*-C was the third *Ambassador*-class ship built by Starfleet. Other ships in the class included the *U.S.S. Adelphi* NCC-26849, the *U.S.S. Zhukov* NCC-26136, and the *U.S.S. Excalibur* NCC-26517. Measuring 526 meters from bow to stern, it was about twice the length of the *Constitution*-class *Enterprise* NCC-1701. With 36 decks and a crew of 530, it was one of the largest ships that Starfleet had built to date.

In terms of design, the *Ambassador* class was a clear midpoint between the *Constitution* and *Galaxy* classes. The engines benefited from a number of advances in warp technology that came about during Starfleet's unsuccessful

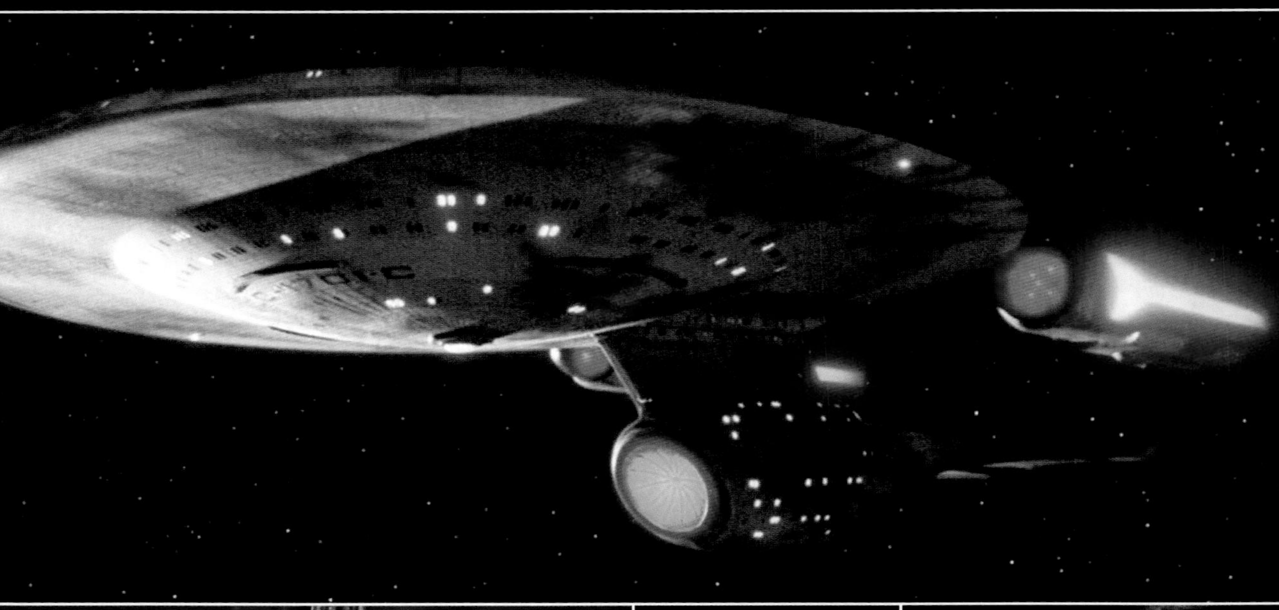

▶ After the *Enterprise*-C was removed from history, the timeline was altered. Knowing nothing of the ship's sacrifice, the Federation went to war with the Klingons. In that time, Starfleet ships were designed for combat rather than exploration and the crew of the *Enterprise*-D were soldiers not explorers.

▶▶ By 2366, the Federation was losing the war with the Klingons, and Picard expected Starfleet to surrender within six months.

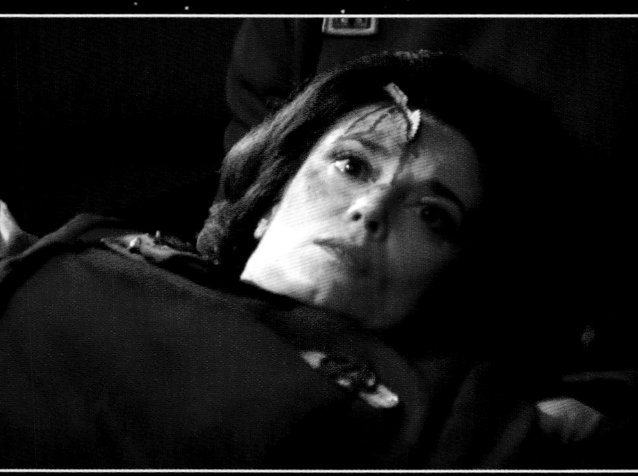

▲ An antimatter explosion during the battle for Narendra III created a temporal rift that sent the *Enterprise*-C 22 years into the future. Here it encountered the Galaxy-class *Enterprise*-D.

▶ Most of the crew were killed, and after Garrett's death the helmsman Richard Castillo became the senior officer.

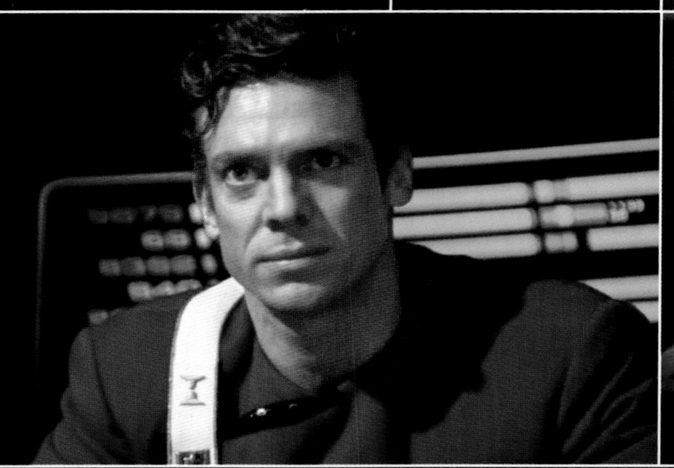

▲ Captain Garrett was preparing to take the *Enterprise*-C back in time when it was attacked by three Klingon ships. She was killed by a piece of exploding shrapnel.

transwarp development program of the 2280s. The *Enterprise*-C was capable of sustaining speeds of warp 8.4 on the newly redrawn warp scale. It was also extremely maneuverable, easily outperforming Romulan vessels of a comparable class. To deal with emergencies, such as a matter/antimatter containment failure, the *Ambassador* class was one of the first to be designed with a vertical warp core that could be ejected from a hatch in the ventral hull.

The sensor systems were concentrated in a sensor dome on the underside of the saucer directly below the main bridge and in pallets mounted on deck 2, with the main deflector providing long-range scans.

The single point phaser emitters used on previous *Enterprises* were replaced by five dorsal and three ventral type-7 phaser emitters. These weapons represented a significant upgrade, since they could generate a beam from many more origin points than before. The *Enterprise*-C also had forward and aft torpedo launchers.

MANY SHUTTLECRAFT

As the *Enterprise*-C was intended for deep space exploration, it was equipped with a large number of shuttles. These were housed in two shuttlebays, one located at the rear of the ship and one in the saucer section. Several of these shuttles were specifically designed for cataloging stellar phenomena at close range, but they were also frequently needed for missions where gaseous environments made the use of the transporters impossible.

The *Enterprise*-C spent most of its years in service on peaceful scientific and exploration missions, but in the 2330s and 2340s galactic politics were still fraught. In 2344, the ship was making its way

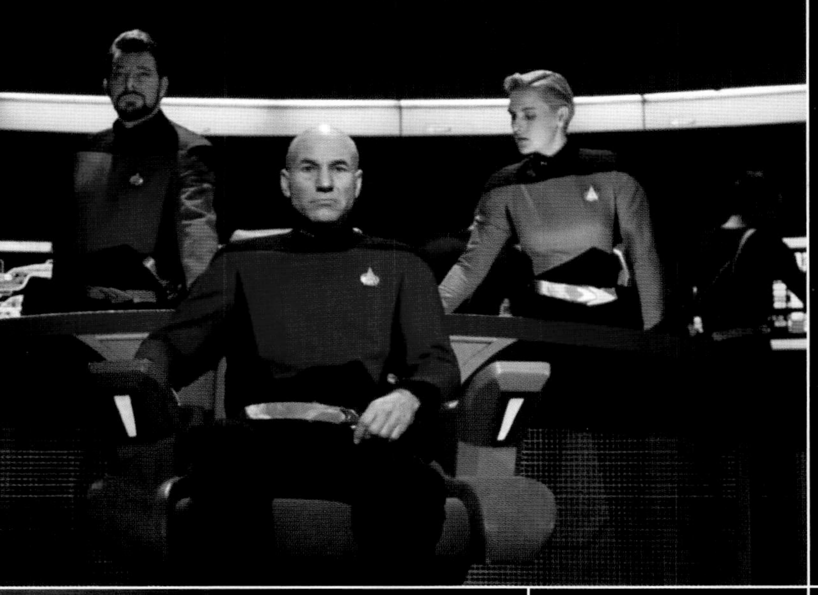

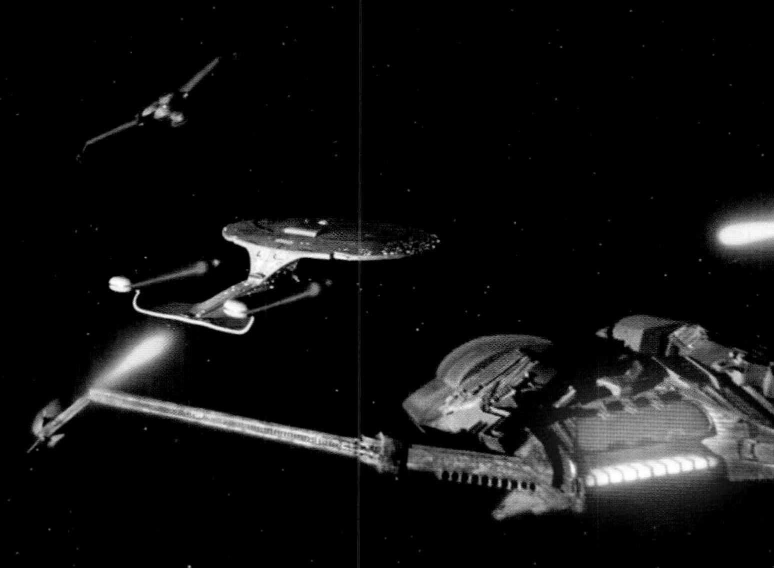

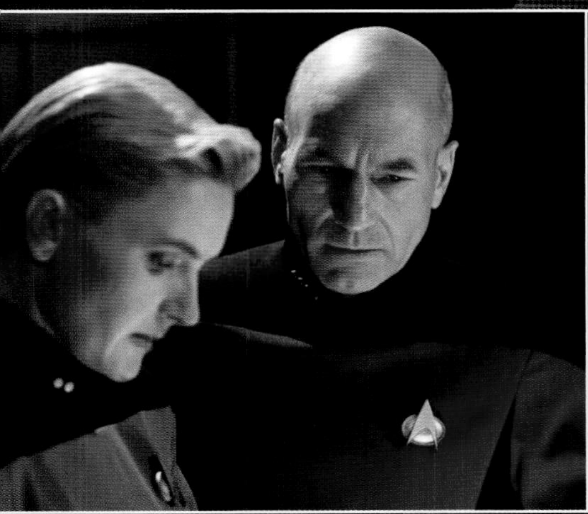

◀ In the altered version of the timeline, Tasha Yar was still alive, but when she realized that this was "wrong," she volunteered to return with the crew of the *Enterprise*-C in the hope of balancing out Garrett's death.

▶ When the *Enterprise*-C returned through the temporal rift, it restored the "correct" timeline.

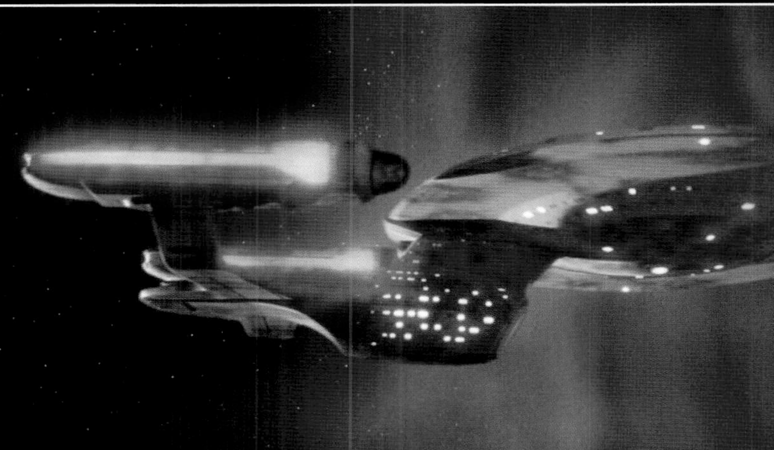

to the planet Archer IV when it responded to a distress call from the Klingon outpost at Narendra III. When the *Enterprise*-C arrived, it found the outpost under a massive Romulan attack and attempted to defend it.

The Starfleet ship was lost during the battle, but what no one realized was that, before it was destroyed, it was thrown through a temporal rift that sent it 22 years into an alternate future where its heroic sacrifice had not been recorded. As a result, in this altered timeline, the Federation and the Klingons were at war. The *Enterprise*-C crew made the choice to return to certain death in their own time, in the hope that their sacrifice would engender a better future.

After the loss of the *Enterprise*-C, it would be another 20 years before a new *Enterprise*, in the form of the *Galaxy*-class *U.S.S. Enterprise* NCC-1701-D, was commissioned.

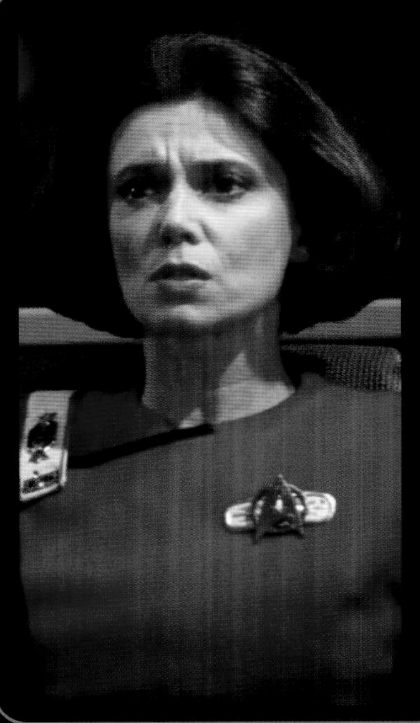

DATA FEED

Captain Rachel Garrett spent 12 years commanding the *Enterprise*-C. She took command in late 2332, when she was promoted to captain after a well-regarded tour as the first officer of the *U.S.S. Hood*. She spent the first six months of her command supervising the final testing of her new ship, before it was commissioned and assigned to an ongoing mission of deep space exploration.

Garrett died in an alternate future, when the *Enterprise*-C was propelled to the year 2366 and attacked by Klingons. Before she died, she had decided to return to certain death in her own time, hoping that her crew's sacrifice would help to avert a war.

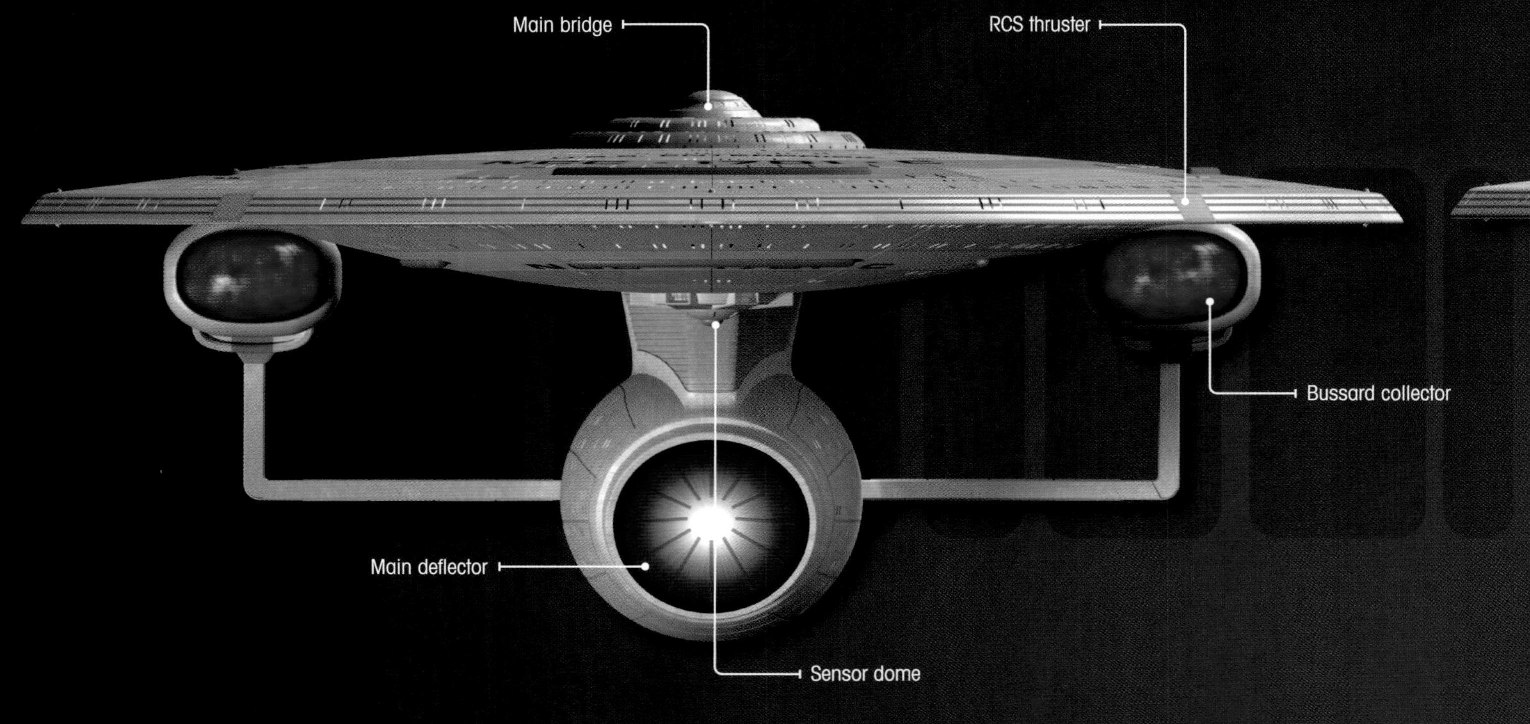
Main bridge
RCS thruster
Bussard collector
Main deflector
Sensor dome

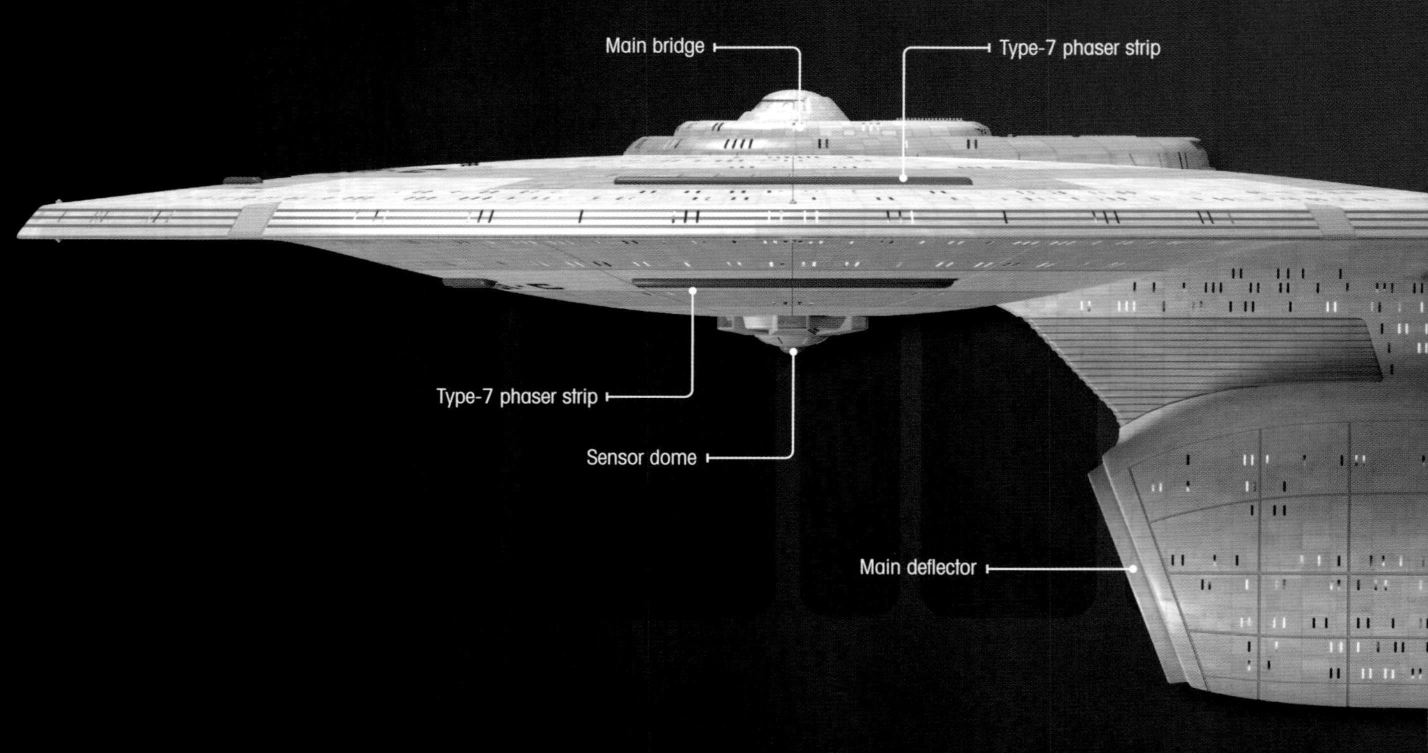
Main bridge
Type-7 phaser strip
Type-7 phaser strip
Sensor dome
Main deflector
Warp core ejection hatch

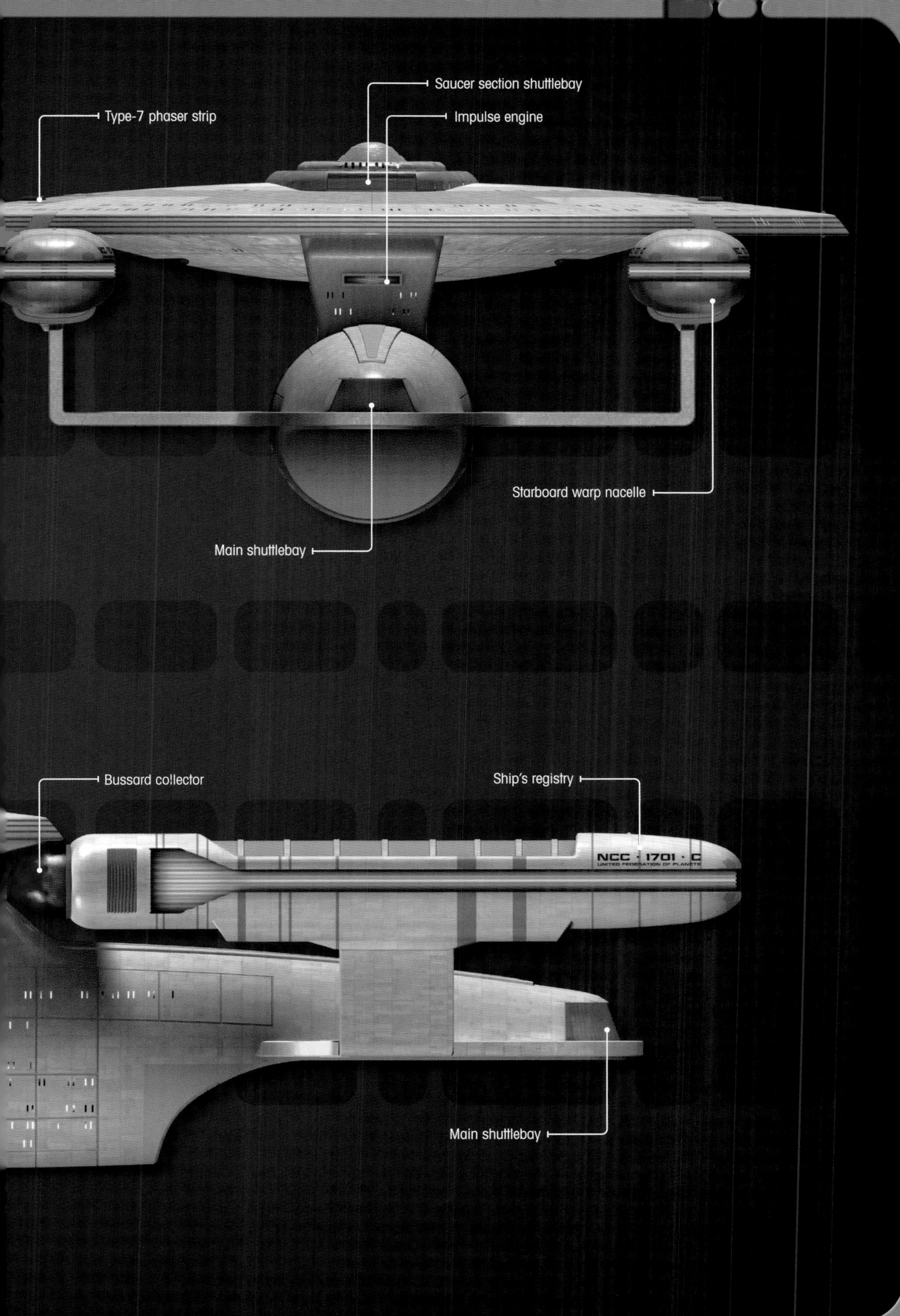

WARP FIELD

Advances in warp field technology meant that the nacelles on the *Ambassador* class were in a lower position relative to the saucer section than on earlier starship vessels.

FIGHTING VESSELS

Although primarily designed for exploration, *Ambassador*-class ships fought in the Dominion War and helped to establish the barricade that restricted Romulan involvement in the Klingon civil war.

TACTICAL ADVANTAGE

When the *Enterprise*-C returned to its own time, its systems had been repaired but only to the standards of its own time. It did, however, have the advantage of Tasha Yar's tactical experience.

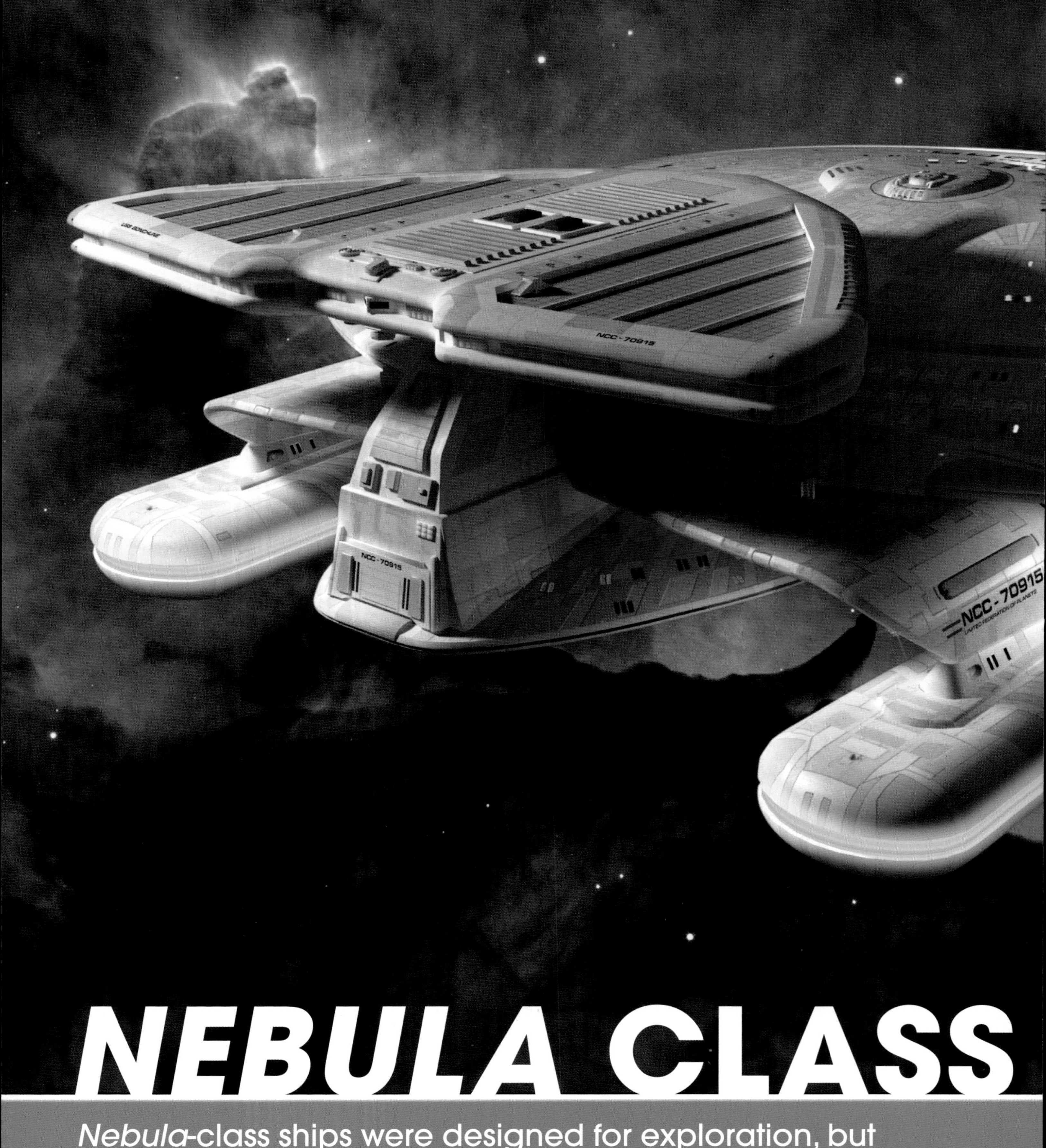

NEBULA CLASS

Nebula-class ships were designed for exploration, but were often diverted to patrol and combat duties.

◀ The *Nebula* class's most distinctive feature was an upper equipment module that could be configured for different mission profiles.

This type of starship was designed by Starfleet in the latter half of the 24th century, primarily to carry out scientific and exploratory roles. In addition, these ships often took on patrol and transport duties, and could ably perform combat assignments when required.

The *Nebula* class was a contemporary of the *Galaxy* class and they shared several design features, including a very similar saucer section. There were, however, several significant differences between them. At 442.23 meters long, the *Nebula* class was about 200 meters shorter than its *Galaxy* counterpart, and its crew complement was normally around 750, compared to 1,000 aboard the larger vessel. The engineering hull on *Nebula*-class vessels was also slightly more curved and rounded than it was on *Galaxy*-class ships. While the two classes of ship shared a similar design for the warp nacelles, these hung beside the engineering hull on the *Nebula* class, rather than being supported above the secondary hull, as on the *Galaxy* class.

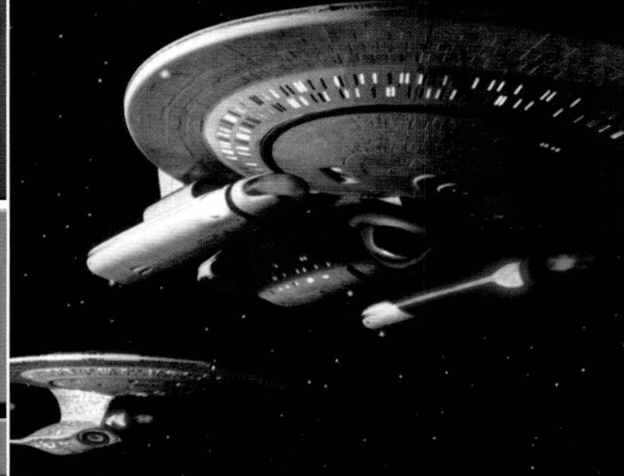

ADAPTABLE MODULE

The most significant difference between the two classes was that *Nebula*-class ships featured a large equipment module at the rear, which rose up behind the saucer section. This module could be outfitted for specific assignments, but usually carried an array of sensor equipment, although it could also be customized to carry more weapons.

Reflecting its versatile role, the equipment module did not look the same on all *Nebula*-class ships. For example, on the *U.S.S. Phoenix* NCC-65420, the pod rose high above the saucer section

◀ The *Nebula* class was designed and constructed in the 24th century, around the same time as the larger *Galaxy* class. As a result, they shared similar technology and components. In particular, the *Nebula* class had a saucer section that was almost identical in design and size to that of *Galaxy*-class ships.

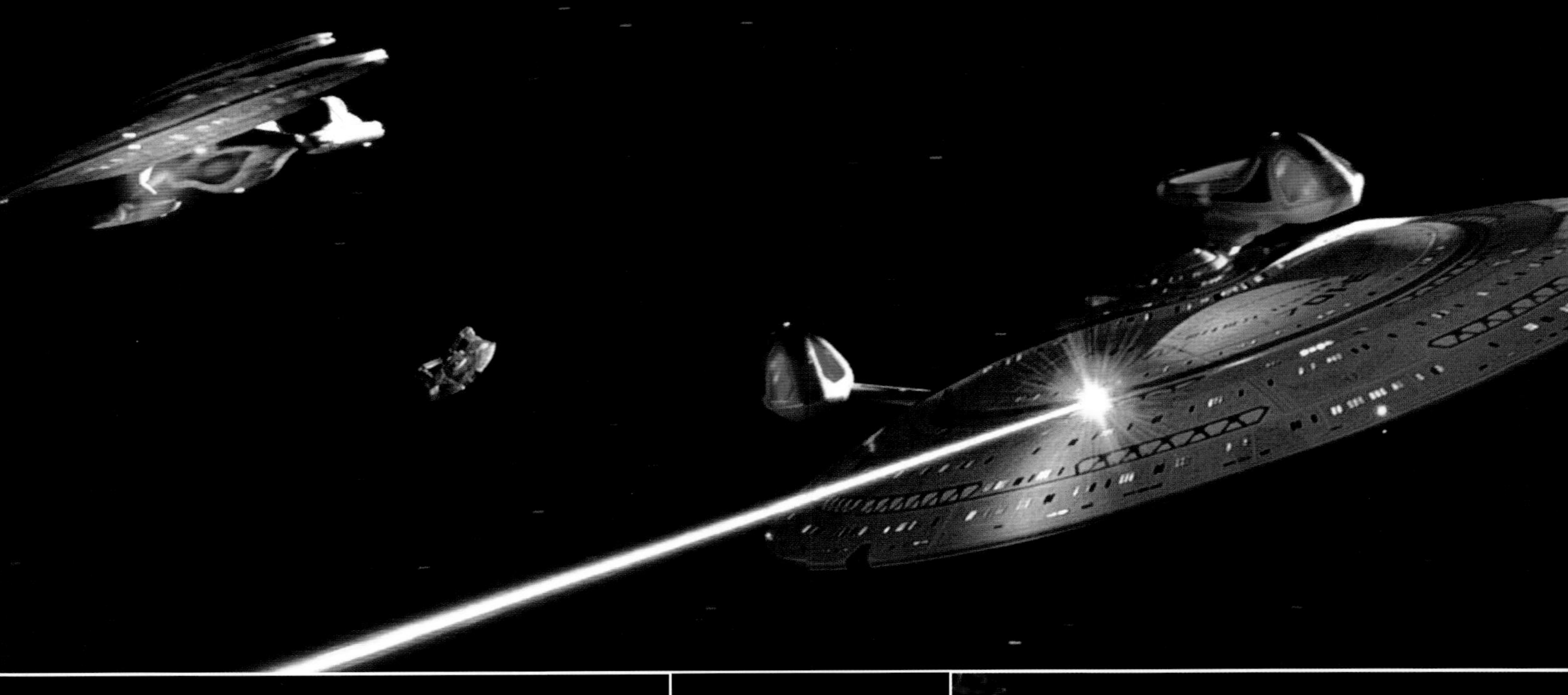

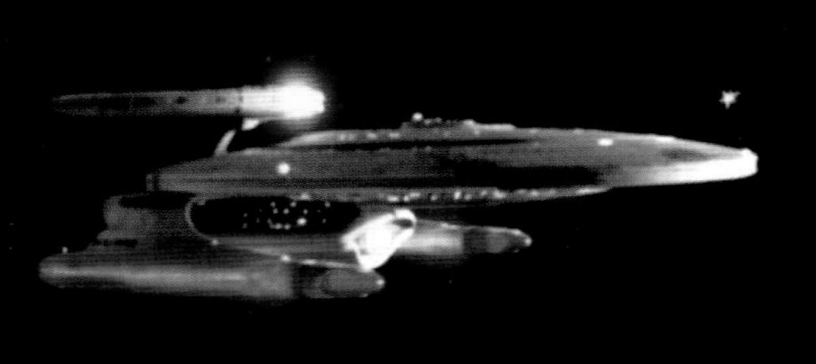

▶ *Nebula*-class ships swapped their normal exploratory duties for a combat role during the Dominion War. They fought alongside the *U.S.S. Defiant* NX-74205 in several major engagements of the war, inlcuding the final assault on Cardassia.

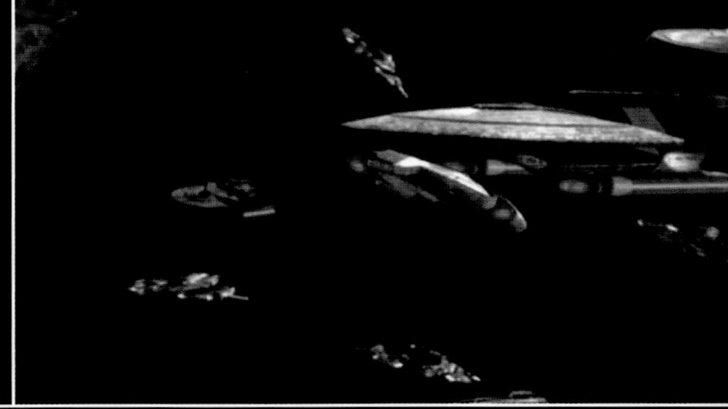

▲ The *Nebula* class was equipped with two torpedo launchers as standard. The equipment module could be configured to carry additional torpedo launchers, thereby increasing its firepower. The *U.S.S. Sutherland* is seen here firing a torpedo from its adaptable superstructure.

and was elliptical, while on the *U.S.S. Sutherland* NCC-72015, it was positioned lower and was more triangular in shape.

Like all Starfleet ships, the *Nebula* class was constantly upgraded. In 2368, its top speed was warp 9.3, but by 2370, this had risen to warp 9.5. Chief Miles O'Brien even managed to eke out more power from the engines of the *Nebula*-class *U.S.S. Prometheus* NCC-71201 so that it could reach warp 9.6 for a short time.

The standard weaponry aboard *Nebula*-class vessels included eight type-10 phaser emitters and two torpedo launchers, while some versions also had extra launchers in the equipment modules.

The shields on *Nebula*-class ships were highly effective and could withstand a direct hit from a Cardassian warship's disruptor weapon, but they did have one slight weakness. Every five-and-a-half minutes, a *Nebula*-class ship would perform a high-energy sensor sweep, but between the sweep ending and another one starting, the shields would have to be realigned. This left the ship unprotected for a fiftieth of a second.

Overall, *Nebula*-class vessels were designed primarily for exploration, as were *Galaxy*-class ships, but they were smaller and slightly less powerful. Serving on board a *Nebula*-class vessel was still regarded as a plum assignment.

PRESTIGIOUS POSITION

Dr. Elizabeth Lense, the valedictorian of Dr. Bashir's Starfleet Medical School class, chose to join the crew of the *Nebula*-class *U.S.S. Lexington*, much to the envy of her classmates. She spent several years on board the *Lexington* on a deep space mission charting unexplored planets.

Ships of this class were also used for specific scientific missions. In 2370, the *U.S.S. Prometheus*

◀ In 2373, *Nebula*-class ships battled the Borg alongside the *U.S.S. Enterprise* NCC-1701-E.

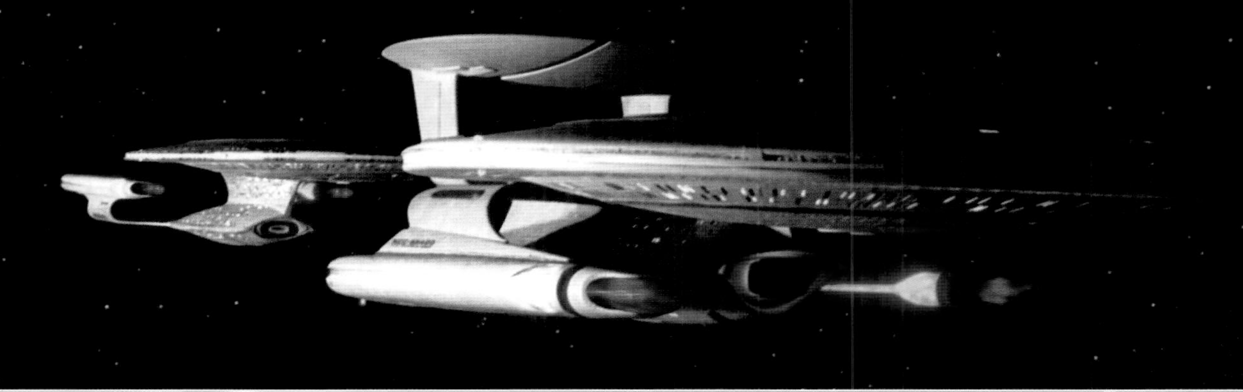

▶ The *U.S.S. Phoenix,* commanded by Ben Maxwell, was fitted with an elliptical equipment module that rose high above the primary hull.

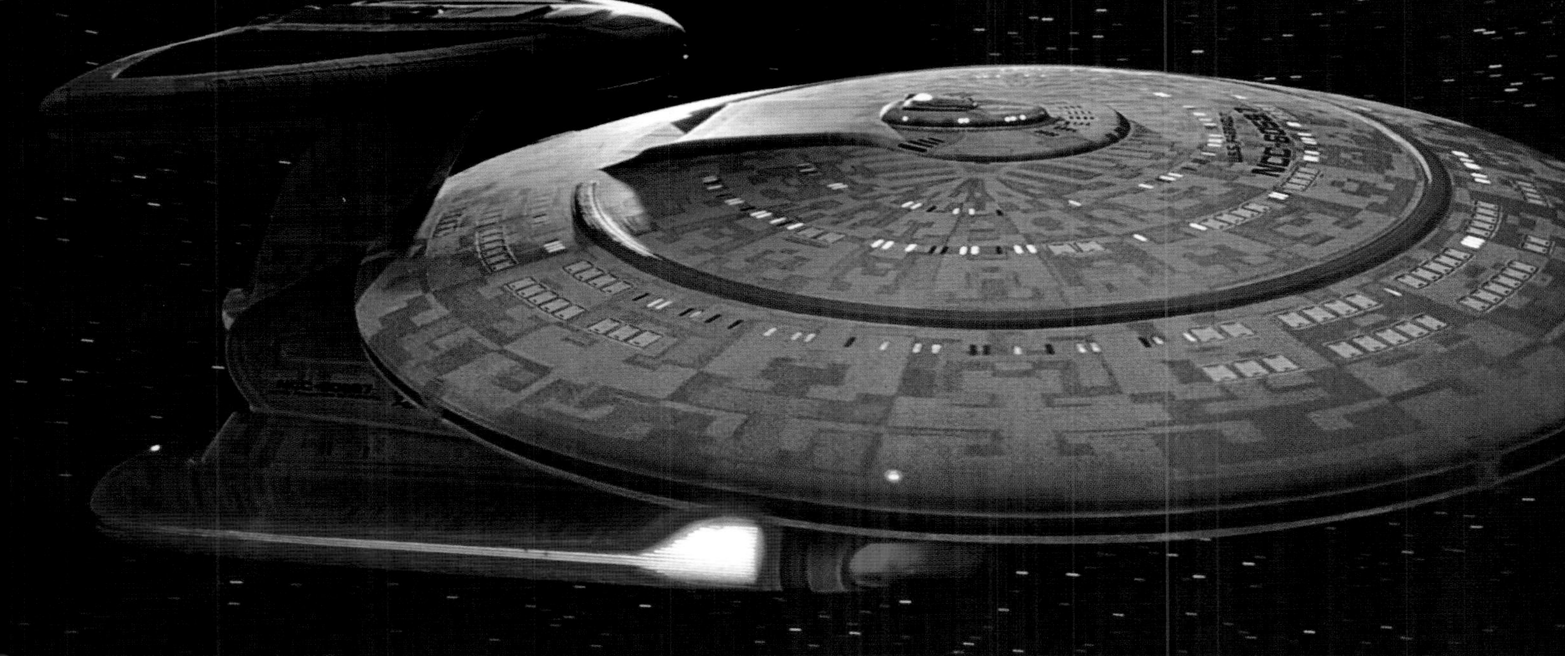

NCC-71201 was assigned to Gideon Seyetik, and aided in his experiment to find out if protomatter could be used to reignite a dead star.

Nebula-class vessels were also deployed on patrol duties to help protect Federation borders. In the 2360s, the *U.S.S. Monitor* NCC-61826 was used to safeguard the Romulan Neutral Zone, while the *U.S.S. Phoenix* performed a similar role in the Demilitarized Zone between Federation and Cardassian space.

Increasingly, *Nebula*-class vessels were seconded to a combat role. At least one was involved and destroyed in the Battle of Wolf 359 against the Borg, and more took part in the later Borg invasion at the Battle of Sector 001.

In 2367-68, when the *U.S.S. Sutherland* NCC-72015 was under the temporary command of Lieutenant Commander Data, it was used as part of a blockade to stop Romulan ships supplying the House of Duras with weapons and supplies during the Klingon civil war.

Nebula-class ships also played a large part during hostilities with the Dominion. The *U.S.S. T'Kumbra,* which had an all-Vulcan crew, spent six months fighting on the front lines, while the *U.S.S. Sutherland* was part of the Ninth Fleet that saw action in most of the major battles of the Dominion War.

▲ The *U.S.S. Farragut* NCC-60597 was a *Nebula*-class ship that helped recover the crew of the *U.S.S. Enterprise* NCC-1701-D after its saucer section crash-landed on Veridian III.

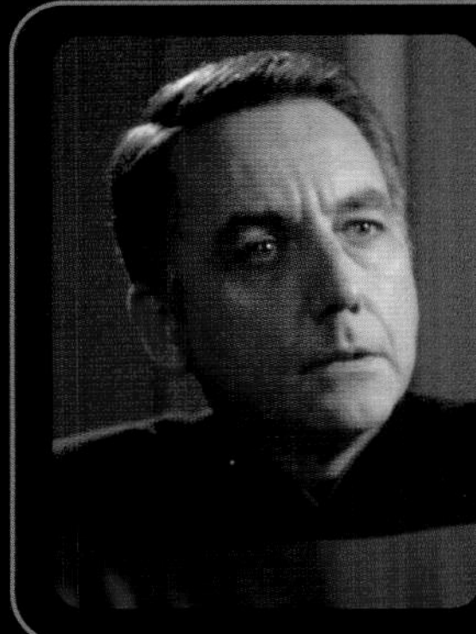

DATA FEED

In 2367, Benjamin Maxwell, captain of the *Nebula*-class *U.S.S. Phoenix* NCC-65420, went rogue and used his ship to destroy a Cardassian outpost. When the *U.S.S. Enterprise* NCC-1701-D caught up with him, Maxwell claimed that the Cardassians were stockpiling weapons in preparation for war. Although Maxwell was brought to justice, his accusations against the Cardassians ultimately proved correct.

NEBULA-CLASS BRIDGE

As on most other classes of Starfleet vessel, the bridge on *Nebula*-class ships was located on deck 1 at the top of the saucer section. There were three entrances to the bridge: one on each side of the room and a third at the rear. The captain's chair was in the center of the room with two free-standing consoles on either side: one was the science station, while the other could be used to remotely control the ship's shuttlecraft. Separate conn and ops stations were on a lower level in front of the command chair and, as always on Starfleet vessels, the main viewscreen was at the front where all the bridge crew could see it.

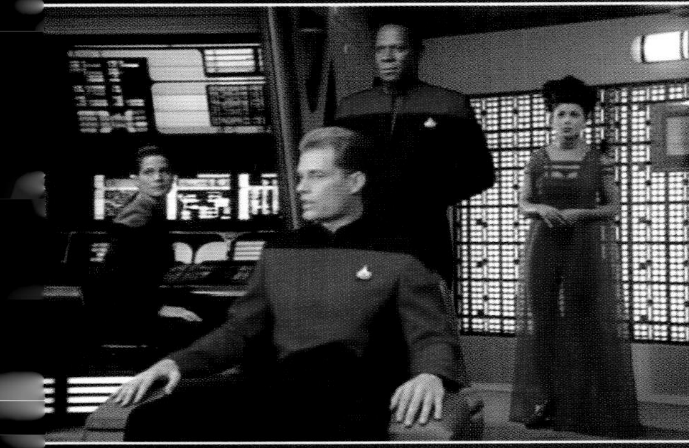

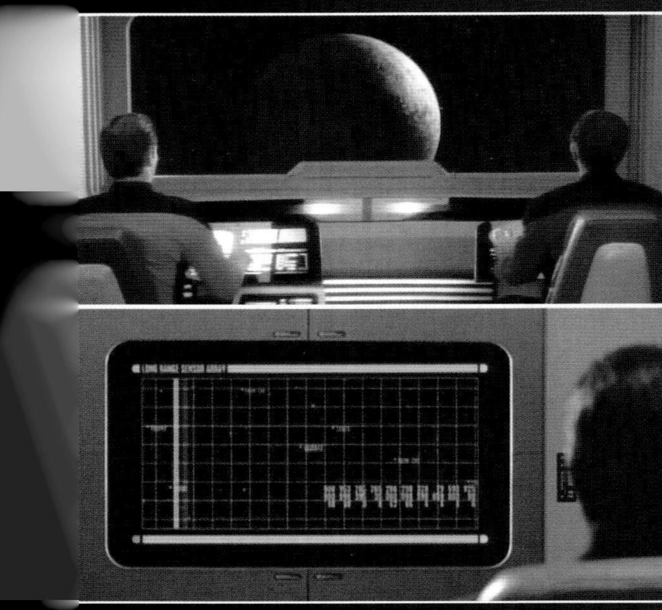

▲ The viewscreen on the *U.S.S. Prometheus* (middle picture) was similar to the viewscreens aboard *Galaxy*-class ships, whereas the viewscreen on the *U.S.S. Sutherland* (above) was much smaller.

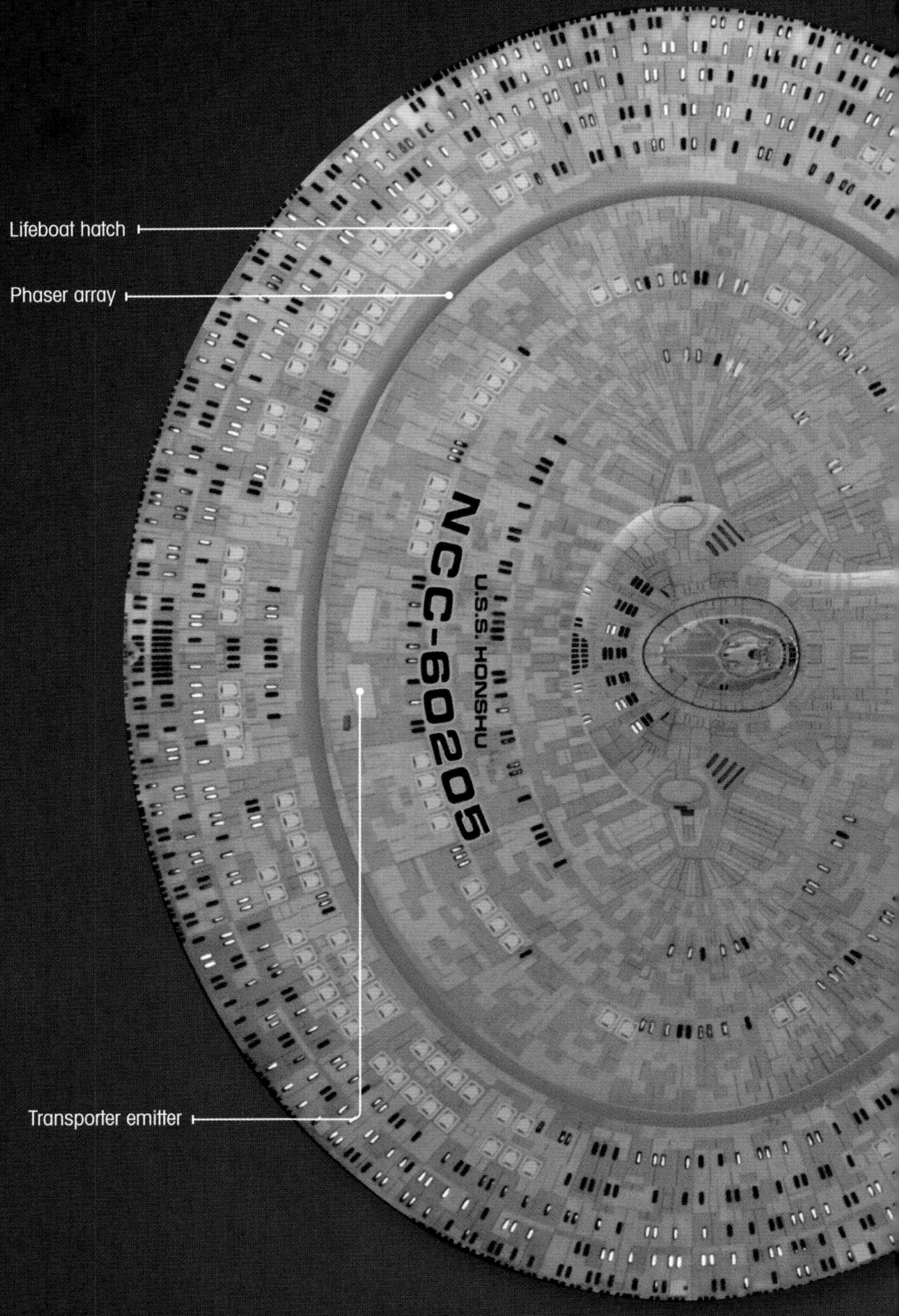

Lifeboat hatch

Phaser array

U.S.S. HONSHU

NCC-60205

Transporter emitter

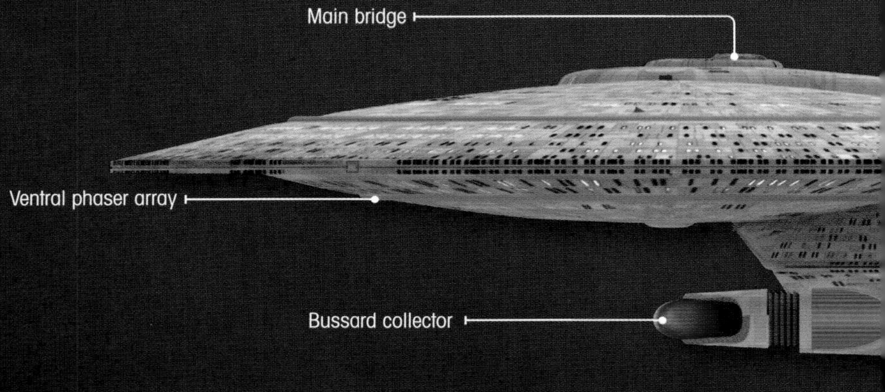

Main bridge

Ventral phaser array

Bussard collector

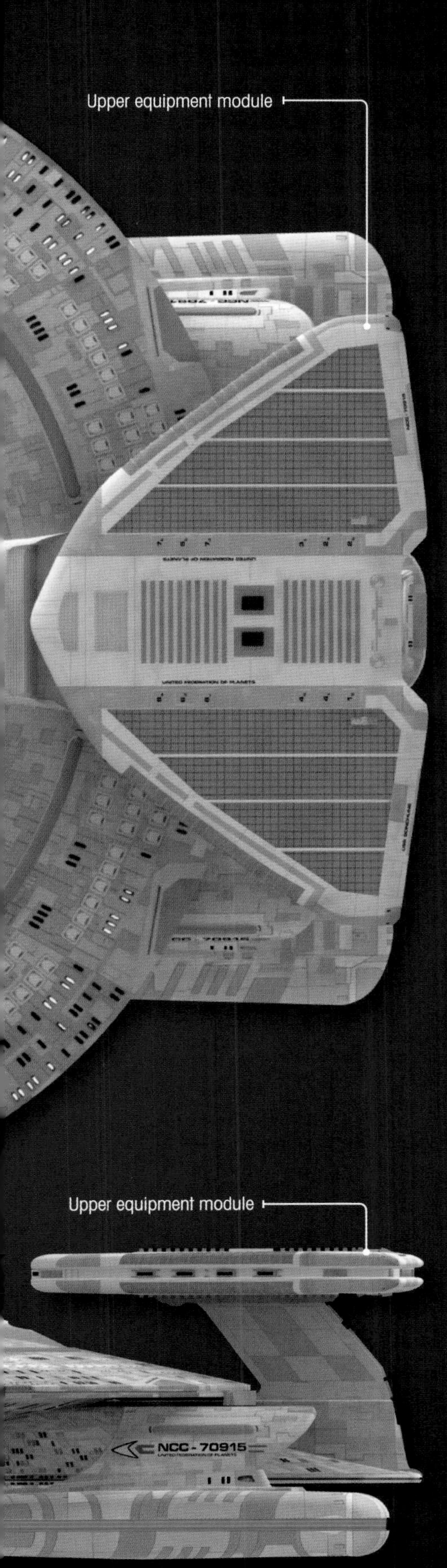

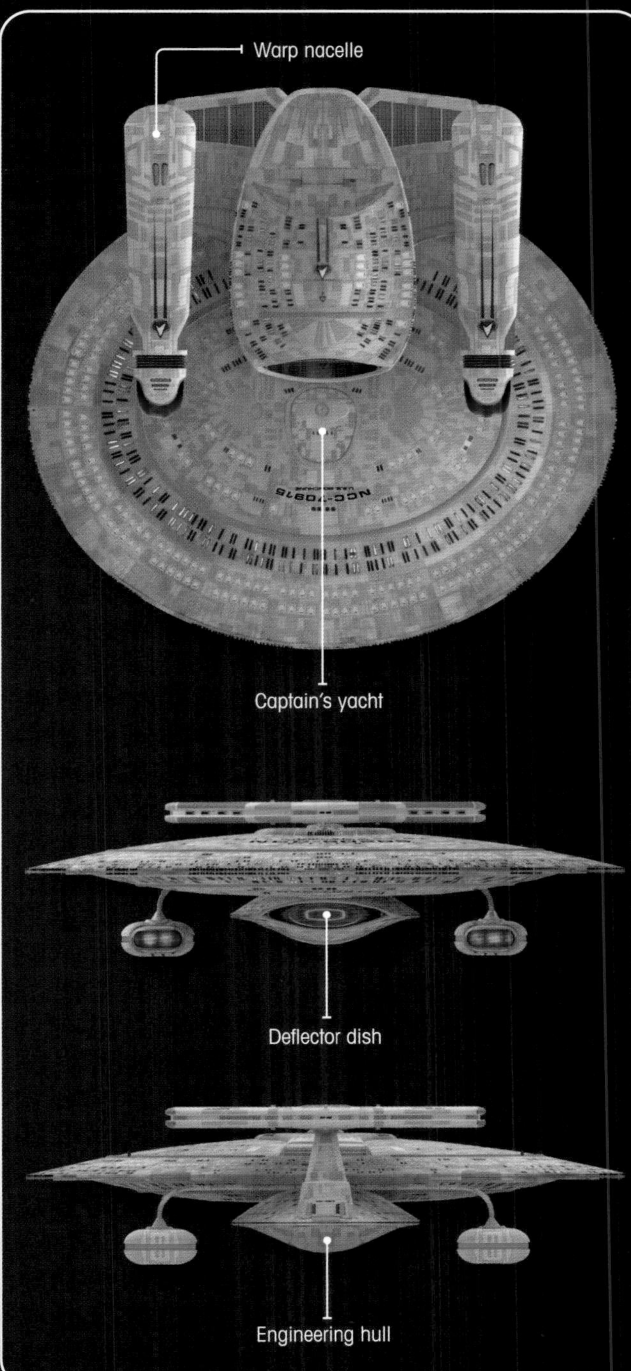

VULCAN CREW

The *Nebula*-class *U.S.S. T'Kumbra* was commanded by Captain Solok and had an all-Vulcan crew. It spent six months fighting on the front lines during the war with the Dominion.

MISSING IN ACTION

Geordi La Forge's mother, Silva La Forge, captained the *Nebula*-class *U.S.S. Hera* NCC-62006. It was on a routine courier run when it went missing. Despite a massive search, the *Hera* was never found.

DATA FEED

***Nebula*-class starships were equipped with a variety of auxiliary craft, including type-6 and type-7 shuttlecraft, as well as the smaller type-15 shuttlepod.**

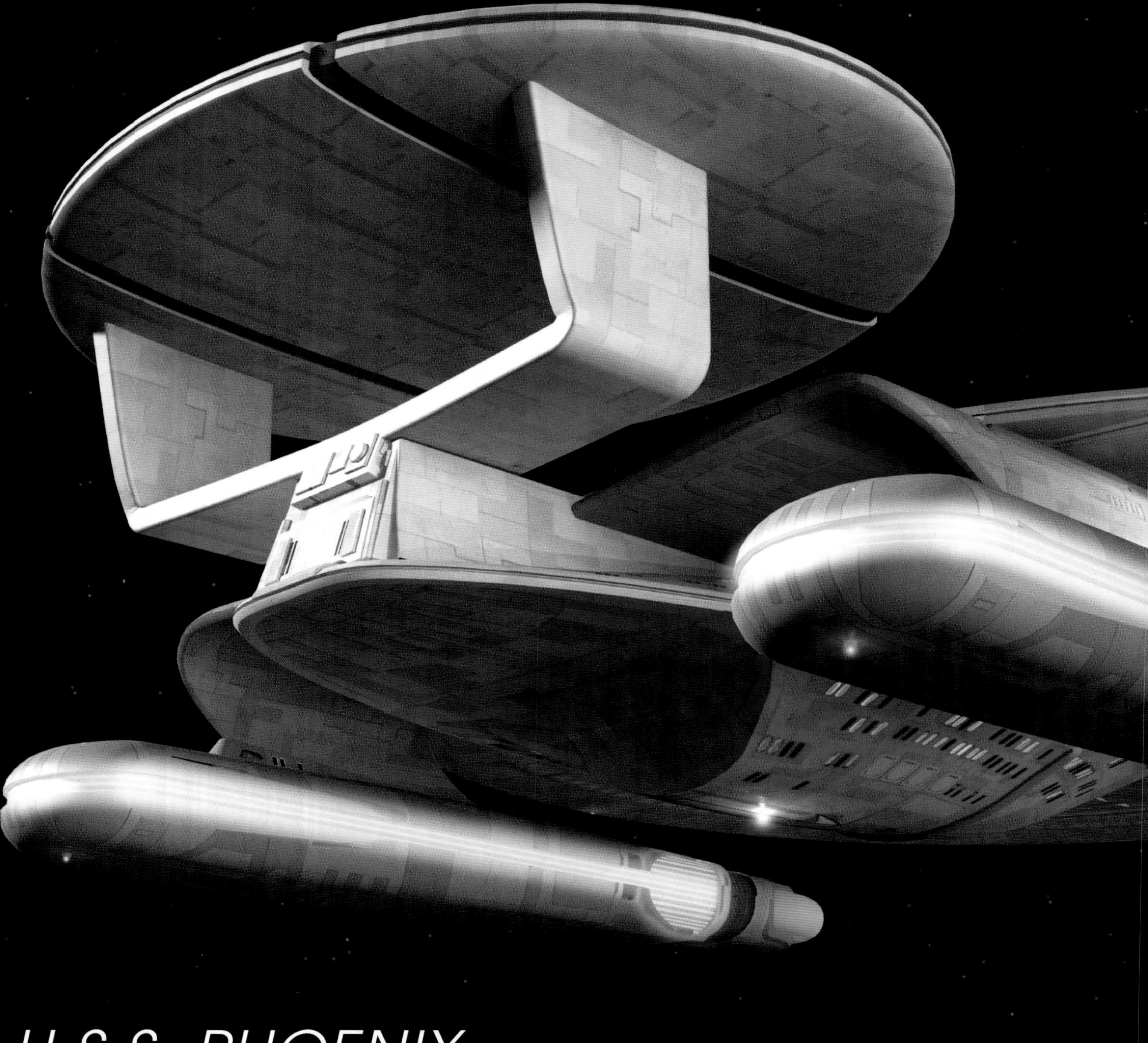

U.S.S. PHOENIX

NCC-65420

In 2367, Captain Maxwell of the *U.S.S. Phoenix* went rogue and led his ship on several attacks against the Cardassians.

◀ On the *U.S.S. Phoenix*, the elliptical module attached above the rear of the engineering hull was equipped with additional sensor equipment.

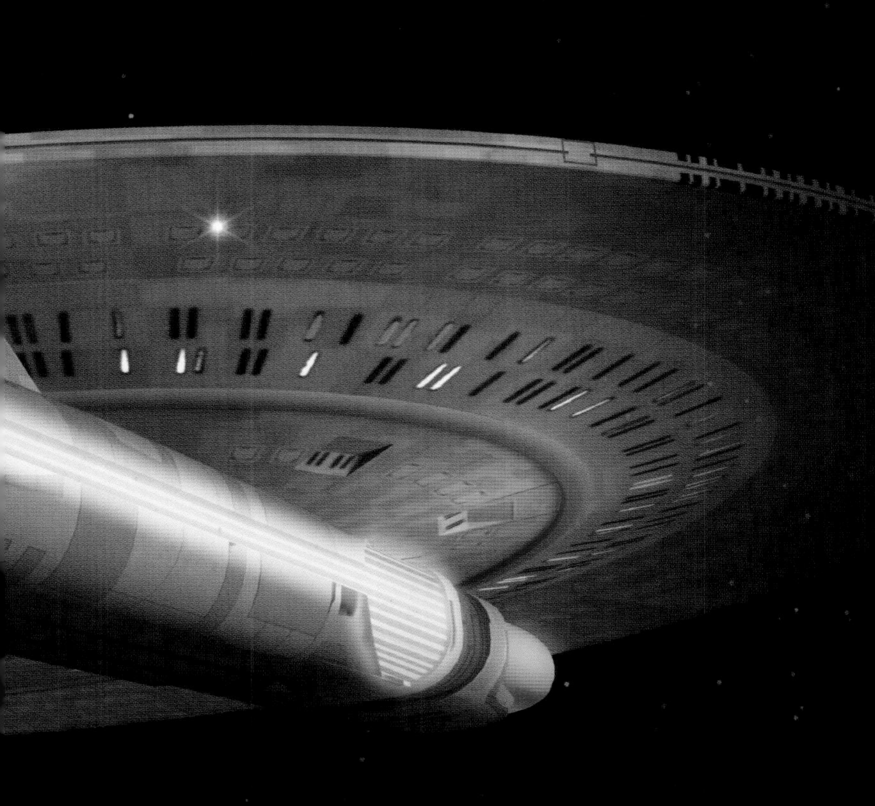

The *Nebula*-class *Phoenix* NCC-65420 was built in 2363 by the Yoyodyne Division at 40 Eridani A Starfleet Construction Yards in the Vulcan system in operation in the 2360s, and in service over the following years.

The *Phoenix* was constructed around the same time as the *U.S.S. Enterprise* NCC-1701-D, and they shared many design features. For example, the *Phoenix* had an almost identical saucer section and warp nacelles to the *Enterprise*-D's, although the *Phoenix*'s secondary hull was different, being shorter and more curved.

At approximately 465 meters in length, the *Phoenix* was roughly two-thirds the length of the *Enterprise*-D, and looked more compact when seen in profile. This was because the *Phoenix* did not have a neck section between the primary and secondary hulls. Instead, the saucer sat directly on top of the engineering section, while the nacelles were suspended just below the secondary hull.

ADDITIONAL MODULE

The *Phoenix* featured an elliptical module that rose up on two supports from the back of the engineering hull and looked over the saucer section. This module could be configured to carry a variety of equipment depending on mission requirements. On the *Phoenix*, this superstructure was outfitted with extra sensor equipment, but on other *Nebula*-class ships, it carried additional weaponry.

The *Phoenix* was a multipurpose ship and was normally assigned to scientific and exploratory

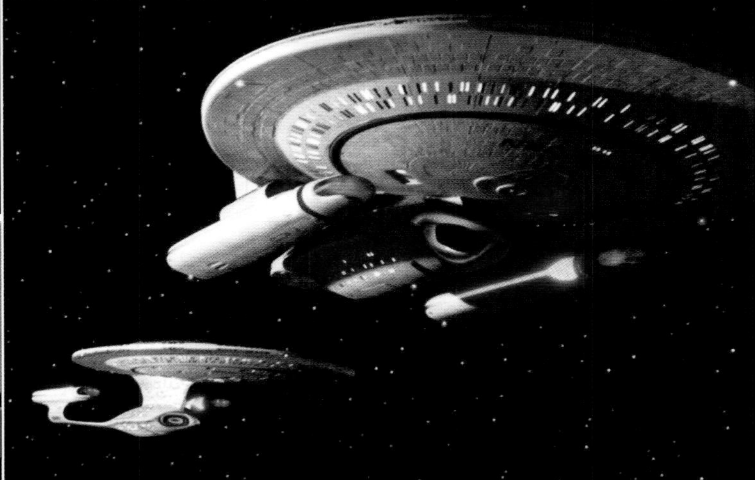

◀ The *Phoenix* was roughly two-thirds the length of the *U.S.S. Enterprise* NCC-1701-D, and was outfitted with many of the same components. The saucer section and warp nacelles appeared to be exactly the same on both vessels, but the engineering hull was shorter and more curved on the *Phoenix*, while its deflector dish was squarer.

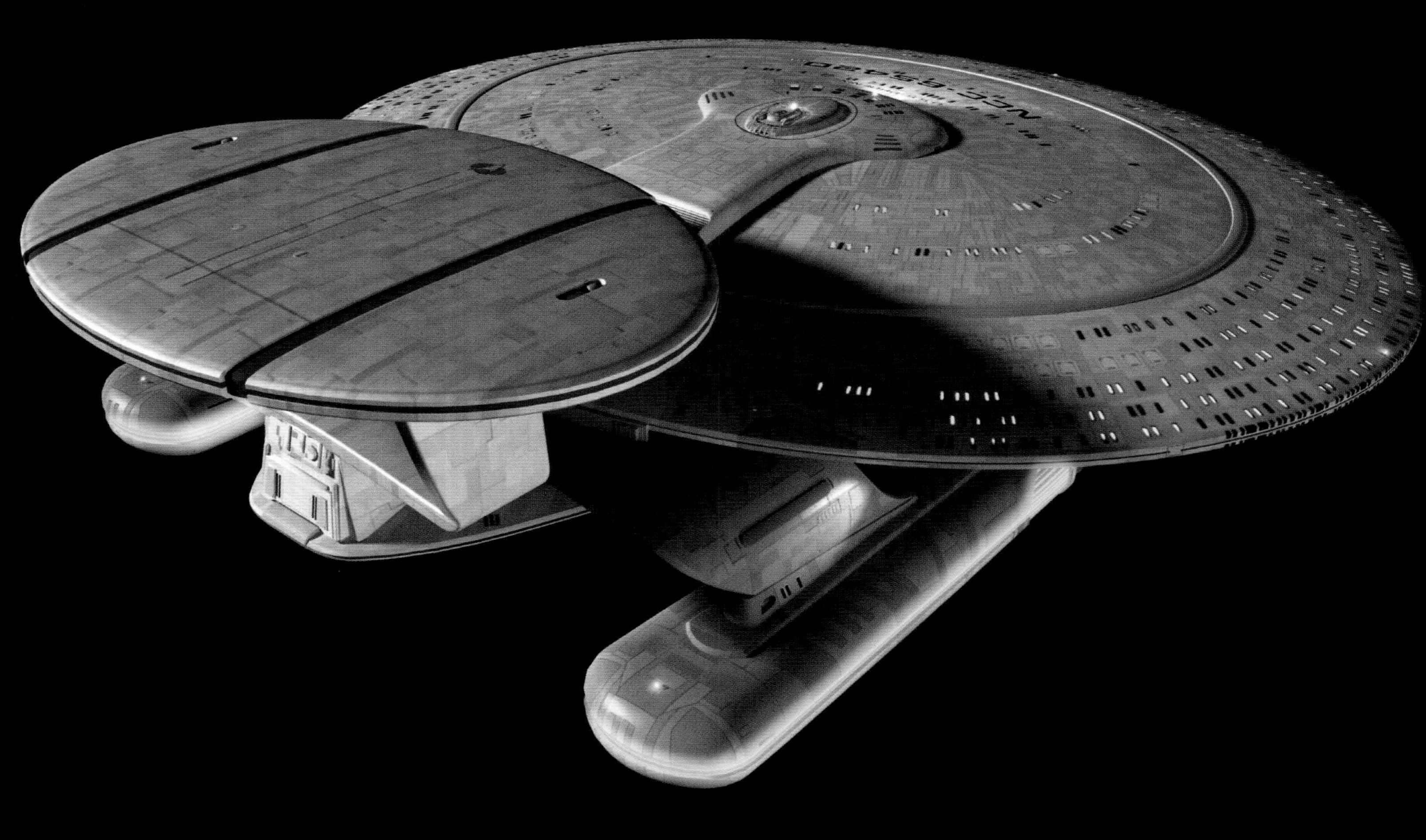

▲ Apart from the large sensor module that rose up from the back of the secondary hull, the *Phoenix* was very similar to the *Enterprise*-D. It may not have been quite as large as Starfleet's flagship, nor have as many facilities, but it was still a powerful ship. The *Phoenix* had no trouble destroying a Cardassian warship, even after the prefix code had been used to lower the *Phoenix*'s shields.

missions, but it was equally suited to transportation and defensive patrol duties. It had a crew complement of around 750, but other *Nebula*-class ships such as the *U.S.S. Hera* NCC-62006 were known to operate with a crew of just 300.

The typical offensive arsenal of the *Phoenix* included a torpedo launcher located just above the deflector dish on the secondary hull. It also had multiple phaser arrays, with one positioned below the deflector dish and others at various points around the primary hull. Its maximum effective weapons range was just under 300,000 kilometers. The *Phoenix* was fitted with warp and impulse drives, and was capable of maintaining a top speed of warp 9.5 for short periods.

In 2367, the *Phoenix* was under the command of Captain Benjamin Maxwell, one of the most highly regarded officers in Starfleet. The ship had been assigned patrol duties near the recently established Demilitarized Zone between Federation and Cardassian space, following a long conflict between the two powers.

ROGUE CAPTAIN

It came to Starfleet's attention that the *Phoenix*, apparently without provocation, had destroyed an unarmed Cardassian science station. To avoid a major diplomatic incident, the *Enterprise*-D was tasked with taking three Cardassian officers onboard in a transparent effort to show them that they were doing everything to locate the *Phoenix*.

Not long after, the *Phoenix* destroyed a Cardassian warship, taking 600 lives in the process. It then turned its attention to a smaller supply ship and annihilated that too, taking a further 50 lives.

When the *Enterprise*-D eventually caught up with the *Phoenix*, Captain Maxwell explained that the Cardassians were arming again in anticipation

▶ The *Enterprise*-D was escorting the *Phoenix* back to Federation space when Captain Maxwell's ship broke off to pursue another supply ship. Maxwell was determined to prove the Cardassians were rearming for war.

▼ The crew of the *Enterprise*-D watched helplessly on their monitors as the *Phoenix* bore down on two Cardassian vessels. First the *Phoenix* destroyed a warship, then it wiped out a supply ship.

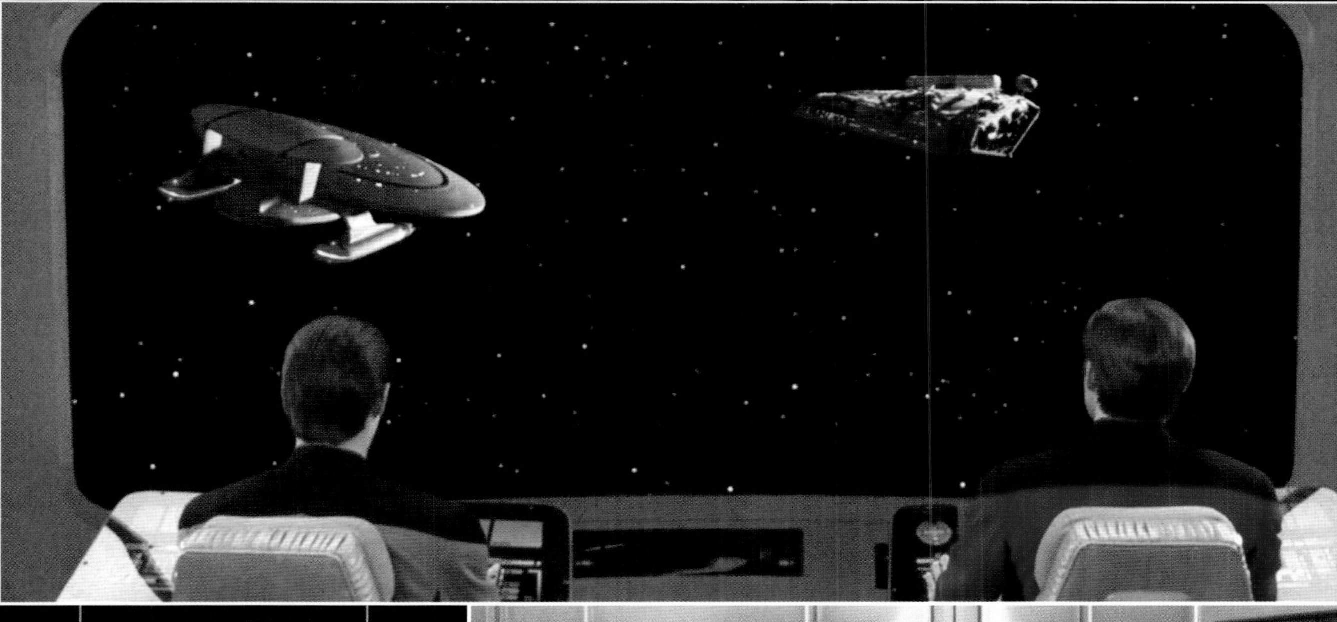

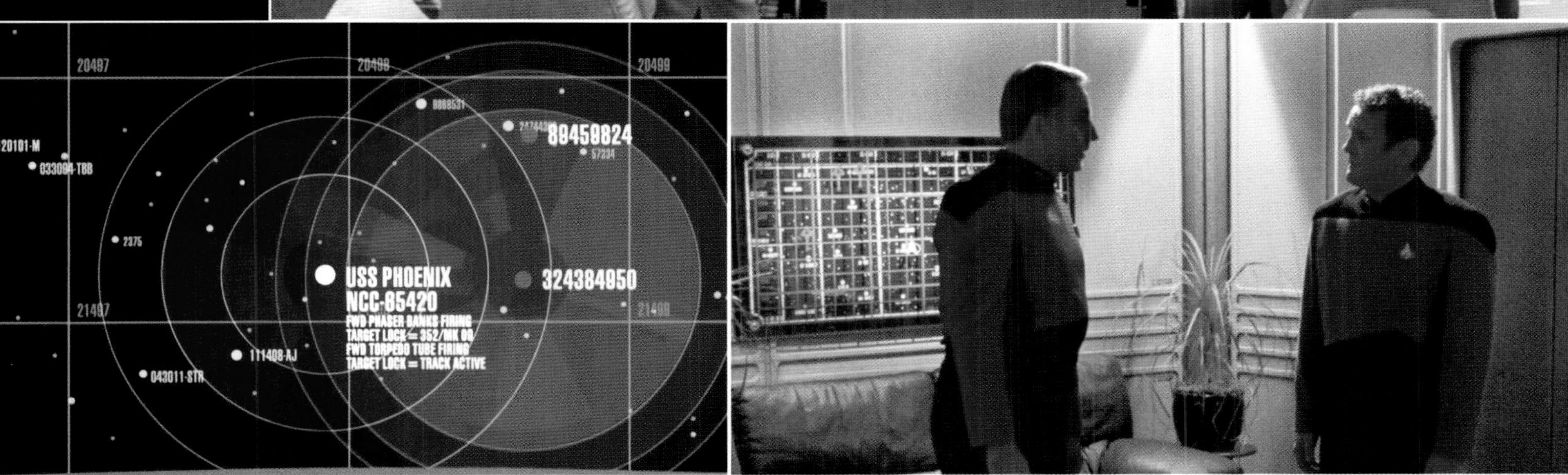

of renewing hostilities with the Federation. He claimed that the science station he destroyed was a military supply port.

When Captain Picard refused to listen to these unsubstantiated accusations, Maxwell went after another Cardassian supply ship. Faced with the prospect of having to fire on a Starfleet ship, Picard called on the advice of Chief Miles O'Brien, who had previously served with Maxwell.

O'Brien believed he could beam over to the *Phoenix* and talk Maxwell down, even though the *Phoenix*'s shields were still raised. O'Brien maintained that he could beam through them because of the high-energy sensor sweep the *Phoenix* was using. This sweep took five and a half minutes, after which it reset and began the cycle again. At the moment it reset, the shields also went down for a fiftieth of a second, giving O'Brien a tiny window in which he could beam through. It required a precise fix on the shield modulation of the *Phoenix*, but O'Brien's theory was correct and he managed to beam over.

He talked Maxwell around, and the captain agreed to stand down. The command of the *Phoenix* was handed over to the first officer, and it returned to Federation space while Maxwell was confined to quarters aboard the *Enterprise*-D.

▲ After performing a precise transport through the *Phoenix*'s shields, Miles O'Brien confronted Maxwell in his ready room. O'Brien convinced his former captain to give up his vendetta against the Cardassians.

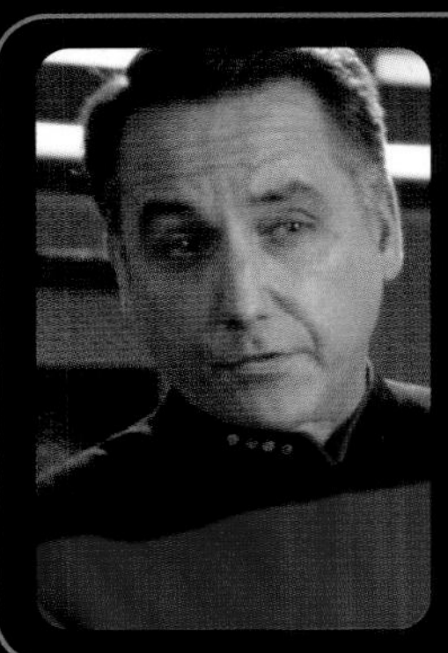

DATA FEED

Captain Benjamin Maxwell was twice decorated with the Federation's highest citations for courage and valor during the Federation-Cardassian War of the 2340s and 2350s. He felt animosity toward the Cardassians after a sneak attack by their military resulted in the deaths of nearly 100 civilians on Setlik III, including his wife and children. He never trusted the Cardassians after this, and later took it upon himself to destroy their supply ships because he believed they were gearing up for war again.

WATCHFUL EYE

Thanks to the actions of Chief Miles O'Brien, Captain Maxwell was taken into custody without further loss of life, and the peace treaty between the Federation and the Cardassians remained intact.

Captain Maxwell's actions were reckless in the extreme, but that did not mean Captain Picard did not believe him. In fact, Picard was sure that the Cardassians were rearming. It made no sense that so many Cardassian supply ships were visiting a "science" station that was within easy reach of three Federation sectors, nor that these ships were running with high-energy subspace fields that prevented sensors from reading what they were carrying.

Picard did not want to search those ships because he knew it would end the peace, and he wanted to preserve it at all costs. He told the Cardassians that they would be watching them closely from now on, with the tacit threat that if they truly wanted peace they should cease what they were doing.

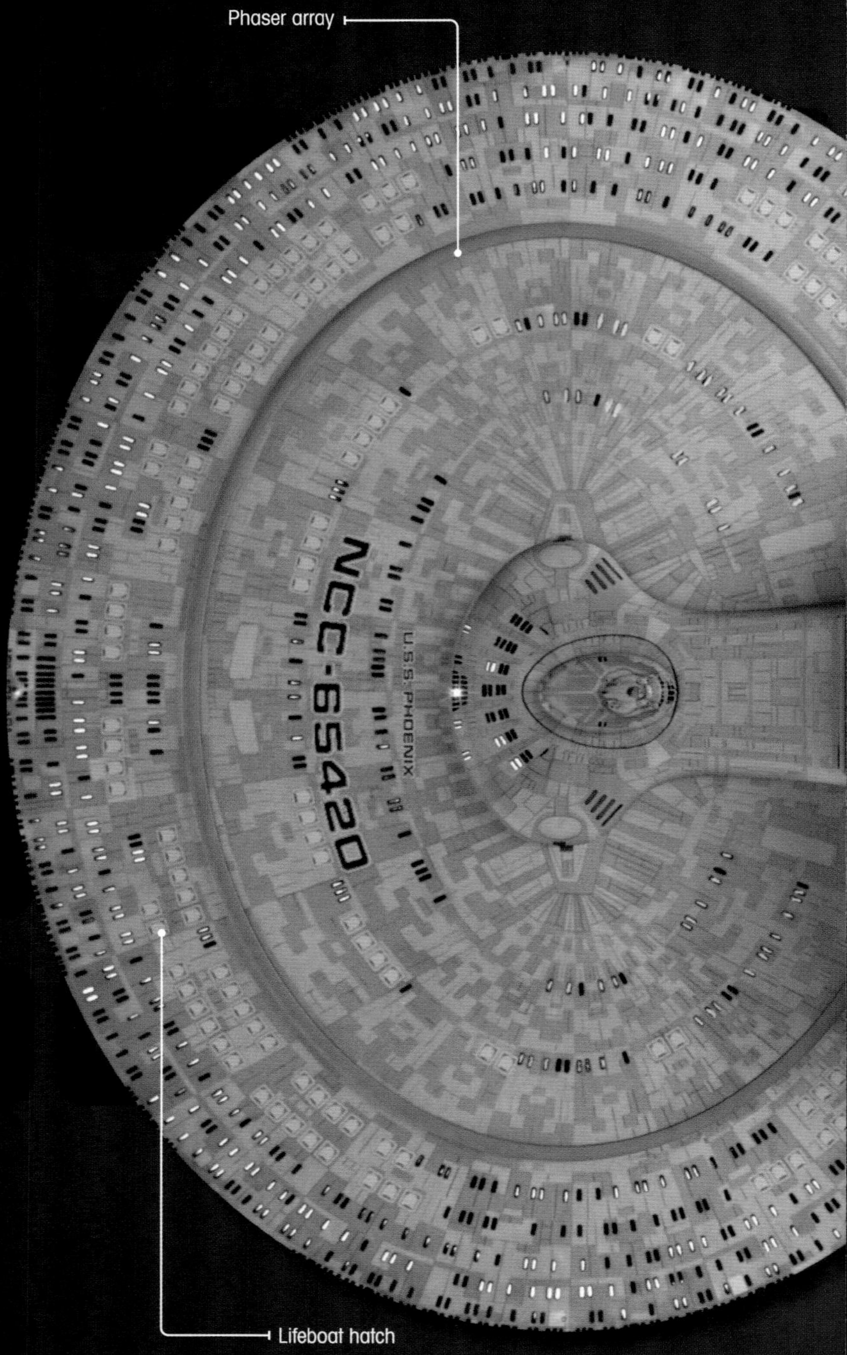

Phaser array

NCC-65420

U.S.S. PHOENIX

Lifeboat hatch

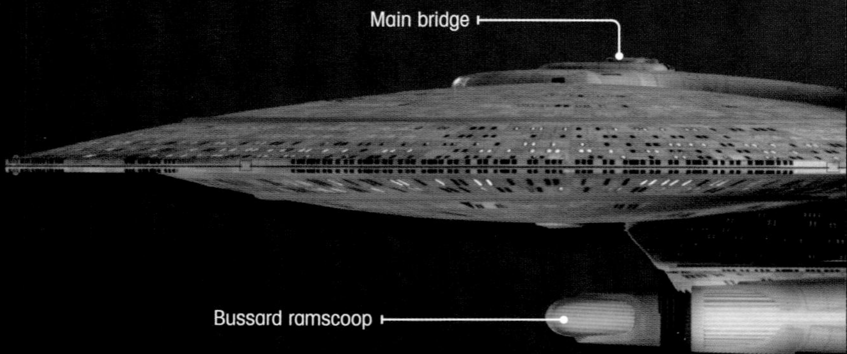

Main bridge

Bussard ramscoop

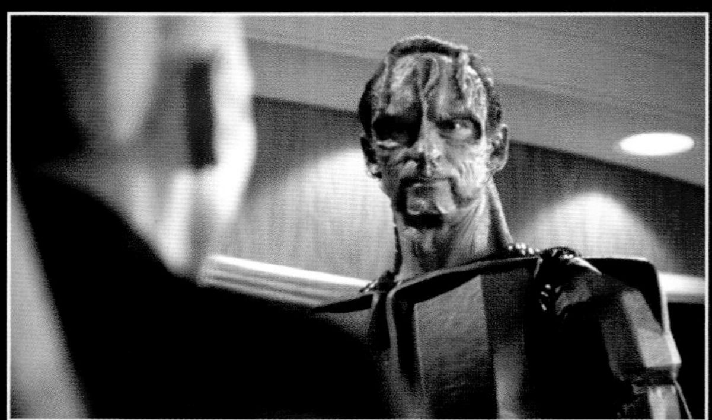

▲ Captain Picard left Gul Macet under no illusion that he believed Captain Maxwell's accusations that the Cardassians were rearming, and he made it clear Starfleet would be keeping a close eye on them.

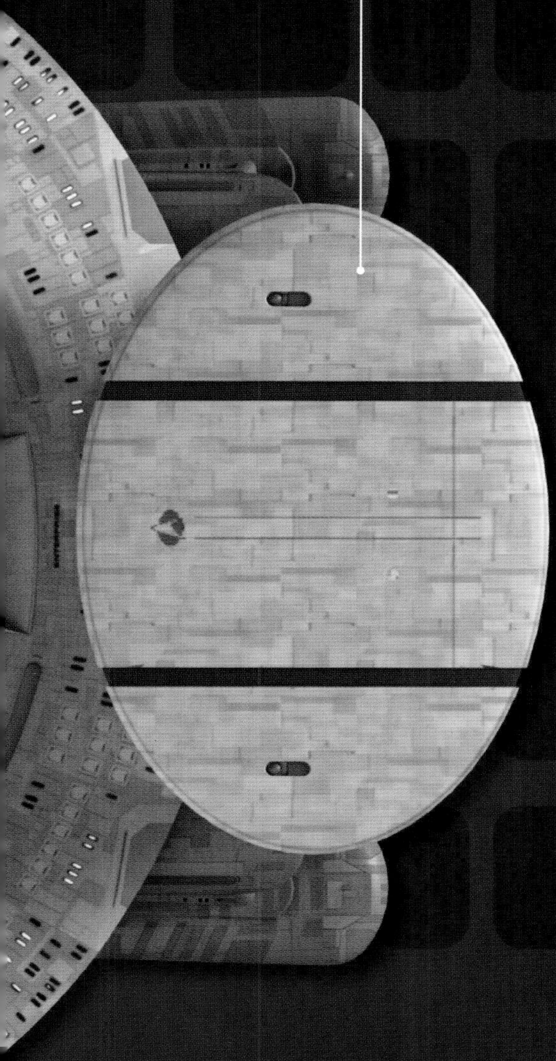

Sensor module

DATA FEED

When the *Phoenix* threatened two more Cardassian ships, Captain Picard reluctantly agreed to give them the *Phoenix*'s transponder and prefix codes. This allowed the Cardassian warship to precisely locate the *Phoenix* and remotely lower its shields. Despite this, the *Phoenix* was still able to come out on top and destroy both Cardassian vessels.

VENTRAL VIEW

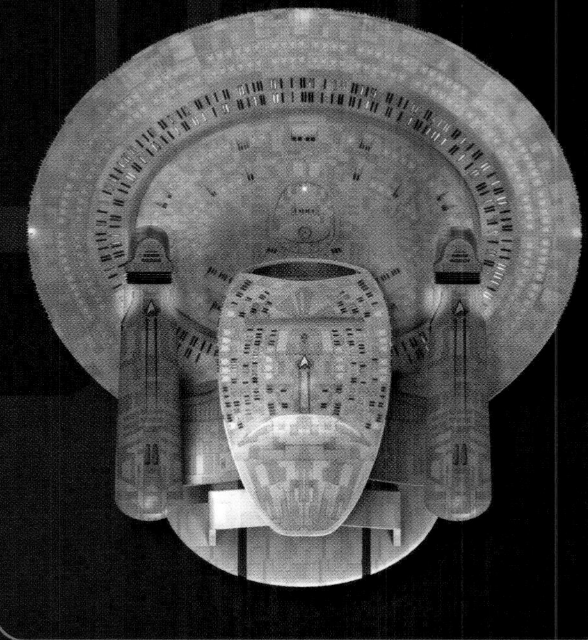

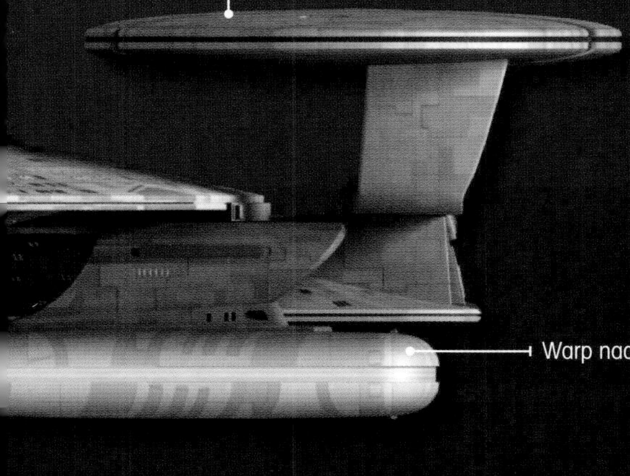

REAR VIEW

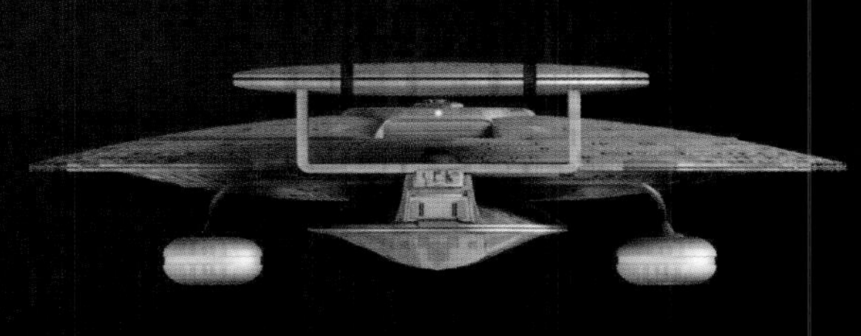

Sensor module

Warp nacelle

PLAQUE LOCATION

The *U.S.S. Phoenix*'s dedication plaque hung on the wall of Captain Maxwell's ready room. This was unusual, since most ship plaques were to be found on the wall of the main bridge.

CRITICAL POSITION

The unarmed Cardassian science space station obliterated by the *Phoenix* was in the Cuellar system. Captain Maxwell was sure this was a military supply post as it held a good strategic position to launch an invasion of three Federation sectors.

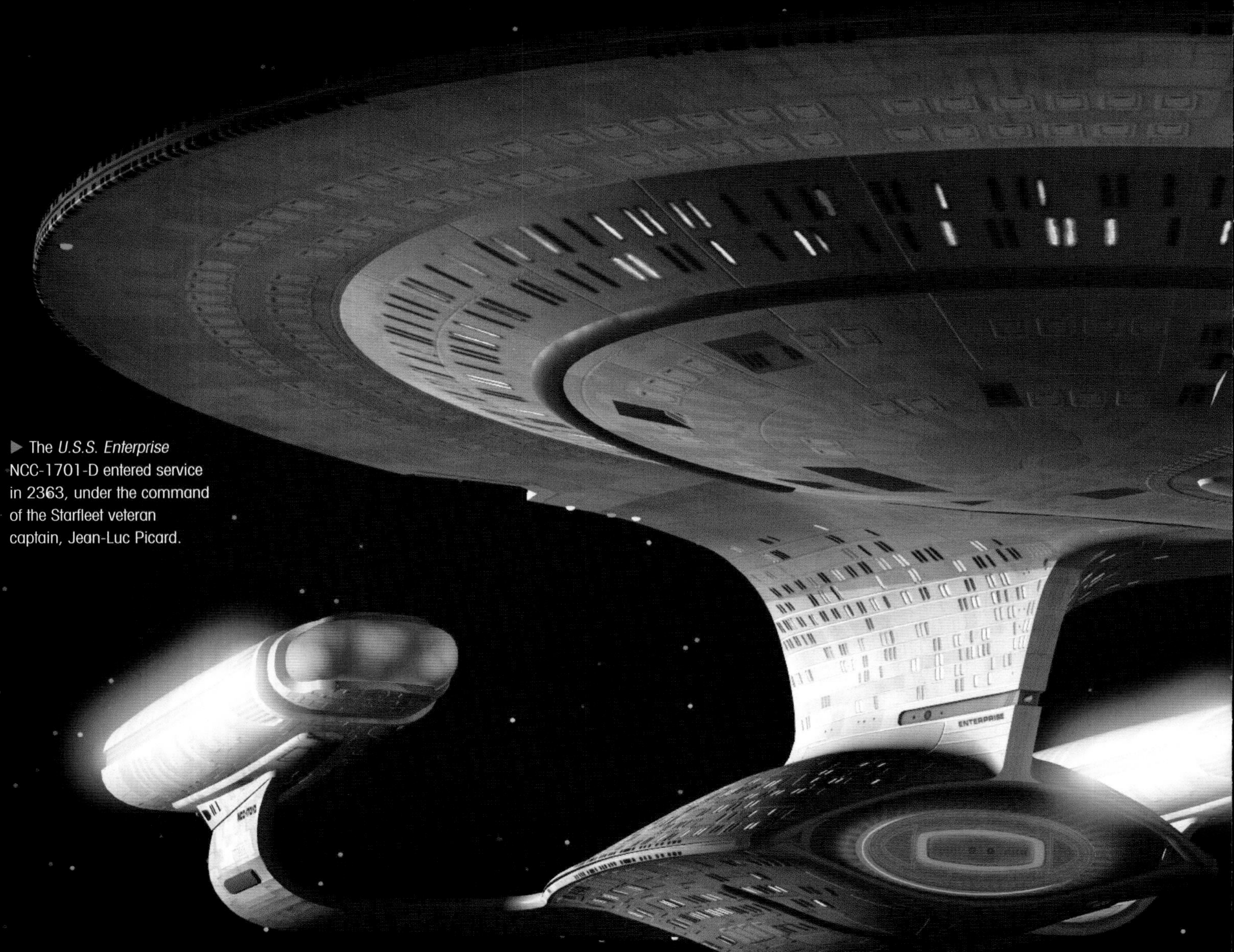

▶ The *U.S.S. Enterprise* NCC-1701-D entered service in 2363, under the command of the Starfleet veteran captain, Jean-Luc Picard.

U.S.S. ENTERPRISE NCC-1701-D

A technical marvel, the *Enterprise*-D was more than half a kilometer long and had a crew of over 1,000 people.

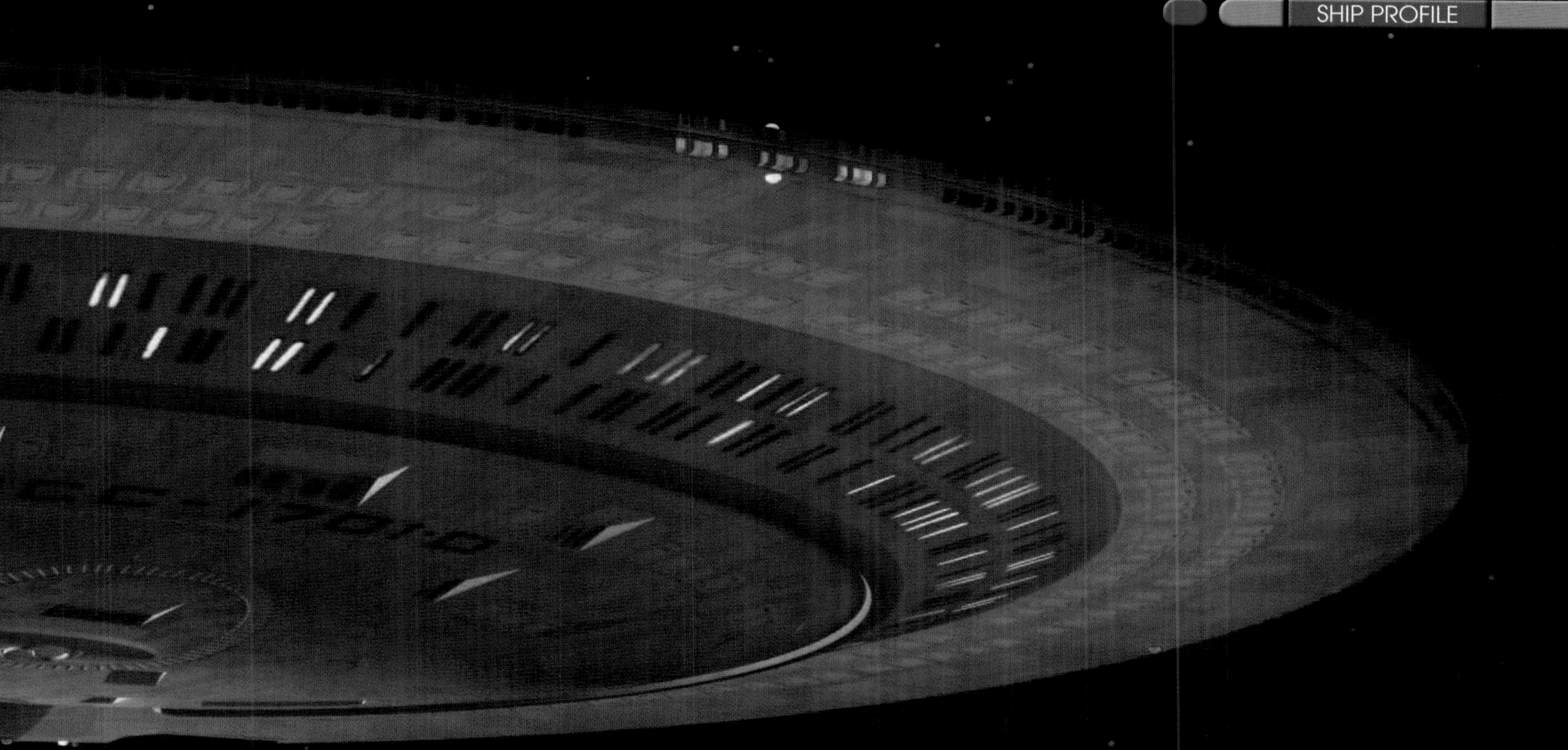

When the *Galaxy*-class *Enterprise*-D was launched in 2363 – 94 years after Captain James Kirk completed his first, legendary, five-year mission on the *U.S.S. Enterprise* NCC-1701 – it was the largest, most advanced vessel Starfleet had ever constructed.

The *Enterprise*-D was an awe-inspiring technical achievement, the result of 20 years' development work from the finest engineering minds of the Federation Advanced Starship Design Bureau, They included Dr. Leah Brahms, who was largely responsible for the design of the warp engines.

The *Enterprise*-D followed the same basic design layout as previous *Enterprises,* but it was sleeker, due to advances in hyperflight dynamics, and the saucer section was larger in proportion to the secondary or engineering hull. At 641 meters in length and with 42 decks covering 3.5 million square meters, it had eight times as much interior space as Captain Kirk's *Enterprise.* This meant there was 110 square meters of living space per person.

SCIENTIFIC MARVEL

The *Enterprise*-D's specifications were mind-boggling: it had more than 4,000 internal systems, including two LF-41 warp engines that gave it a top sustainable speed of warp 9.6 (1,909 times the speed of light). It was equipped with a high-capacity shield grid, 12 type-X phaser arrays, three torpedo launchers, and a complement of 250 photon torpedoes.

Facilities onboard included three sickbays, 20 transporter systems, and more than 100

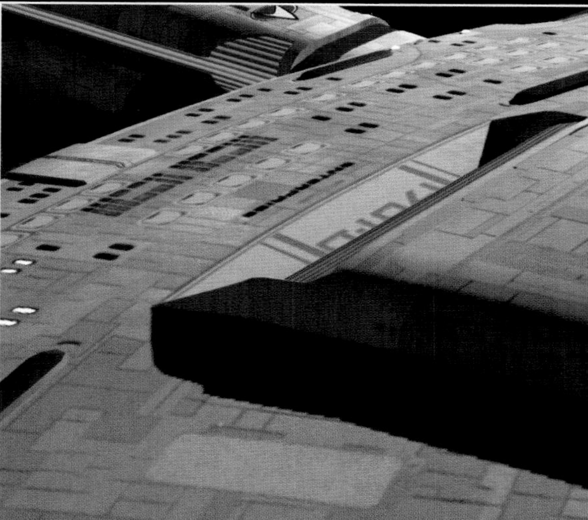

◀ The outer surface of the *Enterprise*-D featured phaser strips, transporter emitter pads, subspace radio antennae, active energy forcefields, navigational sensors, escape pod hatches, and hundreds of viewports. The outermost hull layer was made up of AGP ablative ceramic fabric segments approximately 3.7 square meters in size.

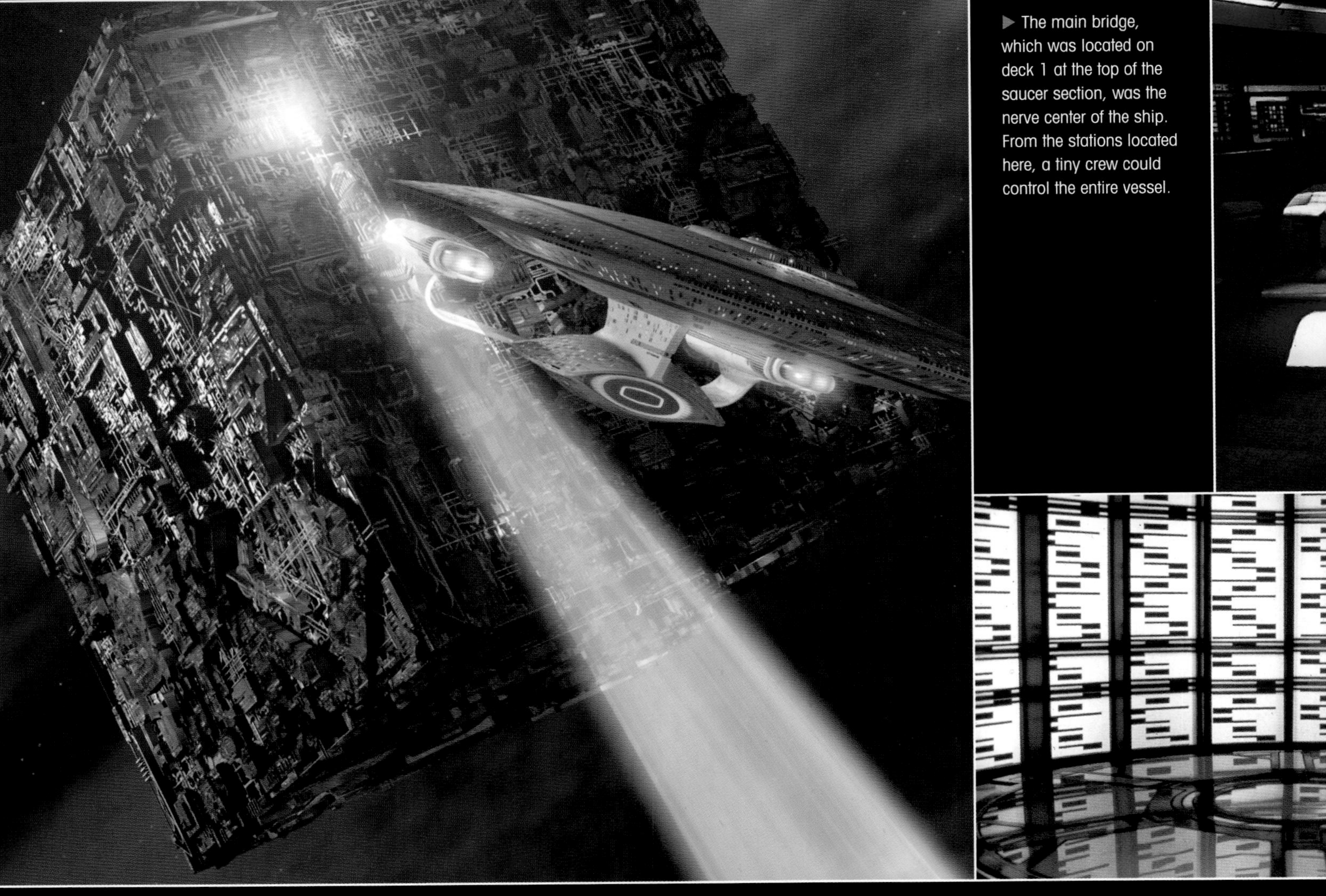

▶ The main bridge, which was located on deck 1 at the top of the saucer section, was the nerve center of the ship. From the stations located here, a tiny crew could control the entire vessel.

▲ Although the *Enterprise*'s primary mission was deep space exploration, it was involved in a number of significant conflicts. It was the first Starfleet vessel to survive an encounter with the Borg, and two years later, the crew was the last line of defense when the Federation repelled the Borg invasion of 2367.

research labs dedicated to disciplines such as stellar cartography, exobiology, cybernetics, astrophysics, geosciences, archaeology, cultural anthropology, and botany.

Amenities included 16 holodecks, a phaser range, theater, gym, salon, and restaurant/bar called Ten-Forward, as well as classrooms and even an arboretum. In other words, the ship offered everything the crew of 1,012 could need; it could also operate for up to seven years without having to return to a starbase for refurbishment. Even Captain Picard was "in awe of its size and complexity." A person could live on it for years and still not know their way around all of it.

The unprecedented size of the *Enterprise*-D and its comprehensive facilities reflected Starfleet's decision that the crew would include families and children. It was felt that Starfleet personnel were far more likely to sign up for exploratory missions, which often continued for years, if they could take their families with them and think of the ship as home.

There are always inherent risks involved in space exploration, but this was a period of unprecedented peace for the Federation. The threat of war with the Klingons and the Romulans had been removed by the Khitomer Accords (2293) and the Treaty of Algeron (2311), while new dangers – in the shape of the Borg and the Dominion – had not yet emerged. It was therefore felt safe enough at this time to accommodate families onboard, especially as *Galaxy*-class starships had a neat trick in an emergency: they could split into two autonomous spacecraft.

All nonessential personnel could be evacuated to the saucer section, which would detach from the engineering hull and retreat to safety under its own impulse power. Meanwhile, the remaining

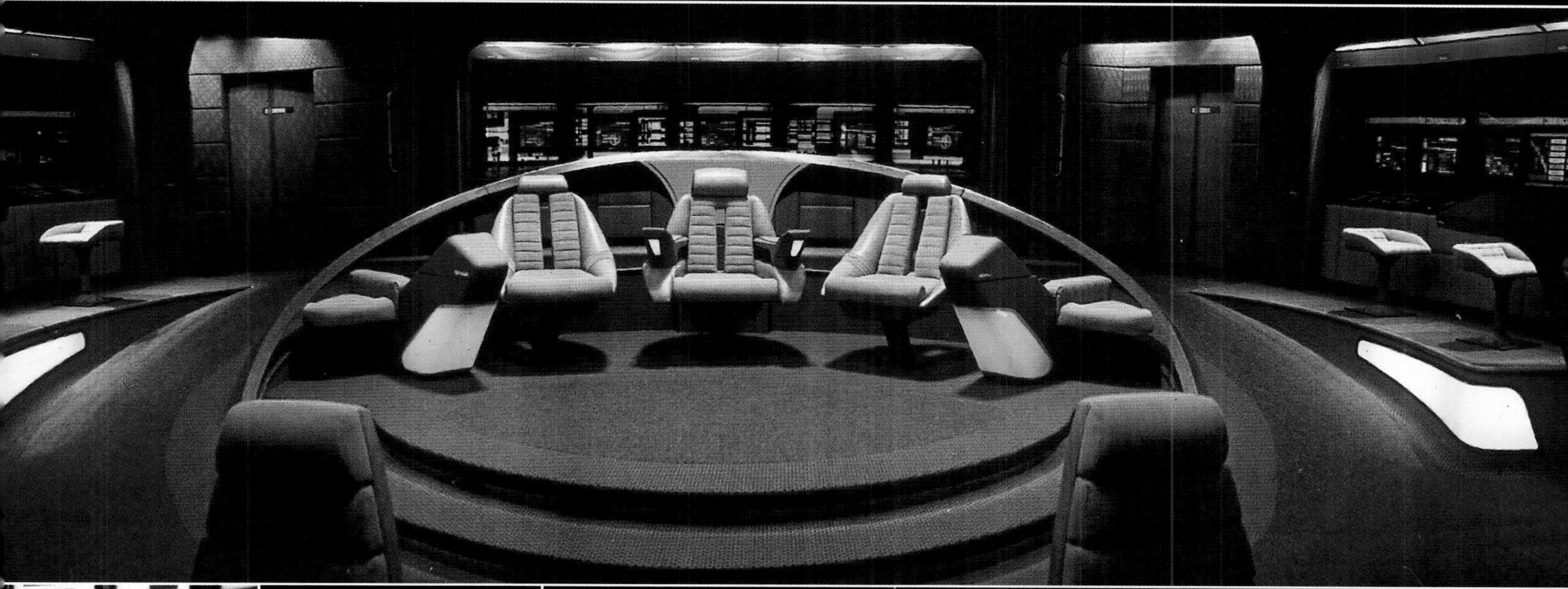

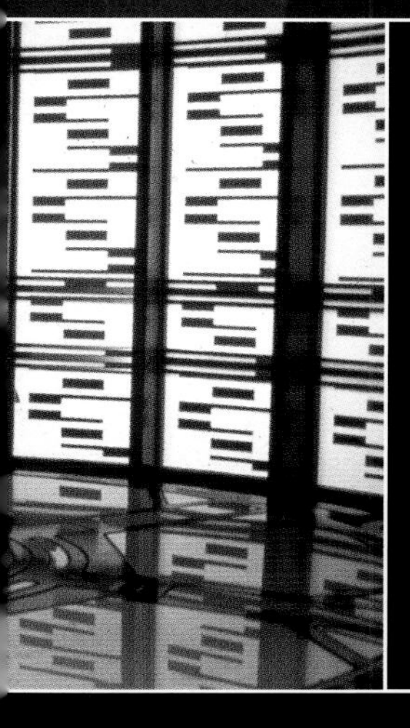

◀ The *Enterprise*-D had 20 transporter rooms, including six main personnel transporters. They were capable of beaming individuals distances of up to 40,000 kilometers almost instantaneously.

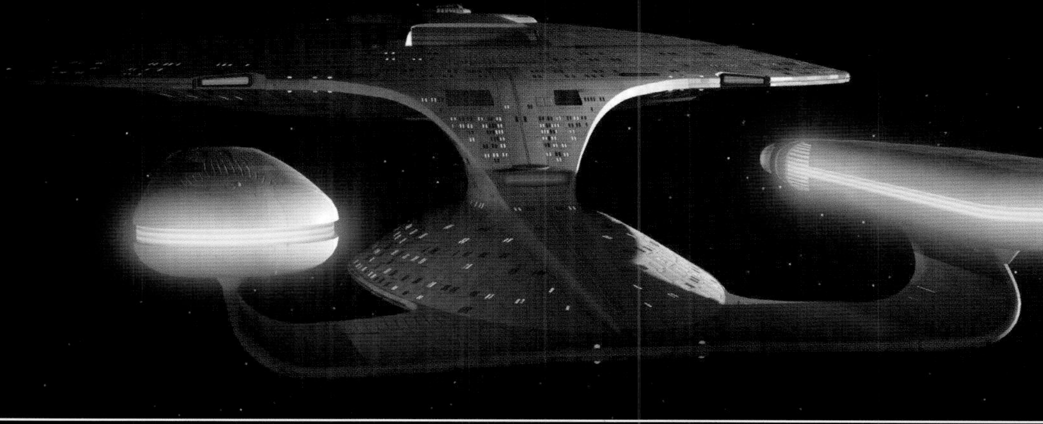

▲ The *Galaxy* class followed the same design principles that Zefram Cochrane established on Earth's first faster-than-light ship, and used twin nacelles to generate fields that warped space.

stardrive section, which was capable of warp flight and optimized for combat, would engage the threat. The two sections could then reattach once the danger was over.

PICARD'S STARSHIP

The *Enterprise*-D was constructed under the supervision of Commander Orfil Quinteros at the Utopia Planitia Fleet Yards, 16,625 kilometers above Mars. Its primary mission was one of exploration, but it was also regularly tasked with diplomatic and humanitarian assigments and with defending the security of the Federation.

The ship remained under the command of Captain Picard throughout its career, apart from one brief period when Captain Edward Jellico took command while Picard was on a covert mission. It played a major role in defending the Federation against the Borg (when Riker was given a field promotion to captain) and in the blockade of Klingon space during the Klingon civil war.

The *Enterprise*-D was designed to be operational for approximately 100 years, with major refits scheduled for every 20 years. However, it was in service for just eight years before being destroyed in the Veridian System in 2371, by a renegade Klingon vessel led by the Duras sisters.

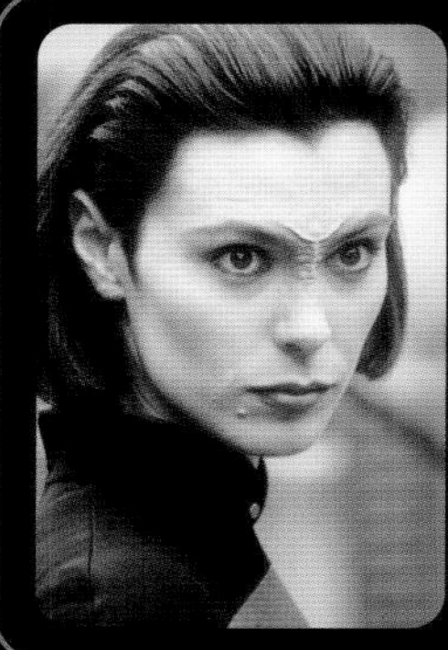

DATA FEED

The *Enterprise*-D's crew of 1,012 included a significant number of civilians, such as Mot the Bolian barber and the botanist Keiko O'Brien. As was typical with a Federation ship, the crew comprised people from many different planets and species. In 2366, there were said to be 13 species represented onboard, while in 2369, there were 17 crewmembers from non-Federation worlds, including the Bajoran Ro Laren.

DEFLECTOR DISH

One of the most important features of the *Enterprise*-D was its navigational deflector. This oval-shaped device was located on the front of the stardrive section and pushed space debris clear of the ship's path. At warp speeds, even microscopic particles of asteroids or other particulates could cause massive damage if they collided with the ship's hull. The deflector dish projected a powerful graviton beam that swept large objects, such as asteroids, out of the way. At the same time, a low-power beam created a shield nearly two kilometers ahead of the ship that deflected the microscopic interstellar debris away from its path.

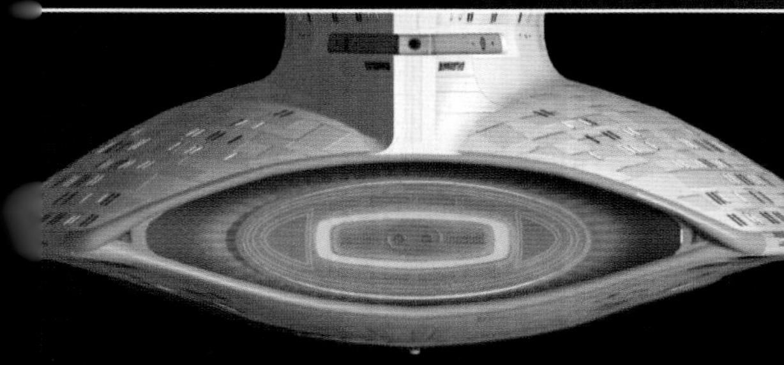

The long-range sensors were directly behind the deflector dish. These were located on decks 32–38 and were the most powerful scientific instruments aboard the *Enterprise*-D.

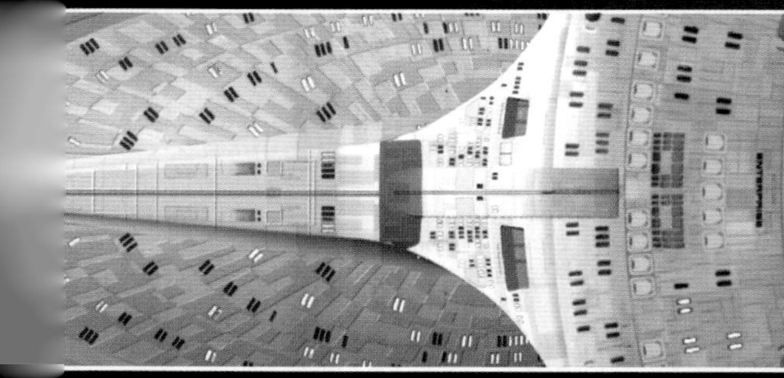

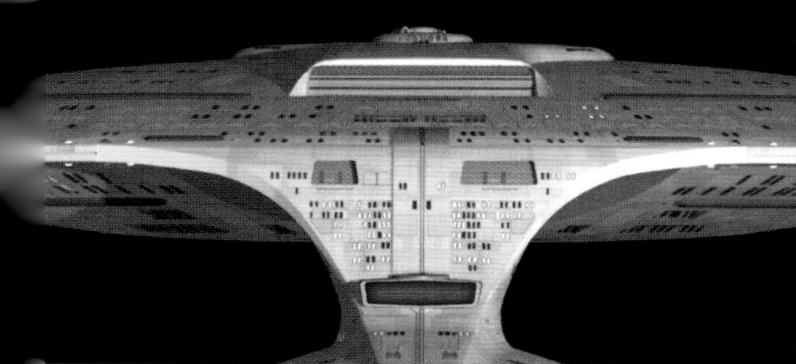

▲ The impulse engines were marked by a red glow on the rear of the saucer section and at the back of the stardrive section, below the doors for shuttlebays 2 and 3.

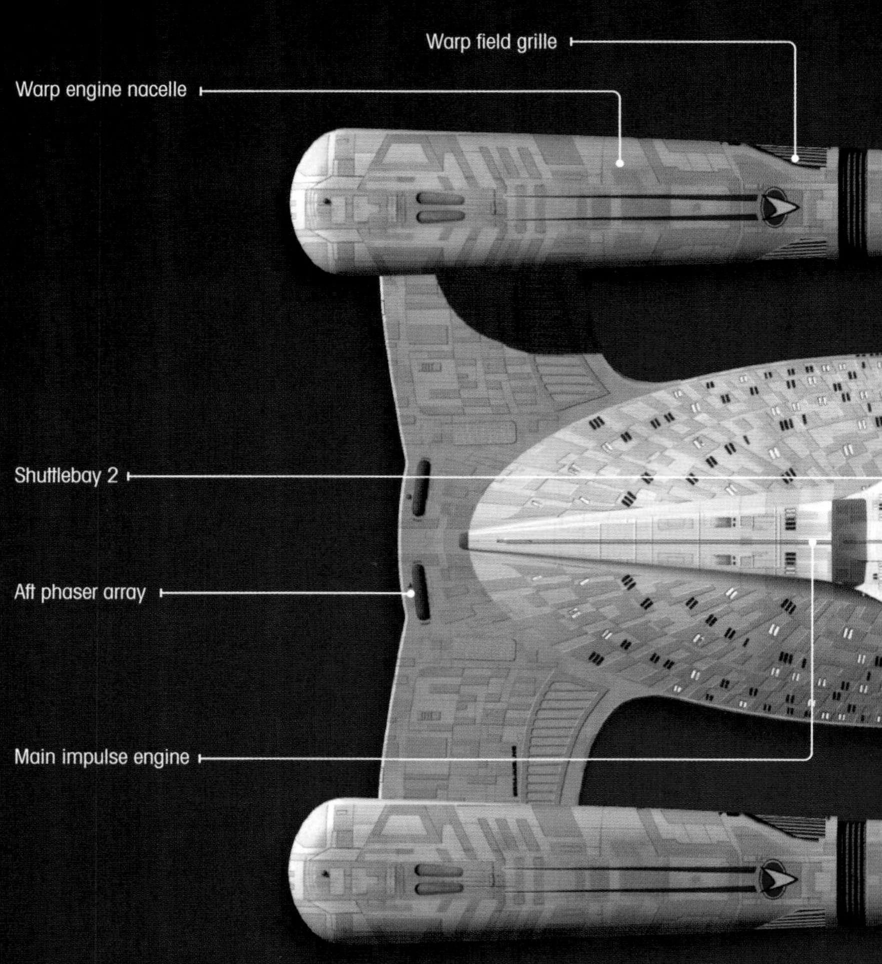

DATA FEED

The *Enterprise*-D's most powerful weapons were its photon torpedoes. Each one had a yield of 18.5 isotons and a range of 3.5 million kilometers. Launchers were fitted to the neck and the rear of the stardrive section, between the nacelle pylons.

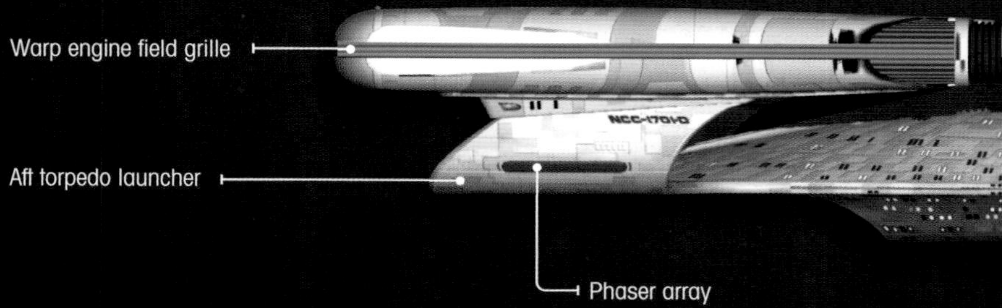

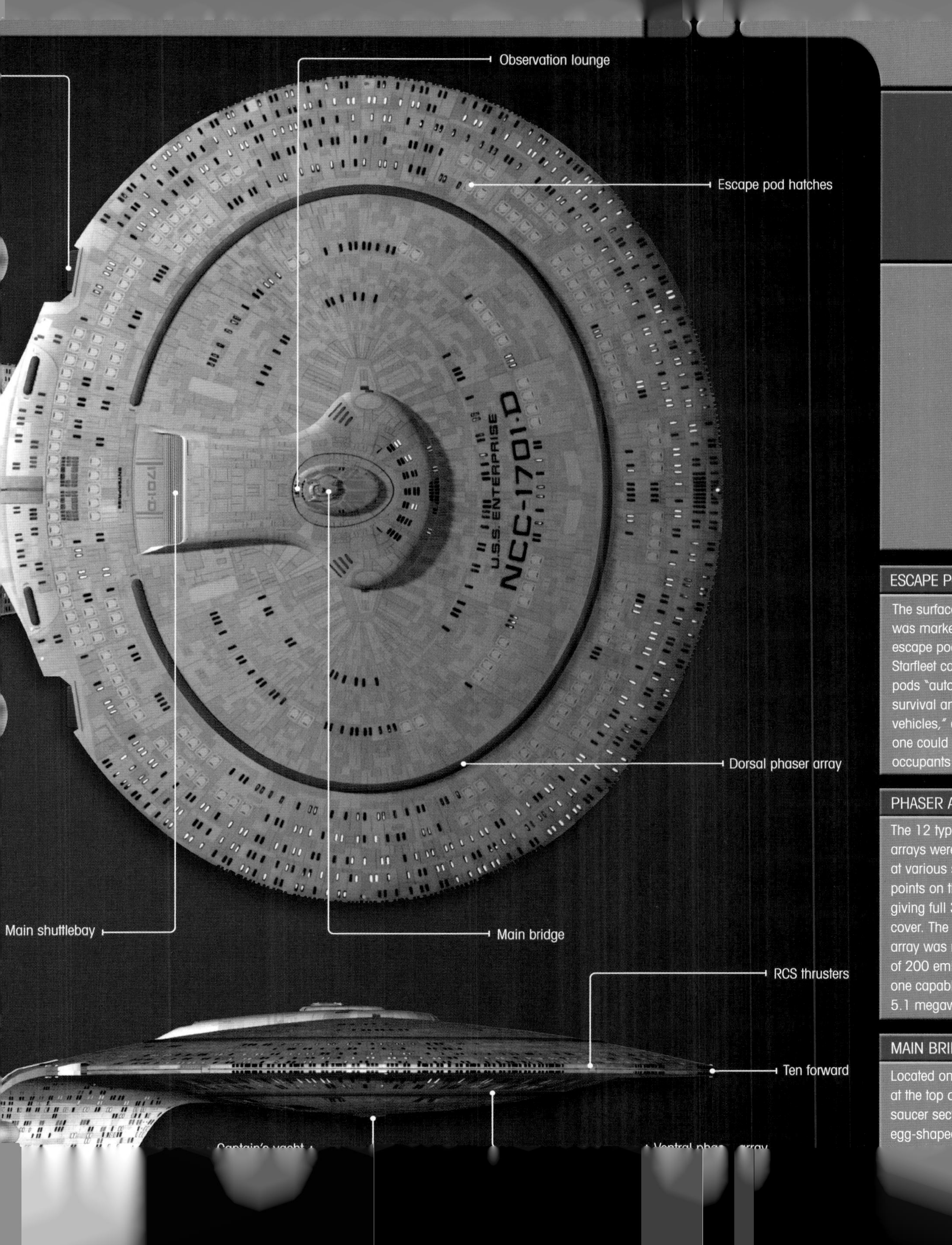

ESCAPE POD HATCHES

The surface of the hull was marked by 400 escape pod hatches. Starfleet called the pods "autonomous survival and recovery vehicles," and each one could sustain four occupants for 86 days.

PHASER ARRAYS

The 12 type-X phaser arrays were located at various strategic points on the hull, giving full 360-degree cover. The main dorsal array was made up of 200 emitters, each one capable of a 5.1 megawatt burst.

MAIN BRIDGE

Located on deck 1 at the top of the saucer section, this egg-shaped room was

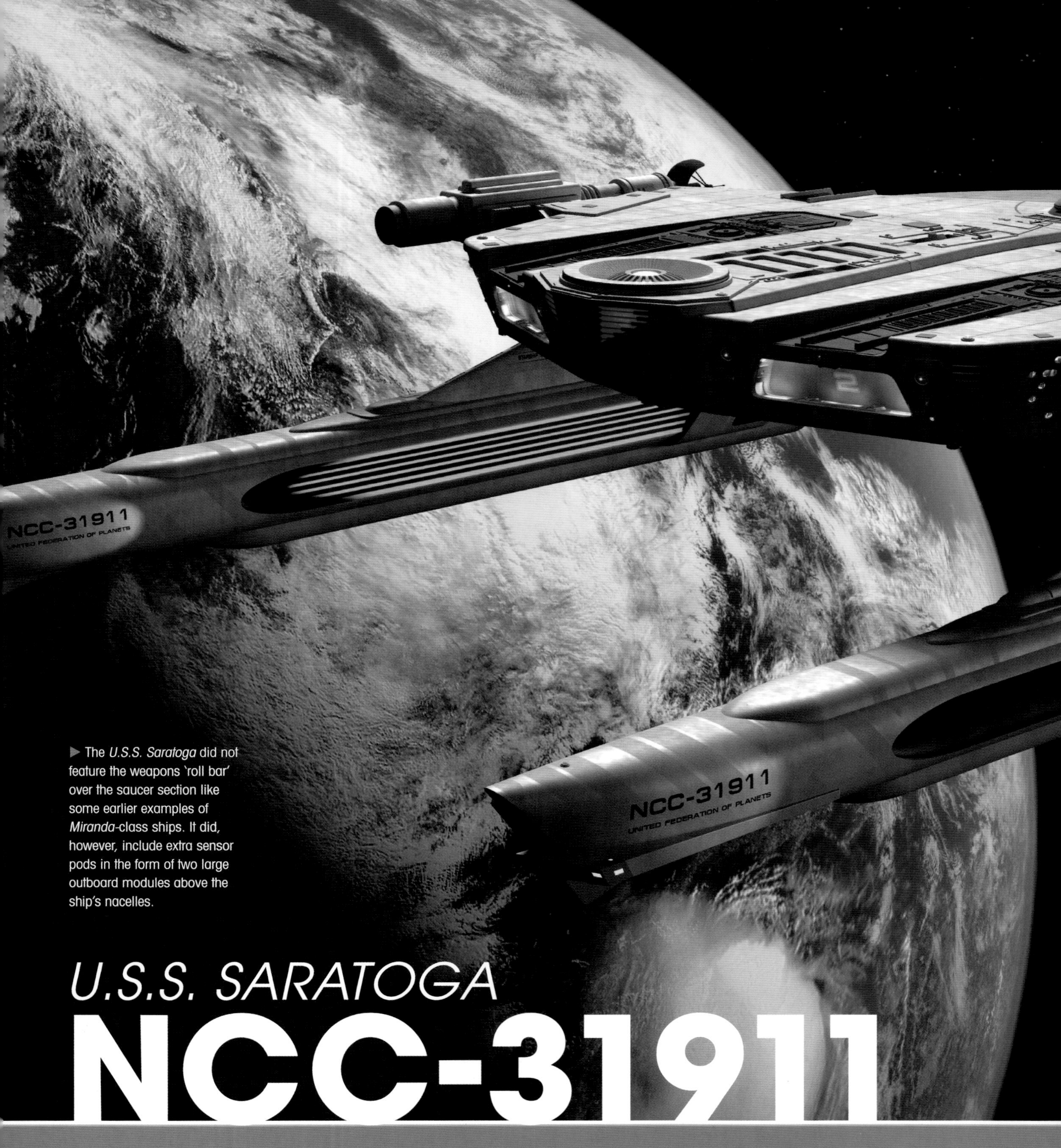

▶ The *U.S.S. Saratoga* did not feature the weapons 'roll bar' over the saucer section like some earlier examples of *Miranda*-class ships. It did, however, include extra sensor pods in the form of two large outboard modules above the ship's nacelles.

U.S.S. SARATOGA
NCC-31911

This *Miranda*-class ship formed part of the fleet that fought a Borg cube at the Battle of Wolf 359.

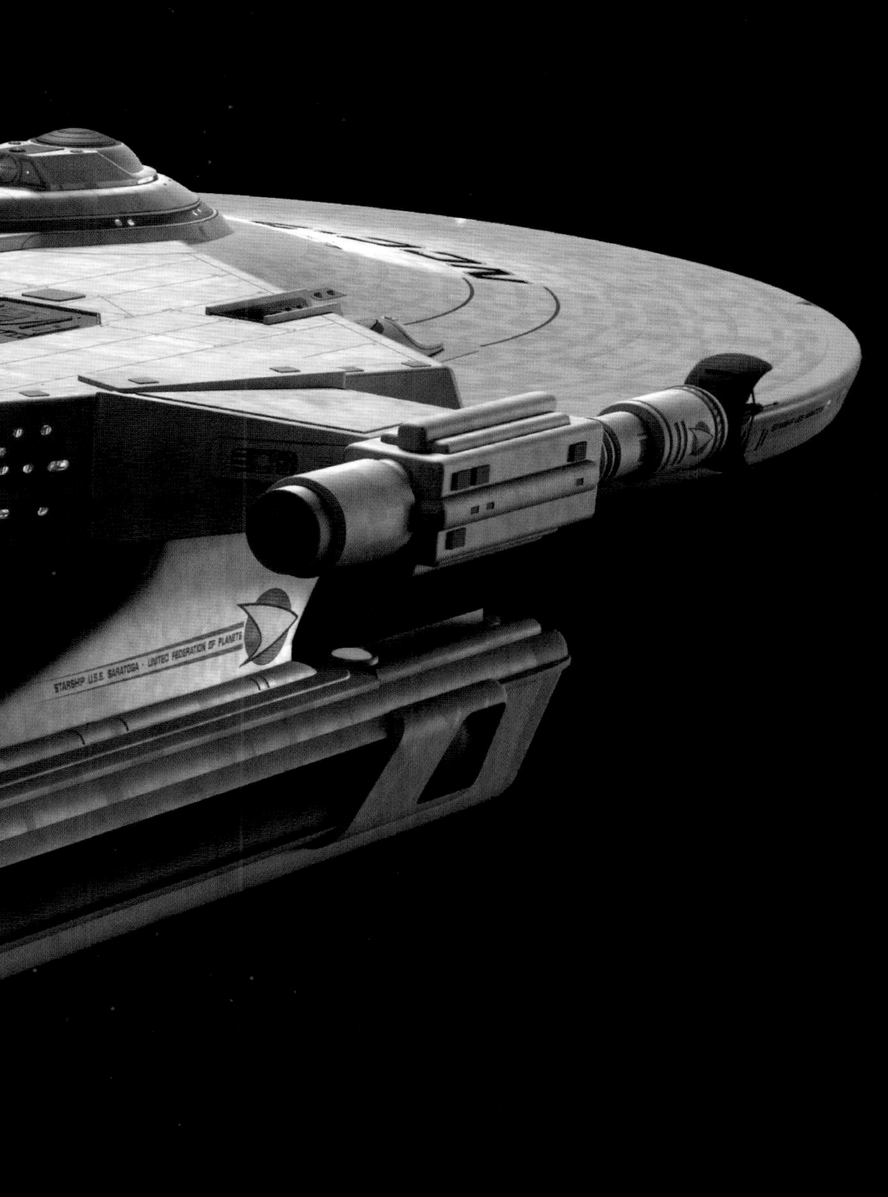

While the *U.S.S. Saratoga* was in service with Starfleet during the 24th century, this class of starship had been operating since at least the 2280s, which made it one of the longest serving and most successful types of vessel to be used by Starfleet.

Miranda-class ships were designed and mainly used for science and patrol missions, but could also be deployed on combat duty if the need arose. They normally had a crew complement of around 200, and by the middle of the 24th century, they also accommodated crewmembers' families.

Over the years, the *Miranda* class featured slightly different hull configurations, but their overall shape remained basically the same. Like all vessels of this type, the *Saratoga* was 243 meters in length and did not have a separate secondary engineering hull. Instead, an enlarged, squared-off section was fitted to the rear of the saucer. This area housed the ship's warp core and impulse engines, as well as two shuttlebays. Both of the shuttlebays also contained escape pods capable of transporting several personnel off the ship in an emergency.

LOCATION OF WEAPONS

Some *Miranda*-class vessels were equipped with a weapons roll bar that was fitted above the rear section of the saucer and carried additional phasers and torpedo launchers. The *Saratoga* did not have this feature, but was just equipped with the standard number of phasers and torpedo launchers. They included six type-7 phaser emitters, three mounted on top of the saucer and three below, including one on the sensor dome. There

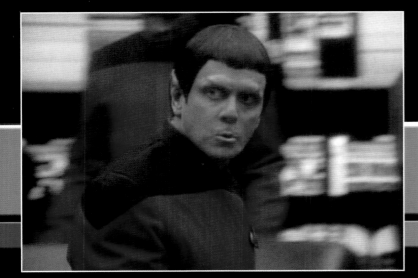

◀ By early 2367, a Vulcan captain had taken command of the *Saratoga*-NCC-31911, with Lieutenant Commander Benjamin Sisko as first officer. The captain and most of his crew were among almost 11,000 lives lost at the Battle of Wolf 359.

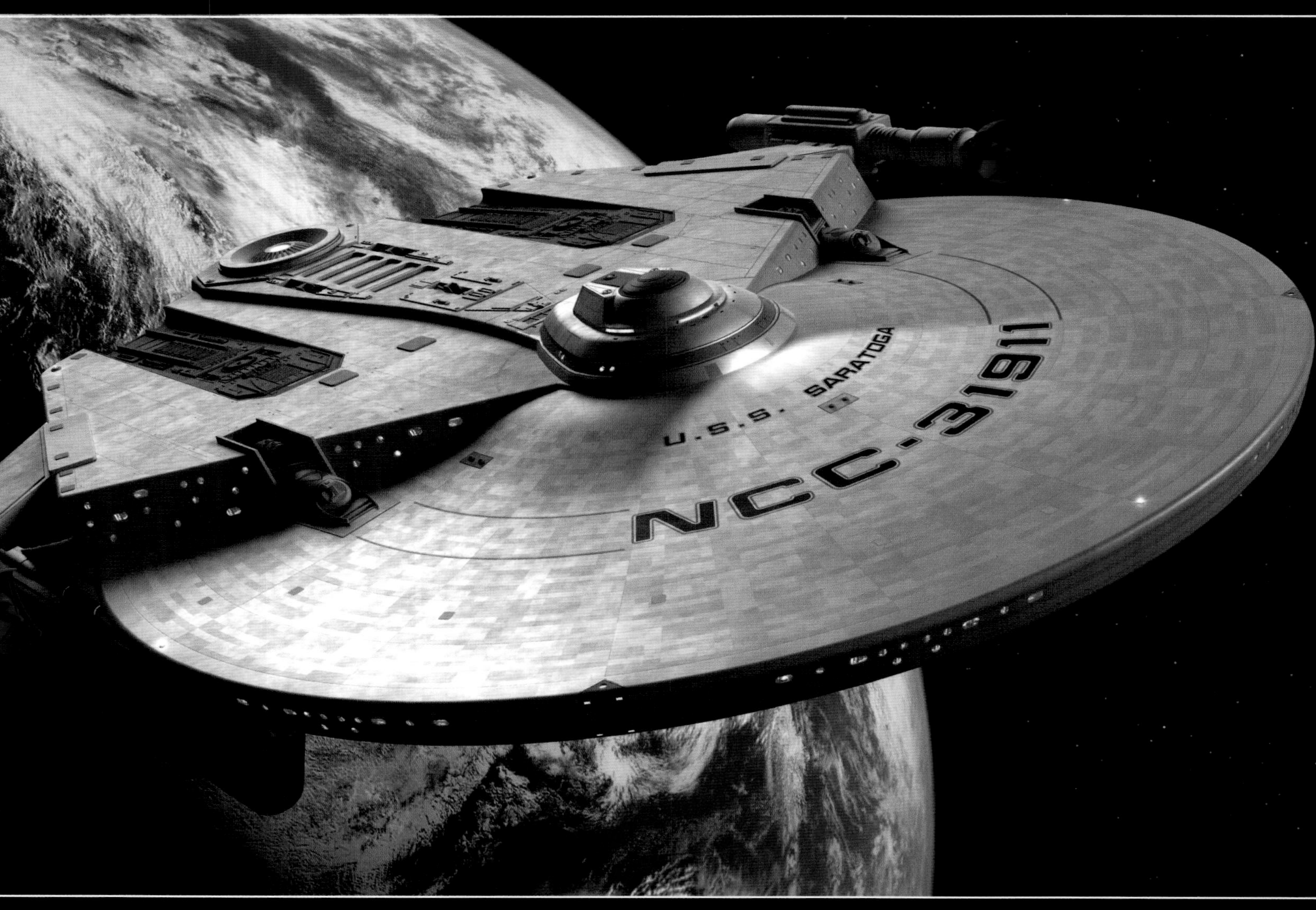

▲ *Miranda*-class vessels, such as the *Saratoga,* were normally used for scientific or supply missions. They featured a host of upgraded sensor equipment to help them carry out their primary tasks. They were not really designed for combat, but they could be pressed into action if the need arose.

were also two phaser emitters located just below the impulse engines at the rear.

The *Saratoga* had additional cylindrical sensor pods below the port and starboard side of the saucer section. These were not standard equipment on all *Miranda*-class vessels, and obviously enhanced the scanning ability of the *Saratoga,* providing additional scientific data.

The *Saratoga*'s vertically installed warp core spanned several decks, and the warp nacelles hung down below the saucer section. The ship was capable of attaining a top speed of warp 9.2 for short periods, but its standard cruising speed was closer to warp 6.

The main bridge was located on deck 1 at the top of the saucer section. The layout was similar to that found on *Constitution*-class ships, with the flight controller and operations stations at the front and the captain's chair in the middle. Two additional standing consoles were positioned behind the captain's chair; the tactical station was on the port side of the bridge, with the science and communications stations on the starboard side.

SERVICE RECORD

In 2365, according to a starship deploy status chart on display in a courtroom of Starbase 173, the *Saratoga* was under the command of Captain Martin Jedlicka. It was assigned to a deep space exploration mission of Sector 002, along with the *U.S.S. Apollo* NCC-30000.

By 2367, the *Saratoga* was under the command of a Vulcan captain and its first officer was Lieutenant Commander Benjamin Sisko, who would later become the commander of Deep Space 9. During that year, the ship was part of a fleet of at least 40 starships that massed at

▶ The *Saratoga* engaged the Borg cube at the Battle of Wolf 359. It fired a full salvo of phasers, but they had no effect. The *Saratoga* was then held in a Borg tractor beam, while its shields were drained.

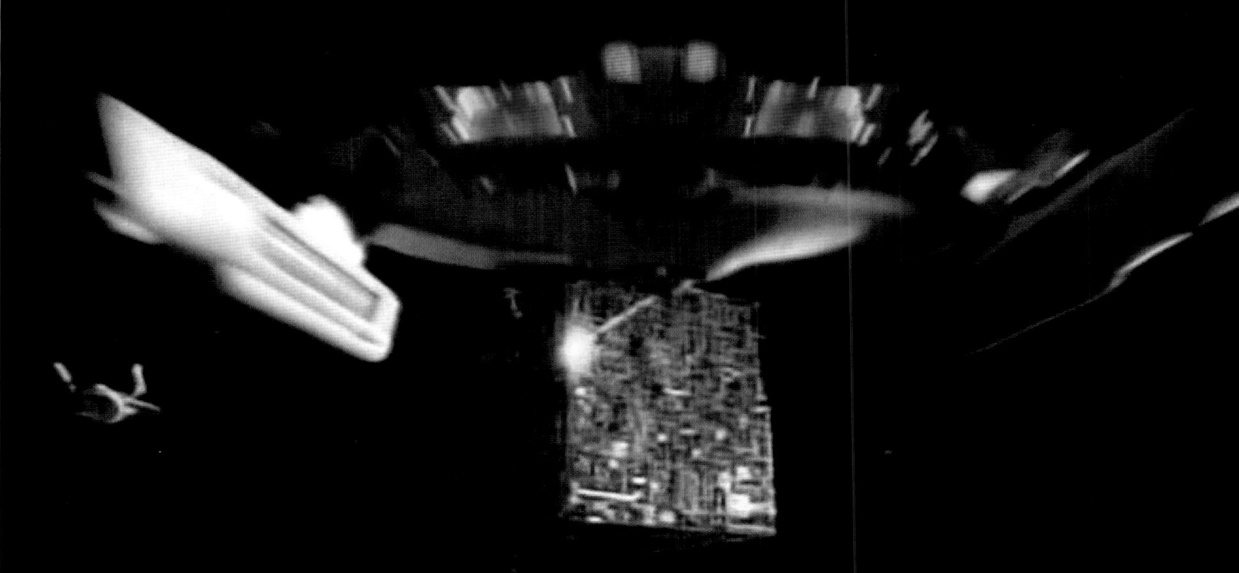

▼ During the encounter with the Borg, the tactical officer aboard the *Saratoga* was a heavily muscled Bolian. He, along with Sisko, were the only members of the bridge crew to survive the Borg attack.

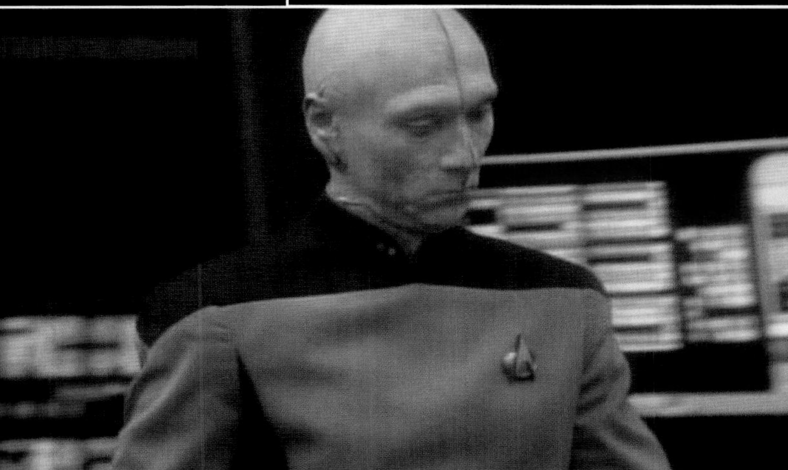

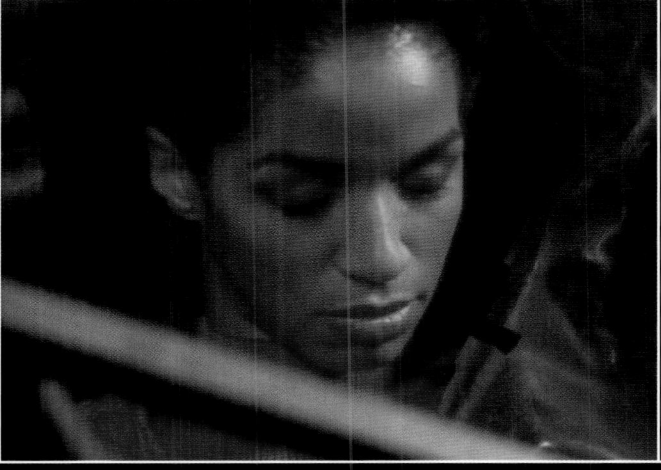

Wolf 359 to protect Earth and the surrounding sector from an invasion by a Borg cube.

During the battle, the *Saratoga* unleashed a full spread of phasers and photon torpedoes at the Borg cube, but they had no effect. The *Saratoga* was rendered immobile by a tractor beam emitted by the cube, while its shields were quickly drained of power.

With no defenses, the *Saratoga* was helpless against the cube's cutting beam, which sliced apart the hull through decks 1 to 4 and caused a massive explosion. The warp core also suffered heavy damage, leading to an antimatter containment failure. Apart from Sisko and the Bolian tactical officer, the entire bridge crew were killed in the attack, while chaos and fires raged all around them. The entire ship leaned to the left as the stabilizers failed, and it was clear that the *Saratoga* could not be saved.

Sisko tried to get as many survivors to the escape pods as he could, before rushing back to his quarters. He managed to rescue his barely conscious son, Jake, but he was too late to save his wife, Jennifer, who died in the attack. As they left in an escape pod along with a dozen others, the *Saratoga*'s warp core breached and the ship exploded in a massive fireball.

▲ Sisko's wife, Jennifer, had taken refuge in their personal quarters, along with their son, Jake, during the battle. Jake survived the encounter, but Jennifer was killed when an explosion tore through the floor.

DATA FEED

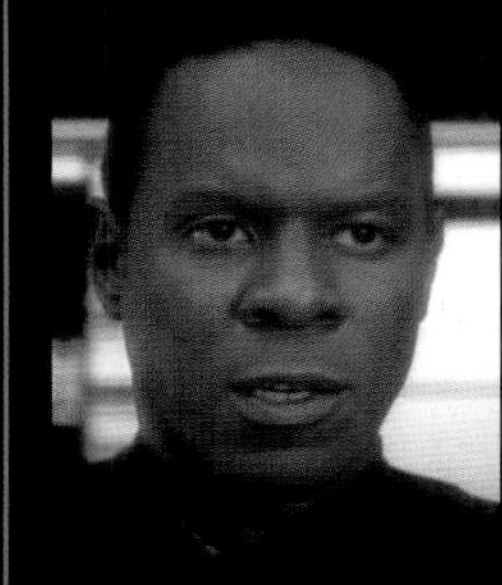

Following the Battle of Wolf 359 and the death of his wife, Benjamin Sisko took up a posting at Utopia Planitia Fleet Yards on Mars. Emotionally devastated, Sisko poured his energy into helping design a prototype *U.S.S. Defiant*. Design flaws emerged and the project was halted, leaving him on the verge of resigning. It was then that one of his former commanding officers, Captain Leyton, recommended Sisko for a command position on Deep Space 9.

BATTLING THE BORG

The *U.S.S. Saratoga* was one of at least 40 Starfleet ships that fought an invading Borg cube at the Battle of Wolf 359 in 2367.

Early in the battle, the *U.S.S. Melbourne* NCC-62043 was caught in the cutting beam weapon from the Borg cube. As the *Melbourne*'s shields were being drained, the *Saratoga* rushed in to help the stricken vessel, but it was too late. Half the *Melbourne*'s saucer was blown away, and the burning hulk of what remained was rammed by the cube as it pursued the *Saratoga*. The Starfleet ship was soon caught in the cube's tractor beam, while its shields were quickly drained. Once they failed, there was a massive explosion that caused huge damage from decks 1 to 4.

After the smoke had cleared, First Officer Benjamin Sisko realized that he and the Bolian tactical officer were the only bridge crew still alive. Damage reports revealed that a warp core containment failure would destroy the rest of the ship in just four minutes. Sisko had no option but to issue the order to abandon ship. He then went to his crew quarters to find his wife and child, and while Jake was still alive, his wife Jennifer had been killed by flying wreckage.

Numb and with badly burned hands, Sisko found his way to an escape pod where he joined Jake and about a dozen other survivors. The escape pod was launched and a few seconds later, they watched through the window as the *Saratoga* blew to pieces.

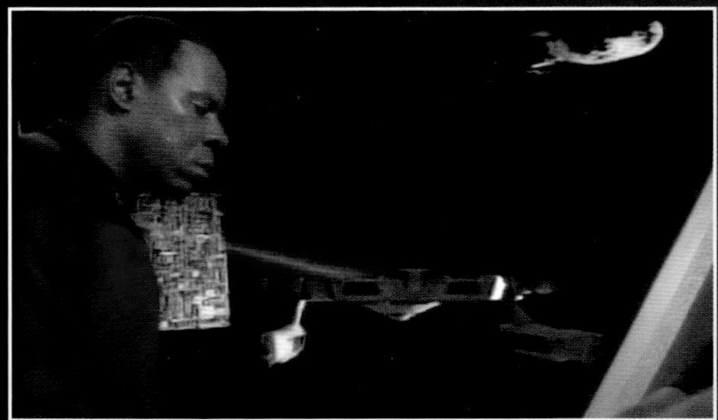

▲ Sisko was lost in his thoughts about his deceased wife as he fled the *Saratoga* in one of its escape pods. Seconds later, the *Saratoga*, which could be seen through the window, erupted in a huge fireball.

DATA FEED

The *U.S.S. Saratoga* NCC-31911 was not the first *Miranda*-class vessel to bear this name. In 2286, the *U.S.S. Saratoga* NCC-1887 was patrolling near the Neutral Zone when it encountered a whale probe on a direct course to Earth. The crew attempted to make contact, but it was neutralized by the probe, which was transmitting an amplification wave of enormous power.

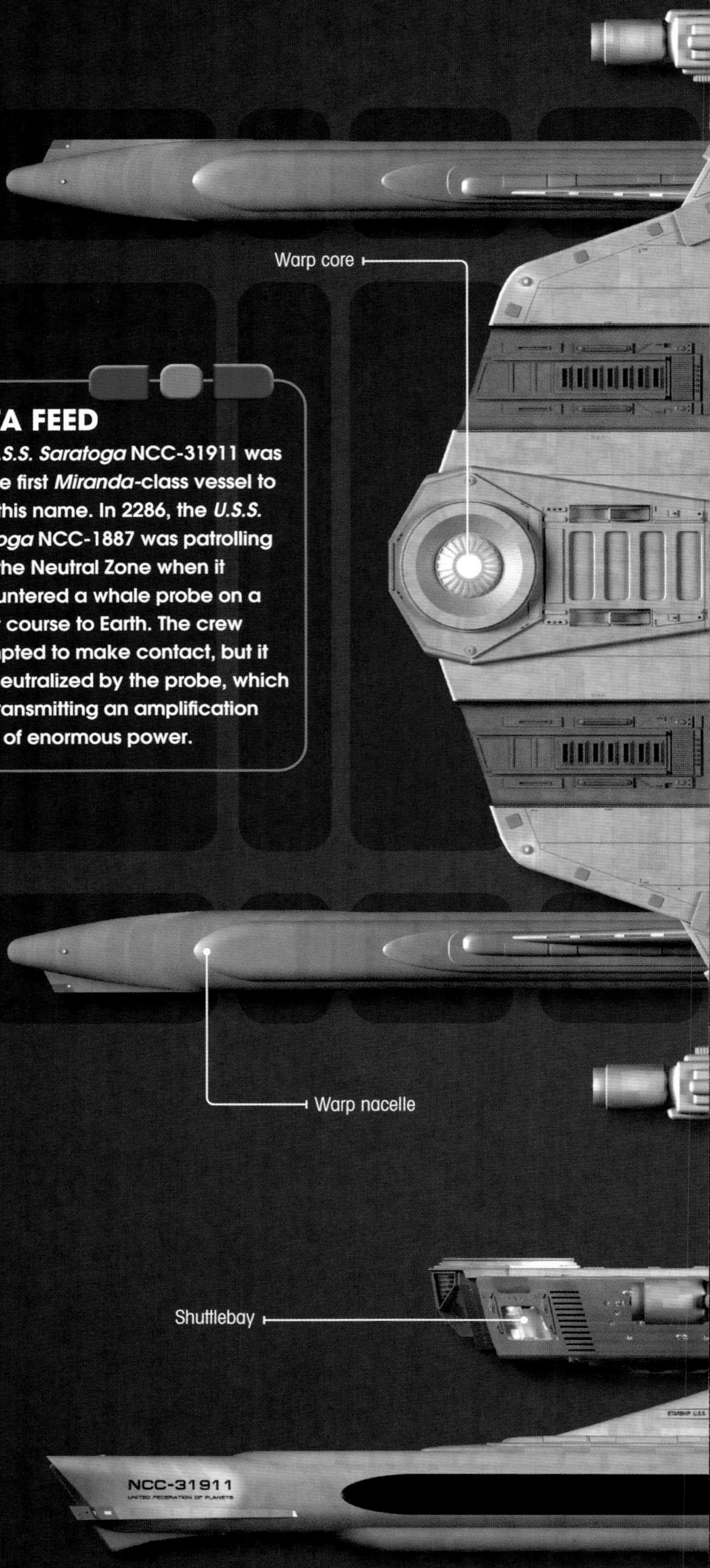

Warp core

Warp nacelle

Shuttlebay

NCC-31911

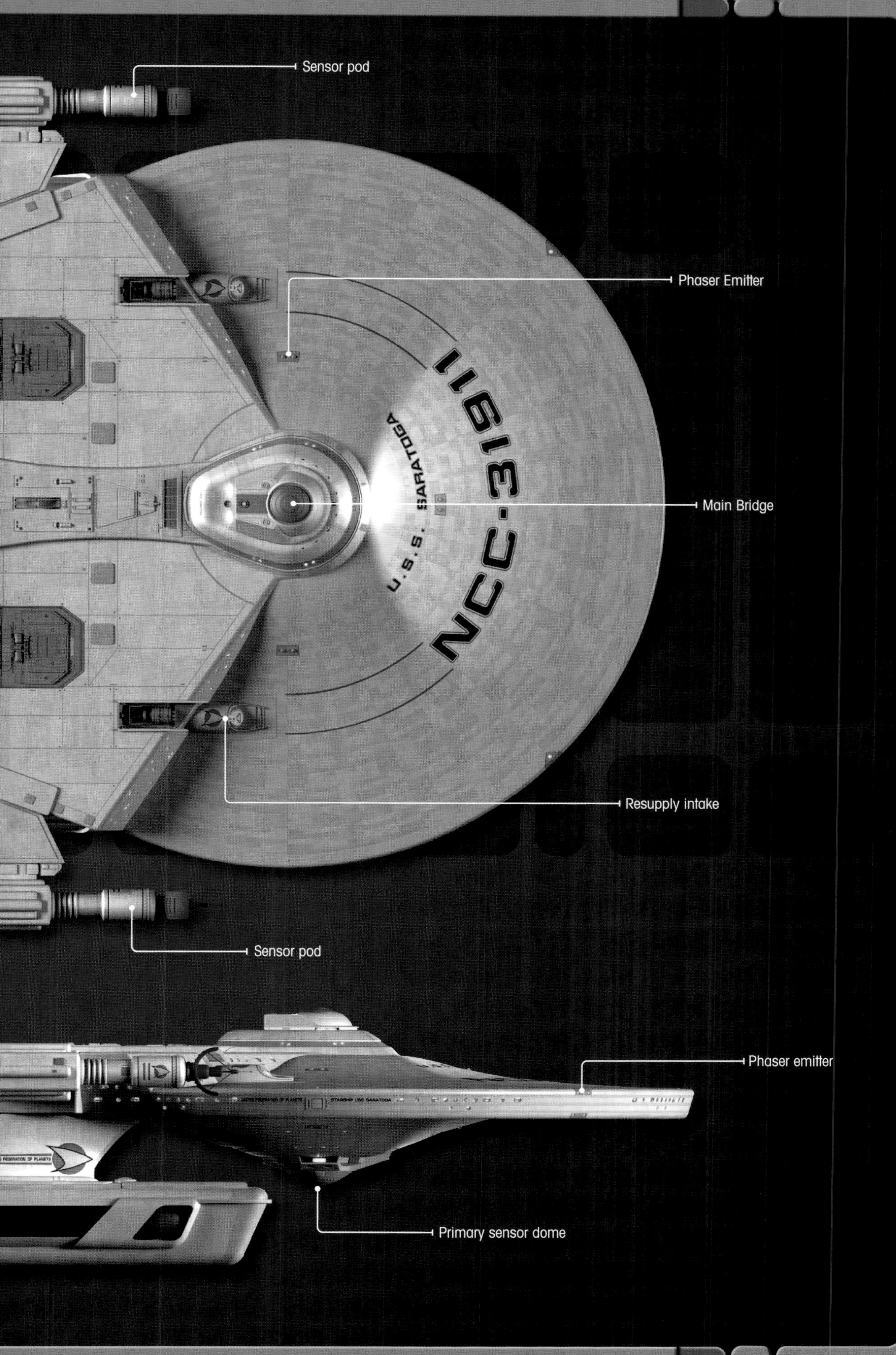

BATTLE SITE

Wolf 359 was the primary star in the Wolf system and 7.8 light-years from Sol – aka Earth's Sun – in Sector 001. The battle was triggered when a Borg cube demanded that the assembled Starfleet ships disarm and escort it to Sector 001. Its target was Earth.

▶ Instead of the secondary engineering hull often seen on other Starfleet ships, the *Akira* class had a large saucer section with a catamaran-style double hull on top. These ships were well defended and armed, their arsenal including quantum torpedoes.

STARFLEET

AKIRA CLASS

This class was designed to carry and launch shuttles, performing great service on combat and rescue missions.

The *Akira* class entered Starfleet service in the latter half of the 24th century and was built in response to the urgent threats posed by both the Cardassian Wars and the Borg. While exploration remained important to Starfleet, Federation space had become potentially much more dangerous and the fleet had to be equipped to meet these darker times. Therefore, the *Akira* class was designed with a strong bias toward patrol and combat duties.

While many Starfleet ships incorporated a secondary engineering hull, the *Akira* class instead featured a single primary saucer section, on which was positioned a split, catamaran-style hull. The beams extended back past the rear of the saucer to a spar that carried a weapons pod. The warp nacelles hung down below on either side, attached to the ends of the spar.

NARROW PROFILE

Despite the lack of a secondary engineering hull, the *Akira* class was still 464.43 meters long, indicating that the saucer section was of a similar size to that of the U.S.S. *Enterprise* NCC-1701-E, which was about one third longer overall. With no dedicated engineering hull, the *Akira* class presented a much narrower profile, and was thus less of a target in combat. The absence of this hull in no way diminished the speed of the ship, since it was capable of a top velocity of warp 9.8.

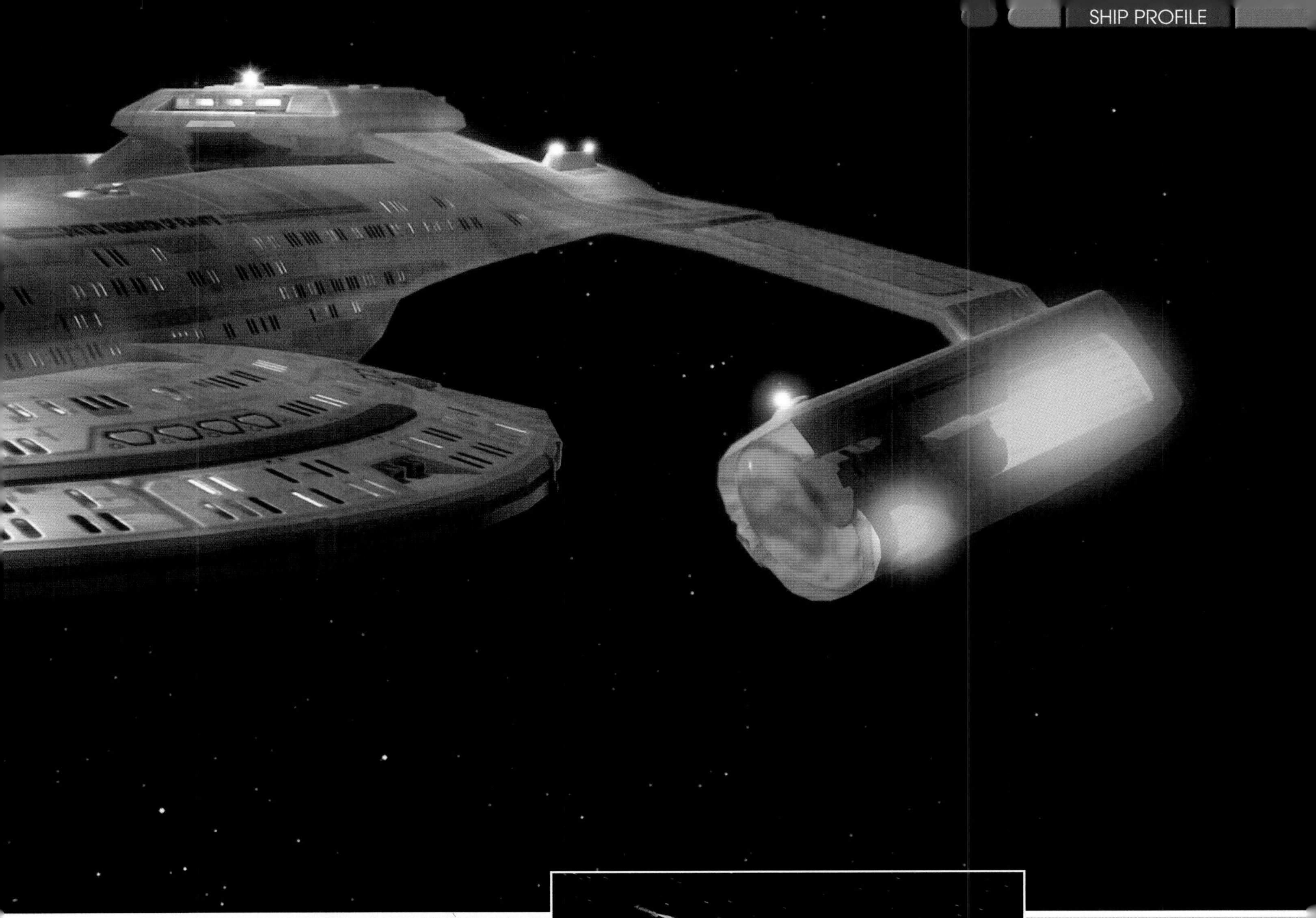

One of the main features of the *Akira* class was the weapons pod situated on top of the boom that connected the two warp nacelles. This pod carried an extraordinary array of weaponry, including seven forward-facing torpedo launchers, with a row of four positioned directly above a row of three. The two central launchers on the top row were designed for the more advanced quantum torpedoes, the rest for photon torpedoes.

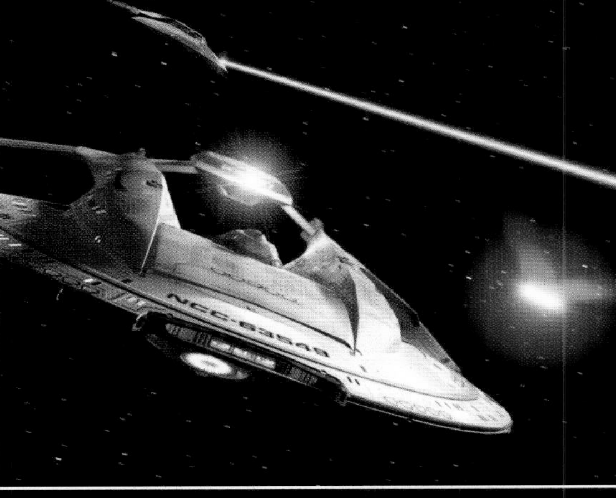

◀ The weapons pod on top of the spar behind the bridge featured multiple torpedo launchers, providing additional firepower to the phaser strips and launchers on the saucer. The *Akira* class also featured a fly-through shuttlebay, so that auxiliary craft could be launched via the nose of the ship and return through doors at the rear.

The weapons pod also featured a further six launchers toward the rear, with three on each side providing comprehensive defensive coverage to the aft of the ship. In addition, the pod was equipped with tactical sensors, and for more exploration- and research-oriented missions, it could be converted to carry more specialized science sensor equipment.

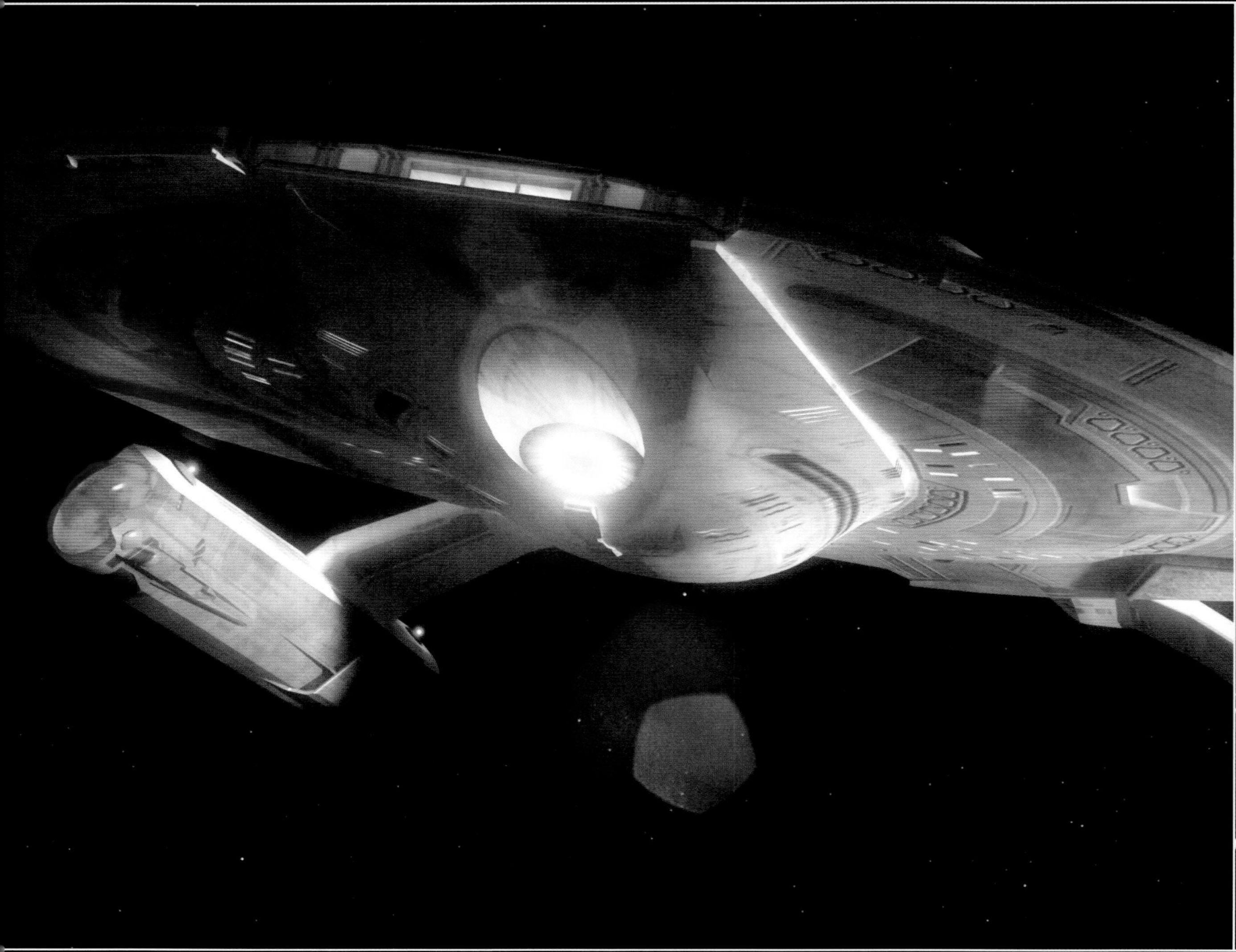

▶ Several *Akira*-class ships were part of the Starfleet armada that fought the Borg at the Battle of Sector 001, with at least two being destroyed.

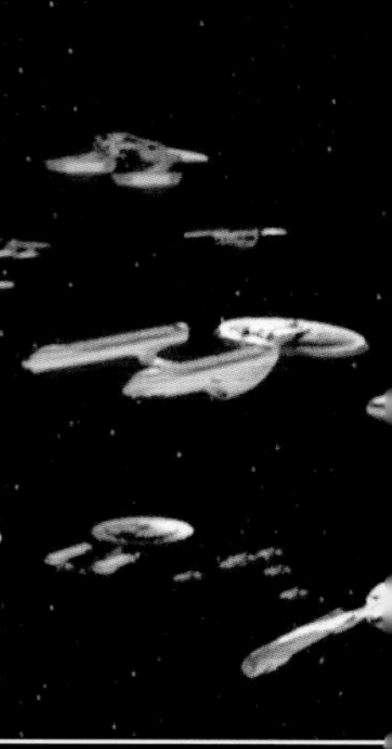

▲ The *Akira* class had three shuttlebay doors at the front of the saucer. This enabled the simultaneous deployment of multiple shuttlecraft, which saved vital time in an emergency or combat situation.

Supplementary to the weapons pod was a number of torpedo launchers on the saucer section itself. The main ones were located on the ventral side, above and below the deflector dish. Unusually, two more launchers were fitted on each side of the saucer, firing out to port and starboard.

There were also six type-10 phaser emitters, with the main ones encircling most of the saucer section on both the dorsal and ventral sides.

FLY-THROUGH SHUTTLEBAY

One of the reasons why the *Akira* class was so heavily defended was because it acted as a carrier, housing a large number of shuttlecraft. It was designed with a fly-through shuttlebay, so that multiple auxiliary craft could be launched simultaneously through three adjacent doors sited in the notch at the front of the saucer. The shuttles could then return to the ship in quick succession through doors at the rear of the saucer, behind the bridge. The ability to launch and dock shuttles at great speed was a major advantage in a combat situation, where smaller, more maneuverable fighter craft proved vital.

This was particularly true during the Cardassian Wars, because Starfleet had to respond quickly to Cardassian incursions into disputed territories. *Akira*-class ships were likewise very effective in pursuing the vessels of the renegade Maquis organization. The Maquis often hid in the Badlands, where larger ships did not cope nearly so well with the plasma storms and gravitational anomalies of that region.

Because *Akira*-class ships carried so many shuttles, they made excellent rescue vessels for evacuation efforts. This was particularly useful in areas where transporters did not work; the shuttles could be rapidly deployed to pick up survivors or

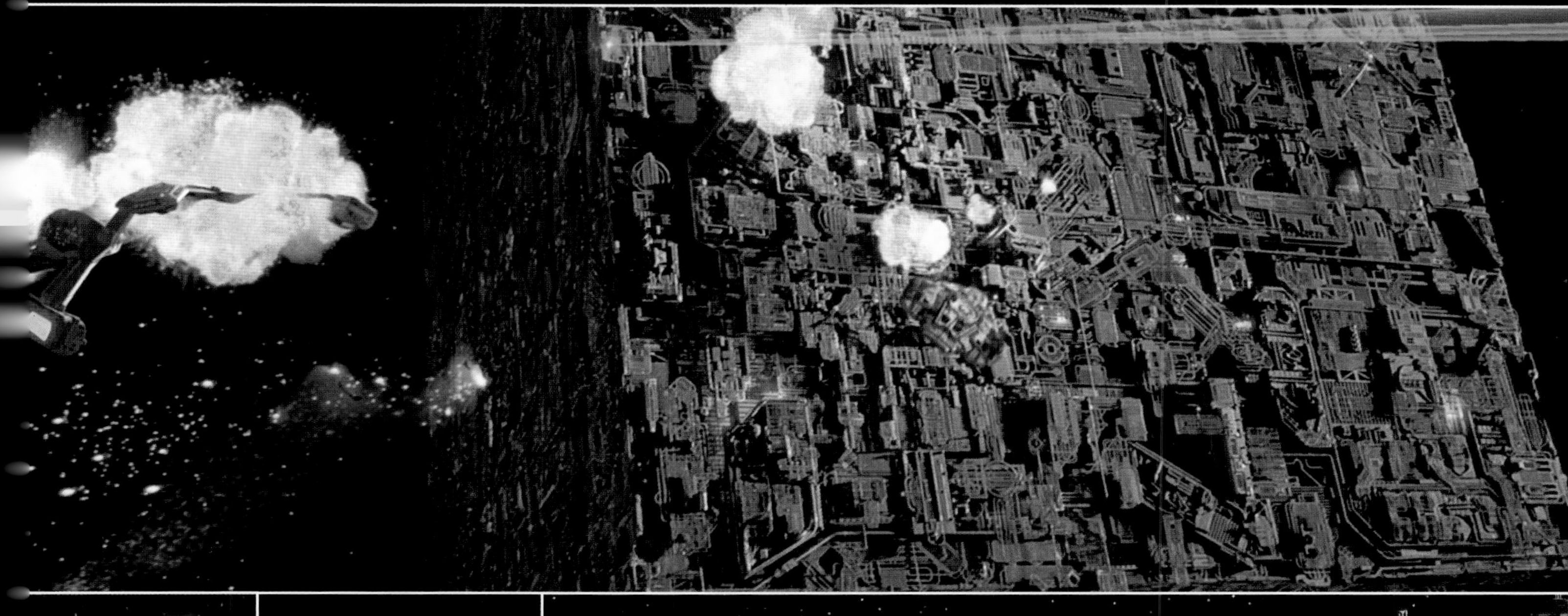

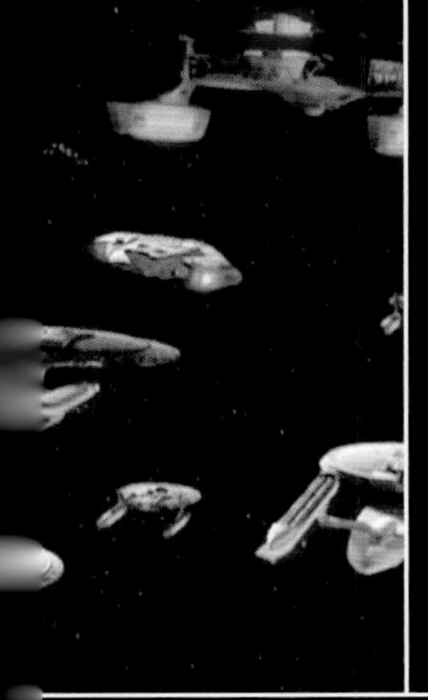

◀ In 2374, more than 600 ships, including *Akira*-class vessels, took part in Operation Return, a successful offensive to retake Deep Space 9 from Dominion control.

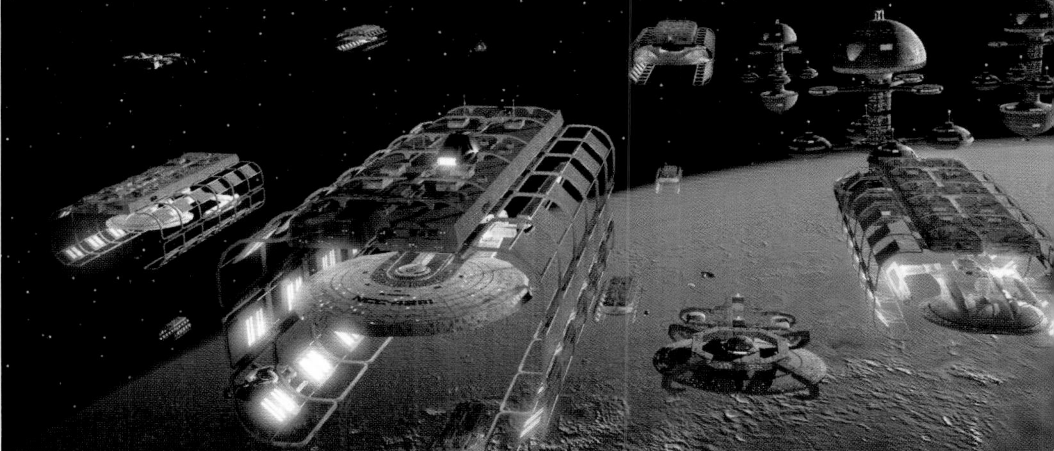

▲ One of the sites for the construction of the *Akira* class was the Utopia Planitia Fleet Yards, a dry dock facility above the Utopia Planitia region on Mars.

vulnerable colonists, return quickly to the mother ship, then be launched again.

The overall layout of the *Akira* class was designed with the protection of its shuttlecraft very much in mind. Extra defensive shield emitters were positioned on either side of the launch bay doors at the front of the saucer, while the rear shuttle doors provided a secure entry point, since they were protected by being tucked down within the split hull. The main bridge, too, was afforded extra protection by the design of the raised double hull. It was shielded between the twin structures, rather than being exposed on top of the saucer as on most other Starfleet ships.

All these attributes meant that the *Akira* class proved very effective during the Cardassian Wars, performing patrol and protection missions among outer Federation territories, and thereby helping to defend vulnerable colonies. It was also invaluable in safeguarding Federation outposts and carrying out emergency evacuations. *Akira*-class vessels, which included the *U.S.S. Thunderchild* NCC-63549, also formed part of the fleet that engaged the Borg at the Battle of Sector 001 in 2373, and they played a significant role in several conflicts during the Dominion War.

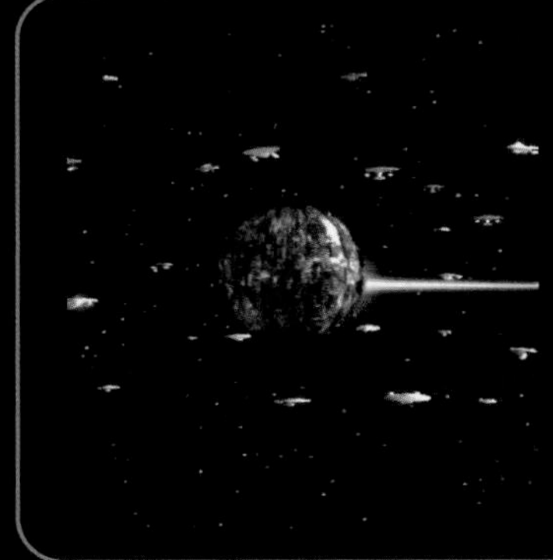

DATA FEED

In 2378, an emergency defensive force of 27 vessels, including several *Akira*-class ships, was hastily assembled to intercept the Borg when a transwarp conduit was detected opening less than a light-year from Earth. As it turned out, the Borg sphere that emerged from the conduit was destroyed from within by the *U.S.S. Voyager* NCC-74656, and the fleet merely had to escort the starship home.

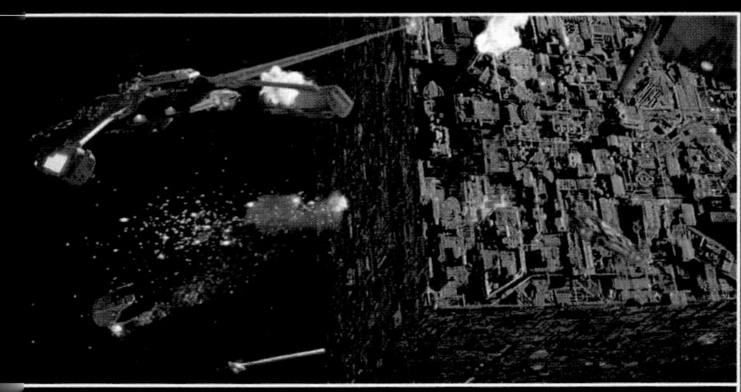

AKIRA CLASS IN ACTION

As a ship designed for patrol and combat duties, the *Akira* class saw much action in the later 24th century. In 2373, several such ships, including the *U.S.S. Thunderchild* NCC-63549, were part of the Starfleet task force that defeated the Borg at the Battle of Sector 001.

In late 2374, several *Akira*-class ships joined the fleet of the Federation Alliance that fought at the First Battle of Chin'toka, during the Dominion War. Three were destroyed by the orbital weapons system there, but the Alliance finally scored a tactical victory and succeeded in landing ground troops.

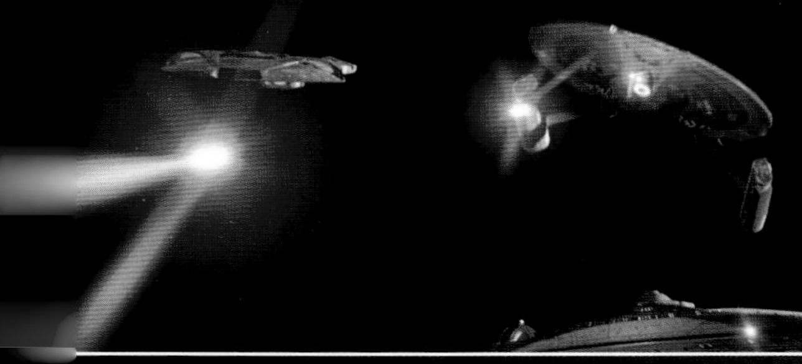

▲ An *Akira*-class ship helped to target the Borg cube with a volley of torpedoes during the Battle of Sector 001. The *Akira* class's combat capabilities proved a major asset for Starfleet in the late 24th century.

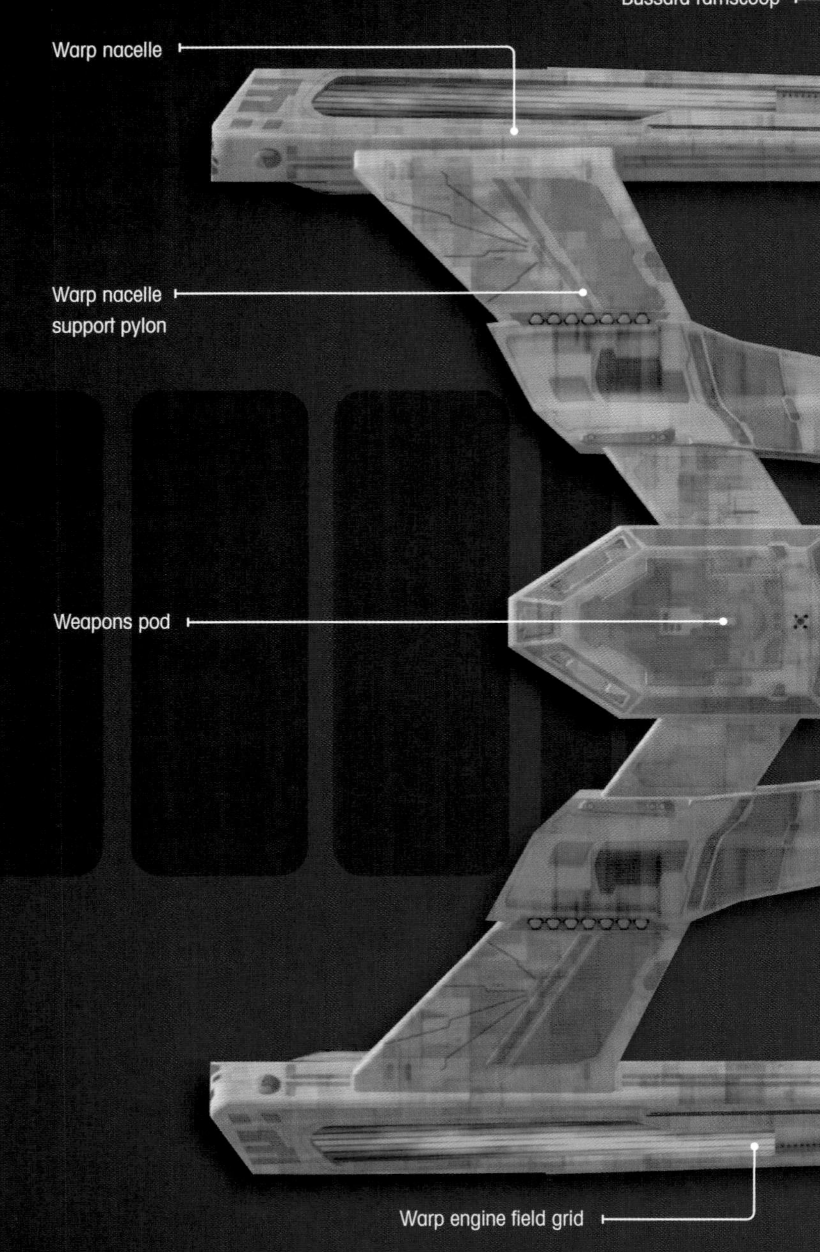

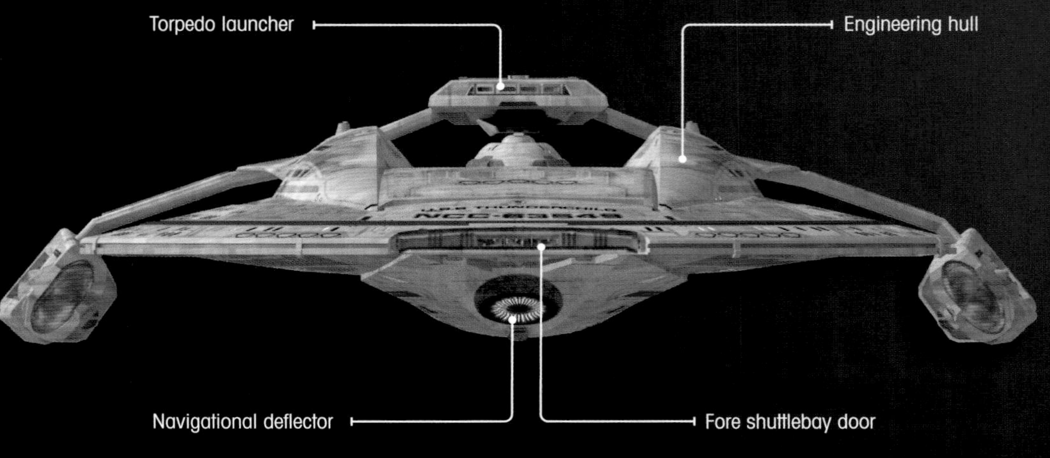

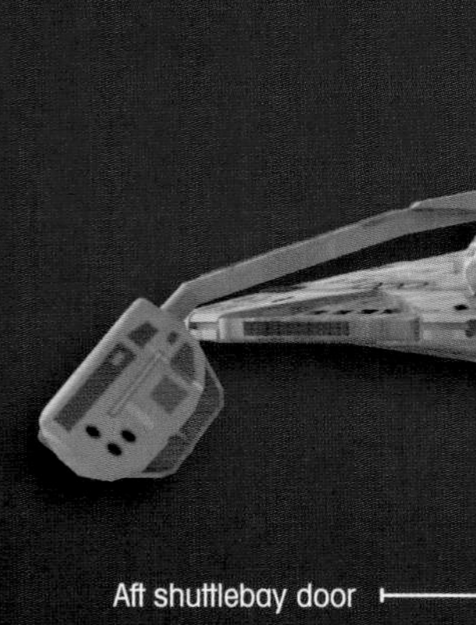

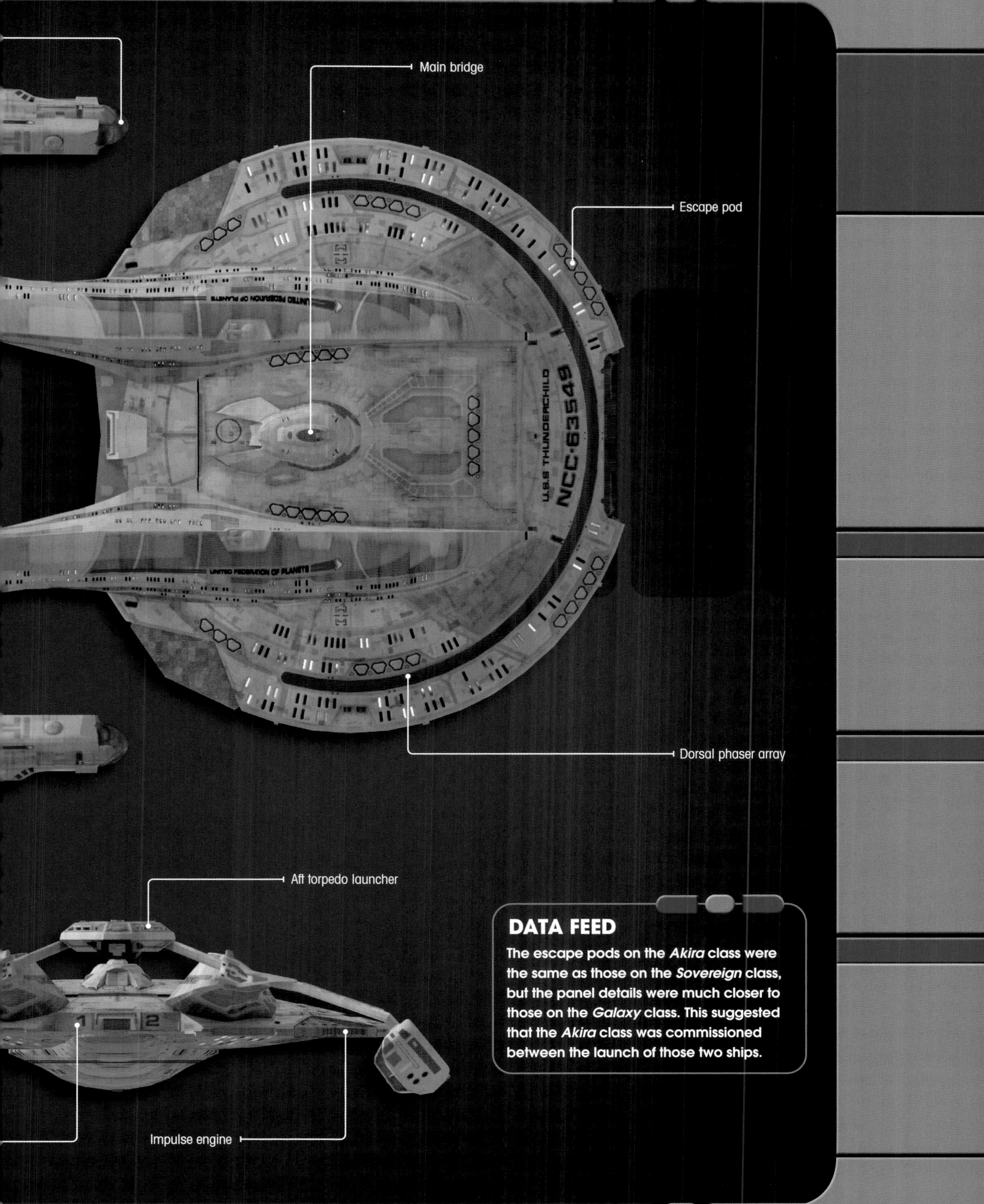

DATA FEED

The escape pods on the *Akira* class were the same as those on the *Sovereign* class, but the panel details were much closer to those on the *Galaxy* class. This suggested that the *Akira* class was commissioned between the launch of those two ships.

▼ The *Defiant* may have been small but it was one "tough little ship," as once described by Commander Riker. Designed in response to the Borg threat, the *Defiant* was a no-frills battleship and Starfleet's most powerfully weaponized vessel.

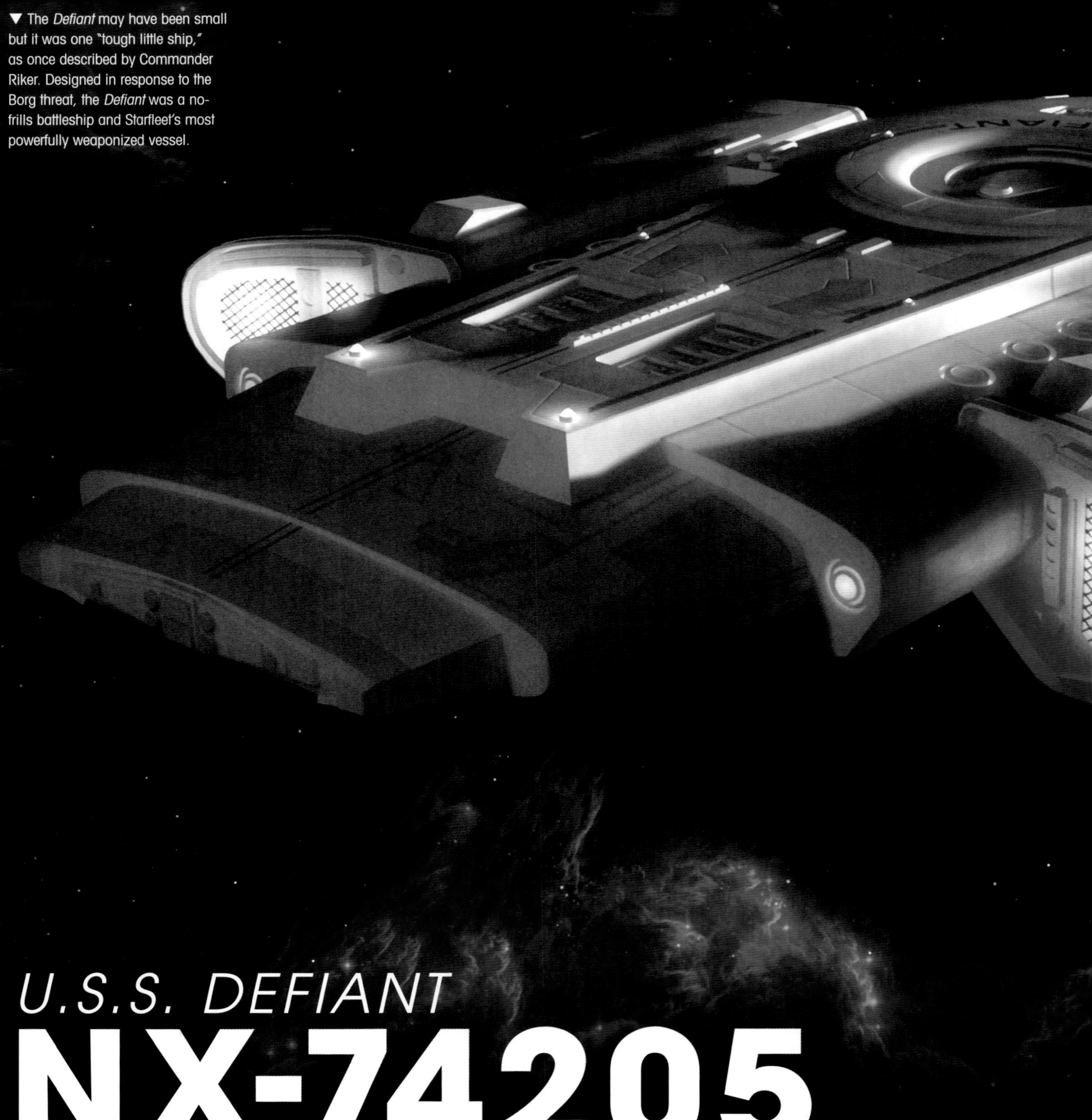

U.S.S. DEFIANT NX-74205

Built for battle, the *U.S.S. Defiant* was armed with pulse phaser cannons, quantum torpedoes, and a cloaking device.

DATA FEED

The *U.S.S. Defiant* was the first Starfleet ship to be equipped with ablative armor plating. This was a type of protective skin that covered the hull plating. It was designed to disperse the energy from weapons fire, thus protecting the ship even if its shields were down. Ablative armor was added to the *Defiant* after its deployment to Deep Space 9 and the technology was so secret that almost no one in Starfleet knew it had been installed.

Officially classed as an escort ship, the *U.S.S. Defiant* NX-74205 was a prototype vessel designed to be Starfleet's first dedicated warship. Developed in response to the threat of a Borg invasion, the *Defiant* was a heavily armed, highly maneuverable, stripped-down vessel designed for combat rather than exploration.

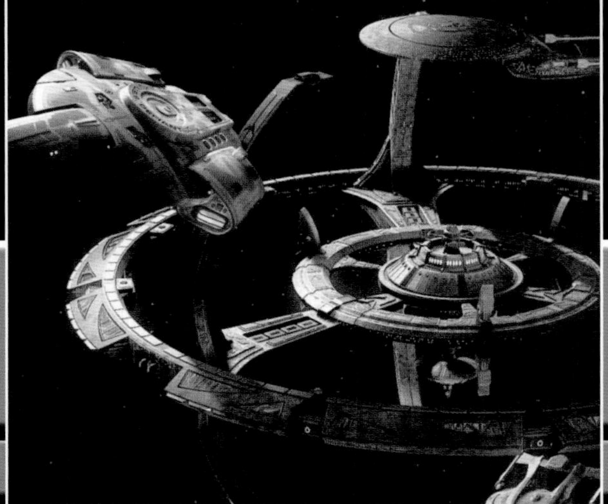

◀ Although it still had design flaws, the *Defiant* was assigned to Deep Space 9 in 2371. The space station's commander, Benjamin Sisko, who had worked on the development of the *Defiant*, requested its use to help protect the station from the threat posed by the Dominion.

At just 170.68 meters long and with a standard operational crew of 40 people, the *Defiant* was undoubtedly a small ship, but it packed a considerable punch. Armed with advanced quantum torpedoes, as well as Mark-VIII and Mark-IX photon torpedoes and four twin-pulse cannon phasers, the *Defiant* was the most destructively powerful ship Starfleet ever produced for its size.

In addition to its formidable weaponry, the *Defiant* was covered in ablative armor, a protective skin on the hull of the ship that dissipated the energy of weapons fire. This was an extra layer of defense that meant the ship still had some protection, even if the conventional shields failed.

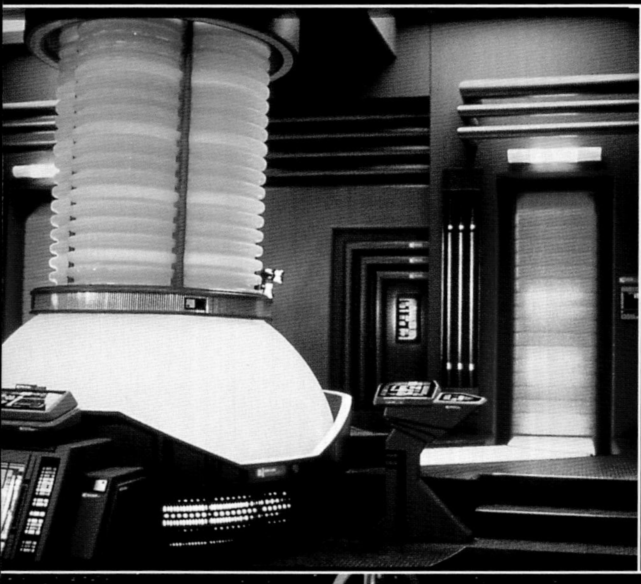

◀ The class-7 warp core ran up through three decks of the ship, while a master systems display was located on the wall of main engineering.

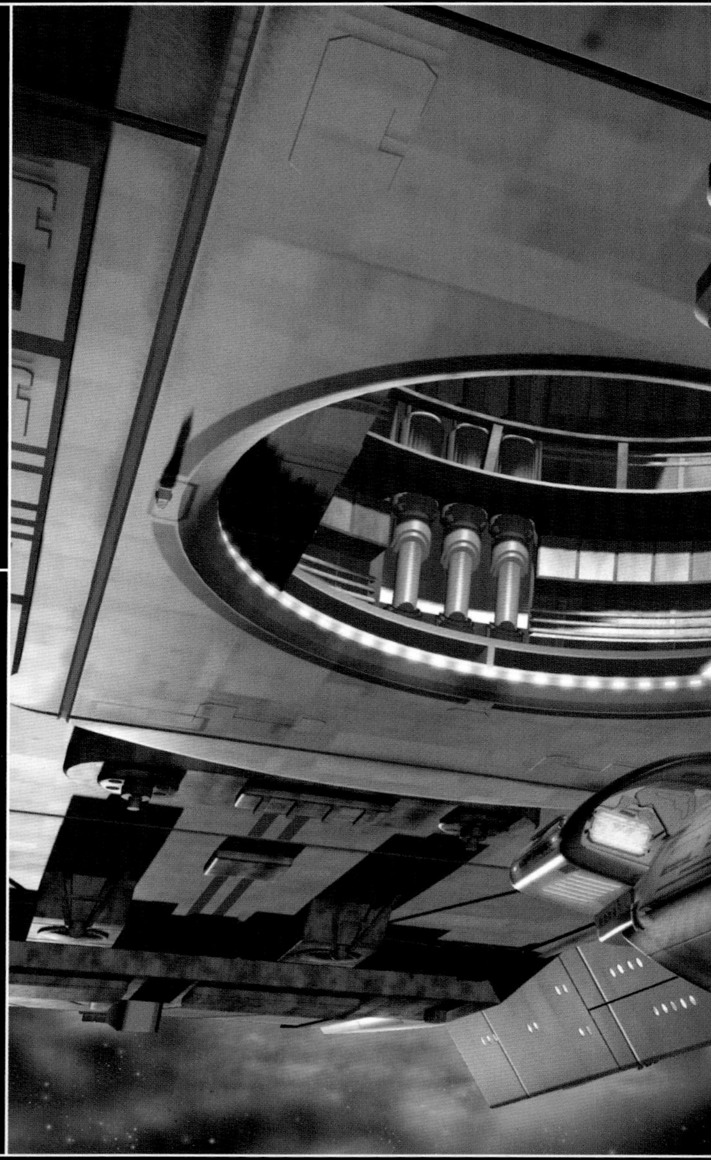

▶ Despite the *Defiant*'s relatively small size, it had provision for several shuttlecraft, which were launched from a circular hatch on the ventral side.

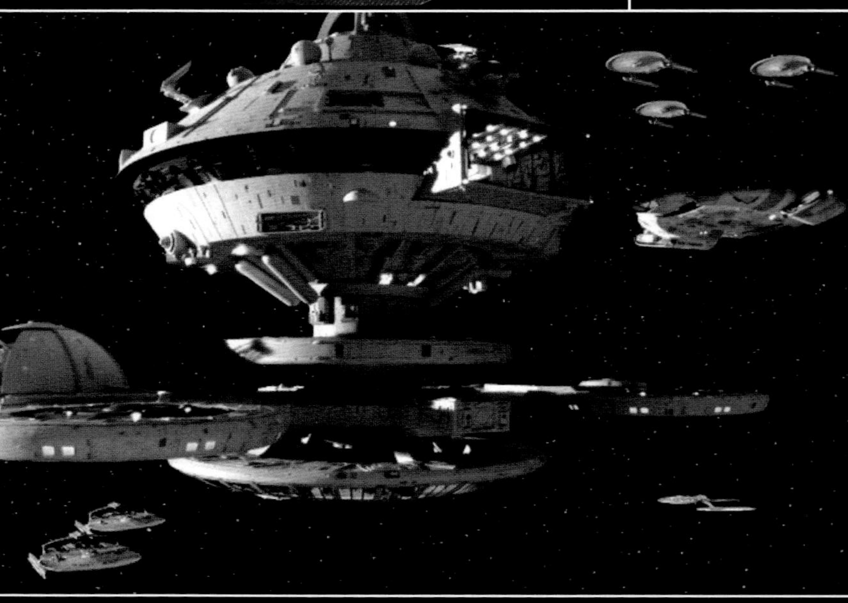

▲ After Starfleet lost control of Deep Space 9 to Dominion forces in late 2373, the *Defiant* was reassigned to the Second Fleet, which operated out of Starbase 375. This facility acted as a base of operations for the *Defiant* for several months, until a combined Federation force retook Deep Space 9 and the *Defiant* was once again tasked with protecting the station.

The *Defiant* marked a radical change in policy by Starfleet in that it had previously only designed ships for exploration, peace-keeping, or scientific purposes. The *Defiant* was a response to the threat posed by the Borg after their invasion of the Alpha Quadrant and the massacre at the Battle of Wolf 359, in which Starfleet lost 39 ships and 11,000 lives.

TOO POWERFUL

Development of the *Defiant* began in 2367, with the then Lieutenant Commander Sisko assisting in design work and flight tests. Launched in 2370 from the Antares Fleet Yards, the *Defiant* proved too heavily weaponized and overpowered for its size, and its structural integrity field struggled to prevent the ship from tearing itself apart in battle drills.

Despite the *Defiant*'s enormous potential, after several years of development its design flaws had still not been overcome and the project was mothballed, especially as the perceived threat from the Borg seemed to have diminished.

It was not until in 2371, when the *Defiant* was assigned to Deep Space 9 – now with Commander Sisko in charge – that its design faults were resolved and it became a vital component in the station's defenses against the Dominion and its allies.

On Deep Space 9, the *Defiant* was granted special dispensation to be equipped with a Romulan cloaking device. The Romulans agreed to supply the cloaking technology in return for all intelligence gathered on the Dominion.

The *Defiant* was equipped with a class-7 warp

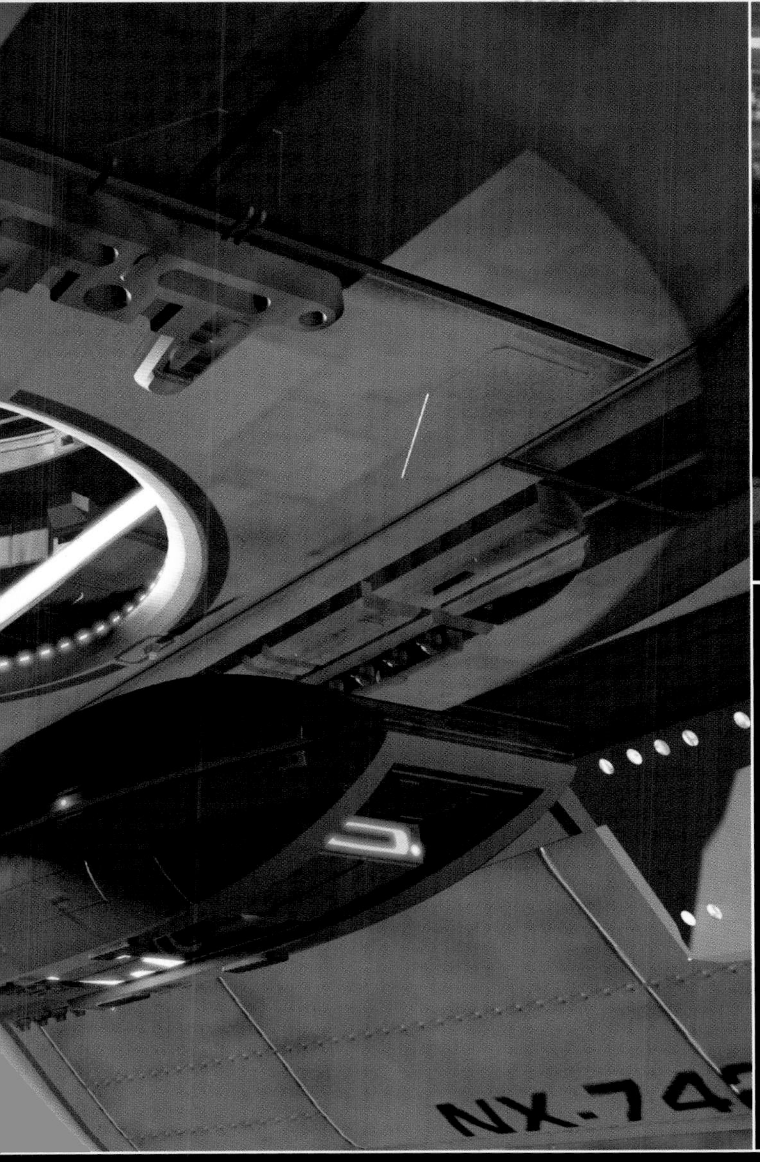

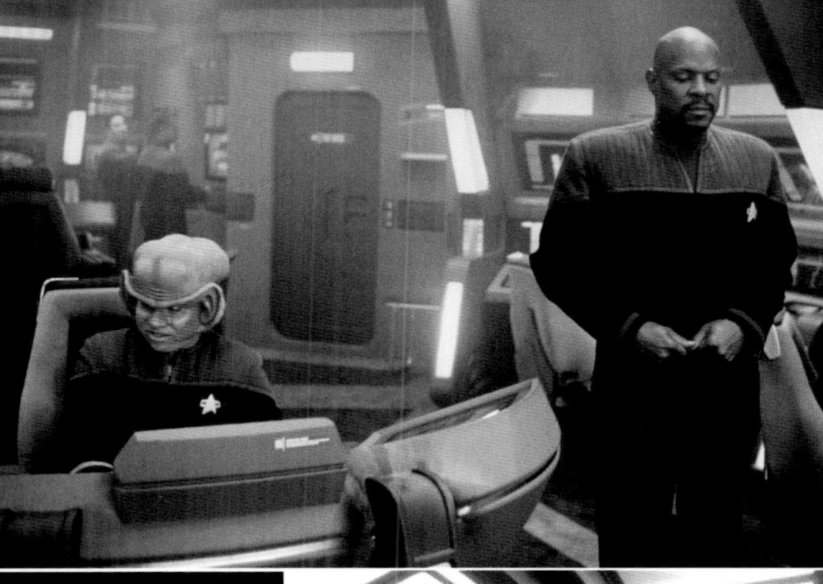

▲ Like the rest of the ship, the bridge on the *Defiant* was configured for maximum efficiency in battle, with the flight control and operations stations combined into one console.

▶ The sickbay was extremely rudimentary, much to Dr. Bashir's annoyance. It contained just four standard biobeds and was ill-equipped to do much more than stabilize a seriously injured patient.

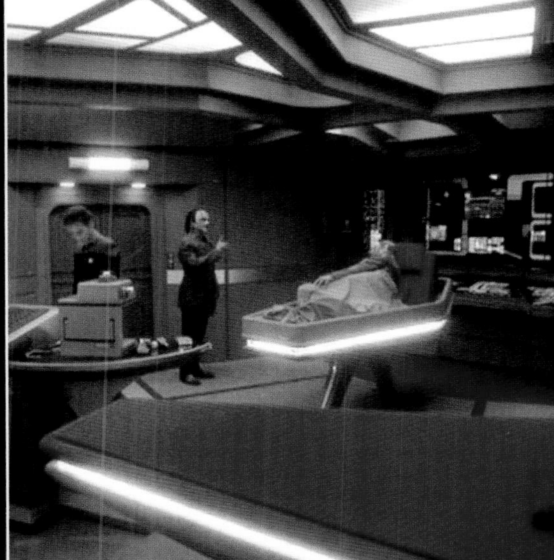

drive and the core spanned three decks in the aft section of the ship. It was extremely powerful for a ship of this size and it could propel the ship at speeds of warp 9.5 for extended periods and even reach warp 9.982 for limited bursts.

SPARTAN STARSHIP

As a combat vessel, the interior of the *Defiant* was extremely functional and had no provision for families or recreational activities. Even the science and medical facilities on deck 2 were extremely limited. One of the few communal areas of the ship was a mess hall where the crew could gather and eat meals dispensed from replicators.

The main bridge was the nerve center, but it was positioned differently from that of other Starfleet

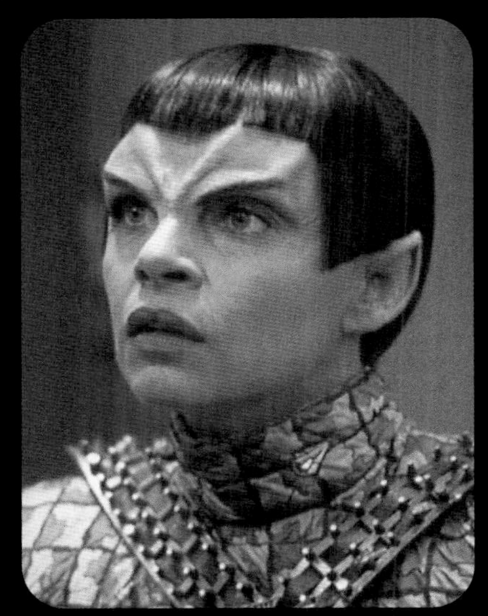

DATA FEED

A special amendment to the Treaty of Algeron allowed for the *Defiant* to be fitted with a Romulan cloaking device. The treaty stipulated that the Federation could not develop cloaking technology. In this instance, the Romulans loaned the *Defiant* a cloaking device, provided it was used only in the Gamma Quadrant and that its operation was overseen by Subcommander T'Rul (pictured). In return, Starfleet shared all intelligence the ship gathered.

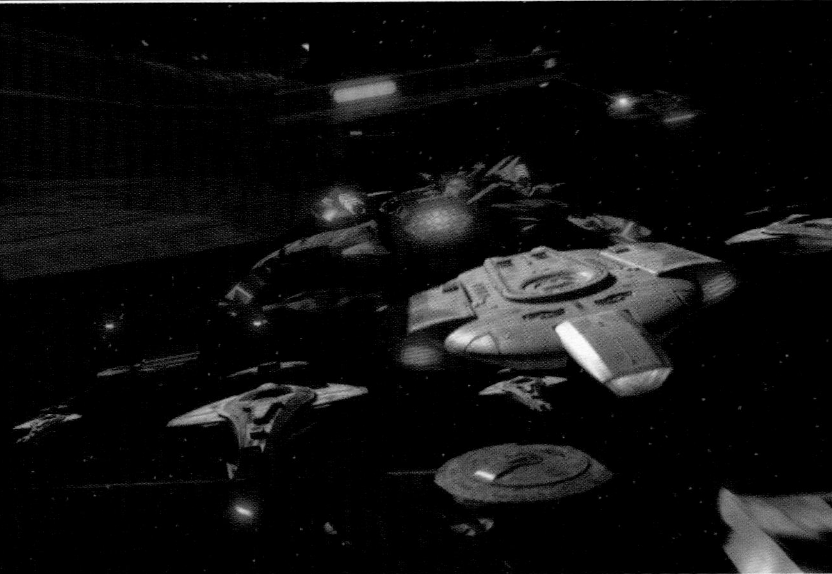

◀ In one of the pivotal battles of the Dominion War, the *Defiant* led a combined Starfleet and Klingon force in an attempt to win back control of Deep Space 9. Although the Dominion had twice the number of ships, the operation was successful and Captain Sisko was once again back in charge of the station.

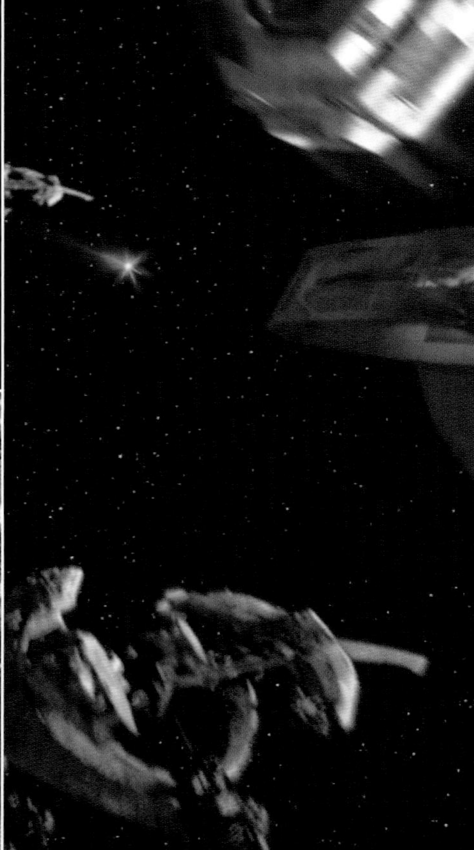

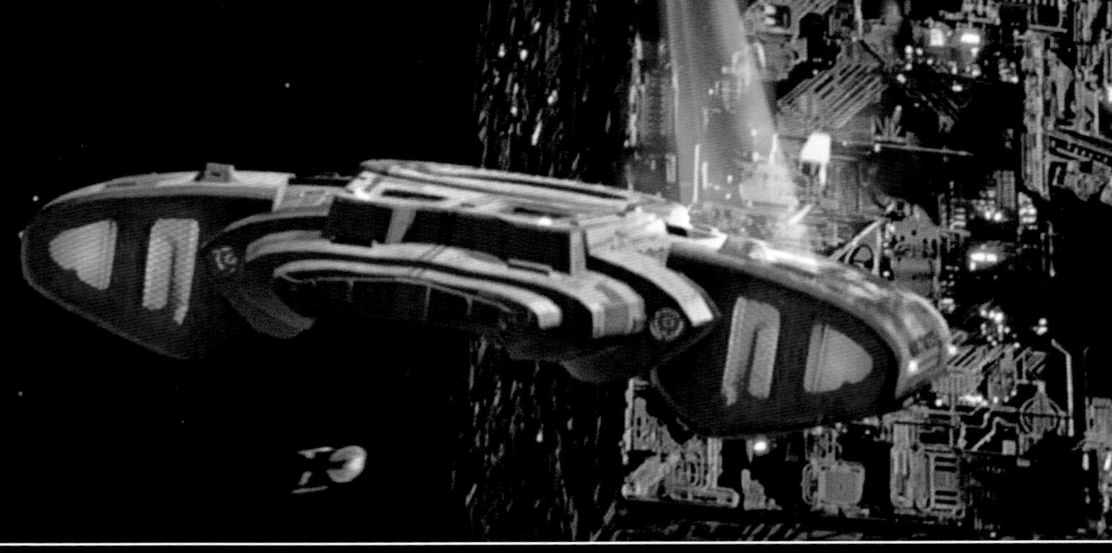

▲ The Borg's second major incursion into Federation space culminated in the Battle of Sector 001, when the *Defiant* and about 30 other Starfleet ships engaged a Borg cube. The fleet was successful in destroying the cube, and although the *Defiant* took heavy damage it was ultimately salvageable and was soon back in service at Deep Space 9.

ships; it was sunk into the center of the vessel, which afforded it more protection than was possible on the top of the ship.

LAST RESORT WEAPONRY

In addition to the *Defiant's* state-of-the-art weaponry, the entire front "nose" section, which contained several torpedo warheads, could detach and be used as a missile, as a last resort. If this function was activated, the main body of the ship could then no longer travel at high speeds, but it was equipped with landing gear so it could set down on a planetary surface in an emergency.

The *Defiant's* active service began in early 2371, when it was assigned to Deep Space 9 to help protect the station from the escalating threat posed by the Dominion. Their genetically engineered army, the Jem'Hadar, had recently destroyed a *Galaxy*-class ship, the *U.S.S. Odyssey* NCC-71832, and Sisko felt that the station needed an extra line of defense.

It was not long before Chief Miles O'Brien managed to iron out most of the *Defiant's* flaws and the ship proved vital, both in the defense of Deep Space 9 and in the later Dominion War.

BATTLING THE BORG

In 2373, the *Defiant* was forced into action to serve its original purpose, when the Borg returned. While many Starfleet ships were destroyed early in the engagement with the Borg cube at Sector 001, the *Defiant* managed to keep fighting for some

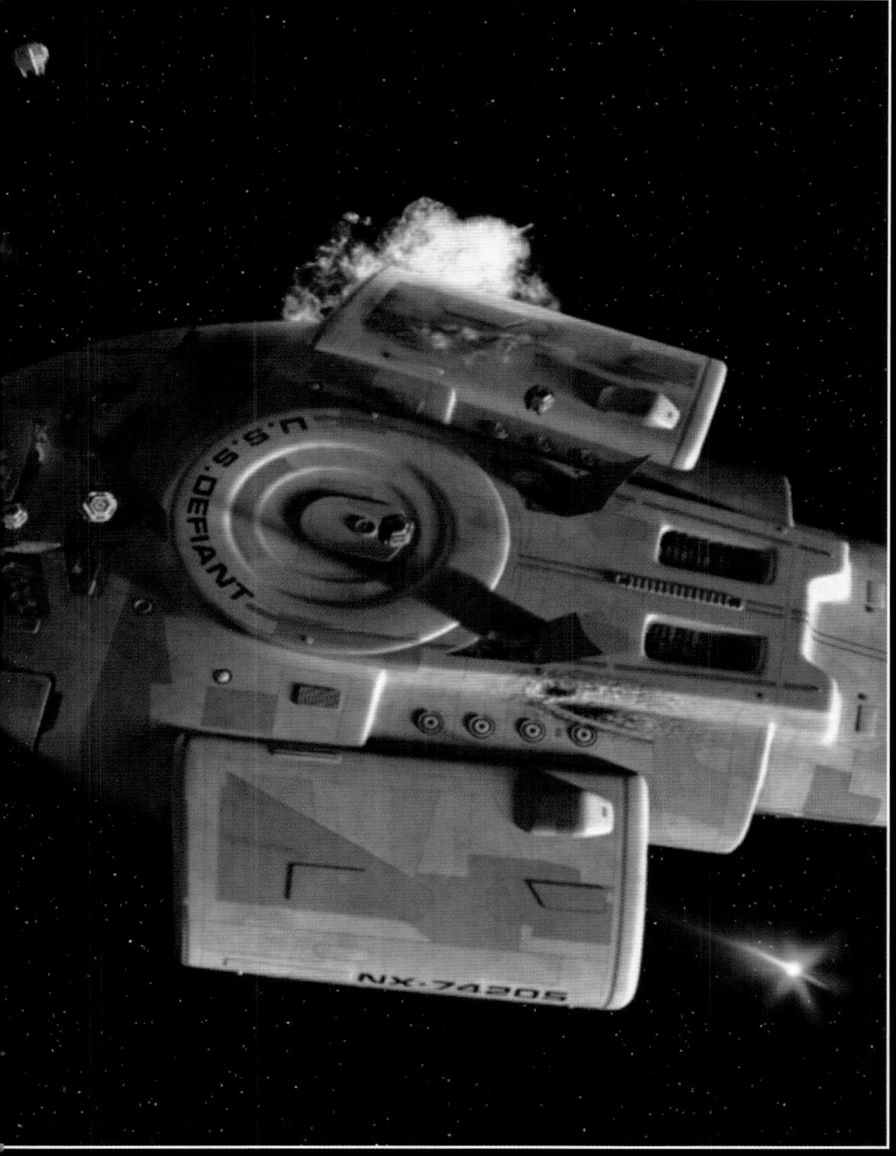

▲ The Breen entered the war alongside the Dominion at the Second Battle of Chin'toka. The Breen's potent energy-dampening weapon proved decisive in the battle, because it completely disabled all the Allied ships' primary systems, leaving them totally exposed. The Allied force was wiped out, and even the *Defiant* was destroyed, although the crew managed to eject in escape pods.

time and inflicted heavy damage on the cube. But the *Defiant* took serious fire, leading to a loss of main power, and it was left adrift in space, but not before the crew were beamed to safety aboard the *U.S.S. Enterprise* NCC-1701-E.

THE DOMINION WAR

The *Defiant* was soon repaired, and later the same year was used to mine the Bajoran wormhole to stop the Dominion's military build-up in Cardassian space. Although this prevented more Dominion forces from entering the Alpha Quadrant, it could not prevent the Dominion from taking control of Deep Space 9, and all-out war soon followed.

For several months, the *Defiant* fought as part of the Second Fleet, operating out of Starbase 375.

DATA FEED

The *U.S.S. Sao Paulo* NCC-75633 was almost identical to the *Defiant*. But it was upgraded with redesigned deflector shield generators to counteract the Breen energy-dampening weapon that had been responsible for the destruction of the first *Defiant*. The bridge was also modified, with some of the consoles being redesigned and the aft operations table replaced with a free-standing console.

The fighting was long, arduous, and at times seemingly hopeless, but the *Defiant* continued to survive against the odds and won many vital engagements during the war. In mid-2374, the *Defiant* led a force that retook control of Deep Space 9 and by the end of the year, the war finally seemed to be turning in their favor when the *Defiant* led another fleet to victory in the First Battle of Chin'toka.

DEFIANT'S DESTRUCTION

Unfortunately, in 2375 a new alliance between the Dominion and the Breen tipped the balance back again, and the *Defiant* was among a toll of 311 Federation Alliance ships destroyed in the Second Battle of Chin'toka.

A new *Defiant*-class vessel, the *U.S.S. Sao Paulo* NCC-75633, was assigned to Deep Space 9, and Captain Sisko received special dispensation from Starfleet Chief of Operations to rename the ship after its illustrious predecessor. This second-generation *Defiant* was upgraded with new deflector shield generators that counteracted the Breen energy-dampening weapon that had decimated the allied fleet at Chin'toka.

The upgraded *Defiant* participated in the final battle of the Dominion War in late 2375, when the Federation Alliance launched an invasion of Cardassia, where the Dominion had centered its operations in the Alpha Quadrant.

The *Defiant* found itself in the thick of the action and, despite taking heavy fire, managed to help the Alliance forces punch a hole through the Dominion's defensive perimeter. The Alliance lost more than a third of its fleet in the battle, but the *Defiant* survived and the Dominion was defeated, declaring an unconditional surrender of all their forces in the Alpha Quadrant.

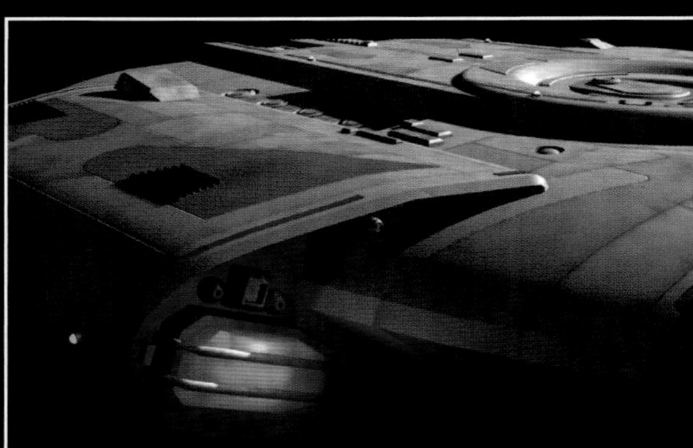

WEAPONRY AND FIREPOWER

Because its original purpose was to defend the Federation against the Borg, the *U.S.S. Defiant* was very heavily armed. It was equipped with four forward-facing phaser cannons, two located on each side of the ship on the nacelles. They were usually deployed in short, rapid-fire bursts, but they could also be fired as a continuous beam. In addition to these cannons, the *Defiant* featured conventional phaser emitters as found on other Starfleet vessels.

The *Defiant* was also equipped with four forward-facing and two aft-facing torpedo launchers. These could be used to fire photon torpedoes or quantum torpedoes. The latter contained a plasma warhead and were more effective than conventional antimatter explosives in penetrating deflector shields.

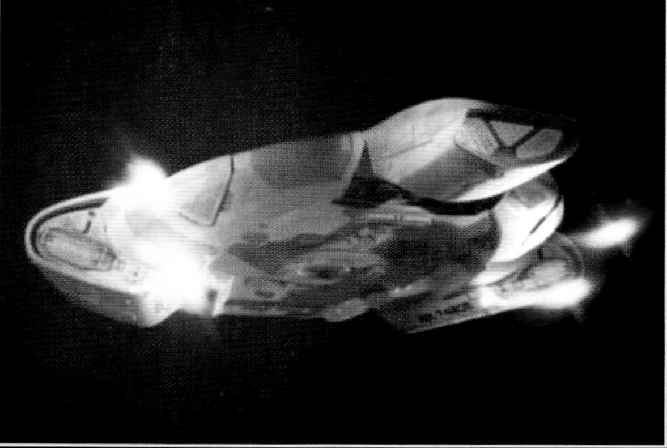

▲ The *Defiant* was the most heavily armed vessel in Starfleet and played a vital role in numerous battles during the Dominion War.

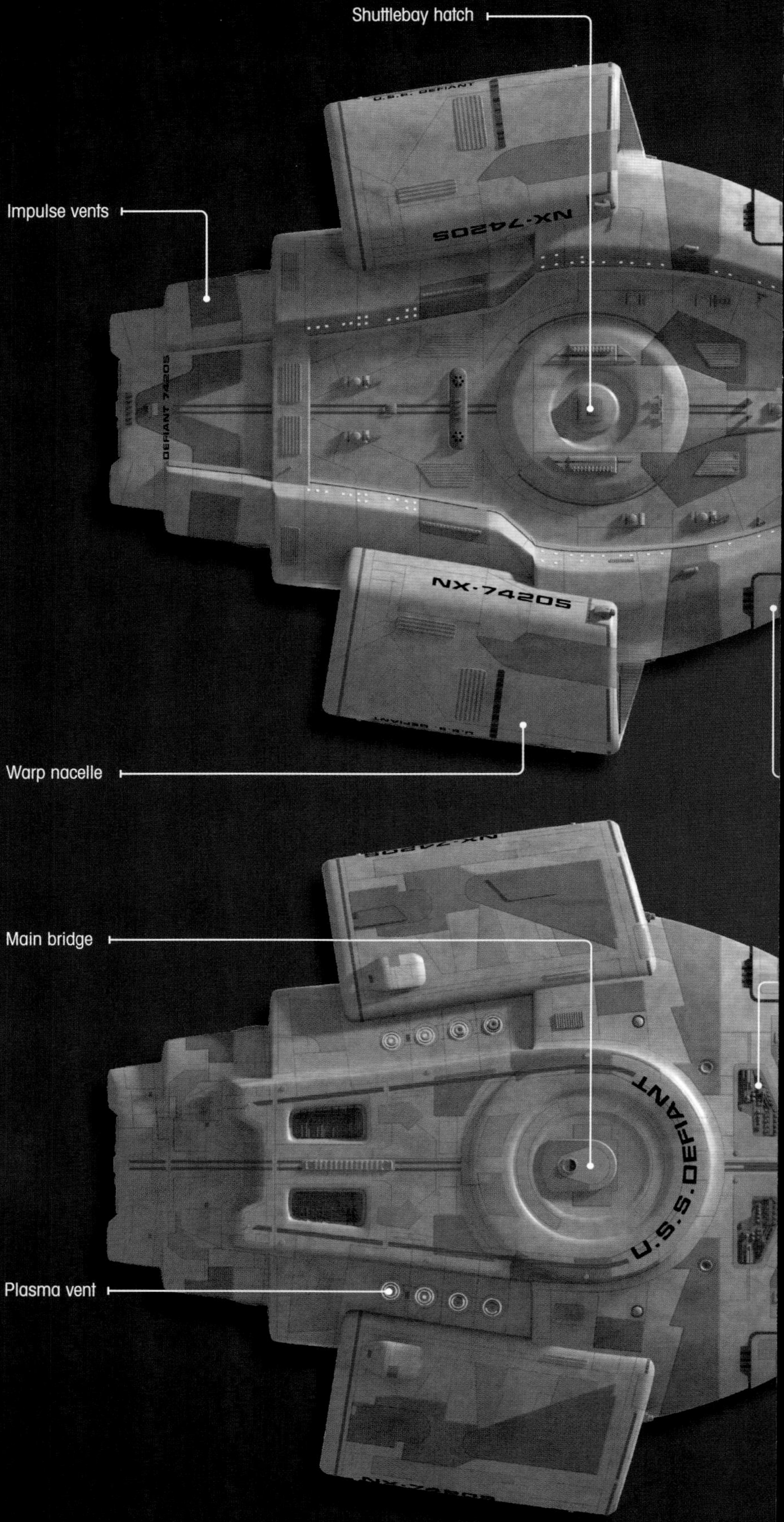

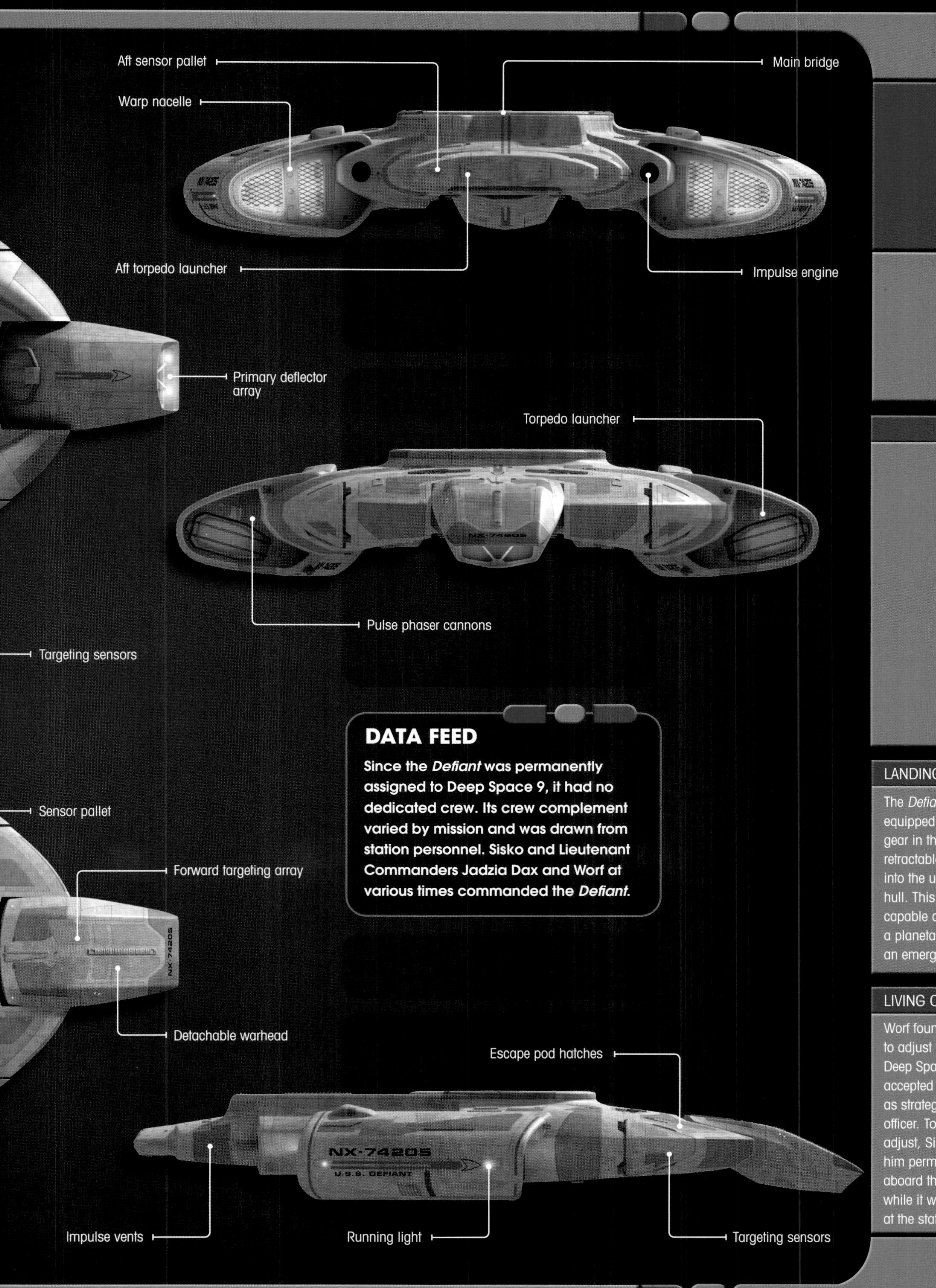

DATA FEED

Since the *Defiant* was permanently assigned to Deep Space 9, it had no dedicated crew. Its crew complement varied by mission and was drawn from station personnel. Sisko and Lieutenant Commanders Jadzia Dax and Worf at various times commanded the *Defiant*.

LANDING GEAR

The *Defiant* was equipped with landing gear in the form of four retractable struts built into the underside of the hull. This meant it was capable of landing on a planetary surface in an emergency.

LIVING ONBOARD

Worf found it difficult to adjust to life aboard Deep Space 9 after he accepted a post there as strategic operations officer. To help him adjust, Sisko granted him permission to live aboard the *Defiant* while it was docked at the station.

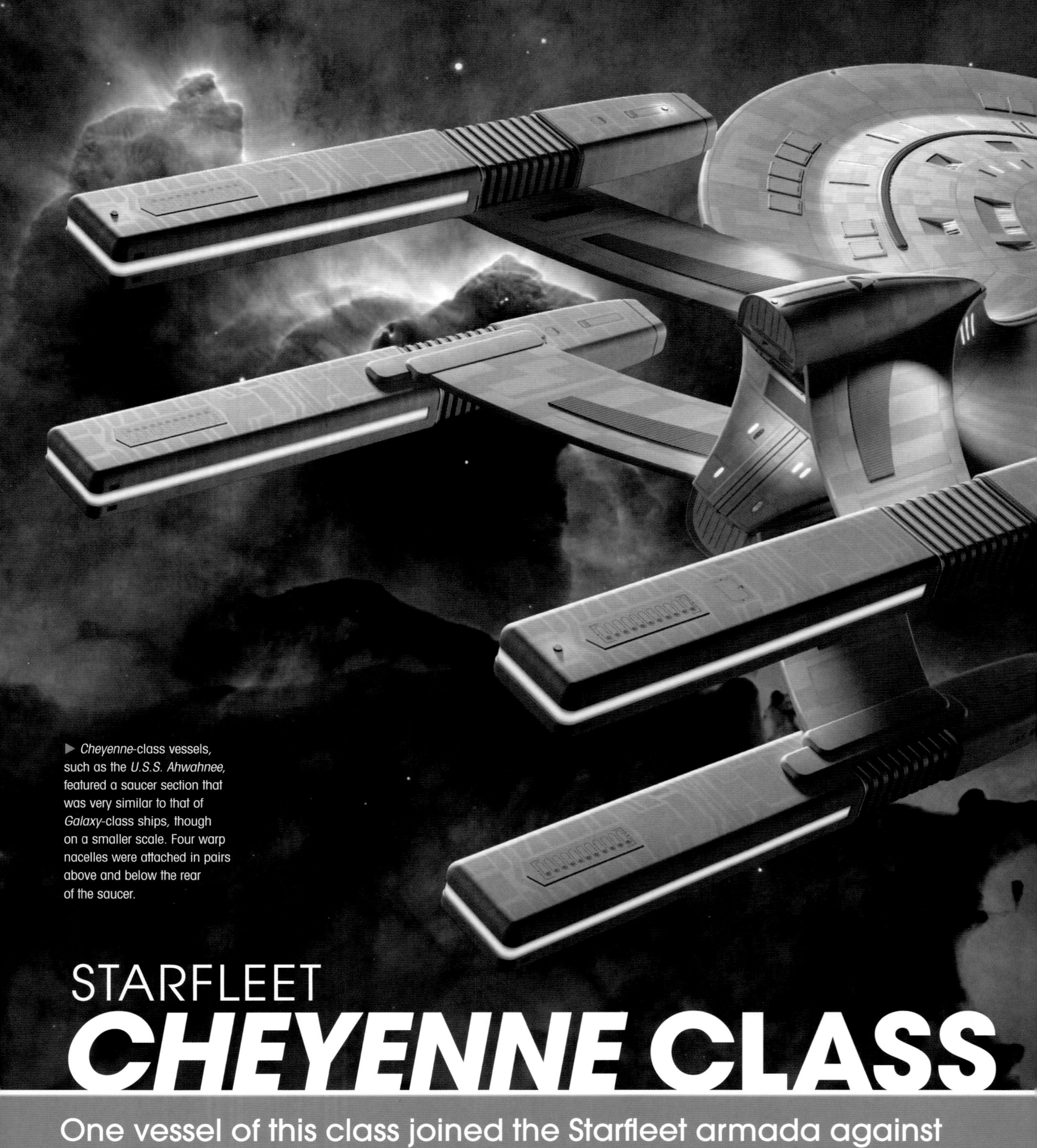

► *Cheyenne*-class vessels, such as the *U.S.S. Ahwahnee*, featured a saucer section that was very similar to that of *Galaxy*-class ships, though on a smaller scale. Four warp nacelles were attached in pairs above and below the rear of the saucer.

STARFLEET
CHEYENNE CLASS

One vessel of this class joined the Starfleet armada against the Borg in 2367 – and survived to tell the tale.

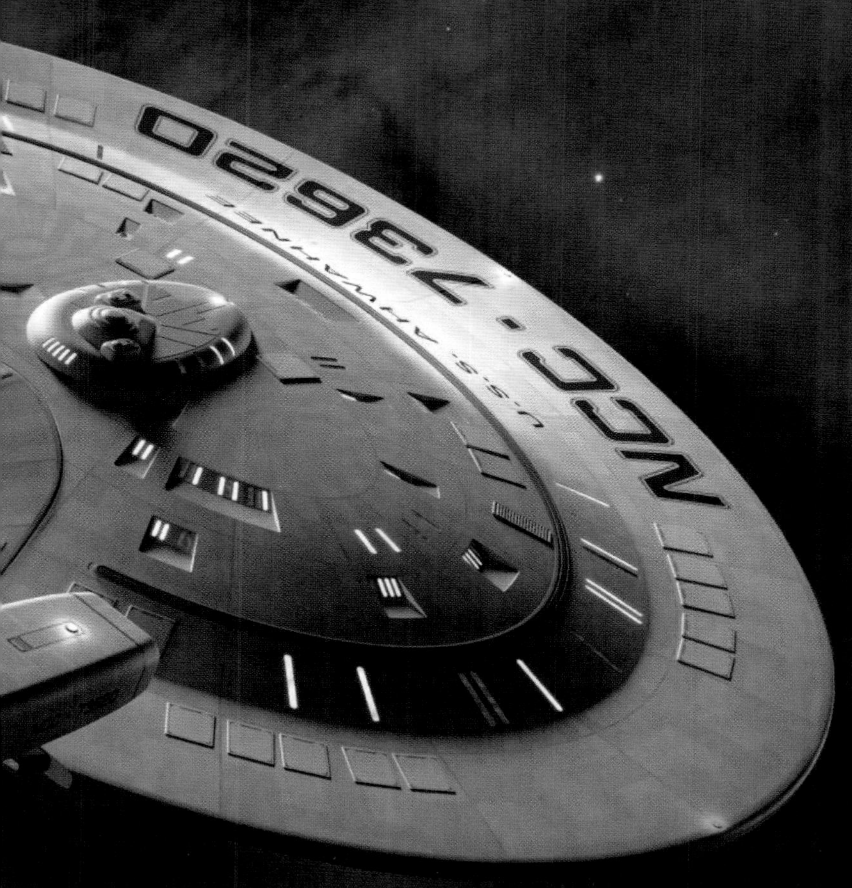

Ships of the *Cheyenne* class, such as the *U.S.S. Ahwahnee* NCC-73620, were light cruisers, suitable for deep space exploration and defensive patrol duties. Their most distinctive design feature was the ships' four warp nacelles.

The *Cheyenne* class could therefore be seen as an evolution of the *Constellation* class, which was in service between the 2280s and 2370s and also incorporated four warp nacelles. They were attached to a structure at the back of the saucer section on the *Cheyenne* class. Despite their extra nacelles, however, ships of this class were no faster than other Starfleet ships of the time – their top velocity was warp 9.6.

SIMILARITIES AND DIFFERENCES

The elliptical saucer section of the *Cheyenne* class was almost identical to that on *Galaxy*-class ships, but on a smaller scale. The overall length of the *Cheyenne* class was about 362 meters, making these ships just over half the length of their *Galaxy*-class counterparts. They did, however, feature a bridge module that from the exterior was a very similar size to the *Galaxy*-class design.

The rear end of the saucer section on the *Cheyenne* class was indented. Two structures, similar to the neck section on a *Galaxy*-class vessel, were fitted here to both the top and bottom of the saucer section on the *Cheyenne* class. Pylons swept out of these structures, which attached to the four warp nacelle; these were shorter and thinner than those found on the *Galaxy* class.

The *U.S.S. Ahwahnee* was part of the fleet of 40 ships that fought the Borg at the Battle of Wolf 359 in 2367. It was disabled in this encounter, but unlike all the other ships in the fleet, it was not so badly damaged that it could not be repaired.

The following year, the *Ahwahnee* was part of the fleet of 23 ships that attempted to blockade the Klingon-Romulan border during the Klingon civil war. It was one of 17 vessels chosen to form a tachyon network, in the hope that this would detect and expose cloaked Romulan ships that were secretly running supplies to the Duras faction.

The Romulans disrupted the tachyon grid with a high-energy burst, however. This forced the fleet, including the *Ahwahnee*, to retreat and regroup at Gamma Eridon, where they intended to reestablish the tachyon net.

◀ The *Ahwahnee* was the only Starfleet ship put back into service after being damaged at the Battle of Wolf 359. The following year, it formed part of a tachyon network set up by Starfleet to try and stop cloaked Romulan ships from resupplying the Duras sisters in the Klingon civil war.

FLEET FAILURE

Captain Jean-Luc Picard and his crew learned of the Borg threat when Q whisked off the *U.S.S. Enterprise* NCC-1701-D to the Delta Quadrant in 2365. After this, Starfleet Tactical ordered a review of their defenses. Admiral J.P. Hanson was put in charge of developing defensive strategies and new technologies to combat a potential incursion by the Borg.

Under Admiral Hanson's supervision, Lieutenant Commander Shelby was put in charge of tactical analysis and defensive planning. Together, they developed what they thought would be adequate preparations to repel a Borg invasion.

Unfortunately, it would transpire that they had severely underestimated the Borg. In late 2366, the *U.S.S. Lalo* NCC-43837 reported that it had come under attack from a cube-shaped vessel while it was on a freight run. This was the first sign that the Borg had invaded the Alpha Quadrant. Admiral Hanson quickly amassed a fleet of 40 ships at Wolf 359, 7.8 light years from Earth, to meet the Borg.

Utilizing the tactical knowledge of Captain Picard, who had earlier been assimilated and given the designation "Locutus," the Borg wiped out the fleet in a matter of minutes. Admiral Hanson's ship was destroyed along with 38 others, and only the *U.S.S. Ahwahnee* was salvageable after the battle.

EM field coils

Warp nacelle

DATA FEED

The *U.S.S. Ahwahnee*'s name originated from a Native American word for the Yosemite Valley. Other Starfleet ships with Native American names included the *U.S.S. Crazy Horse*, the *U.S.S. Lakota*, the *U.S.S. Malinche*, and the *U.S.S. Pueblo*.

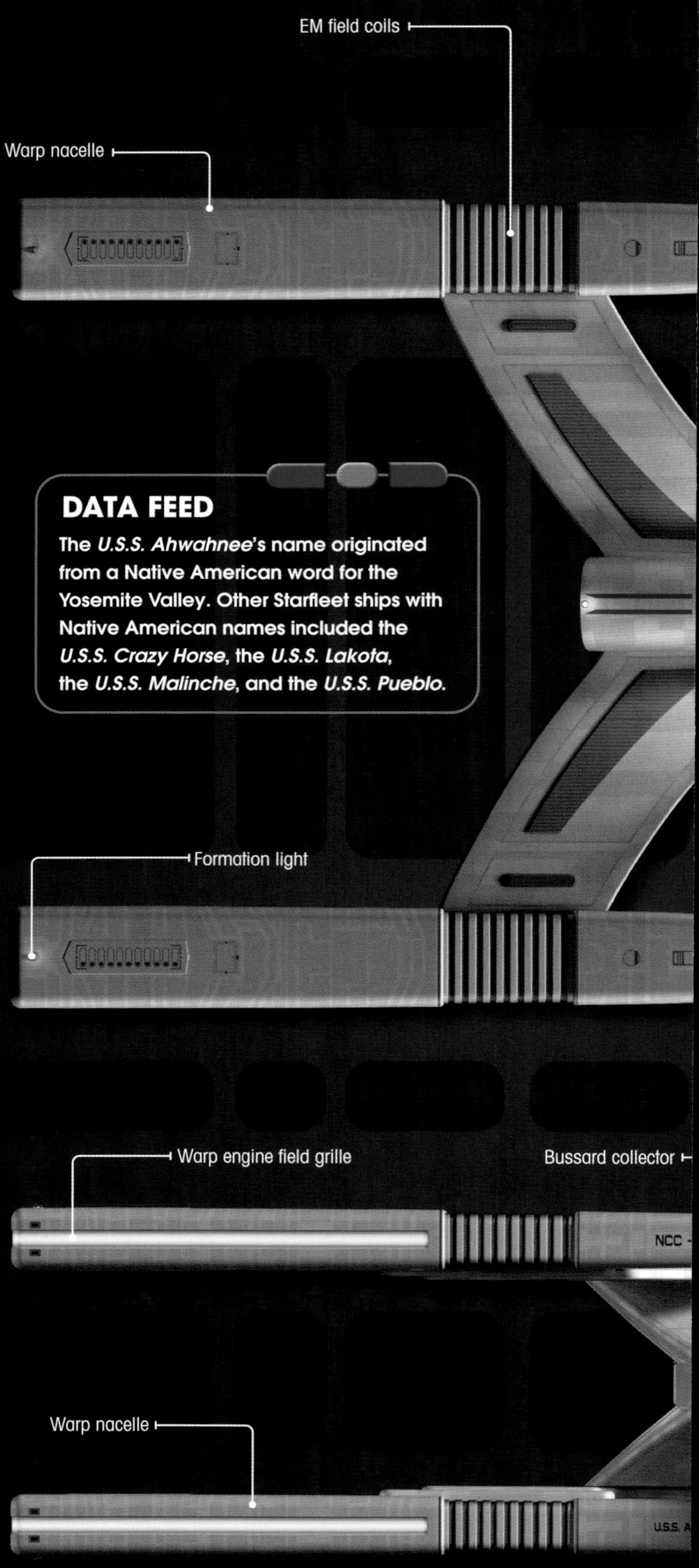

Formation light

Warp engine field grille

Bussard collector

NCC

Warp nacelle

U.S.S. A

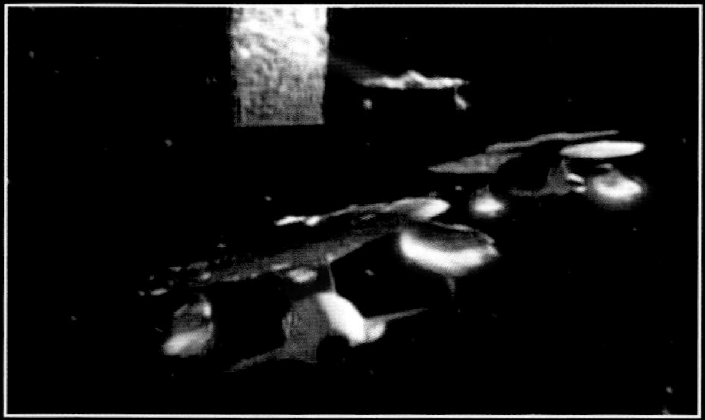

▲ The *U.S.S. Bellerophon* and *U.S.S. Yamaguchi* rushed to the aid of the *U.S.S. Saratoga* after it was held in the Borg's tractor beam, but their efforts were in vain as the cube easily destroyed all three ships.

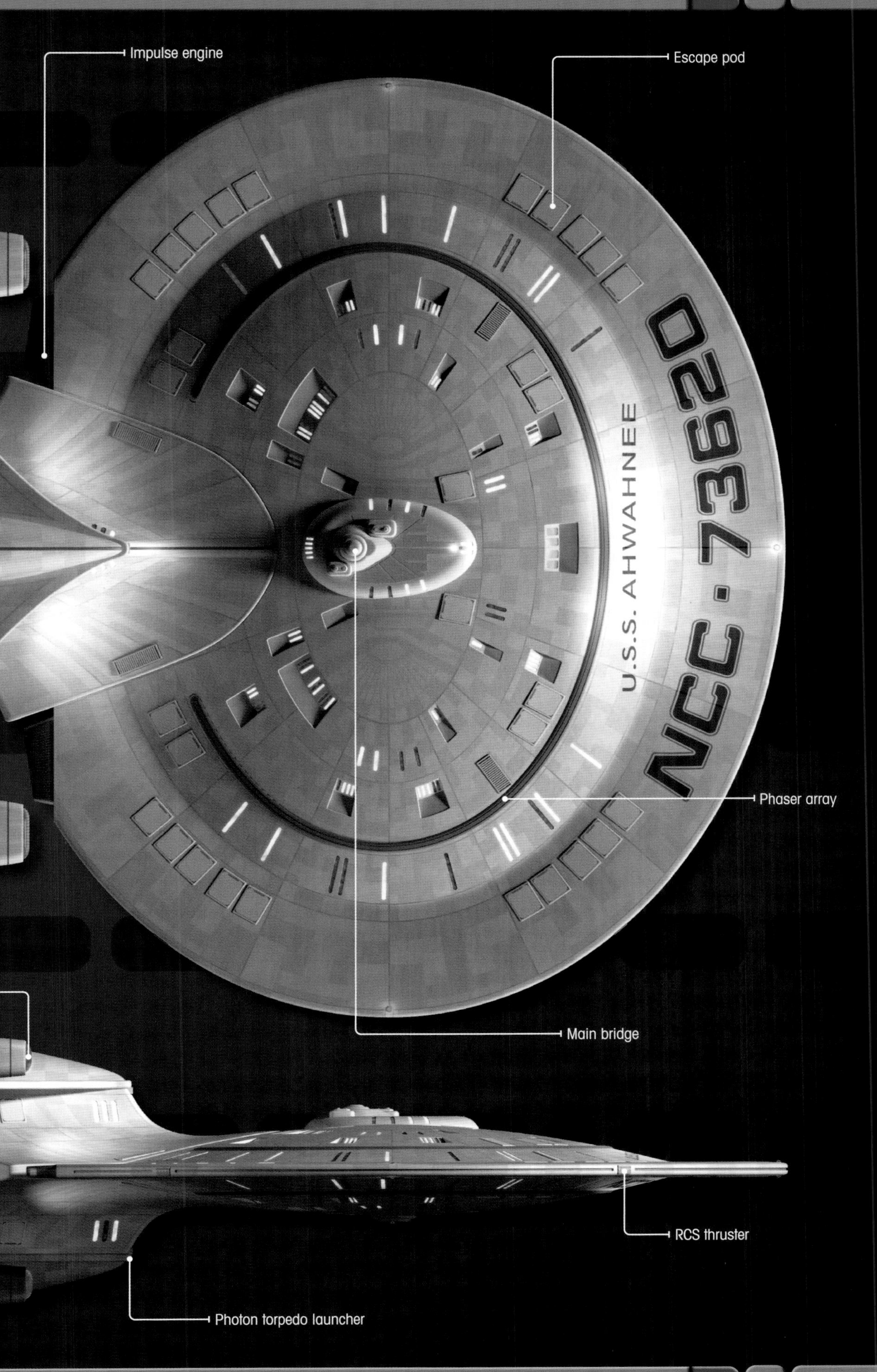

FOUR NACELLES

The *Cheyenne* class was one of the few types of Starfleet ship to have four rather than two warp nacelles. Besides the *Constellation* class, this design was only found on ships of the *Prometheus* class.

BORG ASSIMILATION

During their incursion into the Alpha Quadrant, the Borg assimilated various species, including Klingons, Romulans, Cardassians, and Humans. Commander Chakotay encountered all these in a Borg collective in the Delta Quadrant in 2373.

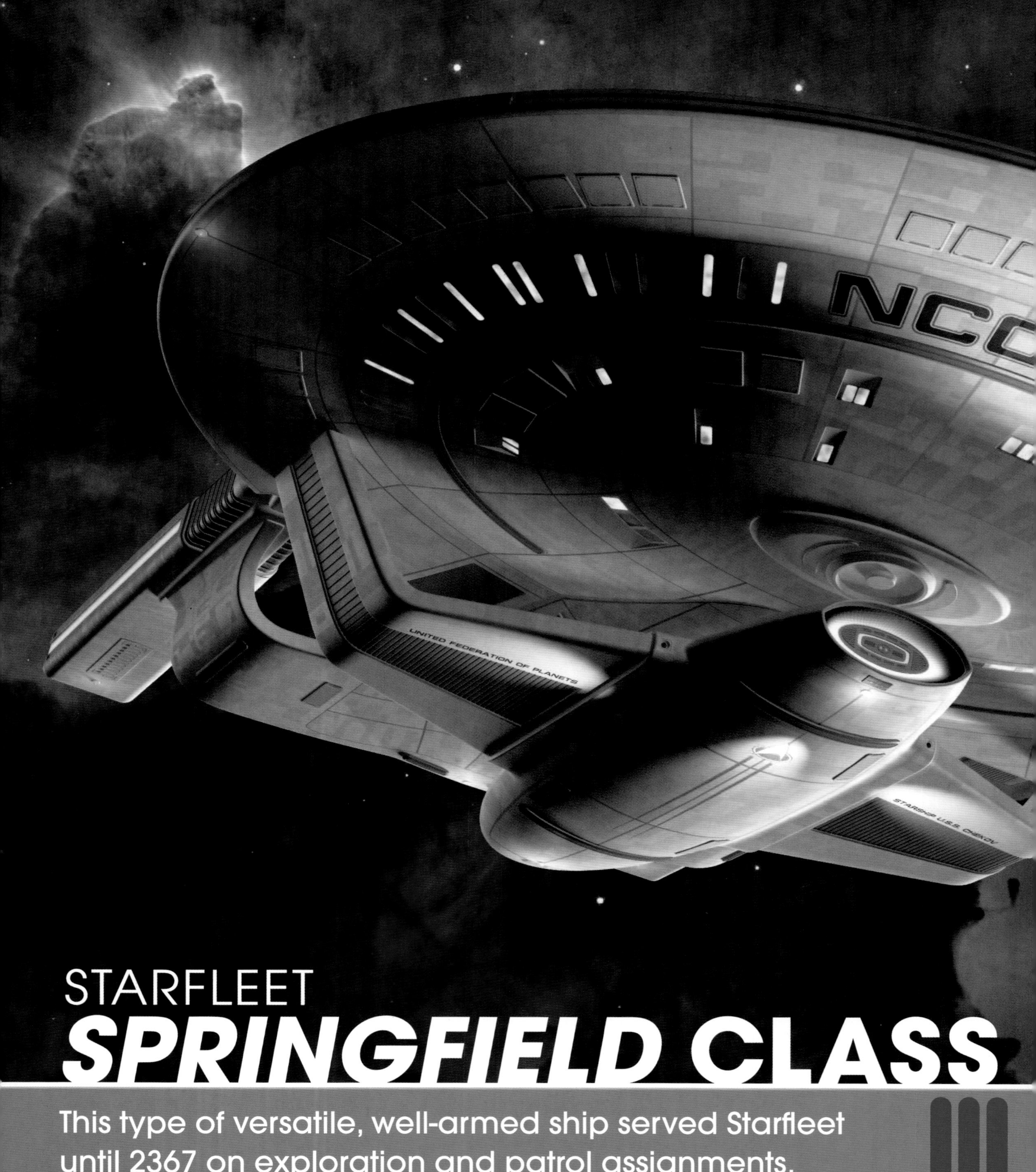

STARFLEET

SPRINGFIELD CLASS

This type of versatile, well-armed ship served Starfleet until 2367 on exploration and patrol assignments.

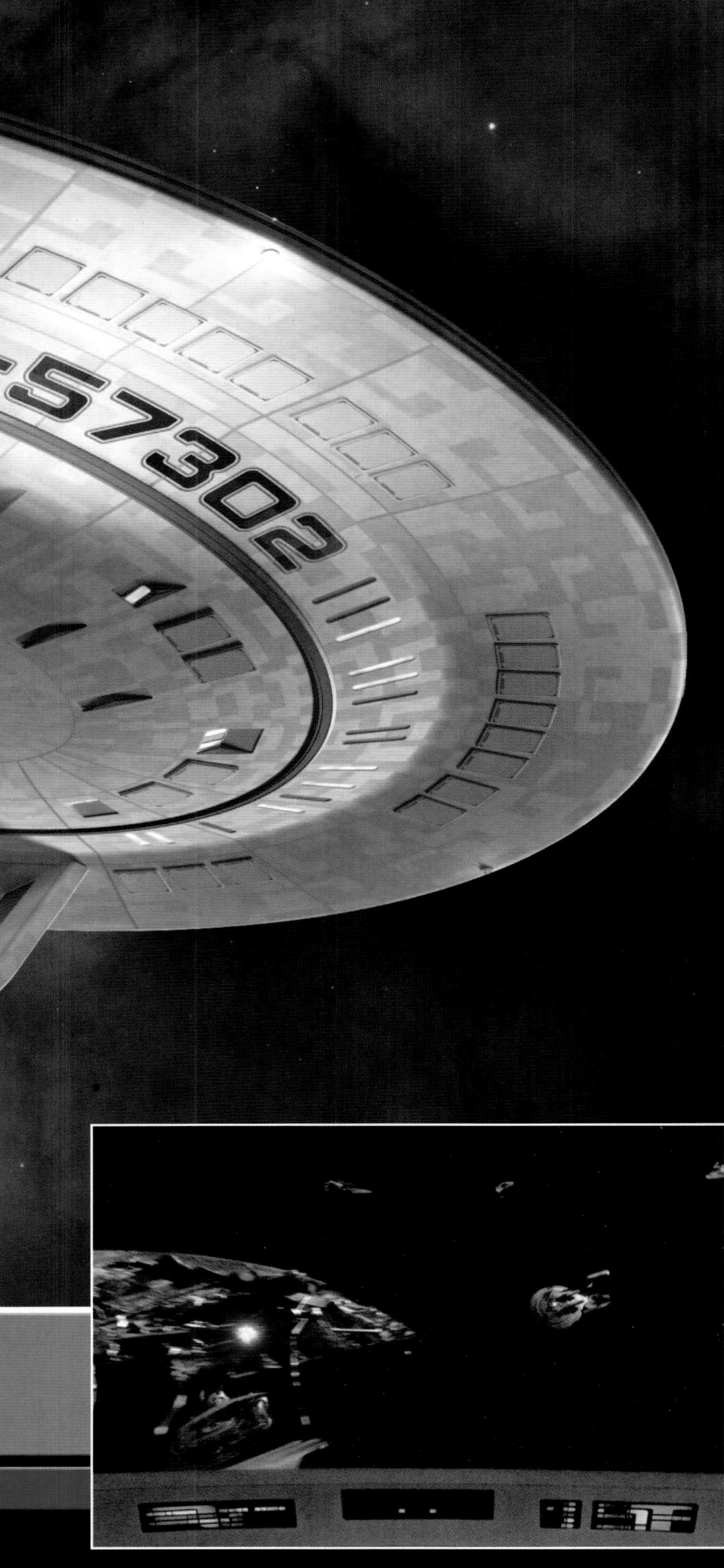

◀ The saucer section on *Springfield*-class ships was similar in shape to the *Galaxy* class's saucer. These ships also had a lozenge-shaped secondary hull and warp nacelles that were the same style and shape as those found on the *Cheyenne* class.

The *Springfield* class was a frigate design, such as the *U.S.S. Chekov* NCC-57302. In the 24th century, these ships were mostly tasked with deep space exploration and patrol duties.

The class was 325 meters in length and carried a standard crew complement of around 430. It was capable of a top speed of warp 9.2 for short periods, while its maximum sustainable speed was warp 7.5. It was armed with several phaser banks, distributed in phaser arrays at various points along its hulls, and two photon torpedo launchers.

The *Springfield* class comprised a saucer section that was a scaled-down version of the saucer on *Galaxy*-class ships. It also had a V-shaped structure cut into the back of the saucer. This provided a link to a mission-specific module that sat above and behind the saucer. It could be configured to carry more sensors, cargo, or weapons, depending on the ship's assignment. Two thin warp nacelles, similar in style to those fitted on *Cheyenne*-class starships, were positioned on either side of the module and attached by winglike pylons.

A secondary hull was suspended below the saucer via downward-turned pylons. This section contained main engineering, while the main navigational deflector was built in at the front.

In 2367, the *Chekov* was part of the fleet of 40 ships gathered together to fight the Borg cube at the Battle of Wolf 359. The *Chekov* appeared to be the only *Springfield*-class vessel in the fleet, and it was obliterated by the Borg along with the other Starfleet ships during the engagement.

◀ When the *U.S.S. Enterprise* NCC-1701-D arrived in the aftermath of the Battle of Wolf 359, it navigated slowly through the wreckage of dozens of Starfleet ships scattered by the Borg cube. On the viewscreen, the bridge crew could just about make out the remains of the *Springfield*-class *Chekov* on the upper left.

LAST OF ITS KIND?

By the time the *U.S.S. Enterprise* NCC-1701-D reached Wolf 359, the 40-strong fleet of Starfleet ships had been decimated by the Borg cube. The eerie, devastating sight of the entire fleet reduced to lifeless hulks floating in space stunned the crew of the *Enterprise*-D into silence, as they tried to take in the enormity of what had just happened. In a matter of minutes, 39 vessels had been damaged beyond repair and around 11,000 lives lost to the Borg.

The *U.S.S. Chekov* was one of the ships that had been destroyed, its wreck forming part of the annihilated fleet. While it was seemingly the only *Springfield*-class vessel that had taken part in the battle, there were so many items of scattered debris , it was difficult to identify which class of ship the various shattered remnants had originally belonged to.

A *Springfield*-class ship was never seen again, not even during the Dominion War, perhaps indicating that this class was retired from service and replaced by another class dedicated to combat.

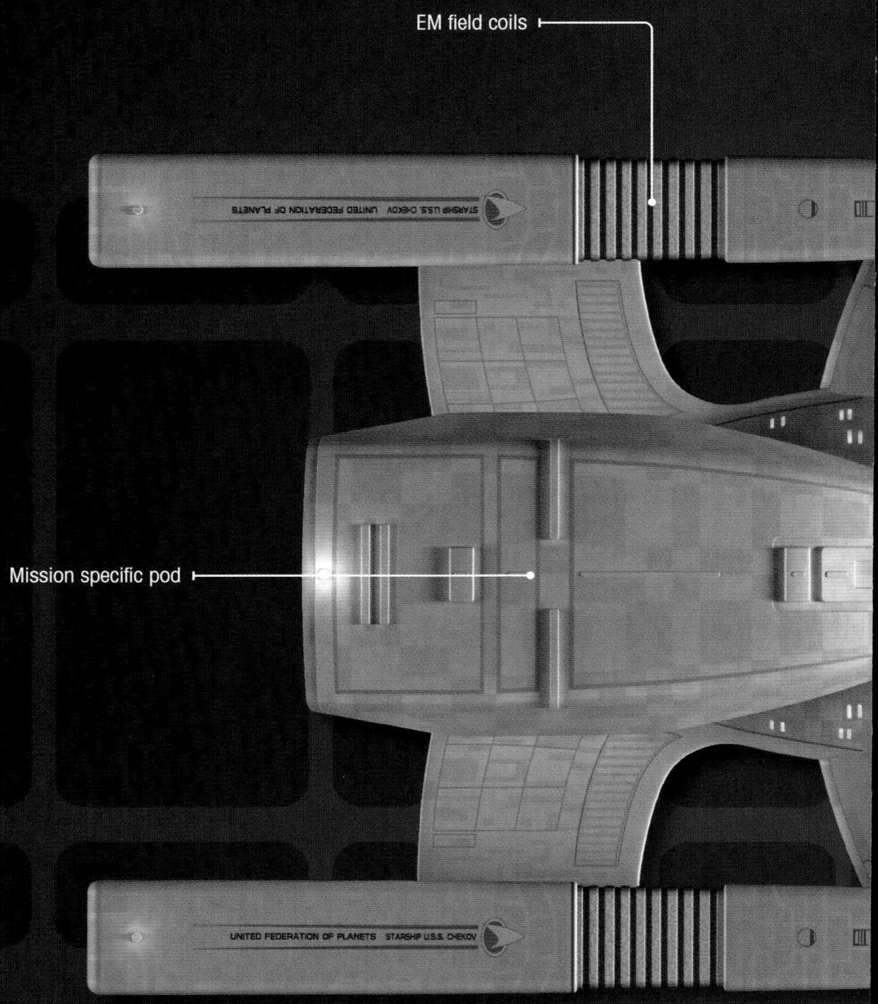

EM field coils

Mission specific pod

Warp engine field grille

Warp nacelle pylon

Engineering hull

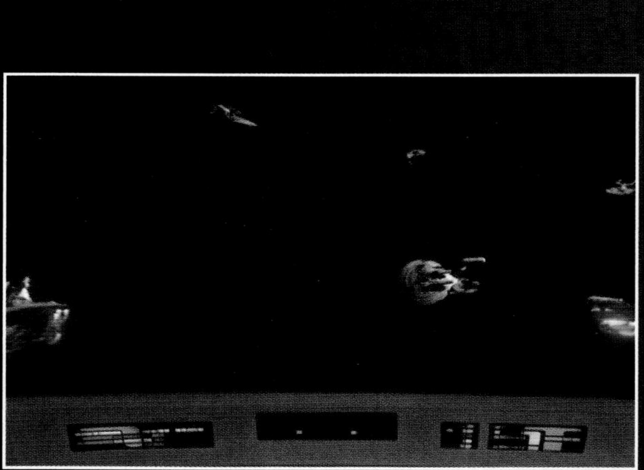

▲ By the time the *Enterprise*-D had repaired its deflector dish and reached Wolf 359, it was already too late. It was met by the chilling sight of the fleet either on fire or floating uselessly in space.

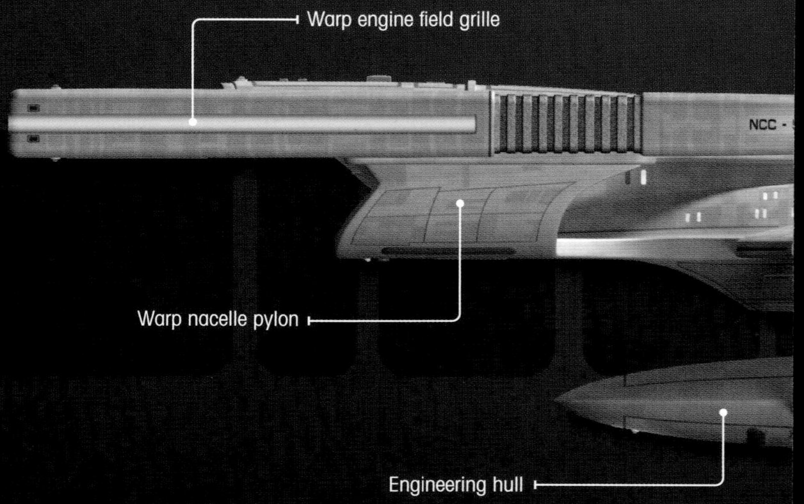

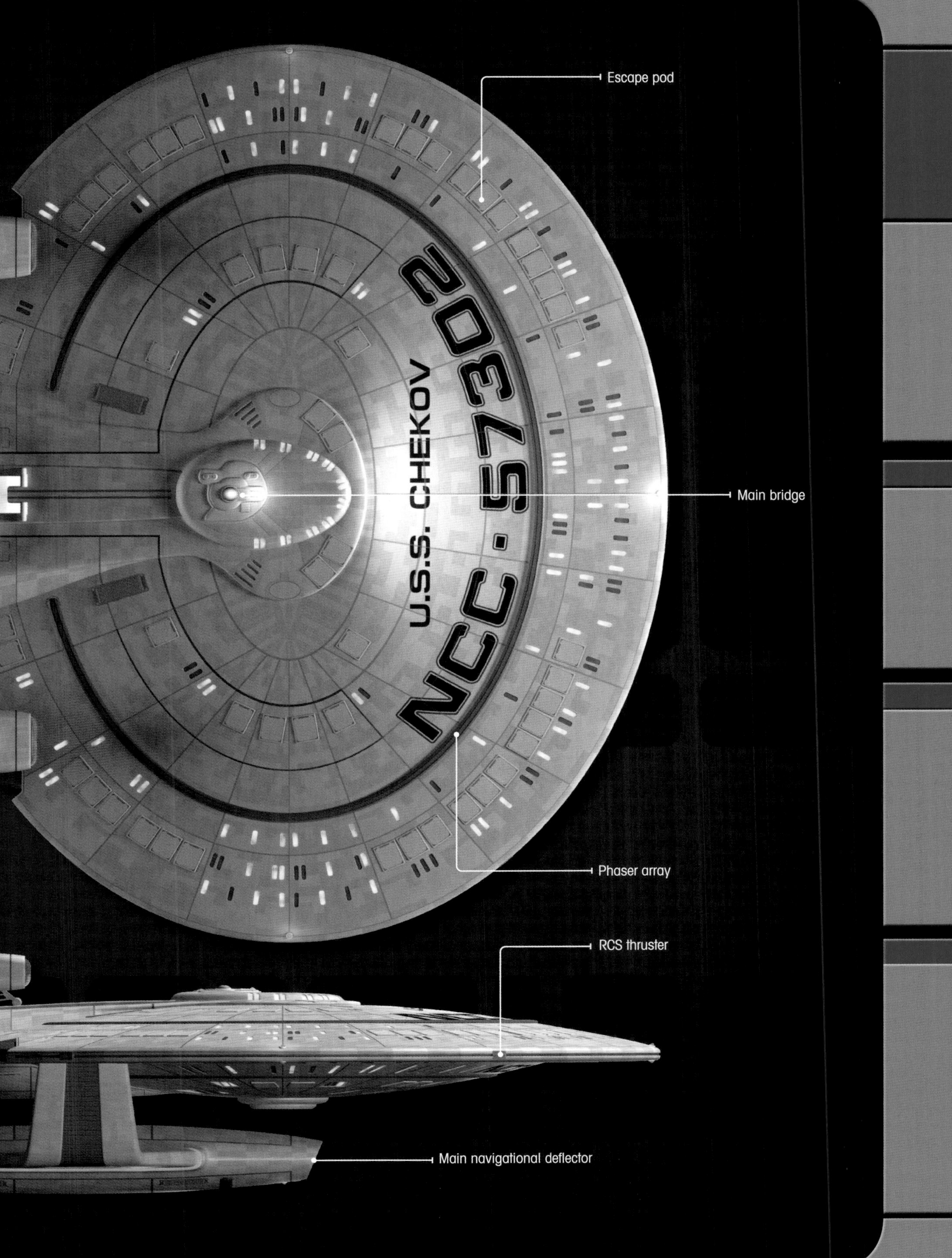

Escape pod
U.S.S. CHEKOV
NCC-57302
Main bridge
Phaser array
RCS thruster
Main navigational deflector

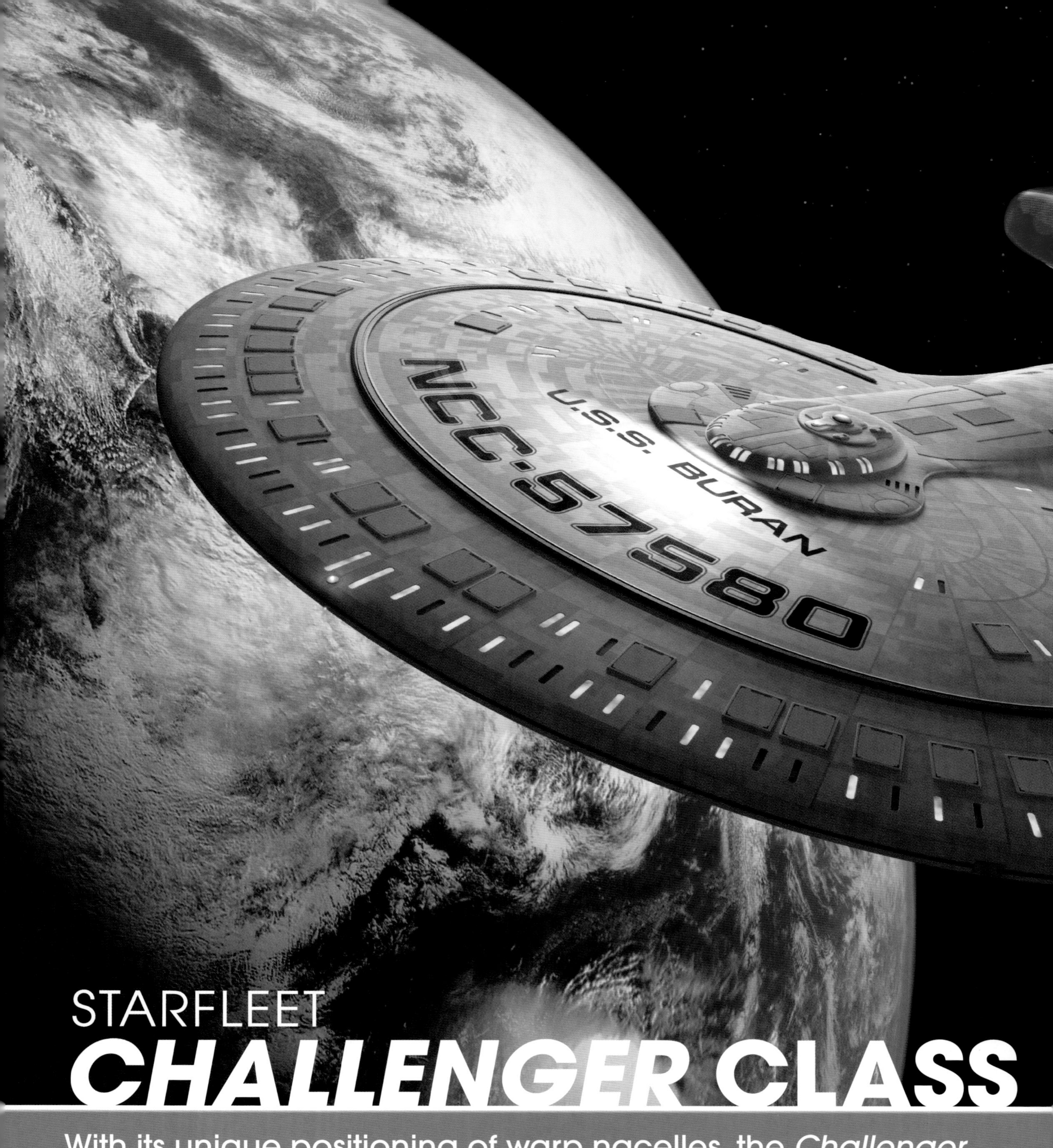

STARFLEET

CHALLENGER CLASS

With its unique positioning of warp nacelles, the *Challenger* class was a distinctive Starfleet design of the 24th century.

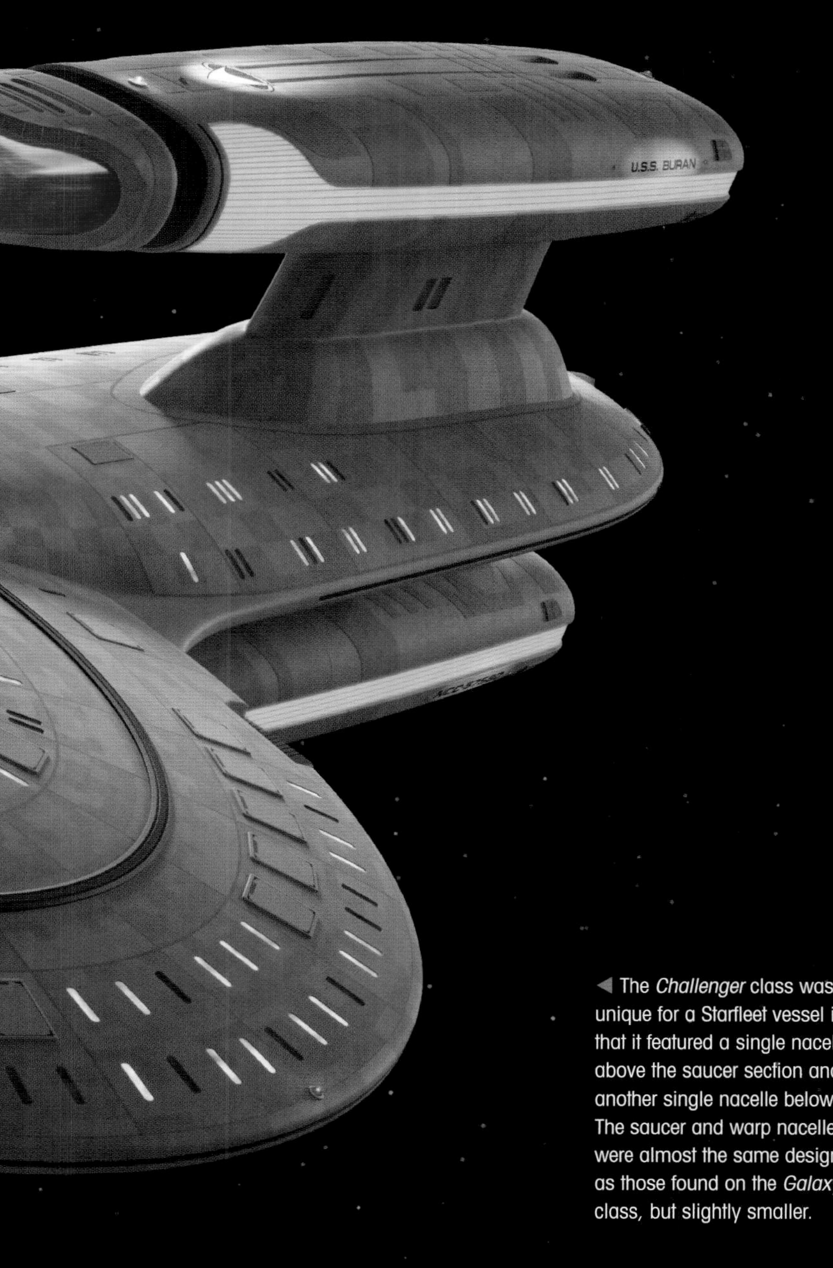

◀ The *Challenger* class was unique for a Starfleet vessel in that it featured a single nacelle above the saucer section and another single nacelle below. The saucer and warp nacelles were almost the same design as those found on the *Galaxy* class, but slightly smaller.

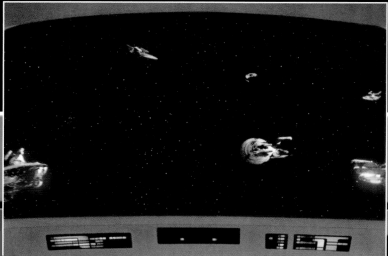

A contemporary of the *Galaxy* class, the *Challenger* class shared the same saucer and nacelle design, except that they were scaled down to about two thirds of the size. *Challenger*-class ships were about 390 meters in length, and mainly used for exploration and diplomatic duties.

The most distinctive feature of the *Challenger* class was that although the ships had two warp nacelles, one was positioned above the saucer and one below. It was the only known class of Starfleet vessel that had this configuration.

Another unusual aspect of the design was that the secondary hull was attached directly to the rear of the saucer. This contained the engineering section, which was slightly longer than the saucer hull, but much thinner.

NACELLE PYLONS

A small, thin pylon attached the lower warp nacelle to the bottom of the secondary hull, while a longer, wider, more substantial element connected the top nacelle to the ship. This part was far more than a pylon, and resembled the neck section found between the saucer and secondary sections on other Starfleet vessels.

The *Challenger* class had similar abilities and facilities to the *Galaxy* class, meaning it could attain a top speed of warp 9.6 for short periods and was armed with multiple phaser arrays and at least two photon torpedo launchers.

The *U.S.S. Buran* NCC-57580 was a *Challenger*-class vessel that fought the Borg at the Battle of Wolf 359 where it was destroyed along with 38 other Starfleet ships.

◀ Arriving after the devastating Battle of Wolf 359, the *U.S.S. Enterprise* NCC-1701-D was in time to see the fire that raged through the *U.S.S. Buran* after it engaged the Borg cube. Its remains could just be seen in the bottom right of the viewscreen, while other Starfleet ships had already burned out and hung lifelessly in space.

CARNAGE AT WOLF 359

In 2366, the Federation lost all contact with the New Providence colony on Jouret IV, a settlement on the border between the Alpha and Beta Quadrants. The *U.S.S. Enterprise* NCC-1701-D was sent to investigate the cause. On arrival, the crew discovered that the entire outpost had been scooped from the planet's surface, as had happened in the earlier attack by the Borg on System J-25. This was the first sign that the Borg were on the doorstep of Federation space and planning an invasion.

Admiral J. P. Hanson, who had been working on countermeasures for just such an attack, made his way to Starbase 324 to discuss strategy with Starfleet Command. He put together a fleet of 40 starships and in early 2367, led them into battle against the Borg cube at Wolf 359, a star system about eight light-years from Earth.

The fleet did not stand a chance and all but one of the Starfleet ships, including the *U.S.S. Buran*, were sliced apart in a matter of minutes by the Borg cube. It was only the heroic efforts of the crew of the *Enterprise*-D that eventually brought the Borg incursion to an end.

The wreck of the *Buran* was later towed to Surplus Depot Z15 in orbit of the planet Qualor II, where it was seen by the crew of the *Enterprise*-D in 2368.

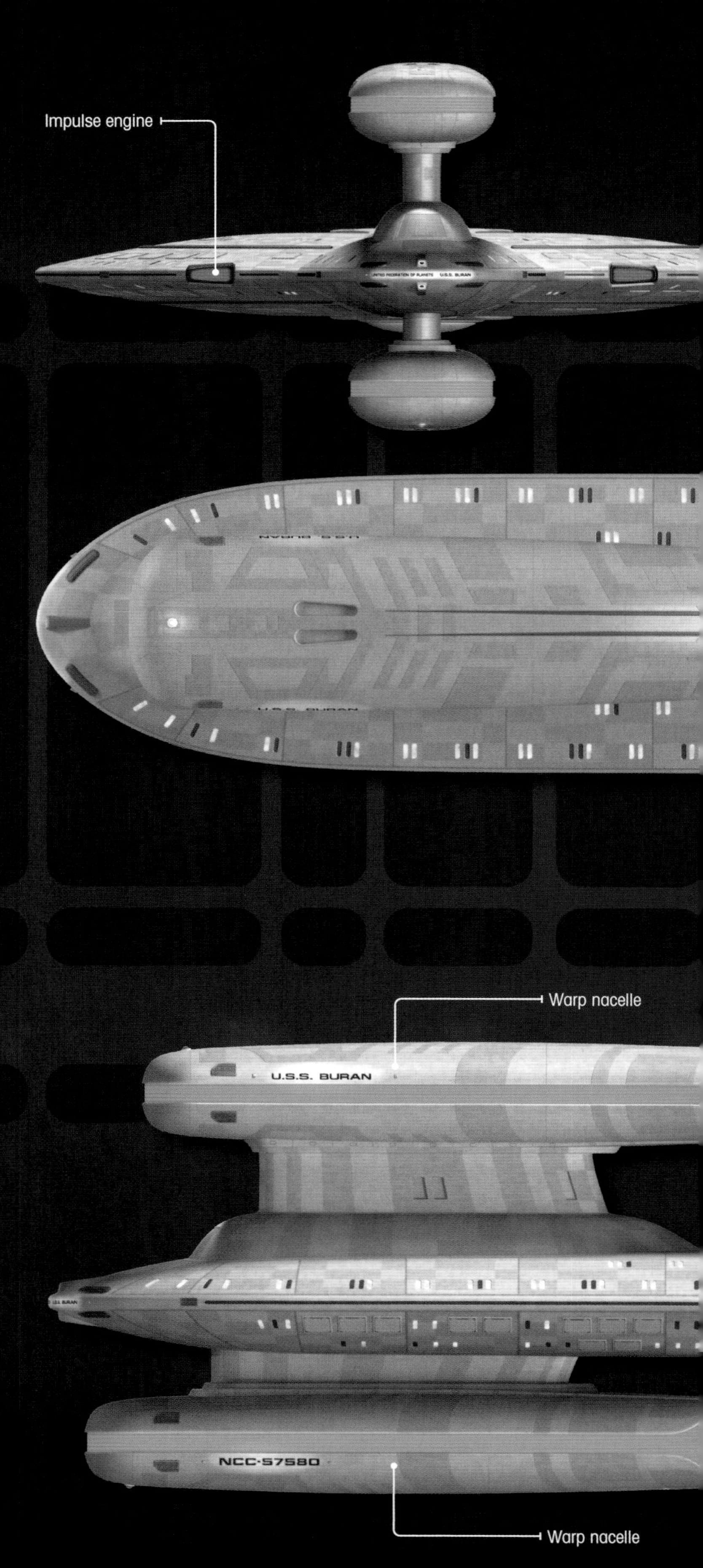

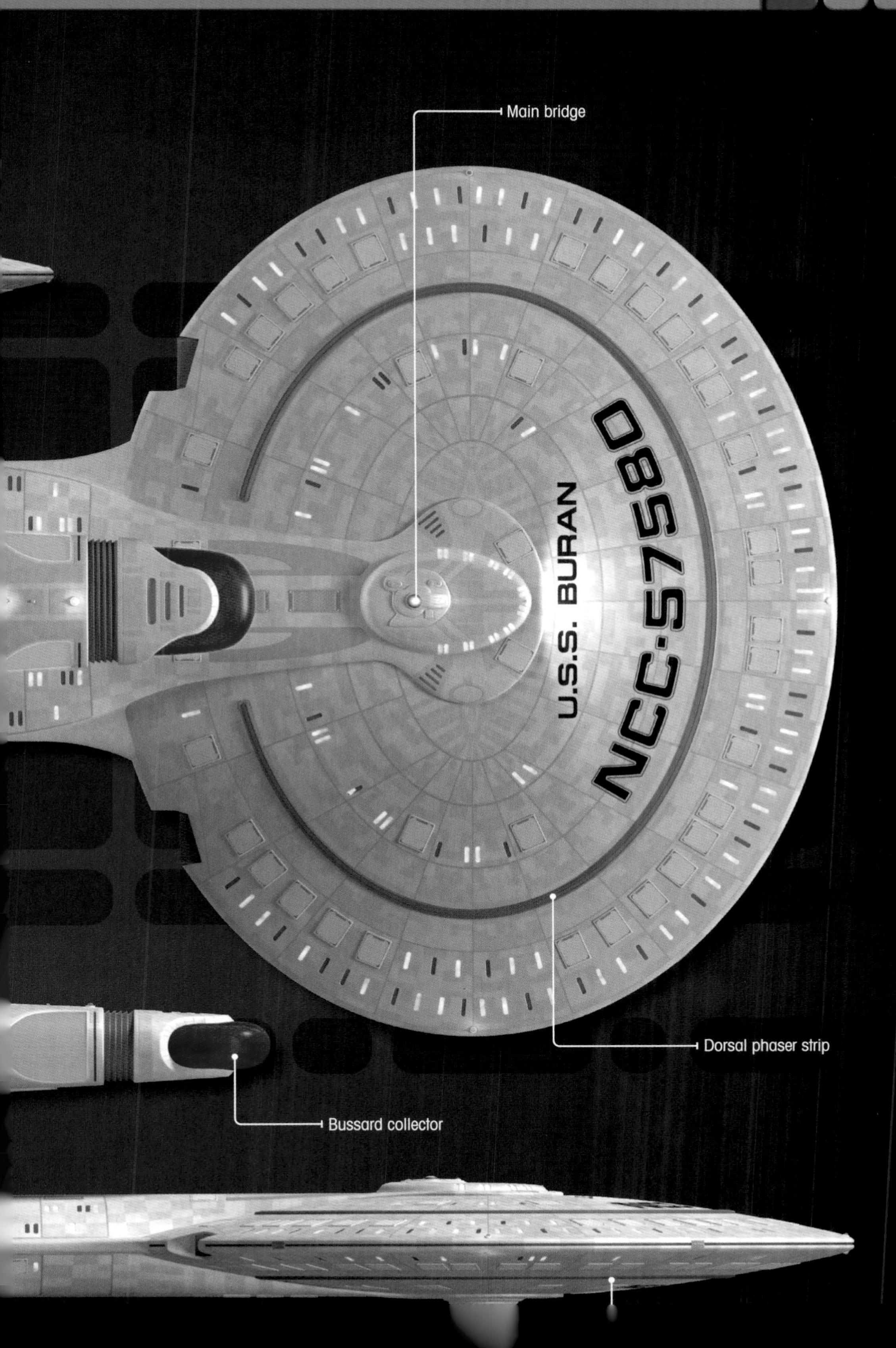

UNEVEN NACELLES

The *Challenger* class was the only known type of Starfleet vessel where the warp nacelles did not exactly line up. Although they were the same length, the top nacelle was mounted several meters further forward than the lower nacelle.

SAME CLASS

Other vessels of the *Challenger* class included the *U.S.S. Armstrong* NCC-57537 and the *U.S.S. Kearsarge* NCC-57566. The *Armstrong* suffered

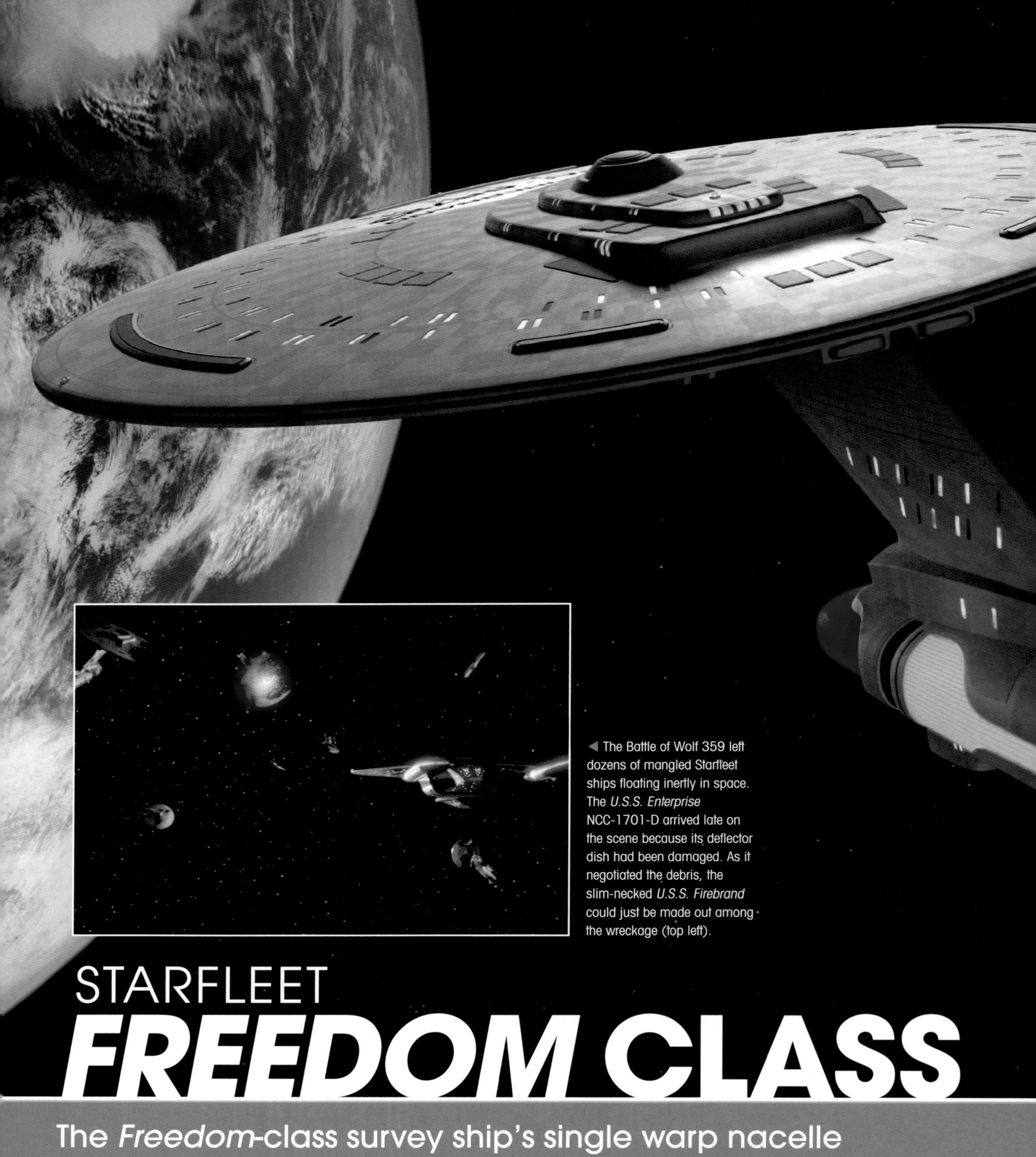

◀ The Battle of Wolf 359 left dozens of mangled Starfleet ships floating inertly in space. The *U.S.S. Enterprise* NCC-1701-D arrived late on the scene because its deflector dish had been damaged. As it negotiated the debris, the slim-necked *U.S.S. Firebrand* could just be made out among the wreckage (top left).

STARFLEET

FREEDOM CLASS

The *Freedom*-class survey ship's single warp nacelle was a rare feature that lent it an unmistakable profile.

Freedom-class ships, such as the *U.S.S. Firebrand* NCC-68723, were in operation in the second half of the 24th century and designed to carry out tasks such as light exploration and planet survey. They were also capable of defending Federation borders and guarding supply convoys.

This class was highly unusual in featuring just one warp nacelle. It did not have a separate engineering hull, and the single nacelle was attached directly to the neck section, which in turn supported the saucer module.

The nacelle was very similar in appearance to those on *Galaxy*-class ships, while the neck section appeared to have been taken from the late 23rd-century *Constellation* class. The saucer utilized a fairly rare design, oval and somewhat flattened in shape – the only other type of starship this was seen on was the *Niagara* class.

SHUTTLEBAY LOCATION

Because *Freedom*-class ships had no engineering hull, the shuttlebay was repositioned underneath the main bridge at the center of the saucer section.

In 2367, the *U.S.S. Firebrand* NCC-68723 was part of the fleet assembled by Admiral J. P. Hanson to attempt to block a Borg cube that had invaded the Alpha Quadrant and was on its way to assimilate Earth. The *Firebrand* was destroyed with all hands by the cube at the Battle of Wolf 359, a catastrophic encounter that claimed the lives of thousands of Starfleet officers and their families.

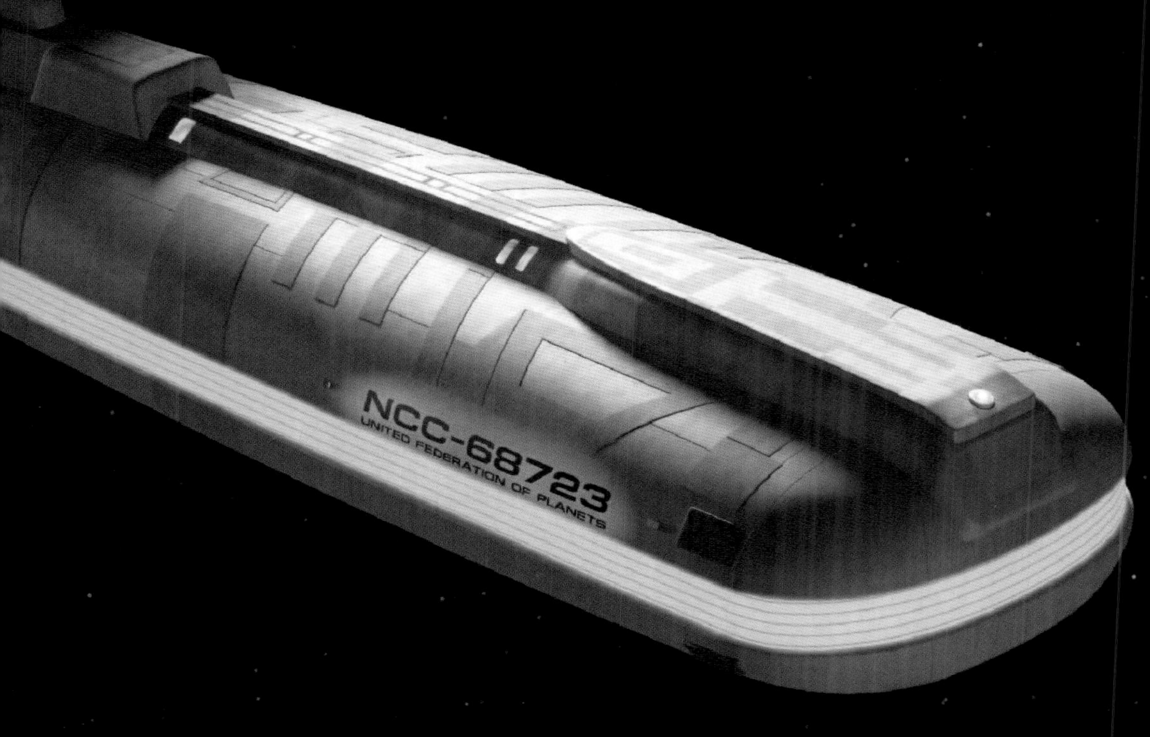

◀ Despite having only one nacelle, *Freedom*-class vessels were still able to reach a top speed of warp 9.2 for limited periods. However, if for some reason the nacelle became inoperable, the ship would only be capable of impulse speeds.

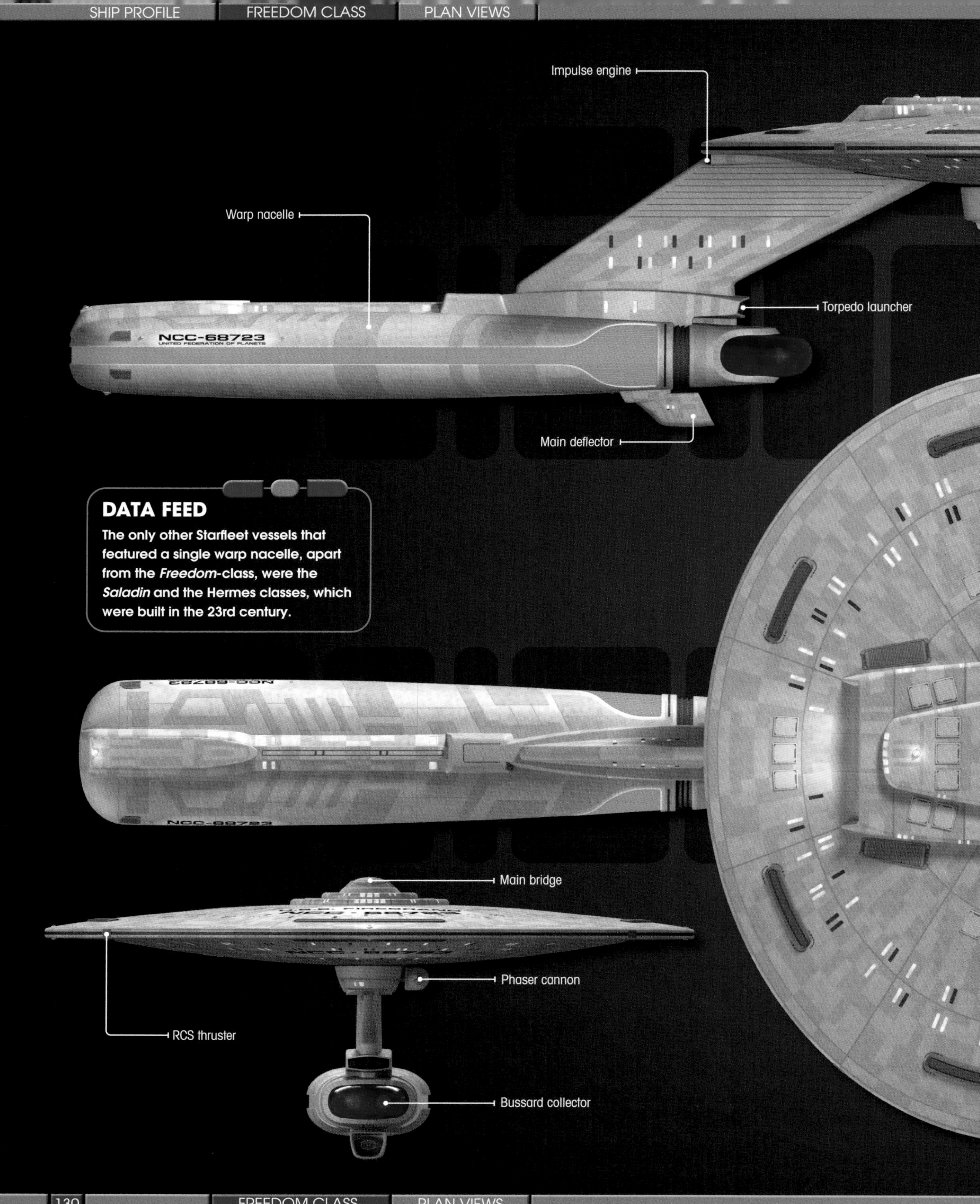

DATA FEED

The only other Starfleet vessels that featured a single warp nacelle, apart from the *Freedom*-class, were the *Saladin* and the Hermes classes, which were built in the 23rd century.

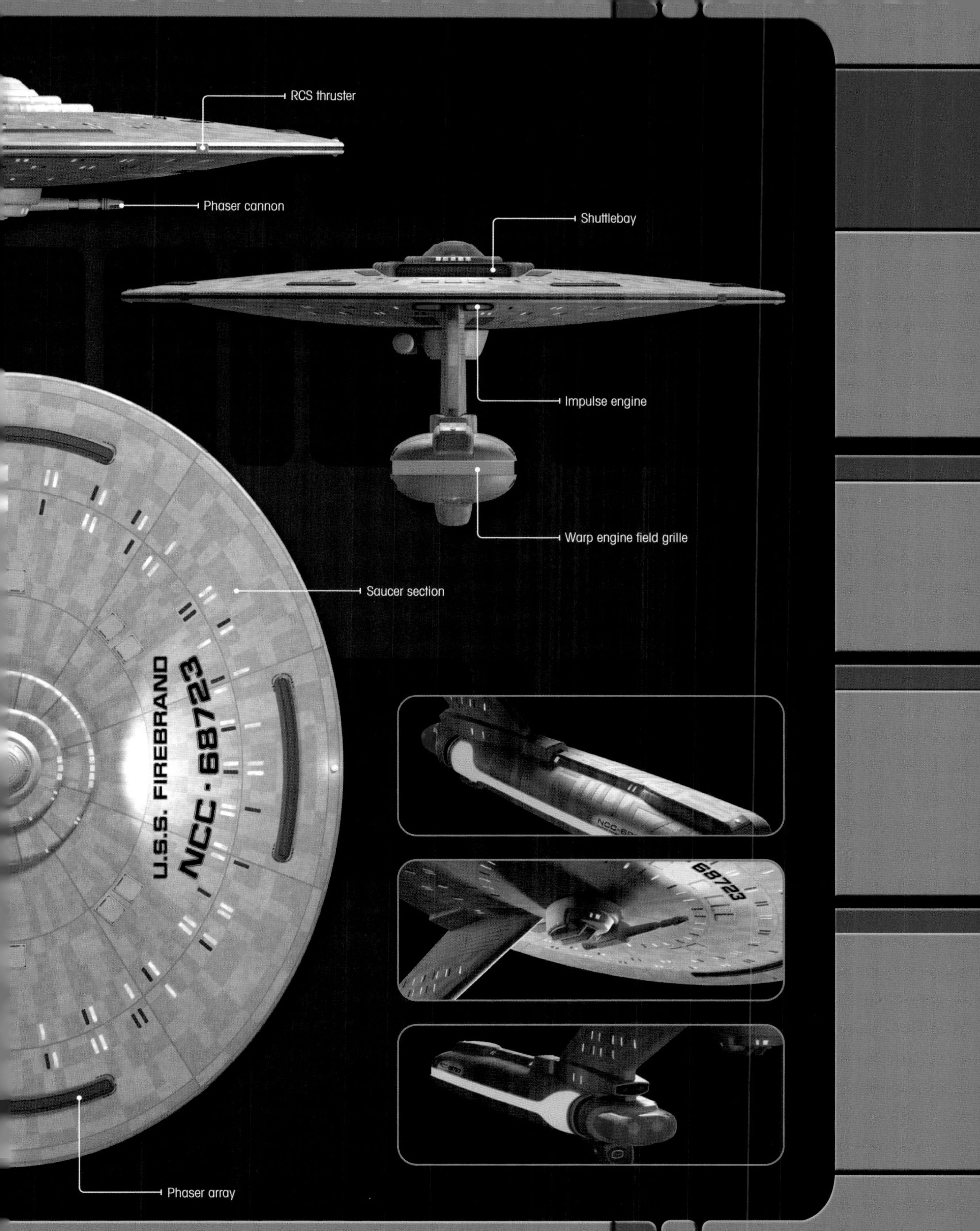
RCS thruster
Phaser cannon
Shuttlebay
Impulse engine
Warp engine field grille
Saucer section
U.S.S. FIREBRAND
NCC-68723
Phaser array

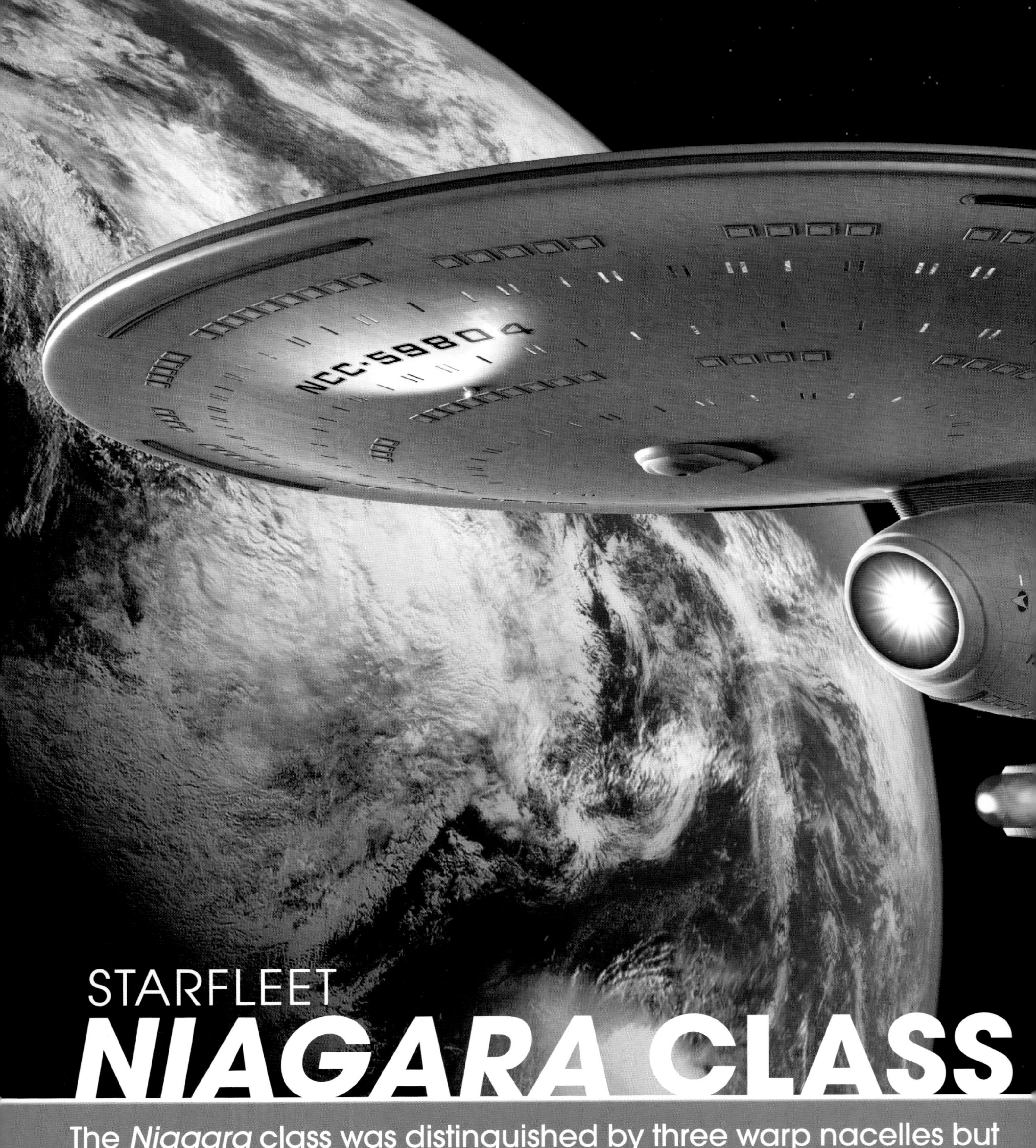

STARFLEET

NIAGARA CLASS

The *Niagara* class was distinguished by three warp nacelles but also shared aspects of both the *Galaxy* and *Ambassador* classes.

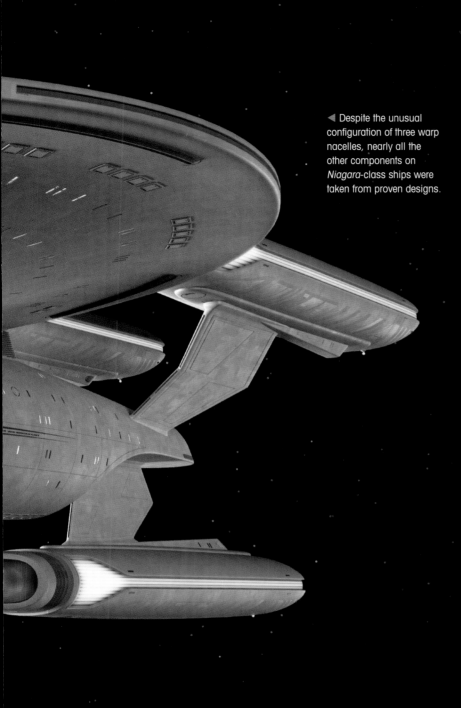

◀ Despite the unusual configuration of three warp nacelles, nearly all the other components on *Niagara*-class ships were taken from proven designs.

The design highlight of the 24th-century *Niagara* class was its three warp nacelles. It was the only known type of Starfleet ship endowed with such an unusual arrangement, and examples included the *U.S.S. Princeton* NCC-59804 and the *U.S.S. Wellington* NCC-28473.

The *Niagara* class was approximately 565 meters in length and carried a crew complement of around 530. It comprised a fairly rare saucer design with an elongated bridge module, and an engineering hull that was identical to that of *Ambassador*-class ships, such as the *U.S.S. Enterprise* NCC-1701-C. The *Niagara* class's warp nacelles were the same design as those found on *Galaxy*-class ships, such as the *U.S.S. Enterprise* NCC-1701-D, but the shape of the *Niagara*'s nacelle pylons was unique.

PRIMARY DUTIES

The *Niagara* class's primary roles were exploration and diplomacy. These ships were equipped with numerous sensor arrays and scientific laboratories to aid in the study of planets and stellar phenomena. They also featured extensive diplomatic facilities, which ensured they were capable of handling multispecies conferences.

Nearly all Starfleet ships featured an even number of warp nacelles. Most had a two-nacelle configuration, since Federation propulsion experts determined that this was the ideal layout for optimal warp field efficiency and vessel control. This did not stop Starfleet experimenting with alternative nacelle configurations, however, and there were also one-nacelle designs, as found on the *Freedom* class, in addition to the three-nacelle layout of the *Niagara* class.

While there were some disadvantages to this

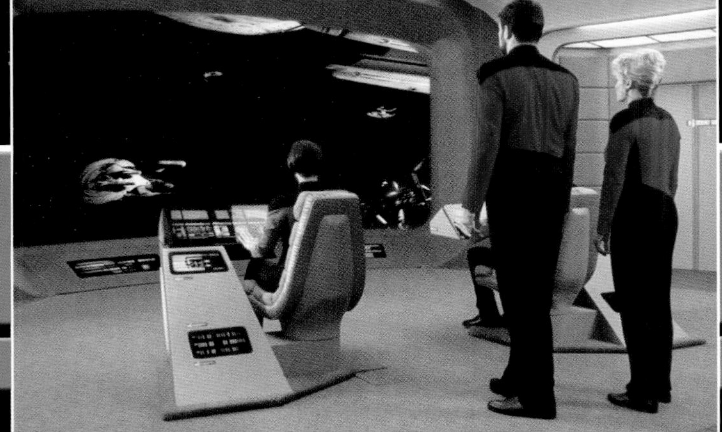

◀ The wreckage of the *U.S.S. Princeton* NCC-59804, a *Niagara*-class ship, filled the top right of the *U.S.S. Enterprise* NCC-1701-D's viewscreen. The *Princeton* was part of the 39-strong ship fleet that had been assembled by Starfleet to stop an invading Borg cube at Wolf 359, but the entire armada was decimated in a matter of minutes.

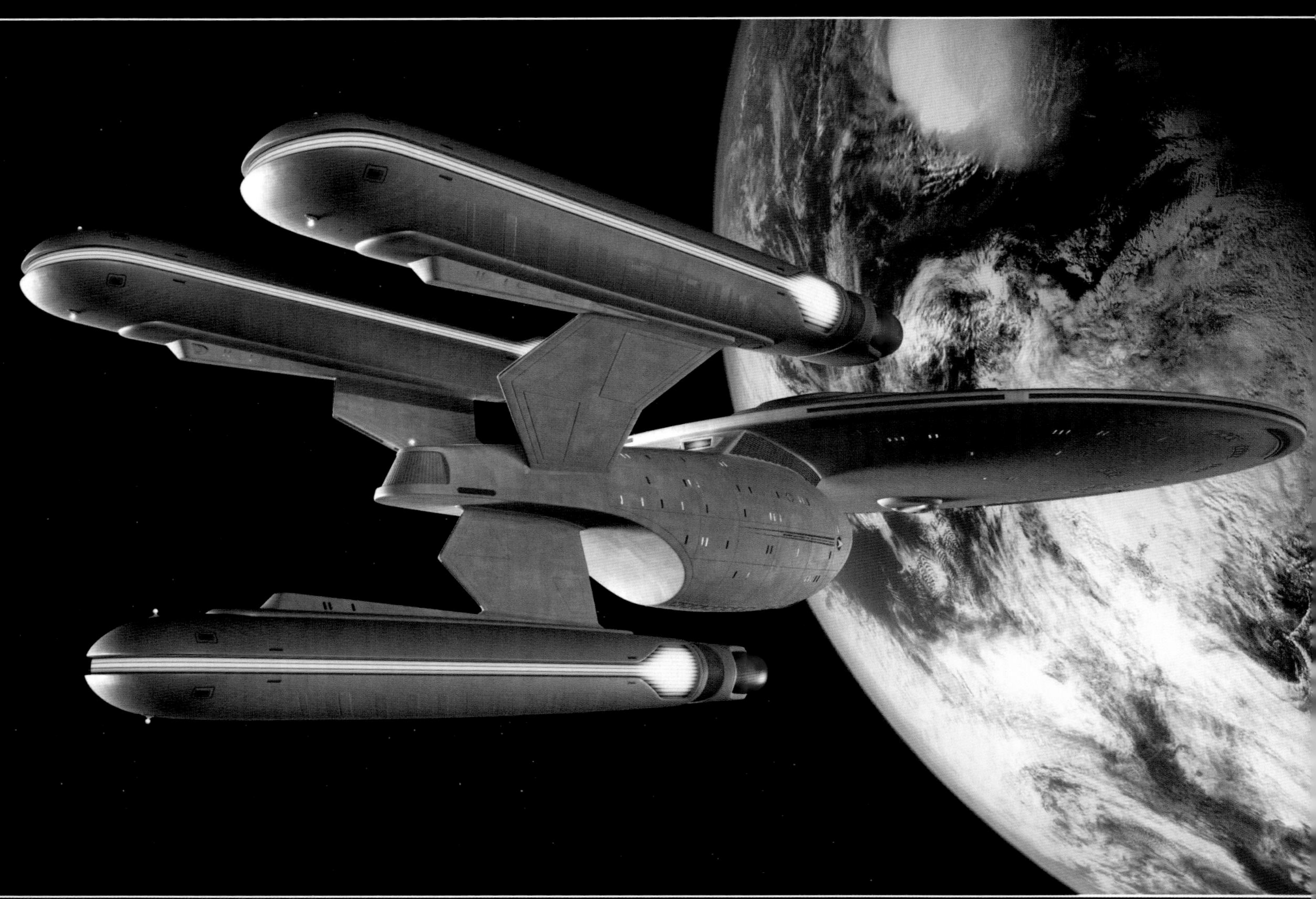

▲ Without the third nacelle hanging below the engineering hull, a *Niagara*-class vessel would have looked like a conventional Starfleet ship of the 24th century. The additional power from the extra nacelle increased the strength of its weapons, shields, and sensor systems.

odd-numbered design, there were certain benefits, too. *Niagara*-class ships were able to operate on their upper nacelle pair only and keep the lower nacelle in reserve, or vice versa. This extended the life of the components, and added another layer of redundancy if a nacelle failed.

The *Niagara* class was therefore more suited to deep space missions far from any starbases or repair facilities, although it did not have a higher top speed than its contemporaries. Like many Starfleet vessels of this era, the *Niagara* class had a maximum velocity of warp 9.6, though its cruising speed was higher than normal, at warp 8.

The architecture of the *Niagara*'s saucer section was found on only one other Starfleet ship design: the *Freedom* class. It was oval in shape and fairly thin compared to other Starfleet ships. The bridge module was located in the middle of the saucer section and sat on top of a secondary shuttlebay. The main shuttlebay was located in the more usual position, at the rear of the secondary hull. The primary hull also featured numerous windows and lifeboat hatches, as well as several type-7 phaser arrays.

SECONDARY HULL

The short neck section that joined the saucer to the rest of the ship was unique to the *Niagara* class, but the engineering hull was the same shape as that found on *Ambassador*-class ships. This was a substantial structure and looked almost round when seen from the front. The warp core ran the entire height of the secondary hull, and it could be ejected in the event of a catastrophic matter/antimatter containment failure.

While the *Niagara* class was mainly deployed on deep space exploration missions, its multiple phaser arrays, as well as fore and aft photon

▶ The engineering hull of the *Niagara* class shared the same outward design as ton *Ambassador*-class ships, such as the *U.S.S. Enterprise* NCC-1701-C seen on the right.

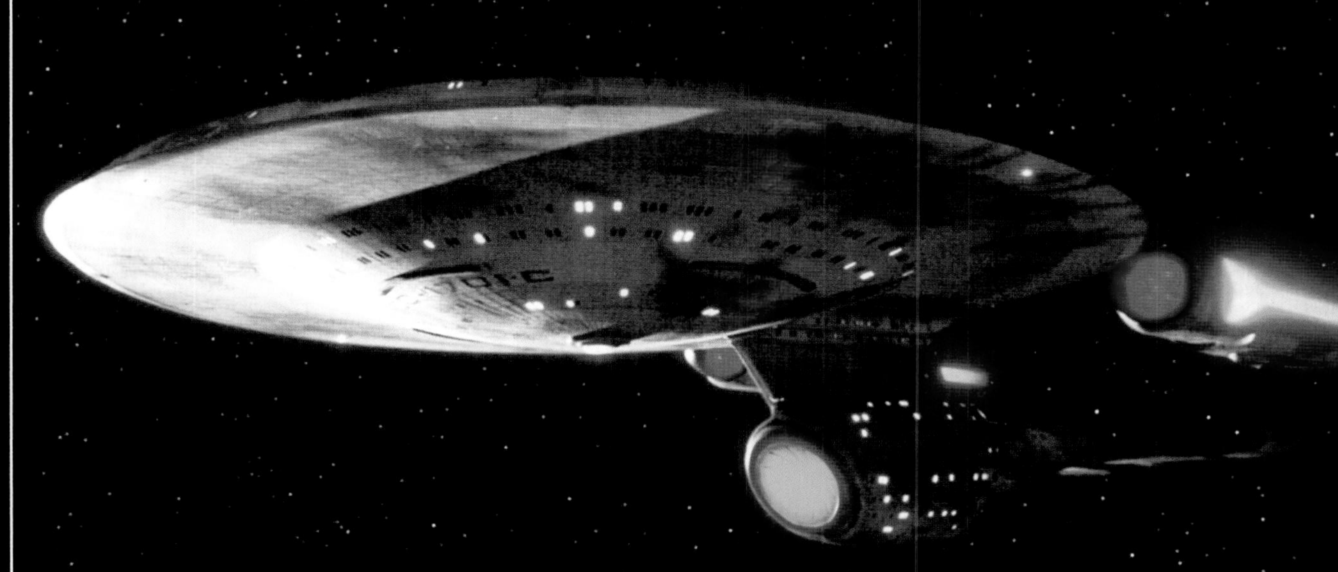

▼ The Borg cube's overwhelming victory at Wolf 359 was helped by Captain Jean-Luc Picard, who had been partially assimilated. His tactical knowledge of Starfleet's battle strategy handed the Borg a huge advantage.

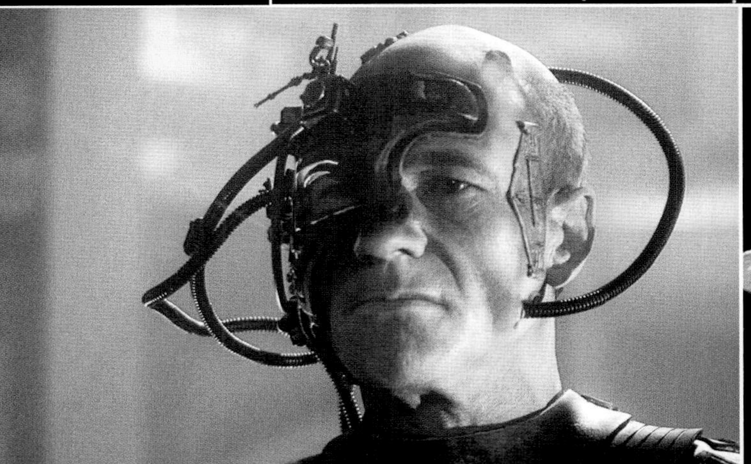

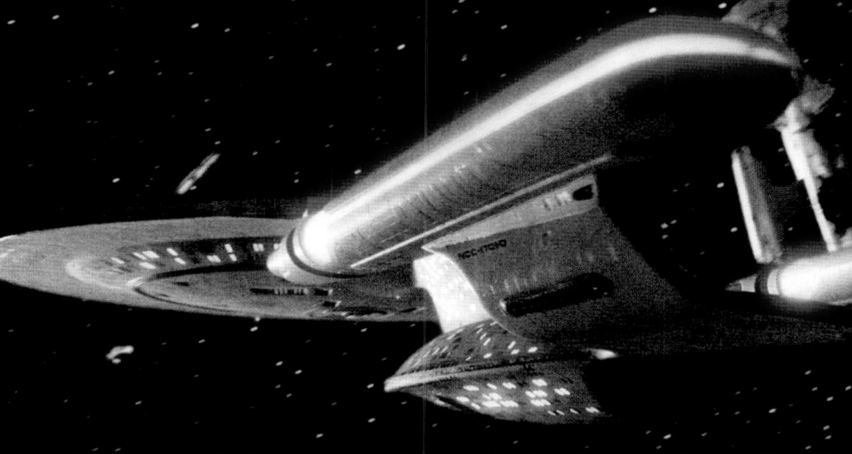

▲ The wreckage of the *Princeton* was later towed to Surplus Depot Z15 near Qualor II. The ship could be seen in a vertical orientation as the *Enterprise*-D passed it on the way to the salvage yard.

torpedo launchers, meant it possessed significant firepower. Add in its robust defensive shields, combined with the extra power generated by its third warp nacelle, and the *Niagara* class was well up to the task of performing combat and defensive duties.

This was certainly needed against the familiar enemies that Starfleet faced in the Alpha and Beta Quadrants, but in 2367, the *Niagara*-class *U.S.S. Princeton* NCC-59804 was heavily outmatched by an invading Borg cube. The *Princeton* lined up with 39 other Starfleet ships to engage the Borg, but It was swatted aside with ease. Almost half its saucer section was torn off by the cube's cutting beam, and all three of its nacelles suffered heavy damage. Most of the crew perished in the attack, and the ship was damaged beyond repair. Its lifeless hull was later towed to the starship junkyard at Surplus Depot Z15 in orbit of Qualor II.

The *U.S.S. Wellington*, the other known *Niagara*-class ship, had its computers upgraded in 2364 at Starbase 74 by Bynar technicians. Lieutenant Ro Laren served on the *Wellington* and provoked an incident on Garon II that resulted in the death of eight fellow officers. She was court-martialed for her actions, demoted to the rank of ensign, and sentenced to imprisonment on Jaros II.

DATA FEED

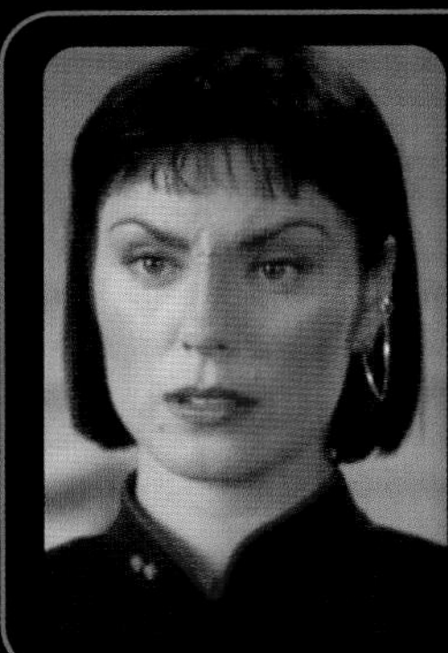

While serving aboard the *Niagara*-class *U.S.S. Wellington*, Ro Laren attained the rank of lieutenant. In the mid-2360s, she took part in a fateful away mission to Garon II. The specifics of the assignment were vague, but she disobeyed direct orders and as a direct consequence, eight members of the away team lost their lives. Ro refused to speak in her own defense at the trial, leaving the court to find her guilty and sentencing her to prison on Jaros II.

NACELLE OPERATION

The warp nacelles were the most important part of a Starfleet ship's propulsion system. They were even given their own series of internal ship coordinates to help the engineering staff pinpoint any potential problems, and their operation and maintenance was overseen from a warp nacelle control room.

Like the rest of the ship, the nacelles were constructed from duranium, and overlaid with gamma-welded tritanium that was 2.5 meters thick. The pressures exerted on the nacelles were extreme, and this was countered by three levels of cobalt cortenide that lined the structures' inner hulls. The power contained within the nacelles was so intense that they could be extremely dangerous if they malfunctioned. Safety features were incorporated that enabled them to be jettisoned in an emergency; explosive structural latches could be fired, driving the nacelles away from a ship at a rate of 30 meters per second.

Most Starfleet ships had two warp nacelles and maneuvered in space by creating slight imbalances in the warp field produced by each nacelle; in simple terms, this was the same principle upon which a kayak is maneuvered, by paddling more quickly on one side than the other.

Complications arose with a three-nacelle design, but a well-balanced warp field was made to work on the *Niagara* class. The idea did not catch on though, since the extra resources needed for an additional nacelle did not justify the slight increase in power.

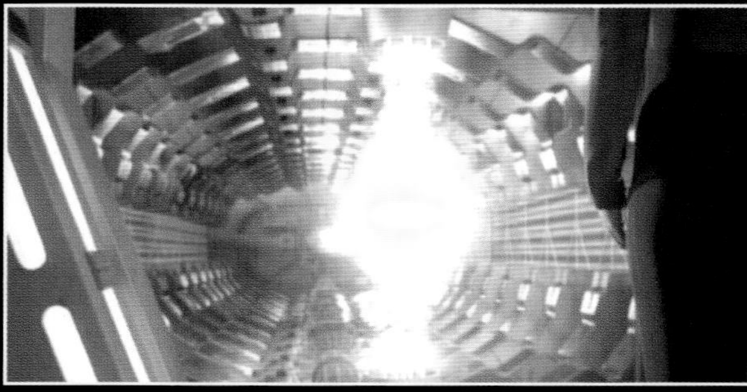

▲ The interior components of the warp nacelles on the *Niagara* class were the same as those on *Galaxy*-class ships. This meant that there were 18 warp field coils, arranged in pairs, on the inside.

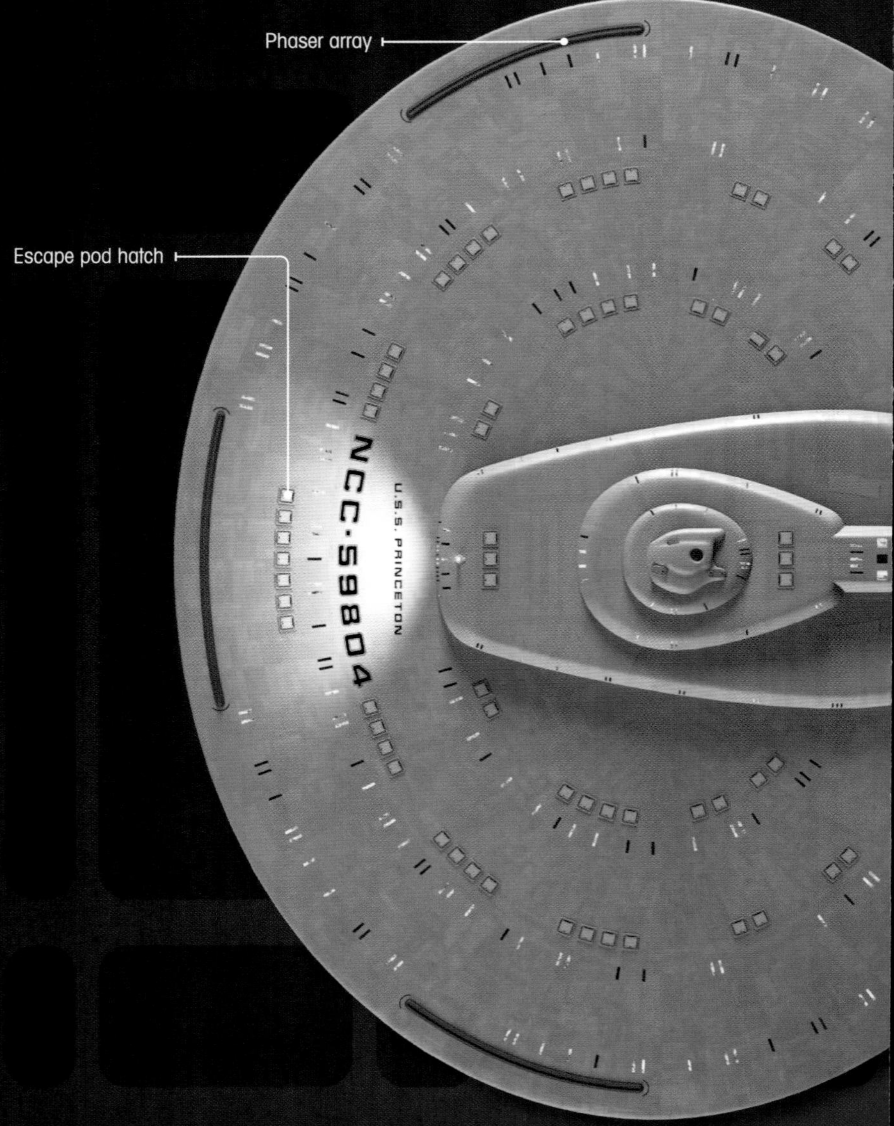

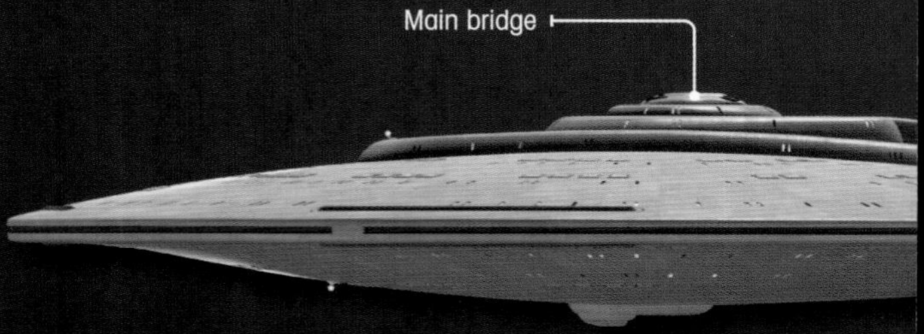

DATA FEED

Most Starfleet vessels had two nacelles, although they could operate with one nacelle at reduced speed. There were Starfleet vessels built with just one nacelle such as the *Freedom* class. The *Niagara* class was the only type of Starfleet ship that had three nacelles in the prime universe, although a schematic seen on a display monitor aboard the *U.S.S. Enterprise* NCC-1701 appeared to show the *Freedom* class as having three nacelles.

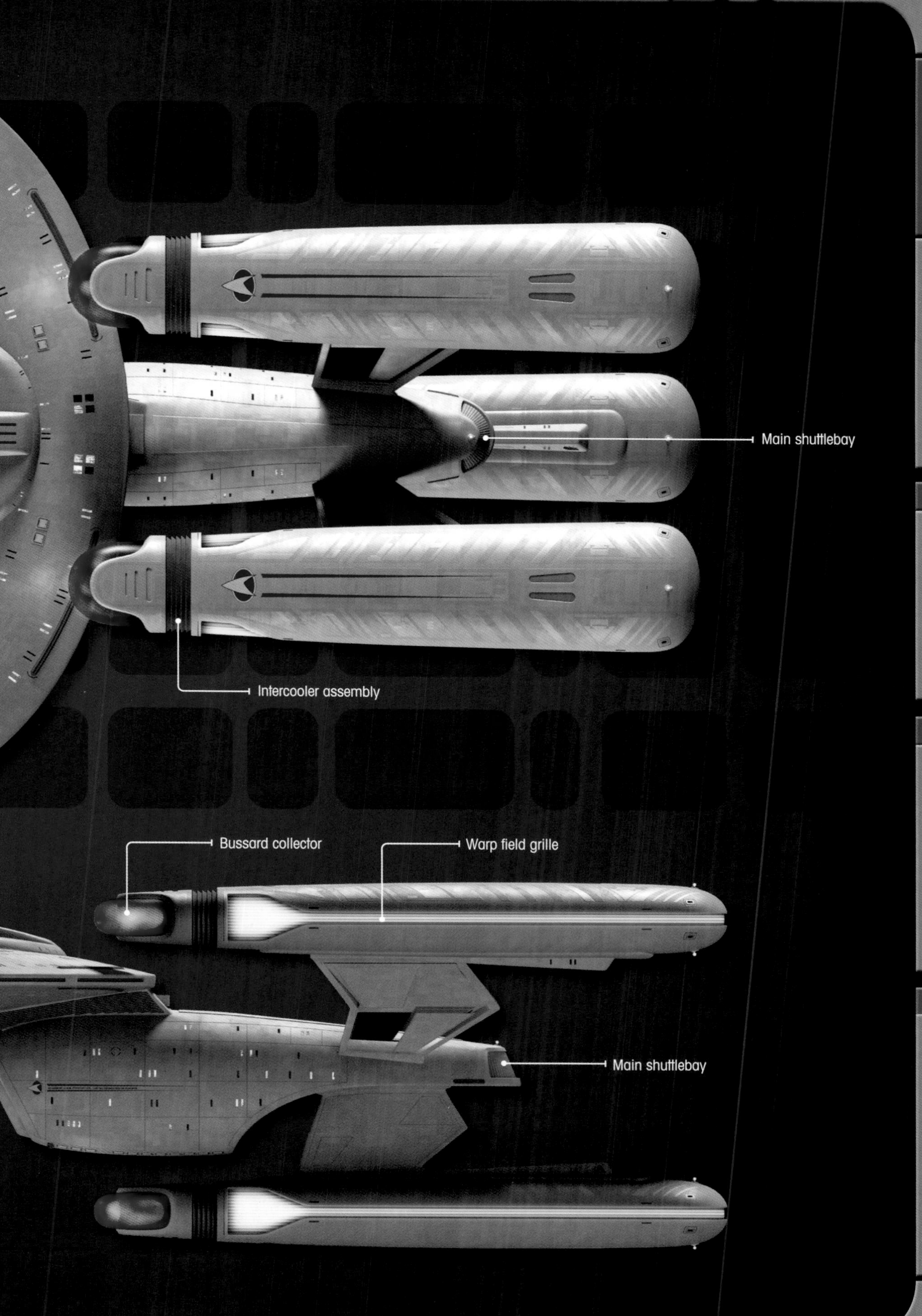

ALTERNATE FUTURE

The only other Starfleet vessel ever seen equipped with three nacelles was a modified *U.S.S. Enterprise* NCC-1701-D from an alternate future created by the Q Continuum.

SAFETY FEATURE

Galaxy-class ships could jettison nacelles in the event of an emergency. Because *Niagara*-class ships were fitted with the same nacelle design as that of the *Galaxy* class, they probably also had this facility.

WELLINGTON CAPTAIN

Captain Thomas Pucer was the commanding officer of the *Niagara*-class *U.S.S. Wellington* in 2365. According to a computer readout screen at Starbase 173, the *Wellington* was assigned to patrol duties in the Neutral Zone in Sector 130.

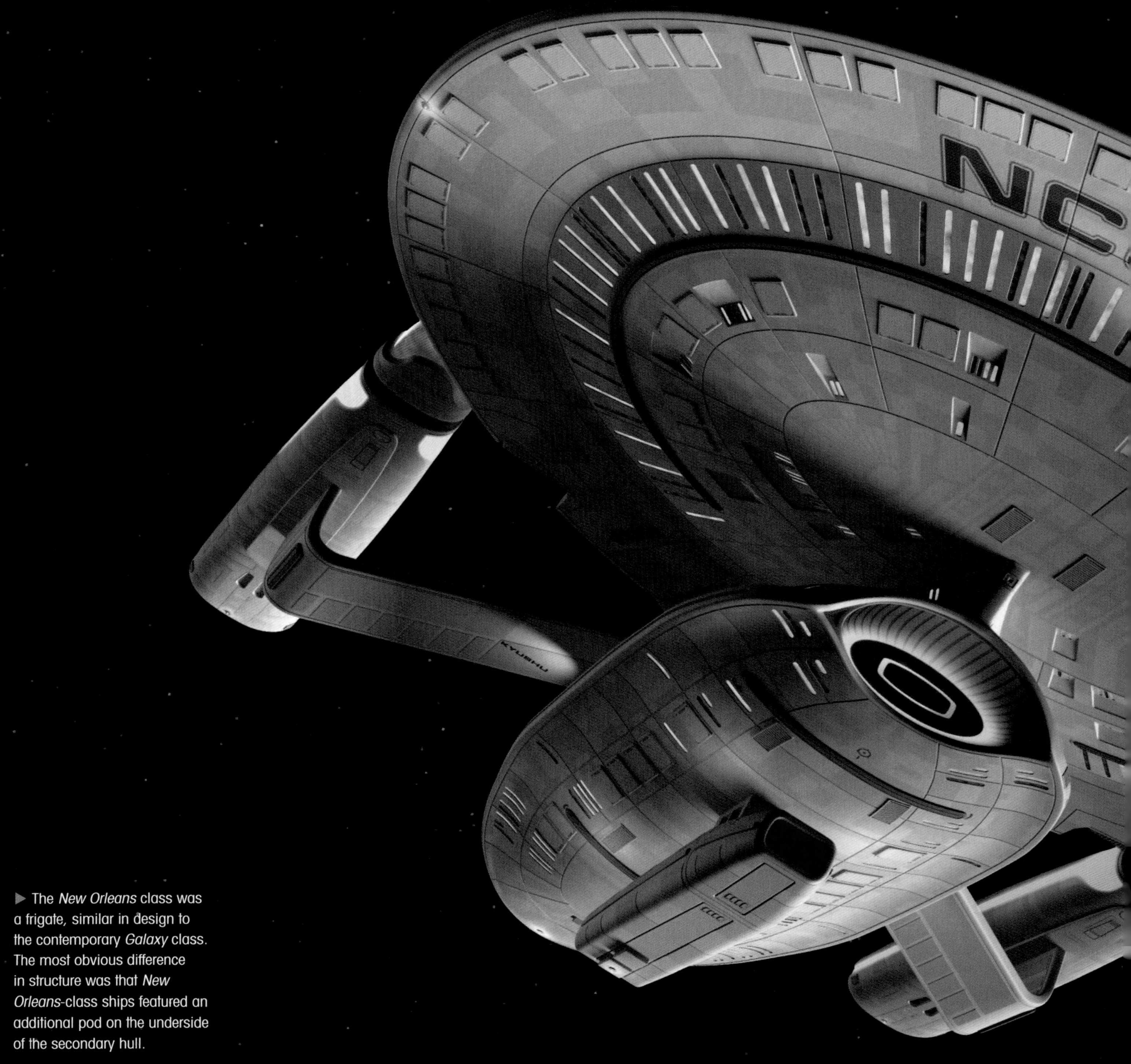

▶ The *New Orleans* class was a frigate, similar in design to the contemporary *Galaxy* class. The most obvious difference in structure was that *New Orleans*-class ships featured an additional pod on the underside of the secondary hull.

NEW ORLEANS CLASS

This adaptable class was well equipped and armed, and one such ship joined the armada that met the Borg in 2367.

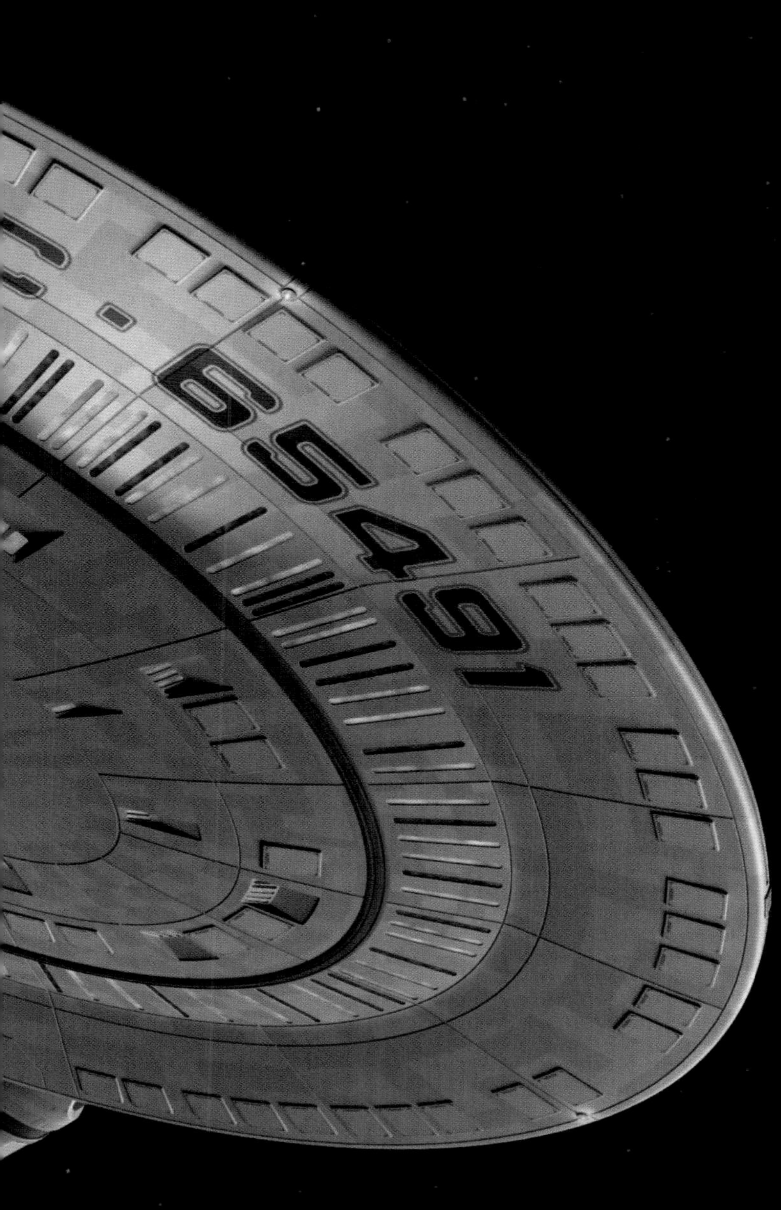

The *New Orleans*-class ship was similar in appearance to its *Galaxy*-class counterpart, but at approximately 340 meters in length, it was significantly smaller – about half the size.

Its saucer section was elliptical in shape and featured the same style of windows and escape pods as on the *Galaxy* class. Given the ship's smaller dimensions, however, the saucer was also on a smaller scale, and had two oblong structures attached on top at the rear. The main bridge was situated on deck 1 in the center of the saucer, but it was slightly larger, relative to that section as a whole, than the bridge on the *Galaxy* class.

FAMILIAR DESIGN

The engineering hull and warp nacelles on the *New Orleans* class were also virtually identical in shape to those on the *Galaxy* class, but were larger in proportion to the rest of the ship.

The most obvious outward difference between the two classes, apart from the size, was that the *New Orleans* class featured a tubular structure on the underside of the engineering hull.

Less obvious differences could also be found in the neck of the ship between the saucer and engineering sections, and in the shape and positioning of the warp pylons. The neck structure was much shorter on the *New Orleans* class, meaning that the saucer and the engineering hulls were much closer together. Meanwhile, the

◀ Captain Rixx was in command of the *New Orleans*-class *U.S.S. Thomas Paine* NCC-65530 in 2364. Rixx was a Bolian and considered one of Starfleet's most accomplished captains at the time. According to records, the *Thomas Paine* was on a diplomatic mission to Epsilon Ashanti III in 2367 and to Alderaan in 2368.

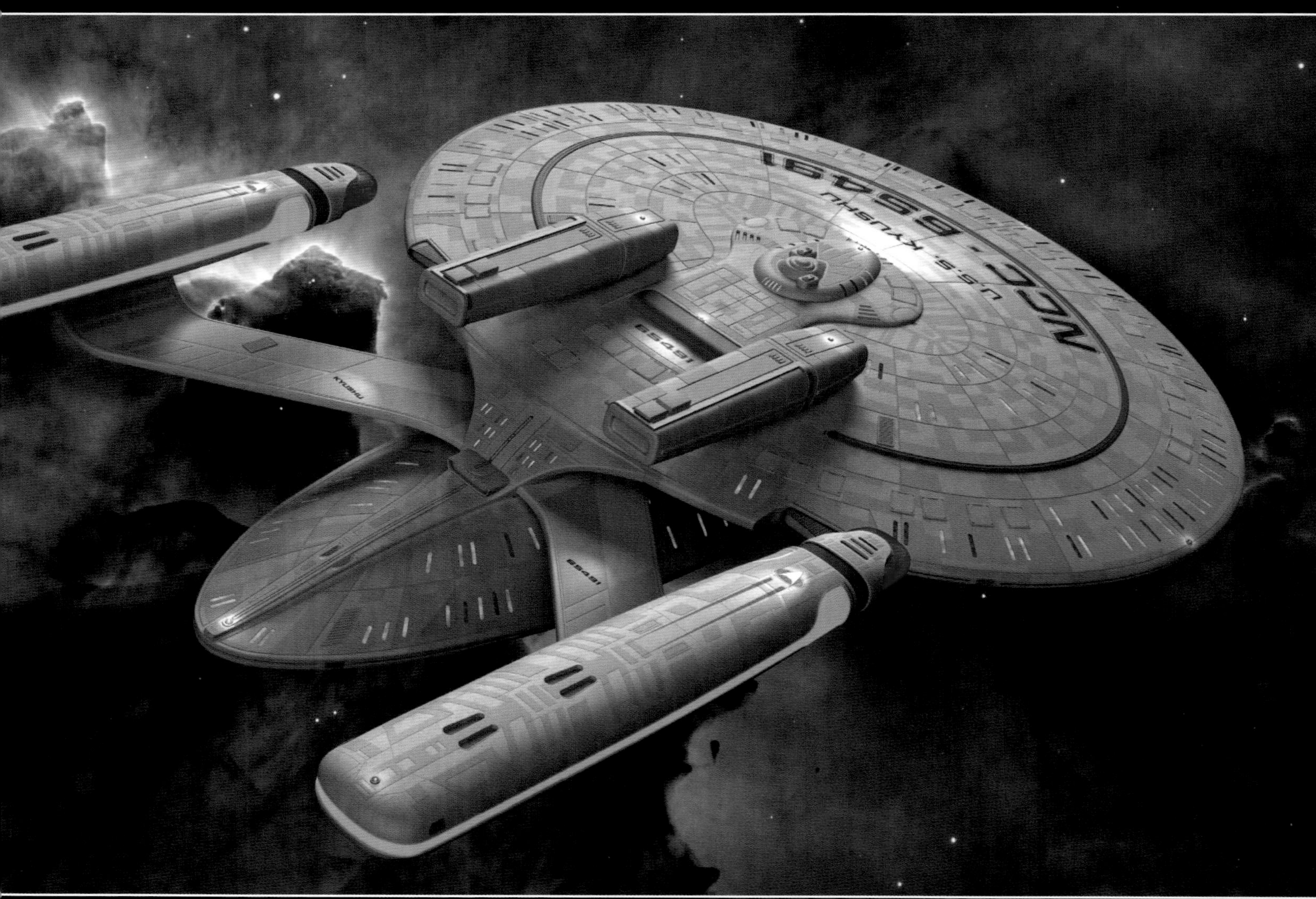

▲ The surface detail on the *New Orleans* class was almost identical to that found on the *Galaxy* class, in particular the windows, escape pods, and phaser strips. Seen from above, however, there were a couple of distinctions: the *New Orleans* class featured two additional structures attached to the rear of the saucer section, and the positioning and design of the warp pylons was different.

nacelle pylons were attached just over halfway along the engineering section and swept back, whereas the pylons on the *Galaxy* class were positioned at the very rear of the engineering hull and extended straight out horizontally.

As the *New Orleans* class was about half the length of the *Galaxy* class, it followed that its crew complement was significantly less. Whereas the *Galaxy* class normally carried just over 1,000 people, the *New Orleans* usually operated with a crew of around 500.

The *New Orleans* class likewise had slightly less powerful engines and armaments than those of the *Galaxy* class. The former's warp engines gave it a top speed of warp 9.3 sustainable for 12 hours, and a cruising speed of warp 6. It was equipped with a high-capacity shield grid, 10 type-X phaser arrays, and three photon torpedo launchers.

Other facilities onboard the *New Orleans* class included sickbays, transporter rooms, holodecks, and several specialized research labs.

ALIEN CONSPIRACY

In 2364, two *New Orleans*-class vessels were summoned to a secret rendezvous at an abandoned mining colony on planet Dytallix B, along with the *U.S.S. Enterprise* NCC-1701-D. Captain Walker Keel of the *U.S.S. Horatio* NCC-10532 called the meeting after he suspected that a neural parasitic alien intelligence was trying to take over Starfleet Command.

The meeting was attended by Captain Jean-Luc Picard, Captain Rixx, and Captain Tryla Scott. Rixx, in command of the *New Orleans*-class *U.S.S. Thomas Paine* NCC-65530, was considered one of Starfleet's best captains, while Scott was captain of the *New Orleans*-class *U.S.S. Renegade*

▶ The drifting wreckage of the *New Orleans*-class *U.S.S. Kyushu* was evidence of the carnage at the Battle of Wolf 359, when a single Borg cube destroyed 39 Starfleet ships on its seemingly inexorable way to Earth.

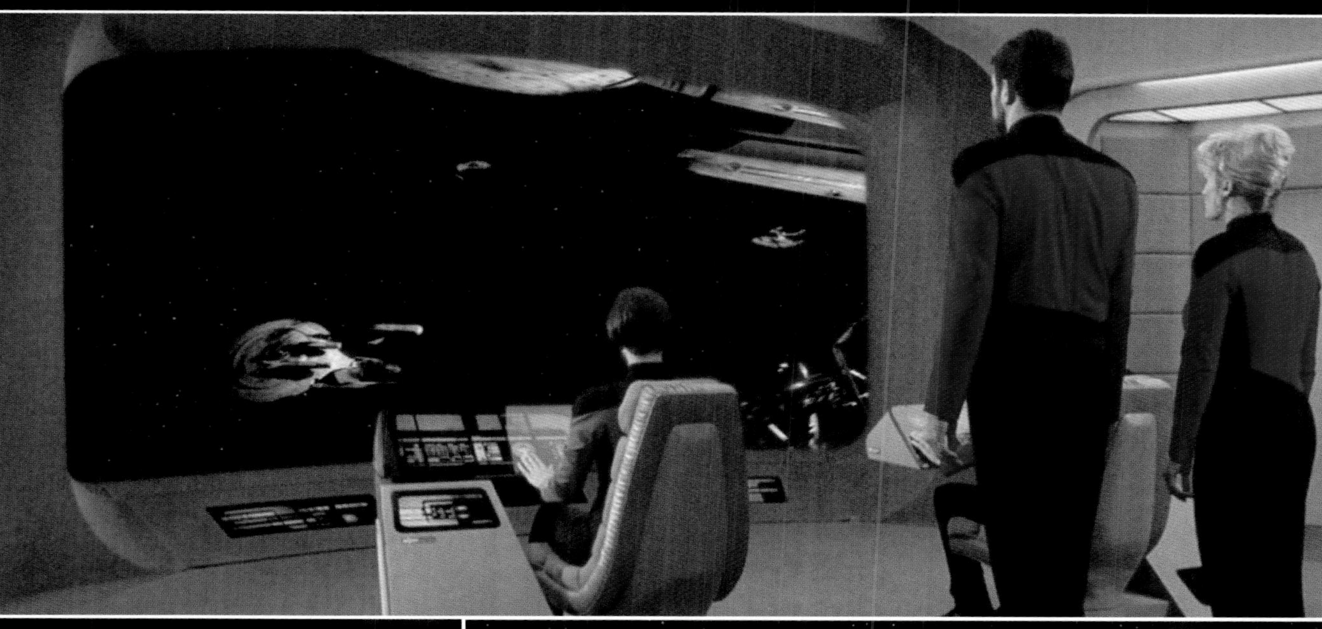

▼ In 2368, the *New Orleans*-class *U.S.S. Thomas Paine* was one of 17 Starfleet ships that formed a tachyon detection grid with the aim of exposing Romulan supply ships entering Klingon space.

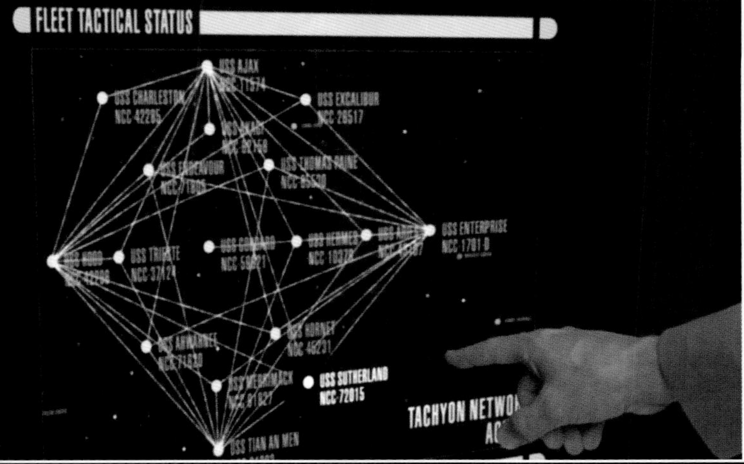

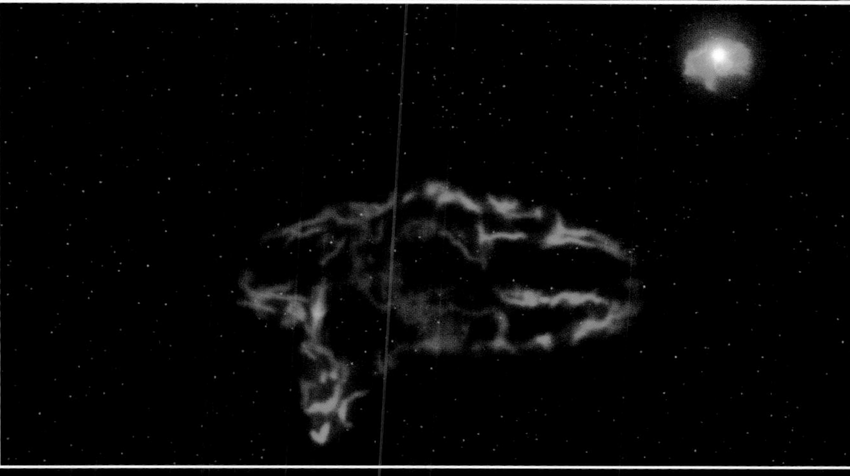

▲ The Romulans tried to aid the House of Duras by supplying weapons for its attempt to take control of the Klingon Empire during the civil war. The Duras were defeated after the Romulan supply ships were discovered.

NCC-63102. She had attained the rank of captain faster than anyone in the history of Starfleet, which made her something of a legend.

Later, in 2367, the *New Orleans*-class *U.S.S. Kyushu* NCC-65491 was called up to join the fleet hastily assembled by Admiral J. P. Hanson to intercept a Borg cube that had invaded the Alpha Quadrant on course for Earth. The ensuing Battle of Wolf 359 very quickly became a massacre, as the cube, armed with the tactical knowledge of the assimilated Captain Picard, ripped through the Starfleet defenses. The toll of 39 ships lost included the destruction of the *Kyushu*.

In 2368, the *U.S.S. Thomas Paine* formed part of a more successful fleet that prevented Romulan warbirds from transporting supplies to the House of Duras during the Klingon civil war. The *Thomas Paine* was one of 17 ships that formed a tachyon grid set up to detect cloaked Romulan warships entering Klingon space. After being exposed, the convoy of Romulan ships was prevented from sending further supplies to the House of Duras, whose attempted coup failed. Gowron was able to hold on to power as the legally appointed leader of the Klingon Empire.

DATA FEED

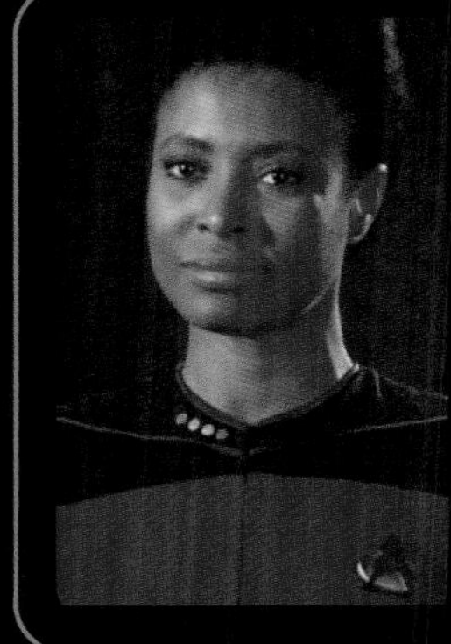

Captain Tryla Scott was in command of the *U.S.S. Renegade* in 2364. She was an outstanding officer, widely celebrated for achieving her rank in an unprecedentedly short time. Along with Captain Picard and Captain Rixx, she was tasked with investigating the infiltration of Starfleet Command by parasitic life-forms. Unfortunately, Scott herself became infested by one of the parasites and Commander Will Riker of the *Enterprise*-D was forced to fire at her with a phaser set to kill.

BATTLE OF WOLF 359

The *New Orleans*-class *U.S.S. Kyushu* NCC-65491 was one of 40 Starfleet vessels that attempted to repel an invading Borg cube at the Battle of Wolf 359, in 2367. Not all the names of the Starfleet ships that made up this armada were known, so it was possible that more *New Orleans*-class vessels were part of this tactical force, but they were not seen and no reference was made to them.

The *New Orleans* class was essentially built for exploration rather than combat, but its offensive and defensive capabilities were considerable, if not quite up to the standard of larger *Galaxy*-class ships. Nevertheless, the *Kyushu*, along with the other ships in the armada, was easily obliterated by the Borg cube. One reason for this was Captain Picard's partial assimilation by the Borg, which gave them access to his invaluable knowledge of Starfleet ships and tactics.

Another reason for the cataclysmic defeat was that the Starfleet armada used the wrong strategy. The ships attacked one at a time because they did not want to risk hitting their own vessels in the crossfire. But this meant the Borg cube could pick them off one by one, with no danger of being overwhelmed itself.

However, even if Picard had not been assimilated or a different strategy had been adopted, the outcome would have been no different. The simple fact was that the Starfleet armada was no match for the Borg.

Warp nacelle

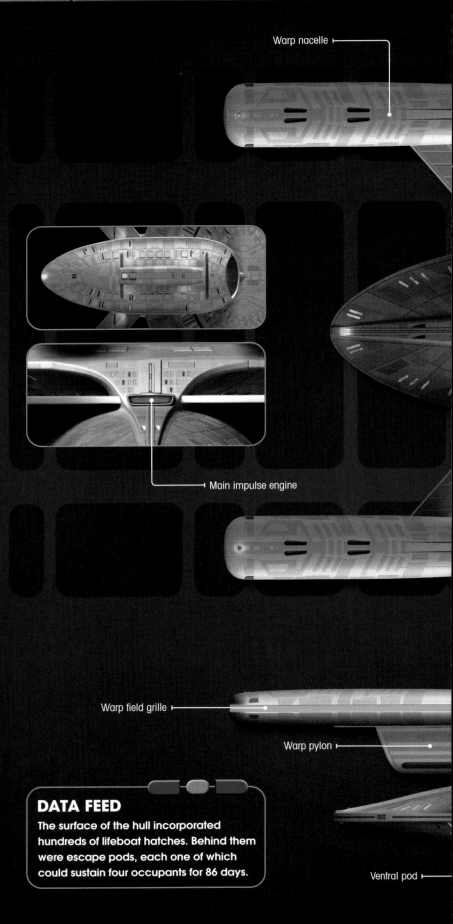

Main impulse engine

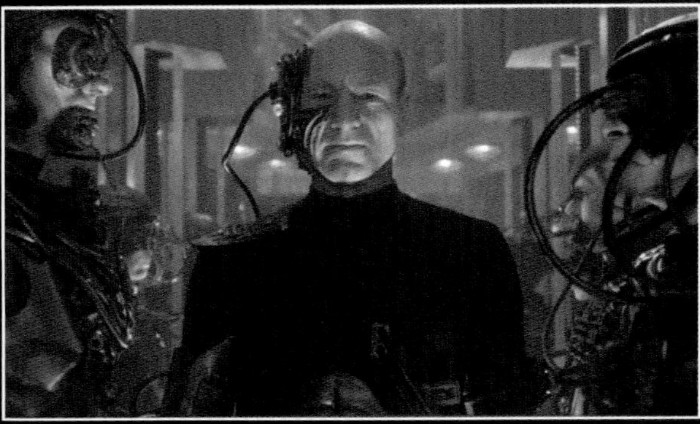

▲ Captured by the Borg, Captain Picard was transformed into Locutus. All his knowledge of Starfleet's defenses was then assimilated by the Borg, making Starfleet's ships even more vulnerable to them.

Warp field grille

Warp pylon

DATA FEED

The surface of the hull incorporated hundreds of lifeboat hatches. Behind them were escape pods, each one of which could sustain four occupants for 86 days.

Ventral pod

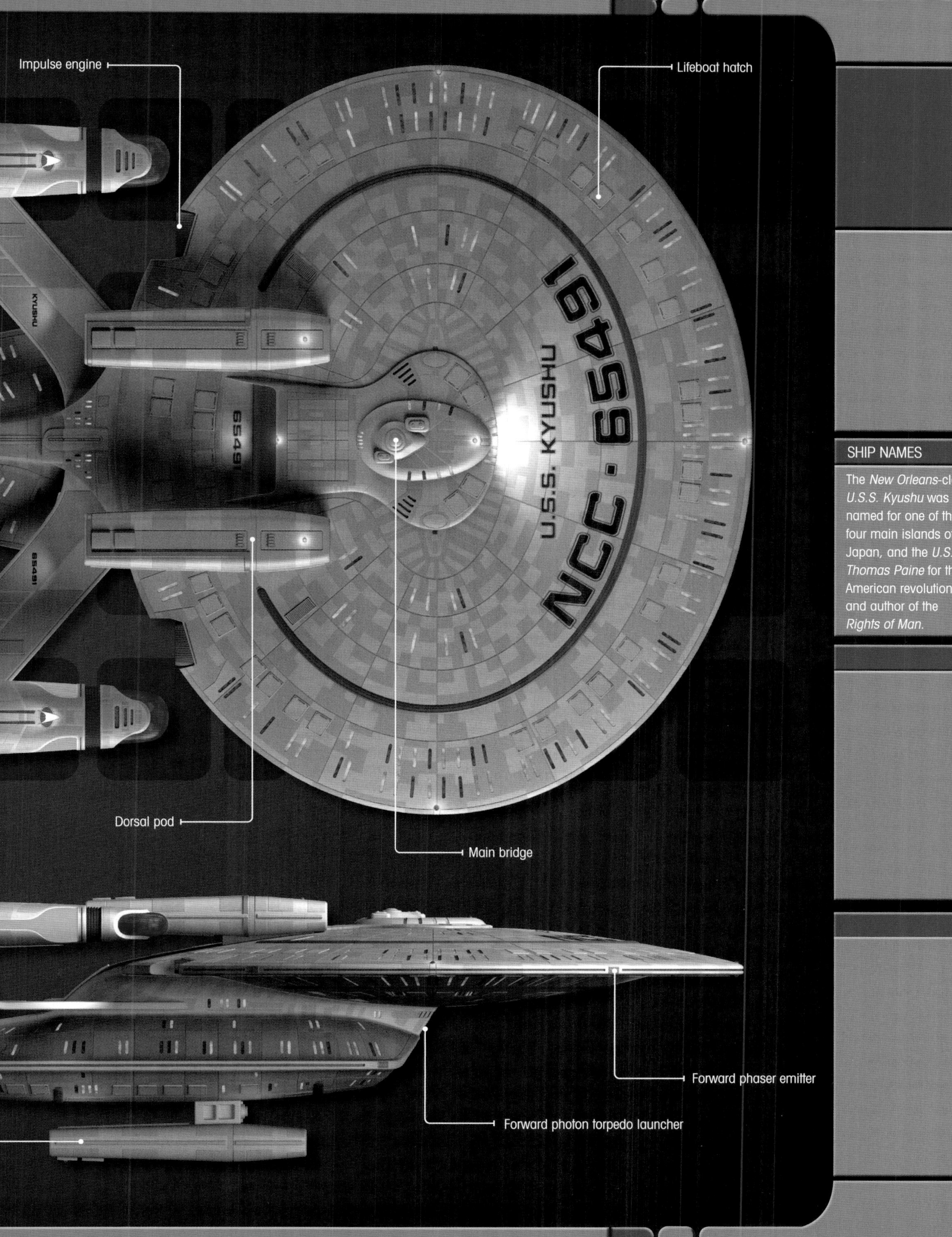

SHIP NAMES

The *New Orleans*-class *U.S.S. Kyushu* was named for one of the four main islands of Japan, and the *U.S.S. Thomas Paine* for the American revolutionary and author of the *Rights of Man*.

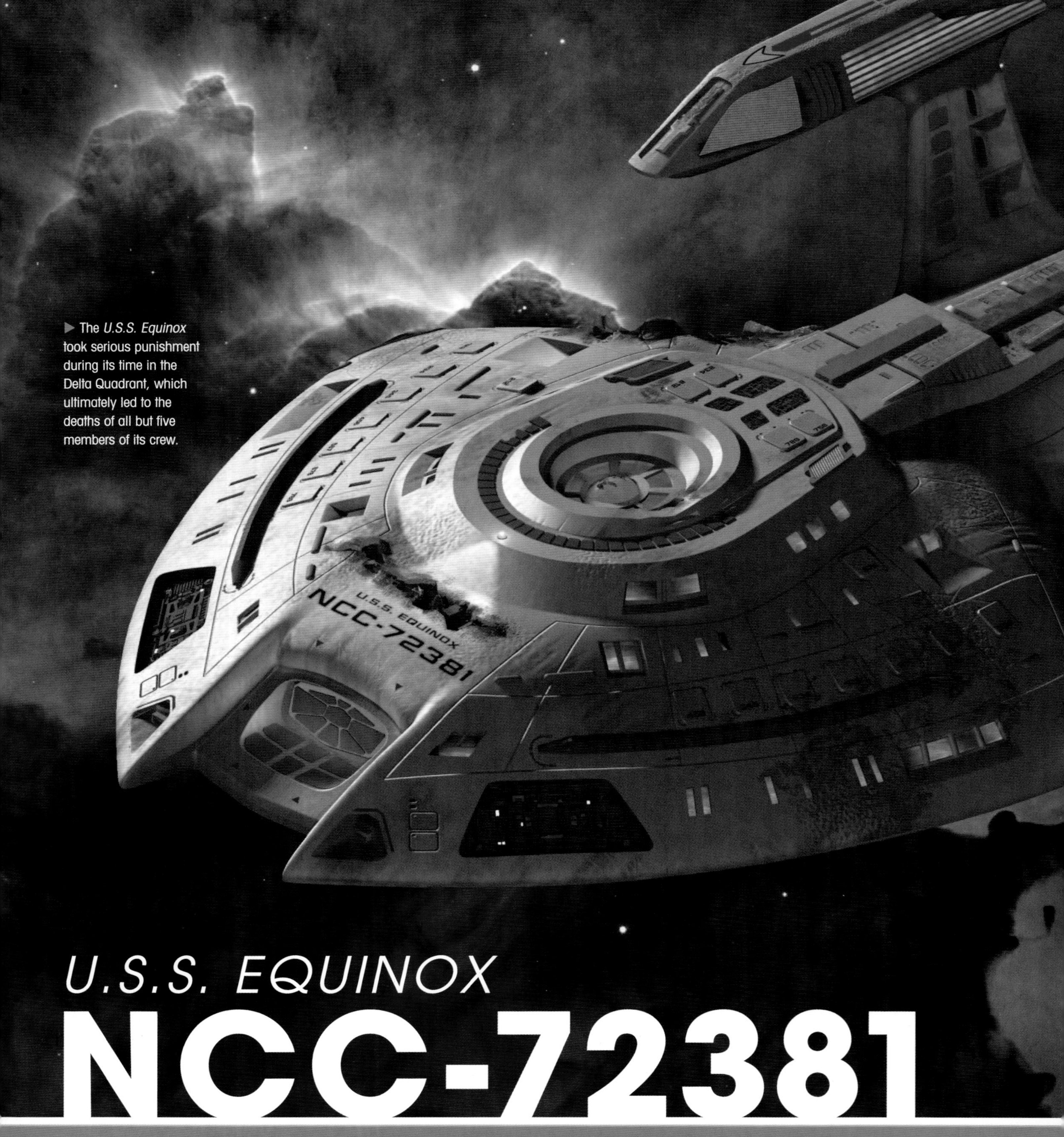

▶ The *U.S.S. Equinox* took serious punishment during its time in the Delta Quadrant, which ultimately led to the deaths of all but five members of its crew.

U.S.S. EQUINOX NCC-72381

This small science vessel was catapulted out of Federation space into a battle for survival in the Delta Quadrant.

DATA FEED

The *Equinox* was one of several ships that the entity known as the Caretaker pulled into the Delta Quadrant. Originally an explorer from another galaxy, the Caretaker had remained in the Delta Quadrant to care for the Ocampa after accidentally ruining the atmosphere on their planet. Close to death, the Caretaker sought to find a successor, so dragged in vessels from anywhere, but he abandoned every species that he deemed unsuitable.

The *Nova*-class *U.S.S. Equinox* was built at the Utopia Planitia Fleet Yards and designed to function as a science and scout vessel. It was therefore perfect for short-term planetary research and analysis rather than long-range tactical missions. As a result, the *Equinox* had a top speed of only warp 8 and was fitted with minimal weaponry, although it was one of the first ships to be equipped with an Emergency Medical Hologram.

Measuring 221.74 meters in length and with eight decks, the *Equinox* was a relatively small vessel. Its *Nova*-class spaceframe was originally developed as part of the *Defiant* project, which was established to deal with the Borg threat in the 2360s. However, when the *Defiant* project took a different approach, the *Nova* prototype was reclassified as a science vessel. Four of its torpedo launchers were removed and replaced with sensor platforms. Additional sensor platforms were located around the perimeter of the saucer section and in the dome on the underside of the saucer. The secondary navigational deflector at the front of the saucer section further enhanced the ship's scanning abilities.

The *Nova* class did retain several design features from its early development, including a recessed bridge protected from conventional attacks by an outer ring. From here, the entire ship could be operated by just two officers.

Like *Intrepid*-class ships, the *Equinox* was designed to land on a planet's surface and was fitted with retractable landing struts in the lower

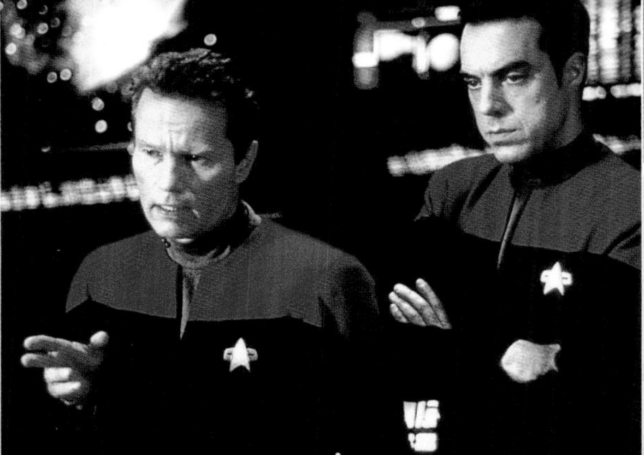

◀ The *Equinox*'s Captain Rudolph Ransom III (far left) and First Officer Maxwell Burke broke many Starfleet rules to survive in the Delta Quadrant. As the ship suffered evermore serious damage, they became less and less concerned with morality and eventually resorted to murder in an attempt to shorten their journey home.

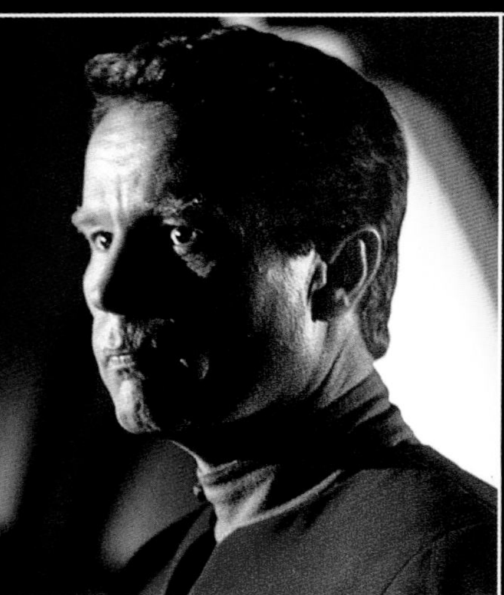

◀ Despite his high reputation as an officer, Captain Ransom made a crucial error of judgment when his ship was first trapped in the Delta Quadrant, which resulted in the loss of many members of his crew.

▶ Meeting a species known as the Ankari led Ransom to discover a nucleogenic life-form.

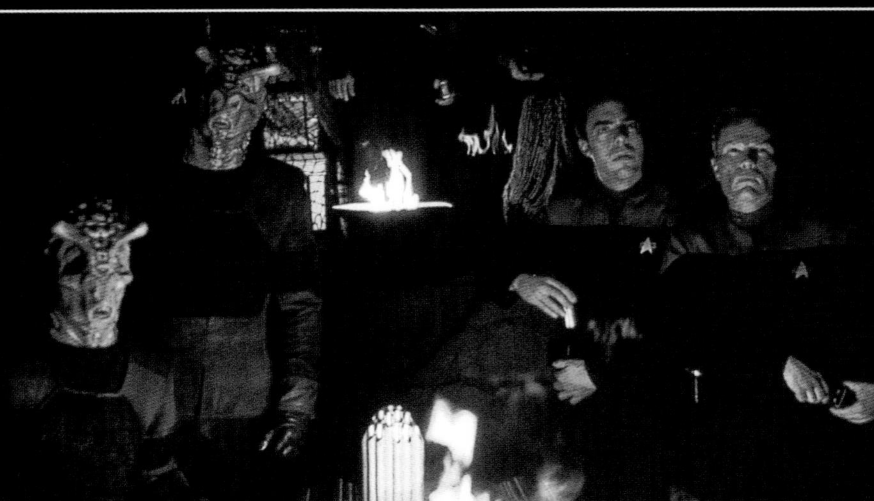

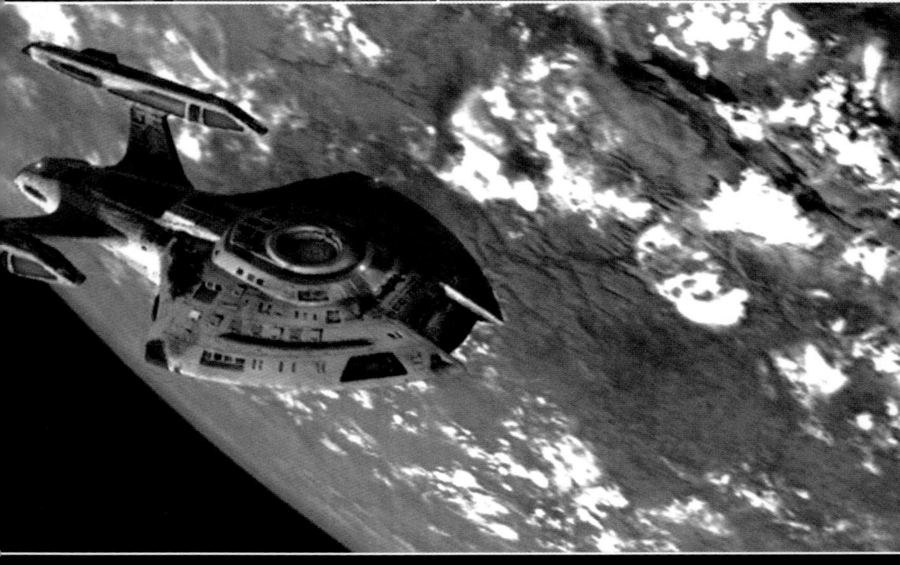

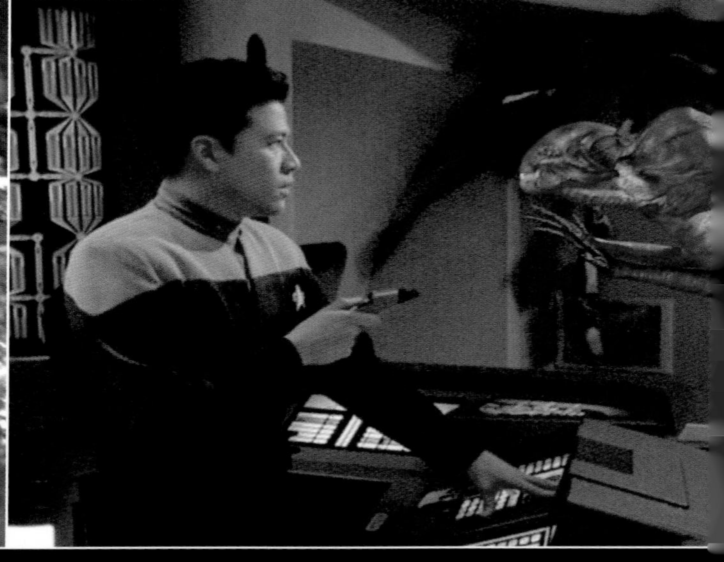

▲ After *Voyager*'s Captain Janeway learned about Ransom's criminal behavior, she tried to arrest him, but he and his surviving crew took the *Equinox* and hid near a planet with a pathogenic atmosphere that masked the ship from sensors.

decks of the engineering hull. The *Equinox* also carried a number of shuttlecraft, including a hypersonic *Waverider* shuttle, which was docked on the underside of the saucer section. Similar to the captain's yachts on *Galaxy*-class vessels, the *Waverider* shuttle was designed to operate within a planetary atmosphere and could reach speeds in excess of Mach 5.

LOST IN THE DELTA QUADRANT

The *U.S.S. Equinox* NCC-72381 was commissioned on Stardate 47007.1 and placed under the command of Rudolph Ransom III, a well-known and admired exobiologist who, after making first contact with the Yridians, a species previously thought to be extinct, was promoted to the rank of captain.

In 2371, the *Equinox* was one of a number of vessels pulled into the Delta Quadrant by the entity known as the Caretaker, who abandoned the crew 70,000 light-years from Earth. Even traveling at its top speed of warp 8, it was clear the ship would not reach home for decades.

Nevertheless, Ransom set a course for Earth. Within a matter of days, the *Equinox* had unwittingly entered an area of space controlled by a species known as the Krowtonan Guard, who ordered them to leave their territory. However, since a detour would add six years to their journey, Ransom opted to maintain course. The Krowtonan Guard launched a series of vicious assaults that resulted in the loss of half the *Equinox* crew and severe damage to the ship. Although the *Equinox* survived, it was not equipped for long-term survival away from Starfleet support facilities.Within a few years, the ship was on the point of collapse and the remaining crew were facing starvation.

The ship managed to enter orbit around an M-Class planet, whose inhabitants, known as the

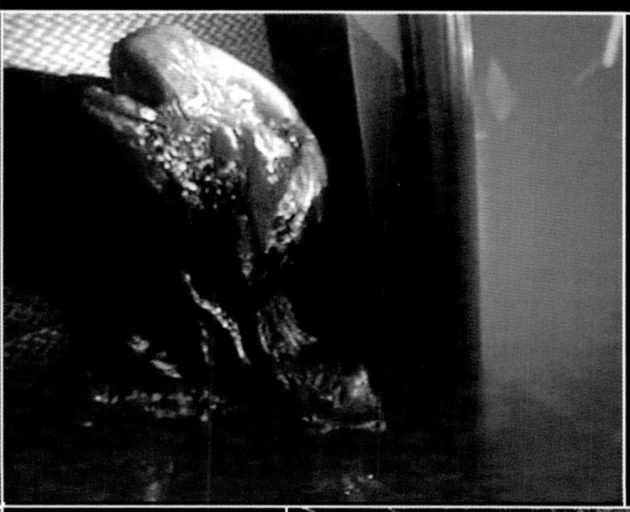

◀ Ransom and his crew hoped to study these life-forms and summoned one onboard. But their attempts to keep it in normal space went wrong and inadvertently caused its death.

▶ The remains of the nucleogenic life-form provided an extremely efficient fuel source that allowed the *Equinox's* engines to reach the high warp 9.9s.

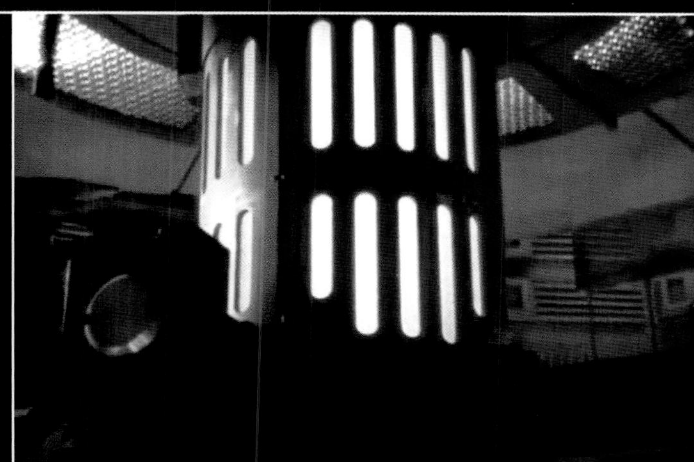

◀ When the *U.S.S. Voyager* came to the *Equinox's* assistance, the nucleogenic life-forms started to attack both ships, convinced that there was no difference between the two crews. *Voyager* eventually managed to communicate with them and promised to punish Ransom.

▶ Janeway pursued Ransom and in the ensuing battle, *Voyager* inflicted serious damage on the *Equinox*.

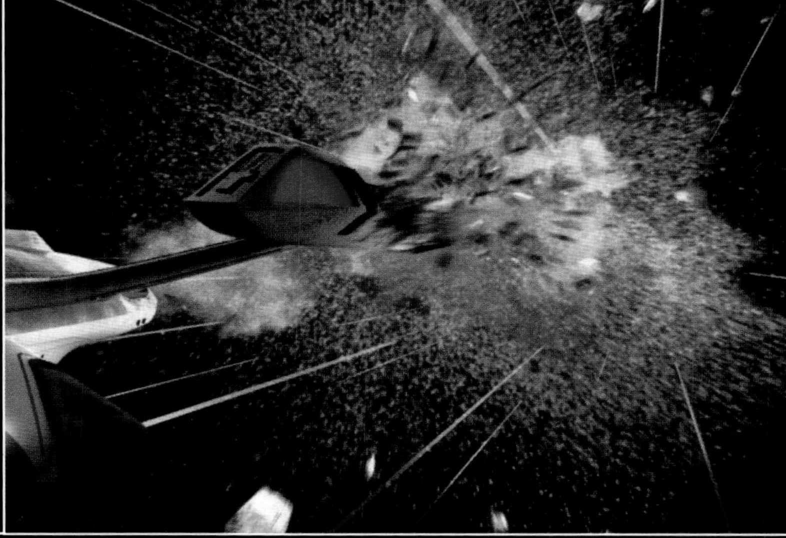

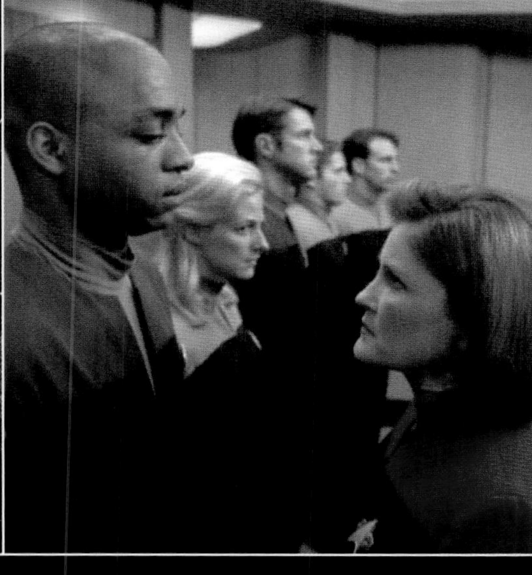

Ankari, summoned their "Spirits of Good Fortune" to bless the crew. Discovering that the spirits were in fact nucleogenic life-forms that emitted high levels of antimatter, Ransom and his crew captured one of the aliens, but then accidentally caused its death. They used the remains to enhance the *Equinox's* warp drive.

MORAL CATASTROPHE

This new power source enabled the ship to travel more than 10,000 light-years in just two weeks. Ransom and his crew continued to capture and kill the aliens in a bid to shorten their journey to Earth. However, the aliens retaliated by attacking the ship, killing many of the remaining crewmembers. In early 2376, after one such attack left the ship almost incapacitated, Ransom sent out a distress call. This was picked up by the *U.S.S. Voyager*, another Starfleet vessel trapped in the Delta Quadrant. Accepting *Voyager's* help, Ransom hid the reason behind the alien attacks. When the truth was exposed, Captain Janeway attempted to arrest him and his crew, and to make peace with the nucleogenic life-forms. The *Equinox* fled and in the ensuing battle, Ransom realized what he had done, beamed his crew to *Voyager*, and destroyed the *Equinox*, with himself aboard.

▲ Ransom was willing to surrender, but First Officer Maxwell Burke was not. Ransom elected to destroy the *Equinox*, killing both himself and Burke. The five surviving crewmembers joined *Voyager's* crew.

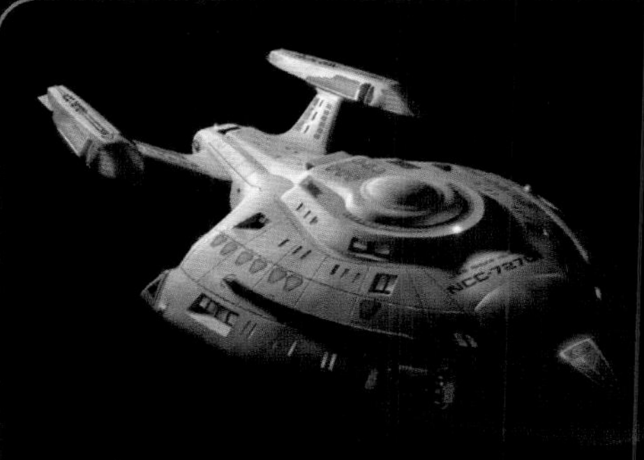

DATA FEED

In one version of the future, *Voyager*'s Ensign Harry Kim was the captain of the *U.S.S. Rhode Island*, a design of Starfleet vessel that had clearly evolved from the *Nova* class. The most obvious difference was that it had a filled-in nose section.

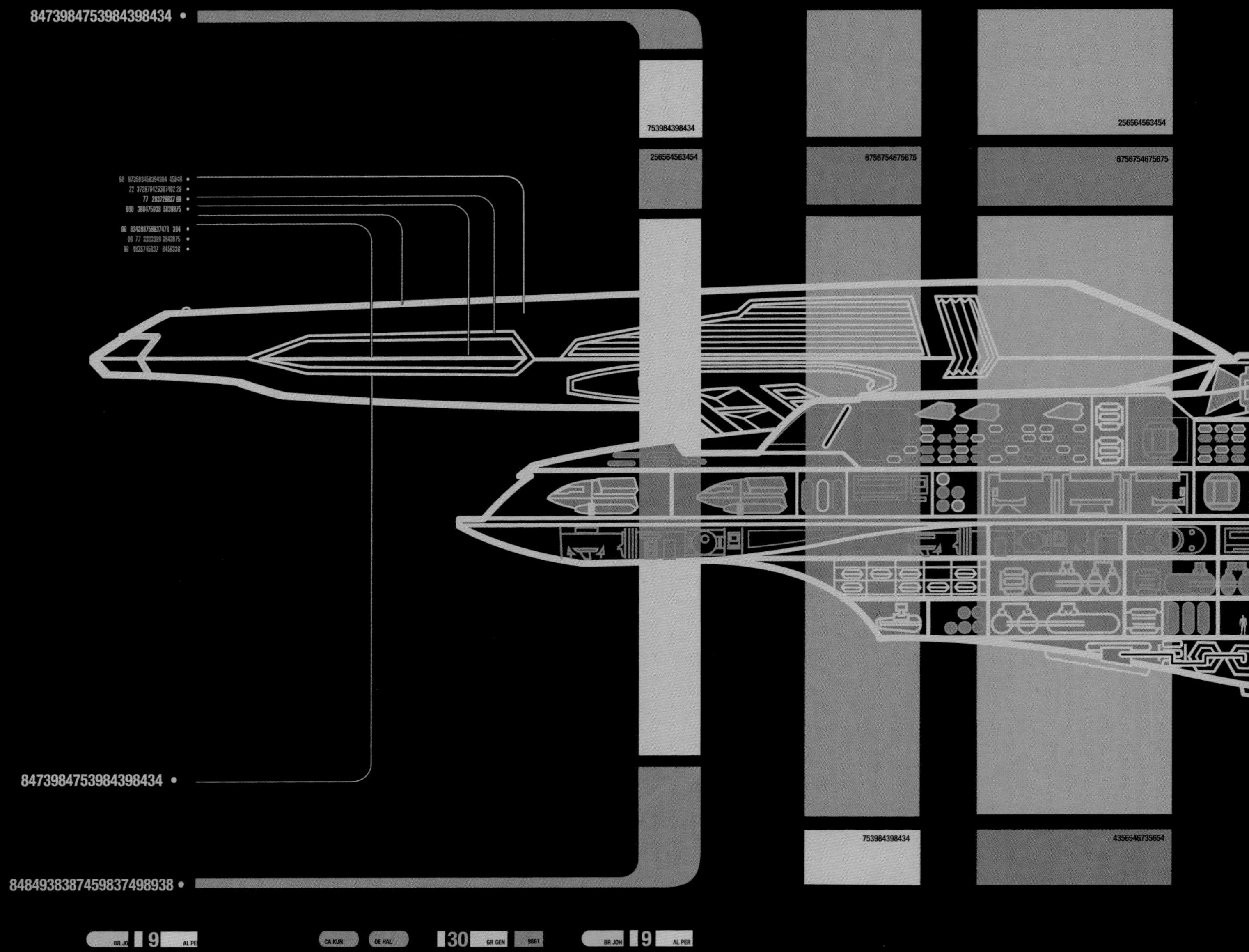

Master Systems Display

The *Equinox* was a small vessel designed for relatively short-range scouting and scientific survey missions. Its eight decks included quarters for a crew of 80, and these were located on the upper decks. The lower decks in the engineering hull were largely taken up by the navigational deflector, which crossed decks 6 and 7 and main engineering, where the vertical warp core ran between decks 5 and 8, with a hatch in the bottom of the hull allowing it to be ejected in an emergency. The impulse engines were on deck 2 at the rear of the saucer section. The main computer core was also located in the saucer section and ran between decks 2 and 4. The *Waverider* shuttle was docked just forward of this on deck 4, where it nestled into the ship behind the secondary deflector dish. Other shuttlecraft were housed in a shuttlebay at the rear of the ship on deck 3, which also housed a variety of science labs.

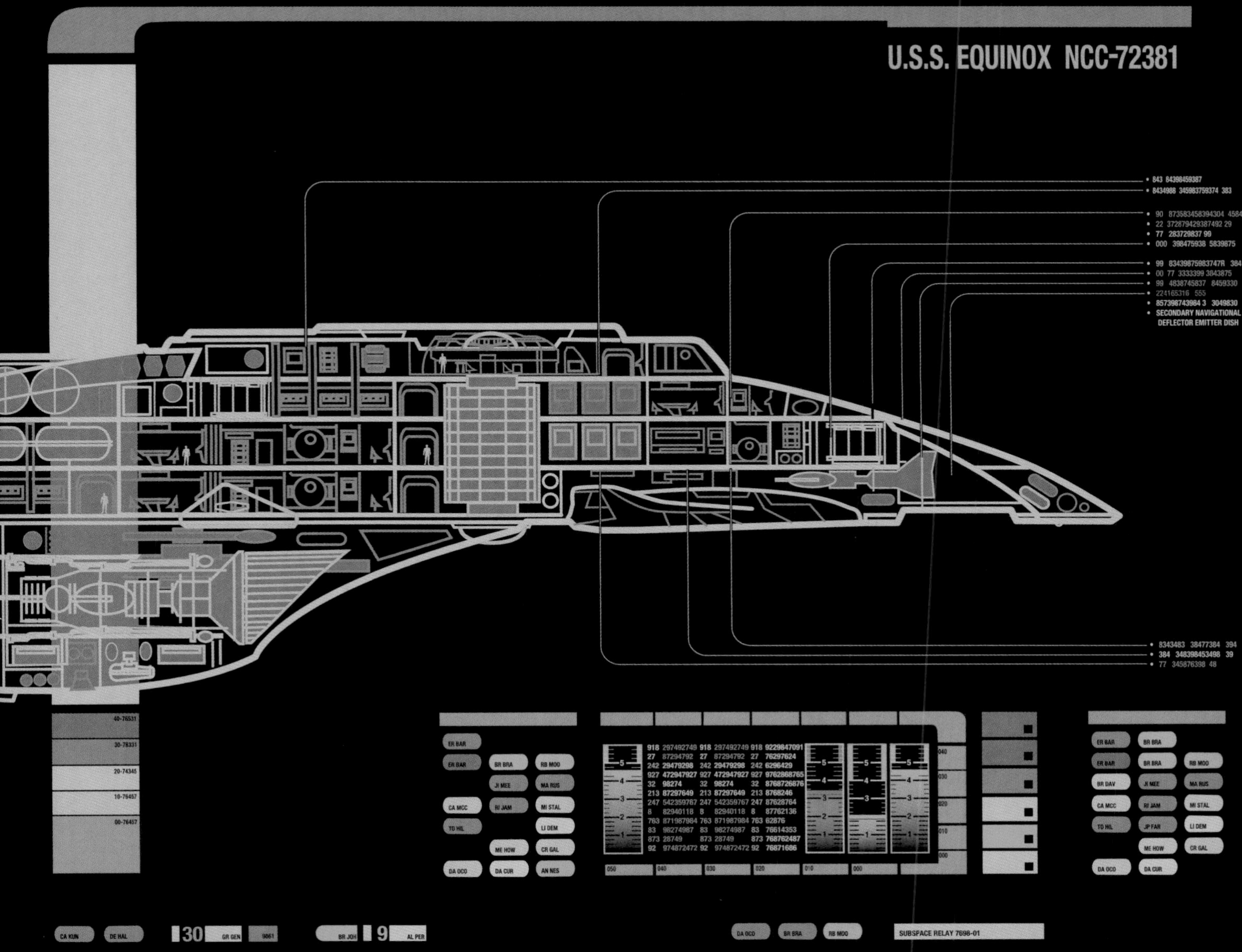
U.S.S. EQUINOX NCC-72381
SECONDARY NAVIGATIONAL DEFLECTOR EMITTER DISH
SUBSPACE RELAY 7698-01

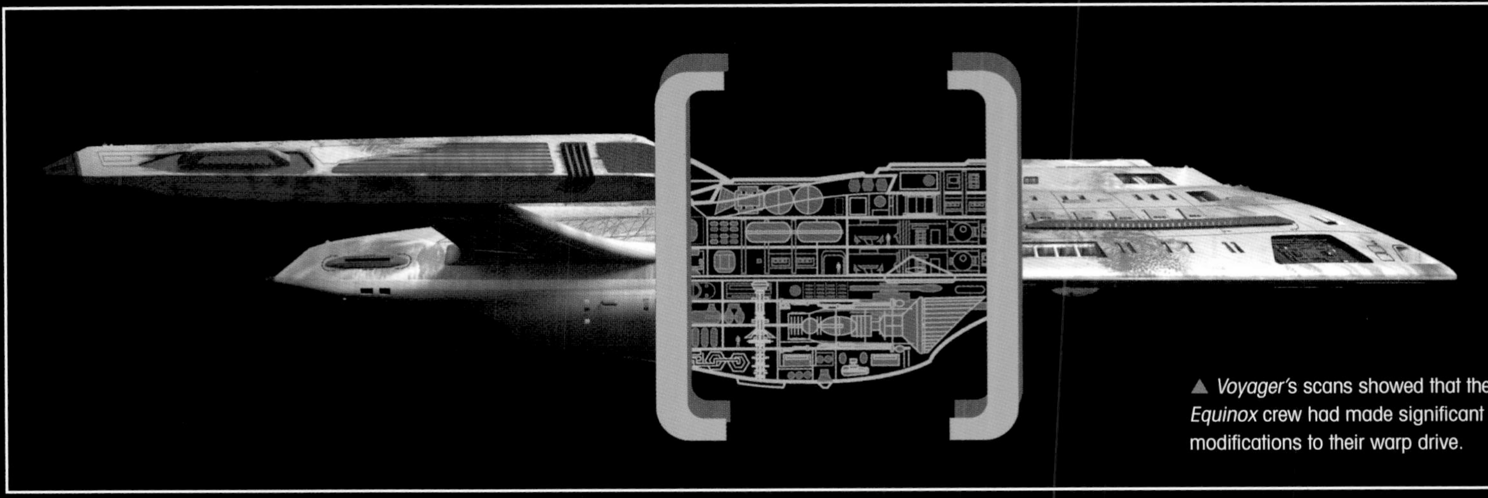

▲ *Voyager's* scans showed that the *Equinox* crew had made significant modifications to their warp drive.

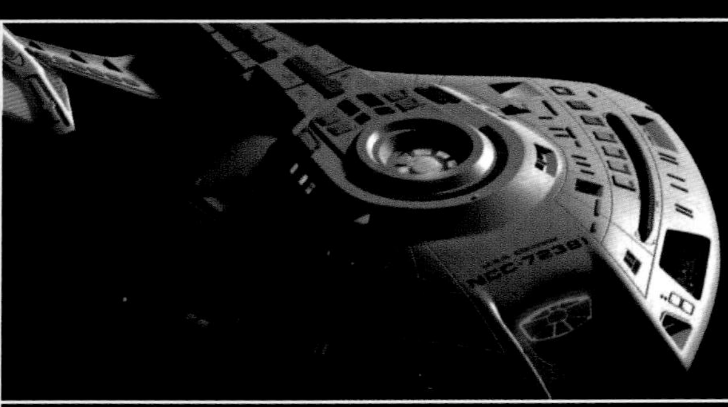

ADVANCED PHASERS

The *U.S.S. Equinox* may have been relatively lightly armed, but it was fitted with the most advanced form of phasers available to Starfleet. These type-Xb phasers were an advance on the type-X phasers in use on *Galaxy*- and *Intrepid*-class starships. This improved design had a new hot-standby feature, where a low-power pulse was constantly running through the central EPS conduits. The design of the type-X phaser had been further refined by the time the *Prometheus* class was being tested. This class of ship was fitted with type-Xc phasers, in which the hot-standby filament was exposed to space and ran at a higher power level.

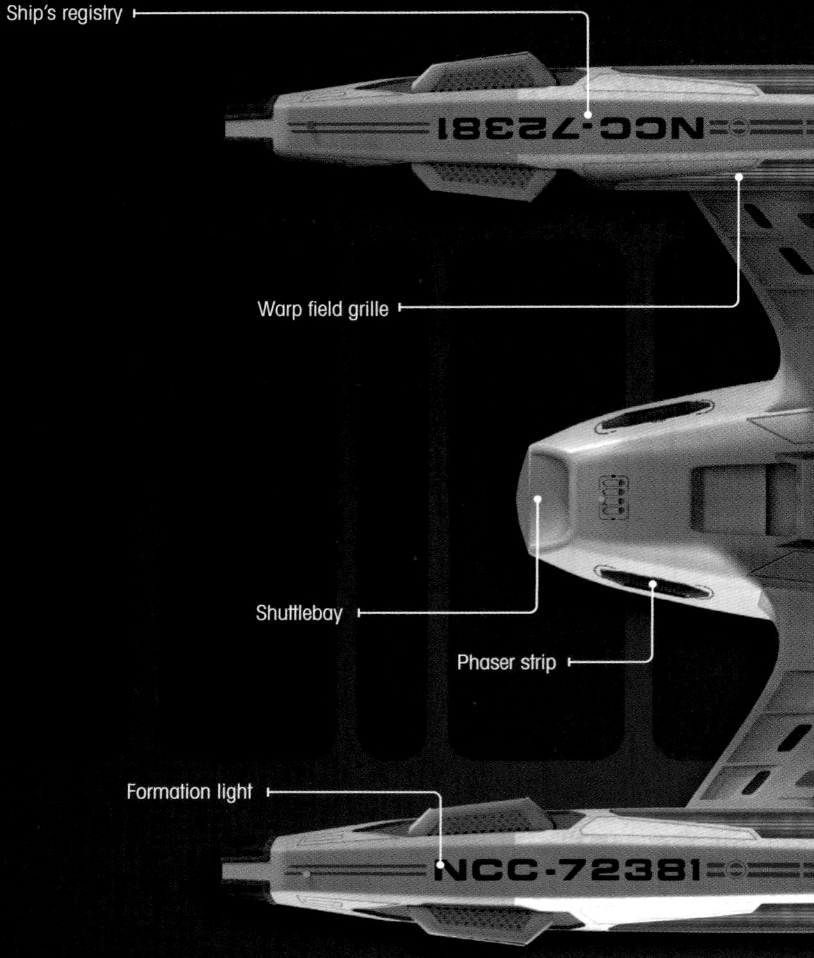

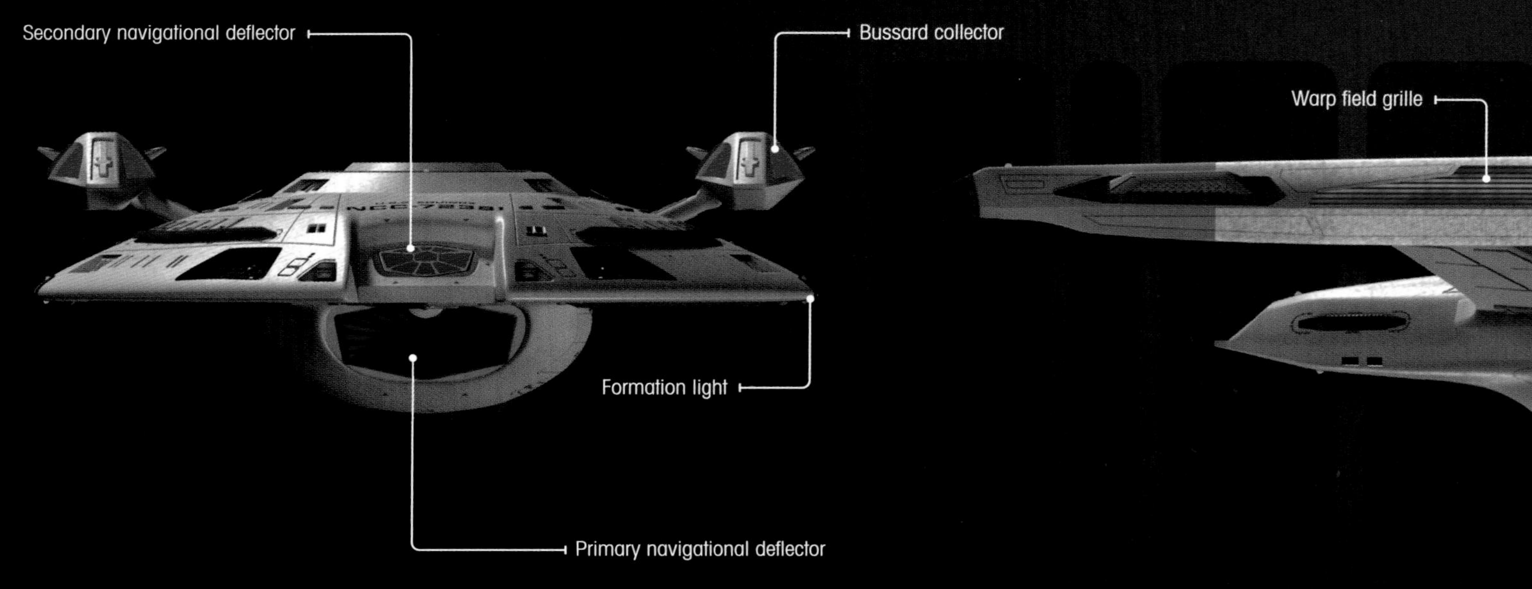

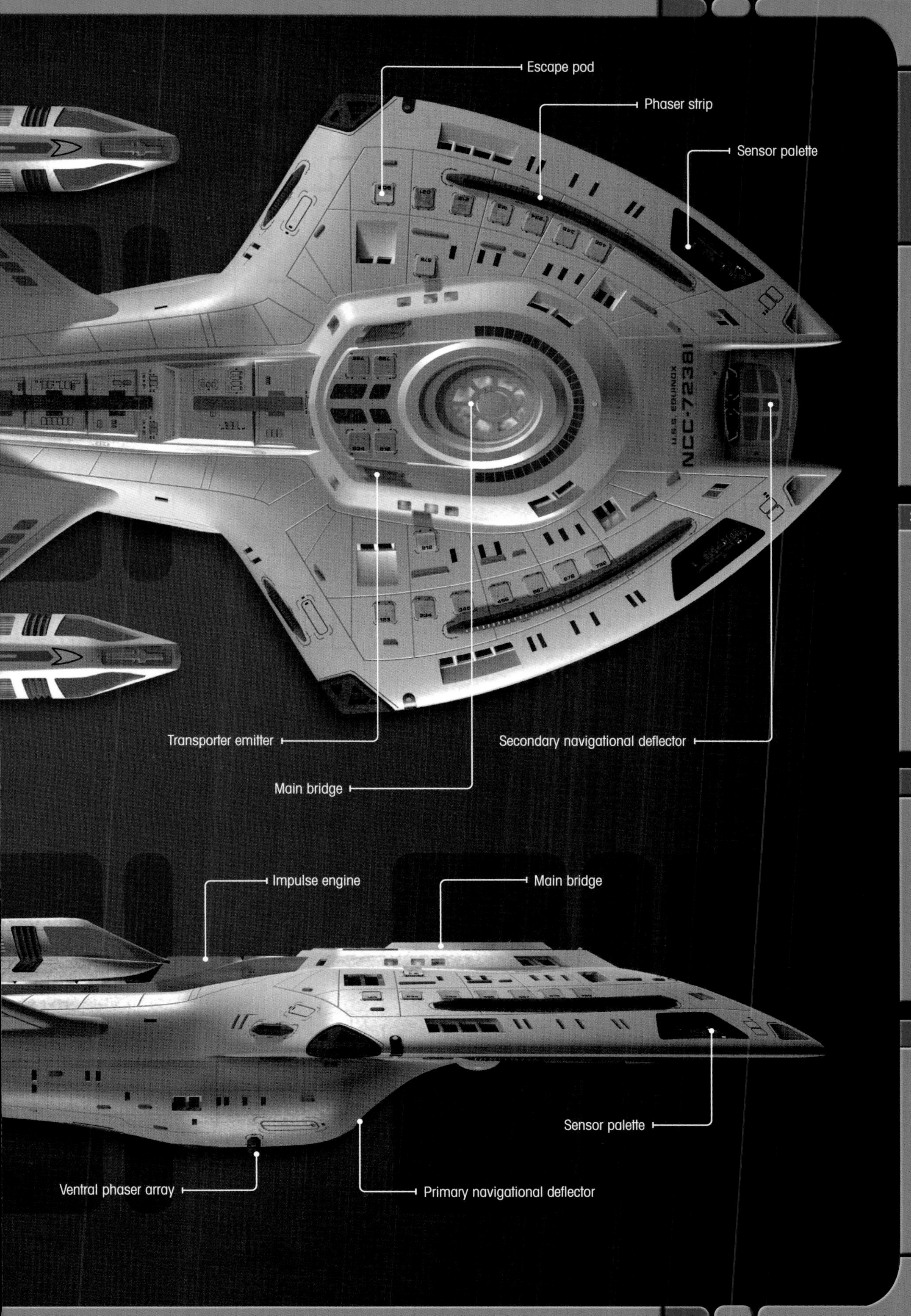

SICKBAY

The majority of the experiments on the nucleogenic life-forms were carried out in the *Equinox's* sickbay on deck 4 and were performed by the ship's EMH. He only cooperated after Ransom deleted his ethical subroutines.

SHIELD MODIFICATION

The *Equinox* crew were able to defend themselves from the alien attacks by establishing a network of multiphasic force fields around the ship. This prevented the aliens moving in and out of normal space.

WAVERIDER

The *Waverider* shuttle was an auxiliary craft docked to the underside of the saucer and accessed from deck 4. Designed for medium-range missions, it was larger and more comfortable than a standard shuttle.

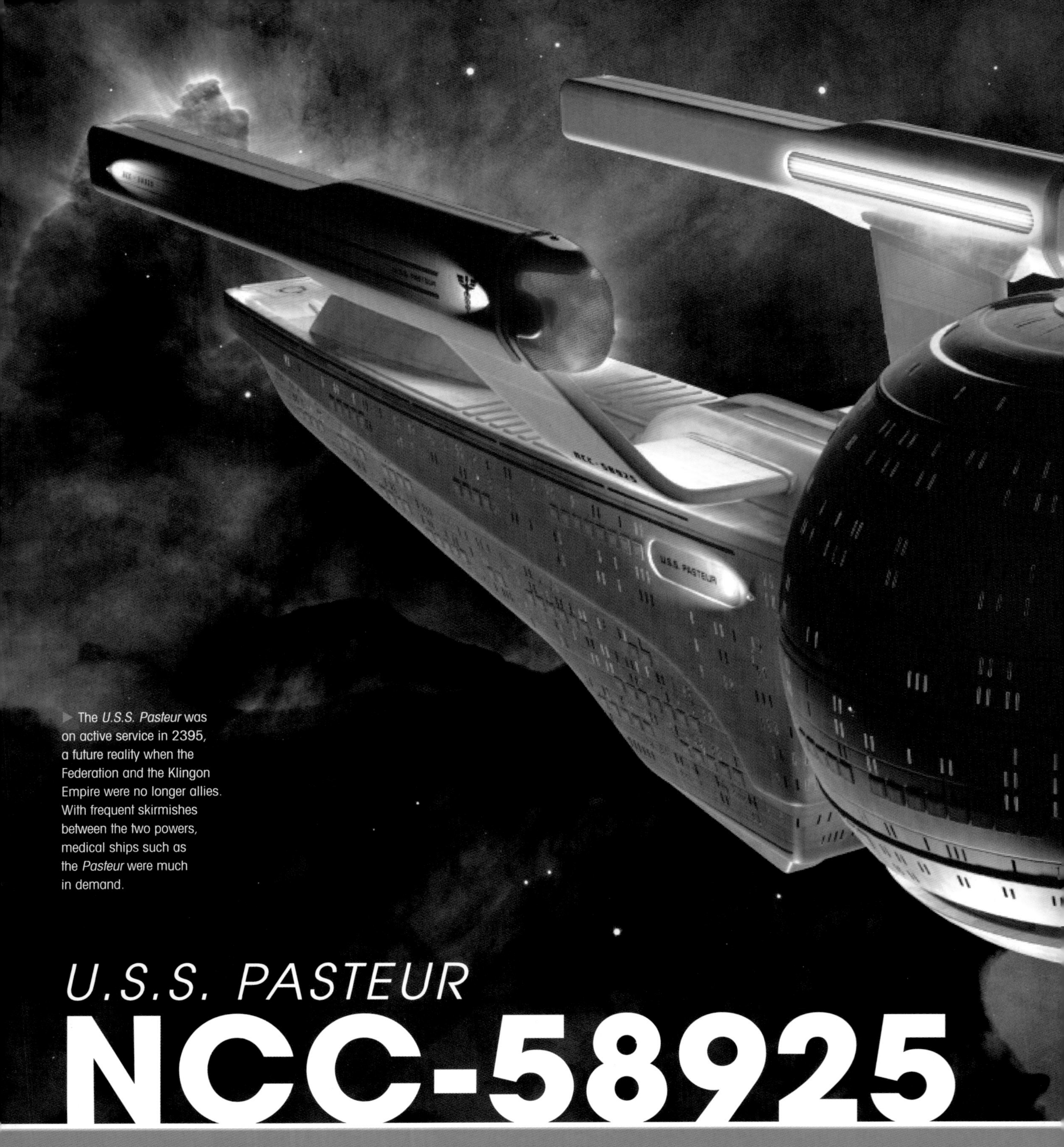

▶ The *U.S.S. Pasteur* was on active service in 2395, a future reality when the Federation and the Klingon Empire were no longer allies. With frequent skirmishes between the two powers, medical ships such as the *Pasteur* were much in demand.

U.S.S. PASTEUR NCC-58925

A medical ship from an alternate future, the *U.S.S. Pasteur* was commaned by Dr. Beverly Picard.

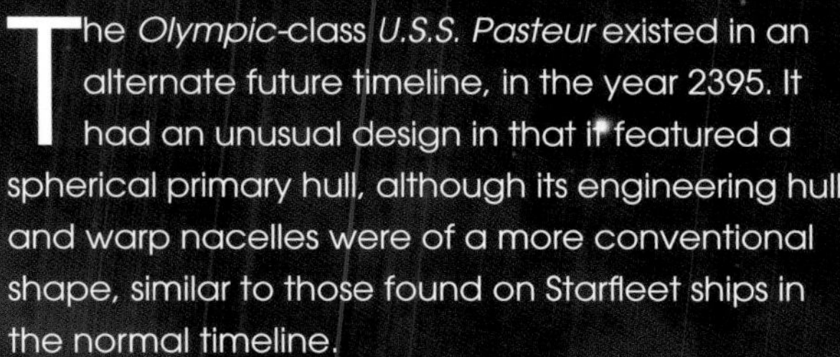

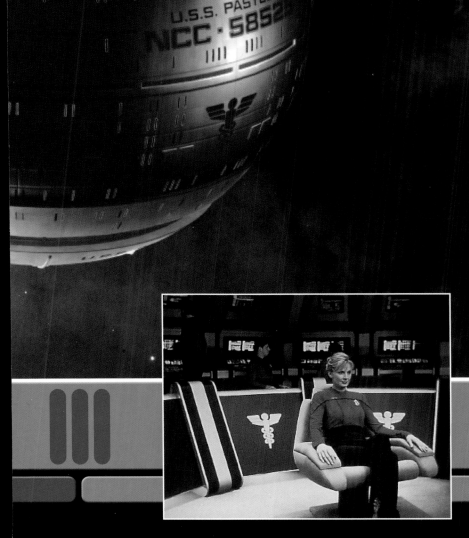

The *Olympic*-class *U.S.S. Pasteur* existed in an alternate future timeline, in the year 2395. It had an unusual design in that it featured a spherical primary hull, although its engineering hull and warp nacelles were of a more conventional shape, similar to those found on Starfleet ships in the normal timeline.

The *Pasteur*'s other distinctive features included a deflector strip, rather than a deflector dish, and a shuttlebay located in a large structure on top of the flat secondary hull.

The *Pasteur* was a purpose-built hospital ship and featured the caduceus, an ancient symbol of medical practice, prominently displayed on its hull in several places, clearly indicating its status as a medical ship. As such, it was designed to deal with medical emergencies rather than exploration or combat missions, and it had several transporter rooms to cope with emergency evacuations, as well as numerous sickbays.

LIMITED TACTICAL ABILITIES

The *Pasteur*'s defenses were minimal, and unlike most Starfleet vessels in this alternate timeline, it was not fitted with a cloaking device, while its sensor sweeping range was limited to one light-year. The ship could, however, travel as fast as warp 13, meaning that in this timeline, warp speeds had once again been redefined.

The interior design was simple and sparse. On the bridge, the caduceus appeared on the front of the control console pedestals. Just off the bridge was Captain (and Dr.) Beverly Picard's ready room, which also doubled as a place for staff meetings.

In the alternate future, Dr. Beverly Picard agreed to take Jean-Luc Picard to the Devron system aboard the *Pasteur,* after he became convinced that there was a spatial anomaly there that

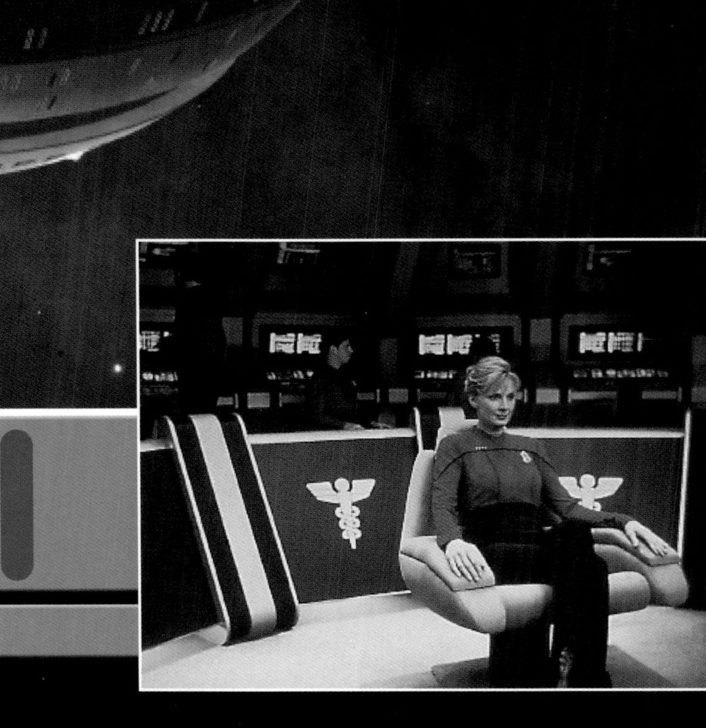

◀ The *Pasteur* was under the command of Captain Beverly Picard, who in this timeline was the ex-wife of Jean-Luc Picard. It was clear that the pair had divorced some years before, but there was still a great deal of affection between the couple and she agreed to help him find the spatial anomaly he was looking for, despite the potential danger.

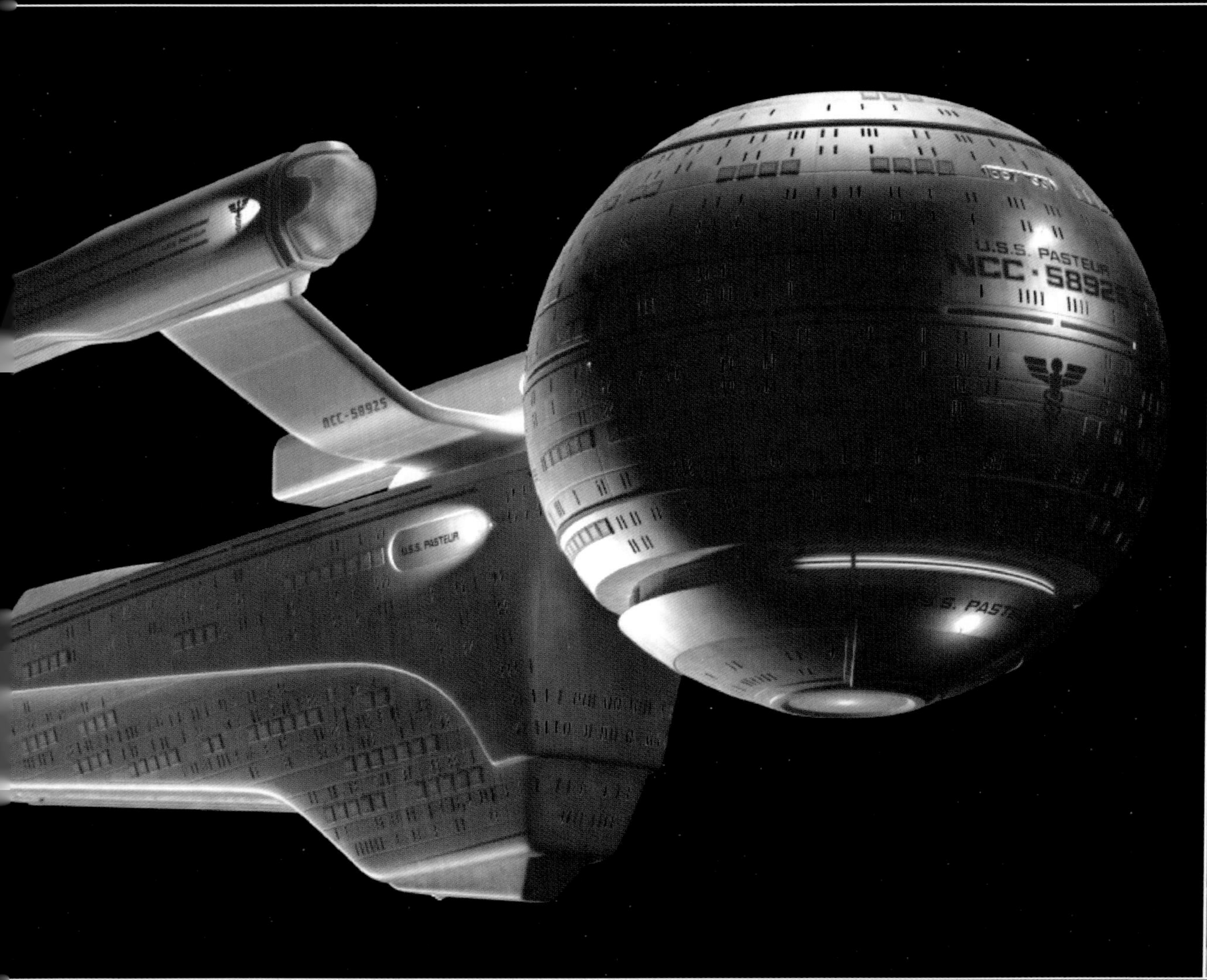

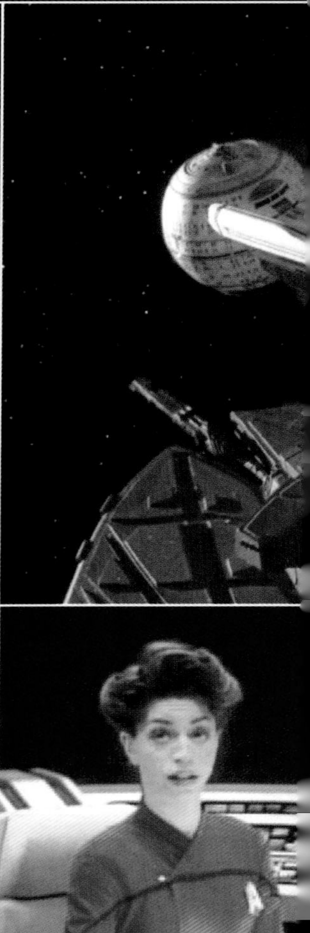

▲ *Olympic*-class vessels, such as the *Pasteur*, were easily identified by their spherical primary hull. The majority of the interior was given over to sickbays and medical labs, showing they were equipped to deal with considerable numbers of casualties.

threatened the very existence of the universe. In the normal timeline, this star system was in the Romulan Neutral Zone, but in the alternate future the Klingons had taken over the Romulan Star Empire. Consequently, this region of space had now become a no-go area for Federation ships, as the Klingons had closed their borders.

The exception to this rule was that medical ships had been granted permission to cross the border to help the Romulans fight off an outbreak of the Terrellian plague. Dr. Picard was far from convinced that her ex-husband was correct about the existence of the spatial anomaly because he was suffering from Irumodic Syndrome, a rare neurological condition similar to Alzheimer's disease. She nevertheless agreed to take him, even though she believed that entering Klingon territory was "insane." Once they were given clearance to cross the border by Worf, who insisted on going with them, Beverly ordered the ship to proceed to the Devron system at warp 13.

This mission was particularly dangerous for a ship such as the *Pasteur*, as it was only lightly armed with phasers and did not appear to carry photon torpedoes. In addition, its shields were not particularly strong and Beverly Picard knew that they would not last long in a fight if they encountered any Klingon ships. She made it perfectly clear to her ex-husband that they would immediately return to Federation space if they encountered any serious opposition.

Once the *Pasteur* reached the Devron system, a full sensor sweep out to one light-year of their location was initiated, but it did not detect any temporal anomalies. At this point, Worf, who had been monitoring Klingon communication channels, heard that several warships had been dispatched to search for a "renegade Federation vessel."

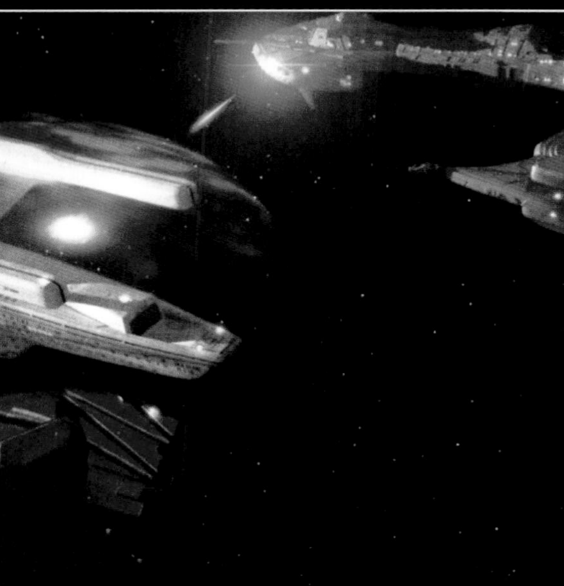

◀ Despite its status as a medical ship, the Klingons attacked the *Pasteur* after it crossed their border. With limited weaponry and very few defensive systems, the *Pasteur* was an easy target for the much more powerful Klingon attack cruisers.

▶ At one point, Q showed Jean-Luc Picard a future reality in which the *Pasteur* was destroyed by the Klingons, but the senior staff beamed to safety on the *Enterprise*-D.

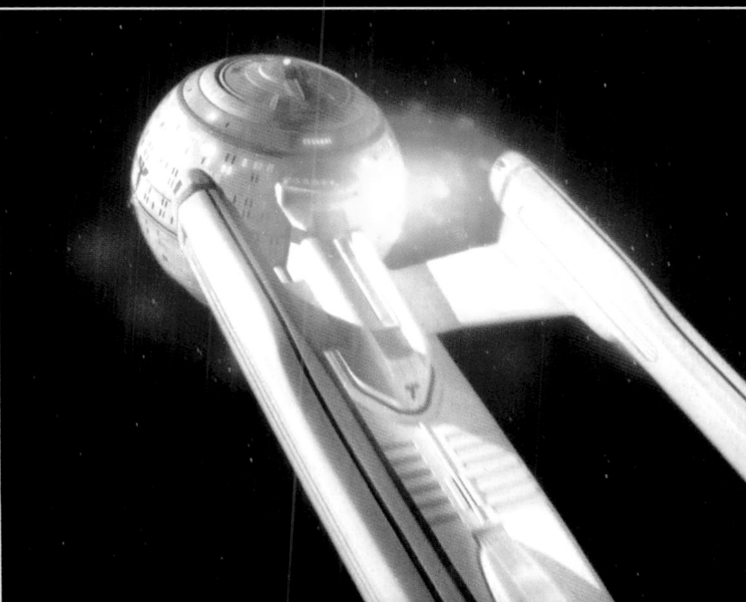

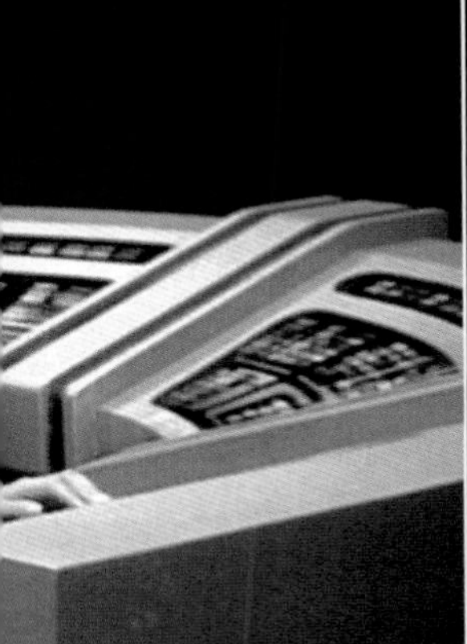

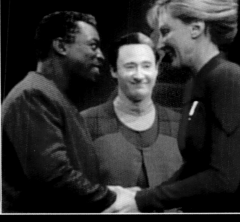

◀ Ensign Nell Chilton was the flight controller on board the *Pasteur*. She was killed when the ship came under attack from the Klingons.

▶ The *Pasteur* was essentially a traveling hospital, and was ideally suited to that task, but it lacked some of the sensor and tactical abilities of other ships.

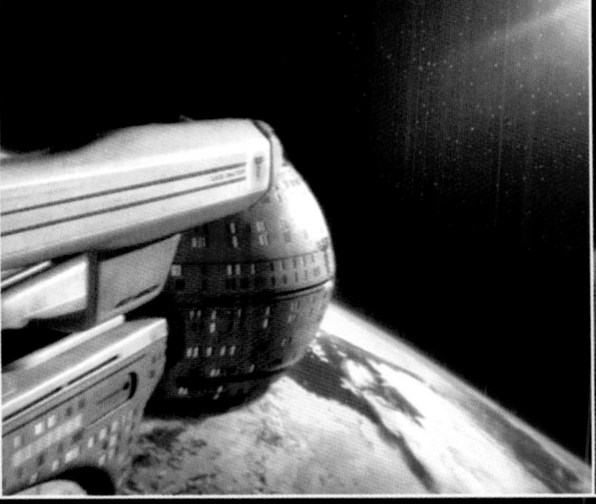

Beverly wanted to leave before the Klingon ships arrived. But Jean-Luc persuaded her to stay a little longer while Data modified the main deflector to increase the limited sensor equipment of the *Pasteur*, so it could scan beyond the subspace barrier.

UNDER ATTACK

Unfortunately, before they could complete the sensor sweep, two Klingon attack cruisers decloaked and attacked the *Pasteur*. In the first volley of disruptor fire, the *Pasteur*'s shield strength was nearly halved and warp power was knocked offline. Its phasers were not powerful enough to penetrate the Klingon ships' shields and in the following wave of attacks, the *Pasteur*'s own shields collapsed, while helm officer Nell Chilton was killed when her console exploded. It looked as if the entire crew would suffer the same fate, when the *U.S.S. Enterprise* NCC-1701-D suddenly arrived and launched a furious volley of phaser fire and torpedoes, which destroyed one Klingon ship and forced the other to retreat. This gave the *Enterprise*-D just enough time to beam the crew of the *Pasteur* aboard before the medical ship's warp core breached, blowing it to smithereens.

▲ Dr. Beverly Picard was delighted to welcome Geordi La Forge and Data aboard her ship. They had all agreed to take Jean-Luc Picard to the Devron system to search for a spatial anomaly.

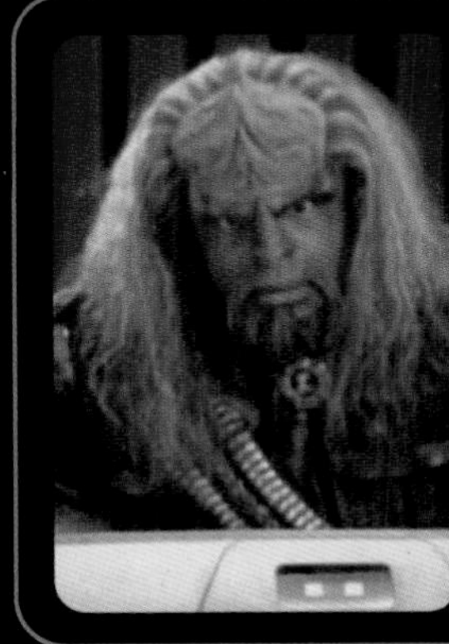

DATA FEED

In the alternate future, Worf was no longer on the Klingon High Council because the House of Mogh had been forced from power. Instead, he was now governor of H'atoria, a small Klingon colony near the border with the Federation. Although this position was largely ceremonial, Worf still had enough influence to grant permission for the *Pasteur* to enter Klingon territory. Also in this future, Will Riker had become an admiral and chosen the refitted *U.S.S. Enterprise* NCC-1701-D as his flagship.

INTERNAL CONFIGURATION

The bridge of the *U.S.S. Pasteur* NCC-58925 was much more compact than those found on other Starfleet vessels. Nevertheless, it conformed to a similar configuration, with the captain's chair in the middle, surrounded by other work consoles, such as the science station, built into the walls of the room. The flight controller sat alone at a large, semicircular workstation at the front of the bridge.

In addition to sickbays and medical labs, the internal layout of the *Pasteur* featured at least two transporter rooms, which could be used for emergency evacuations, and crew quarters located on deck 5.

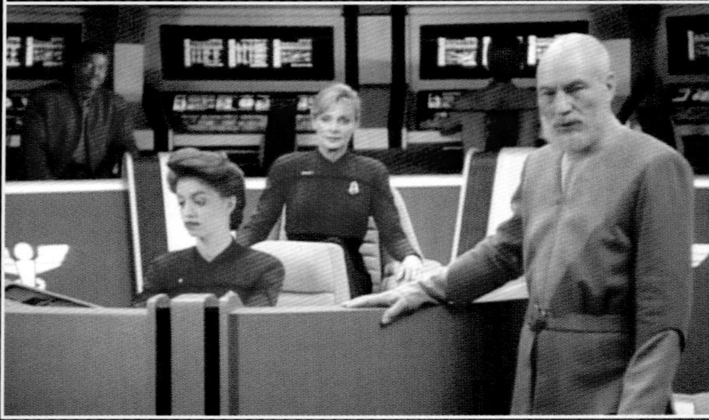

▲ Most of the *Pasteur's* main flight and operational controls could be operated from the semicircular console positioned in front of the captain's chair, facing the main viewscreen.

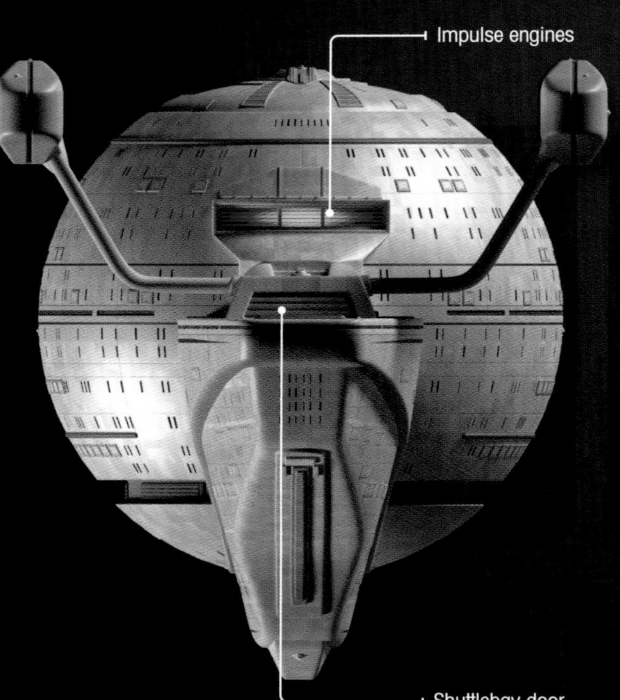

Main bridge

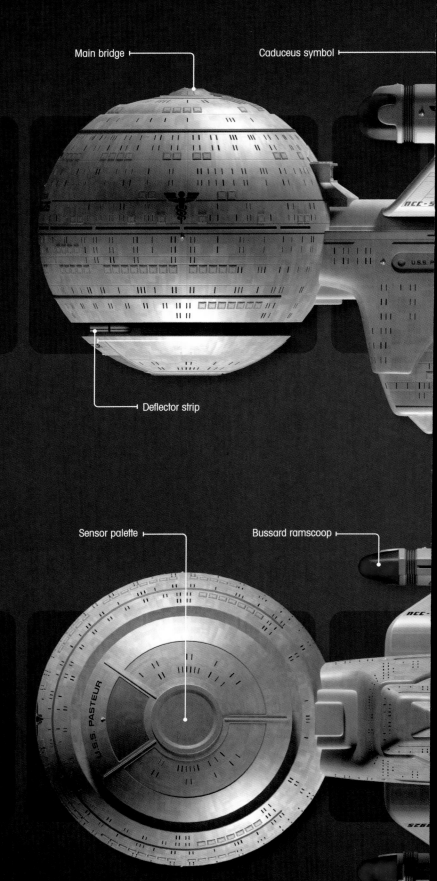

Caduceus symbol

Deflector strip

Sensor palette

Bussard ramscoop

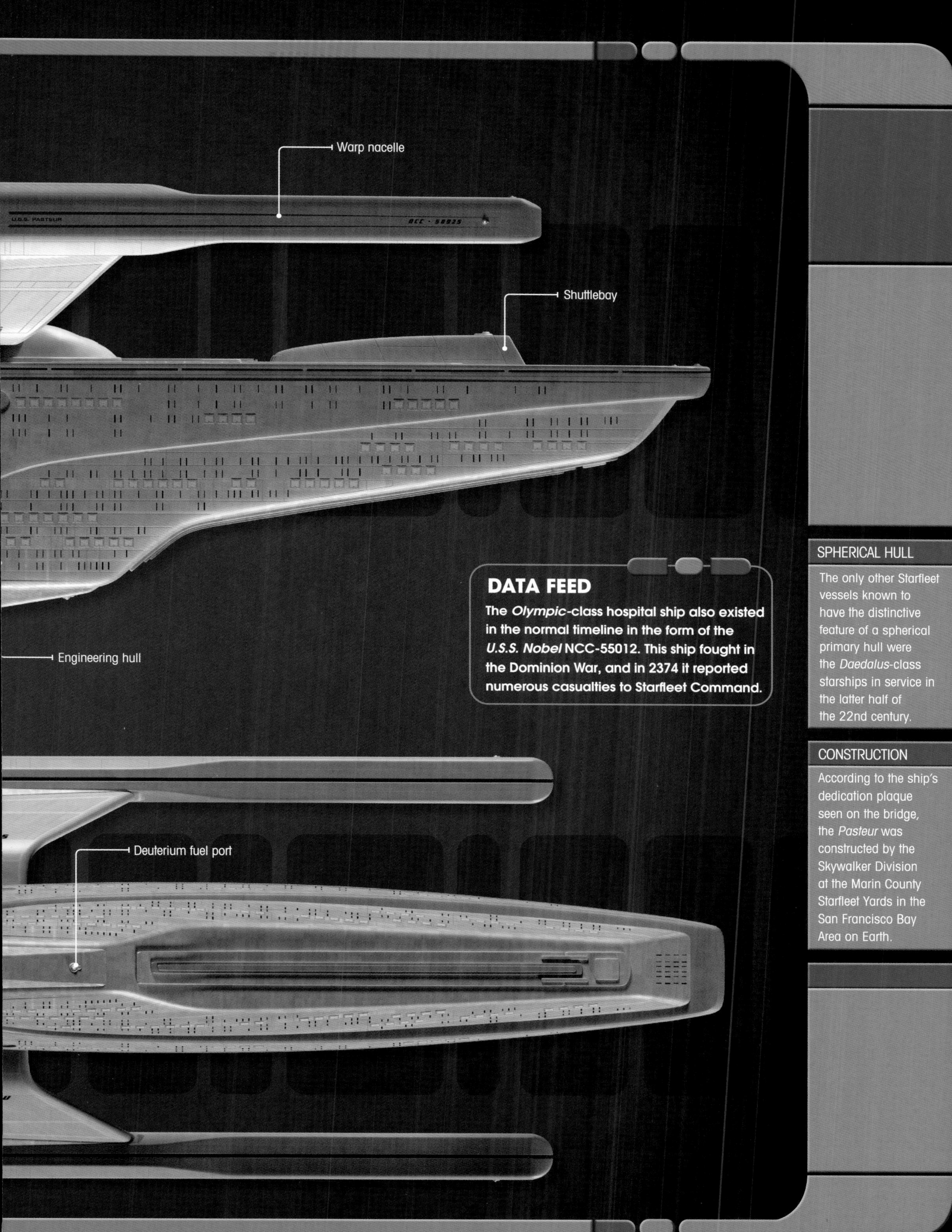

DATA FEED

The *Olympic*-class hospital ship also existed in the normal timeline in the form of the *U.S.S. Nobel* NCC-55012. This ship fought in the Dominion War, and in 2374 it reported numerous casualties to Starfleet Command.

SPHERICAL HULL

The only other Starfleet vessels known to have the distinctive feature of a spherical primary hull were the *Daedalus*-class starships in service in the latter half of the 22nd century.

CONSTRUCTION

According to the ship's dedication plaque seen on the bridge, the *Pasteur* was constructed by the Skywalker Division at the Marin County Starfleet Yards in the San Francisco Bay Area on Earth.

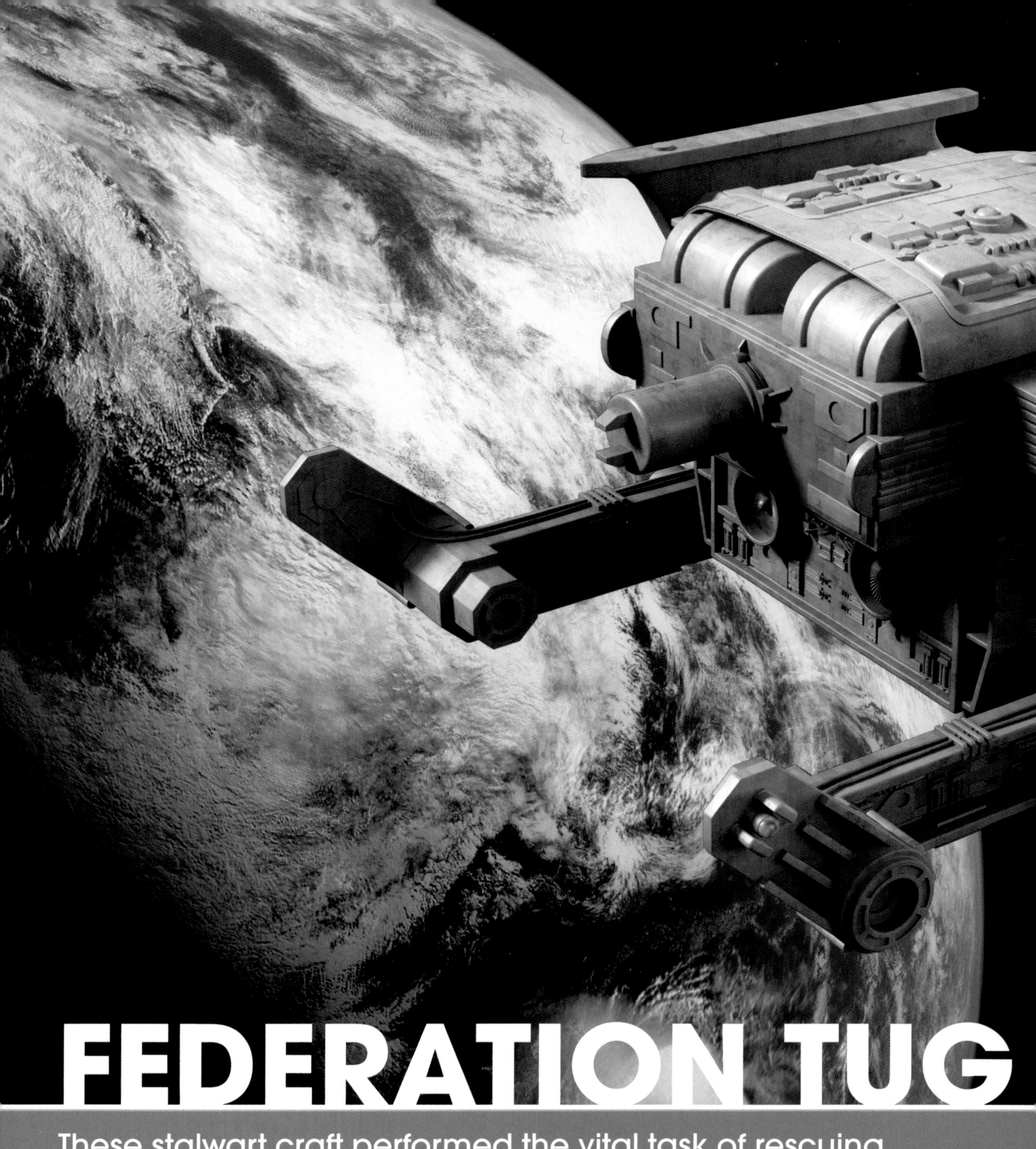

FEDERATION TUG

These stalwart craft performed the vital task of rescuing damaged ships so they could be returned to service.

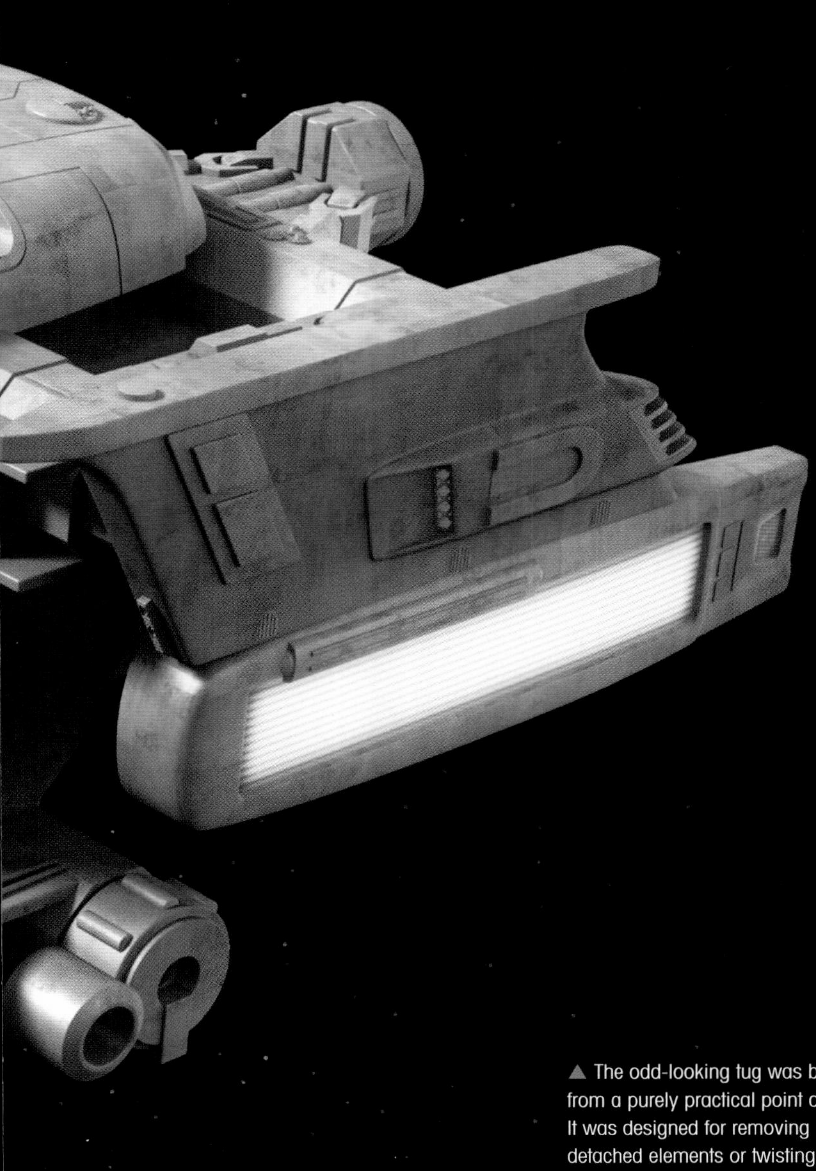

This small, warp-powered ship was designed for towing inoperable or severely damaged starships to a suitable place where they could be restored to full working order. It was used by the Federation and Starfleet in the 24th century, and operated out of starbases and orbital ship-building facilities.

The Federation tug was approximately 90 meters in length, and crewed by a small number of engineering specialists. It could reach low-to-mid warp speeds and was equipped with powerful twin tractor beams capable of towing large vessels over considerable distances. It was also fitted with long mechanical arms that could clamp onto damaged or loose parts and pull them clear, to make a ship safe and ready for towing.

▲ The odd-looking tug was built from a purely practical point of view. It was designed for removing partly detached elements or twisting them back in place with its mechanical arms, to make a stranded ship secure for towing. Its powerful tractor beams could then haul the vessel to safety.

DEEP SPACE RESCUE

A Starfleet ship was able to use its tractor beam to tow another vessel, but normally only at sublight speeds for safety reasons. A specialized Tug could perform the task at warp speeds, meaning it could retrieve a stranded ship that was light years from a starbase. The Tug could also be used to haul large components to space stations, and its repair crew could fit these parts.

In 2364, the *U.S.S. Enterprise* NCC-1701-D requested that a tug be sent to tow the wrecked hulk of the *U.S.S. Stargazer* NCC-2893 back to Xendi Starbase 9 after it had been found adrift by the Ferengi.

Federation tugs were more widely used during the Dominion War when countless ships were disabled by Jem'Hadar forces. In 2374, the *U.S.S. Fredrickson* NCC-42111 was seen being towed away by a tug from a battle zone, after the Second Fleet was forced to retreat in the early weeks of the Dominion War.

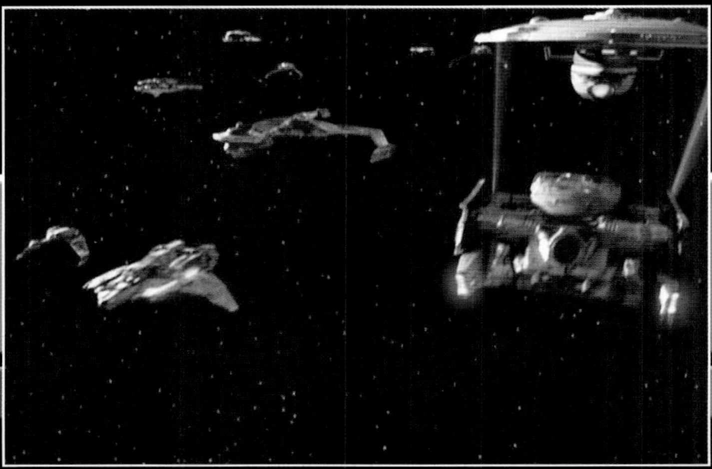

◀ A Federation tug latched onto the saucer section of the *U.S.S. Fredrickson* with two tractor beams and towed it to safety, after the starship had lost propulsion during a battle with Dominion forces. Tugs were worth their weight in gold during the Dominion War, because they could retrieve ships that would otherwise have been lost.

SALVAGING SHIPS

Federation tugs were used so extensively throughout the Dominion War, because it was paramount that Starfleet and its Allies kept starships in working order to fight the might of the Dominion.

For example, the Second Fleet, of which the *U.S.S. Fredrickson* was a part, suffered greatly during the first three months of the war. It was reduced to a third of its original size during these early battles and it was vital to save as many ships as possible. This was the role of Federation tugs, and their invaluable efforts to rescue vessels such as the *Fredrickson* kept Starfleet in the fight at a time when they were suffering one demoralizing defeat after another. Battle-ready ships were in extremely short supply, since Starfleet could not possibly build new ships fast enough to replace those that were lost. It was therefore extremely important to reuse any resources that they had, and thanks to the Federation tugs, very many damaged vessels were saved and repaired to fight another day.

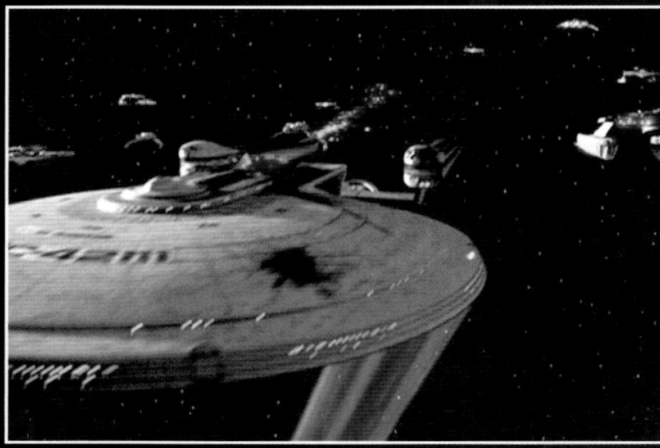

▲ Without the tireless work of the Federation tugs in saving ships, it was very possible that Starfleet might have run out of vessels with which to fight the Dominion during the war's early days.

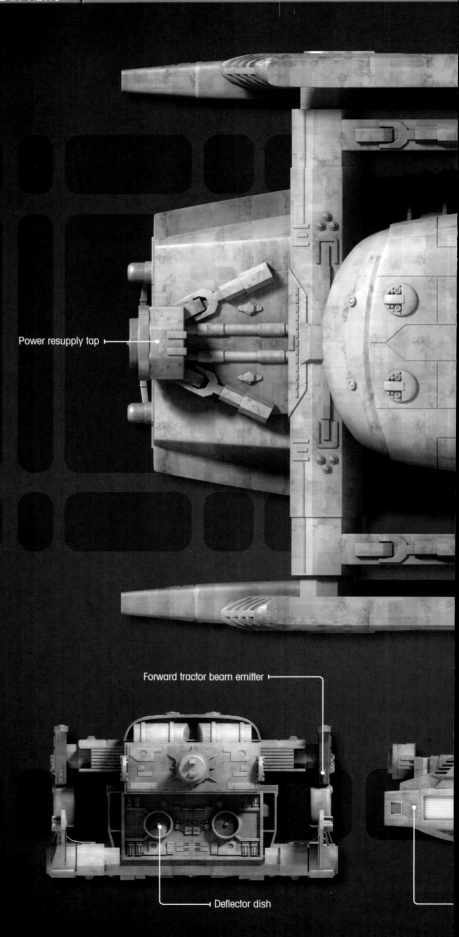

Power resupply tap

Forward tractor beam emitter

Deflector dish

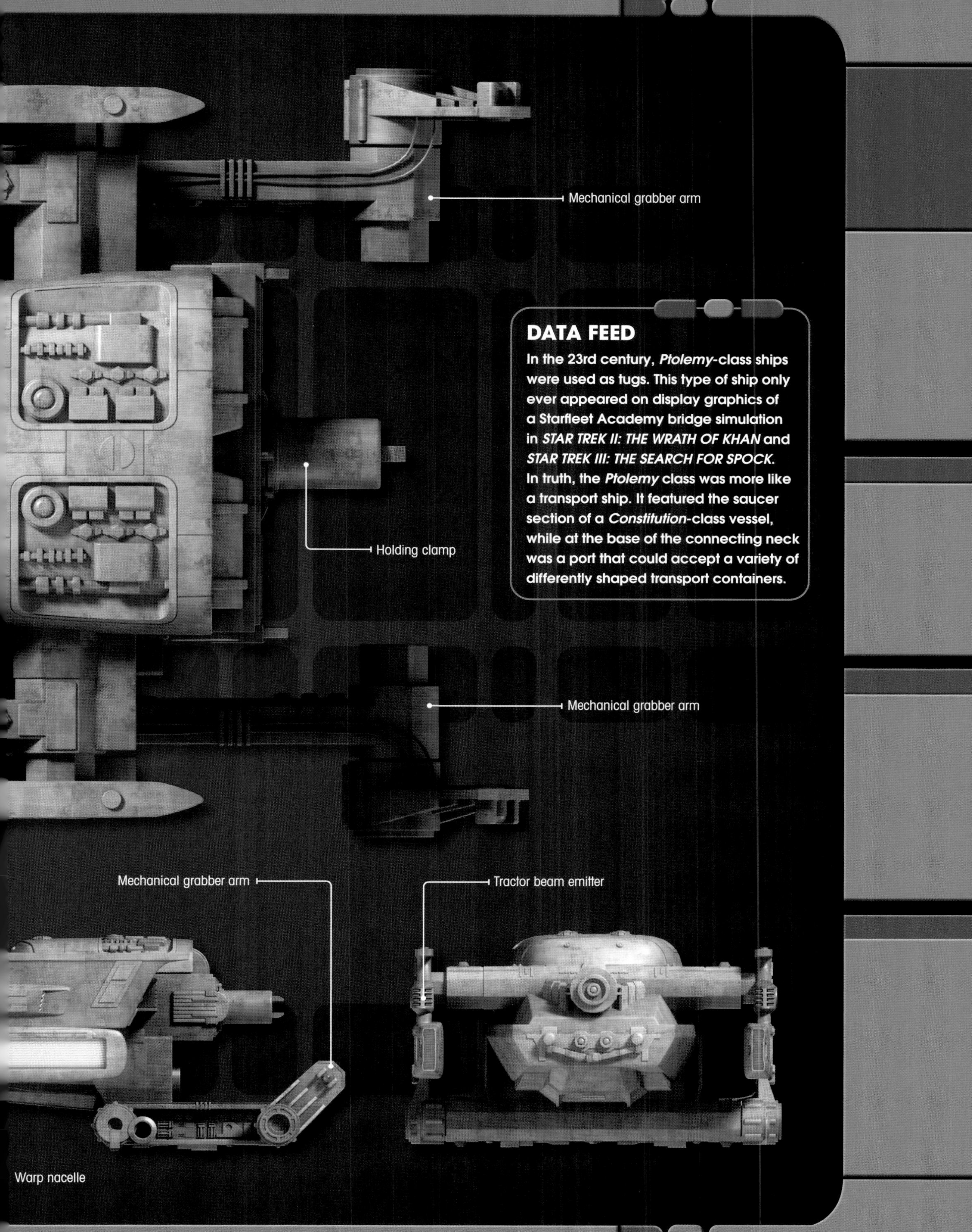

DATA FEED

In the 23rd century, *Ptolemy*-class ships were used as tugs. This type of ship only ever appeared on display graphics of a Starfleet Academy bridge simulation in *STAR TREK II: THE WRATH OF KHAN* and *STAR TREK III: THE SEARCH FOR SPOCK*. In truth, the *Ptolemy* class was more like a transport ship. It featured the saucer section of a *Constitution*-class vessel, while at the base of the connecting neck was a port that could accept a variety of differently shaped transport containers.

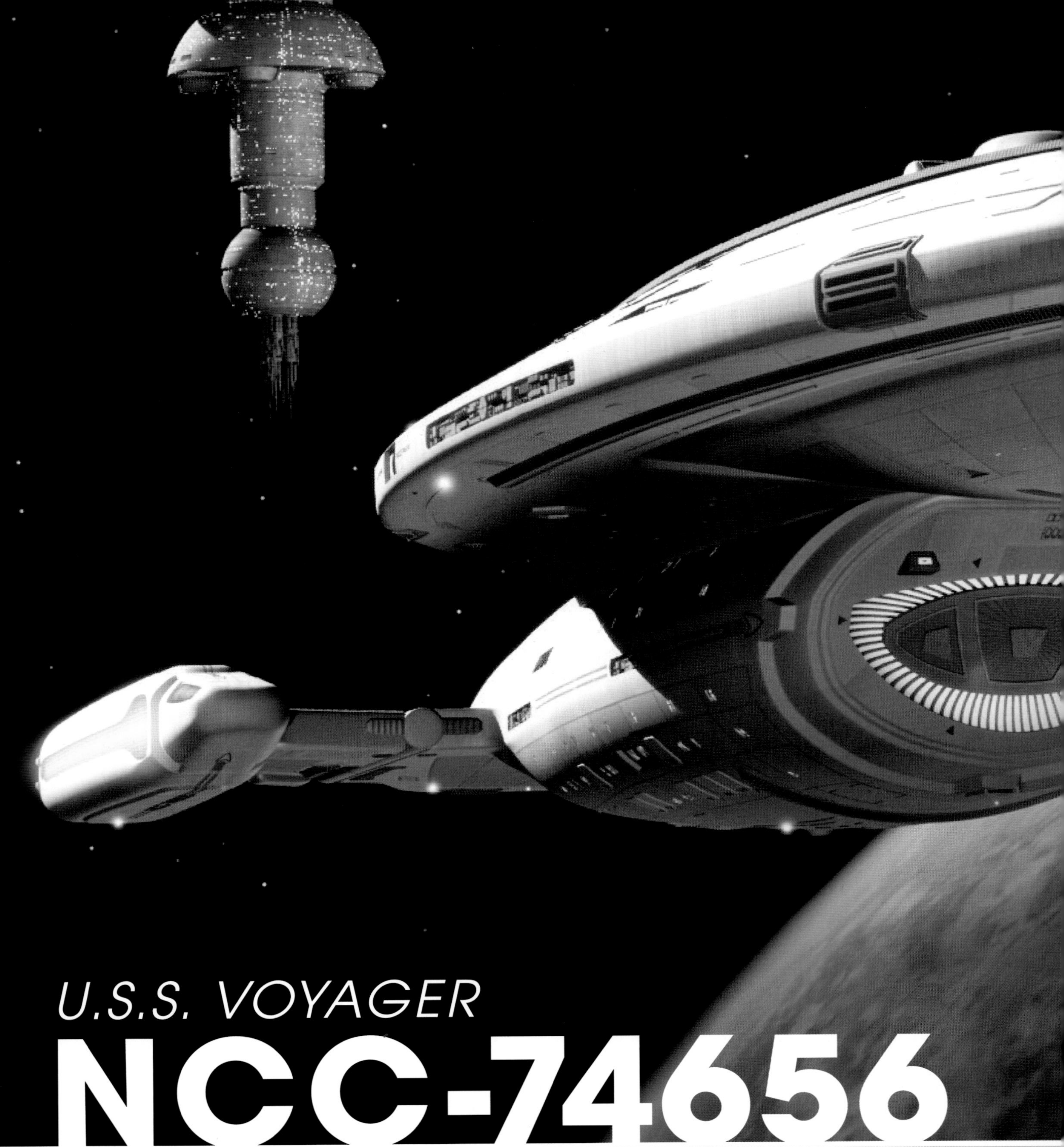

U.S.S. VOYAGER

NCC-74656

After being lost in the Delta Quadrant, 70,000 light-years from Earth, *Voyager* made an epic journey home.

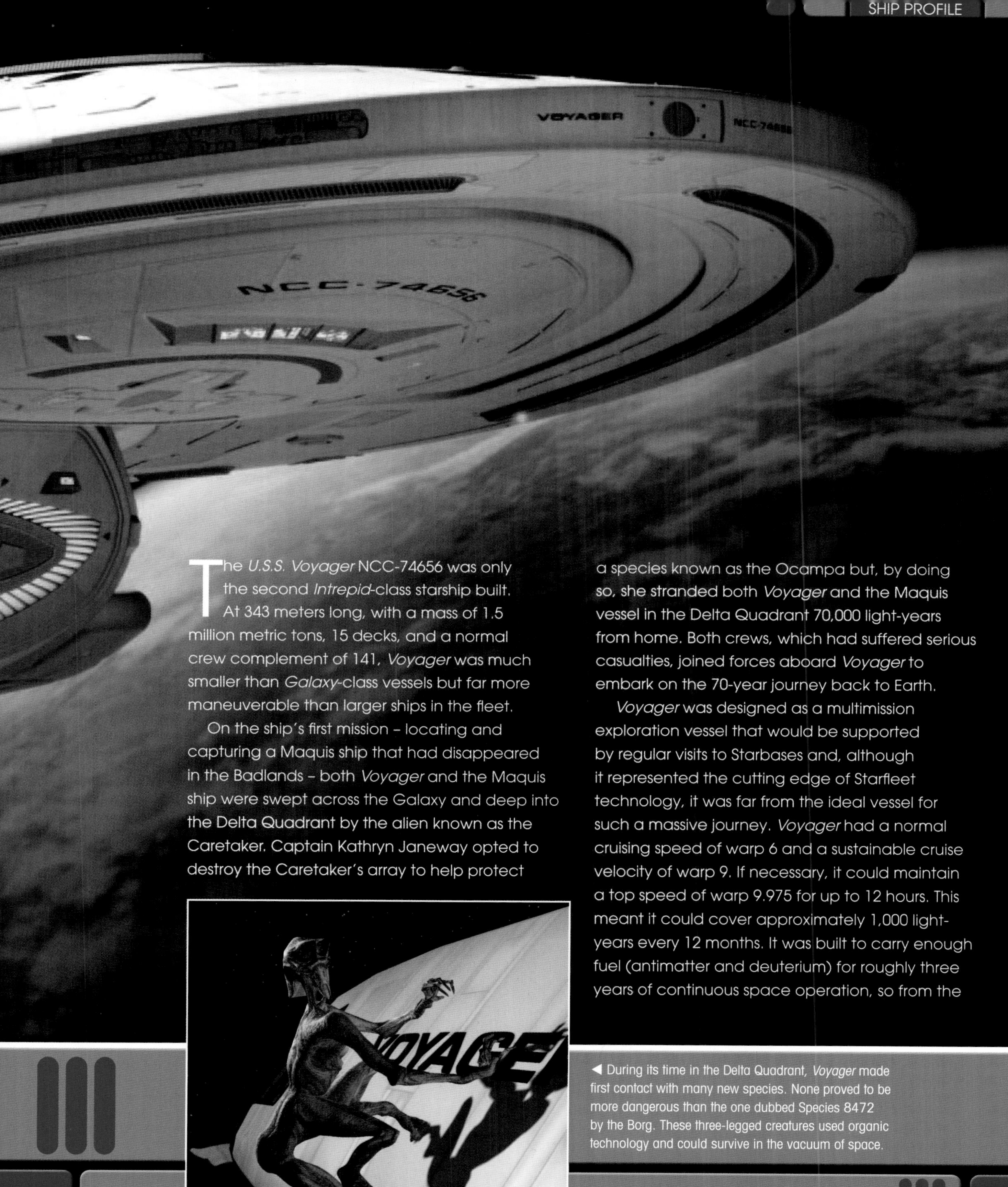

The *U.S.S. Voyager* NCC-74656 was only the second *Intrepid*-class starship built. At 343 meters long, with a mass of 1.5 million metric tons, 15 decks, and a normal crew complement of 141, *Voyager* was much smaller than *Galaxy*-class vessels but far more maneuverable than larger ships in the fleet.

On the ship's first mission – locating and capturing a Maquis ship that had disappeared in the Badlands – both *Voyager* and the Maquis ship were swept across the Galaxy and deep into the Delta Quadrant by the alien known as the Caretaker. Captain Kathryn Janeway opted to destroy the Caretaker's array to help protect a species known as the Ocampa but, by doing so, she stranded both *Voyager* and the Maquis vessel in the Delta Quadrant 70,000 light-years from home. Both crews, which had suffered serious casualties, joined forces aboard *Voyager* to embark on the 70-year journey back to Earth.

Voyager was designed as a multimission exploration vessel that would be supported by regular visits to Starbases and, although it represented the cutting edge of Starfleet technology, it was far from the ideal vessel for such a massive journey. *Voyager* had a normal cruising speed of warp 6 and a sustainable cruise velocity of warp 9. If necessary, it could maintain a top speed of warp 9.975 for up to 12 hours. This meant it could cover approximately 1,000 light-years every 12 months. It was built to carry enough fuel (antimatter and deuterium) for roughly three years of continuous space operation, so from the

◄ During its time in the Delta Quadrant, *Voyager* made first contact with many new species. None proved to be more dangerous than the one dubbed Species 8472 by the Borg. These three-legged creatures used organic technology and could survive in the vacuum of space.

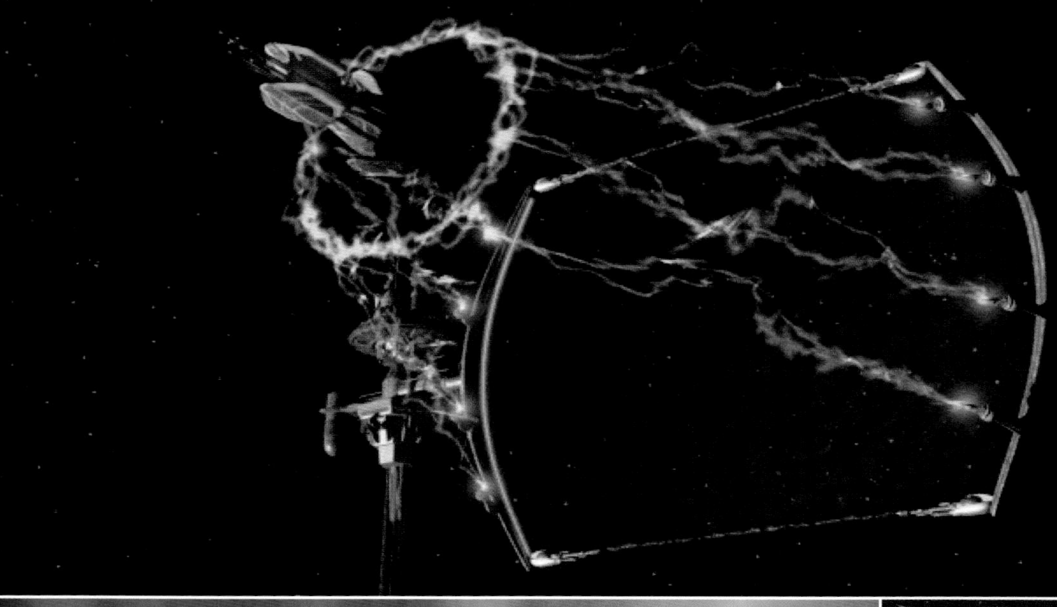

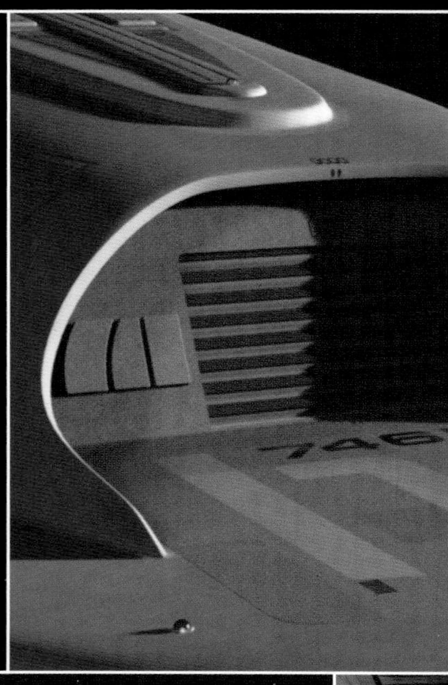

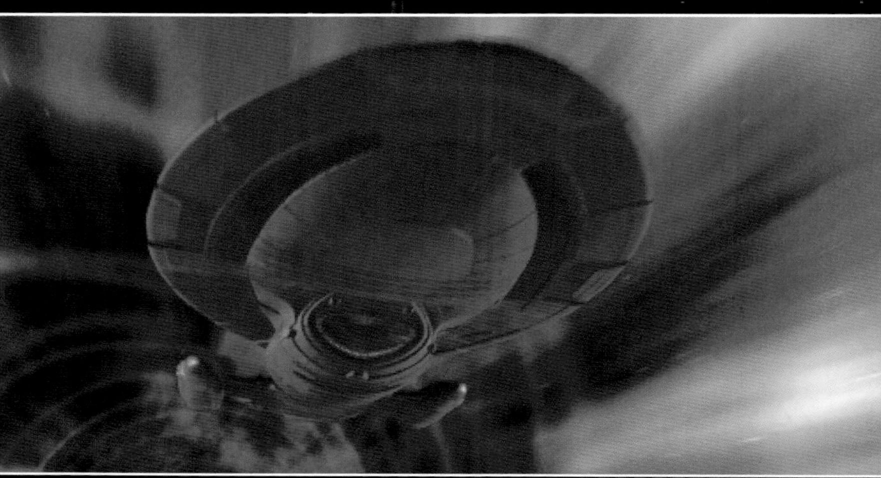

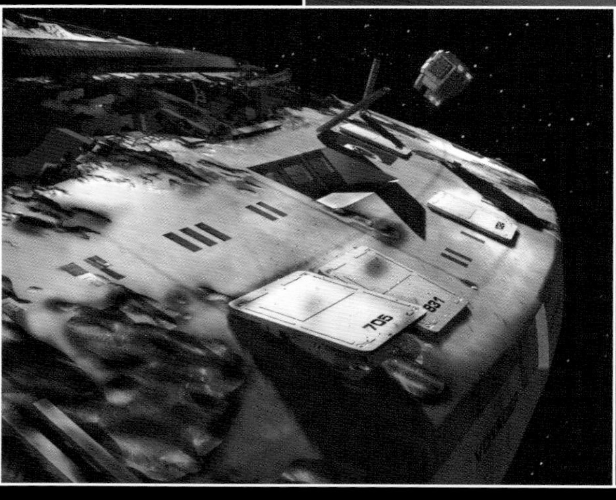

▲ *Voyager* adopted a number of advanced technologies to make the 70,000 light-year journey to Earth in a relatively short time. They used a graviton catapult to cut three years off the journey and completed the last leg by means of Borg transwarp conduits.

beginning it was clear that the crew would have to modify their ship for the long journey home.

Systems were rerouted to conserve as much power as possible. In particular, the use of replicators was severely restricted. The captain's private dining room was removed and replaced with a galley that provided the crew with freshly cooked meals using vegetables grown in the hydroponics garden, which had been established in the cargo bays. The mess hall doubled as a reception area for diplomatic events and was also used by crewmembers as a rec room. For further relaxation, they were able to use *Voyager's* two holodecks, albeit on a strictly rationed basis.

Crew quarters were also affected by the modifications. *Voyager* had never been intended to accommodate families, so quarters located on decks 3 to 6 were modified so that crewmembers could have the option of marrying and raising children during the 70 years it would take for them to return to Federation space.

The most serious casualties involved the loss of the ship's entire medical staff. Fortunately, *Voyager's* state-of-the-art sickbay incorporated advanced holographic systems that generated an Emergency Medical Hologram. The EMH, which was programmed with the experience of 47 doctors, was left active and developed an unexpected level of independence.

Unwilling to accept that the journey would take generations, the crew worked on several engine projects using the ship's holodecks for extensive flight simulations. These were vital to the development of the ground-breaking warp 10 engines that were tested on the *Cochrane* shuttle. In 2375, *Voyager* itself was equipped with a quantum slipstream drive, which enabled it to travel 300 light-years closer to Earth within a short

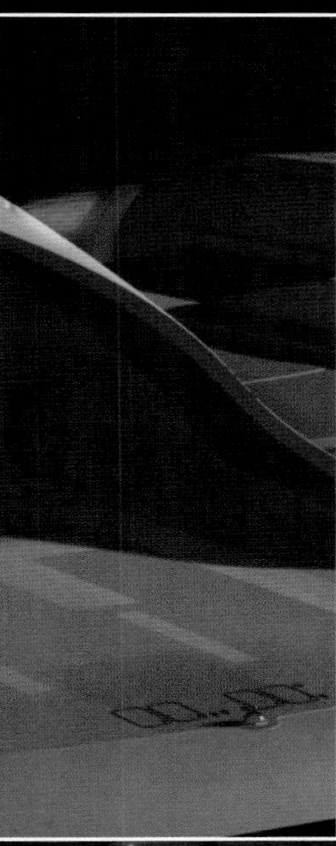

◀ *Voyager's* shuttlebay was located at the rear of the main hull. The ship carried a variety of class-2 and class-6 shuttles, all of which were warp capable. The shuttles were regularly sent on reconnaissance and diplomatic missions.

▶ During the journey home, the crew lost many of their shuttles, but fortunately they had the resources to build new ones. They also built an advanced ship known as the *Delta Flyer* (near right), which incorporated Borg technology provided by Seven of Nine.

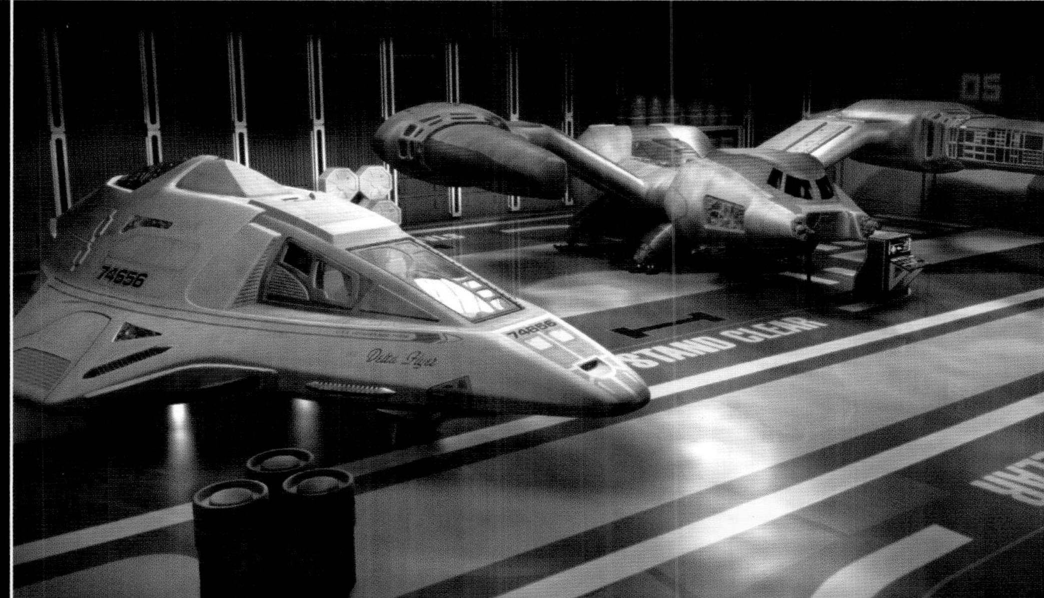

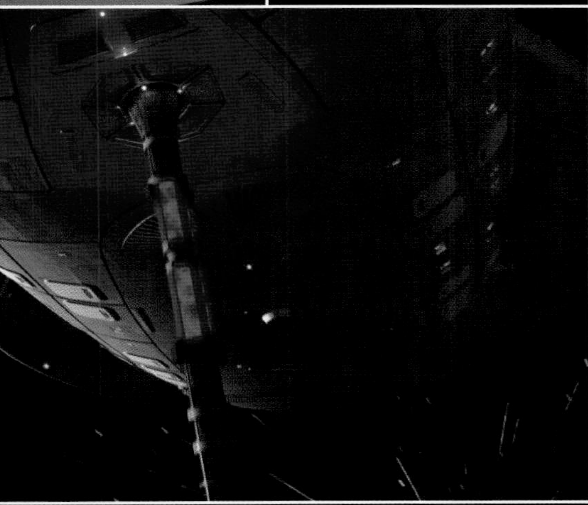

◀ In emergencies, *Voyager* could eject the warp core from a hatch in the underside of the main hull. Assuming the core did not detonate, it could be retrieved, repaired, and reinstalled in the ship.

◀◀ If the ship were lost, the crew could use escape pods housed under small hatches around the hull. Each escape pod had a small engine and enough shielding to allow it to make planetfall.

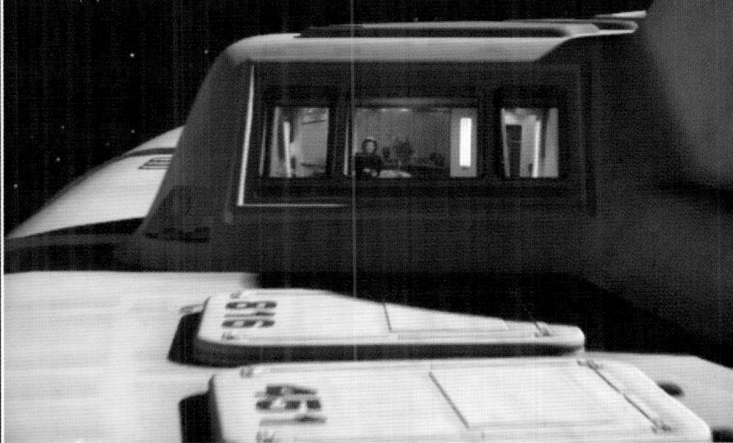

space of time. Both methods of propulsion were, however, ultimately deemed to be too unstable.

The crew also used Borg technology to update *Voyager's* astrometrics laboratory and enhance the ship's navigational sensors. The new astrometric sensors measured the radiative flux of up to three billion stars simultaneously. The upgraded system enabled the crew to plot a new course home that shaved five years off their original projected journey time.

After initially assuming the ship had been lost, Starfleet learned of *Voyager's* fate. A Starfleet project named Pathfinder was quickly put in place, with the aim of making contact with the ship through a Federation communications array known as MIDAS, and via a micro-wormhole and the Hirogen communications network.

From 2377 onward, the crew was able to send and receive orders and instructions from Starfleet, as well as messages to and from their loved ones back home, in the form of monthly data streams. With the help of the Pathfinder project and the use of a Borg transwarp hub whereby vessels could be deployed anywhere in the quadrant within minutes, *Voyager* was finally able to return to Earth a mere seven years after the crew were stranded in the Delta Quadrant.

▲ The Captain's ready room was located on deck 1, to the port of the main bridge. It provided Captain Janeway with a working area where she could perform her administrative duties and talk to crewmembers.

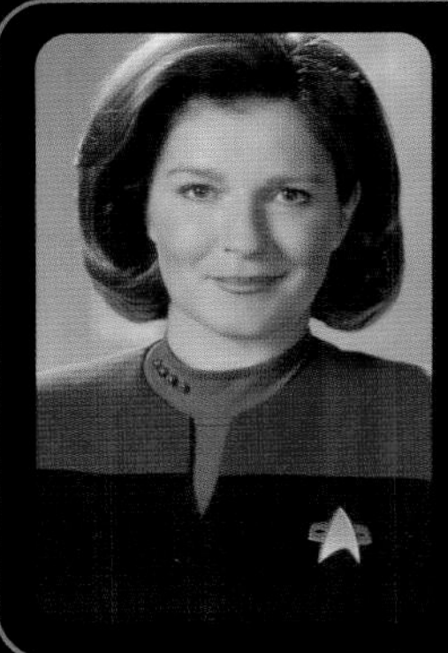

DATA FEED

The *U.S.S. Voyager* was commanded by Captain Kathryn Janeway, who assumed control of the ship as soon as it was launched. The crew was trapped in the Delta Quadrant on the ship's first mission, and she decided it was more important to protect the Ocampa than to get home. Under her command, *Voyager* made the journey to Earth in a tenth of the anticipated time, and on her return she was promoted to Admiral.

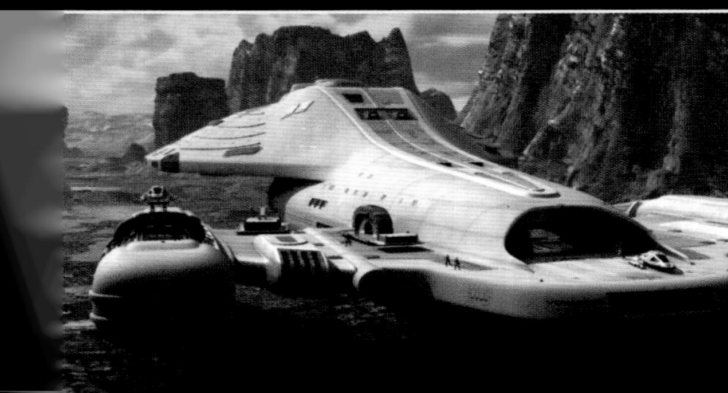

PLANETARY LANDING

Unlike most large Starfleet vessels, *Voyager* was designed to land on a planet's surface. The landing procedure started with the chief engineer taking the warp core offline and venting plasma from the nacelles. The conn officer then brought the landing mechanisms online and set the inertial dampeners and structural integrity fields to maximum. The ops officer monitored for any EM discharges. On the final stage of approach, the four landing struts were deployed and immediately before touchdown, the structural integrity field was adjusted to match planetary gravity. After landing, the engines were disengaged and the thruster exhaust was secured.

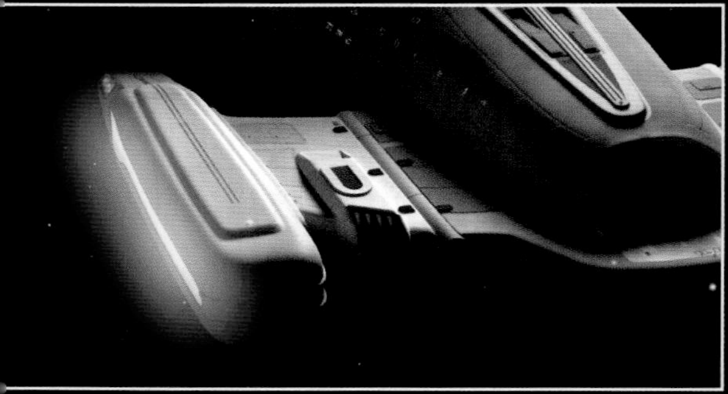

▲ The *U.S.S. Voyager* used variable geometry warp nacelles that swung into position when the ship went to warp. This was part of a redesign that prevented the warp systems from causing permanent damage to the fabric of space.

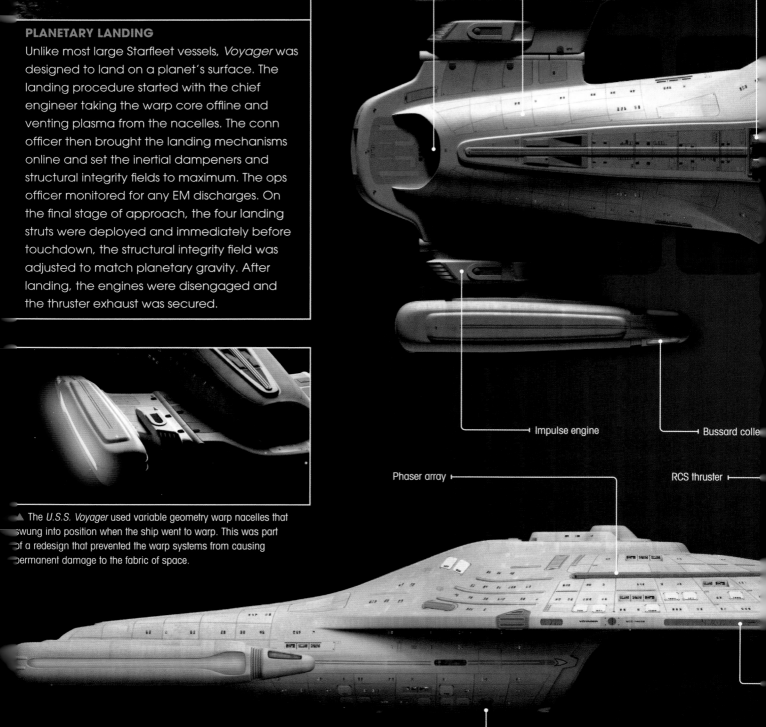

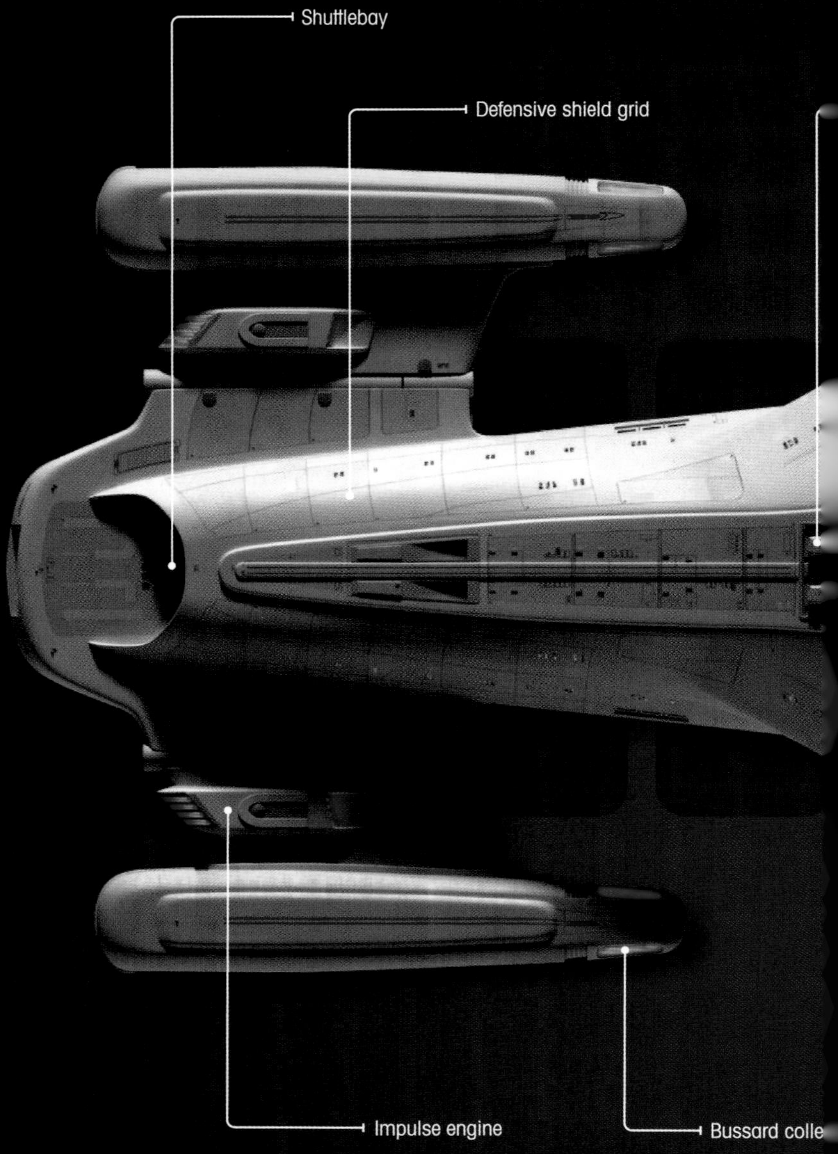

Shuttlebay

Defensive shield grid

Impulse engine

Bussard colle

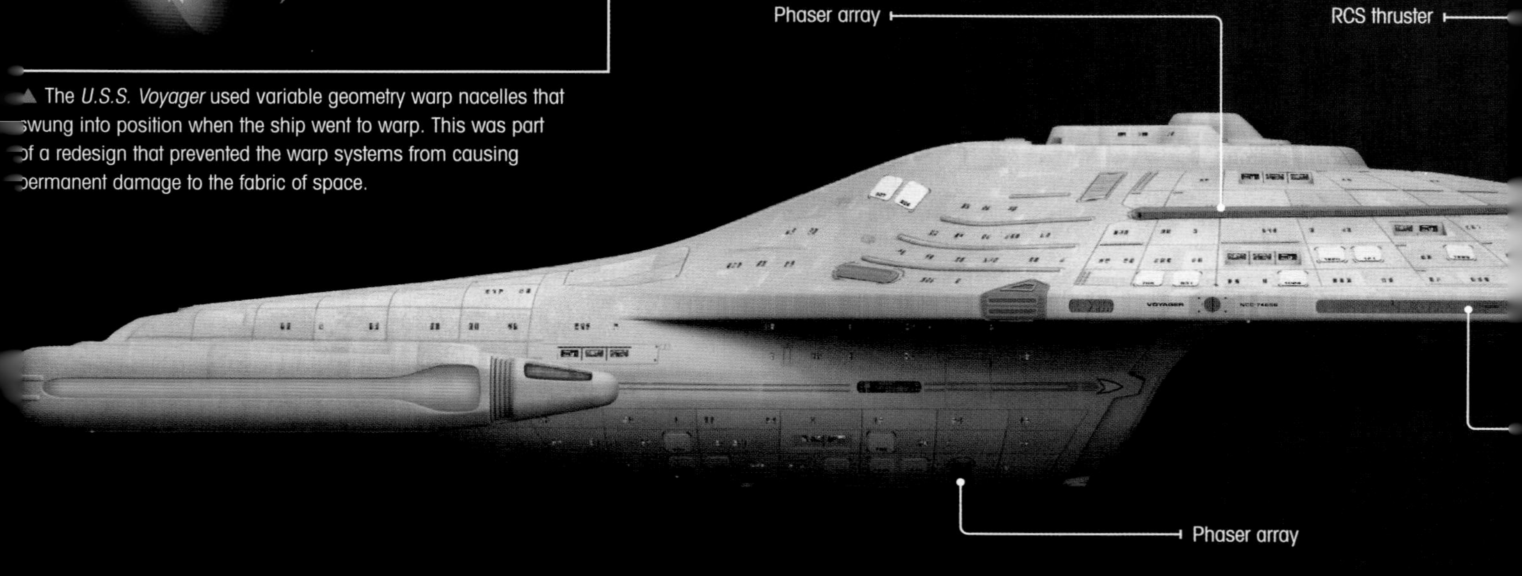

Phaser array

RCS thruster

Phaser array

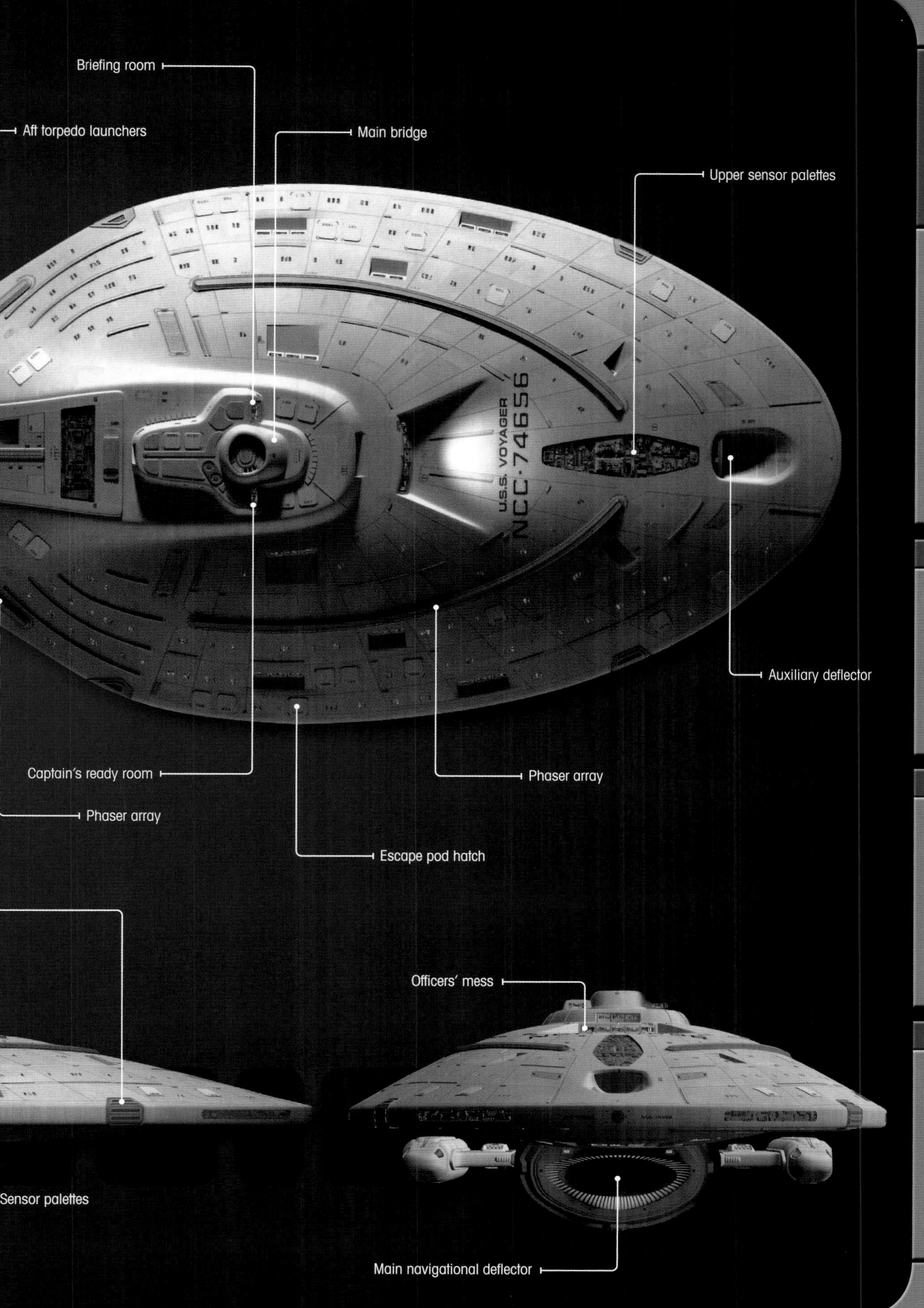

COMPUTERS

Voyager was fitted with state-of-the-art computers that used bio-neural gel packs. These organic components could make extremely fast calculations but were vulnerable to disease.

TORPEDOES

In addition to the regular complement of photon torpedoes, *Voyager* was issued with tricobalt charges, which had a massive explosive yield. Janeway used two of them to destroy the Caretaker's array.

UPGRADES

Voyager completed the journey to Earth with the help of technology that a version of Janeway brought back from the future. The technology included advanced armor and transphasic torpedoes that were a match for the Borg.

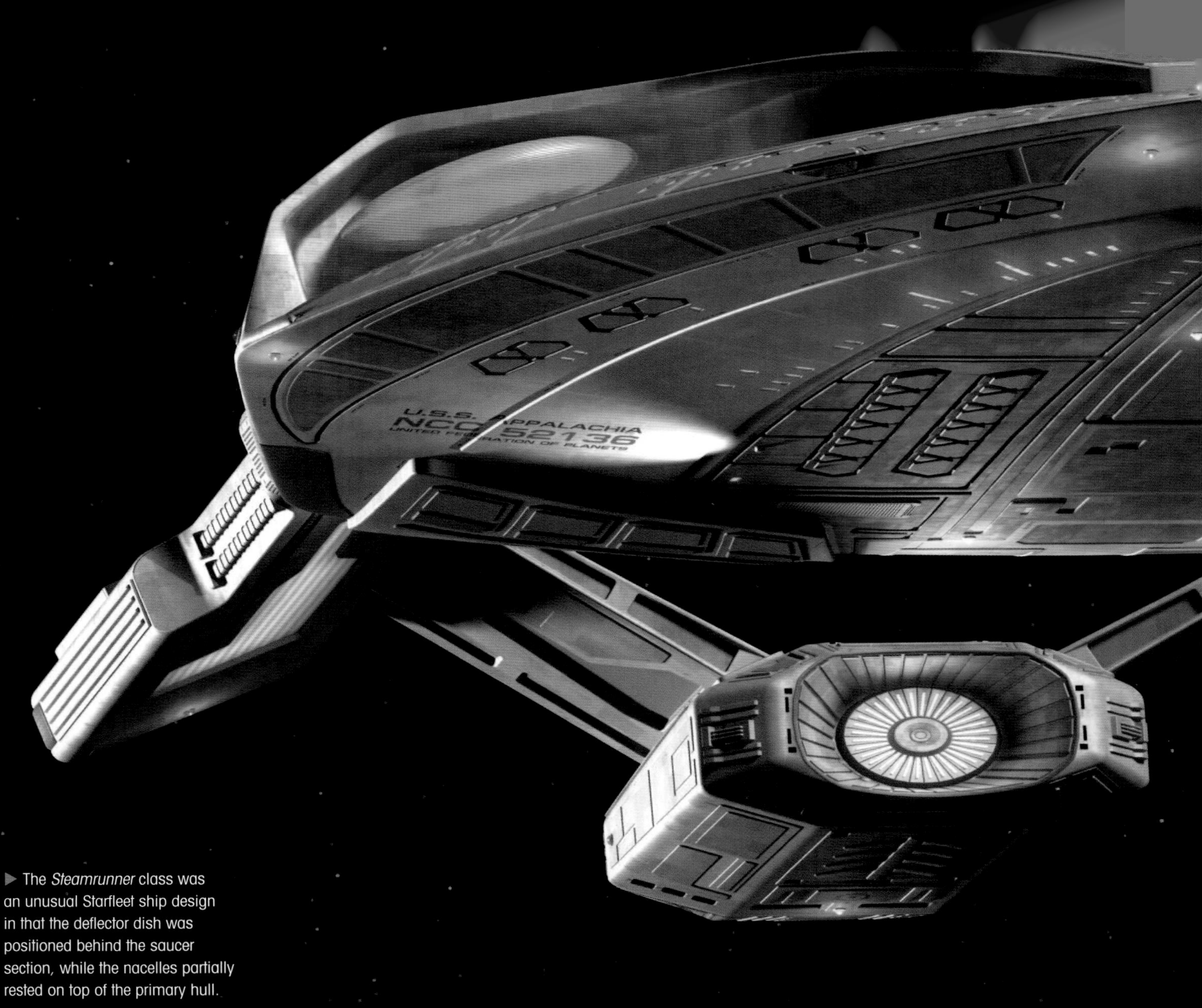

▶ The *Steamrunner* class was an unusual Starfleet ship design in that the deflector dish was positioned behind the saucer section, while the nacelles partially rested on top of the primary hull.

STEAMRUNNER CLASS

This class of ship was involved in crucial battles with the Borg and the Dominion in the late 24th century.

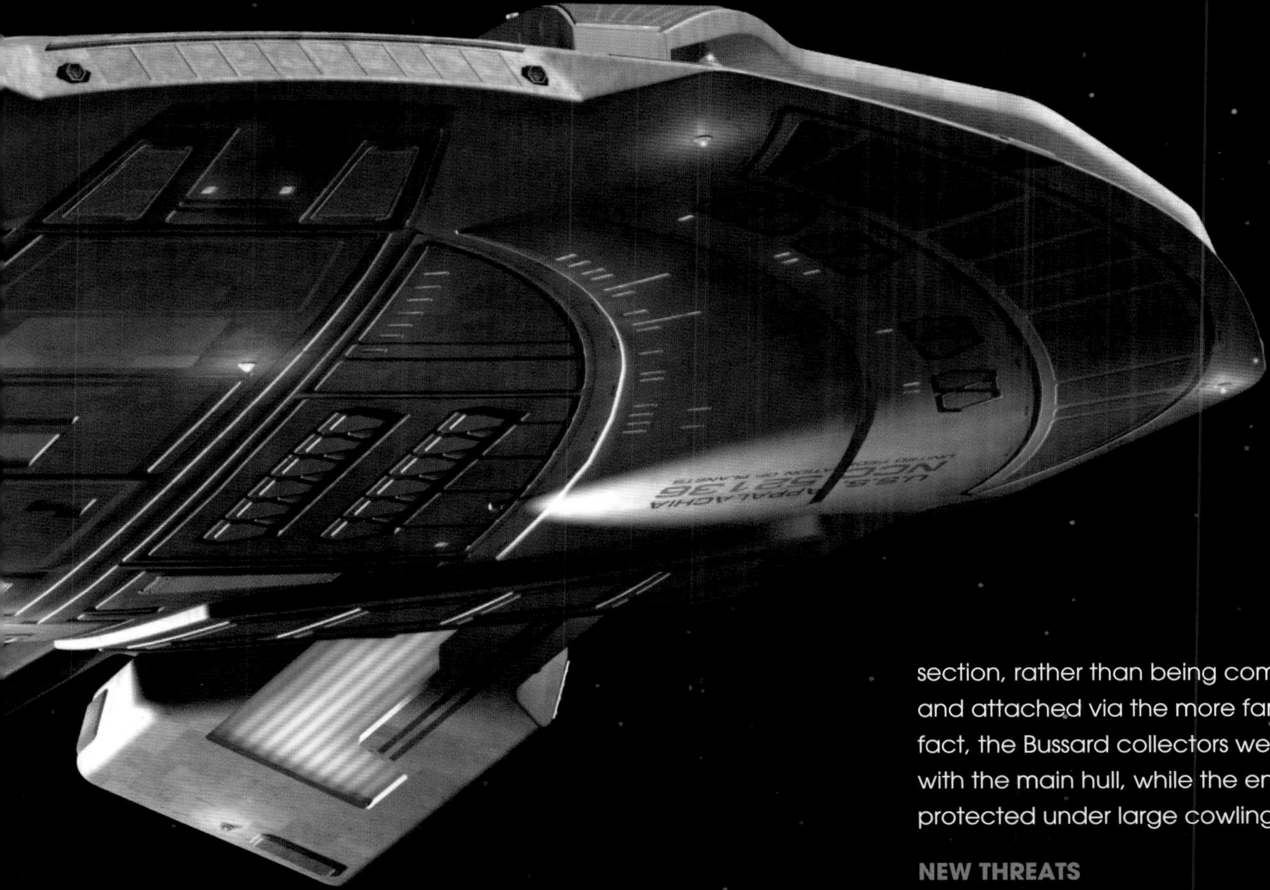

The *Steamrunner* class represented a radical shift from traditional Starfleet ship design. This was partly because the main deflector dish was located on the front of a compact secondary hull that hung down below and behind the saucer section. In addition, the engineering module was not directly connected to the saucer section. Instead, the two hulls were joined together via support struts that angled down between the warp nacelles.

Another unique element of this class was that the warp nacelles were streamlined into the saucer section, rather than being completely separate and attached via the more familiar outriggers. In fact, the Bussard collectors were in direct contact with the main hull, while the entire nacelles were protected under large cowlings.

NEW THREATS

The *Steamrunner* class was first seen in service in 2373, indicating that it was designed in response to the dual threat posed by the Borg and the Dominion. Starfleet had experienced one of its darkest days at the Battle of Wolf 359 in 2367, when a single Borg cube destroyed 39 Starfleet ships with the loss of 11,000 lives. In the wake of this devastation, Starfleet began a major shipbuilding program in case the Borg returned. Realizing that new types of starship were needed to meet the tactical requirements of facing a far superior enemy, Starfleet designed vessels that were more focused on combat than exploration and discovery.

This new type of dedicated combat vessel was best exemplified by the *Defiant* class, the prototype of which was so powerful that it almost shook itself apart during trial runs. Lessons learned

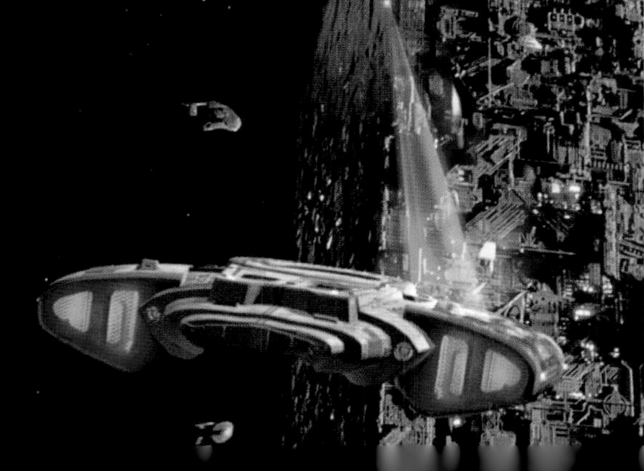

◀ The *Steamrunner* class was just one type of combat ship that was designed and rushed into service by Starfleet, in readiness for an anticipated incursion by the Borg into Federation space. These tactically advanced vessels had their first encounter with an invading Borg cube at the Battle of Sector 001 in 2373.

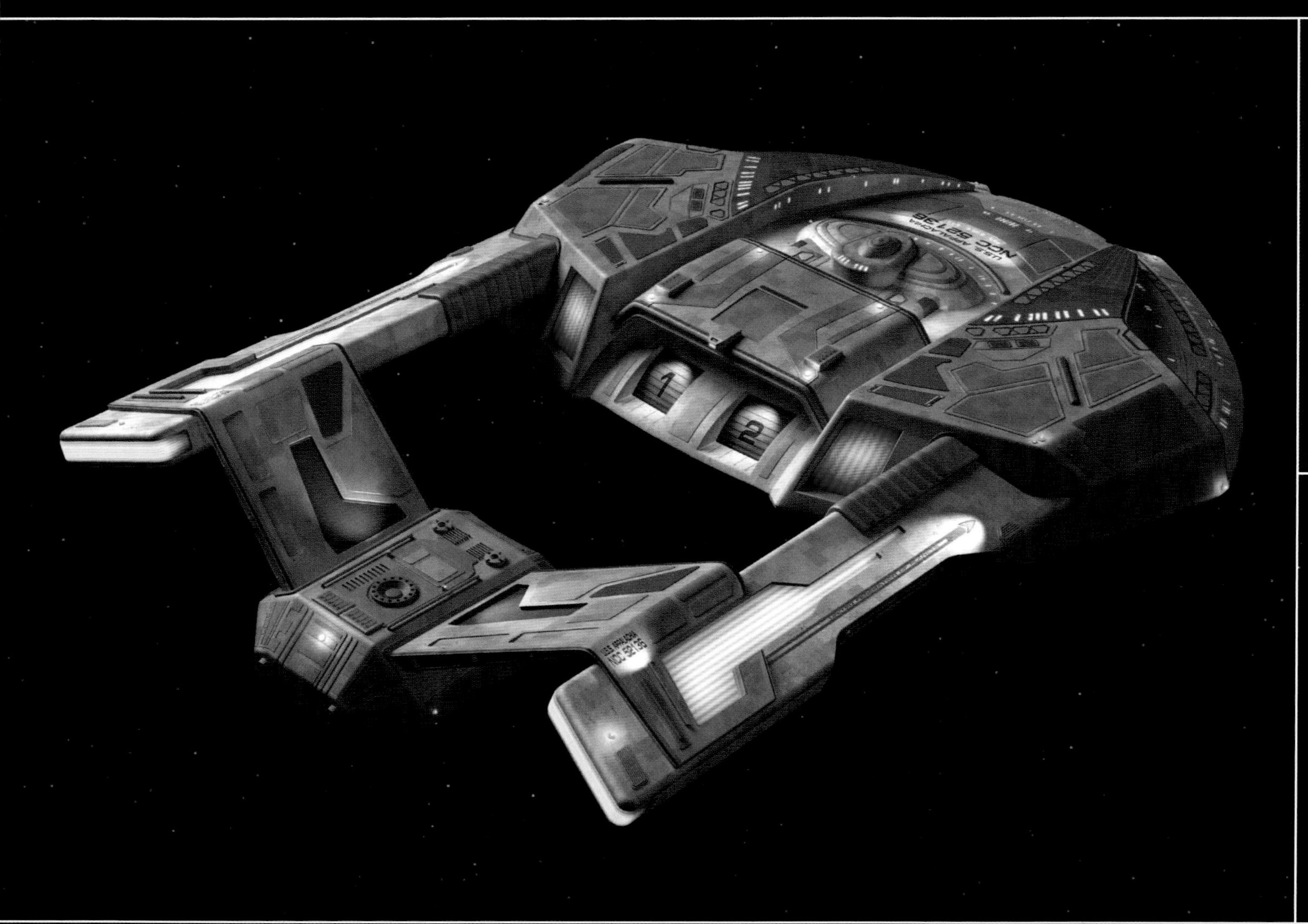

▲ The engineering hull on *Steamrunner*-class ships was much smaller than on earlier Starfleet designs. Despite this, the engineering systems were just as powerful as they had been on larger ships, and *Steamrunner*-class ships were capable of reaching speeds of up to warp 9.6.

during its development filtered down to other designs that were being fast tracked into production. One of these was the *Steamrunner* class.

NARROW PROFILE

Like the *Defiant* class, the *Steamrunner* featured a sleek profile by eliminating the long neck section between the primary and secondary hulls. This much narrower profile meant that the *Steamrunner* class provided less of a target in combat. It was made possible by advances in warp technology, which meant that the engineering hull could be much more compact than on earlier Starfleet ship designs, while providing similar levels of power.

Though the dimensions of the engineering hull on the *Steamrunner* class were greatly reduced compared to earlier designs, there was still enough space to accommodate the deflector dish on the front. Its location towards the rear of the vessel may have appeared odd, especially as its primary function was to clear asteroids and assorted space debris from the ship's path. But because it hung down below the saucer, it still had a "clear line of sight" in front of the ship to do its job. The fact that such a major component as the deflector dish was placed toward the rear of the ship also offered it more protection. This move made a great deal of sense, given the combat design considerations of the class.

The main bridge and shuttlebay on the *Steamrunner* class were also positioned and integrated in such a way as to give them enhanced protection. Although not as protected as the sunken command module on the *Defiant* class, the bridge on the *Steamrunner* class was still partially shielded by the raised sides of the saucer. Meanwhile, the main shuttlebay was located at the rear of the saucer, where its doors offered a

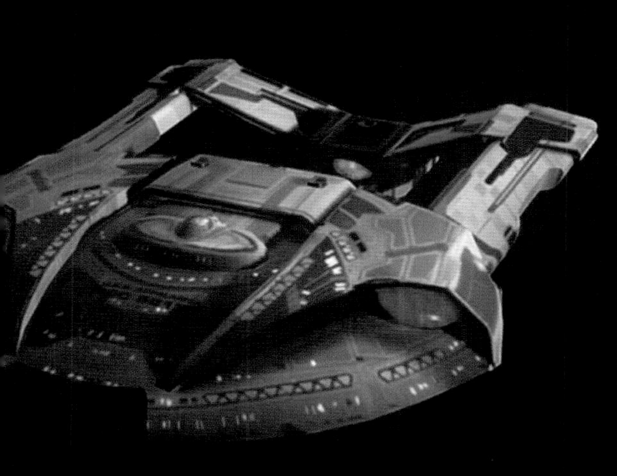

▶ The main shuttlebay was located at the rear of the saucer section. Its position between the nacelles provided a relatively sheltered entry and exit point for shuttles.

◀ The nacelles were embedded in the saucer section to give them greater protection. The bridge was also well sheltered by the raised sides of the saucer.

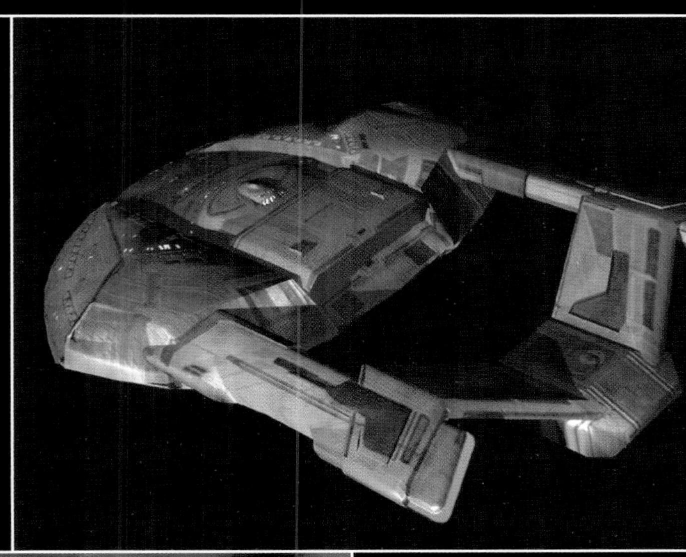

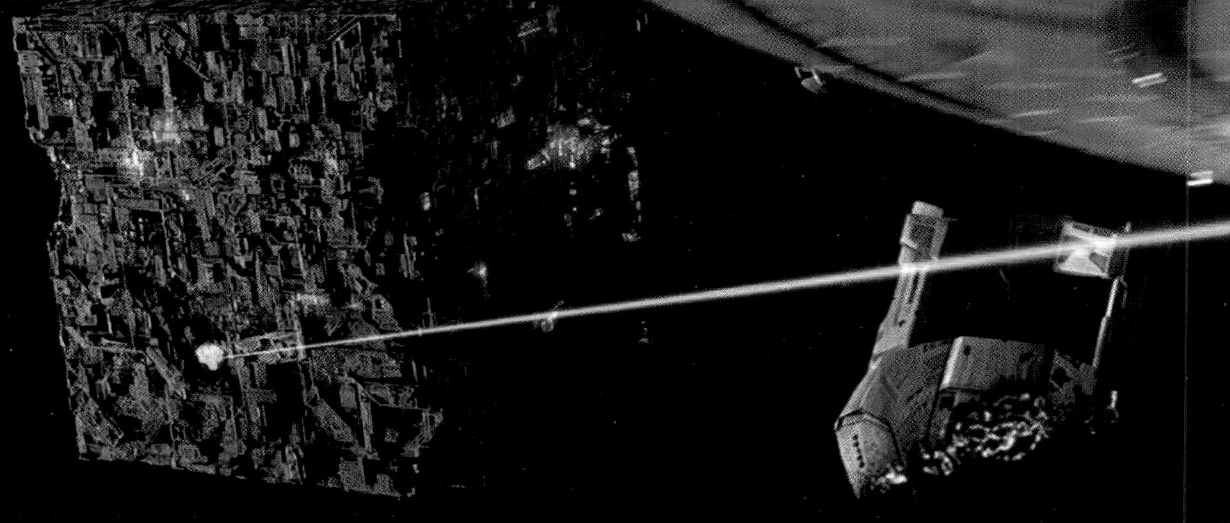

◀ Several *Steamrunner*-class ships were part of the Federation fleet that fought the Borg cube at the Battle of Sector 001. At least one *Steamrunner*-class ship was among the 20 or so Starfleet vessels destroyed during the engagement. The losses were not in vain, however, as their actions bought enough time for the *Enterprise*-E to join the fray and defeat the Borg.

safe and calm entry point, because they were tucked down between the nacelles.

SHARED DESIGN

The shape and design of the hull plating and escape pods on the *Steamrunner* class closely resembled those found on *Sovereign*-class ships, such as the *U.S.S. Enterprise* NCC-1701-E. This clearly indicated that they were contemporary designs, having been developed and constructed around the same time. Indeed, the *Steamrunner* class was seen for the first time at the Battle of Sector 001 against the Borg in 2373, just after the *Enterprise*-E had completed its shakedown tests.

Steamrunner-class ships later saw action in many crucial battles during the Dominion War as part of the Second Fleet. This proved that the *Steamrunner* class, along with other types of Starfleet ship developed in the late 24th century, was a formidable tactical force and a match for some of the most serious threats the Federation had ever faced. They helped to destroy vital Dominion shipyards on Torros III and to take the Chin'toka system from Cardassian control, and were part of the Allied fleet that met the Dominion at Cardassia Prime, inflicting a final defeat.

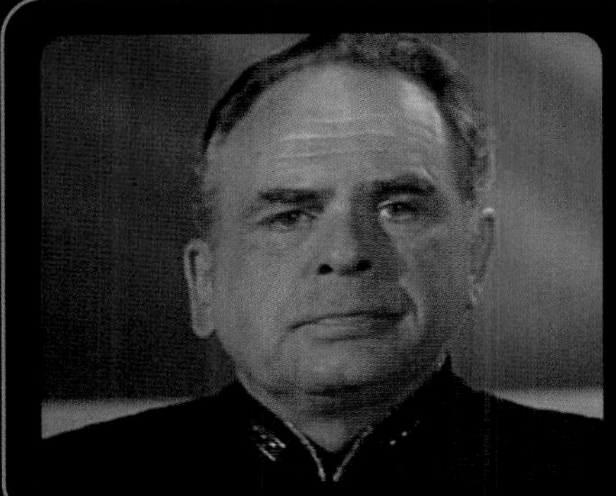

DATA FEED

Vice Admiral Hayes was initially in command of around 30 ships that made up the armada tasked with engaging the Borg cube when it invaded Federation space in 2373. Captain Jean-Luc Picard later took command of the fleet after several Starfleet vessels, including Hayes' flagship, were destroyed.

FIGHTING THE DOMINION

In 2373, several *Steamrunner*-class ships served in the Second Fleet, an alliance of Federation and Klingon ships that fought the Dominion. During the second Battle of Deep Space 9, a number of *Steamrunner*-class ships made up part of a task force that crossed the Cardassian border and delivered a serious blow to the Dominion by obliterating their shipyards on Torros III.

Later, at least one *Steamrunner*-class ship was part of an Alliance fleet that attacked Cardassian space in the Chin'toka system. This invasion was ultimately successful, even though the Cardassians had deployed hundreds of automated orbital weapon platforms in the system. And in late 2375, vessels of this class formed part of the huge Allied fleet that defeated the Dominion in the final battle of the war, at Cardassia Prime.

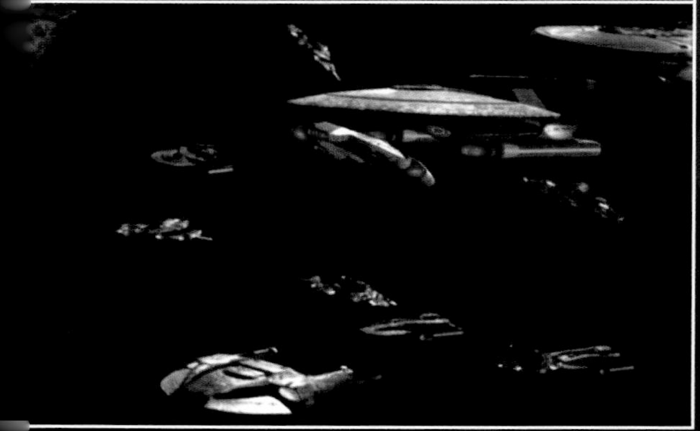

▲ *Steamrunner*-class ships fought alongside several other classes of Starfleet vessel as part of the Second Fleet during the Dominion War.

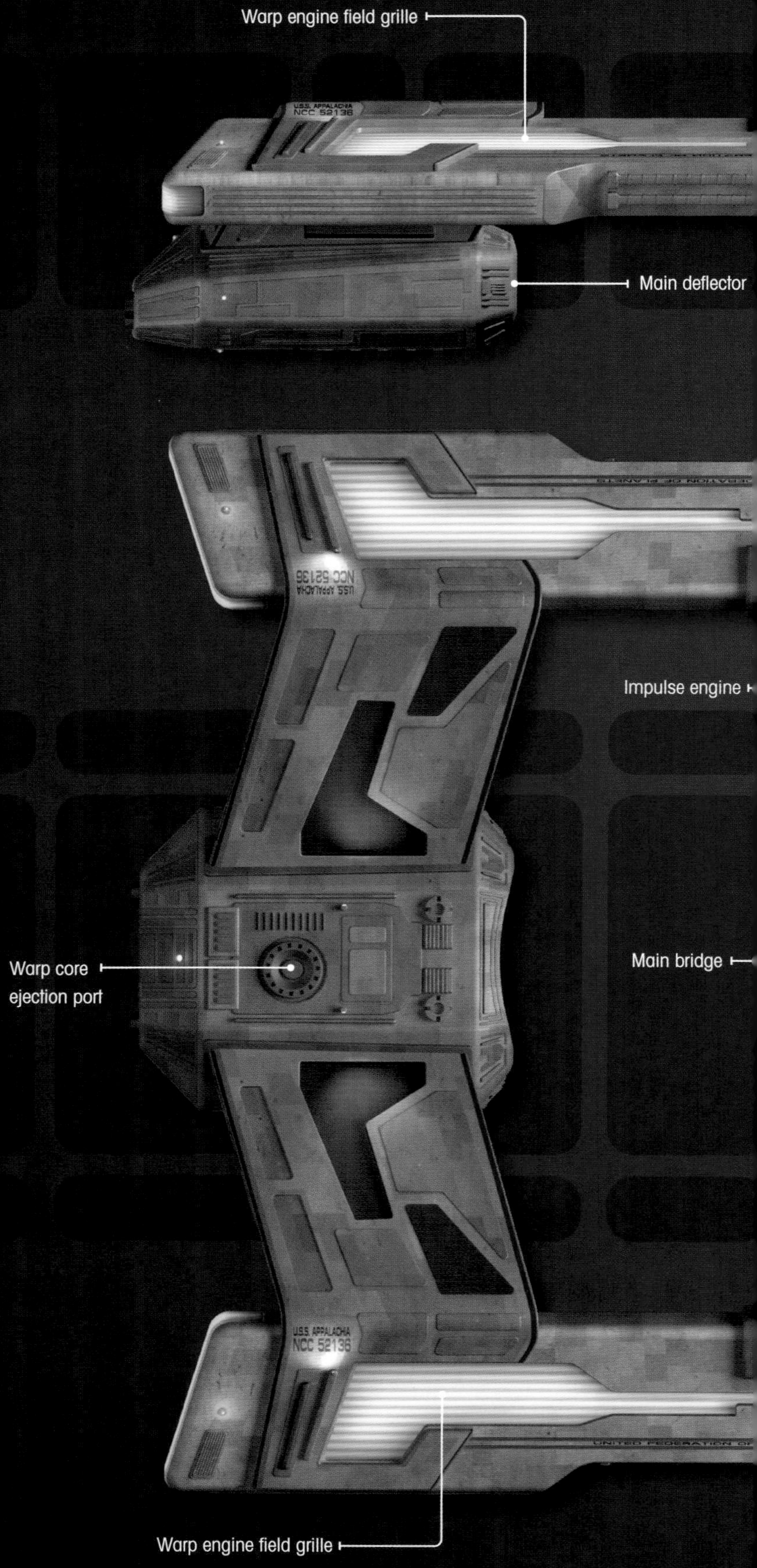

DATA FEED

Despite the loss of Alliance ships during the Battle of Sector 001, the remaining vessels in the fleet managed to coordinate a successful attack on the Borg cube. This was largely due to Captain Picard's knowledge of the precise place where the cube was vulnerable to attack. He had learned this during his time of partial assimilation as Locutus.

Warp engine field grille

Main deflector

Impulse engine

Warp core ejection port

Main bridge

Warp engine field grille

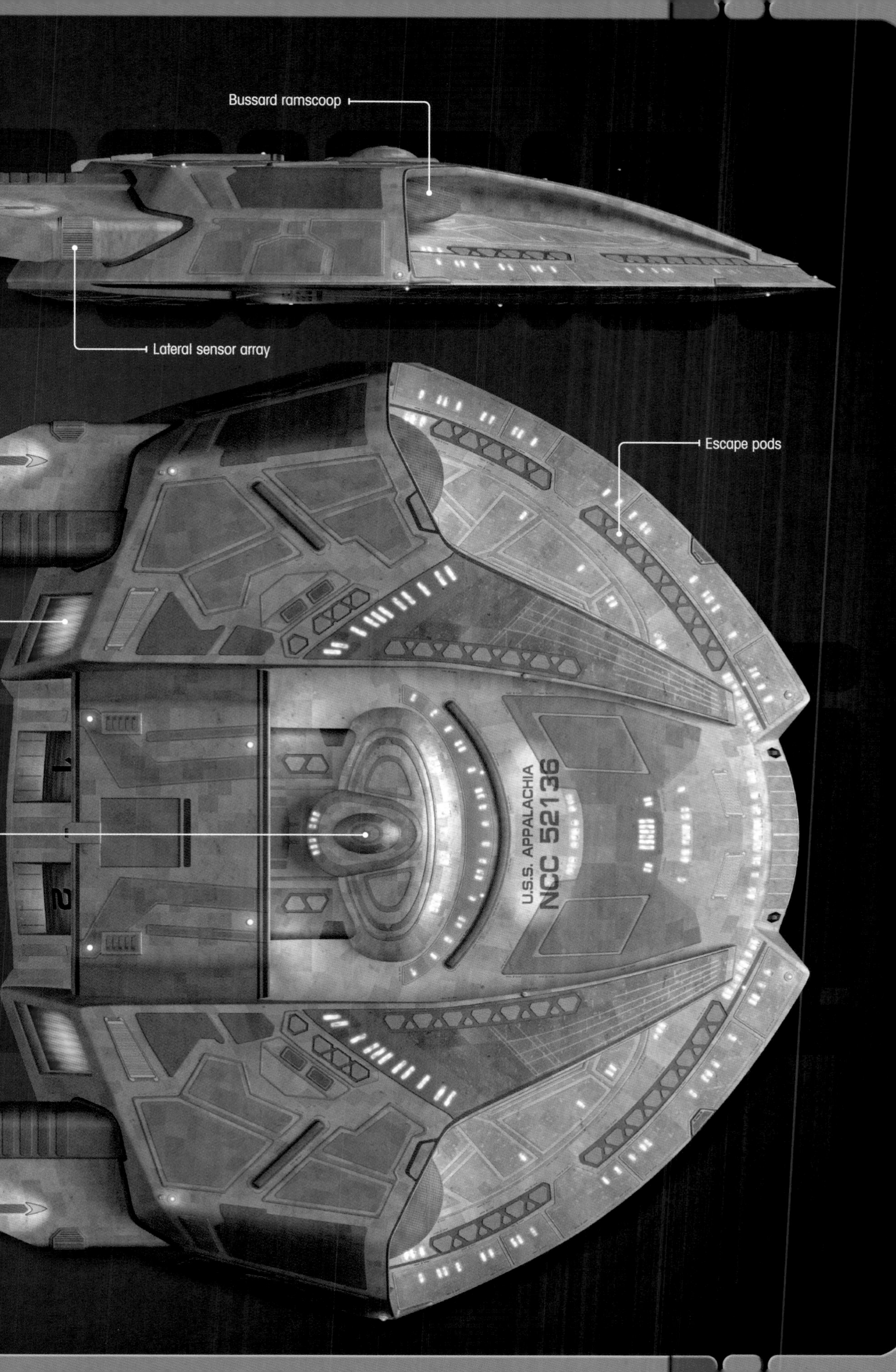

BLOWHARD OFFICER

Vice Admiral Hayes survived the encounter with the Borg, despite his flagship being destroyed. He was later described by Captain Janeway as a "good man, fine officer, a bit of a windbag."

SINGLE NAME

Though several vessels of the *Steamrunner*-class served as part of the Federation-Klingon alliance, the only such ship known by name was the *U.S.S. Appalachia* NCC-52136, lost at the Battle of Sector 001.

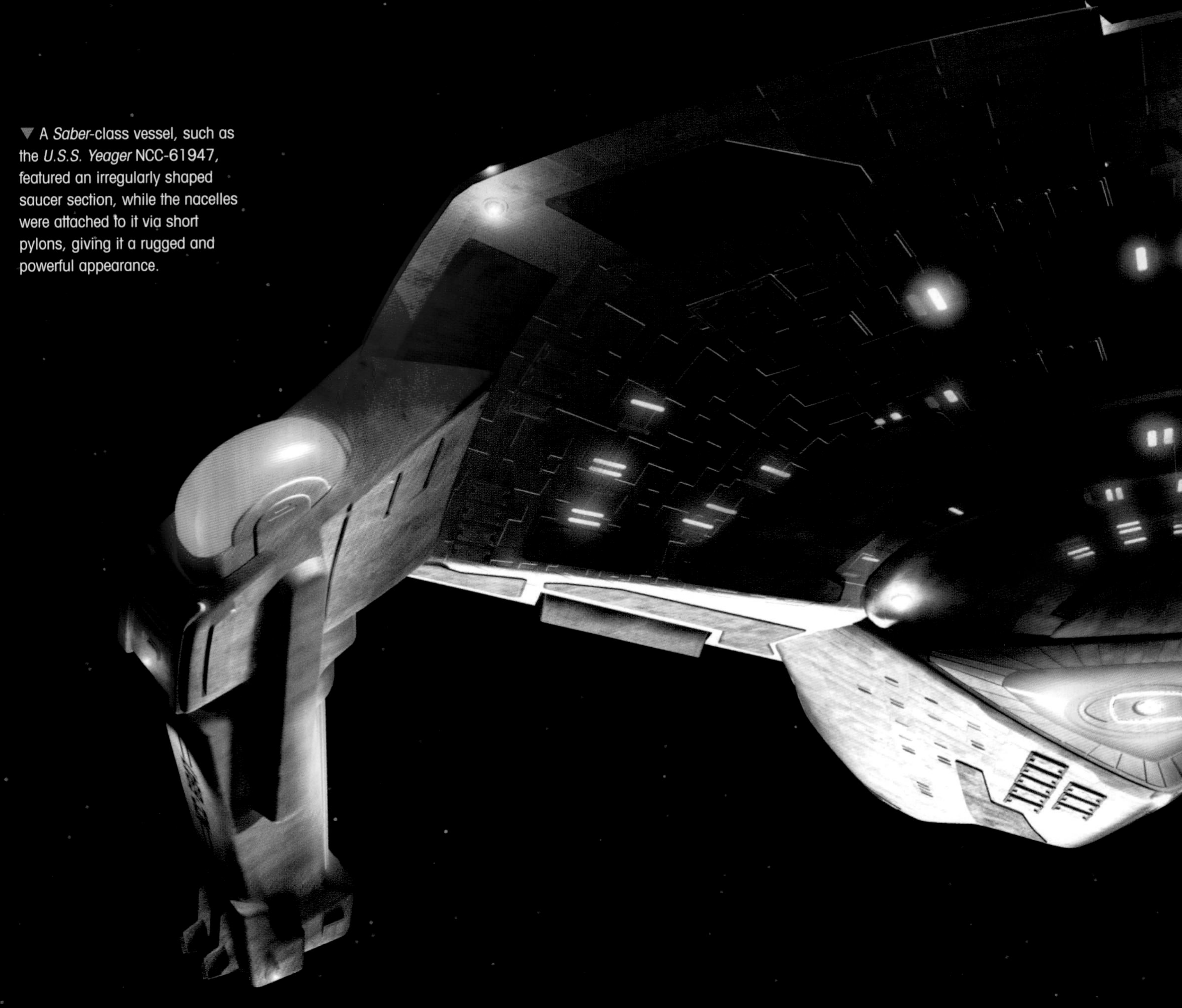

▼ A *Saber*-class vessel, such as the *U.S.S. Yeager* NCC-61947, featured an irregularly shaped saucer section, while the nacelles were attached to it via short pylons, giving it a rugged and powerful appearance.

SABER CLASS

Compact and well-armed, *Saber*-class ships were brought into service in the late 2360s to fight in the Dominion War.

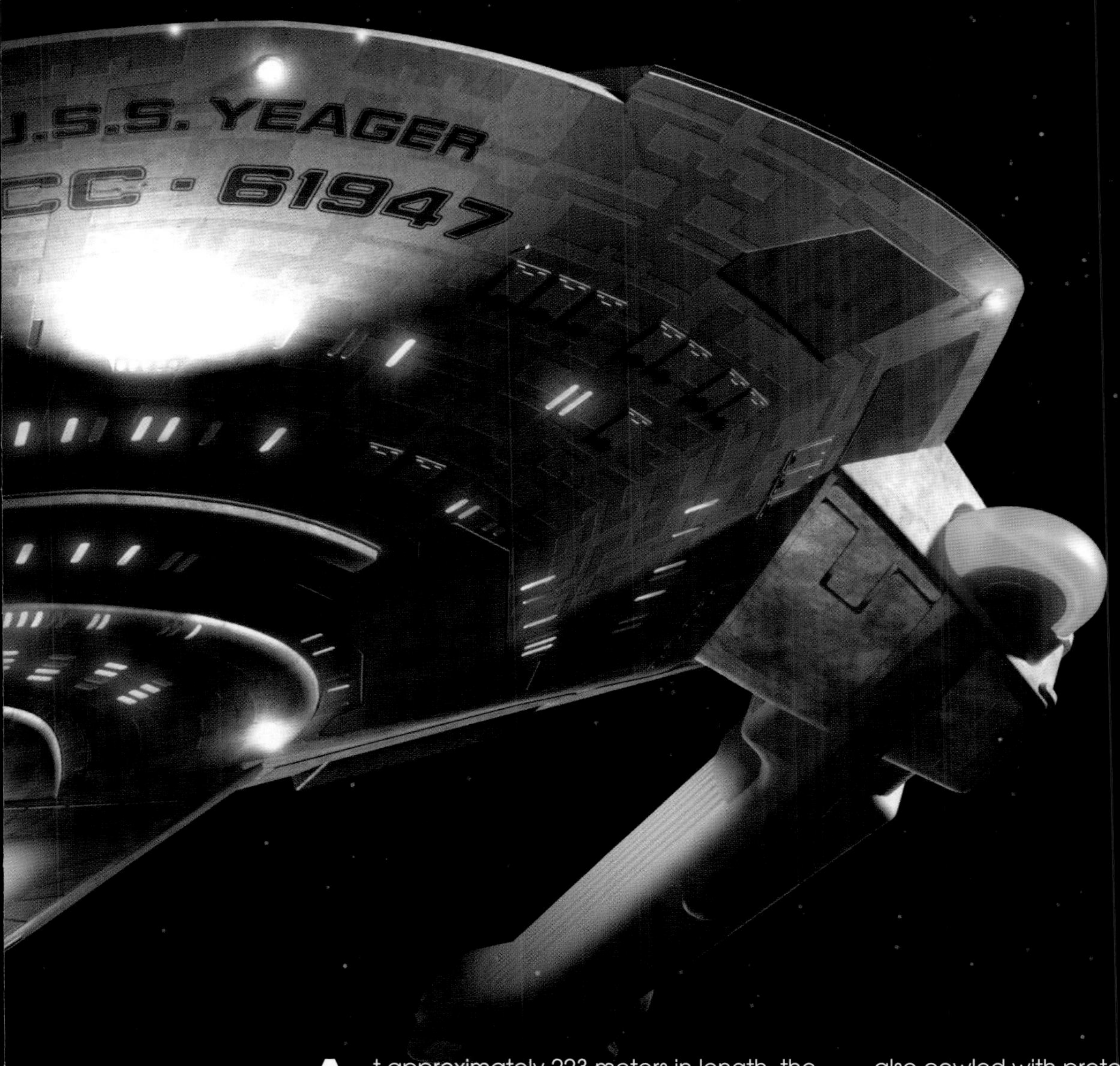

At approximately 223 meters in length, the *Saber* class was a relatively small type of 24th-century Starfleet vessel that operated with a standard crew of 40. The entire ship was a similar size to the saucer section of a *Galaxy*-class starship, while its nacelles were attached to the outer edges of the saucer via short struts rather than on extended outriggers. The nacelles were also cowled with protective plating on the outside, providing them with extra shielding from enemy fire. The ship's engineering section was merged into the back of the saucer section, giving it a robust and compact appearance.

The shuttlebay entrance and exit was located on the leading edge of the saucer, just forward of the main bridge, which retained its standard position on deck 1 toward the center of the primary hull. The deflector dish was also in the usual position at the front of the engineering hull, while the impulse engines were located on the rear of the saucer.

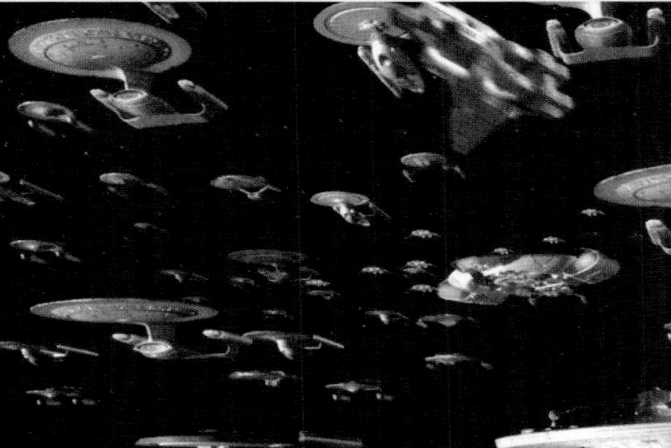

◀ *Saber*-class vessels were part of the Second Fleet, a Federation Alliance force that fought in the Dominion War. This fleet comprised numerous classes of Starfleet ships as well as Klingon vessels. The Second Fleet fought in the second Battle of Deep Space and destroyed the Dominion shipyards on Torros III in Cardassian space.

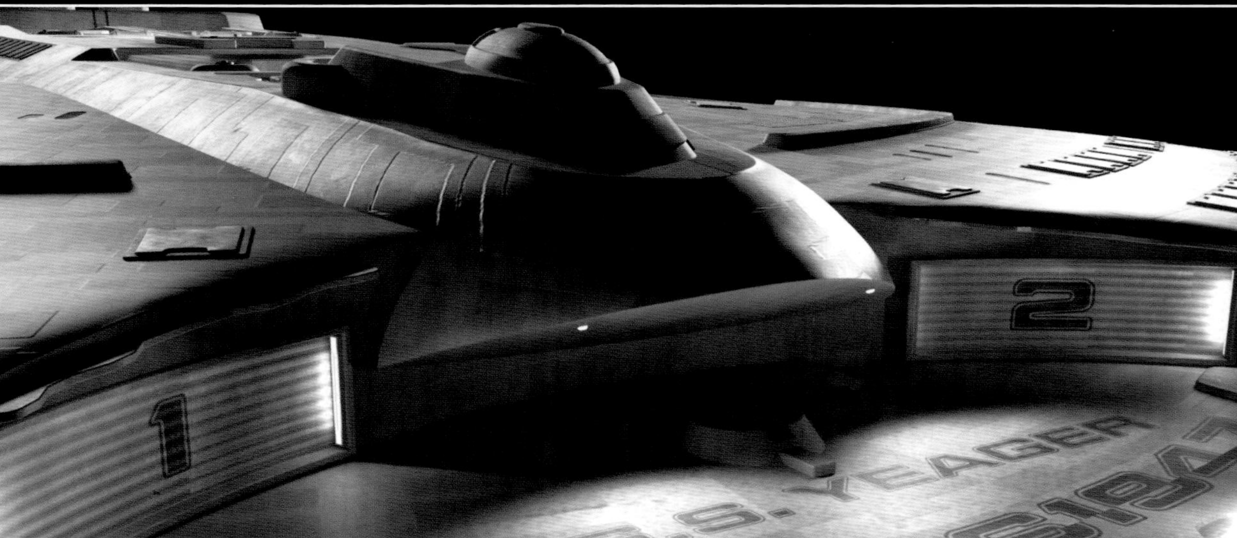

◀ Unlike most Starfleet ships, which sited the shuttlebay at the rear of the engineering section, *Saber*-class ships featured a shuttlebay at the front of the saucer section.

▼ The outer hull of *Saber*-class vessels displayed far more surface detail than many other Starfleet vessels, particularly in the area behind the main bridge.

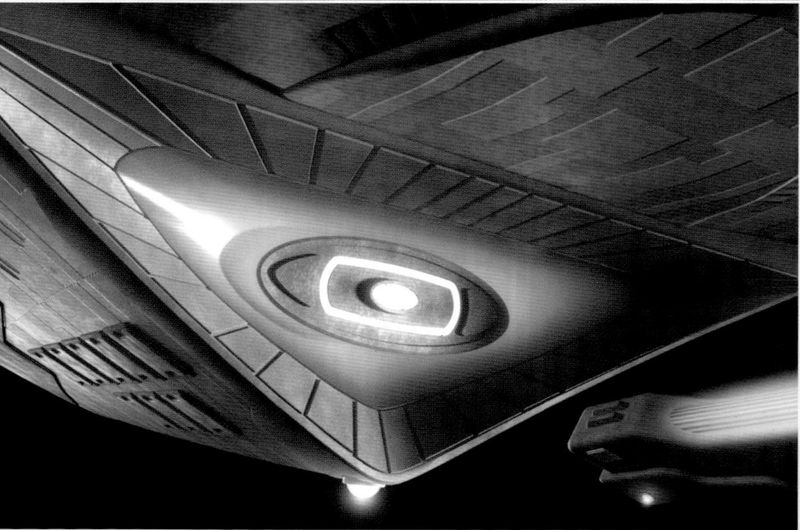

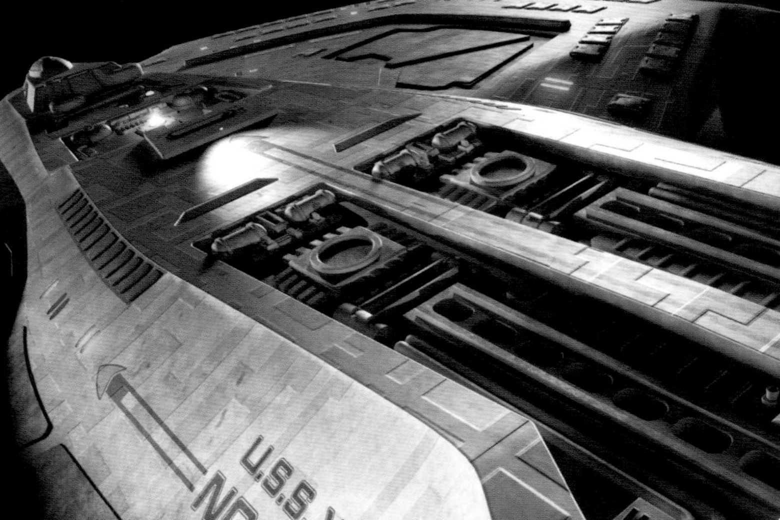

▲ The engineering hull on the *Saber* class had a distinctive triangular shape, while the main navigational deflector was surrounded by copper-colored panels. The surface of the hull featured prominent escape hatches of a similar shape and design to those on the *Defiant* class, indicating the classes were contemporary.

The warp core was sited near the rear of the secondary hull, with the ejection hatch clearly visible on the underside.

The design of the hull plating and escape pods on the *Saber* class was similar to that found on the *Defiant* class. This appeared to indicate that both classes were developed and constructed around the same time, in the late 2360s.

Both classes of ship, as with other Starfleet designs, were built in response to the Battle of Wolf 359 in 2367, when a Borg cube ripped through Starfleet's defenses, destroying 39 starships in minutes. While the Federation had faced threats to its security before, nothing had ever matched the magnitude of the danger presented by the Borg. In response, Starfleet developed new types of starship. While the *Defiant* class was nothing less than a warship, the *Saber* class was more of a light cruiser. Nevertheless, it was heavily armed with numerous type-10 phaser emitters and two photon torpedo launchers. Its compact dimensions meant it offered less of a target, particularly in profile, but it was still capable of a top speed of warp 9.7, ensuring it could respond quickly to emergency situations.

UNDER CONSTRUCTION

The *Saber* class was first seen in 2371 when two of these starships were in dry dock at the Utopia Planitia Fleet Yards in orbit of Mars, while the *U.S.S. Voyager* NCC-74656 was undergoing its final phases of construction.

Two years later, the *Saber* class was on active service, facing the Borg's second invasion of the Alpha Quadrant. Several *Saber*-class ships, including the *U.S.S. Yeager* NCC-61947, made up part of a fleet assembled by Vice Admiral Hayes to intercept a Borg cube at Sector 001.

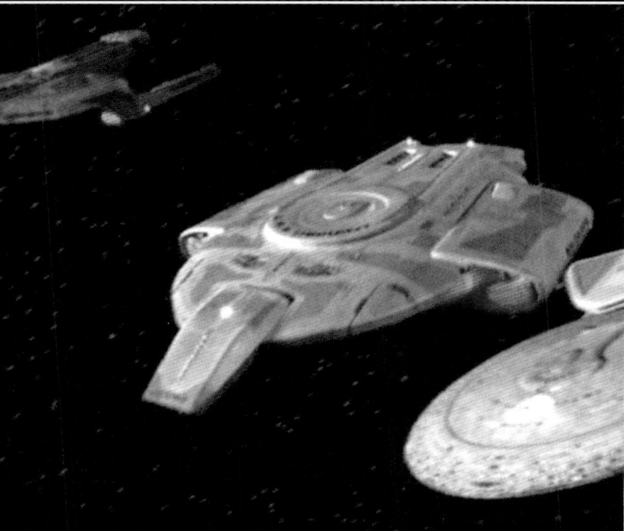

◀ During the Dominion War, small, maneuverable ships of the *Saber* and *Defiant* classes were often used to defend larger vessels from attack, enabling them to concentrate on breaking through enemy lines.

▶ *Saber*-class vessels were among the fastest in Starfleet in the late 24th century. Their nacelles were partly cowled for extra protection against enemy fire.

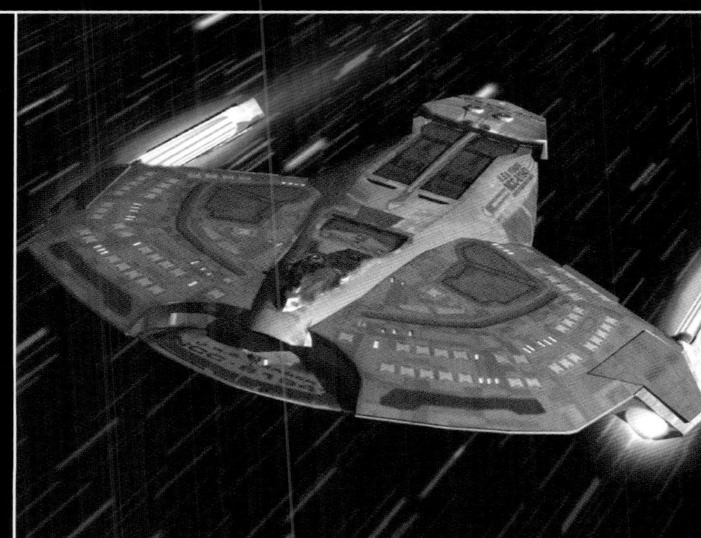

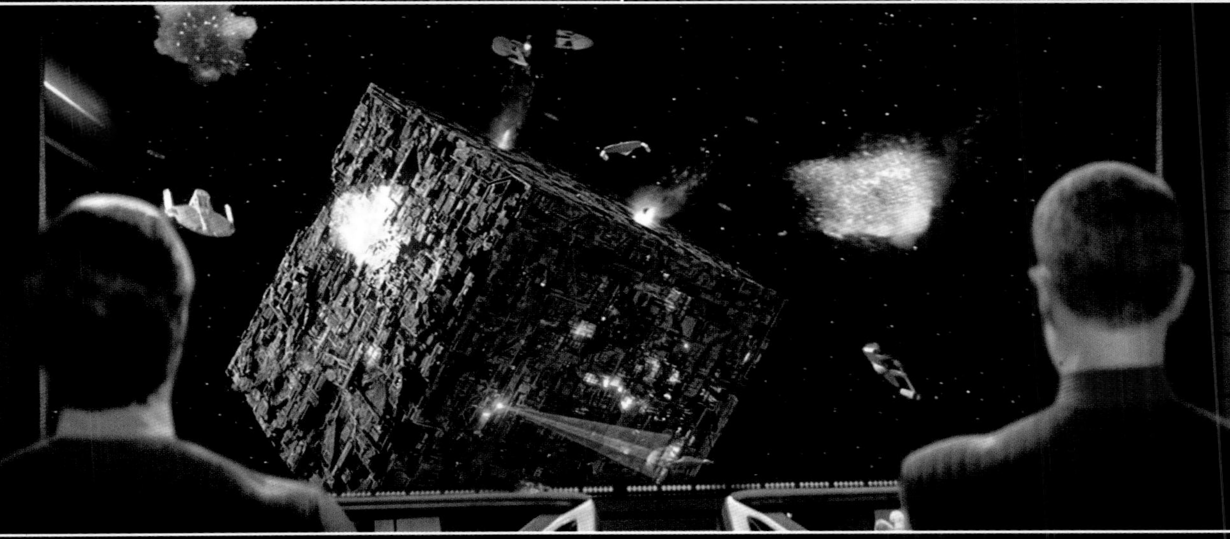

◀ Several *Saber*-class ships were part of the task force that engaged the Borg cube at the Battle of Sector 001. From the perspective of the viewscreen on the *U.S.S. Enterprise* NCC-1701-E, the Starfleet armada could be seen taking heavy losses as it assaulted the cube from all sides. The Borg were only stopped when Captain Picard coordinated the fleet's attack on a vulnerable area of the cube.

Later the same year, a number of *Saber*-class vessels were assigned to the Second Fleet, an alliance of Federation, Klingon, and later, Romulan ships that fought in several crucial engagements during the Dominion War.

Saber-class ships were often used to flank larger starships, helping to draw fire and protect them as they attempted to punch through enemy lines. Among their many encounters, they saw action at the Second Battle of Deep Space 9 – the first engagement of the Dominion War – the raid on the Dominion's shipyards on Torros III, and the First Battle of Chin'toka – the first Federation Alliance offensive into Cardassian territory.

In 2378, *Saber*-class ships were among the fleet that was hastily gathered by Admiral Owen Paris and sent to an area less than a light-year from Earth, where a transwarp conduit had been detected. Starfleet knew that only one species used transwarp conduits: the Borg. Fully prepared to engage whatever Borg vessels emerged from the conduit, the fleet were shocked when first a Borg sphere appeared, only for it to explode and the *U.S.S. Voyager* NCC-74656 to materialize out of the debris. A jubilant fleet then accompanied *Voyager* back to Earth.

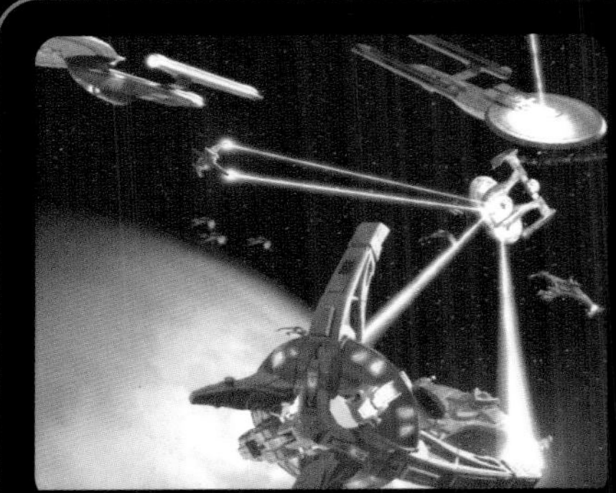

DATA FEED

Saber-class ships made up part of the Second Fleet when it launched an attack on the Chin'toka system. The Federation Alliance fleet had to overcome powerful automated orbital weapon platforms to gain control of this strategically vital system, which was located on the Cardassian border.

MARTIAN SHIPYARDS

Two *Saber*-class vessels were undergoing construction, refitting, or repairs at the Utopia Planitia Fleet Yards in 2371, at the same time as the *U.S.S. Voyager* NCC-74656 was entering the final stages of its construction. These facilities were positioned in synchronous orbit 16,625 kilometers above the Utopia Planitia region on Mars. The shipyards included a number of dry docks and space stations, and were one of Starfleet's largest and most important vessel construction and design facilities in the 24th century. They also included large drafting rooms for starship design, as well as several buildings on the surface of Mars. Much of the design and construction of the *Galaxy* class took place at these shipyards, and later, Lieutenant Commander Benjamin Sisko worked here on the development of the *Defiant* class.

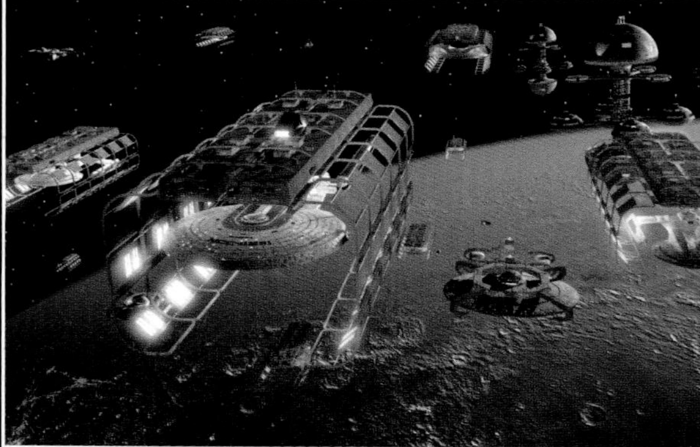

▲ The Utopia Planitia Fleet Yards in orbit of Mars featured mushroom-shaped space docks and dozens of cagelike dry docks, which encased starships while they were being built.

DATA FEED

A human settlement known as the Utopia colony was established on Mars at least as early as 2155. Lieutenant Tom Paris's idea of a perfect date was to visit the hills overlooking the Utopia Planitia plains in a 1957 Chevy. The Doctor took his advice and programmed the scenario into the *U.S.S. Voyager* NCC-74656's holodeck for his date with Denara Pel.

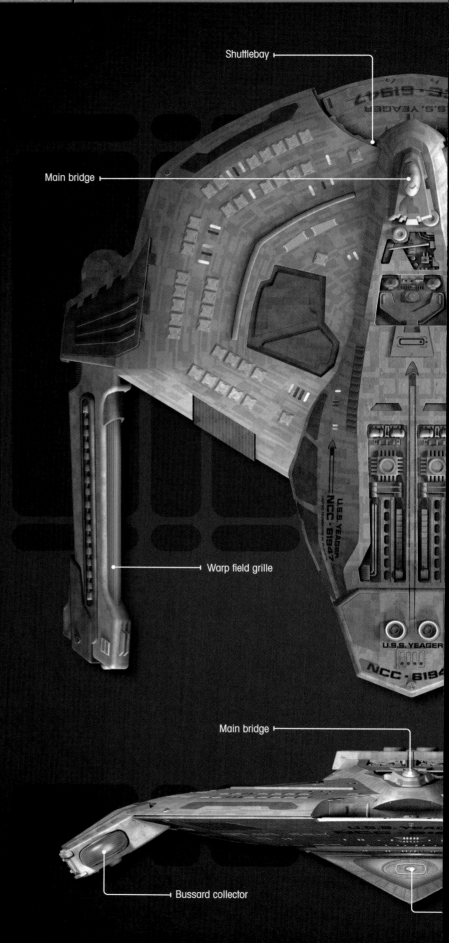

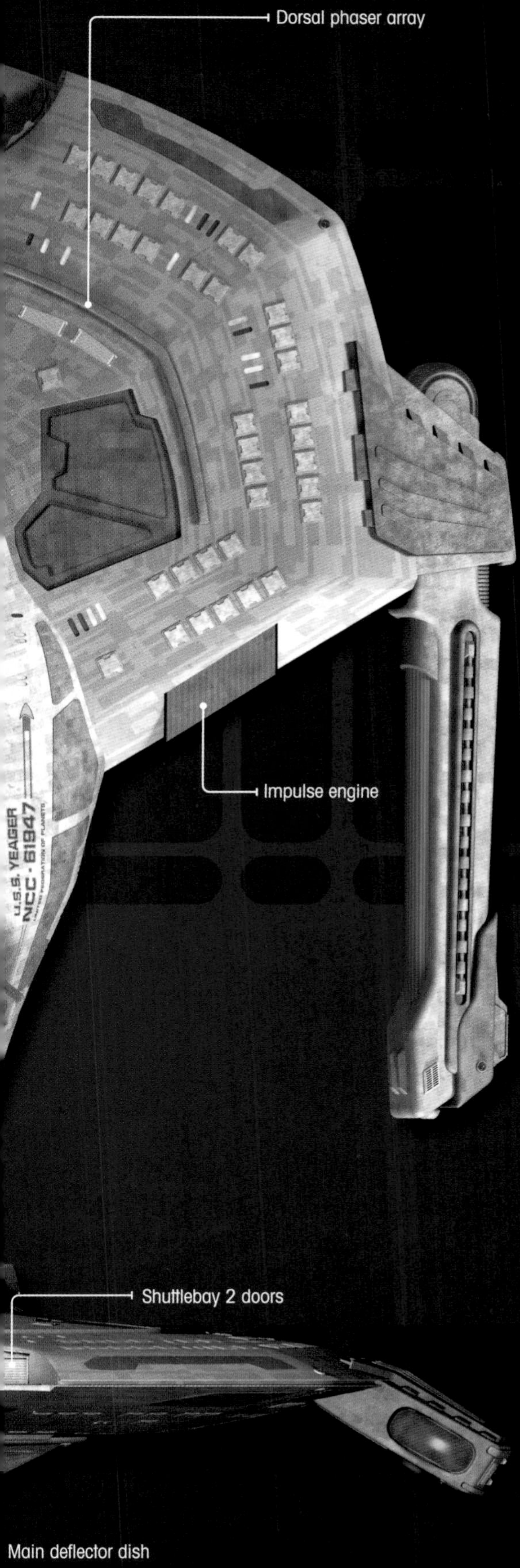

Dorsal phaser array

Impulse engine

Shuttlebay 2 doors

Main deflector dish

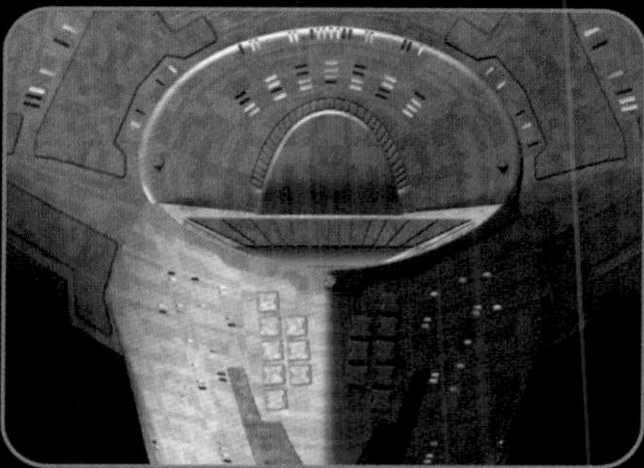

VENTRAL VIEW

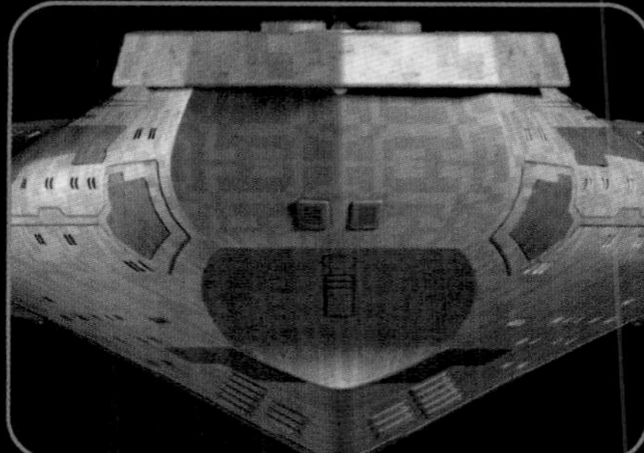

AFT VIEW

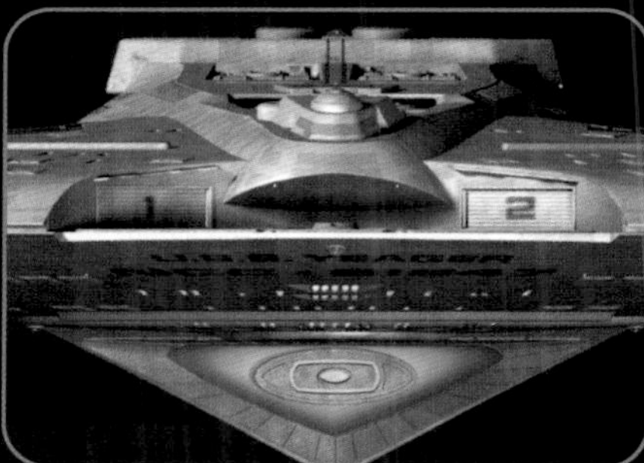

FORE VIEW

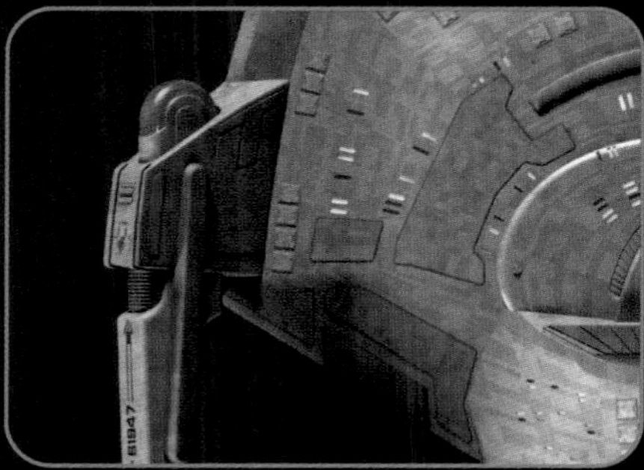

VENTRAL NACELLE VIEW

LEGENDARY NAME

The *Saber*-class *U.S.S. Yeager* NCC-61947 was named in honor of Chuck Yeager, the celebrated USAF test pilot who was the first person to break the sound barrier, on October 14, 1947, in the Bell X-1.

MAJOR BATTLES

Some of the conflicts involving *Saber*-class ships in the Dominion War included the Battle of Torros III, the Battle of the Tyra System, Operation Return – to reclaim Deep Space 9 – and the Battle of Cardassia.

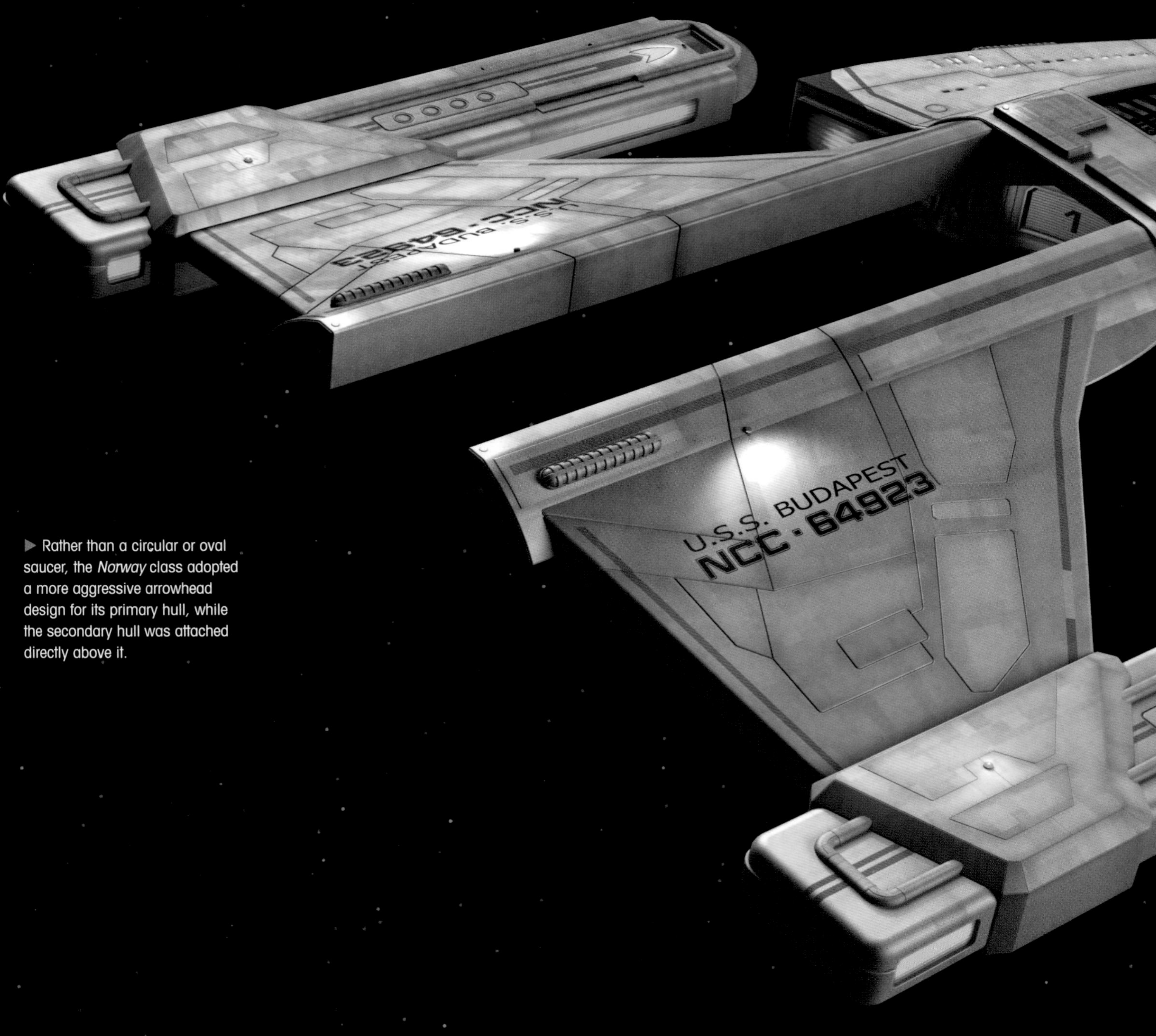

▶ Rather than a circular or oval saucer, the *Norway* class adopted a more aggressive arrowhead design for its primary hull, while the secondary hull was attached directly above it.

NORWAY CLASS

This streamlined type of vessel saw action as part of a strengthened fleet at the Battle of Sector 001.

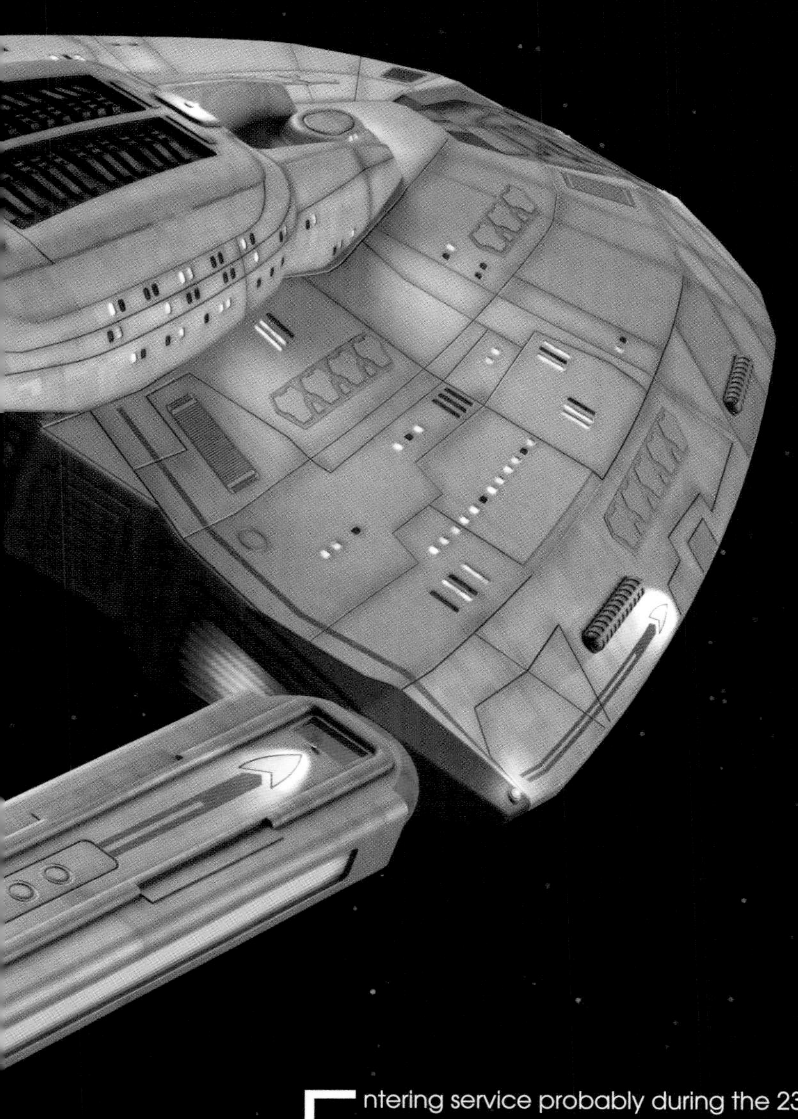

Entering service probably during the 2370s, the *Norway* class was 364.77 meters long and featured a shovel-shaped primary hull, not unlike that found on the *U.S.S. Voyager* NCC-74656. A short engineering hull was built on top of the primary hull, merging into it just behind the bridge, so that it looked as though the two structures were all one section. Two rectangular beams emerged from the rear of the engineering hull in a catamaran-style configuration, to which flat-mounted nacelle struts were attached to support the short nacelles.

The main bridge was located on deck 1 on top of the saucer section, and provided control of all the ship's main systems from engines to weapons. The bridge was partly concealed between the struts of the catamaran-style beams that led back to the nacelles. This meant that the bridge had enhanced protection from the sides, and was not as exposed as it had been on earlier types of ship.

POWERFUL ENGINES

Despite the relatively short engineering section and nacelles, the *Norway* class was still capable of a top speed of warp 9.7. This was thanks to advancements in propulsion technology, which meant powerful engines could be incorporated into a much smaller area.

The deflector dish was inset into the saucer section, not the engineering hull as it had been on many other Starfleet designs. It was also pushed much further back from the leading edge of the ship, but provided it had a "clear line of sight" into open space, this was not a problem.

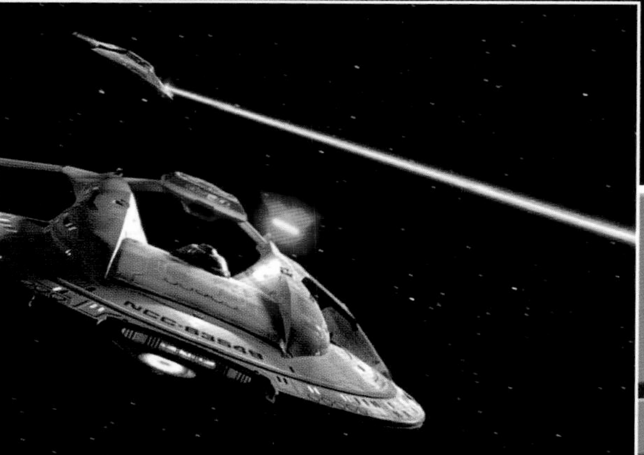

◀ The *Norway* class, seen here above the *Akira* class, was one of several relatively new Starfleet designs that made up an armada of at least 30 ships at Sector 001. Unlike at the earlier Battle of Wolf 359, they opted to swarm the Borg cube, causing serious damage.

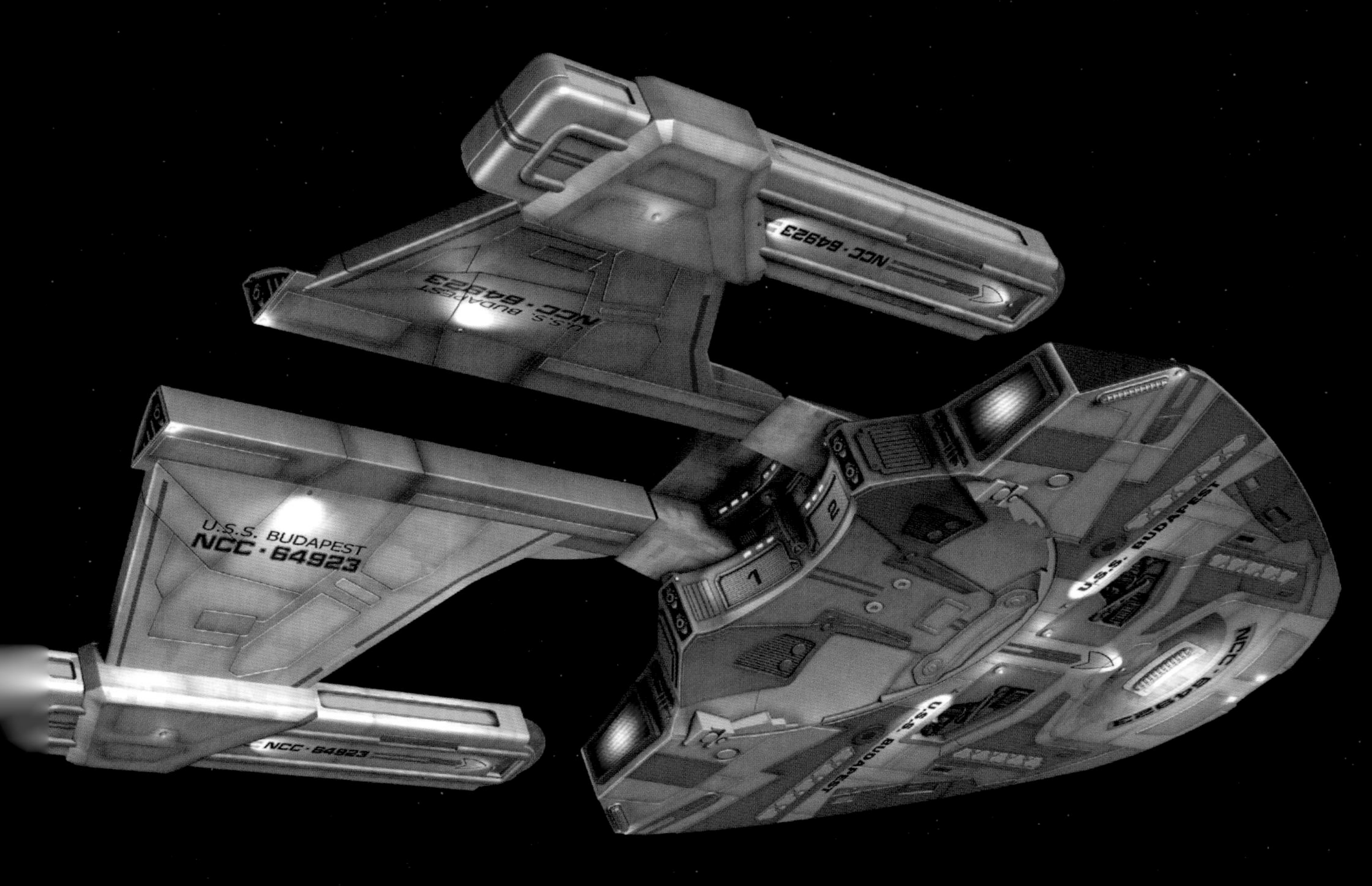

▲ The *Norway* class had a primary saucer very similar in shape to that of the *U.S.S. Voyager* NCC-74656. It also featured an atypically small number of windows on the external hull, while the surface detail echoed both that of the *U.S.S. Enterprise* NCC-1701-D and the *U.S.S. Defiant* NX-74205.

Weapons on the *Norway* class included six type-10 phaser emitters set at various points around the hull, including on the trailing edge of the split hull struts. There were also two photon torpedo launchers, one just below the main deflector dish and another at the rear.

The class's overall design was compact, and from the side it presented a very compressed profile. This made it a much smaller target than earlier Starfleet designs featuring a long neck structure between the saucer and engineering hull, or elongated nacelle struts between the engineering hull and warp nacelles.

The flat design was a very deliberate styling departure by Starfleet. They had an aging fleet, and its combat deficiency was made all too apparent with the disastrous defeat at the Battle of Wolf 359 in 2367, which saw the obliteration of 39 Starfleet ships by a single Borg cube.

The consequent round of shipbuilding brought into service ship classes that were rather more combat-oriented than the average Starfleet design. The preceding centuries had seen periods of conflict and tension for Starfleet, after which a largely peaceful period had prevailed because the Federation had grown to include more than 150 worlds that lived in a spiritof mutu cooperation. Starfleet had developed ships largely for exploratory, scientific, and diplomatic purposes during this time – but the threat of the Borg changed all that.

CALLED INTO ACTION

It was not long before all these new ships saw action at the Battle of Sector 001 in 2373, when reports came in that a Borg cube had destroyed colony on Ivor Prime. Vice Admiral Hayes mobilize a fleet that included at least four *Norway*-class

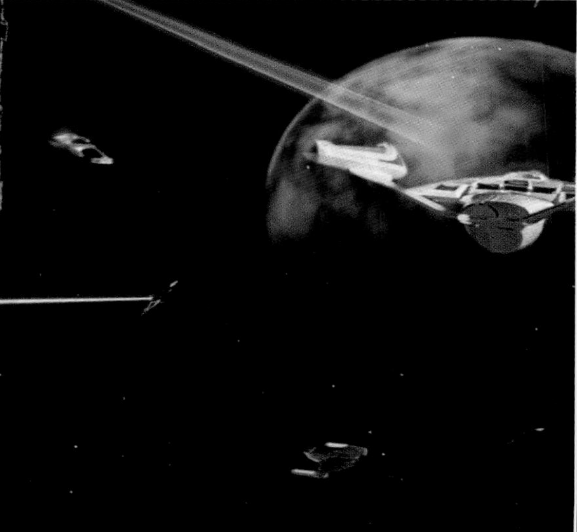

◀ By the time the *U.S.S. Enterprise* NCC-1701-E joined the battle with the Borg near Earth, a large portion of the fleet had been lost – but it had also inflicted damage on the Borg cube's outer hull.

▶ The *Norway* class had a very flat design, the nacelles being aligned with the saucer section. This gave it a linear profile, making it difficult to target and pick off in battle.

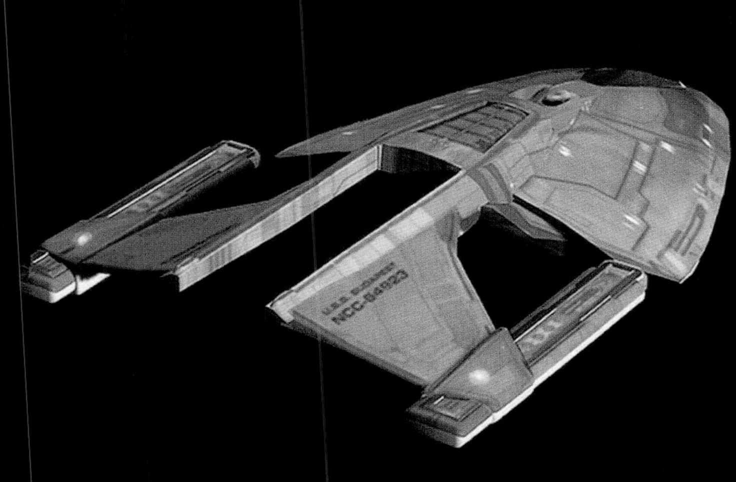

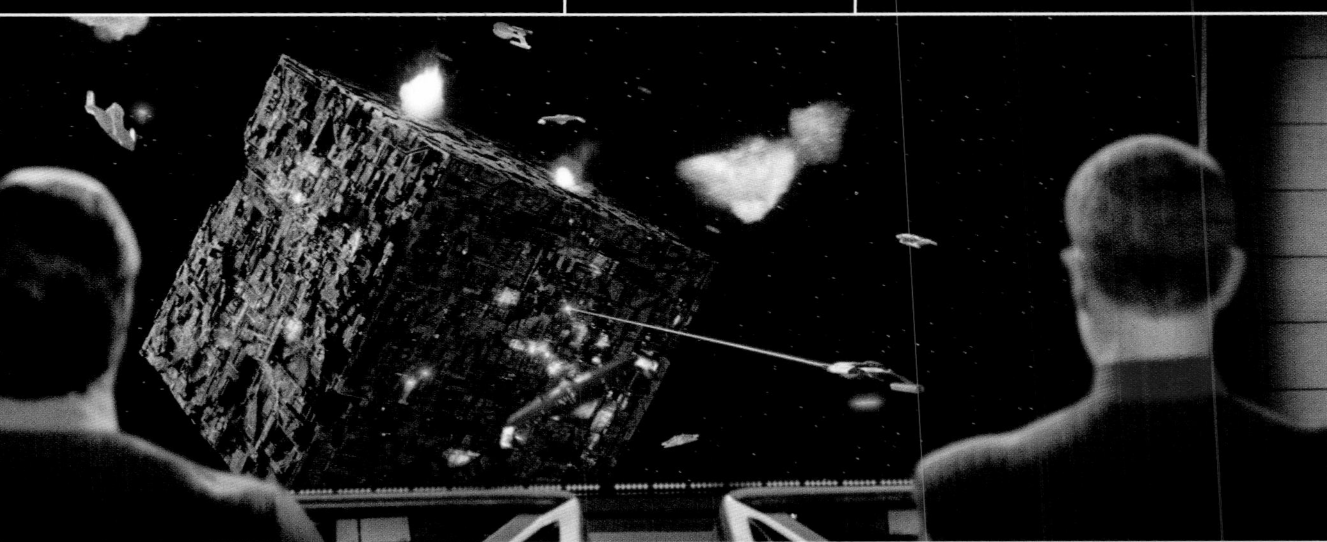

◀ Seen from the *Enterprise*-E's bridge, the battle with the Borg appeared to be a melee, with numerous Starfleet ships, including *Norway*-class vessels, performing strafing runs on the cube. Under Captain Picard's orders, the fleet then targeted a specific area of the cube, causing it to explode.

ships to intercept the Borg in the Typhon sector. The fleet failed to stop the cube, however, and Hayes was forced to request reinforcements as the Borg continued unrelentingly toward Earth.

Many Starfleet ships were disabled or destroyed completely by the time the *U.S.S. Enterprise* NCC-1701-E joined the fight in orbit of Earth. As the battle raged on, the combined force of the fleet slowly wore down the cube's defenses. The crucial factor in the battle was Captain Picard's inside knowledge of the Borg after his earlier assimilation. He directed the fleet to fire on a seemingly unimportant area of the cube, and it was eventually destroyed. This left the *Enterprise*-E free to pursue the sphere that had emerged from the cube shortly before its destruction.

After this, the *Norway* class was not seen in action again, although a computer display graphic did show one of these ships at Starbase 375. This space station acted as a gathering point for the Second and Fifth Fleets prior to Operation Return and the retaking of Deep Space 9 from Dominion forces in late 2373. The fact that the *Norway* class was displayed in a graphic before this battle appeared to indicate that at least some of these ships were present during the engagement.

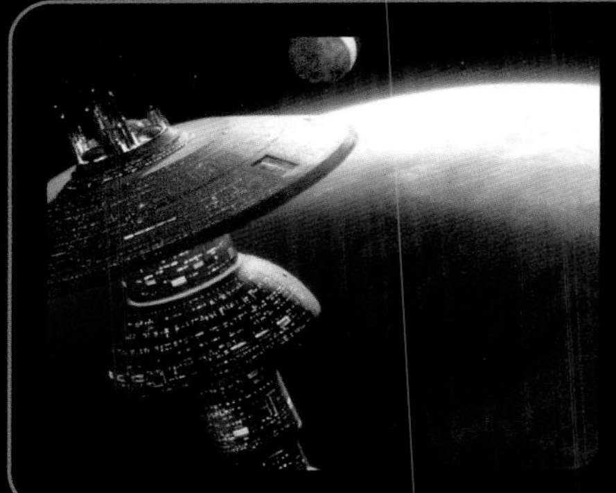

DATA FEED

Sector 001 not only encompassed the Sol system and Earth, but also the 40 Eridani A system, where additional Starfleet construction yards were located. It also included the Tarsas System, where Starbase 74 (left) was positioned, as well as the Federation's Orion Sector Tactical Command outpost.

NEW TACTICS

At the earlier Battle of Wolf 359, roughly eight light years from Earth, the Starfleet armada of 40 ships employed a tactic of attacking the Borg cube in formation, to avoid damaging friendly ships. Unfortunately, this had not worked because it allowed the cube to pick off the Starfleet ships one at a time.

For the Battle of Sector 001, where Starfleet was using a number of relatively new starships, including the *Norway* class, they instead opted for a swarm tactic. This met with some success. After the *U.S.S. Enterprise* NCC-1701-E arrived, Data reported that the cube had sustained heavy damage – something not even closely achieved at the earlier battle. The Starfleet armada still suffered major losses, but eventually, with the help of Captain Picard, they managed to annihilate the Borg cube.

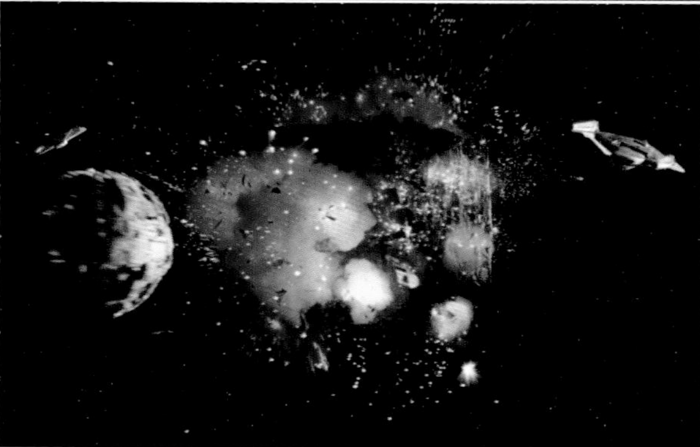

▲ *Norway*-class ships fought alongside several other classes of Starfleet vessel as part of a swarm tactic to defeat the Borg cube.

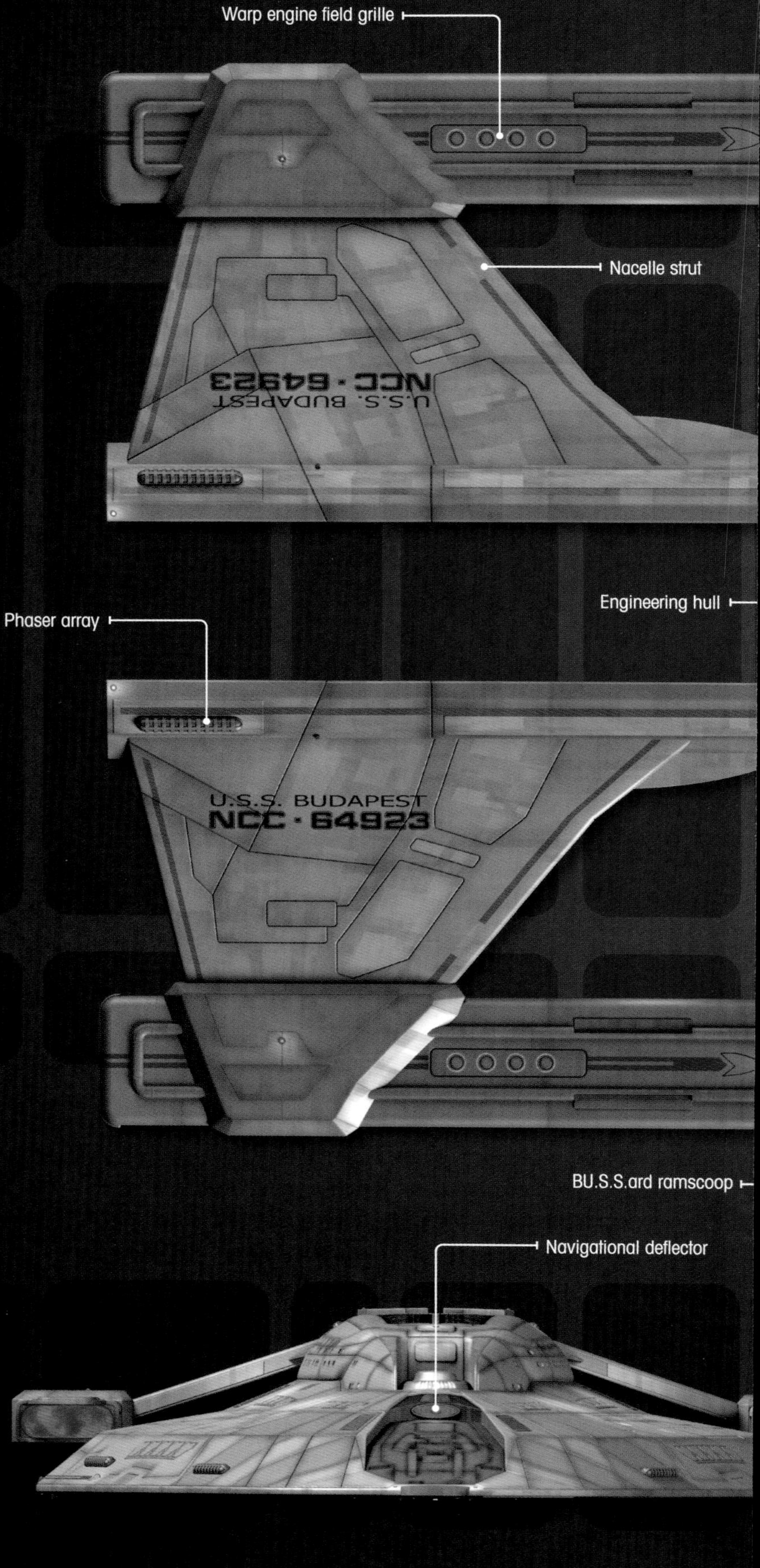

Warp engine field grille

Nacelle strut

U.S.S. BUDAPEST
NCC · 64923

Engineering hull

Phaser array

U.S.S. BUDAPEST
NCC · 64923

BU.S.S.ard ramscoop

Navigational deflector

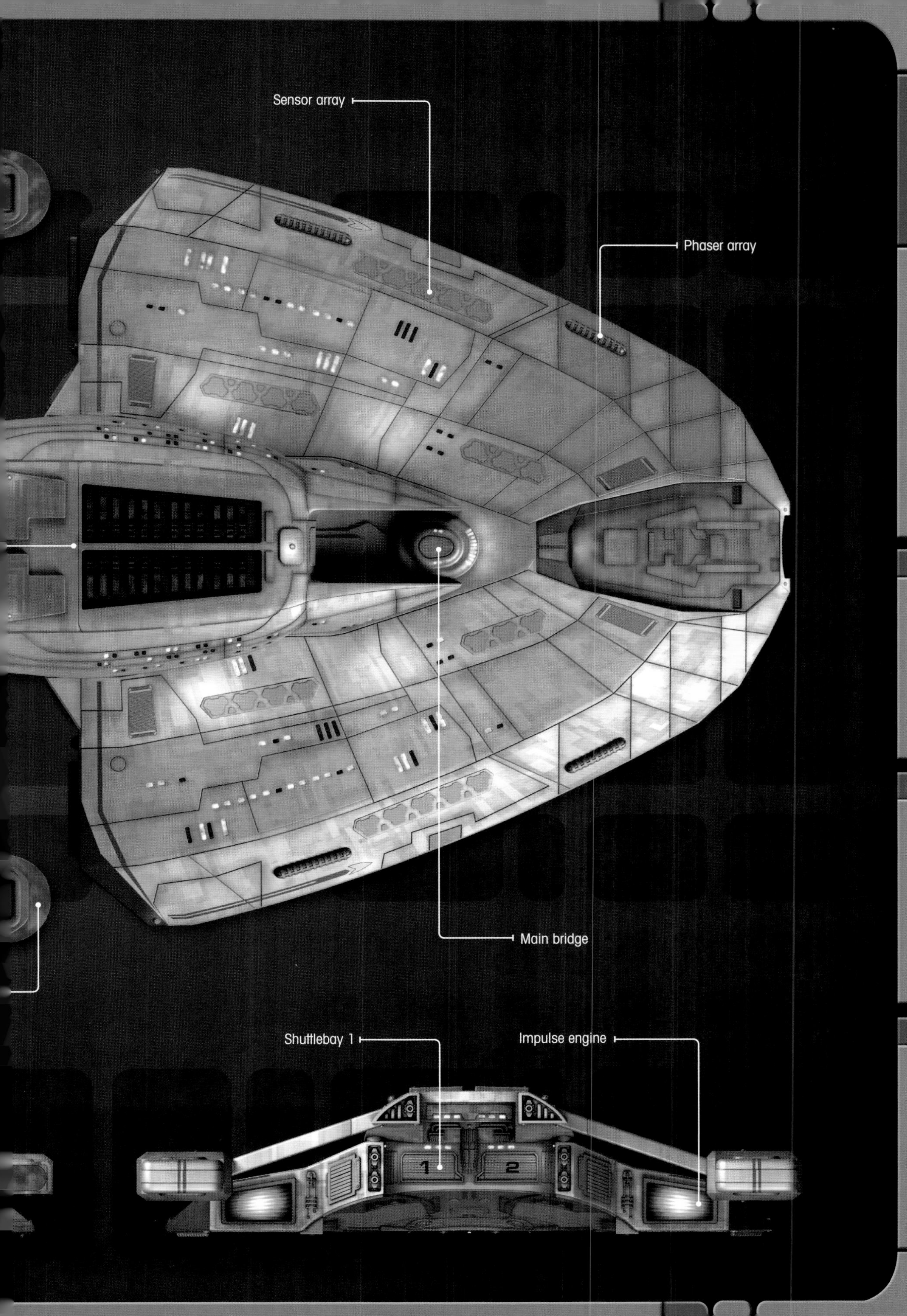

FLEET REBUILDING

Commander Shelby led the task force assigned to build the fleet up to previous deployment levels. Production on the *Norway* class was based at the Advanced Starship Design Bureau Integration Section at Spacedock 1, Earth.

NORWAY NAME

One of the *Norway*-class vessels that formed part of the reinvigorated fleet that fought the Borg at the Battle of Sector 001 was the *U.S.S. Budapest* NCC-64923. It was named after the Hungarian capital.

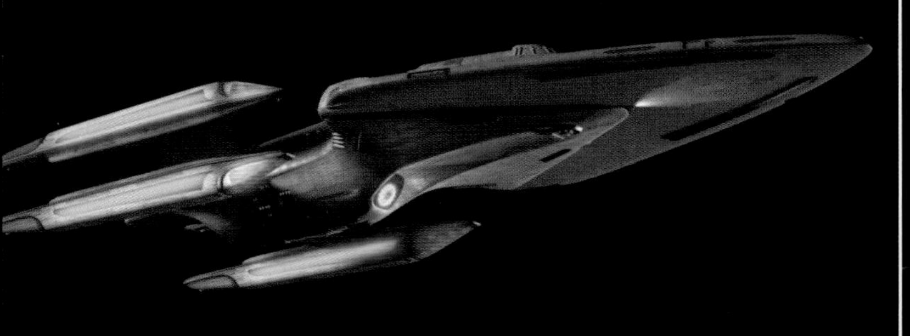

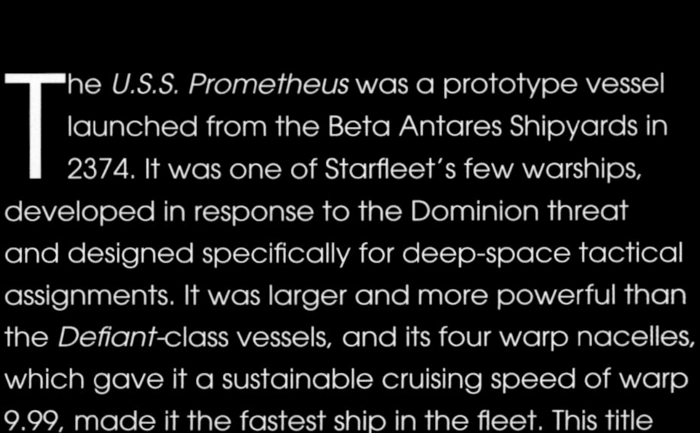

The *U.S.S. Prometheus* was a prototype vessel launched from the Beta Antares Shipyards in 2374. It was one of Starfleet's few warships, developed in response to the Dominion threat and designed specifically for deep-space tactical assignments. It was larger and more powerful than the *Defiant*-class vessels, and its four warp nacelles, which gave it a sustainable cruising speed of warp 9.99, made it the fastest ship in the fleet. This title was previously held by the *Intrepid*-class vessels that were capable of a warp speed of 9.975.

EXPERIMENTAL WARSHIP

At the time of its launch, the *Prometheus* was so highly classified that only four people were trained to operate the bridge. Even access to most onboard systems, including communications, was restricted to personnel with level-four clearance.

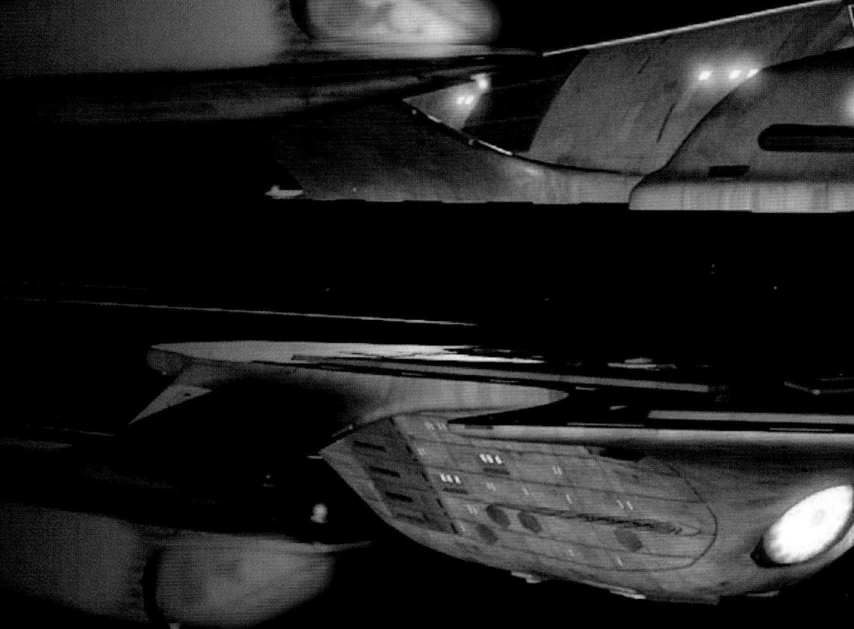

U.S.S. PROMETHEUS NX-59650

This experimental vessel was designed to split into three to mount a devastating attack.

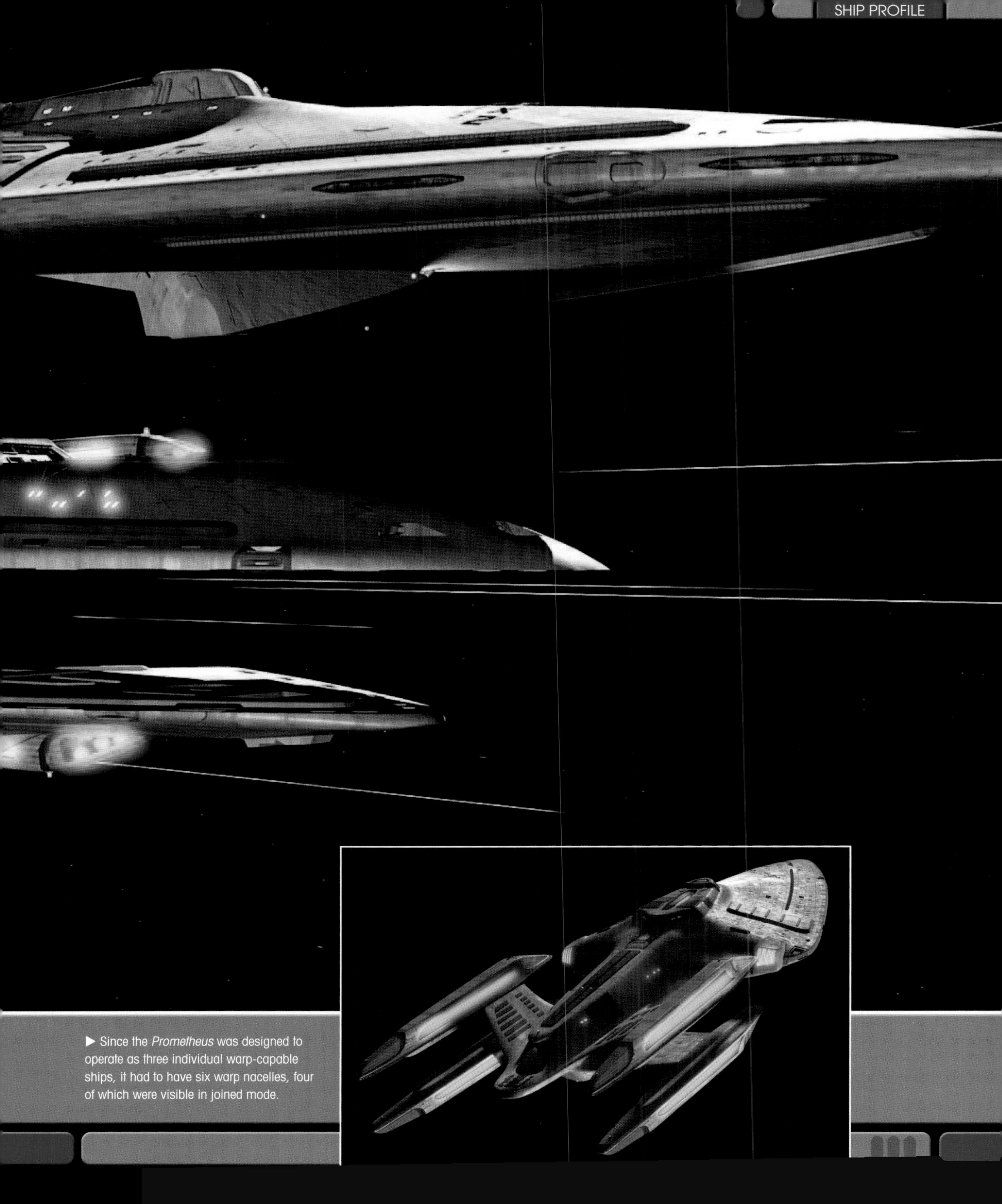

▶ Since the *Prometheus* was designed to operate as three individual warp-capable ships, it had to have six warp nacelles, four of which were visible in joined mode.

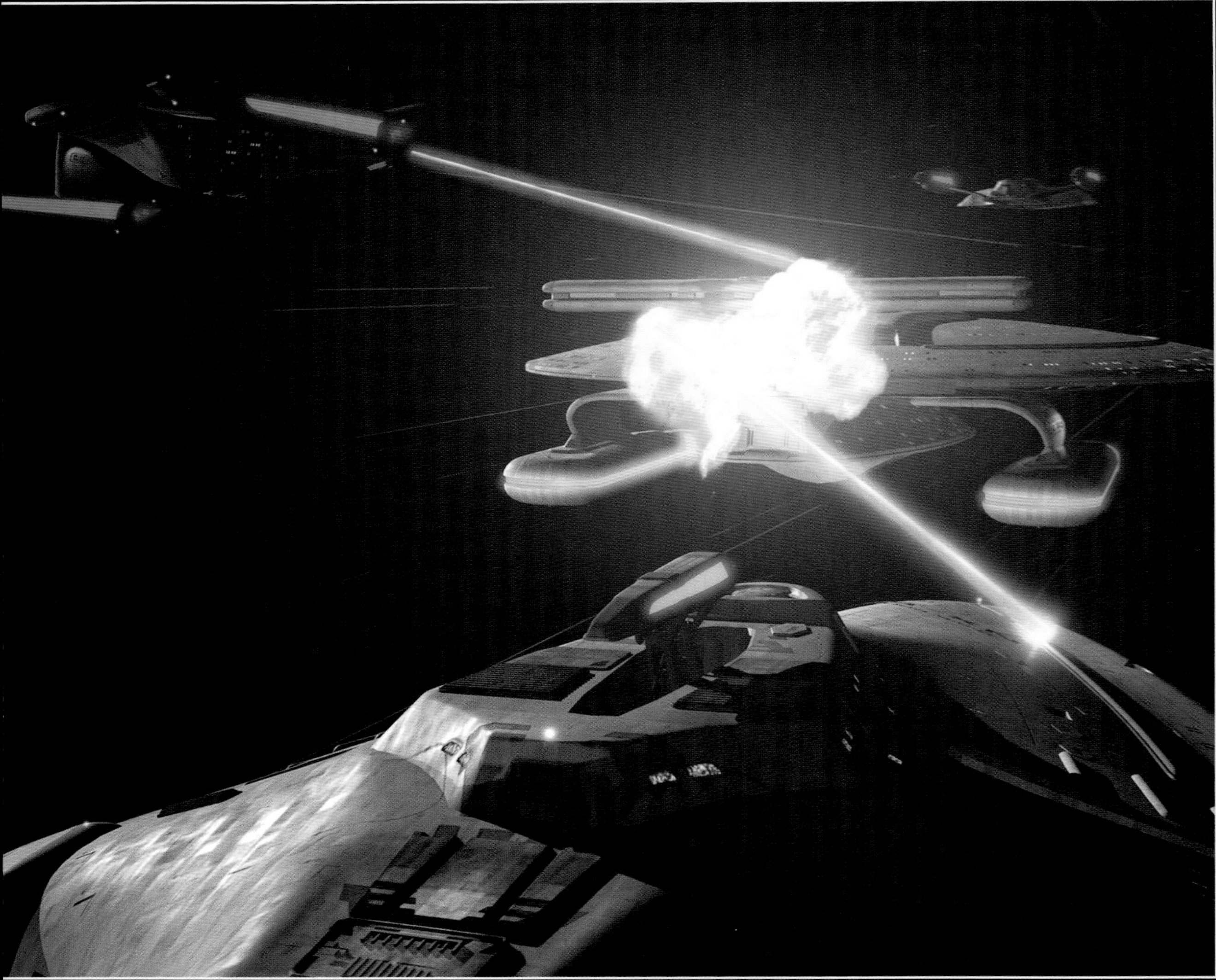

▶ When *Voyager*'s crew made contact with the *Prometheus*, they were able to transmit their EMH. Most of the ship was fitted with holoprojectors and this enabled the EMH and his counterpart on the *Prometheus* to travel to all parts of the ship, including the bridge.

▼ The *Prometheus* was fitted with the latest defensive technologies, including regenerative shields and ablative armor.

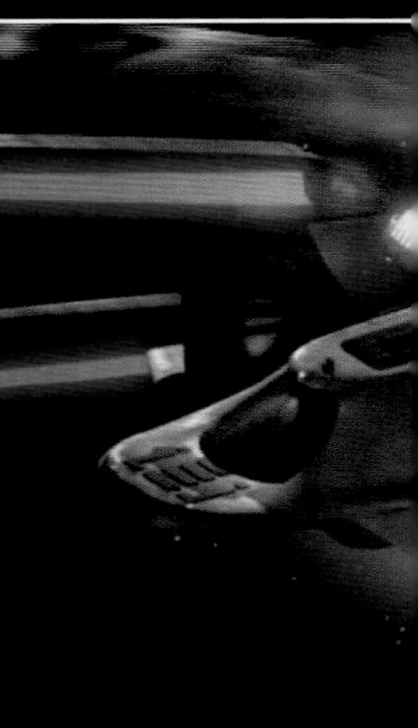

▲ Once the *Prometheus* had separated into three, it was designed to mount a combined assault on an enemy target. All three component vessels were heavily armed and programmed with a variety of attack patterns. The first time the system was operated in field conditions, the ship was under Romulan control and attacked the *U.S.S. Bonchune*.

The high level of security was necessary because the *Prometheus* was equipped with a number of cutting-edge systems. These included regenerative and metaphasic shields augmented by a polaron modulator, ablative hull armor (an outer layer that vaporized under weapons fire, dissipating energy and protecting the ship's interior); and multiple Type-XII phaser arrays, together with photon and quantum torpedoes.

ASSAULT SQUADRON

The ship's most impressive feature, however, was its multivector assault mode. By using advanced compartmentalization and automaton systems, it was able to split into three separate vessels. All three sections were warp capable and had independent maneuvering and attack capabilities. This enabled the *Prometheus* to operate as a mini squadron that could launch a coordinated, three-pronged assault on a target.

By default, each section was remotely controlled by the ship's sophisticated tactical computer, which was based on the main bridge of the main hull. Once the ship had separated, the computer requested an attack pattern and a target. Alternatively, an experienced Tactical Officer could control all three sections, either semi-manually in emergency combat situations, or each section could be manned by a skeleton crew. The decoupling could be achieved in a matter of seconds and reintegrated just as quickly.

The ship boasted 15 decks, comprised of officers' quarters, engineering, and shuttlebays. The sickbay was packed with state-of-the-art technology, including the latest incarnation of the Emergency Medical Hologram – the Mark II program. This improved version of the EMH had an updated subroutine that gave it a friendlier

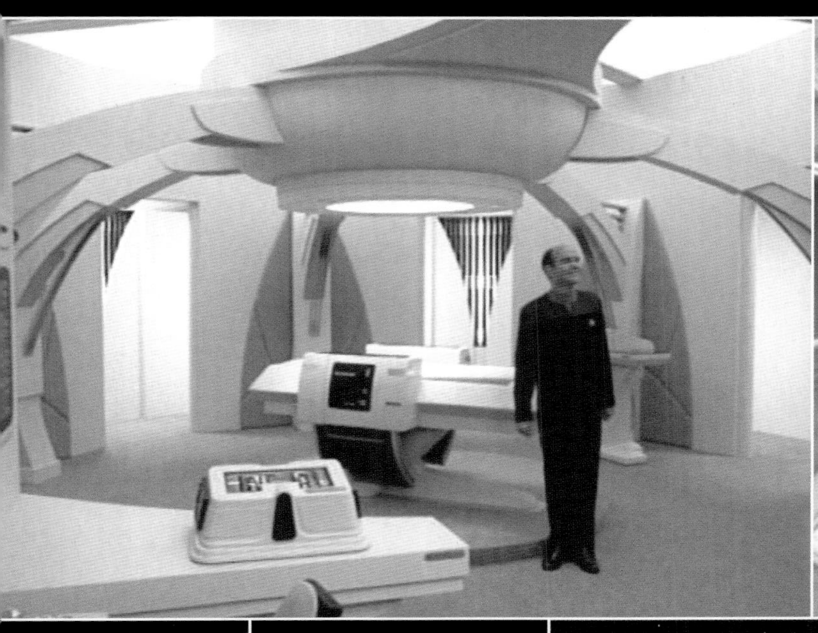

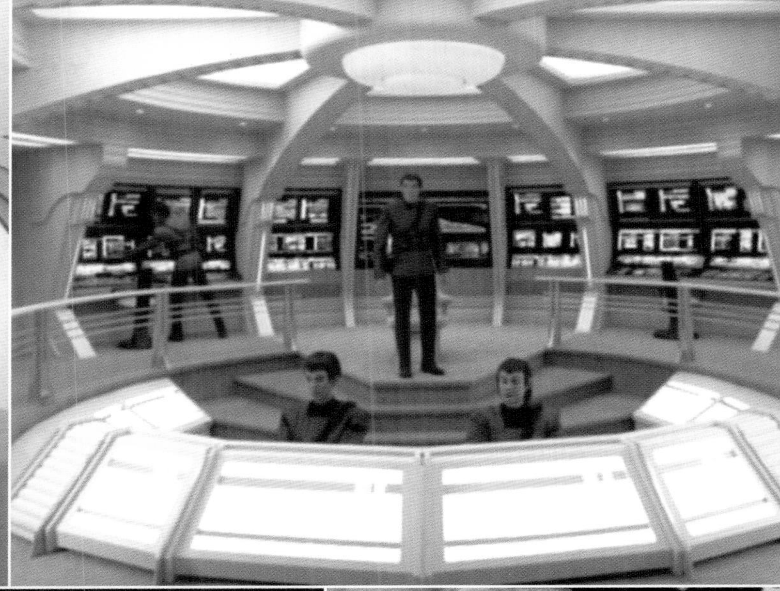

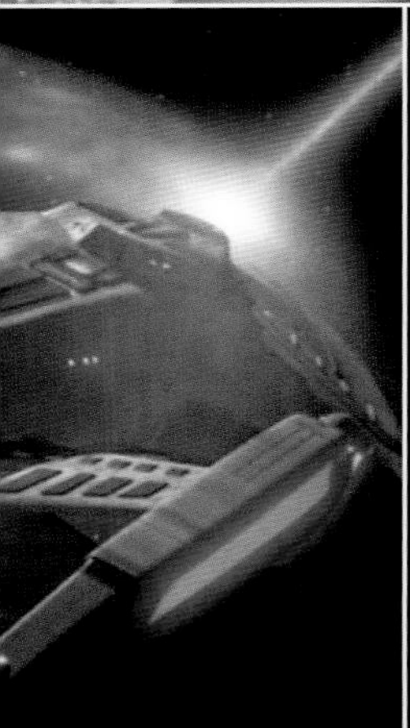

▶ *Voyager* tried to contact the *Prometheus* after the crew found an ancient network of subspace relays. When their initial attempts to contact the ship failed, they sent their EMH through the network. On arival, he discovered the Starfleet crew were dead but managed to work with the *Prometheus*'s EMH to regain control of the ship.

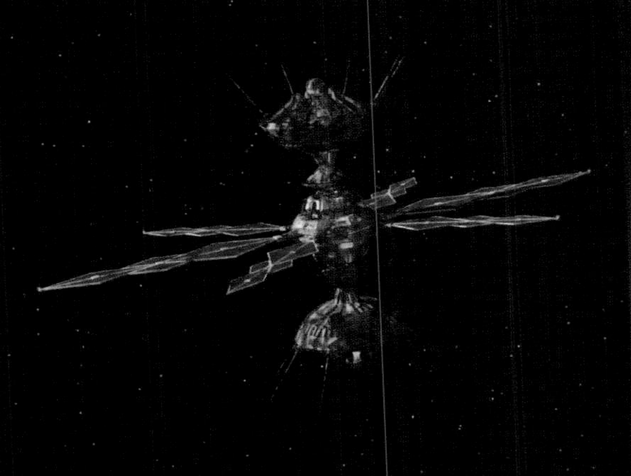

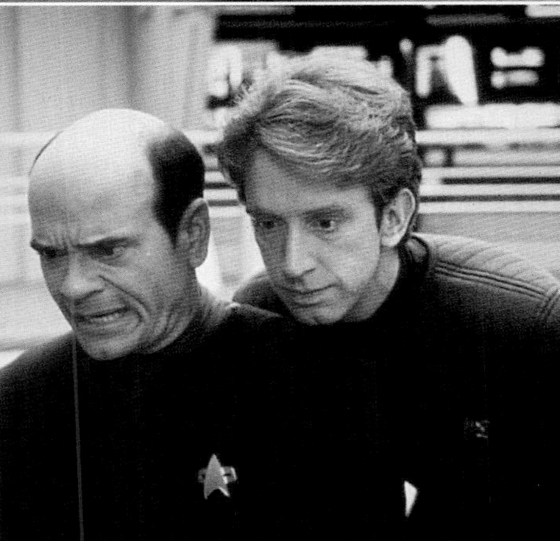

and more approachable bedside manner. It also featured advanced security features.

Thanks to holographic emitters dotted throughout the vessel, the EMH had the ability to operate outside of sickbay, so it could reach any area of the ship in order to treat injuries sustained during battle.

HOLOGRAPHIC RESCUE

The holographic aspect of the design was crucial in recovering the ship when, during a test shortly after its launch in 2374, Romulan hijackers took command of the *Prometheus*. Using the multivector system, they were able to successfully disable the *Nebula*-class *U.S.S. Bonchune*. The *Prometheus* was eventually recaptured with the help of two EMHs, who disabled the attackers and destroyed a *D'deridex*-class Romulan warbird before Starfleet managed to recover the ship.

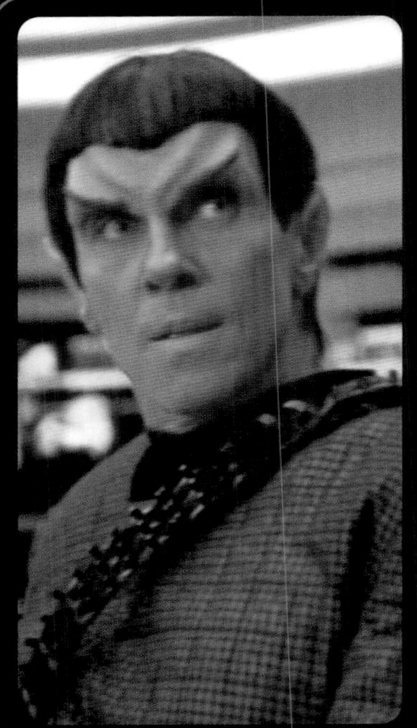

DATA FEED

The *Prometheus* was field-tested on the edge of Federation space in 2374. During the trial, a team of 27 Romulans led by Commander Rekar took control of the ship and killed the Starfleet crew. They were pursued by the *U.S.S. Bonchune* but used the *Prometheus*'s untested multivector assault mode to overpower it. Rekar then planned to enter Romulan space and hand the *Prometheus* over to the Romulan secret police, the Tal'shiar. However, before he could do so, the *Prometheus*'s EMH disabled his team with neurozine gas. The EMH, working with his *Voyager* counterpart, then used the automated systems to destroy one of the Tal'shiar's warbirds, forcing them to retreat.

DATA FEED

All three sections of the *Prometheus* were fitted with state-of-the-art weapons, including yype-XII phaser arrays and photon and quantum torpedoes. During battle, these were linked to a central tactical computer that coordinated their attack pattern to inflict maximum damage on their target.

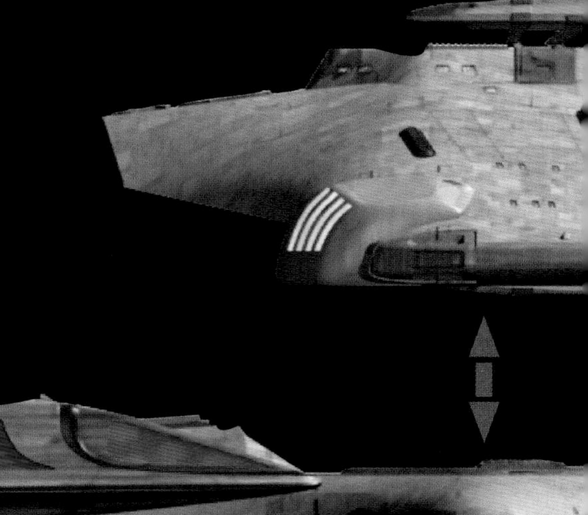

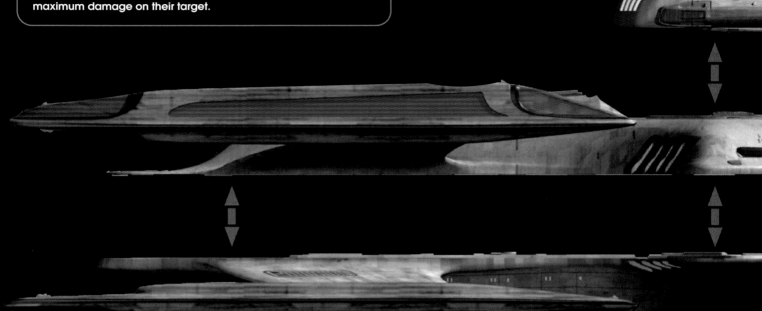

Ship Separation

The *Prometheus*'s ability to split into three required Starfleet's Advanced Starship Design Bureau to radically rethink its design. Vessels had been designed to split in two for many years, but in those cases the intention had always been to use the saucer module effectively as an enormous escape module. For the *Prometheus*, the intention was to create three independent warships.

The biggest challenges involved the design of the Warp Propulsion System (WPS). The system required three reaction chambers. In the engineering section, which split in two, this was achieved by using a unique design of warp core. During normal operation, matter was fed in at the top of the core and antimatter at the bottom. The fuel streams then passed directly through upper and lower reaction chambers before continuing to their meeting point in a conventional central reaction chamber. The central reaction chamber lay on a separation plane, which was shut down when the ship split. Additional matter and antimatter feeds were then activated to feed the now independent reaction chambers.

When separated, the primary hull operated with an independent, horizontal, *Defiant*-style warp core, which was kept in hot standby mode until it was needed. While the combined engineering WPS was able to operate on an efficiency level comparable to and, in fact, in excess of any contemporary starship, in separated mode it lost a degree of efficiency but could still maintain high warp speeds.

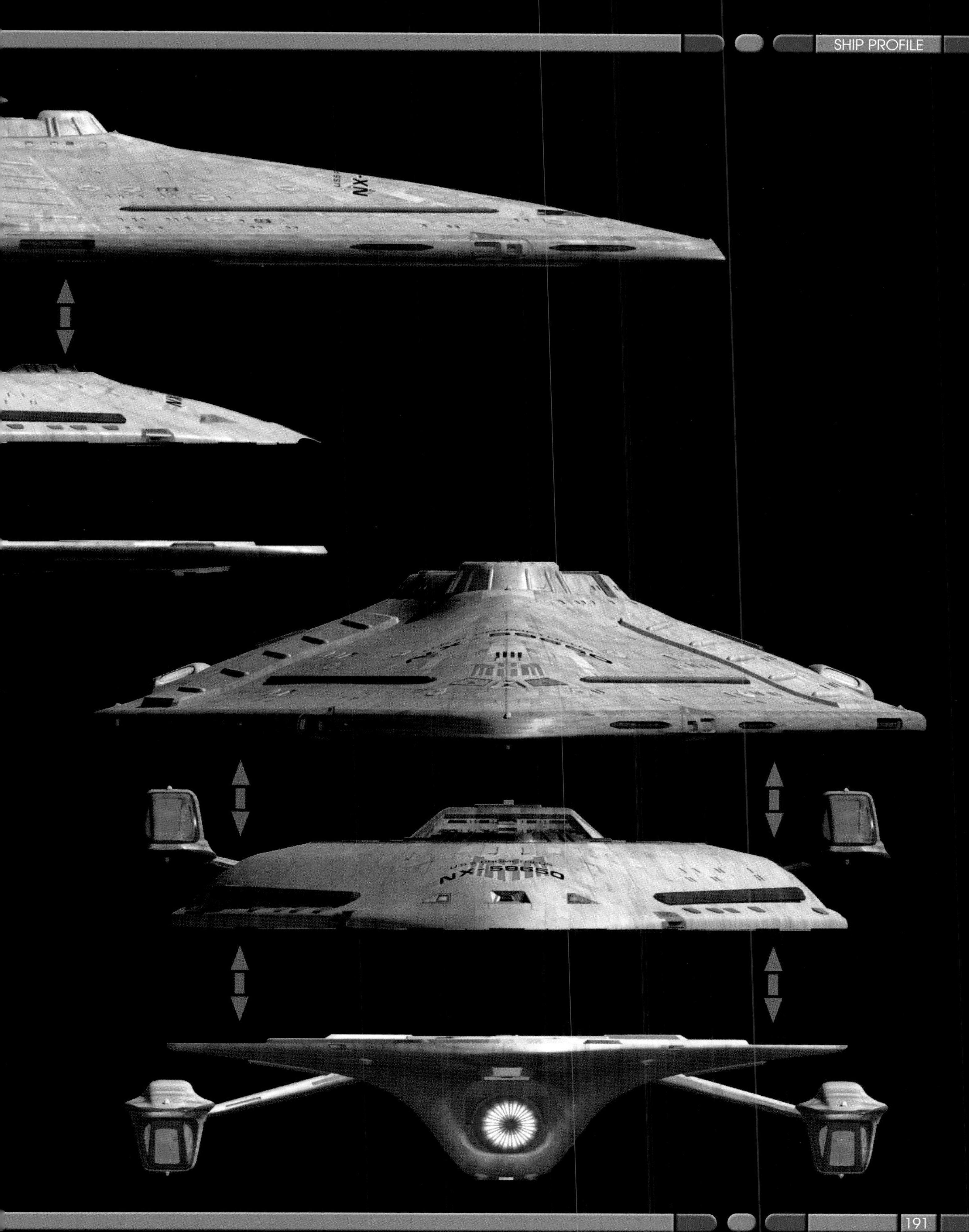
U.S.S. PROMETHEUS
NX-59650

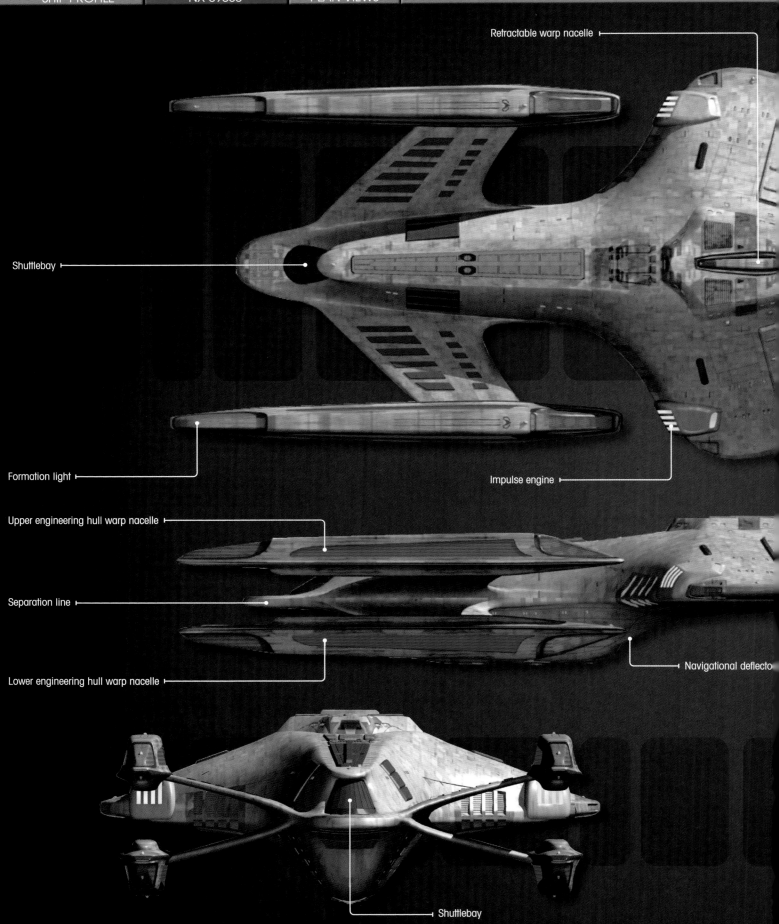

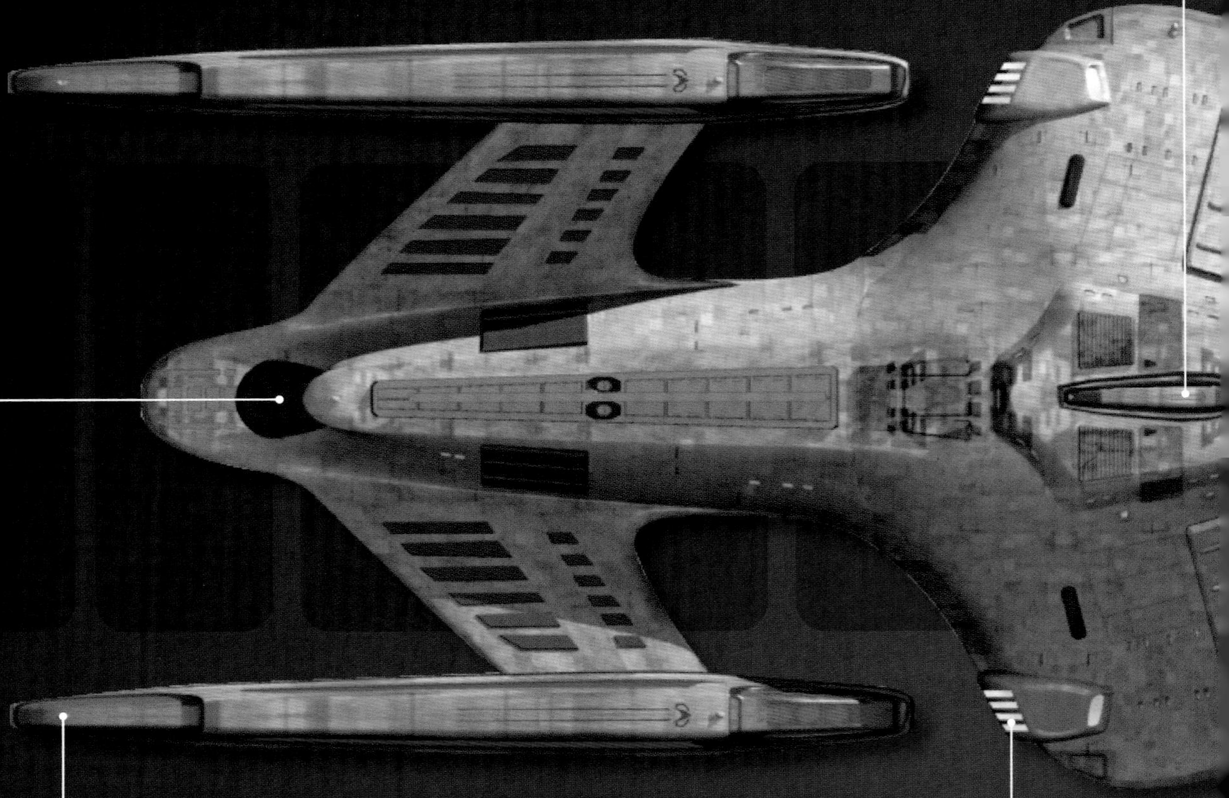

Retractable warp nacelle

Shuttlebay

Formation light

Impulse engine

Upper engineering hull warp nacelle

Separation line

Lower engineering hull warp nacelle

Navigational deflecto

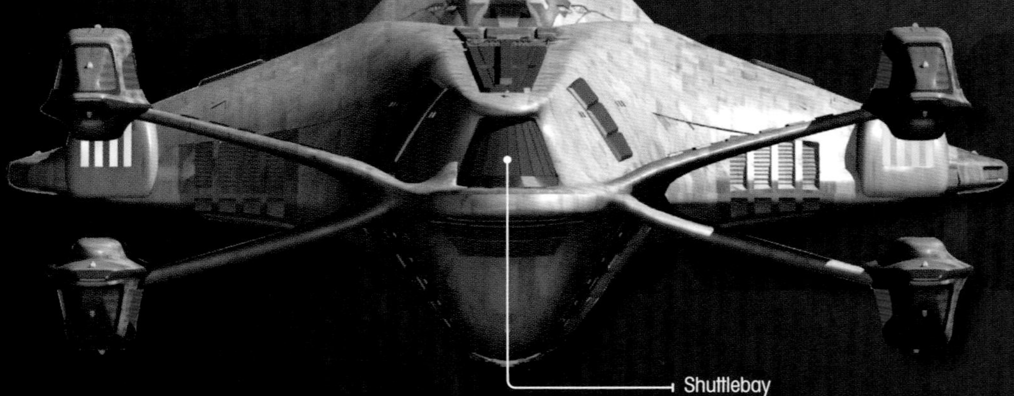

Shuttlebay

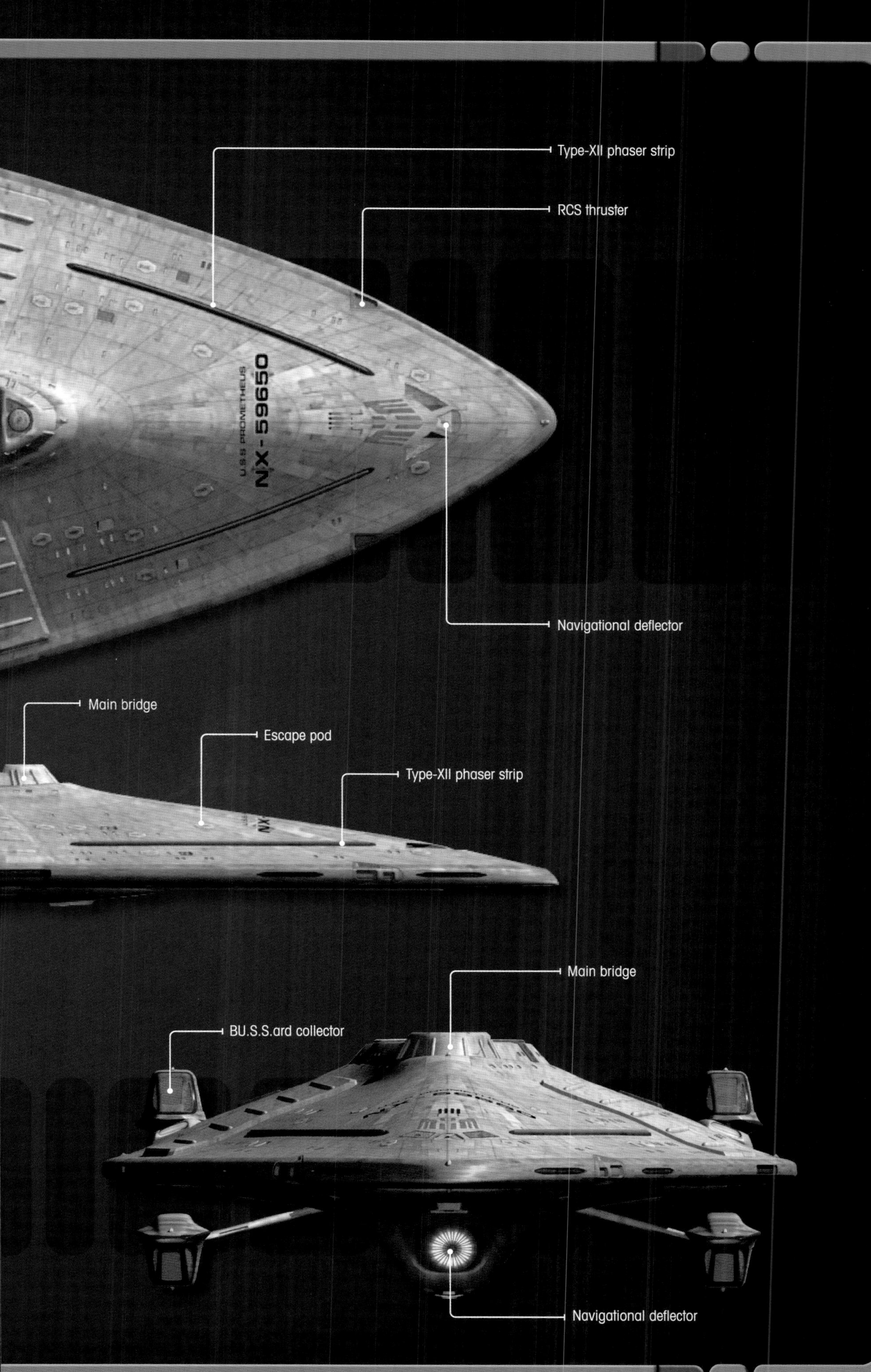

EFFICIENT SYSTEM

It took the *Prometheus* just over 10 seconds to decouple the three sections. While it was in the process of decoupling, warning lights flashed blue throughout the ship.

SAUCER NACELLES

The main hull – or saucer section – used twin retractable warp nacelles that were positioned above and below the hull, rather than on the sides. Only the upper nacelle was visible when the ship was in joined mode.

ABLATIVE ARMOR

The *Prometheus* was equipped with ablative armor, a protective outer layer on the hull that dissipated weapons fire. It was first fitted to the *Defiant* class in 2371. A similar technology was employed by the Borg.

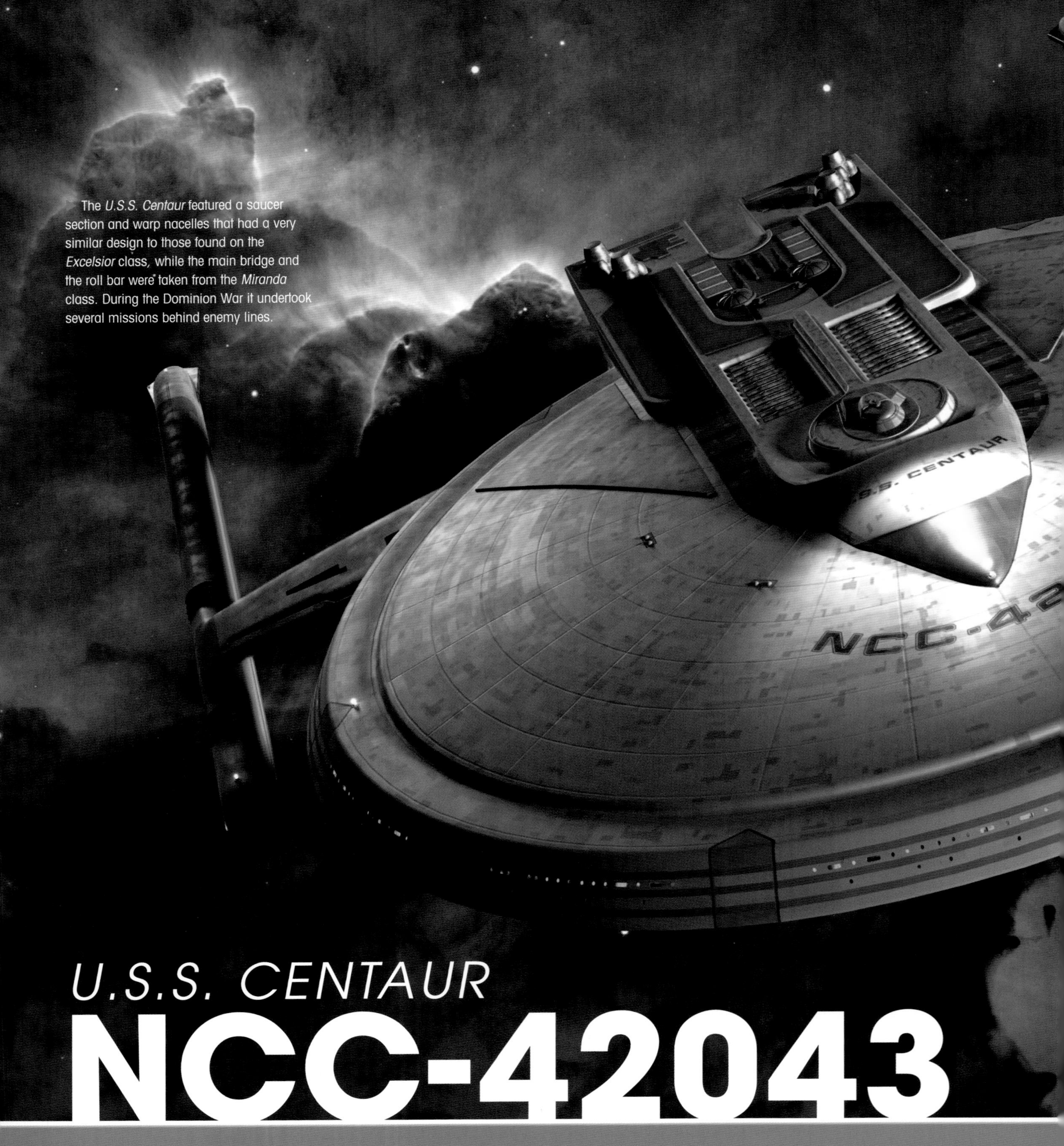

The *U.S.S. Centaur* featured a saucer section and warp nacelles that had a very similar design to those found on the *Excelsior* class, while the main bridge and the roll bar were taken from the *Miranda* class. During the Dominion War it undertook several missions behind enemy lines.

U.S.S. CENTAUR NCC-42043

The *U.S.S. Centaur* was closely related to the *Excelsior* and *Miranda* classes, and saw action in the Dominion War.

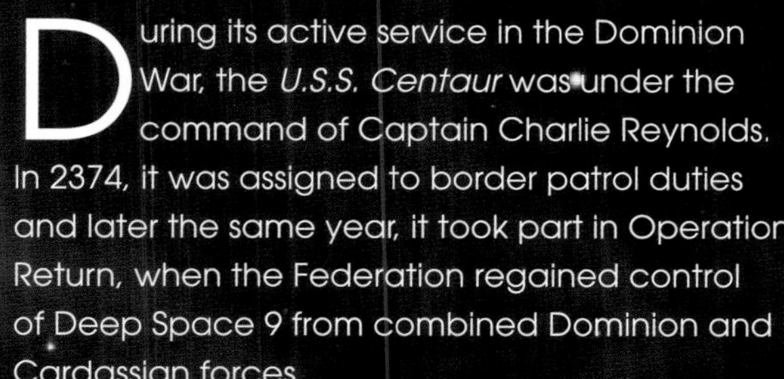

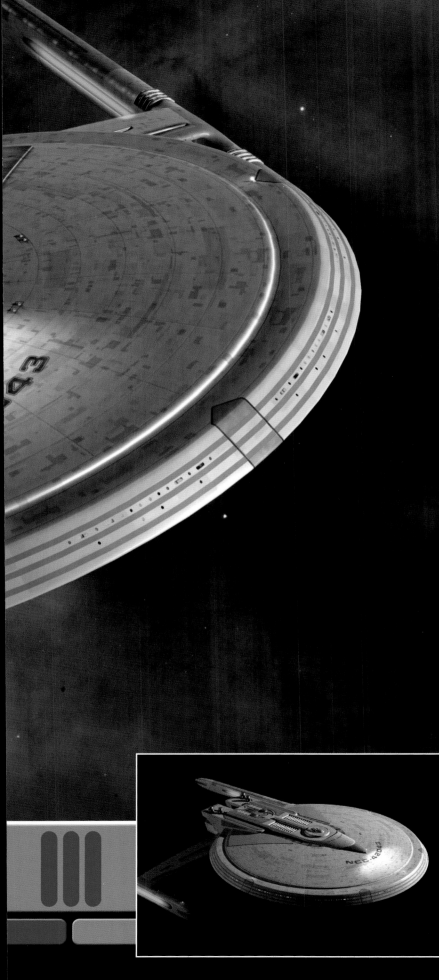

During its active service in the Dominion War, the *U.S.S. Centaur* was under the command of Captain Charlie Reynolds. In 2374, it was assigned to border patrol duties and later the same year, it took part in Operation Return, when the Federation regained control of Deep Space 9 from combined Dominion and Cardassian forces.

The *Centaur* was constructed after Starfleet suffered huge losses in the opening months of the war with the Dominion, leaving its fleets severely depleted. For example, the Seventh Fleet was dispatched to the Tyra system to prevent Dominion forces advancing further into Federation space, but the counteroffensive was nothing short of a disaster. Out of the Seventh Fleet's 112 ships, only 14 survived the engagement and made it back to their lines.

COMPOSITE DESIGN

Devastating losses such as this meant that Starfleet had to accelerate its shipbuilding programs to compensate. With resources stretched thin, this inevitably meant that compromises had to be made and ships had to be constructed from partial builds, salvaged components and serviceable warp engines. The *Centaur* was almost certainly a result of this expedited assembly process, resulting in its hybrid appearance.

The *Centaur*'s design was very similar to that of the *Excelsior* and *Miranda* classes. The saucer section and its long, thin warp nacelles were highly reminiscent of those found on the *Excelsior* class, although much smaller. The main bridge module in the center of the saucer was identical to that of the *Miranda* class. The nacelle pylons on the *Centaur* also echoed the inverted shape of the spars that connected the weapons pod

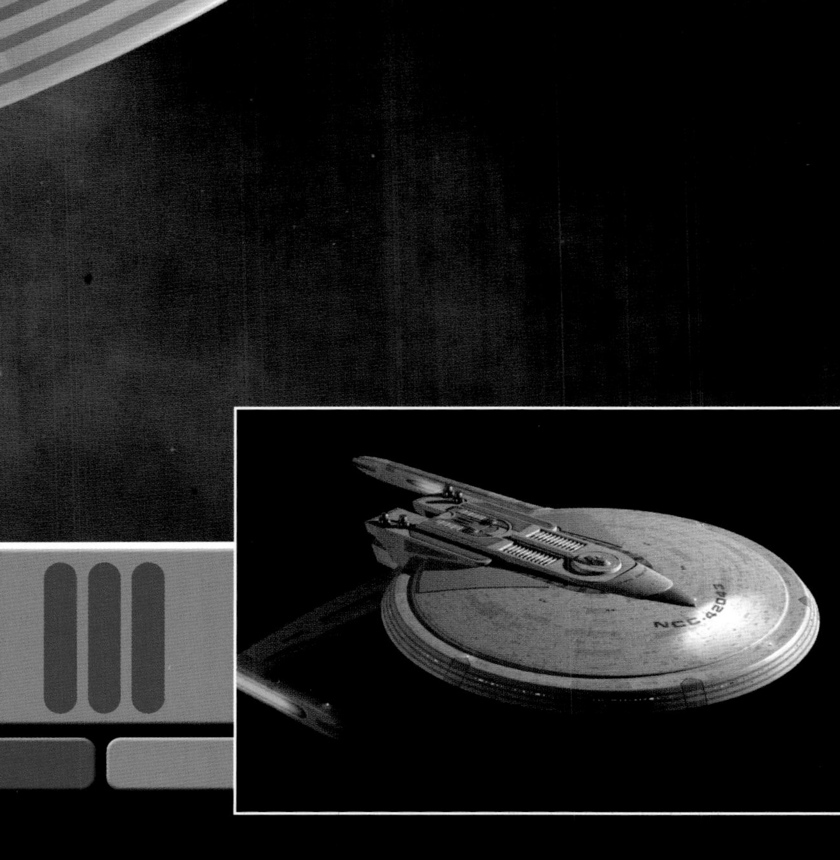

◀ Unusually for a Starfleet vessel, the *Centaur*'s main shuttlebay was not located at the rear of the vessel, but at the front of the saucer, in-between the bridge module and the registry number. The shape of the copper-colored shuttlebay doors was identical to those found at the rear of the *Excelsior* class.

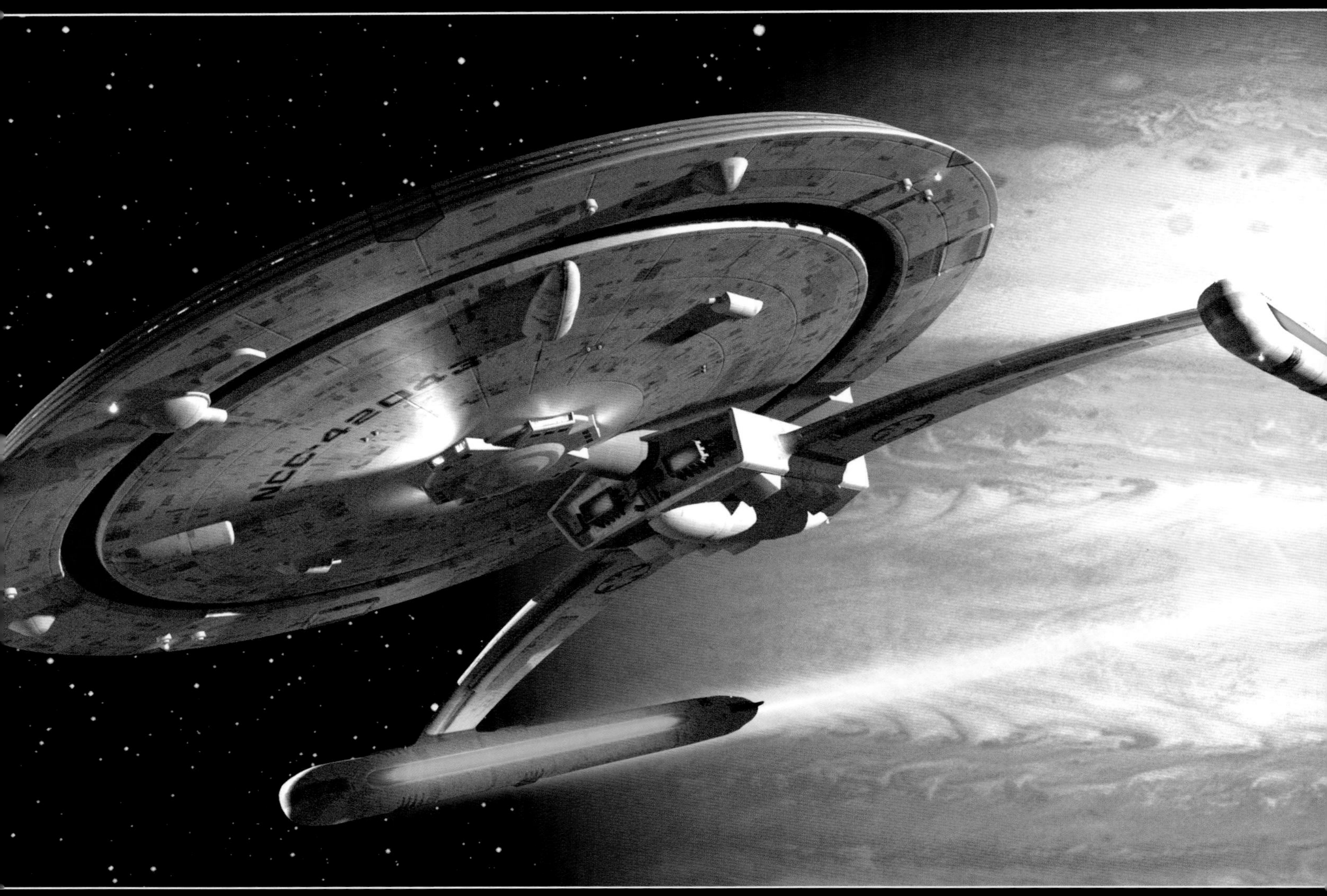

▲ The weapons pod that was located on a roll bar above the saucer on the *Miranda* class was turned upside down for use on the *Centaur*. This pod featured fore and aft torpedo launchers and greatly increased the *Centaur's* firepower.

above the saucer on the *Miranda* class. And the *Miranda* class's whole weapons pod appeared to have been turned upside down and used as the small secondary hull at the rear and below the saucer on the *Centaur*. This module provided two forward- and two rear-facing torpedo launchers, and supplemented the type-9 phaser emitters that provided full, 360-degree covering fire around the hull of the ship.

HIDDEN DEFLECTOR

The *Centaur's* forward-facing shuttlebay was a surprising feature for a Starfleet ship. This was located in front of the bridge module on top of the saucer section. But, while the location was unusual, the shape and design of the copper-colored shuttlebay doors were identical to those found at the rear of the engineering hull on *Excelsior*-class ships.

Despite its overall close similarities to the *Excelsior* and *Miranda* classes, the *Centaur* did possess some unique features. They included some copper-colored arrays behind the bridge module and similarly colored turrets above the impulse engines, all of which were designed for long-range sensing. There were also various raised features on the underside of the saucer, including a sensor dome in the center.

The *Centaur* may have been constructed in haste and featured a mishmash of styles, but it was just as capable as established classes. It had a top speed of warp 9.6, and was equipped with sensitive long-range scanning equipment, as well as a formidable array of weaponry.

All these attributes made the *Centaur* ideally suited to border patrol and incursion, providing early warning and a first line of defense against invading Dominion and Jem'Hadar forces.

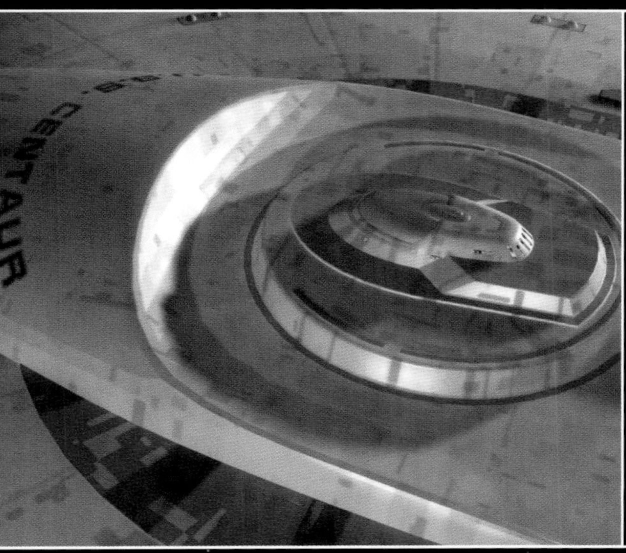

▶ The twin impulse engines on the *Centaur* emitted a deep red glow and were positioned on top of a wedge-shaped structure at the rear of the saucer section.

◀ The *Centaur* had a bridge shaped like the one found on a *Miranda*-class ship. It was positioned behind a raised segment that helped to protect it from enemy fire.

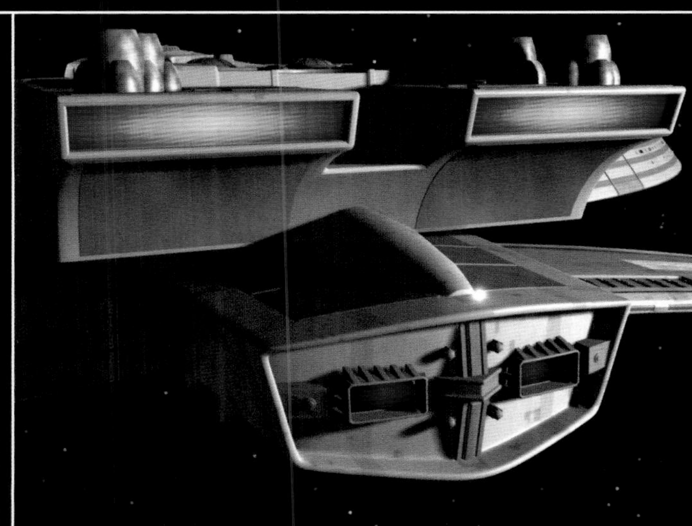

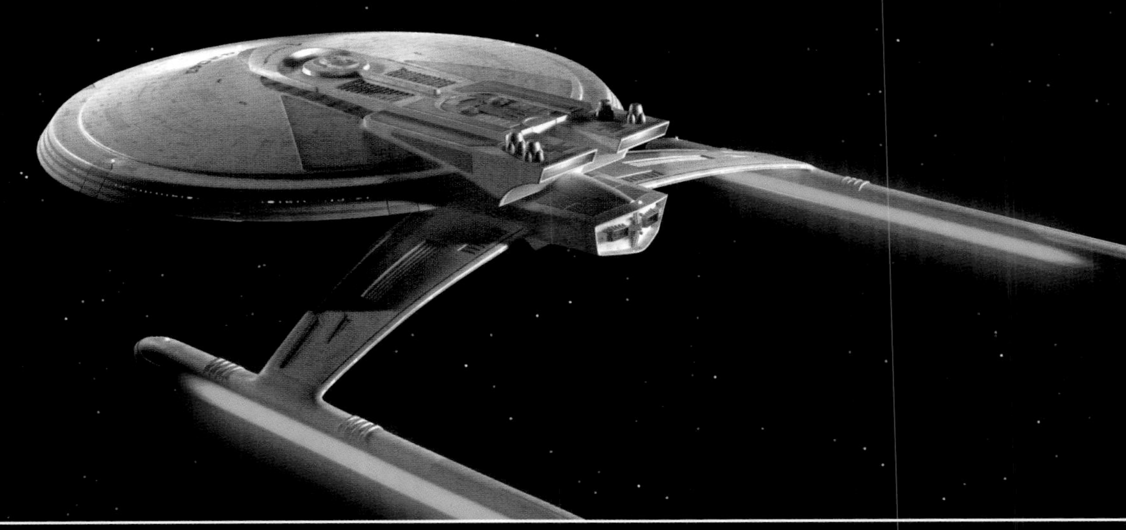

◀ The warp nacelles appeared to be extremely long and thin on the *Centaur* because of its truncated secondary hull. In fact, the nacelles and saucer were in proportion to one another as they were almost identical to those found on the *Excelsior* class. The nacelles and warp engine combined to give the *Centaur* an impressive top speed of warp 9.6.

In 2374, the *Centaur* was on the edge of Federation-controlled space when it encountered what was believed to be a lone Jem'Hadar attack ship returning to Dominion lines.

SPACE BATTLE

Captain Reynolds decided to engage the smaller vessel, and opened fire. However, he did not know that the Jem'Hadar ship was actually under the control of Starfleet officers, led by his old friend Captain Benjamin Sisko, and was on a secret mission to destroy a ketracel-white production facility deep in Cardassian space.

Sisko's mission was so secret that other Starfleet vessels had not been informed of it. A brief dogfight ensued, as Sisko tried not to cause serious damage to the *Centaur*, by targeting just its weapons, not its engines. The battle ended only when three more Jem'Hadar attack ships appeared and Reynolds was forced to retreat at speed back into Federation space.

Later in the Dominion War, the *Centaur* operated out of Starbase 375 along with the Second and Fifth Fleets. Here they fought in several crucial theaters of combat before helping to retake Deep Space 9 from Dominion forces.

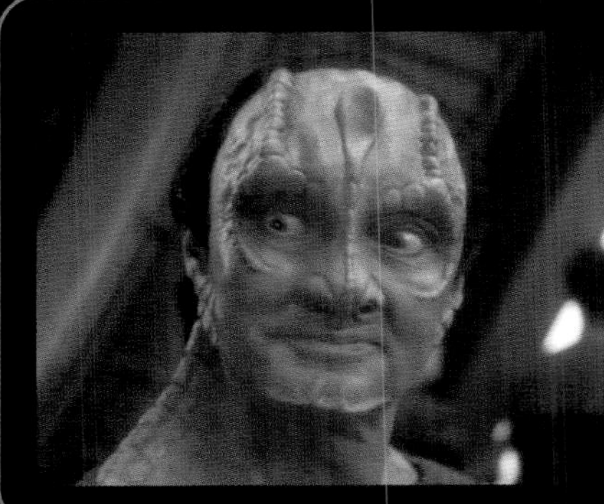

DATA FEED

When Elim Garak was taken prisoner by Jem'Hadar troops in 2374, he claimed that he was Kamar, a member of the Cardassian Intelligence Bureau. He told them he had been working for the Founders when he was captured by the *U.S.S. Centaur*, a story that was completely false.

OPERATION RETURN

The massive military undertaking code-named Operation Return was one of the most important battles of the Dominion War, in which Starfleet and its Klingon allies attempted to retake Deep Space 9 from the Dominion. Captain Sisko assembled a huge task force that combined elements of the Second, Fifth, and Ninth Fleets. Among the Starfleet ships known to have fought in this battle were the *U.S.S. Centaur, U.S.S. Cortez, U.S.S. Galaxy, U.S.S. Hood, U.S.S. Magellan, U.S.S. Majestic, U.S.S. Sarek, U.S.S. Sitak,* and *U.S.S. Venture*. The Allied fleet was confronted by 1,254 enemy vessels and outnumbered by about two to one, but still managed to win back control of Deep Space 9.

DATA FEED

Deep Space 9 became the headquarters of the Ninth Fleet ,and General Martok was made its supreme commander after it was recaptured from the Dominion. Vessels assigned to the Ninth Fleet included the *U.S.S. Akagi*, *U.S.S. Exeter*, *U.S.S. Potemkin*, *U.S.S. Sutherland*, and Martok's bird-of-prey, the *IKS Rotarran*.

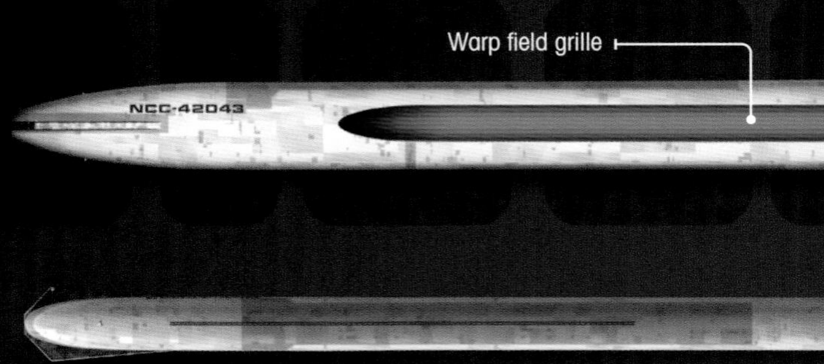

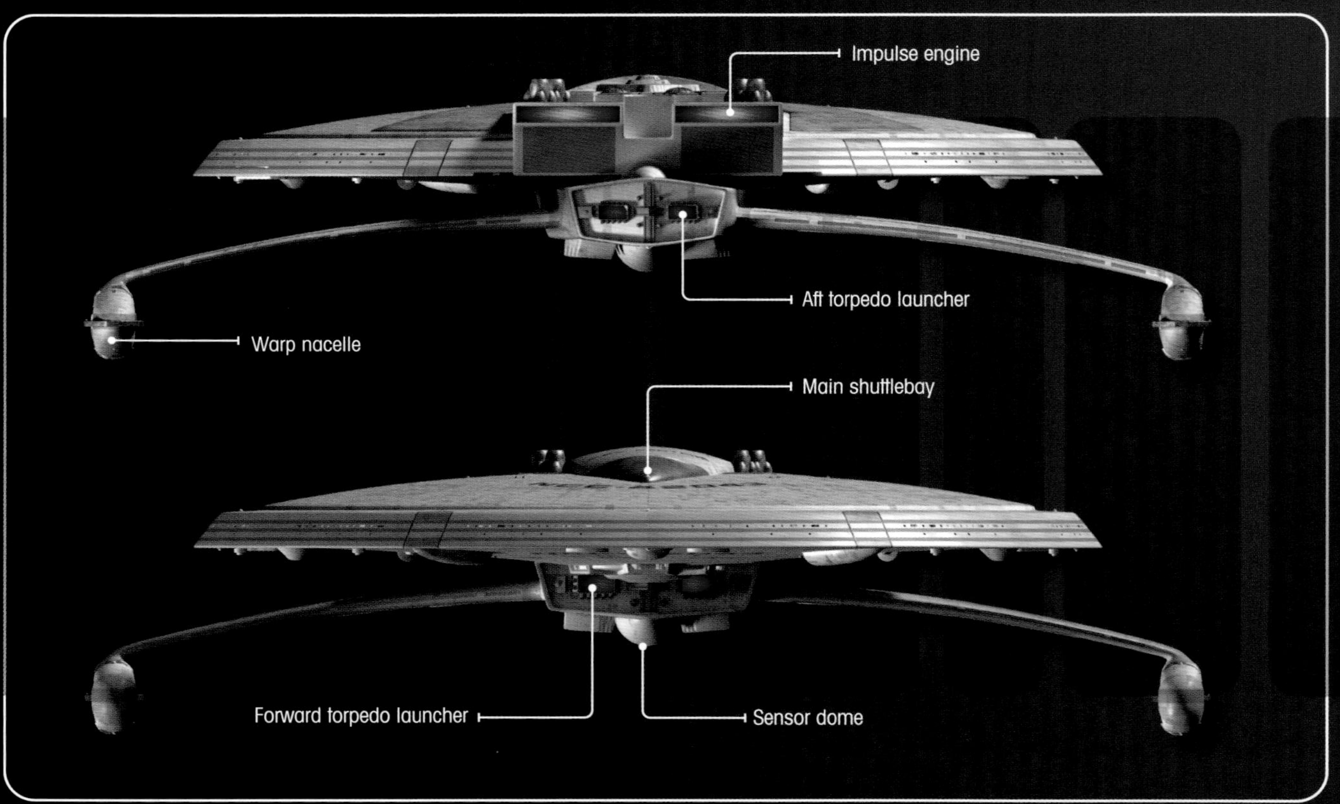

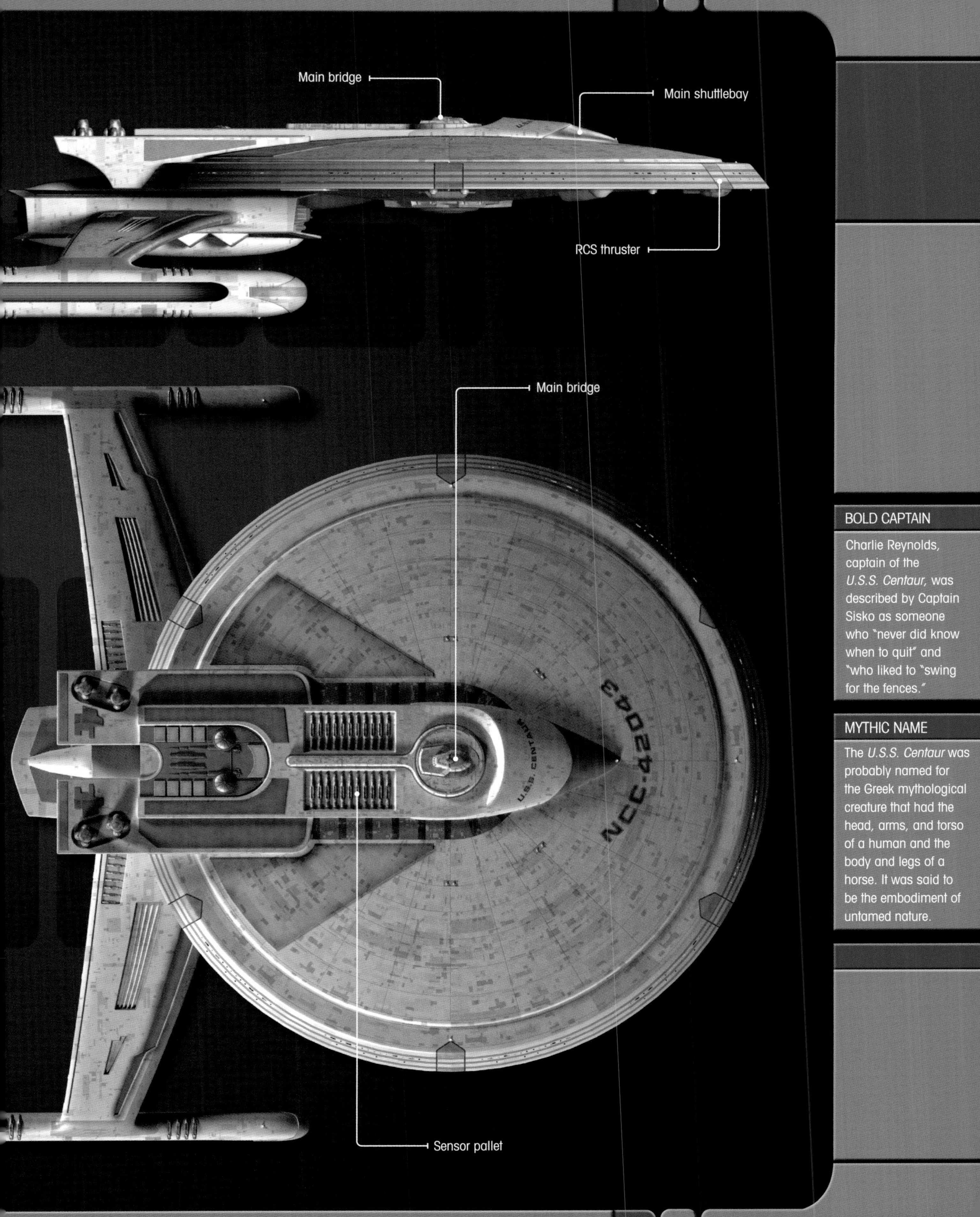

BOLD CAPTAIN

Charlie Reynolds, captain of the *U.S.S. Centaur,* was described by Captain Sisko as someone who "never did know when to quit" and "who liked to "swing for the fences."

MYTHIC NAME

The *U.S.S. Centaur* was probably named for the Greek mythological creature that had the head, arms, and torso of a human and the body and legs of a horse. It was said to be the embodiment of untamed nature.

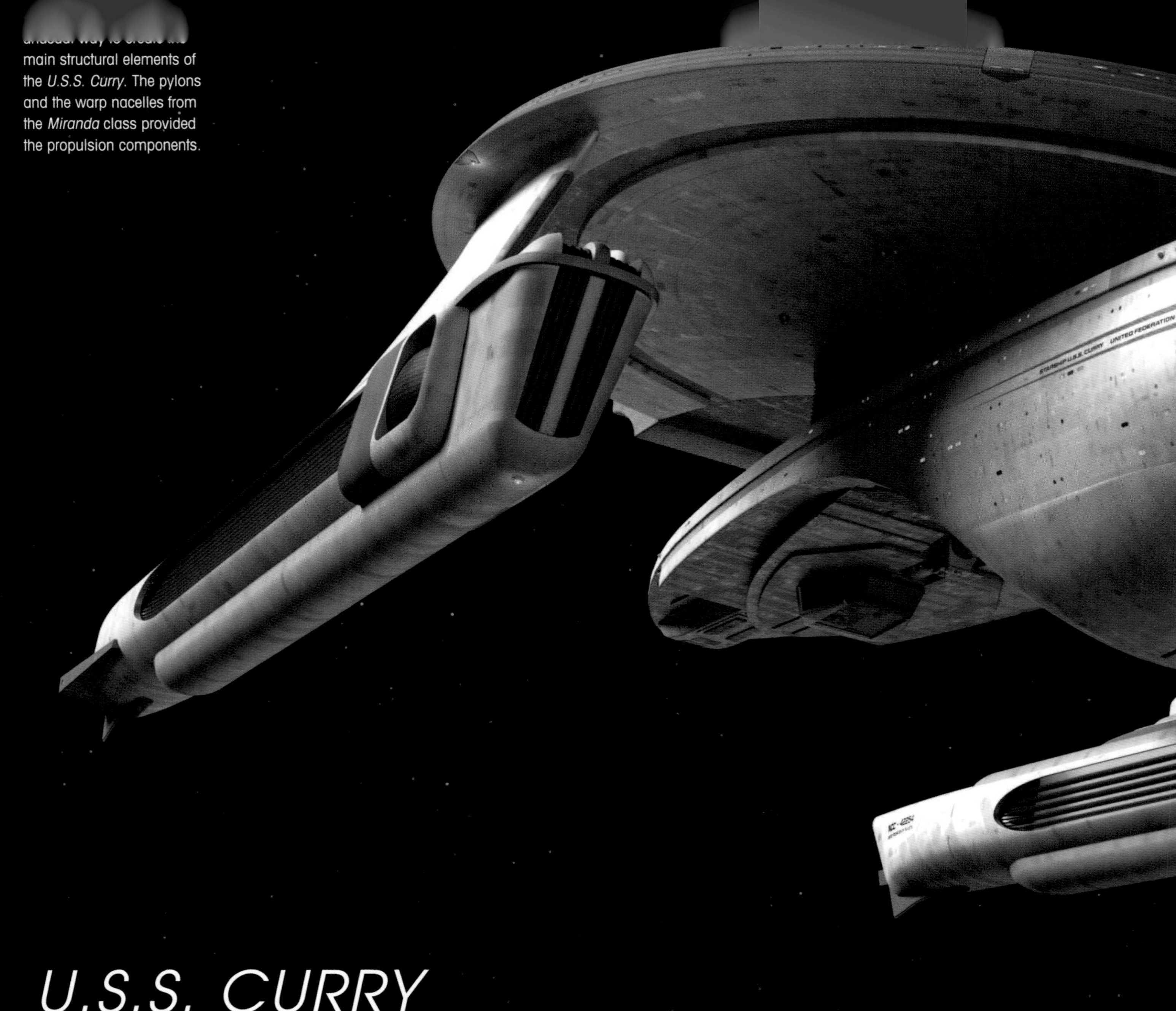

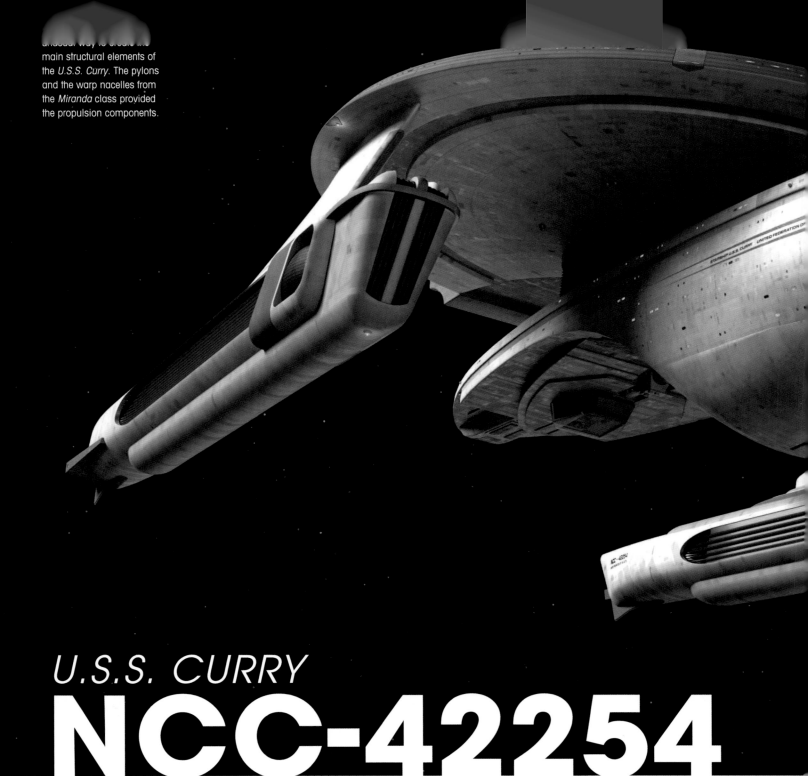

main structural elements of the *U.S.S. Curry*. The pylons and the warp nacelles from the *Miranda* class provided the propulsion components.

U.S.S. CURRY NCC-42254

The *U.S.S. Curry* was hastily assembled from various classes of ship to fight in the war against the Dominion.

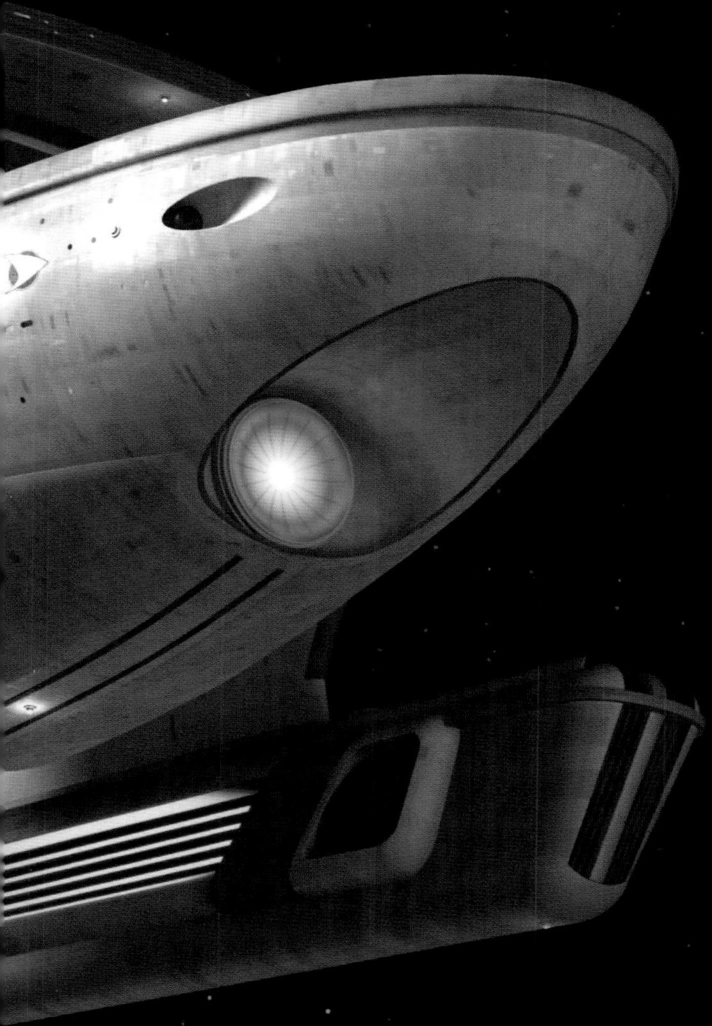

The *U.S.S. Curry* fought with the Second Fleet during the early part of the war with the Dominion, which broke out in 2373. The ship was unusual in being composed of parts taken from different classes so that it could enter service as quickly as possible to meet the Dominion threat.

The *Curry*'s saucer and engineering hulls were the same as those on the *Excelsior* class. However, the secondary hull was moved much further forward, and connected to the middle of the saucer section rather than at the back. This meant that the front of the engineering hull extended out well beyond the front of the saucer, giving the ship a very distinct profile.

UNORTHODOX CONFIGURATION

Another singular feature of the *Curry* was that the shuttlebay and shuttlebay doors were moved from the rear of the engineering hull – as on the *Excelsior* class – to the front.

The warp nacelles and pylons were very similar in shape and style to those found on the *Miranda* class, a type of ship that had first entered service over 100 years earlier. Despite their aging look, the nacelles were fitted with more advanced propulsion technology and were capable of propelling the ship to a top speed of warp 9.6 for short periods.

In fact, although the different elements that made up the *Curry* came from classes that had been in service for a considerable time, many of the systems had been upgraded to late 24th-century specifications. For example, its sensors

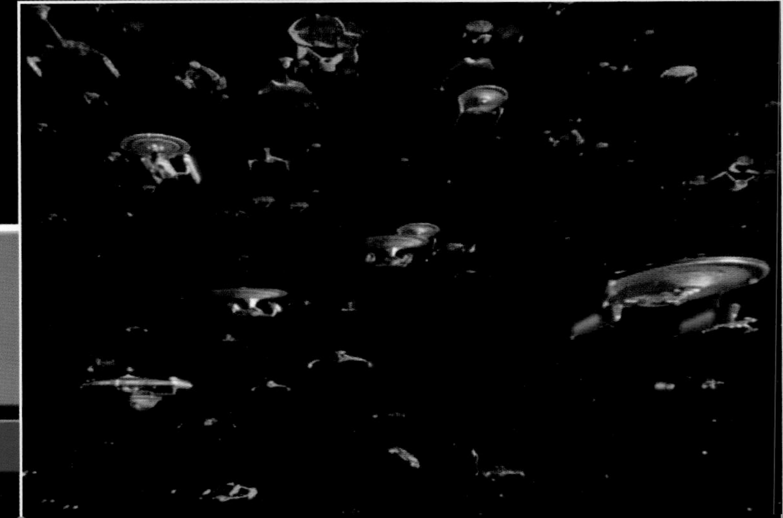

◀ The *U.S.S. Curry* fought with the Second Fleet for a short time during the opening engagements of the Dominion War. This large armada comprised a number of Starfleet and Klingon ships, and included vessels from the *Excelsior*, *Miranda*, *Steamrunner*, *K't'inga*, *Galaxy*, *Vor'cha*, and *Saber* classes.

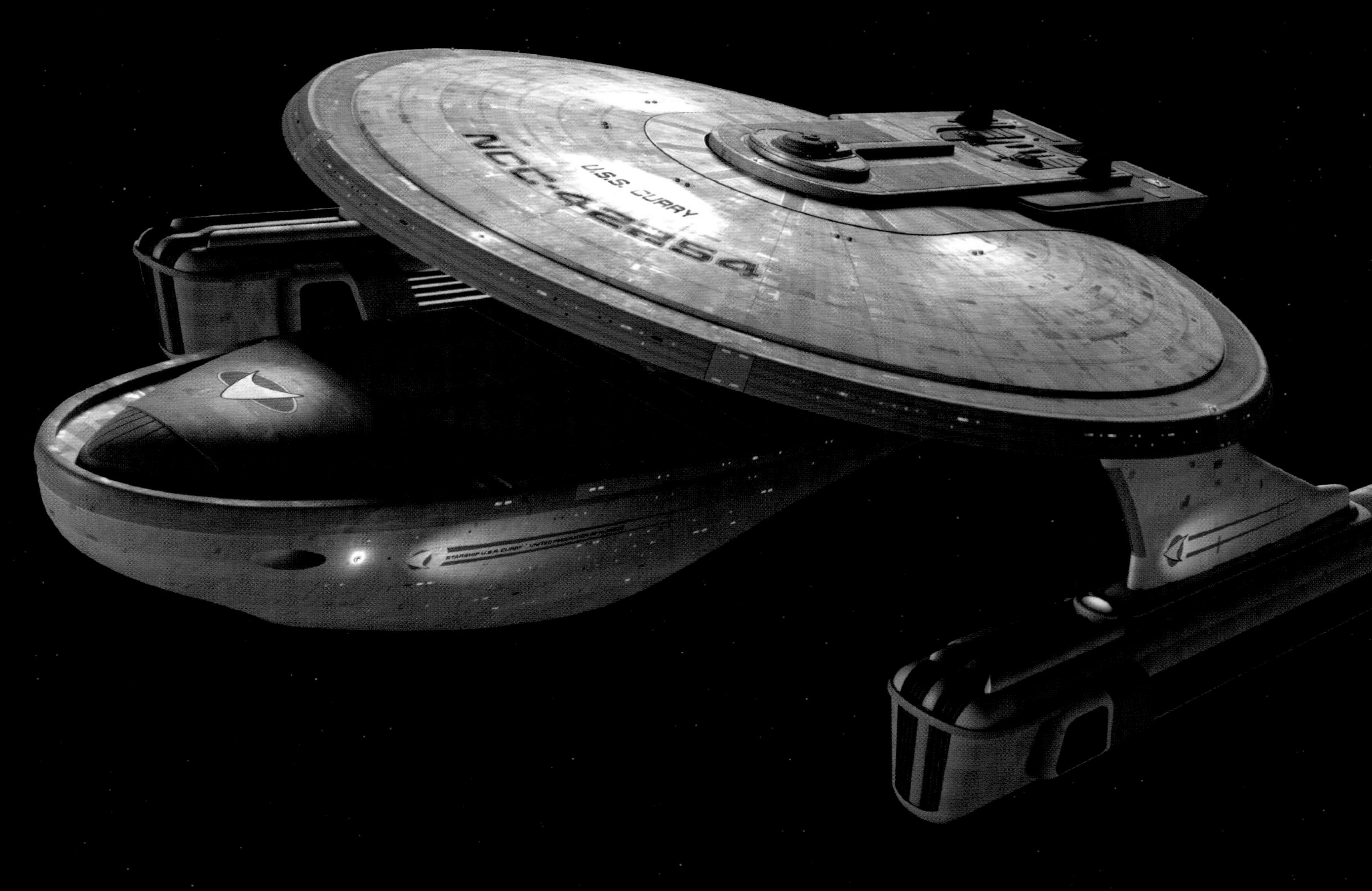

▲ The *Curry* looked somewhat ungainly with its secondary hull jutting out beyond the saucer section, but it was effective. Starfleet needed all the ships it could muster to fight the Dominion, and refurbishing parts from salvaged vessels was a quick way of adding more vessels to the fleets that fought in the war.

had been updated, while its armaments, which included 10 phaser emitters and two photon torpedo launchers, had also been modernized.

The latter feature was of particular importance, given the situation that the Federation found itself in. After first contact had been made with the Dominion in 2370, a state of cold war had developed following the destruction of the *U.S.S. Odyssey* NCC-71832 by the Jem'Hadar. From that point on, many thought it was only a matter of time before the Dominion invaded.

To have any chance of repelling the Dominion's legions of Jem'Hadar soldiers, Starfleet realized it needed ships – and fast. Starship production was ramped up in all fleet yards, with Starfleet engineers using whatever resources they could find. Parts and systems from vessels that were due to be scrapped were instead salvaged, reconditioned, and upgraded.

This led to ships being constructed in the manner of the *Curry*, including elements from several classes. To expedite the building of these vessels, some of the internal layout was left empty. This meant that facilities such as holodecks and research labs were not part of the outfitting, as they normally would have been on Starfleet ships of this time. Instead, the imperative was to launch vessels such as the *Curry* as soon as their defensive and combat systems were ready.

OUTBREAK OF WAR

The *Curry* joined the Second Fleet, an alliance of Starfleet and Klingon vessels that numbered in the hundreds. By 2373, the Second Battle of Deep Space 9 signaled the start of war with the Dominion, who captured the station. However, Captain Sisko was able to evacuate all Starfleet personnel and activate a minefield within the

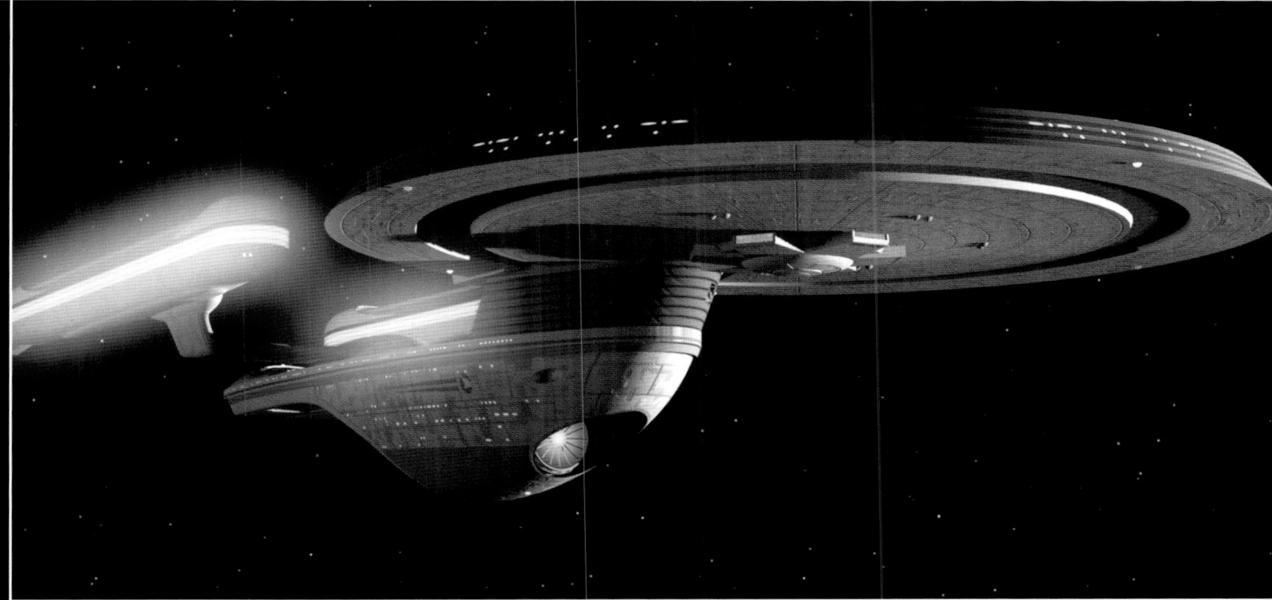

▶ An *Excelsior*-class ship, like the one pictured here, provided much of the framework for the *Curry*, including both the main hulls. The engineering hull was moved much further forward on the *Curry*.

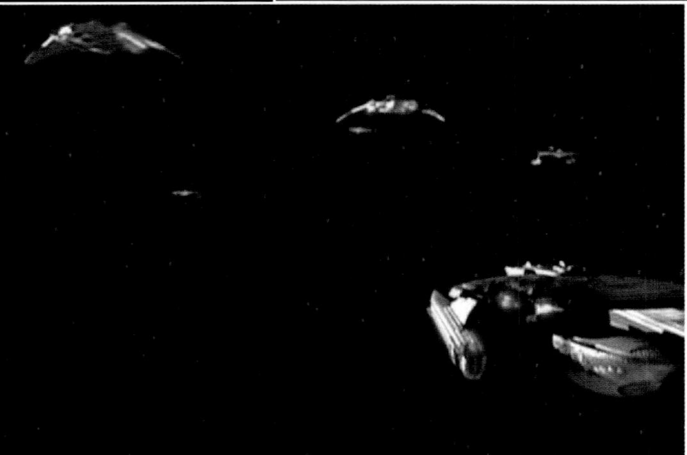

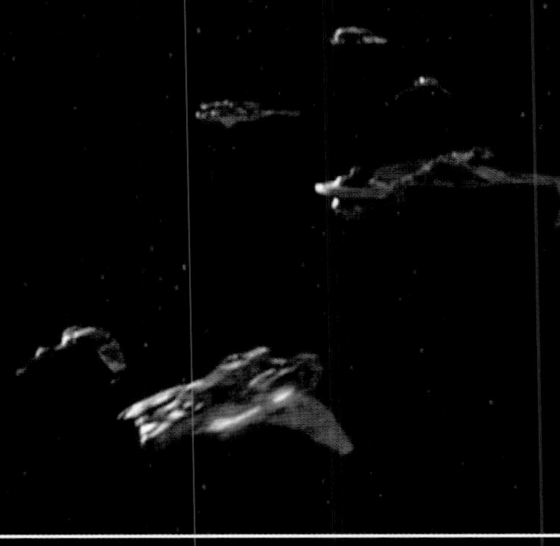

▼ The *Curry*, seen here in the bottom right of the picture, sustained serious damage from the war with the Dominion. A large part of its saucer was blown away, and its secondary hull became etched with scorch marks.

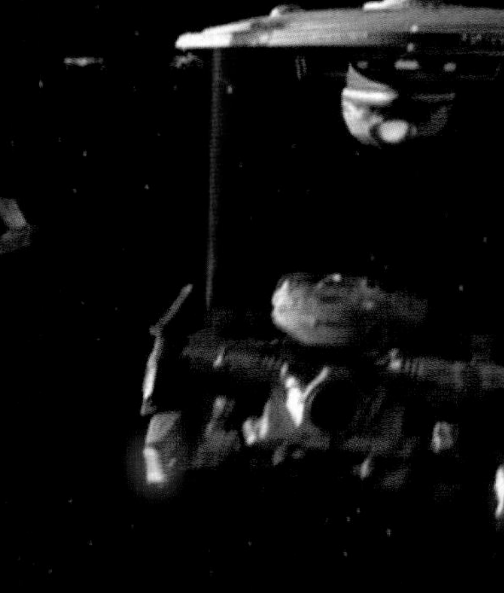

▲ The *U.S.S. Fredrickson* NCC-42111, an *Excelsior*-class ship, fought alongside the *Curry* in the Second Fleet. It suffered even more damage than the *Curry*, and had to be towed back to Federation space.

Bajoran wormhole, which prevented Dominion reinforcements from the Gamma Quadrant joining the war. While this was going on, the Second Fleet crossed the border into Cardassian territory and destroyed a major Dominion shipyard at Torros III.

This proved to be one of the few successes for the Allies at the beginning of the war. Just three months later, Allied fleets were in disarray, continually forced to retreat in the face of overwhelming Dominion opposition. The once proud and powerful armada that made up the Second Fleet had been reduced by the ravages of war to a third of its original size.

After one particular bruising encounter, the remaining ships of the Second Fleet limped back to Federation space, all looking battered and much the worse for wear. Some were leaking plasma, others were towed, unable to proceed under their own power. The *Curry* itself had suffered a massive hull breach to its saucer section and was barely operational.

This was the last time that the *Curry* was seen, even though the Second Fleet took part in many more engagements during the Dominion War. It may have been that the *Curry* was too badly damaged to be repaired, and any parts that were salvageable were used to build more ships.

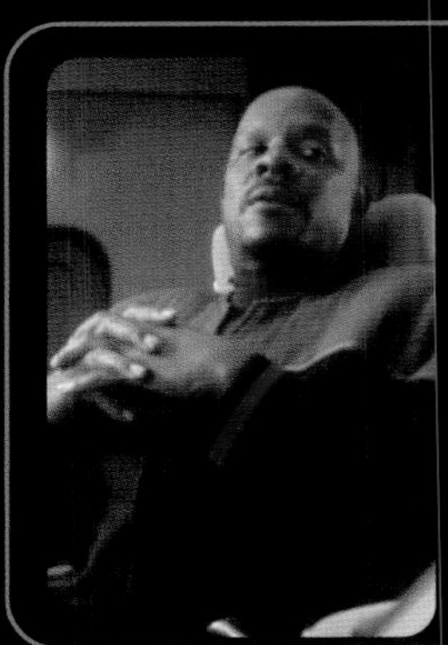

DATA FEED

Captain Sisko commanded the Second Fleet from the *U.S.S. Defiant* NX-74205 in many of the engagements with the Dominion during the first three months of the war. This was a grim time for the Federation and its Allies, as their fleets were constantly pushed back by the Jem'Hadar. Sisko tried to remain positive for the sake of morale, but even he felt hopeless rage when he heard that the Seventh Fleet had been decimated by the Dominion.

MIXED CLASSES

At the time the *U.S.S. Curry* served with the Second Fleet, this task force was made up of different classes of Starfleet and Klingon ships. While many of the Starfleet vessels belonged to familiar, specific classes, a few, like the *Curry*, were an amalgam of components from various classes.

The most notable of these was the *U.S.S. Raging Queen* NCC-42264, which had much in common with the *Curry*. The *Raging Queen* was mainly composed of parts from the *Excelsior* and *Miranda* classes in a similar configuration, but the nacelles were connected at the rear of the saucer with an additional pair of corrugated pylons.

The Second Fleet also included hybrid ships in the shape of the *U.S.S. Centaur* NCC-42043 and the *U.S.S. Elkins* NCC-74112. The *Centaur* was largely made up of *Excelsior*- and *Miranda*-class parts, but it did not feature a secondary hull. The *Elkins*, on the other hand, displayed a very similar saucer hull to that of *Intrepid*-class vessels. This was mated to a secondary hull that looked similar to a Maquis raider's.

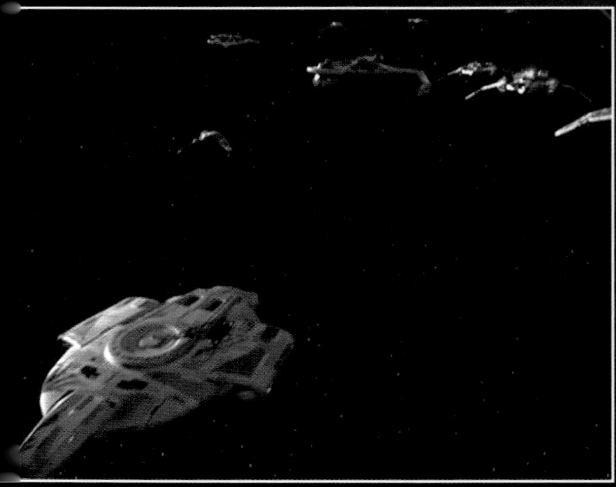

▲ In 2374, the battle-weary Second Fleet retreated to the relative safety of Federation space. The armada included several "mongrel" ships, such as the *Curry*, the *Raging Queen*, the *Centaur*, and the *Elkins*.

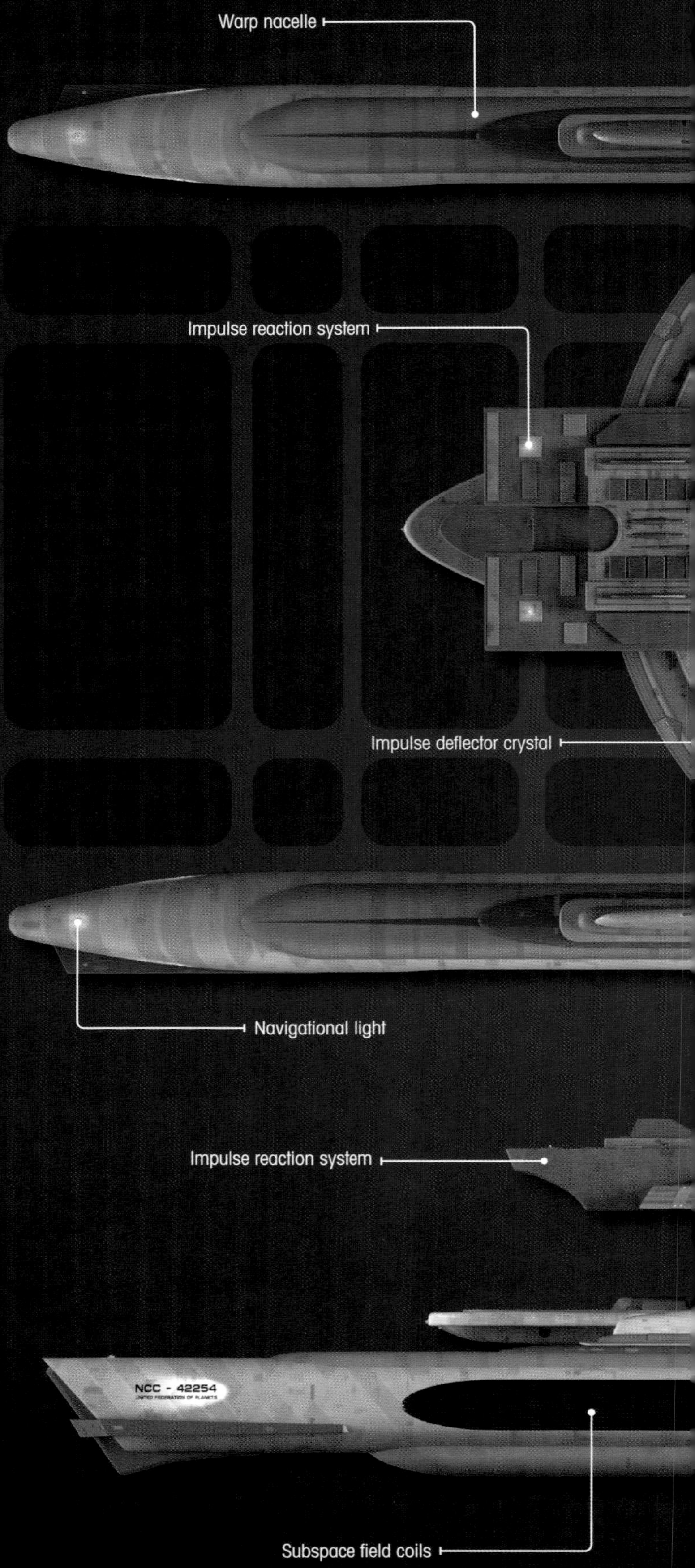

Warp nacelle

Impulse reaction system

Impulse deflector crystal

Navigational light

Impulse reaction system

NCC - 42254

Subspace field coils

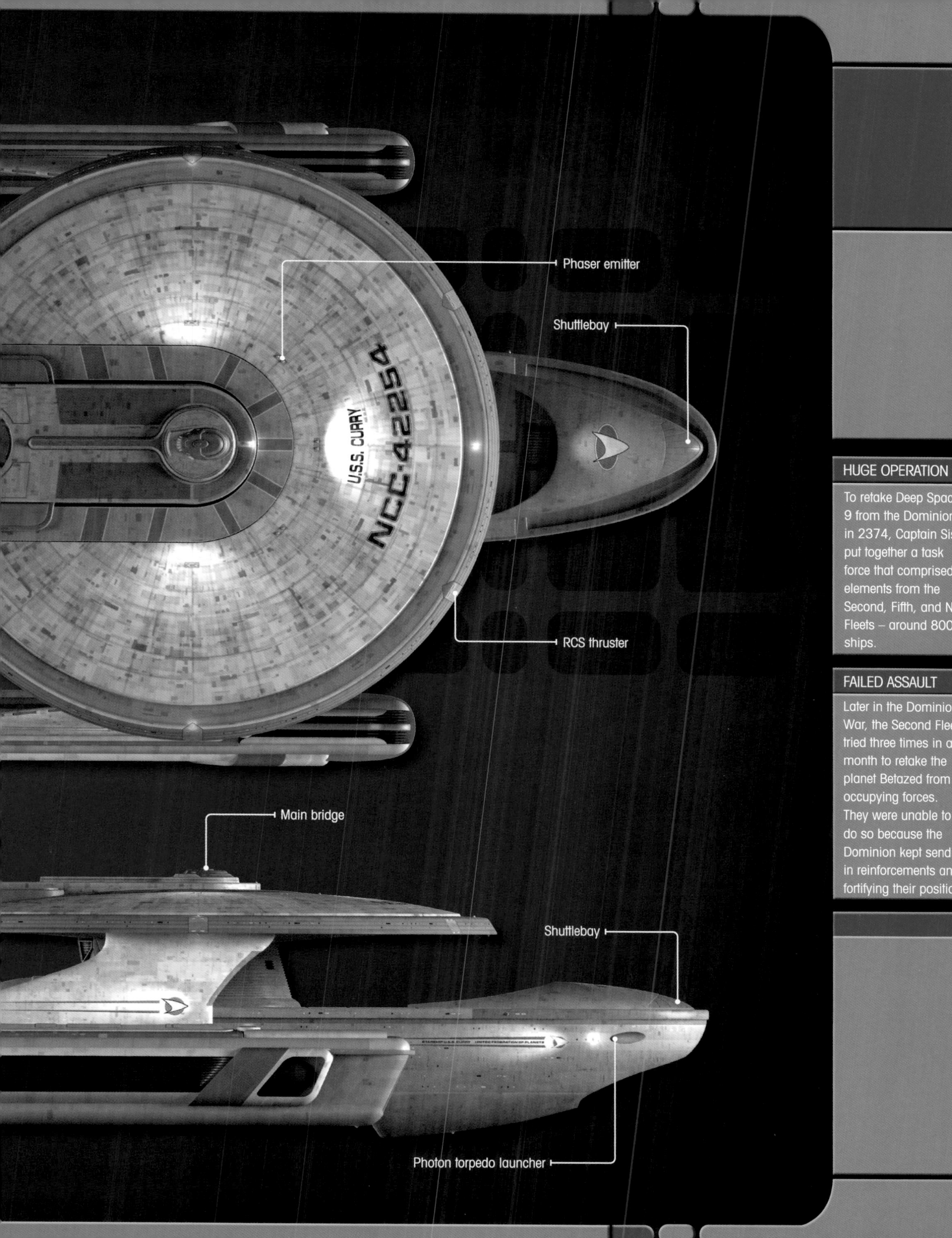

HUGE OPERATION

To retake Deep Space 9 from the Dominion in 2374, Captain Sisko put together a task force that comprised elements from the Second, Fifth, and Nine Fleets – around 800 ships.

FAILED ASSAULT

Later in the Dominion War, the Second Fleet tried three times in a month to retake the planet Betazed from occupying forces. They were unable to do so because the Dominion kept sending in reinforcements and fortifying their position.

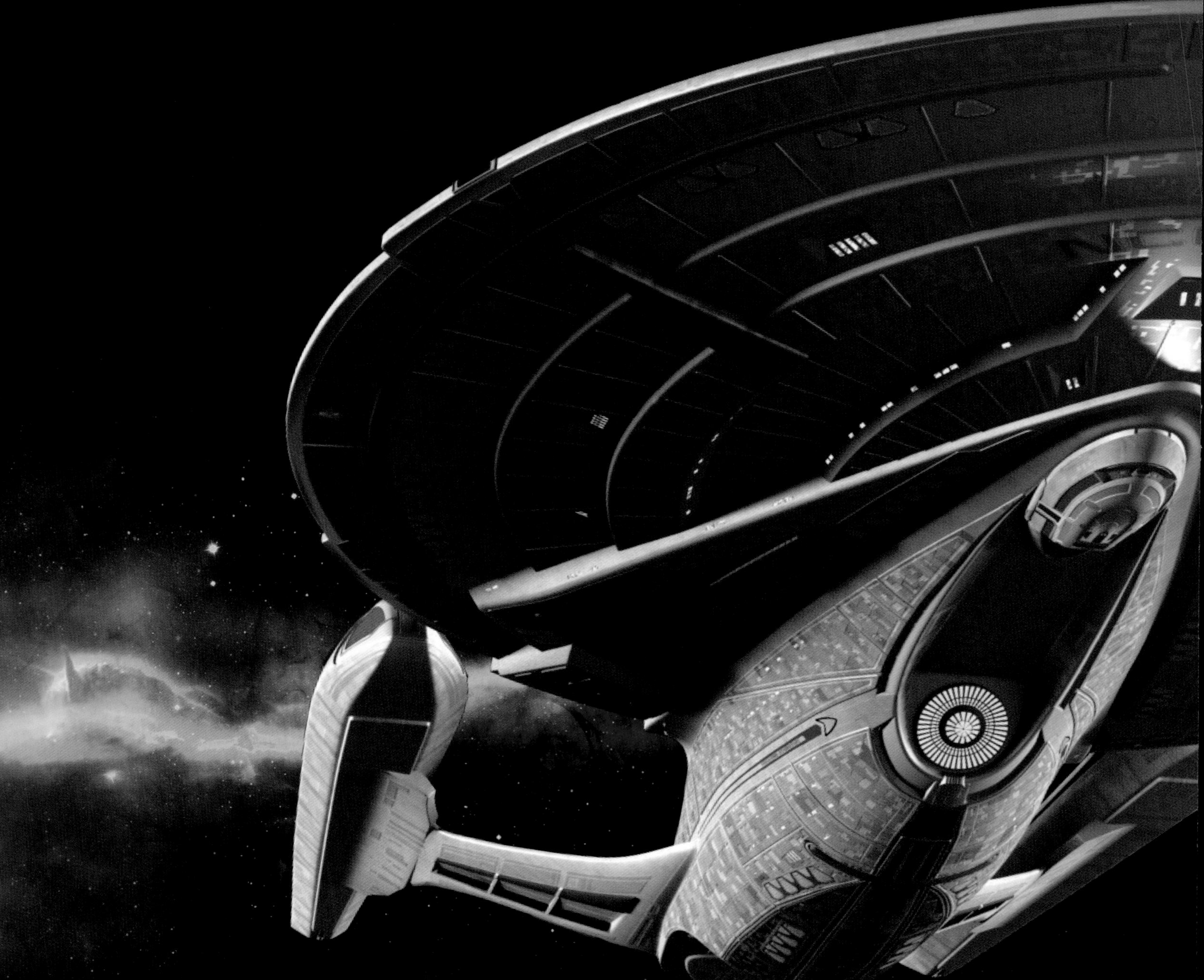

U.S.S. ENTERPRISE

NCC-1701-E

The *Sovereign*-class *Enterprise*-E was designed as a sleek and tough ship, battle-ready to fight the Borg.

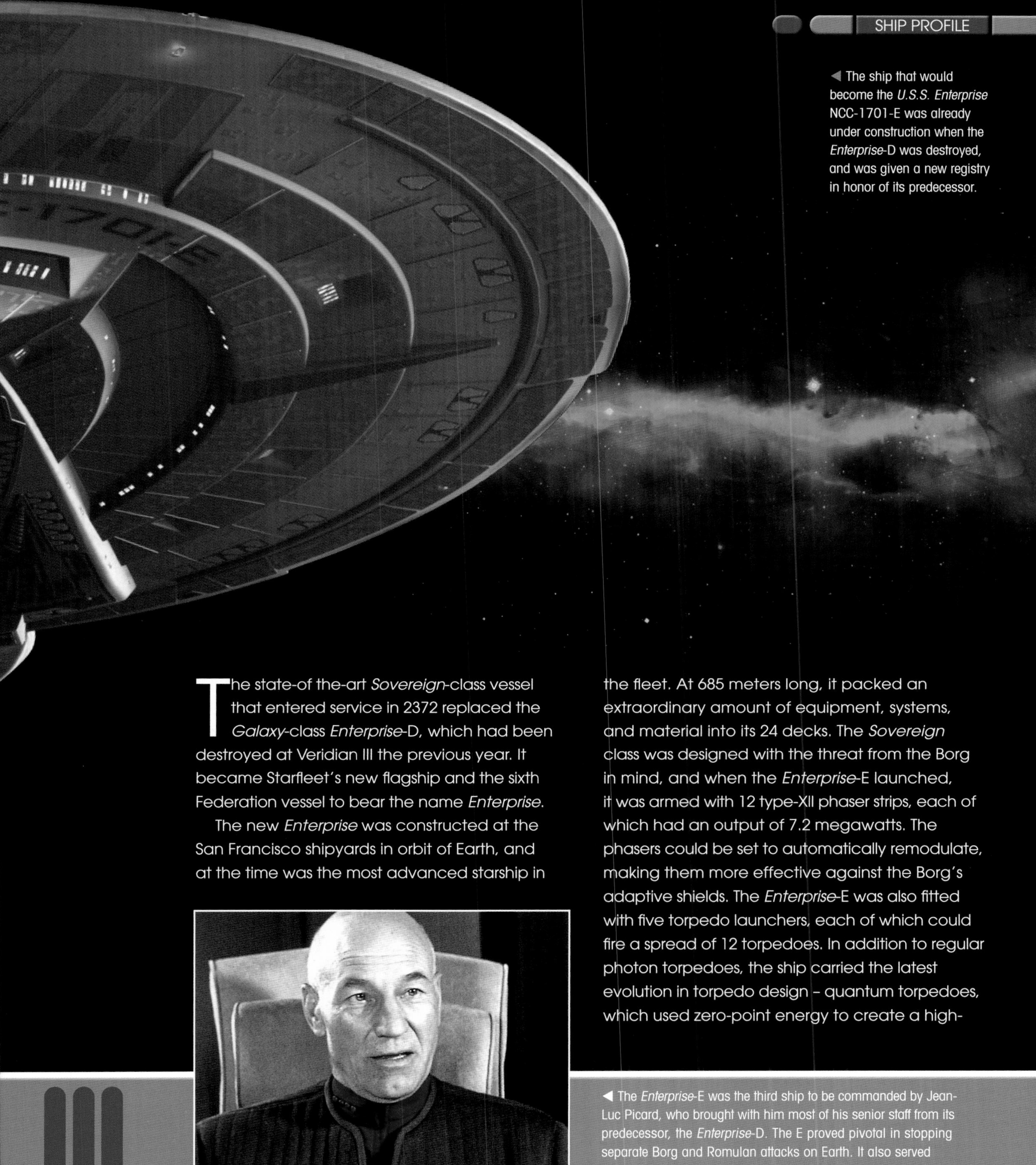

◀ The ship that would become the *U.S.S. Enterprise* NCC-1701-E was already under construction when the *Enterprise*-D was destroyed, and was given a new registry in honor of its predecessor.

The state-of the-art *Sovereign*-class vessel that entered service in 2372 replaced the *Galaxy*-class *Enterprise*-D, which had been destroyed at Veridian III the previous year. It became Starfleet's new flagship and the sixth Federation vessel to bear the name *Enterprise*.

The new *Enterprise* was constructed at the San Francisco shipyards in orbit of Earth, and at the time was the most advanced starship in the fleet. At 685 meters long, it packed an extraordinary amount of equipment, systems, and material into its 24 decks. The *Sovereign* class was designed with the threat from the Borg in mind, and when the *Enterprise*-E launched, it was armed with 12 type-XII phaser strips, each of which had an output of 7.2 megawatts. The phasers could be set to automatically remodulate, making them more effective against the Borg's adaptive shields. The *Enterprise*-E was also fitted with five torpedo launchers, each of which could fire a spread of 12 torpedoes. In addition to regular photon torpedoes, the ship carried the latest evolution in torpedo design – quantum torpedoes, which used zero-point energy to create a high-

◀ The *Enterprise*-E was the third ship to be commanded by Jean-Luc Picard, who brought with him most of his senior staff from its predecessor, the *Enterprise*-D. The E proved pivotal in stopping separate Borg and Romulan attacks on Earth. It also served with distinction during the Dominion War.

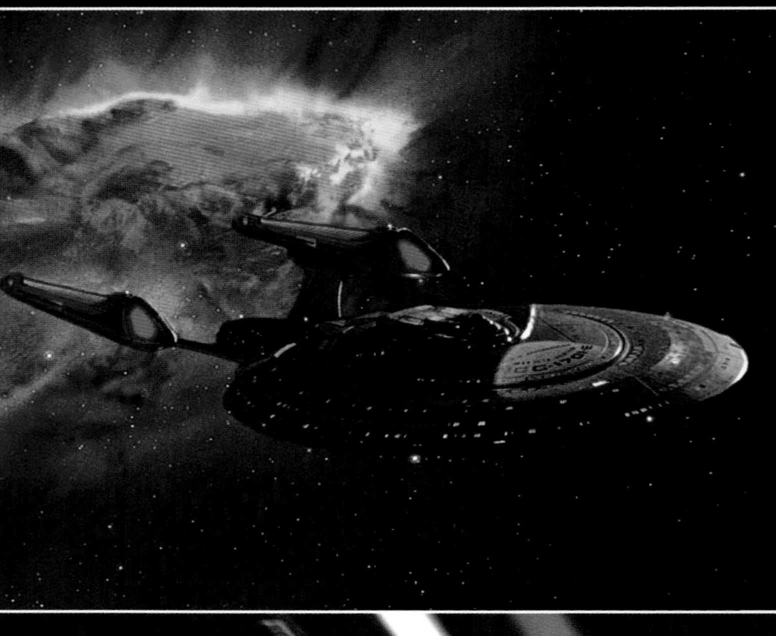

◀ When the Borg attacked in 2372, the *Enterprise*-E was the most advanced ship in the fleet. But since Picard had once been assimilated by the Borg, Starfleet Command feared that the captain might be unreliable and assigned the ship to patrol the Romulan Neutral Zone.

▶ Picard disobeyed orders and the *Enterprise* joined the Battle of Sector 001, taking command of the fleet. Picard's innate understanding of the Borg then proved instrumental in defeating them.

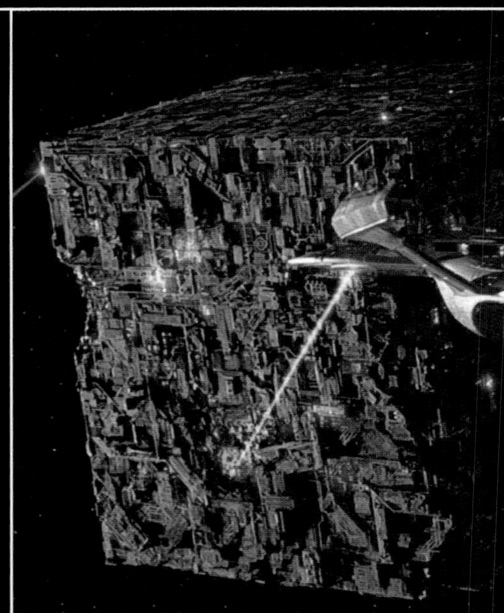

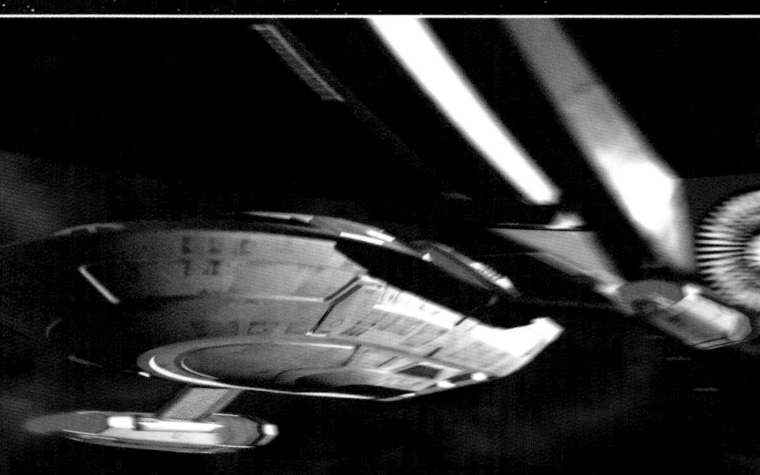

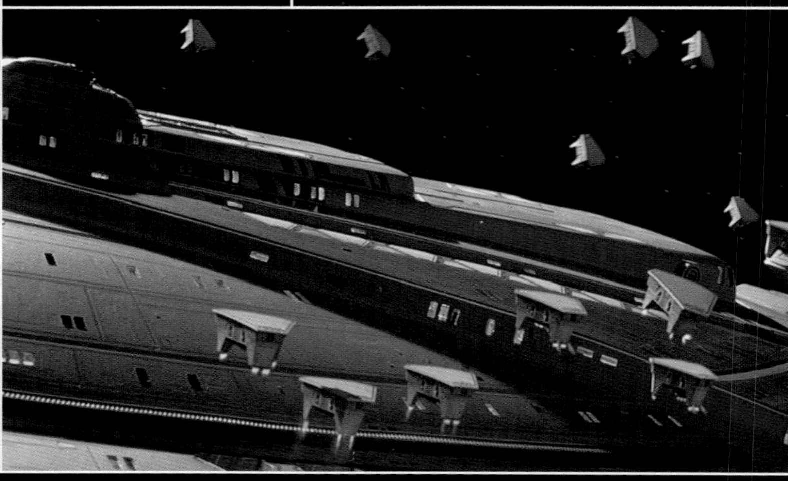

▲ Like the *Enterprise*-D, the *Enterprise*-E was fitted with a captain's yacht, which was docked on the underside of the saucer section. This large and somewhat luxurious shuttle was intended for diplomatic missions.

energy yield. The *Enterprise*'s shields were also designed to remodulate automatically, making them more resistant to Borg weapons' fire. In 2376, the *Enterprise* underwent a refit, which included adding a further four phaser arrays and five more torpedo launchers.

The vessel was equipped with redesigned warp engines and nacelles that were superior to those on the *Galaxy* class. The new design enabled the ship to maintain a cruising velocity of warp 8, while its high warp velocity was around 9.95. Emergency plasma purge vents in the nacelle support pylons provided the ships' engineers with a secondary safety buffer, allowing them to bleed off heated plasma before it reached the warp field coils. In some circumstances, this obviated the need to shut down systems or eject the warp core.

As had become standard practice by the late 24th century, the *Sovereign* class carried a diplomatic shuttle known as the captain's yacht, which was normally docked on the underside of the saucer. It was also able to separate the saucer section from the main engineering hull.

LIVING COMPUTERS

The computer systems featured advanced bio-neural circuitry, which employed synthetic cells rather than optical technology. This semi-organic system could process 6,200 kiloquads of data per second, but it was still in its infancy and was vulnerable to attack and infection. Accordingly, it functioned in concert with a conventional Optical Data Network (ODN).

The *Enterprise*-E was also one of the first vessels to be fitted with an Emergency Medical Hologram (EMH), which was designed to provide short-term assistance by supporting or even replacing the ship's medical staff in an emergency. During an

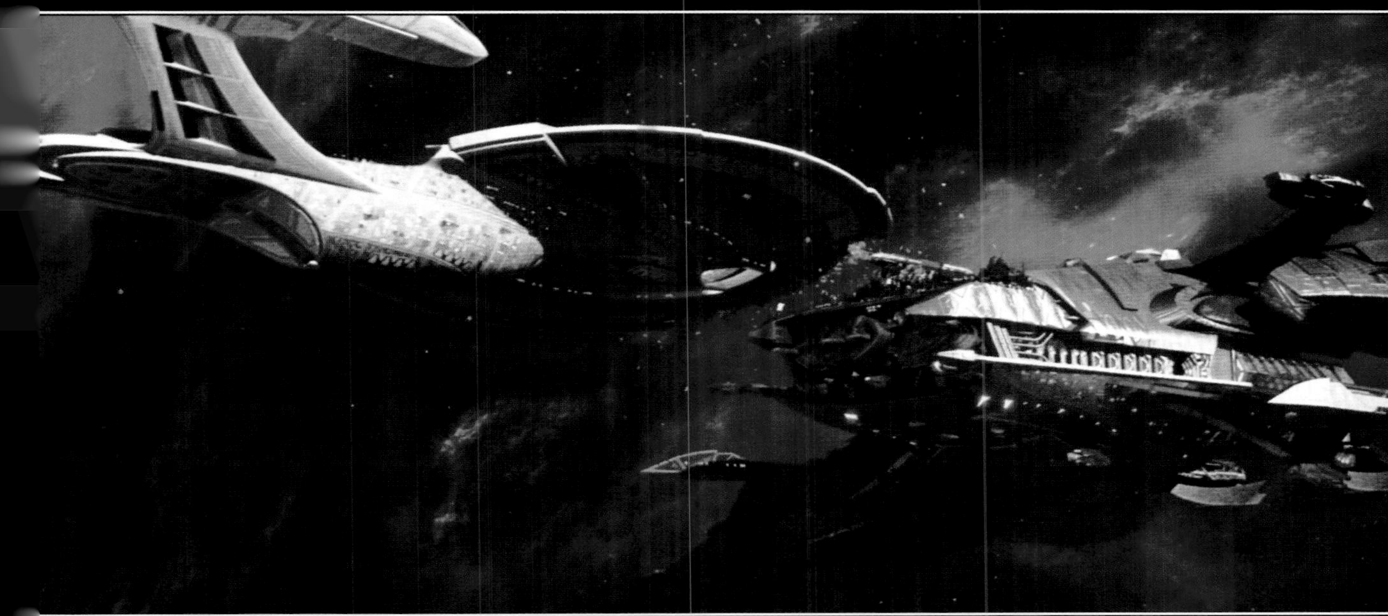

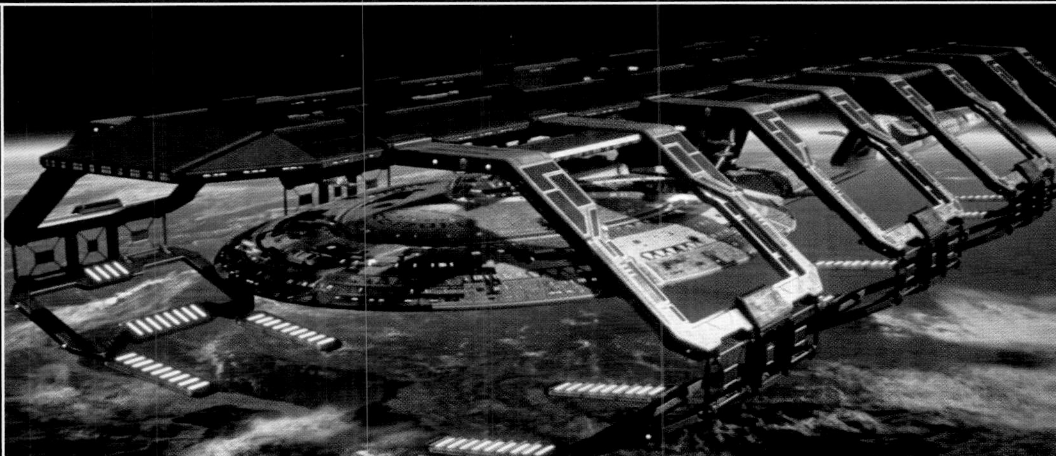

▲ When the Reman leader Shinzon attacked Earth, the *Enterprise*-E was overpowered by his flagship, the *Scimitar*. Picard only managed to stop him by ramming his own ship into the *Scimitar*.

◀ Following the Borg invasion of 2372, the *Enterprise*-E pursued the Borg into the past, where it was temporarily assimilated, forcing the crew to abandon ship.

rprise by the Borg, the EMH was distraction, allowing the medical tients to escape from sickbay. *terprise*-E had the same basic s as its predecessor, it did not or family members. Instead, it ly by Starfleet personnel, who n exploring space and seeking ew civilizations.

AREER

ise had substantially the same s its predecessor. Captain ommand on launch and was eating the Borg invasion of 2373 Ba'ku crisis of 2375. However, by crew were ready to move on, iam Riker was promoted to command of the *U.S.S. Titan*.

On the crew's final mission together, the ship was nearly destroyed by the vast Reman warbird *Scimitar*, and Picard took the radical step of ramming the enemy vessel. Victorious but badly damaged, the *Enterprise* returned to spacedock where it underwent substantial repairs. It also took on a new first officer, Commander Martin Madden, before resuming its mission of exploration.

▲ The *Enterprise* survived its collision with the *Scimitar* and returned to spacedock where it underwent substantial repairs.

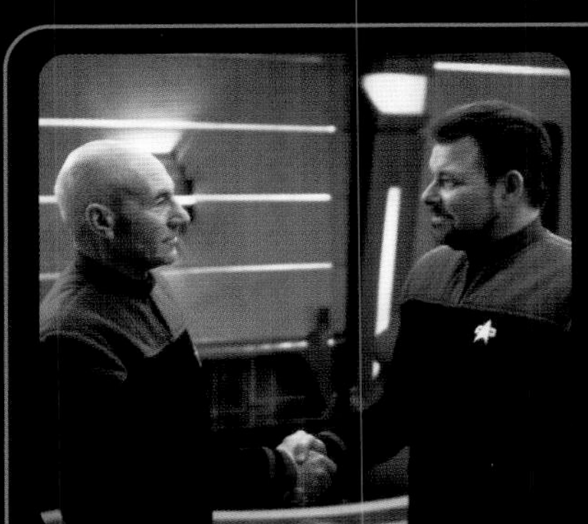

DATA FEED

Though Captain Picard remained in command of the *Enterprise*-E throughout its career, several of his senior staff eventually left the ship. Commander Riker became captain of the *U.S.S. Titan*, while Commander Data was lost in the final battle with the Reman leader, Shinzon.

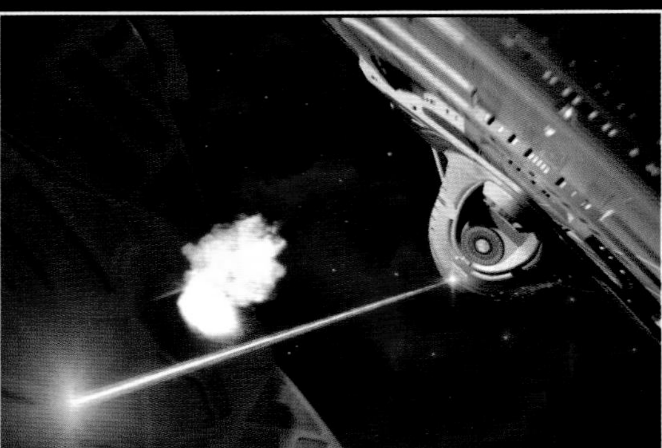

REGULAR REFITS

During its operational life, the *Enterprise*-E received a number of refits and upgrades that increased the amount of weaponry it carried and enhanced the efficiency of its engines. The first refit involved repairing damage inflicted by the Borg and upgrading the ship's weaponry by adding more torpedo launchers. A second refit involved moving and shortening the nacelles, reducing the ship's length from 685 to 673 meters.

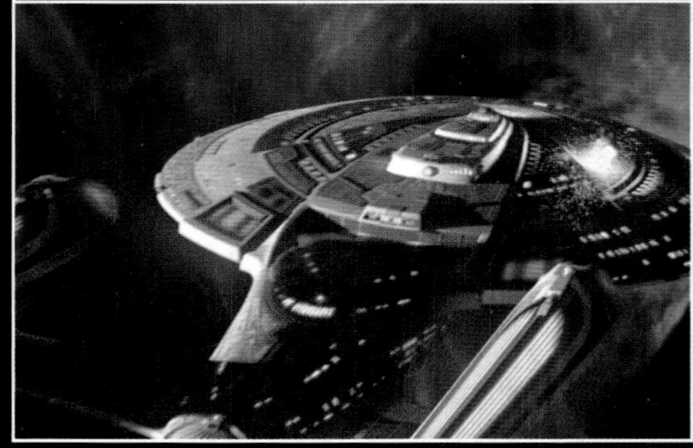

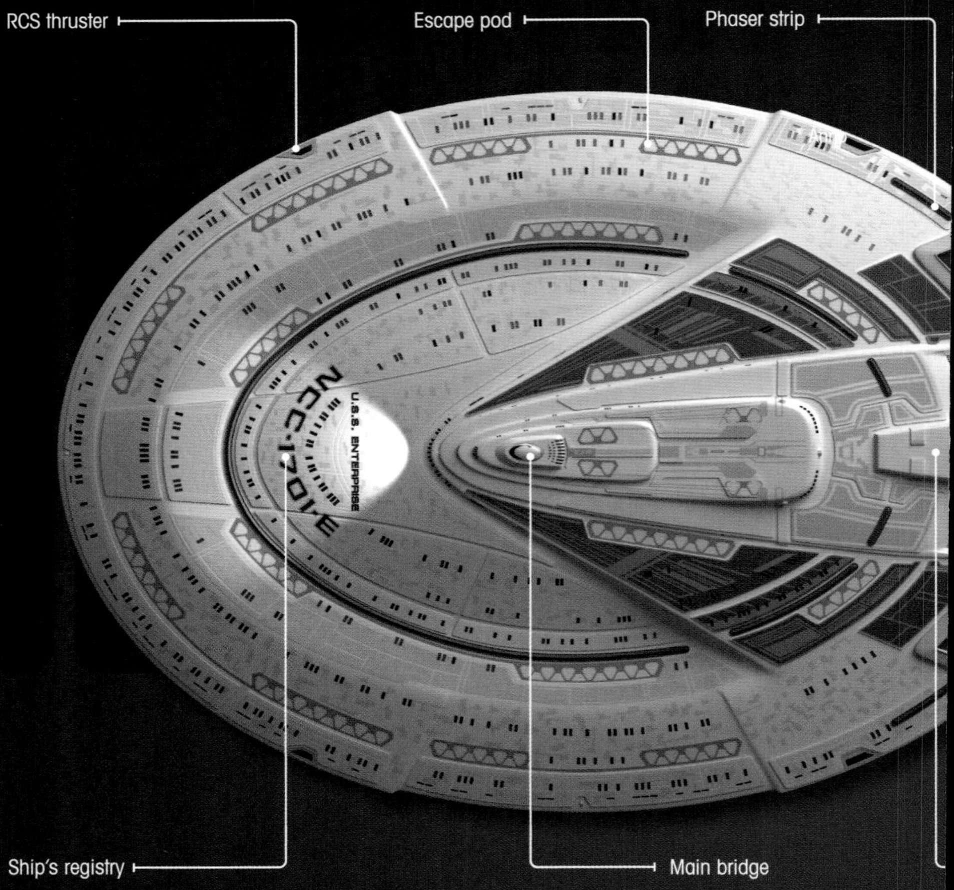

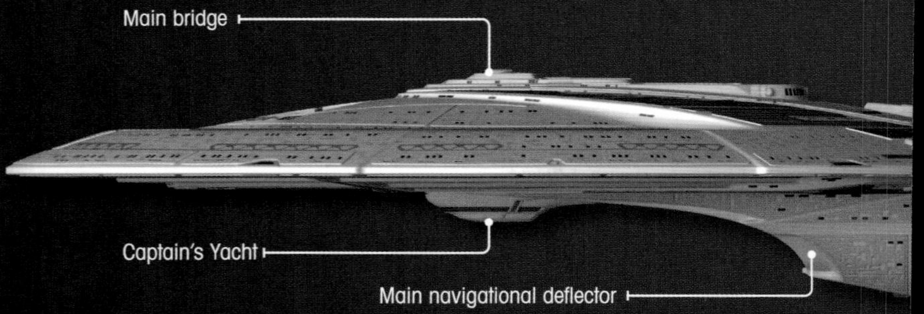

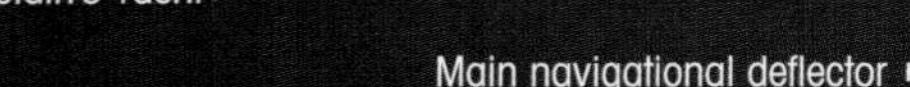

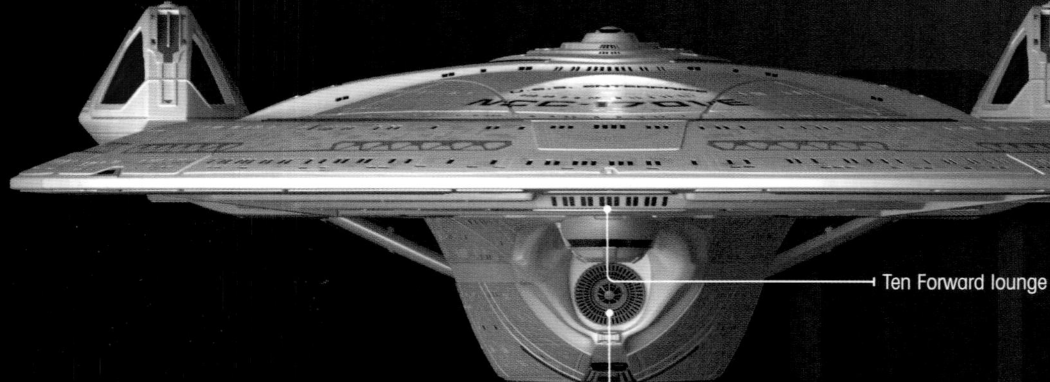

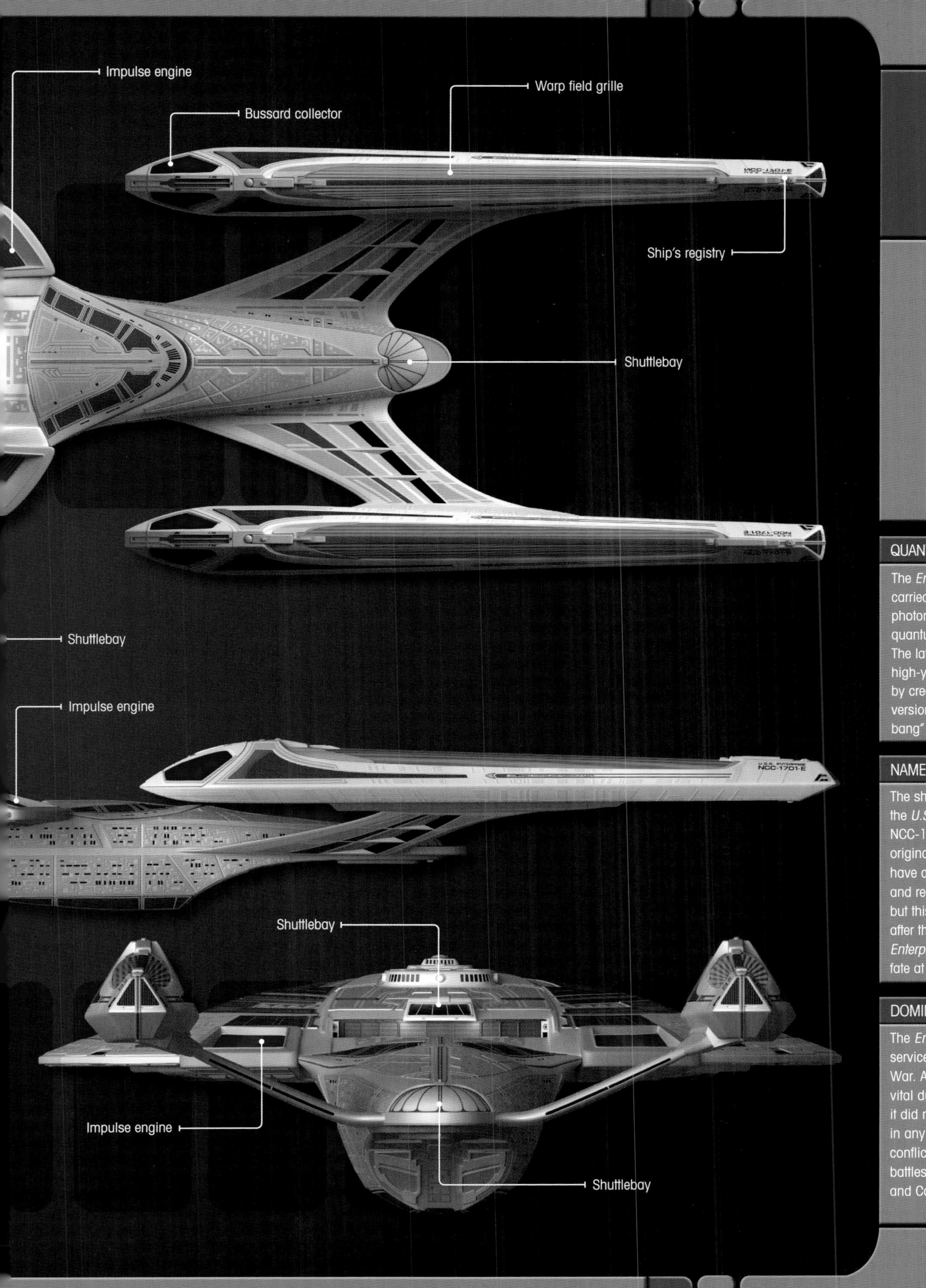

QUANTUM TORPEDOES

The *Enterprise*-E carried both standard photon torpedoes and quantum torpedoes. The latter generated high-yield explosions by creating miniature versions of the "big bang" event.

NAME CHANGE

The ship that became the *U.S.S. Enterprise* NCC-1701-E was originally slated to have a different name and registry number, but this was changed after the *Galaxy*-class *Enterprise*-D met its fate at Veridian III.

DOMINION WAR

The *Enterprise*-E did see service in the Dominion War. Assigned to other vital duties, however, it did not take part in any of the major conflicts, such as the battles of Chin'toka and Cardassia.

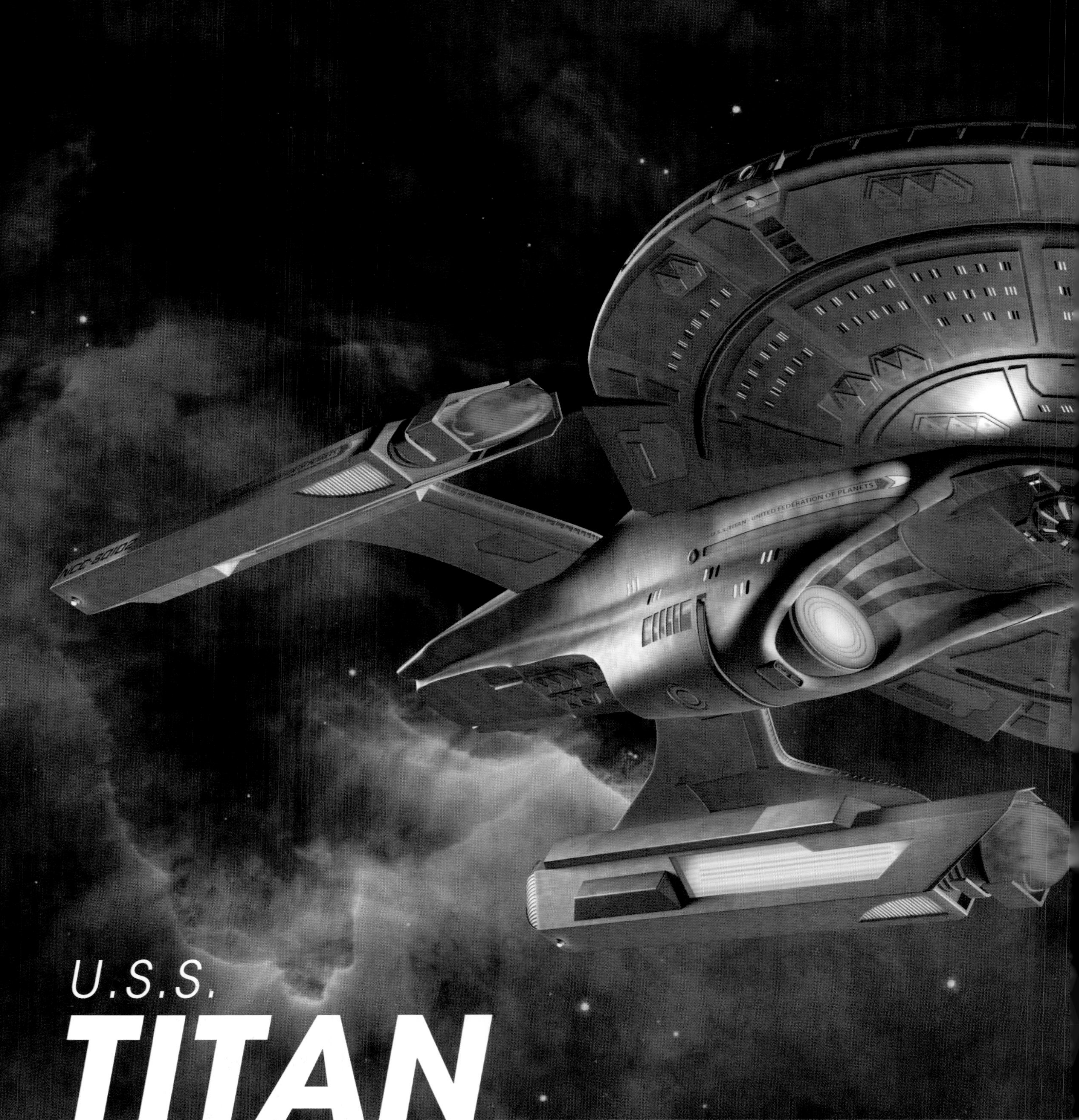

U.S.S. TITAN

Commanded by William T. Riker, the *U.S.S. Titan* NCC-80102 was a formidable vessel of 24th-century Starfleet.

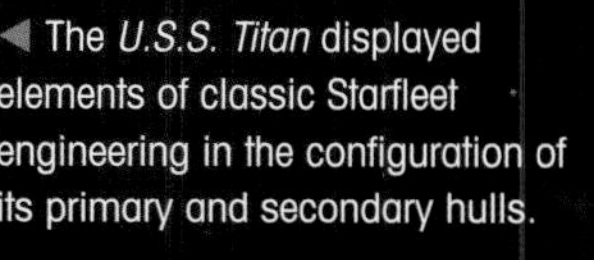

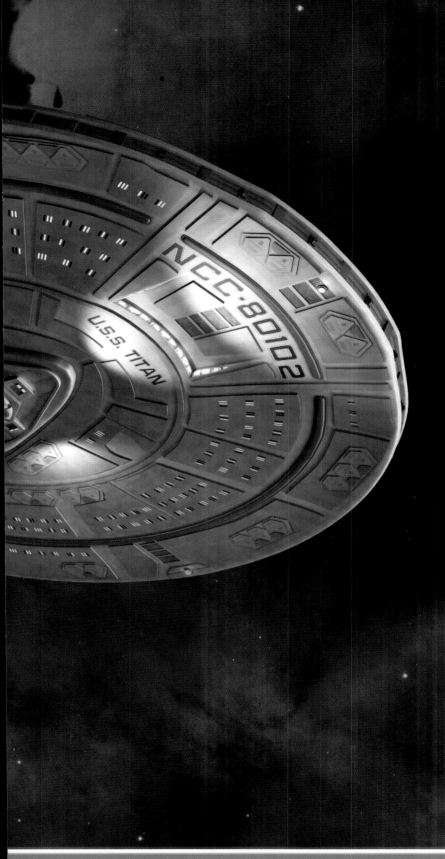

◀ The *U.S.S. Titan* displayed elements of classic Starfleet engineering in the configuration of its primary and secondary hulls.

A *Luna*-class vessel, the *Titan* was adaptable to a variety of mission parameters, its tactical capabilities providing an edge in ship-to-ship combat scenarios. Overall, it ranked as one of Starfleet's finest.

The *Titan*'s configuration adopted a traditional primary hull saucer above a secondary hull and forward deflector dish. Warp nacelles were ranged in compact manner below the primary saucer, anchored by pylons located on the dorsal surface of the secondary hull. Armaments included a saucer-mounted phaser array, torpedo launchers located in an upper roll-bar mounted pod, and twin launchers to port and starboard of the deflector dish.

On an unrecorded stardate in 2380, the *Titan* came to the assistance of the *U.S.S. Cerritos*, which had sustained near-critical damage during an attack by Pakled vessels seeking to harvest Starfleet technology. The *Titan* neutralized the Pakled threat, allowing the *Cerritos* to undergo repairs at a nearby starbase.

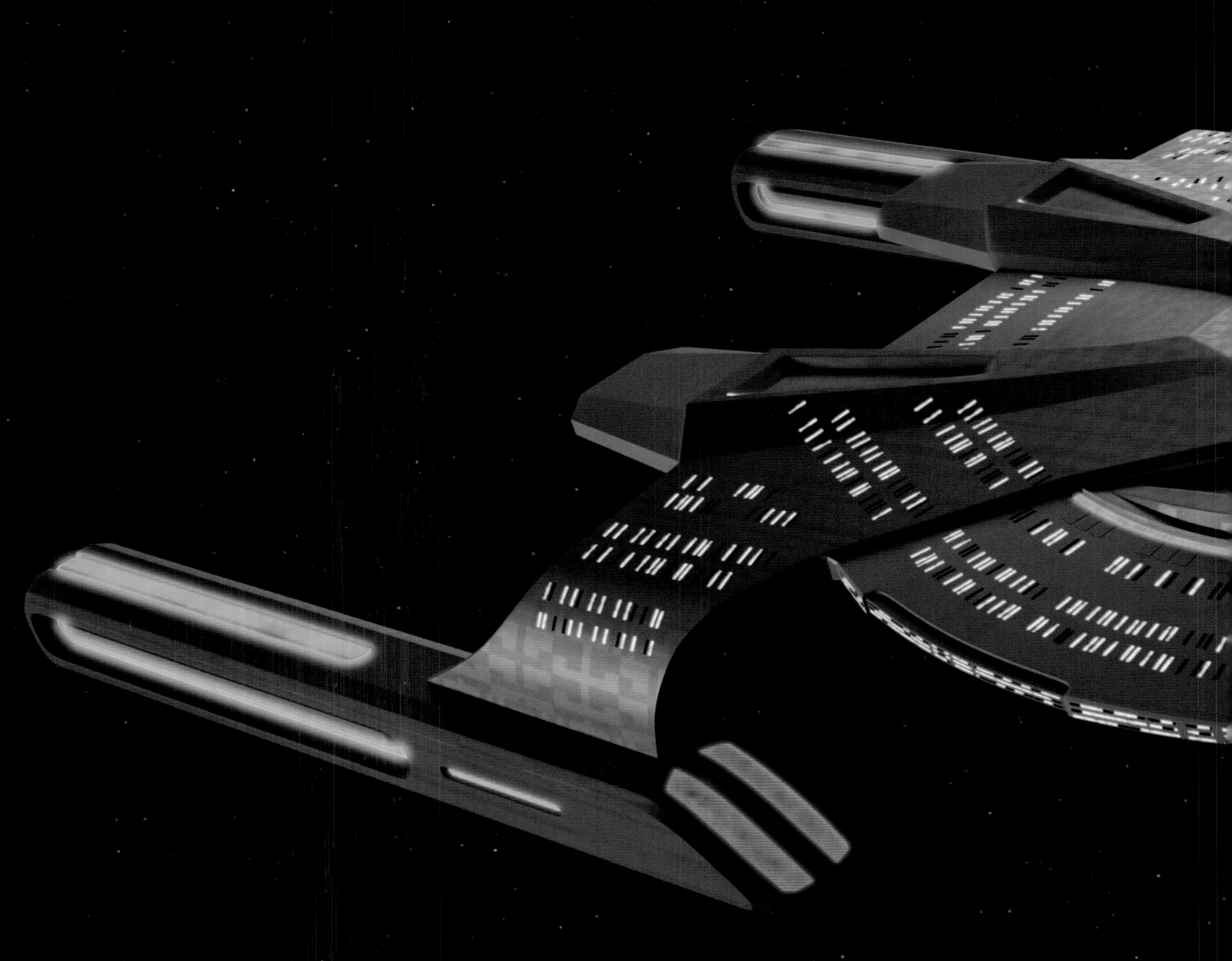

U.S.S. VANCOUVER

As a *Parliament*-class starship, the *U.S.S. Vancouver* NCC-70492 was in the vanguard of 24th-century design.

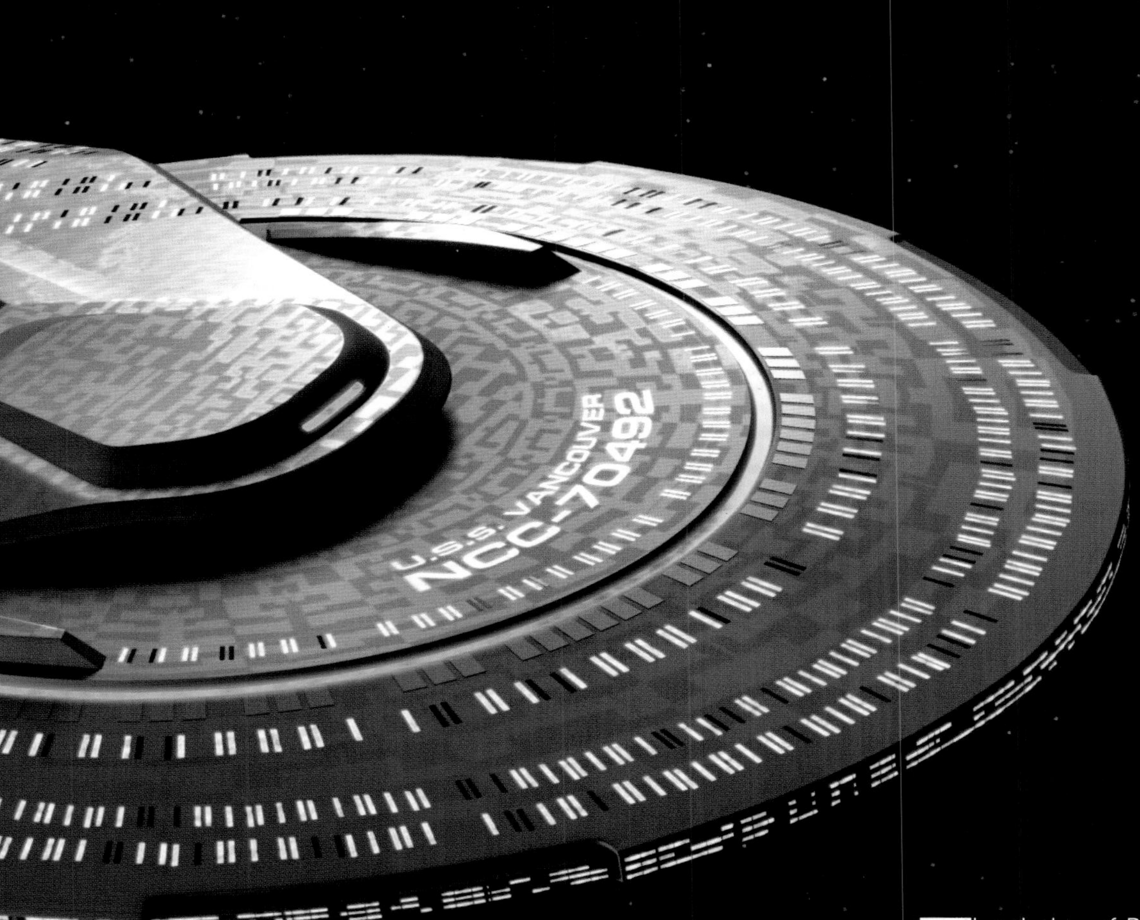

◀ The *U.S.S. Vancouver* was a state-of-the-art starship, its advanced systems geared toward a wide range of large-scale, engineering-based missions.

The design of *Parliament*-class starships was essentially dictated by their role in handling assignments that focused on extensive, complex engineering projects.

Advanced in terms of 24th-century design, the *Vancouver* comprised a large primary saucer section. Its low-slung, aft-ranged warp nacelles were secured by large pylons that formed part of the saucer section's dorsal superstructure. A discrete secondary hull and deflector array was located below and aft of the saucer section.

Around 2380, the *Vancouver* was instrumental in successfully completing an operation to demolish one of the moons of Mixtus III. During the mission, the crew was supported by the *U.S.S. Cerritos*.

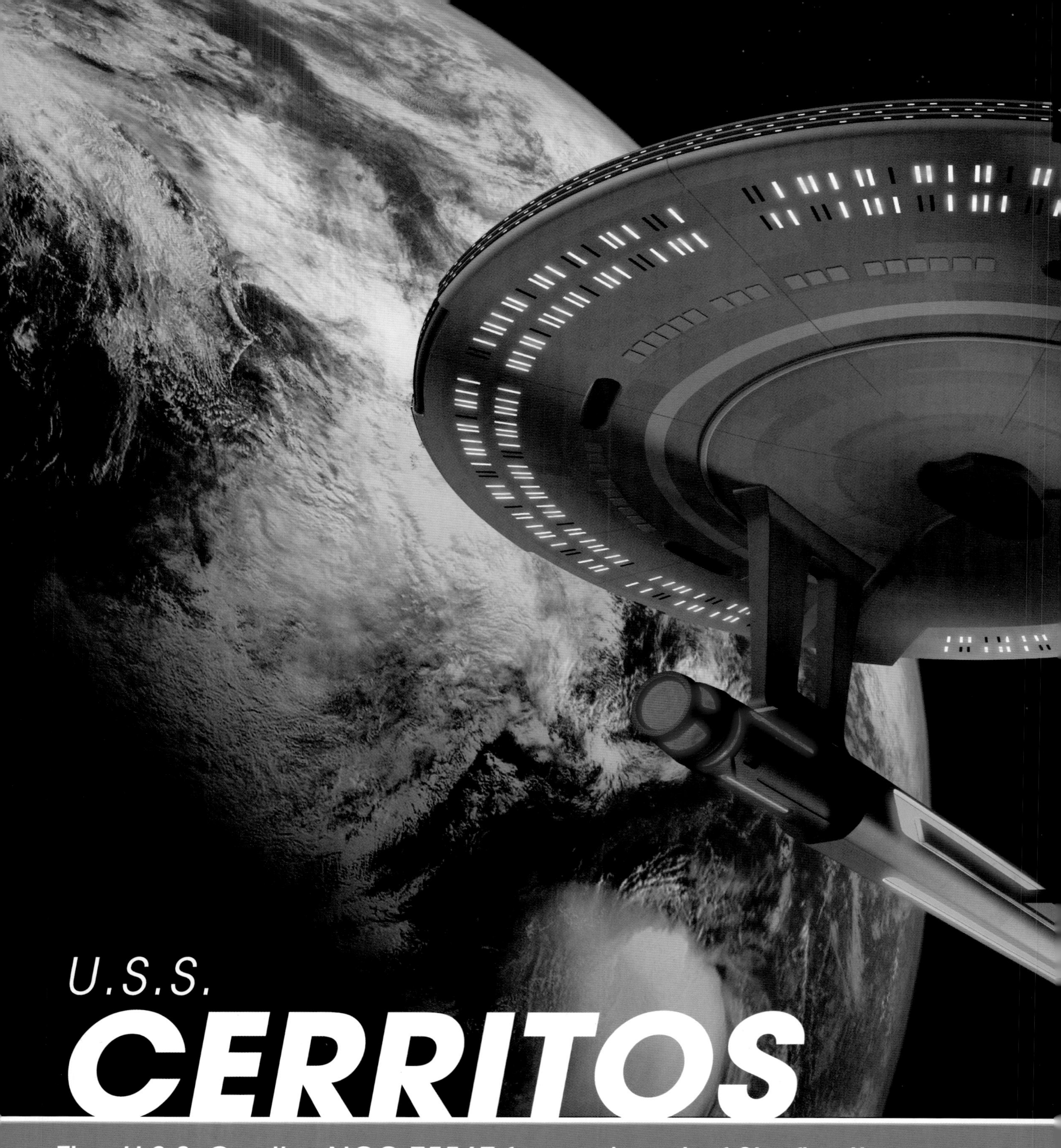

U.S.S. CERRITOS

The *U.S.S. Cerritos* NCC-75567 formed part of Starfleet's complement of 24th-century "second contact" vessels.

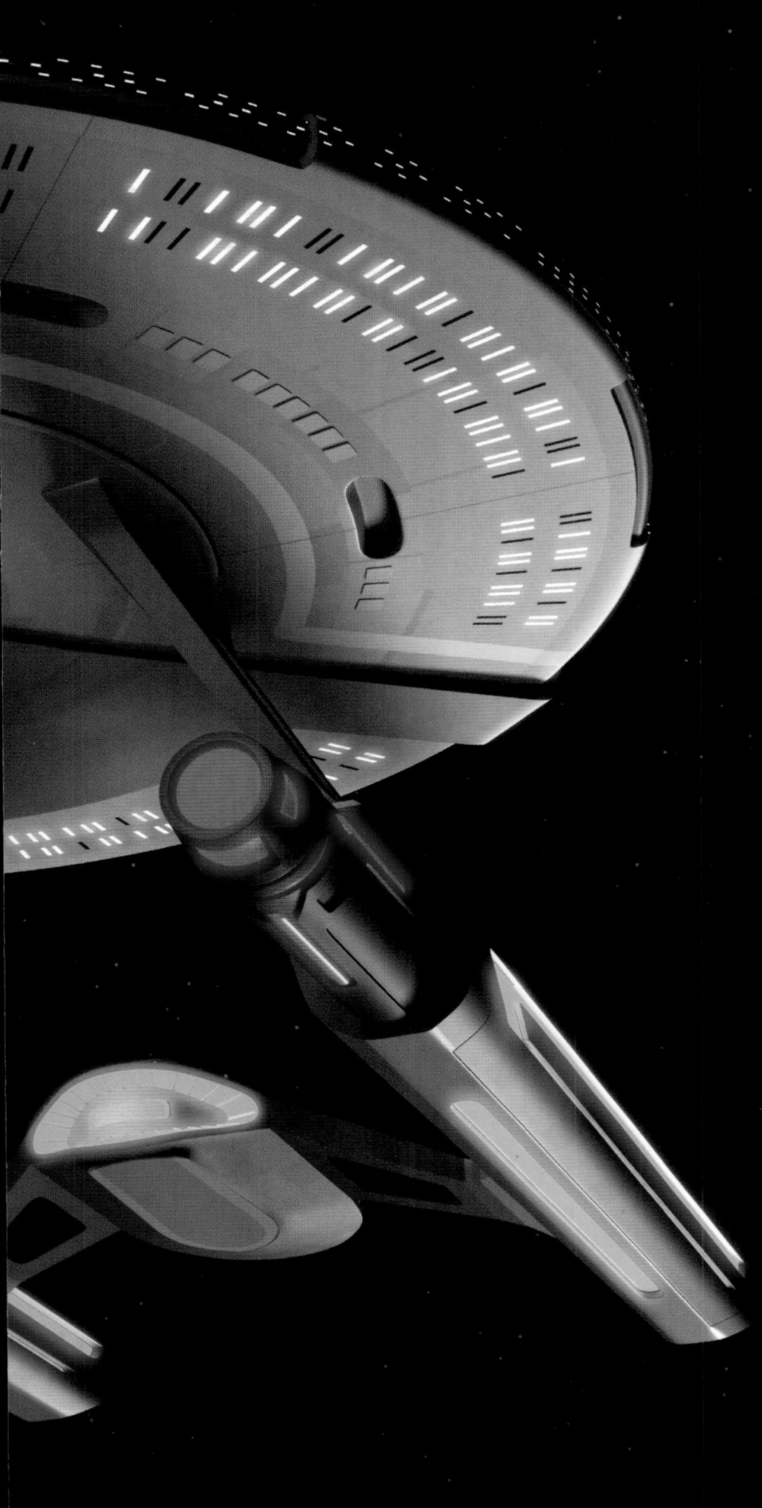

◀ Like all *California*-class starships, the *Cerritos*' saucer section and secondary hull were separated by much longer pylons than seen in other ships of the era.

Starfleet's *California* class of ship equated to a reliable workhorse of the 24th century. As an example of the class, the *U.S.S. Cerritos* logged many mission hours in undistinguished fashion, but gained a reputation under Captain Carol Freeman for getting the job done.

Unremarkable in design – a primary saucer ranged high above a secondary hull with dual warp nacelles – the *Cerritos* was not designed with maneuverability or combat scenarios in mind. Its primary function was to carry out second contact missions, visiting previously charted worlds to assess further needs following first contact.

The *Cerritos* had two shuttlebays to the aft of the saucer, with a complement of shuttles and *Argo*-type vehicles available. Among the *Cerritos*' missions were second contact with the Galardonian High Council, escort assignments, and assisting the *U.S.S. Vancouver* in a moon demolition. In 2380, the *Cerritos* was critically damaged engaging Pakled vessels, resulting in a major repair program. Captain Freeman refused a full refit, however.

Other examples of the *California*-class starship included the *U.S.S. Merced, U.S.S. Rubidoux*, and the *U.S.S. Solvang*. All three were destroyed while on active service.

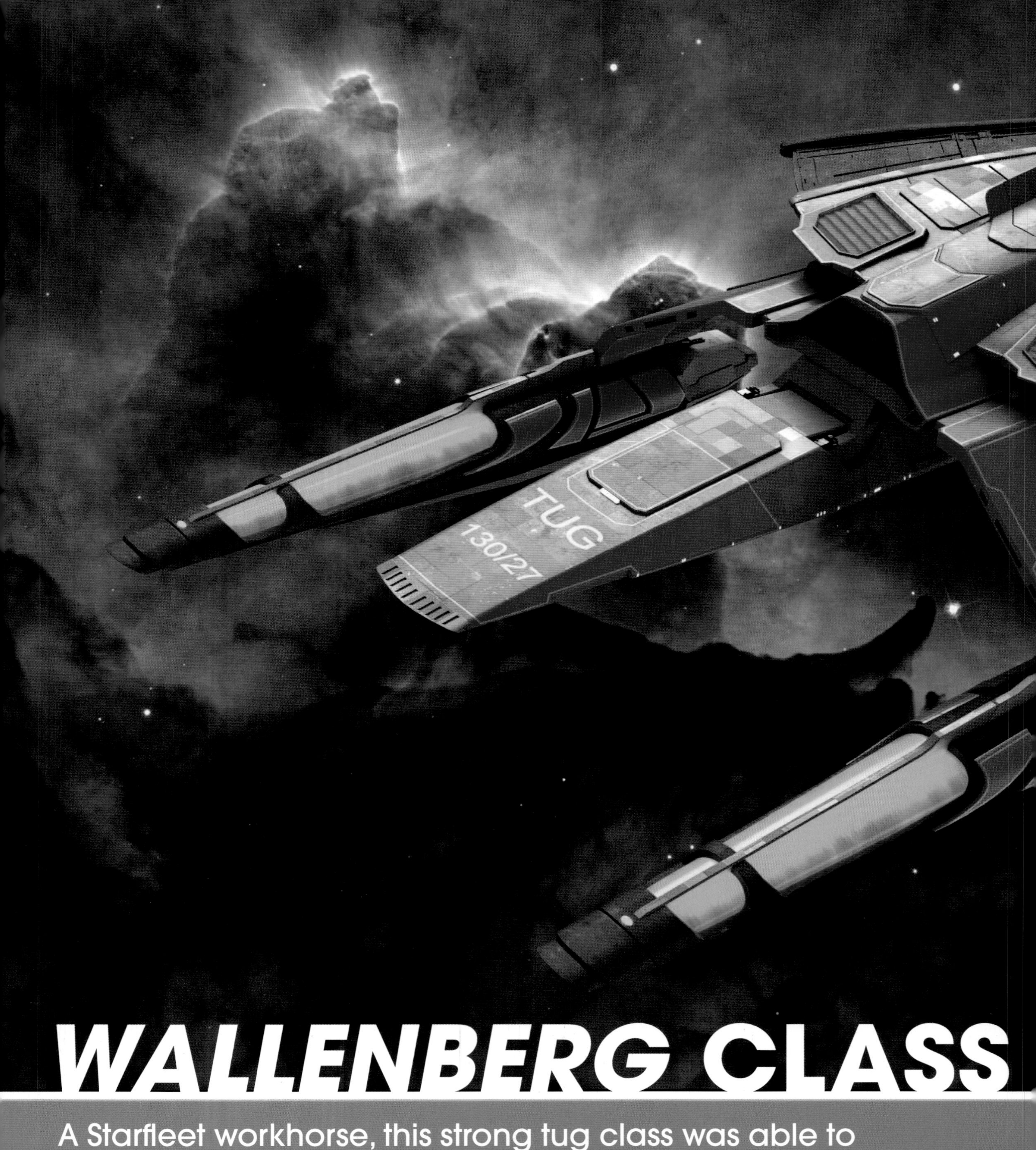

WALLENBERG CLASS

A Starfleet workhorse, this strong tug class was able to provide assistance in a wide range of missions.

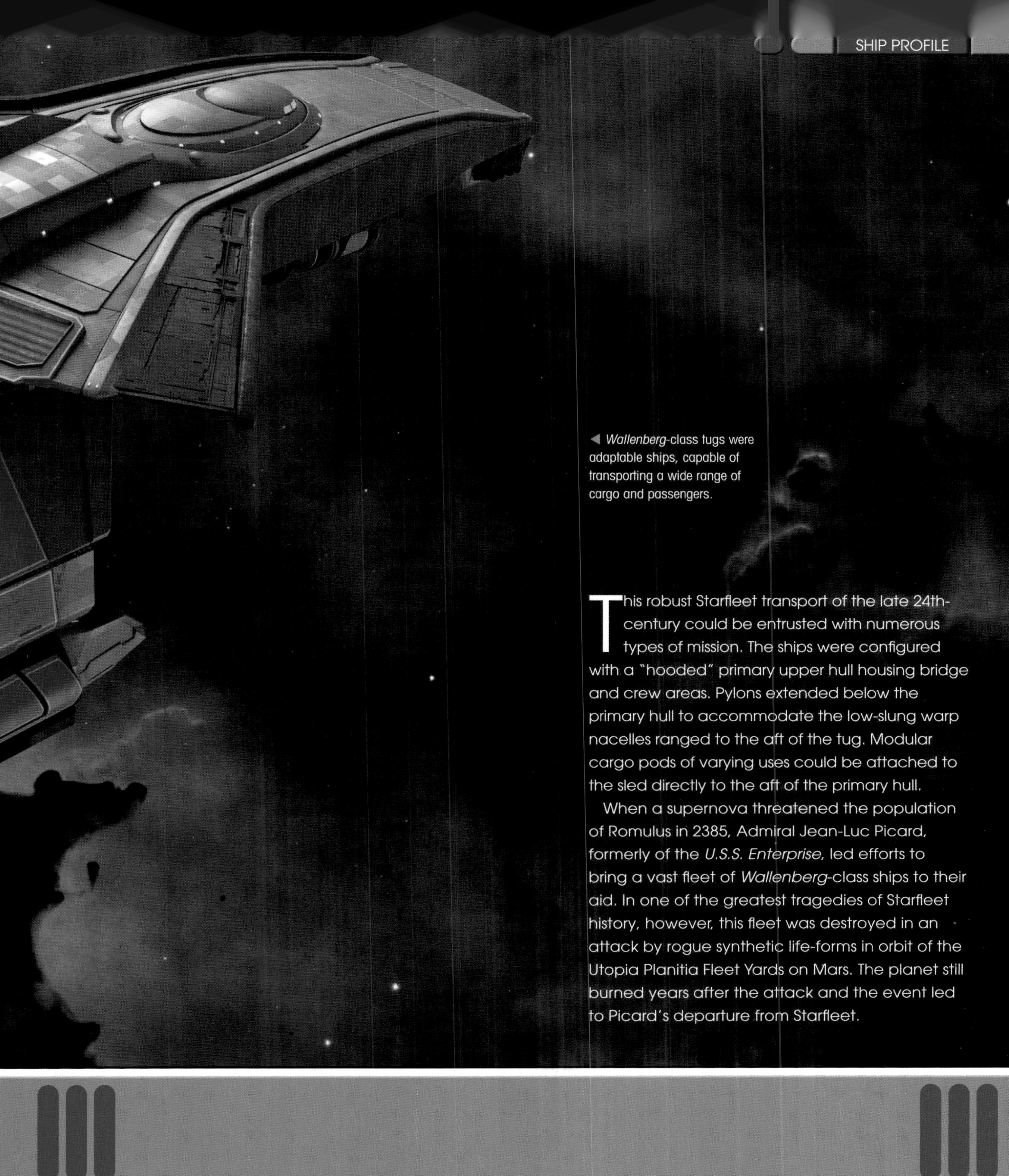

◀ *Wallenberg*-class tugs were adaptable ships, capable of transporting a wide range of cargo and passengers.

This robust Starfleet transport of the late 24th-century could be entrusted with numerous types of mission. The ships were configured with a "hooded" primary upper hull housing bridge and crew areas. Pylons extended below the primary hull to accommodate the low-slung warp nacelles ranged to the aft of the tug. Modular cargo pods of varying uses could be attached to the sled directly to the aft of the primary hull.

When a supernova threatened the population of Romulus in 2385, Admiral Jean-Luc Picard, formerly of the *U.S.S. Enterprise*, led efforts to bring a vast fleet of *Wallenberg*-class ships to their aid. In one of the greatest tragedies of Starfleet history, however, this fleet was destroyed in an attack by rogue synthetic life-forms in orbit of the Utopia Planitia Fleet Yards on Mars. The planet still burned years after the attack and the event led to Picard's departure from Starfleet.

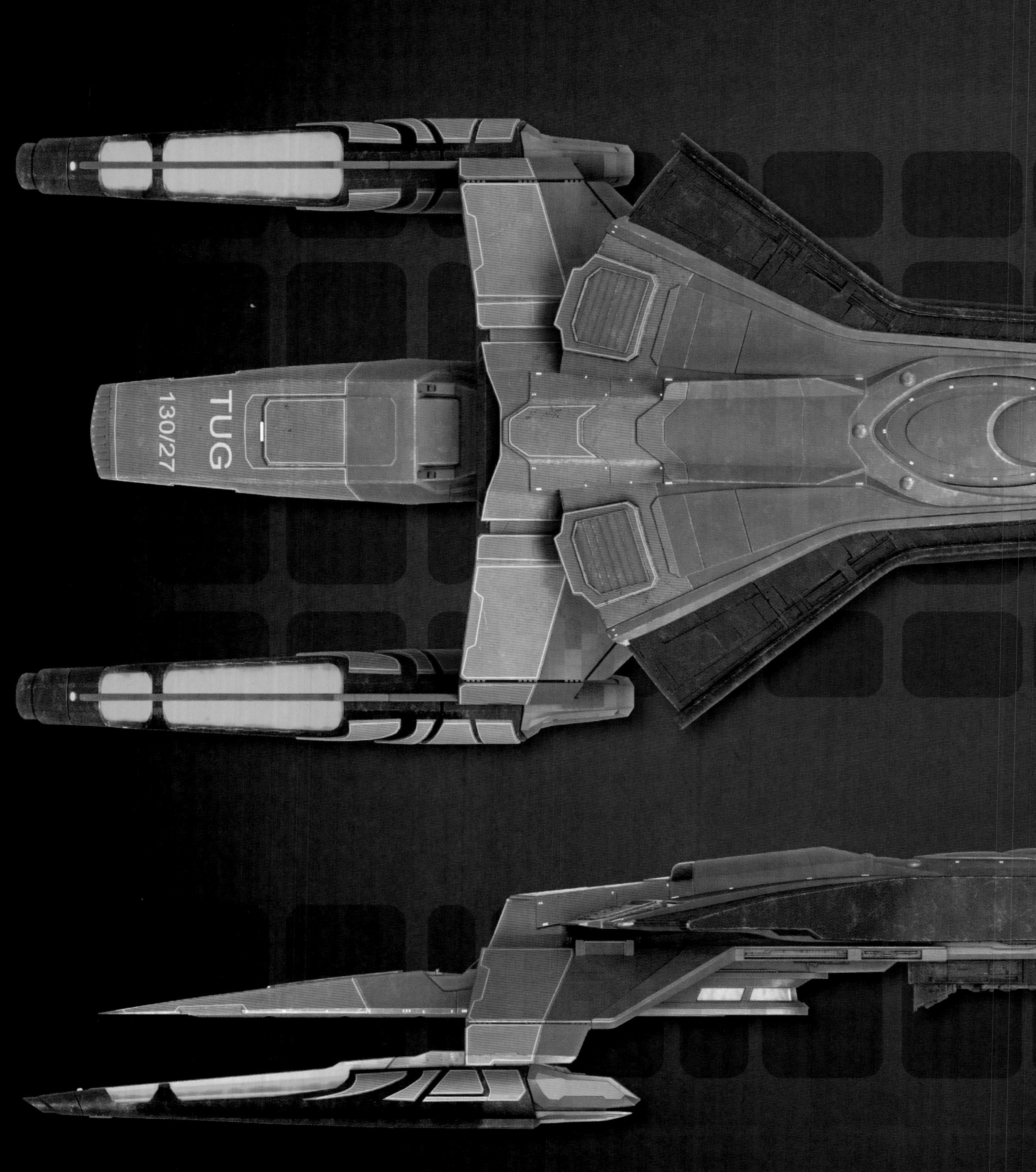
TUG
130/27

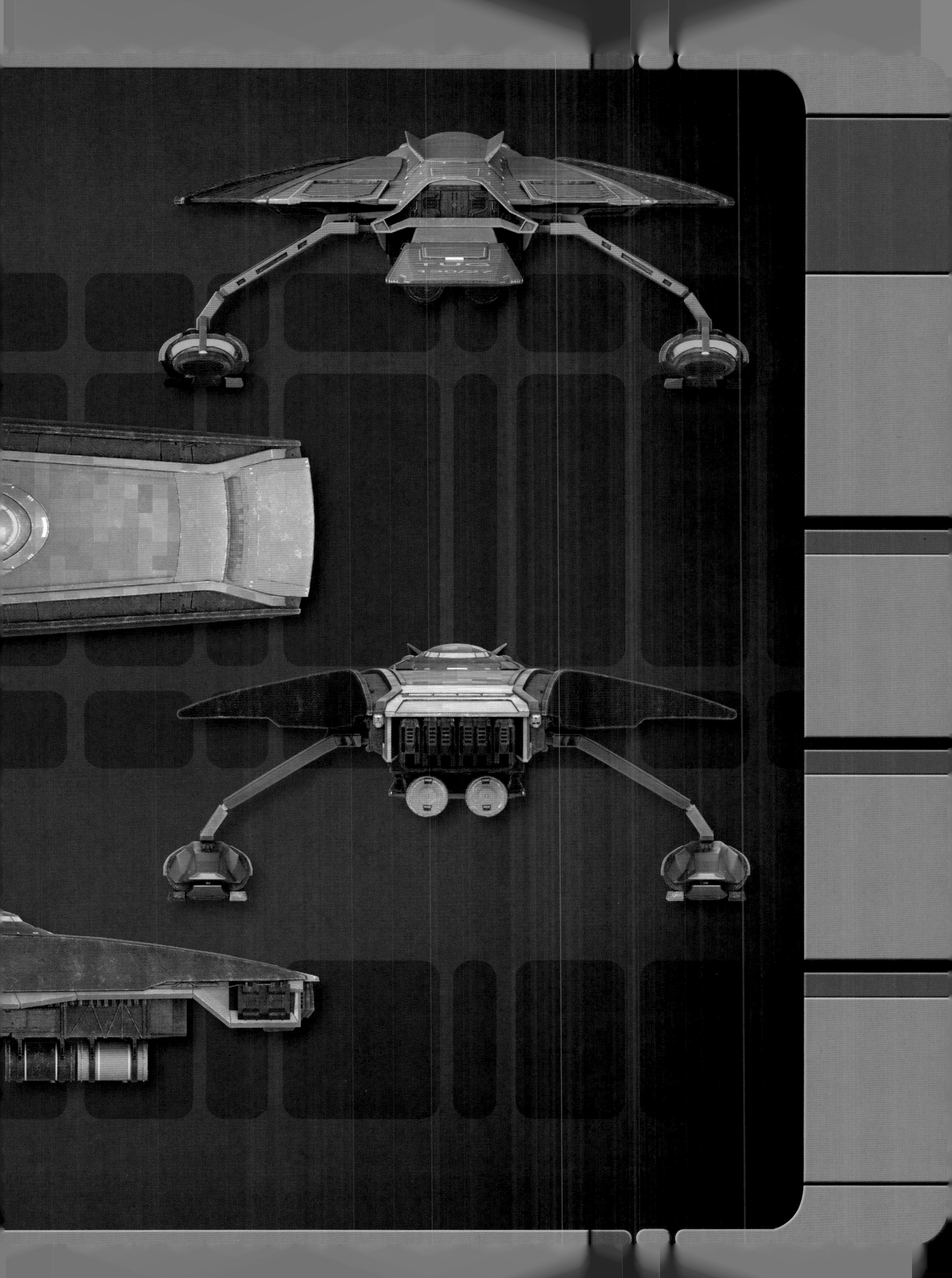

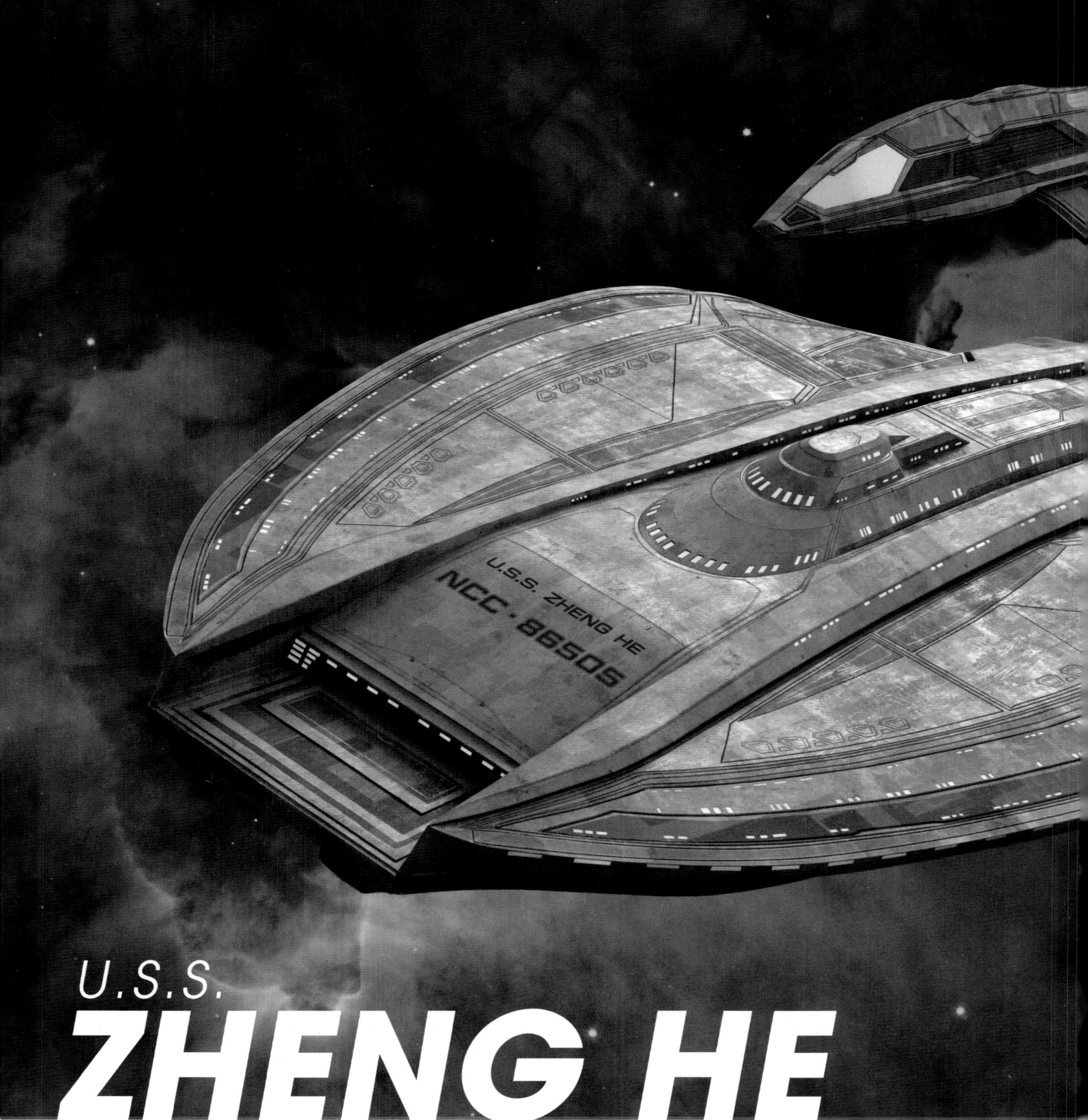

U.S.S. ZHENG HE

When it entered service, the *Inquiry*-class *U.S.S. Zheng He* was deemed Starfleet's toughest, fastest ship.

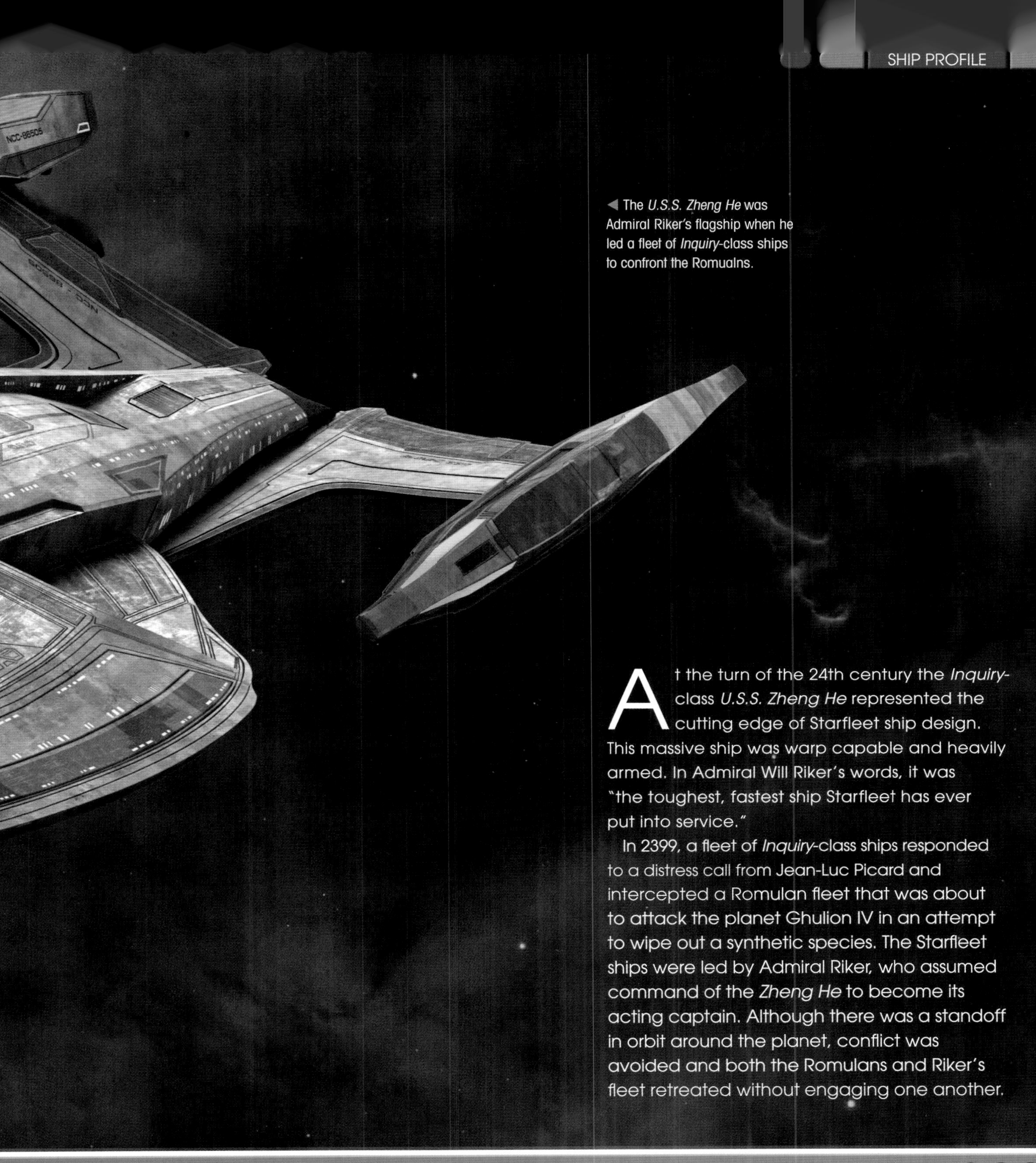

◀ The *U.S.S. Zheng He* was Admiral Riker's flagship when he led a fleet of *Inquiry*-class ships to confront the Romualns.

At the turn of the 24th century the *Inquiry*-class *U.S.S. Zheng He* represented the cutting edge of Starfleet ship design. This massive ship was warp capable and heavily armed. In Admiral Will Riker's words, it was "the toughest, fastest ship Starfleet has ever put into service."

In 2399, a fleet of *Inquiry*-class ships responded to a distress call from Jean-Luc Picard and intercepted a Romulan fleet that was about to attack the planet Ghulion IV in an attempt to wipe out a synthetic species. The Starfleet ships were led by Admiral Riker, who assumed command of the *Zheng He* to become its acting captain. Although there was a standoff in orbit around the planet, conflict was avoided and both the Romulans and Riker's fleet retreated without engaging one another.

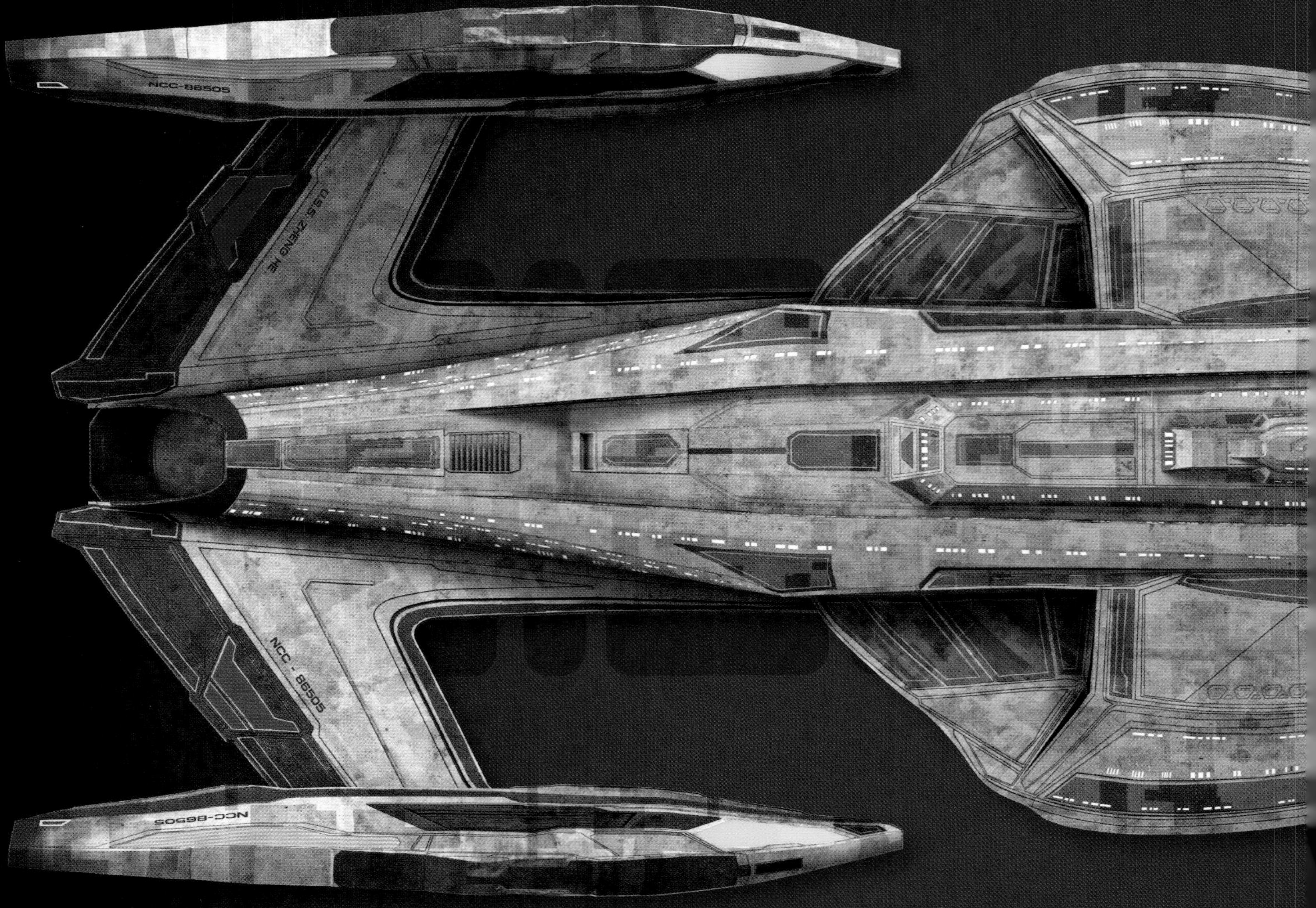

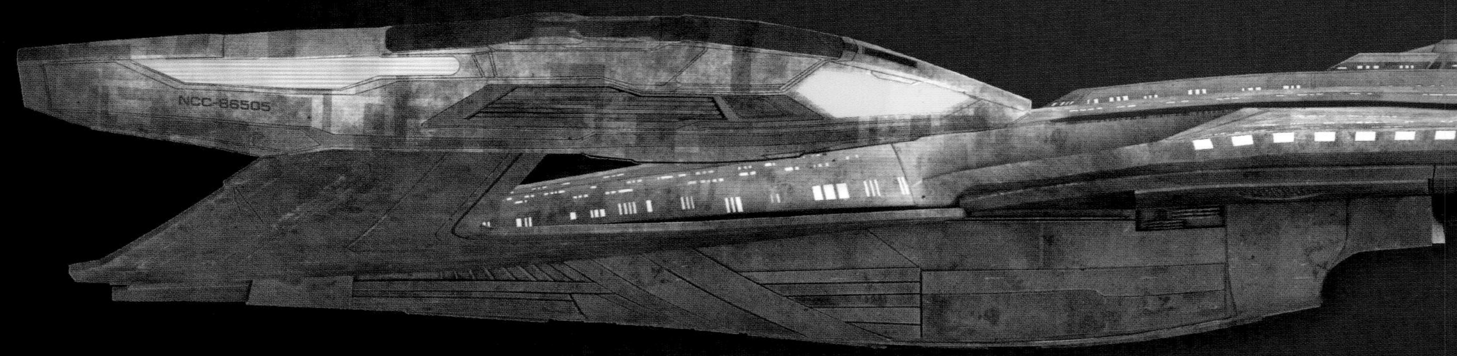
NCC-86505

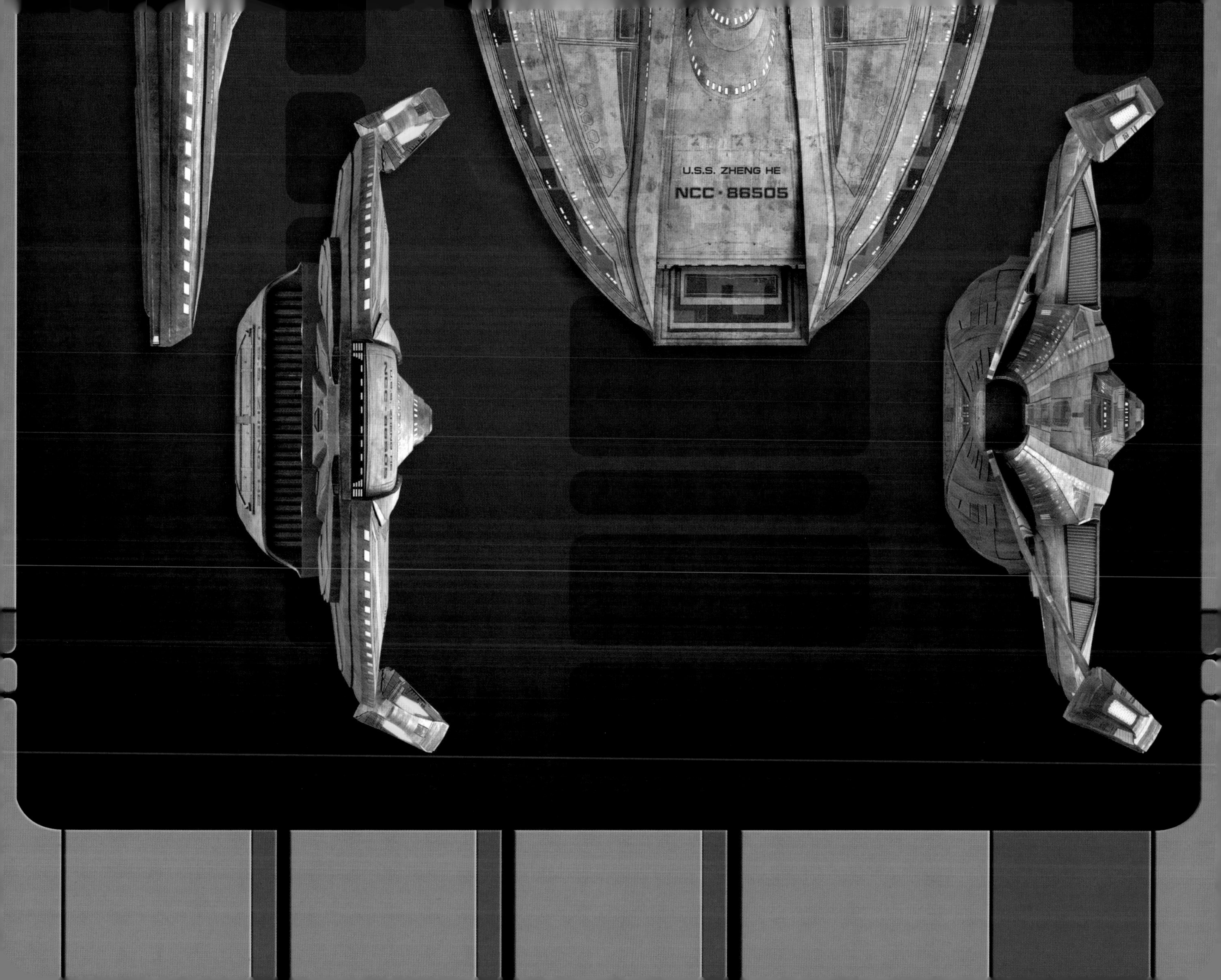
U.S.S. ZHENG HE
NCC-86505

INQUIRY-CLASS VARIANTS

VARIAN FRY

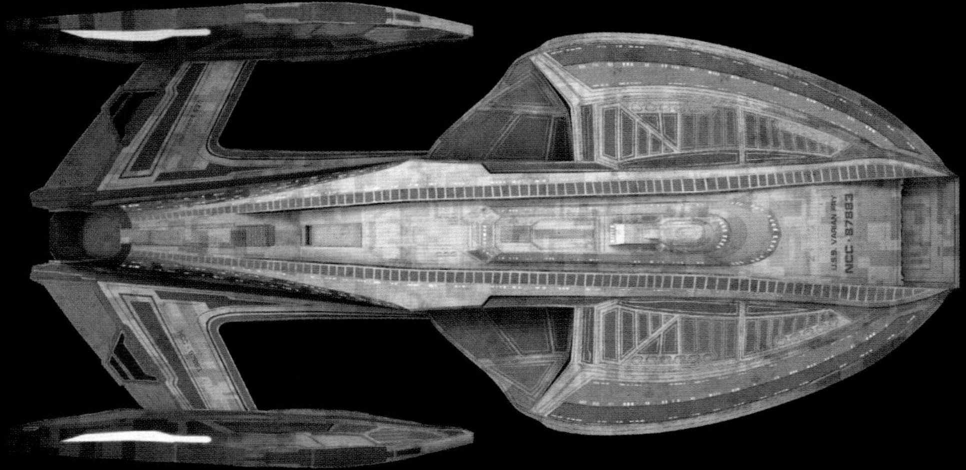

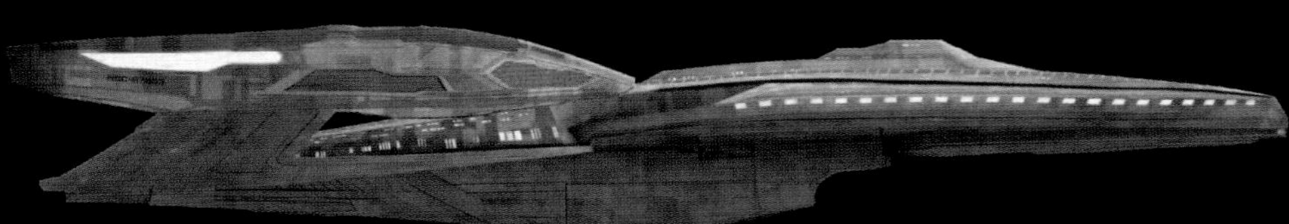

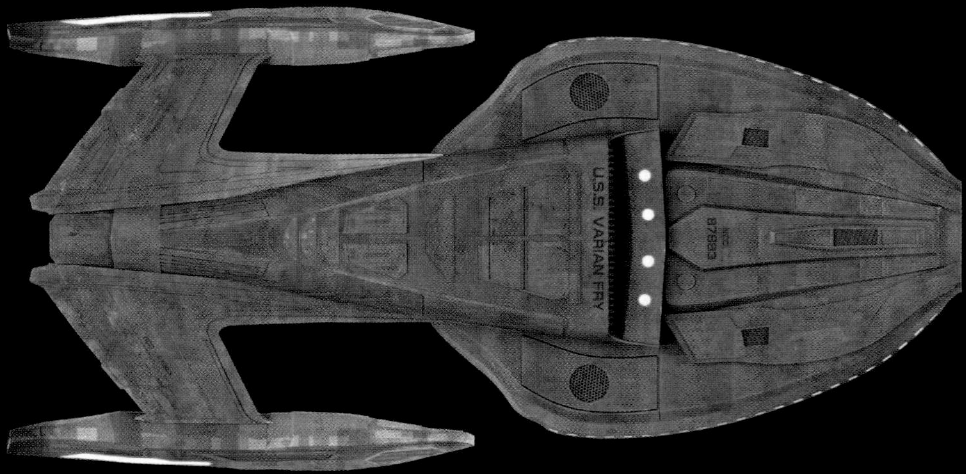

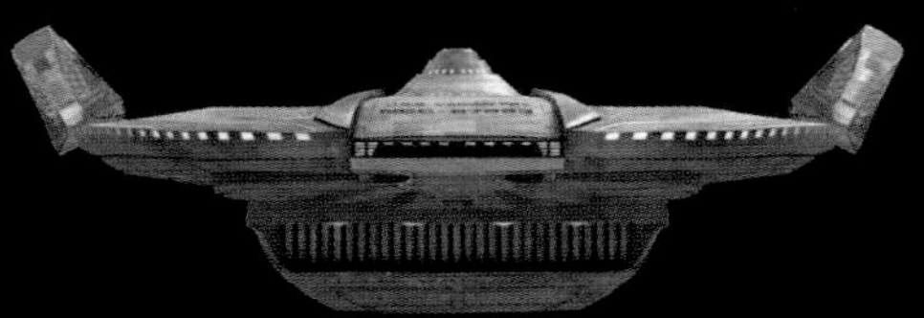

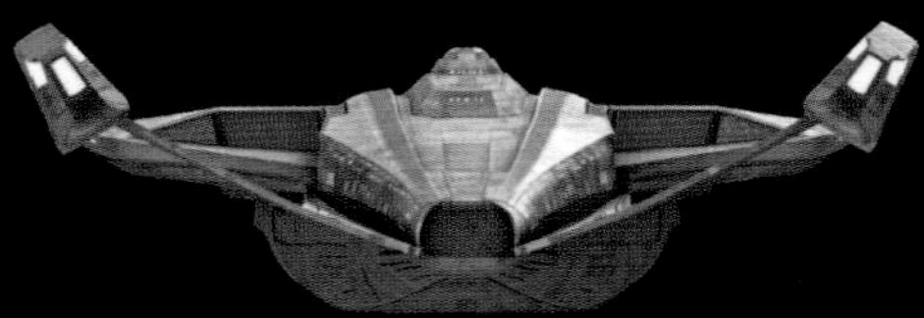

TOUSSAINT

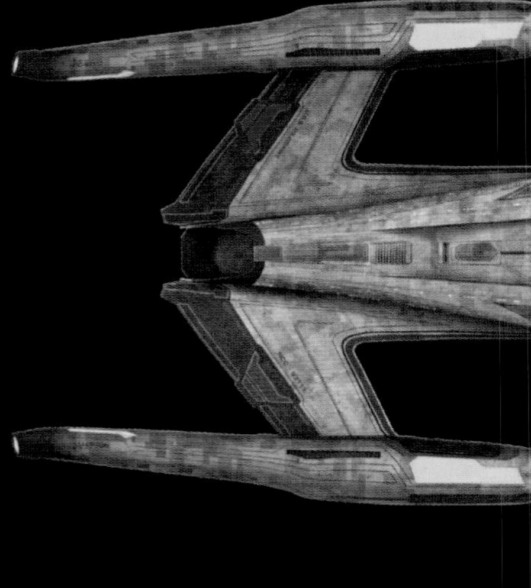

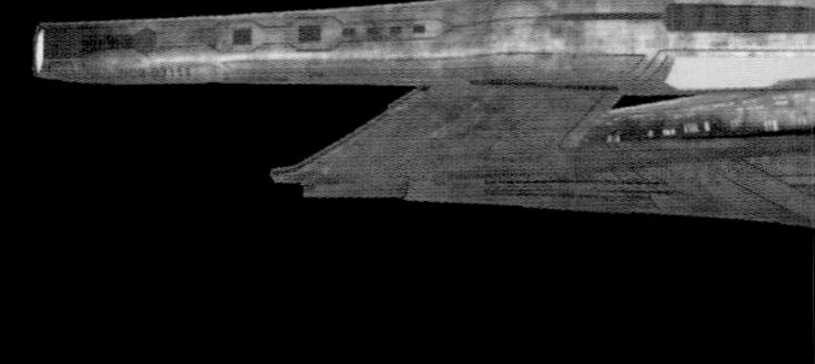

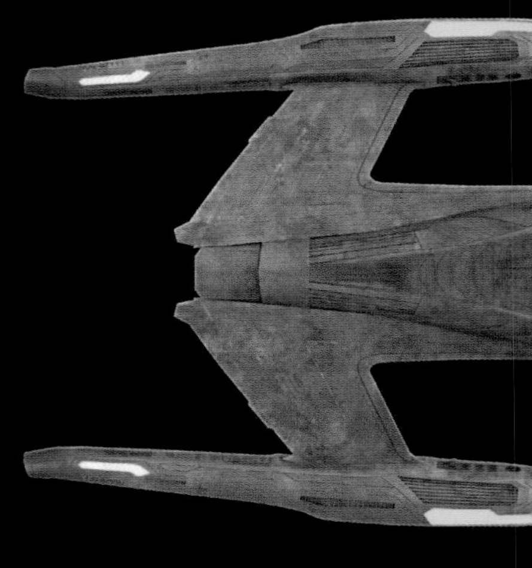

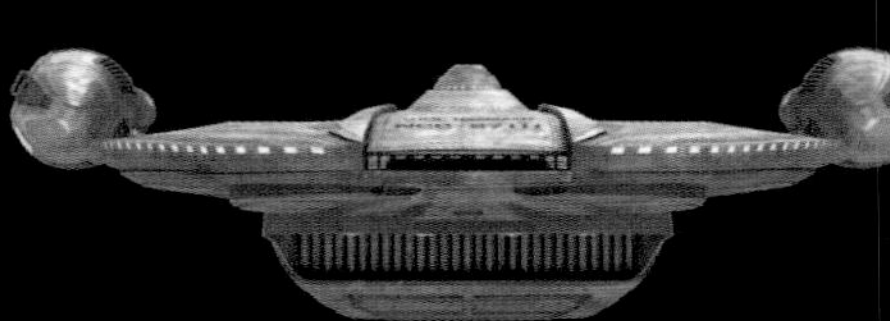

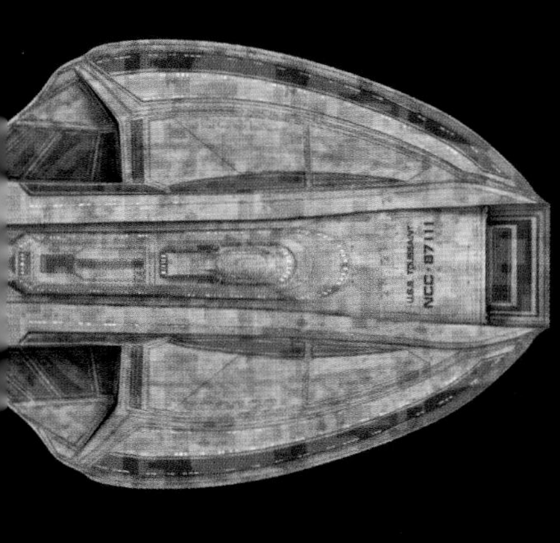

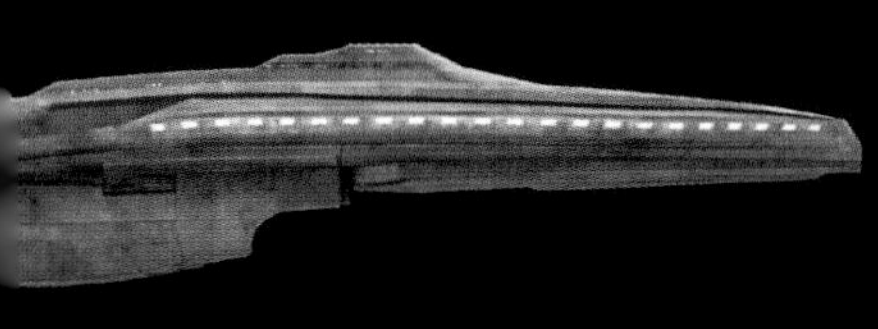

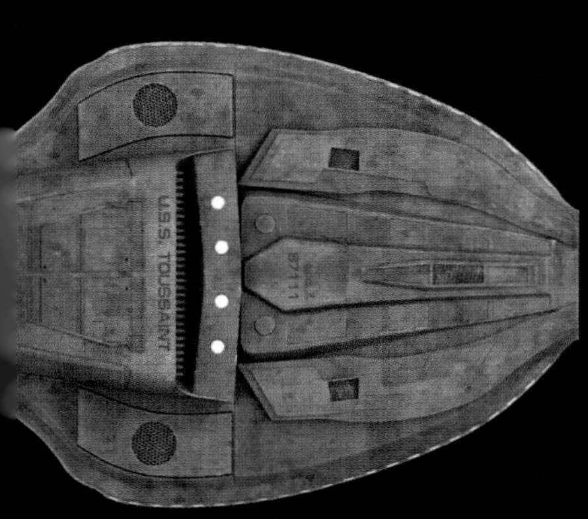

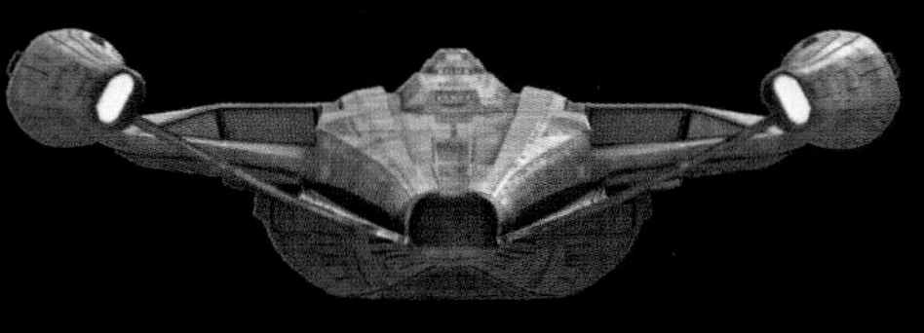

MAUI

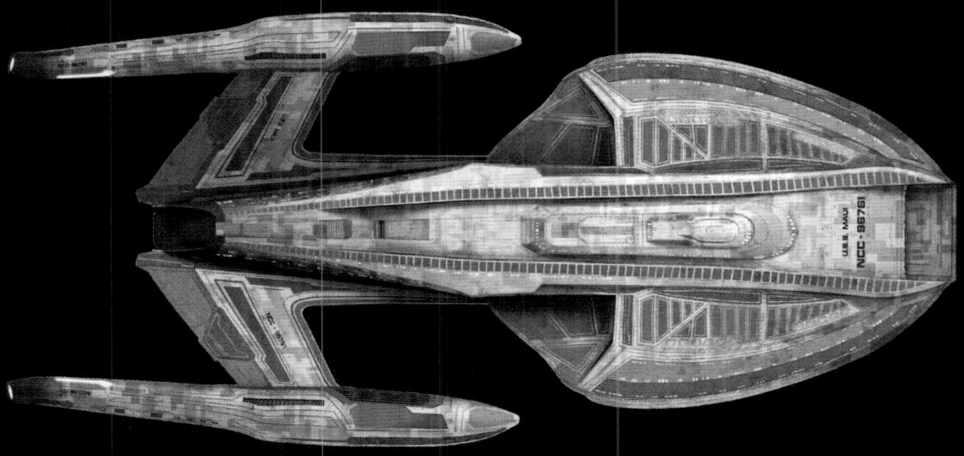

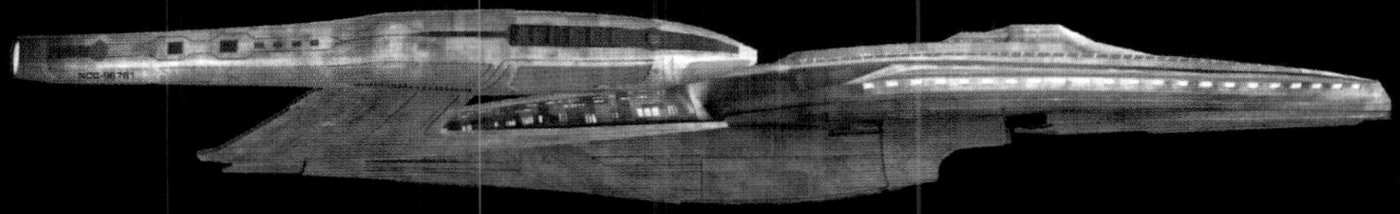

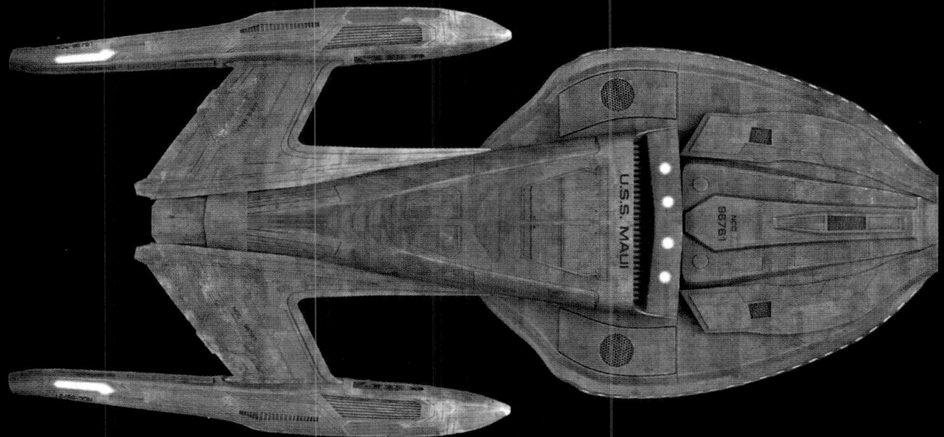

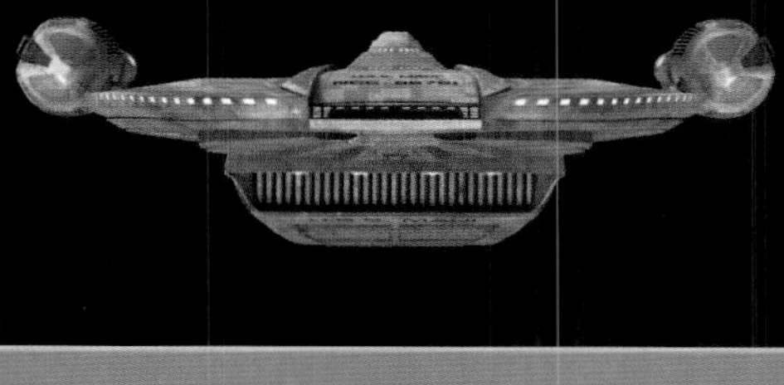

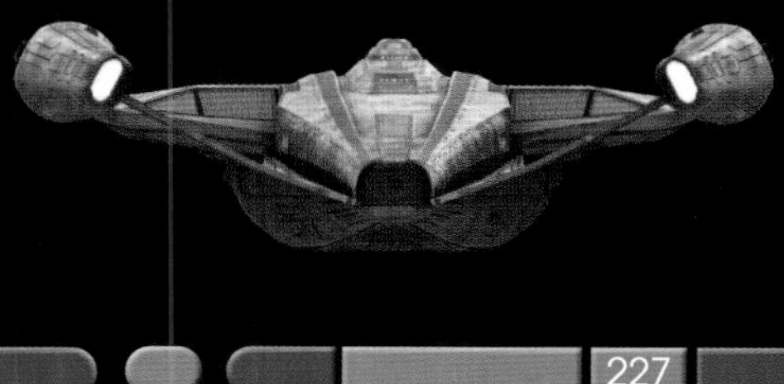

MULTI-MISSION EXPLORERS
SIZE CHART

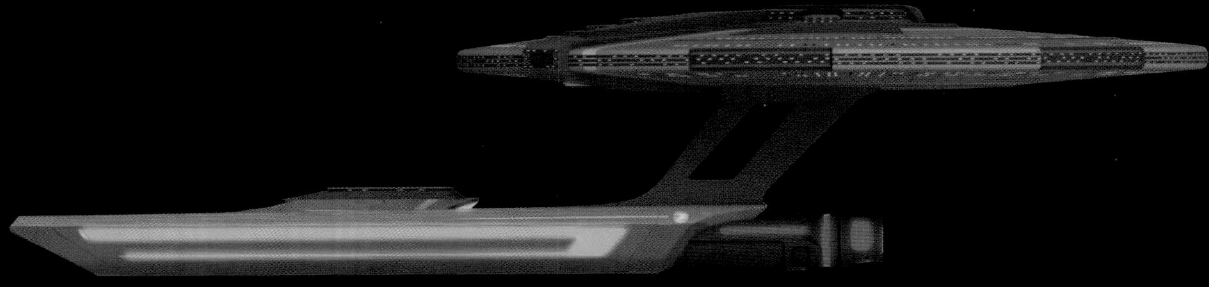

U.S.S. CERRITOS NCC-75567

794m

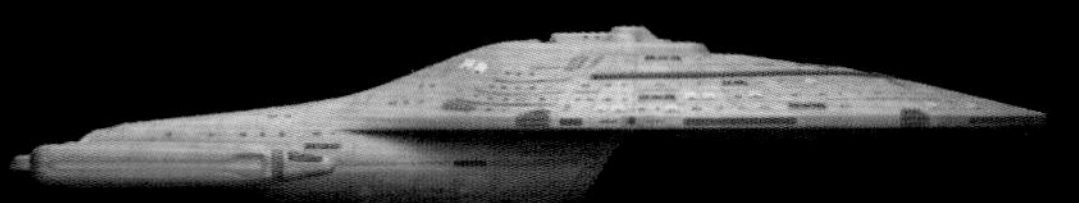

U.S.S. VOYAGER NCC-74656

343m

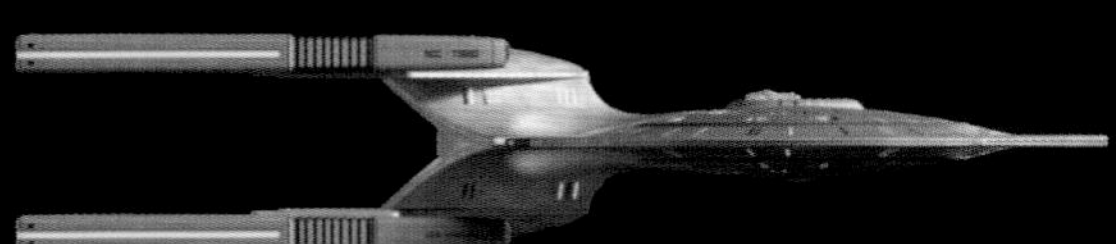

CHEYENNE CLASS

362m

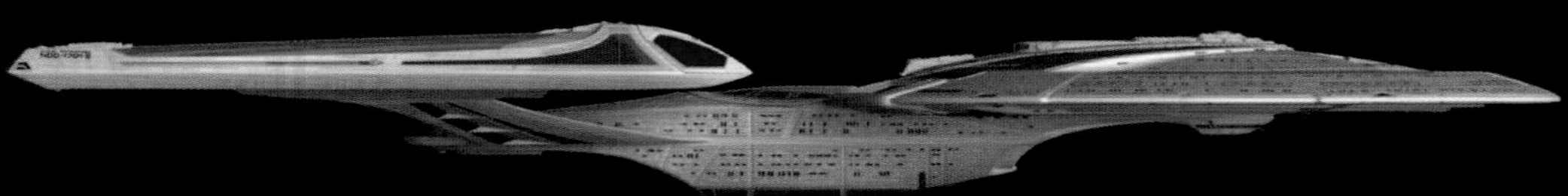

U.S.S. ENTERPRISE NCC-1701-E

685m

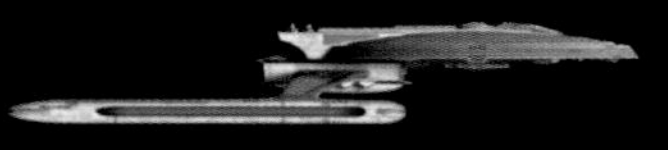

U.S.S. CENTAUR NCC-42043

210m

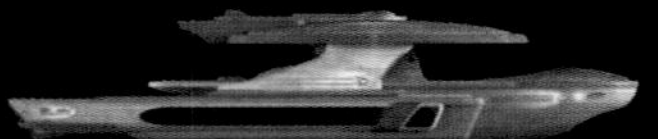

U.S.S. CURRY NCC-42254

210m

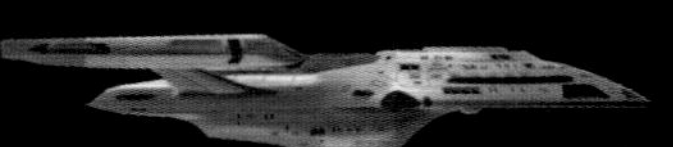

U.S.S. EQUINOX NCC-72381

222m

SCALE: 1:6000

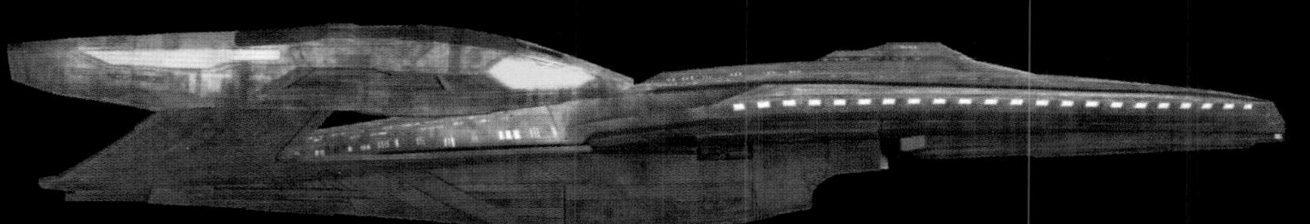

U.S.S. ZHENG HE NCC-86505

630.94m

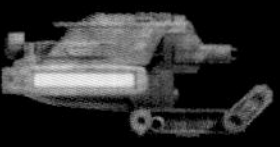

FEDERATION TUG

90m

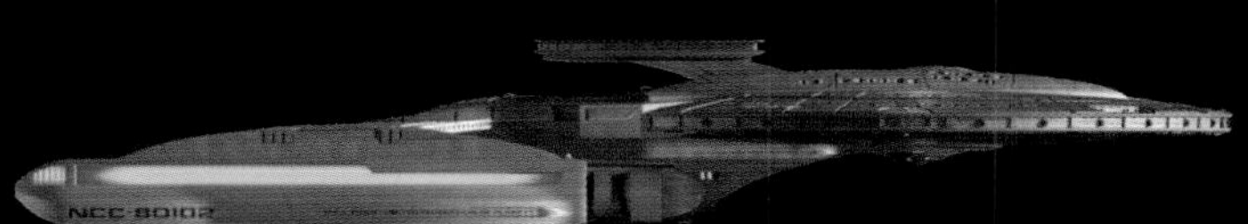

U.S.S. TITAN NCC-80102

454m

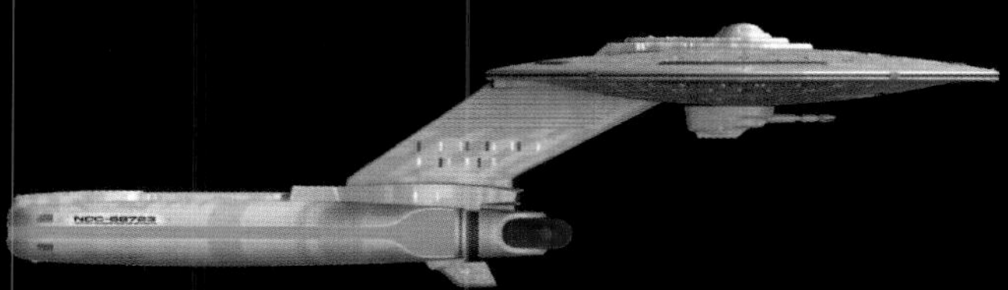

FREEDOM CLASS

430m

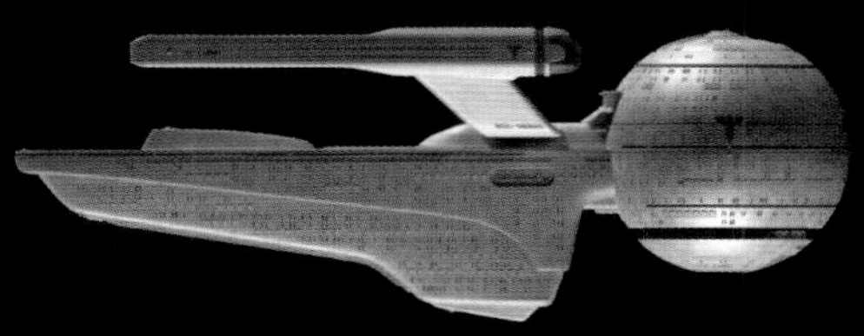

U.S.S. PASTEUR NCC-58925

320m

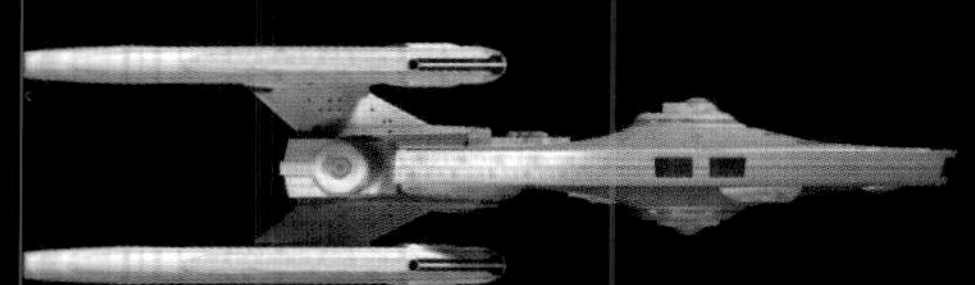

U.S.S. STARGAZER NCC-2893

310m

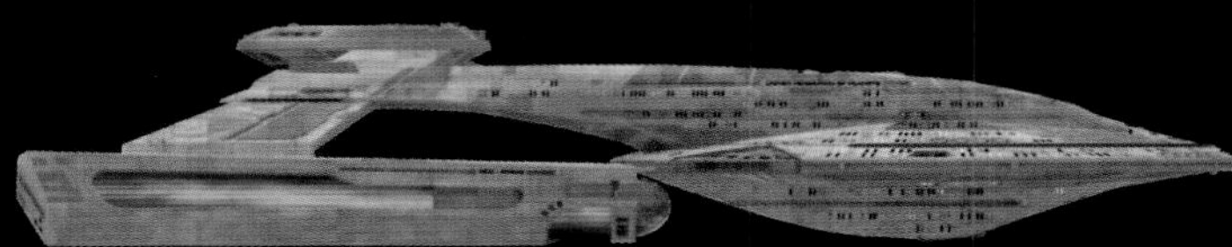

AKIRA CLASS

464.43m

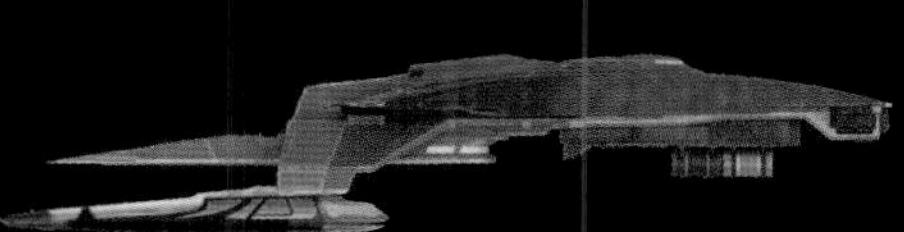

WALLENBERG TUG

298.7m

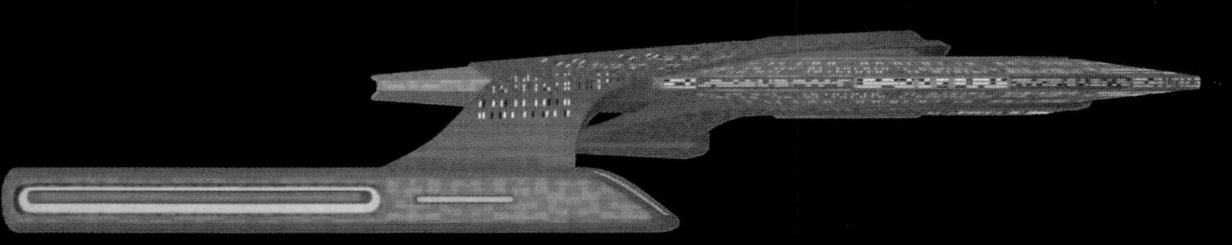

U.S.S. VANCOUVER

641m

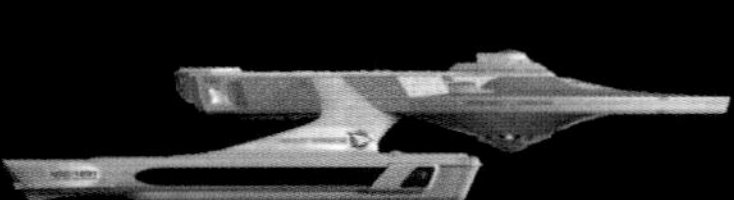

U.S.S. LANTREE

243m

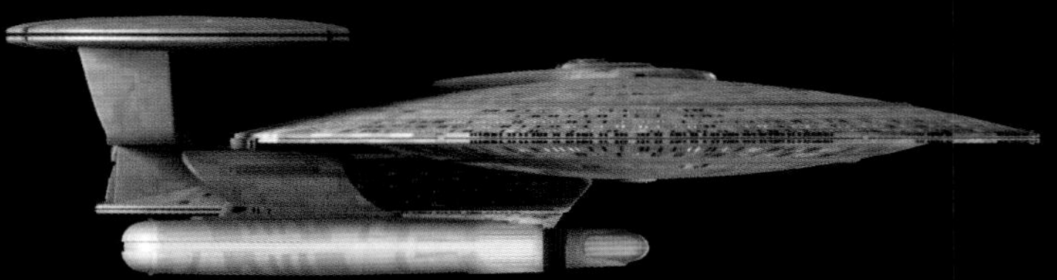

U.S.S. PHOENIX NCC-65420

465m

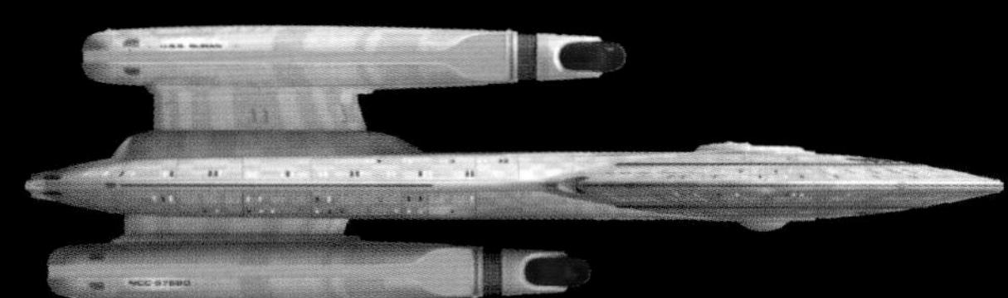

CHALLENGER CLASS

390m

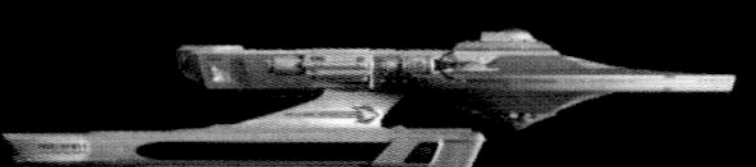

U.S.S. SARATOGA NCC-31911

243m

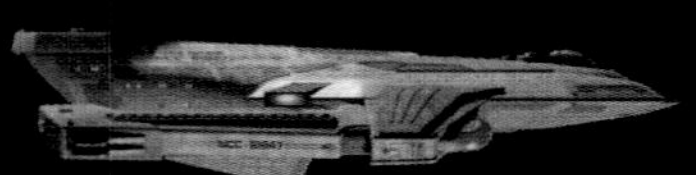

SABER CLASS

223m

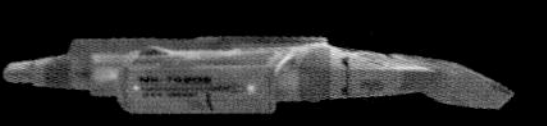

U.S.S. DEFIANT NX-74205

170.68m

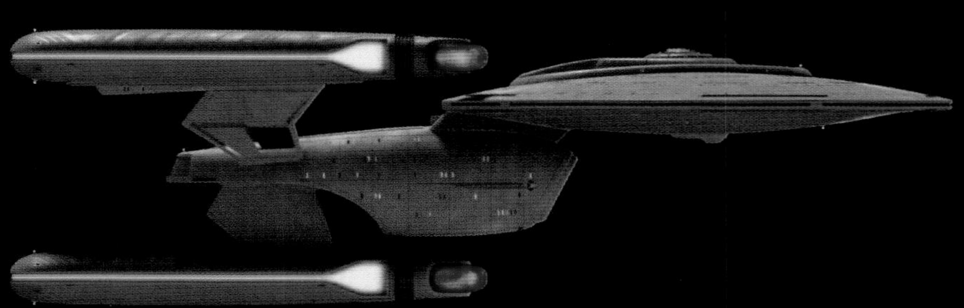

NIAGARA CLASS

565m

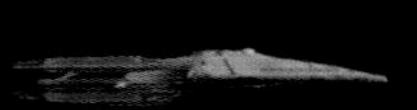

U.S.S. PROMETHEUS NX-59650

126m

SCALE: 1:6000

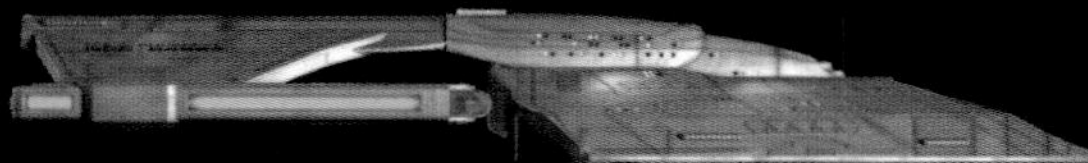

NORWAY CLASS
364.77m

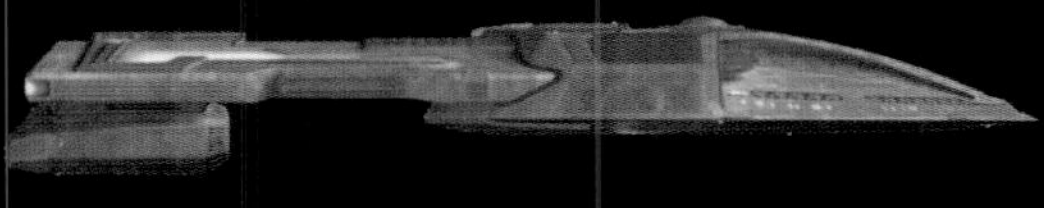

STEAMRUNNER CLASS
343m

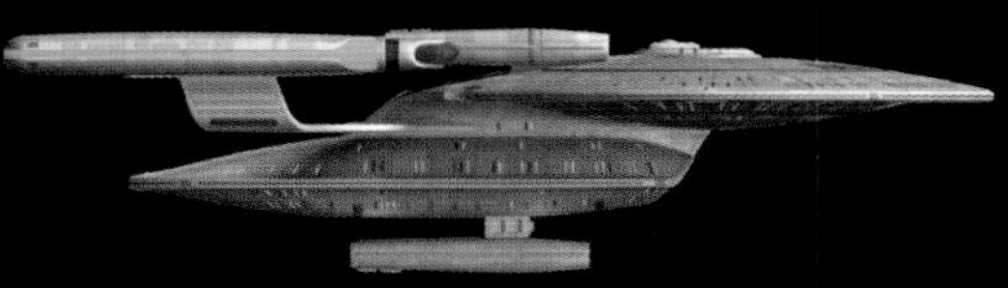

NEW ORLEANS CLASS
340m

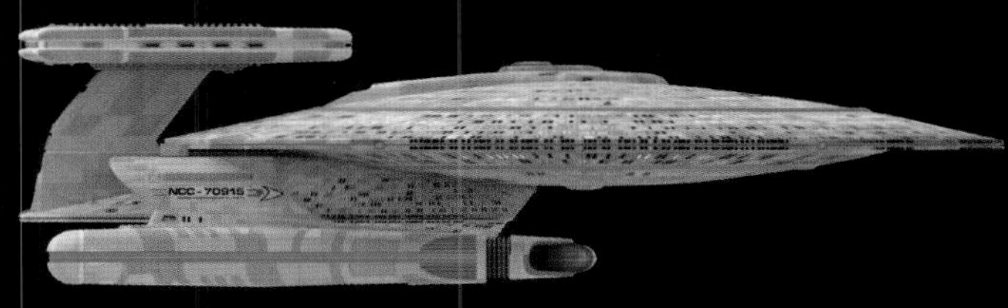

NEBULA CLASS
442.23m

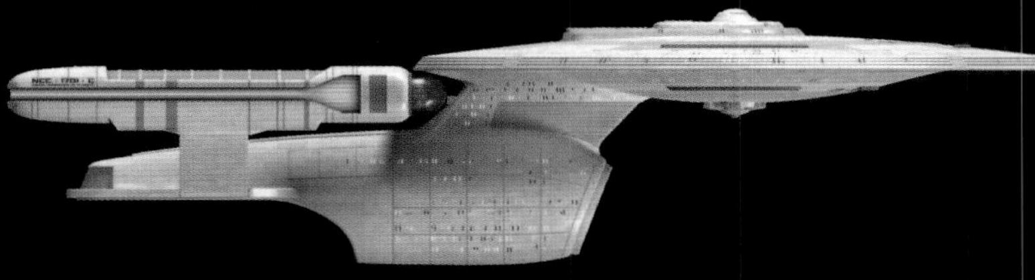

U.S.S. ENTERPRISE NCC-1701-C
520m

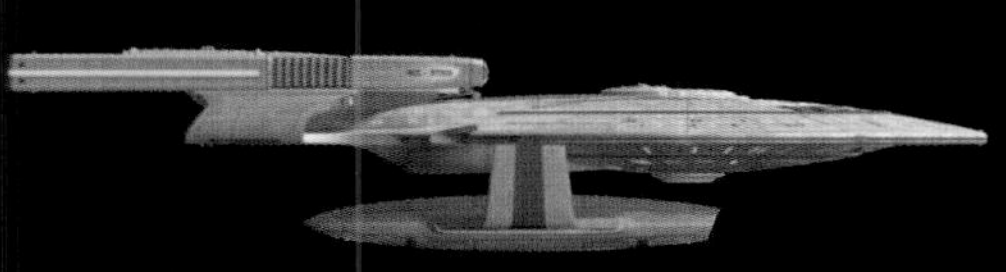

SPRINGFIELD CLASS
325m

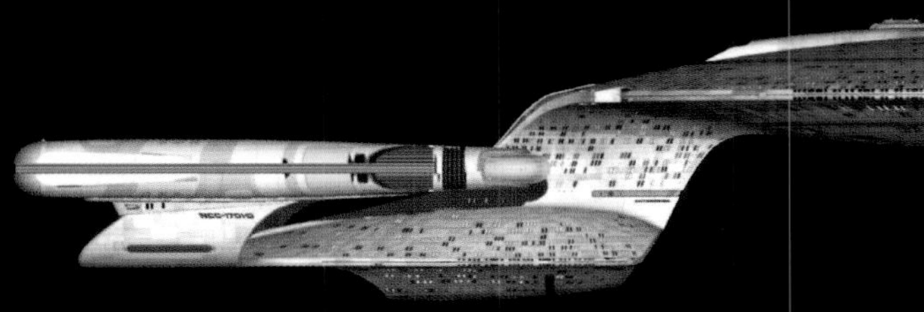

U.S.S. ENTERPRISE NCC-1701-D
641m

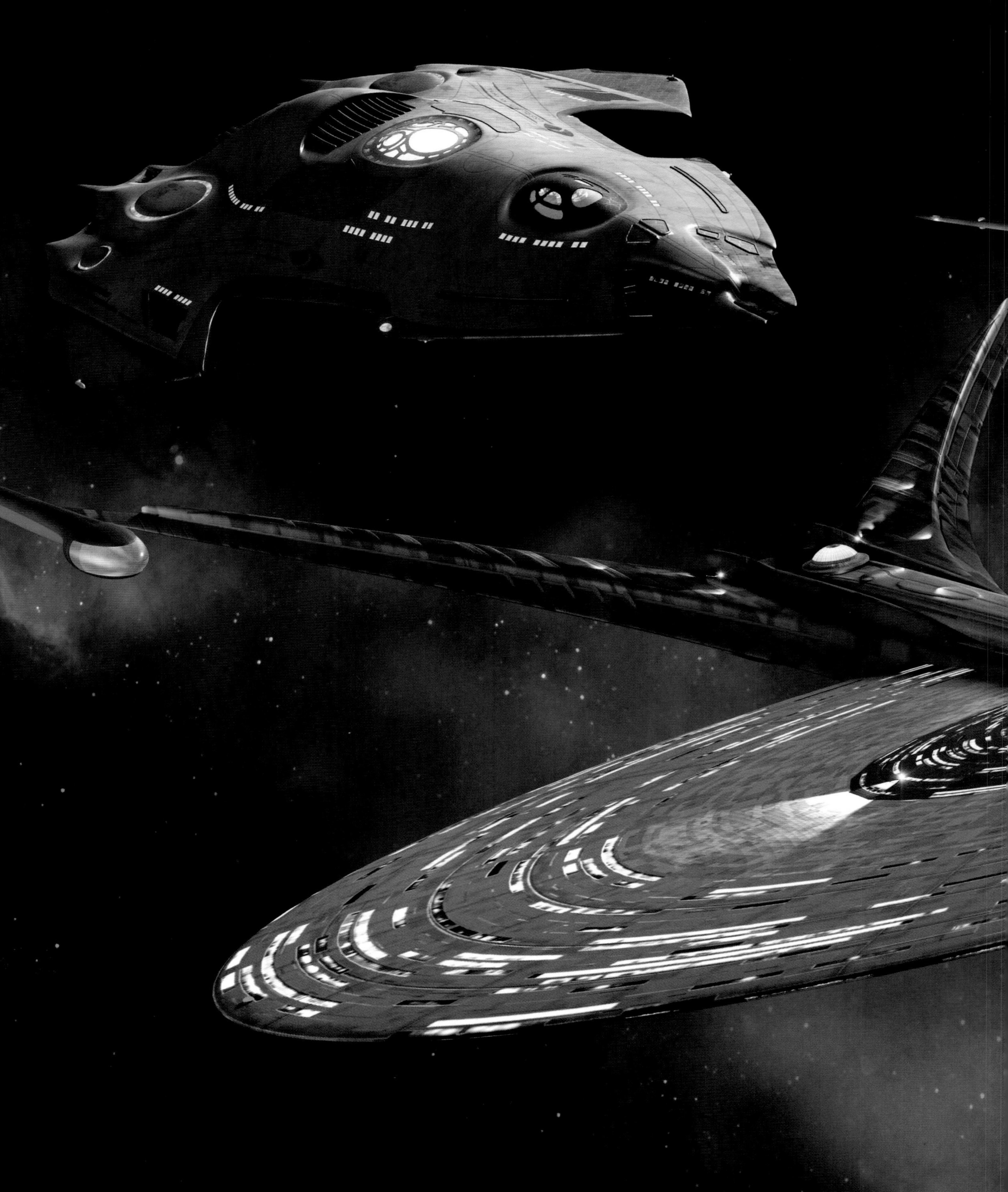

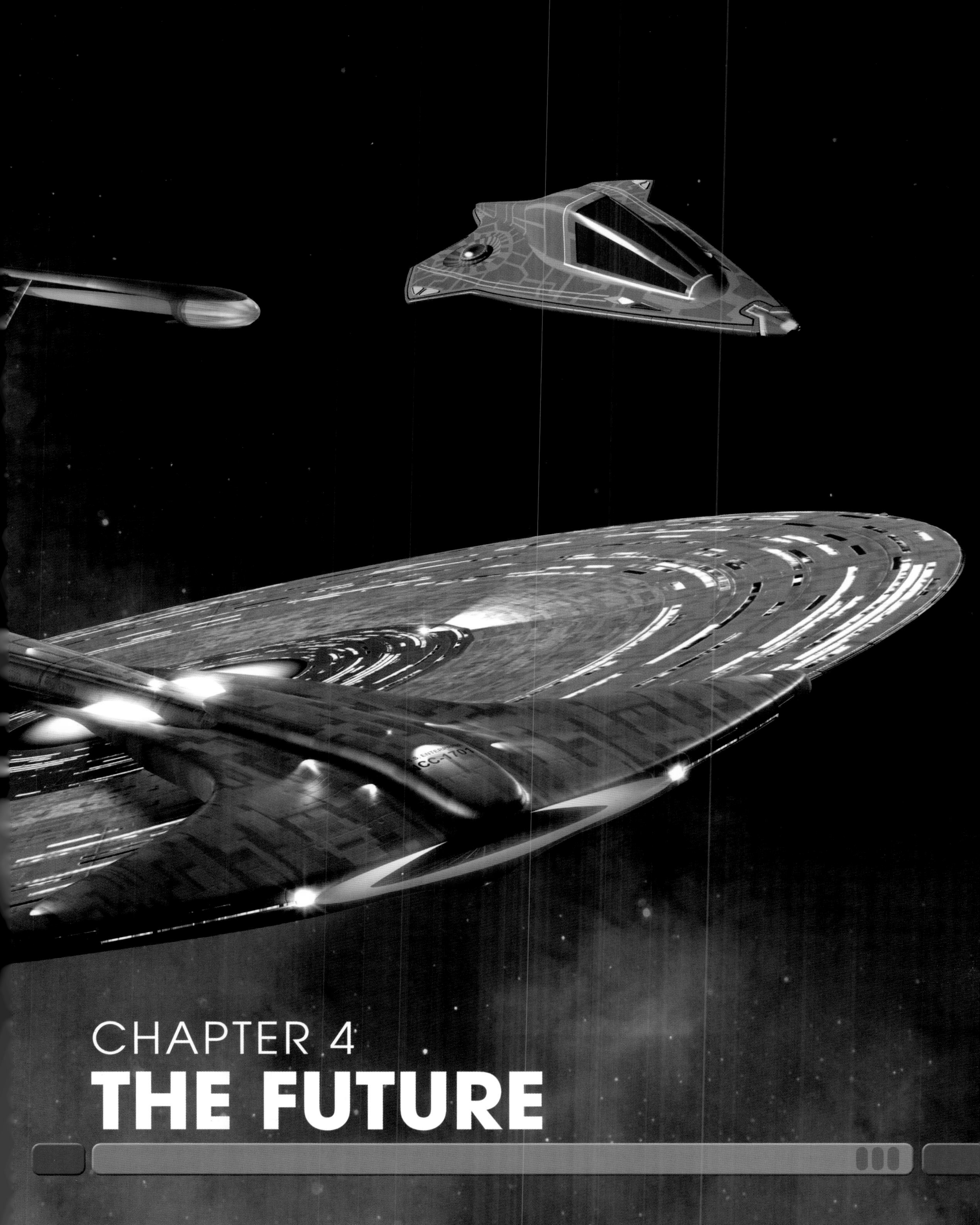

CHAPTER 4
THE FUTURE

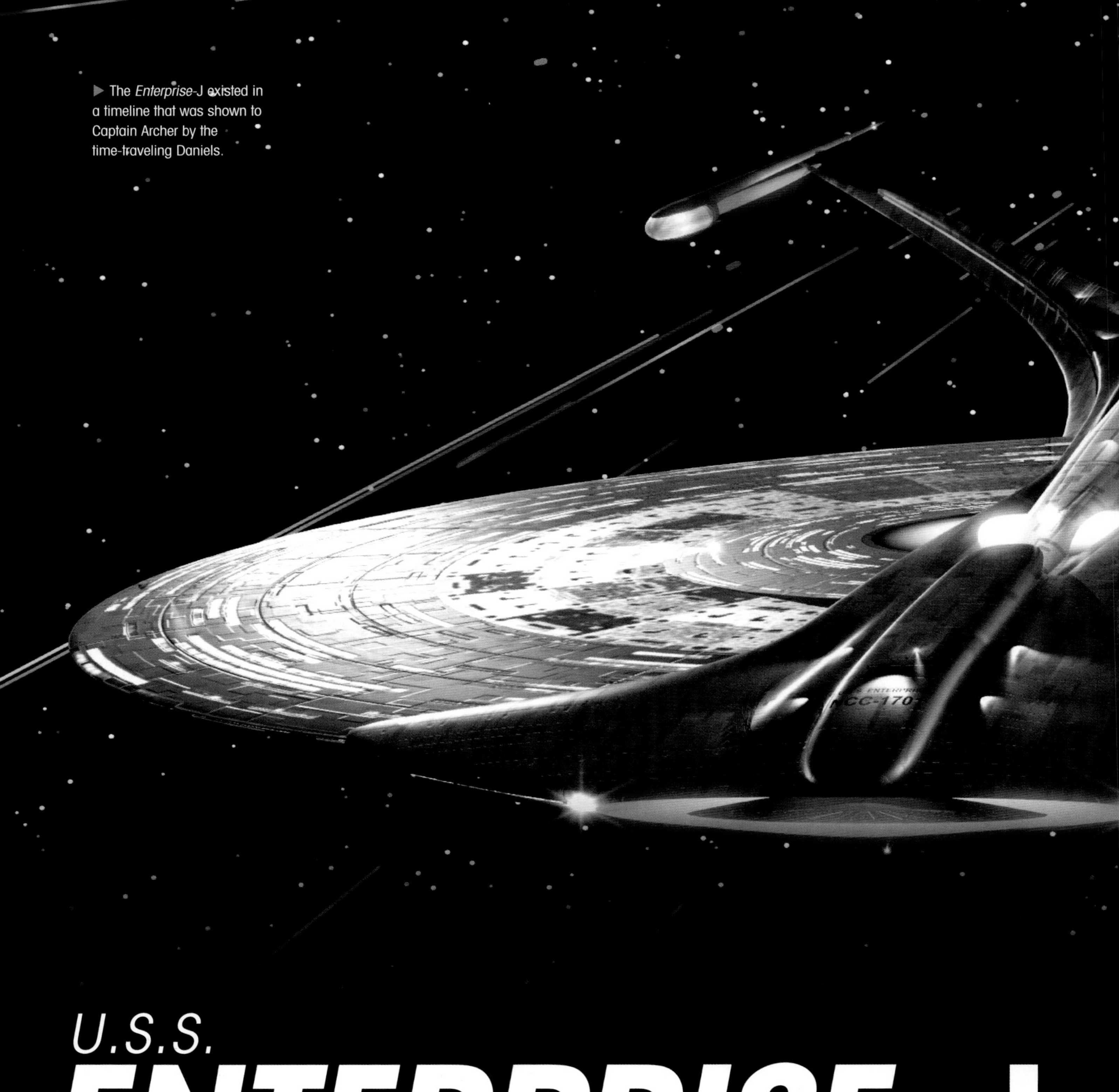

▶ The *Enterprise*-J existed in a timeline that was shown to Captain Archer by the time-traveling Daniels.

U.S.S. ENTERPRISE-J

There was still an *Enterprise* in the 26th century: a massive ship that played a part in a historic battle.

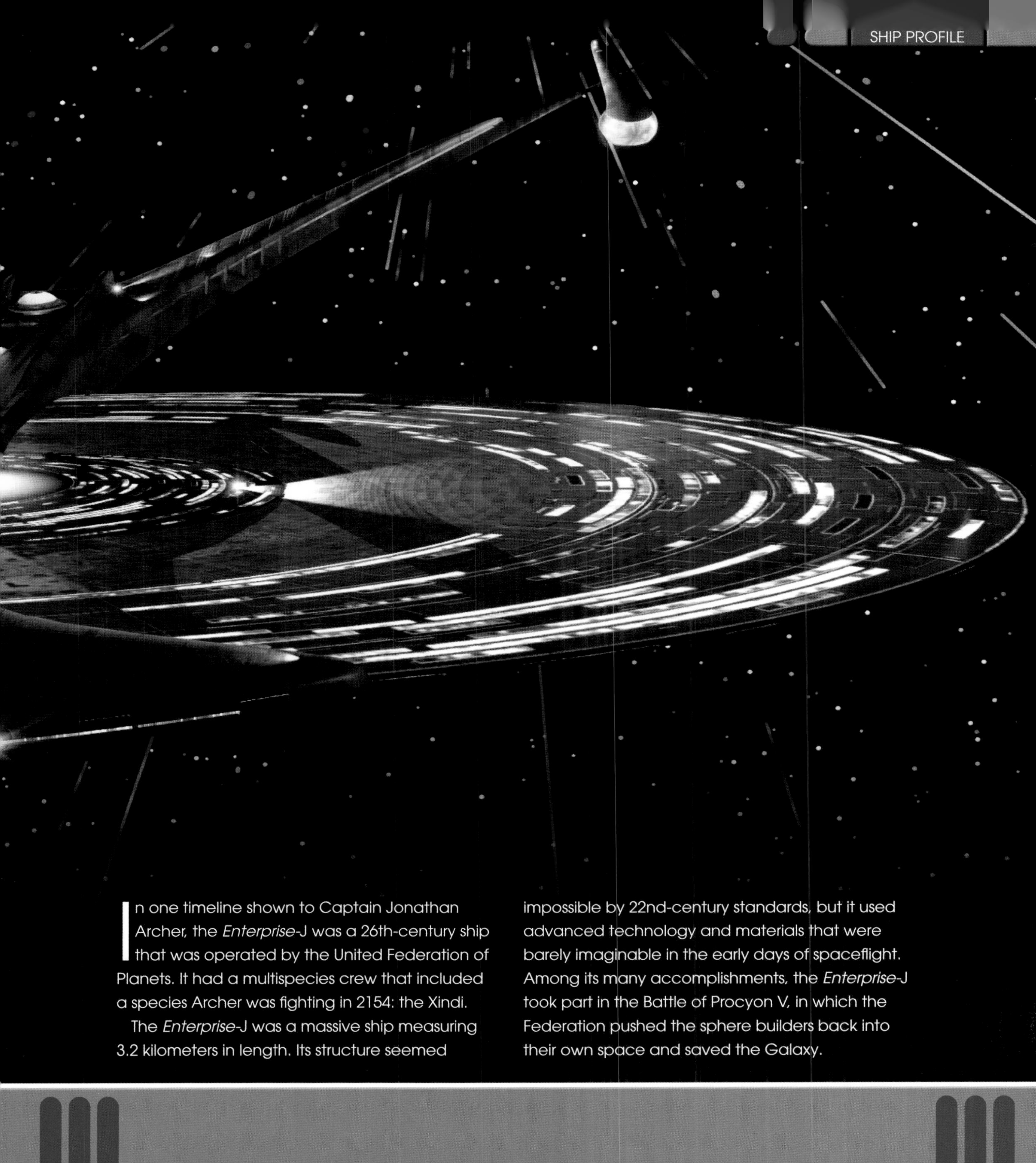

In one timeline shown to Captain Jonathan Archer, the *Enterprise*-J was a 26th-century ship that was operated by the United Federation of Planets. It had a multispecies crew that included a species Archer was fighting in 2154: the Xindi.

The *Enterprise*-J was a massive ship measuring 3.2 kilometers in length. Its structure seemed impossible by 22nd-century standards, but it used advanced technology and materials that were barely imaginable in the early days of spaceflight. Among its many accomplishments, the *Enterprise*-J took part in the Battle of Procyon V, in which the Federation pushed the sphere builders back into their own space and saved the Galaxy.

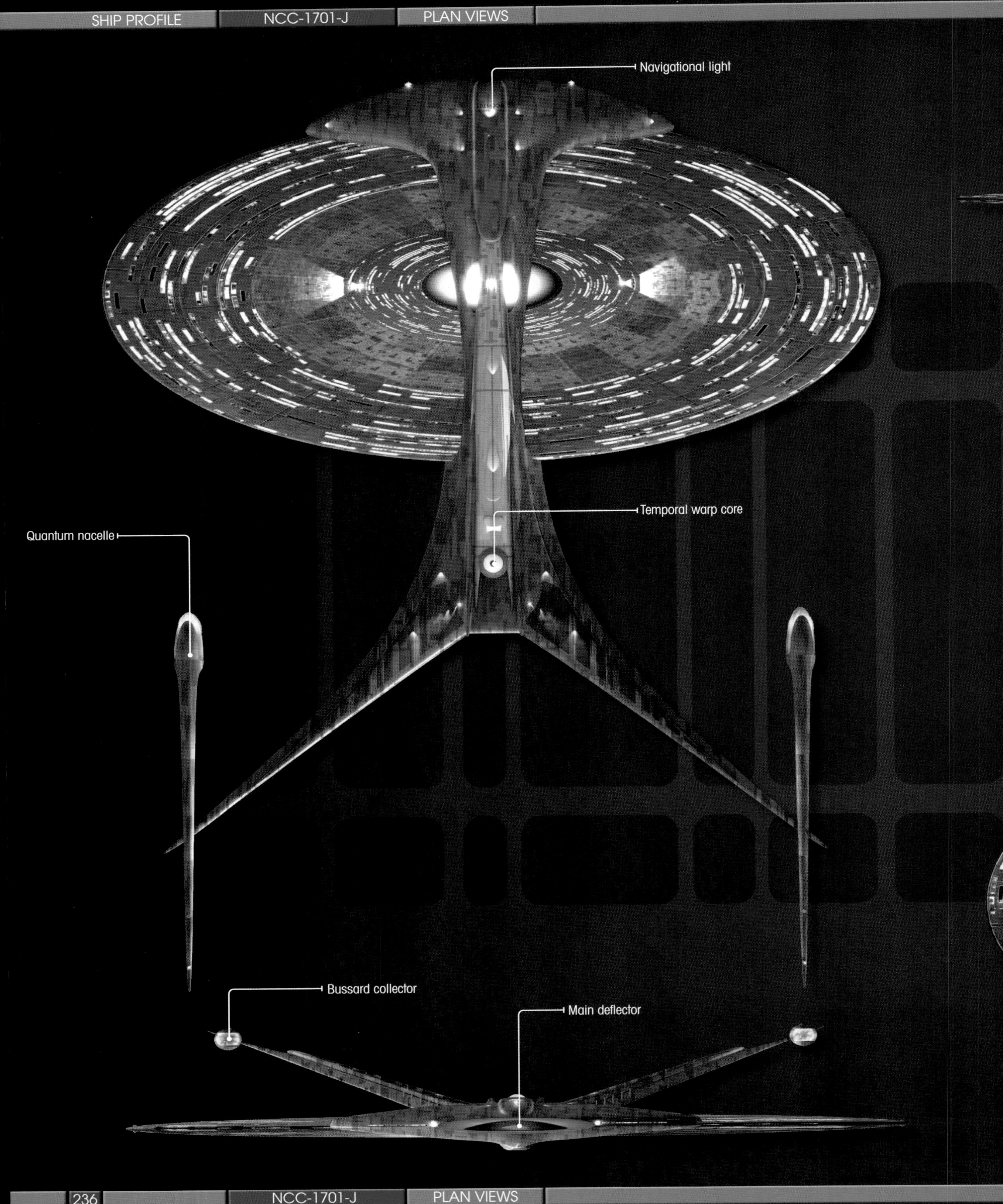
Navigational light
Temporal warp core
Quantum nacelle
Bussard collector
Main deflector

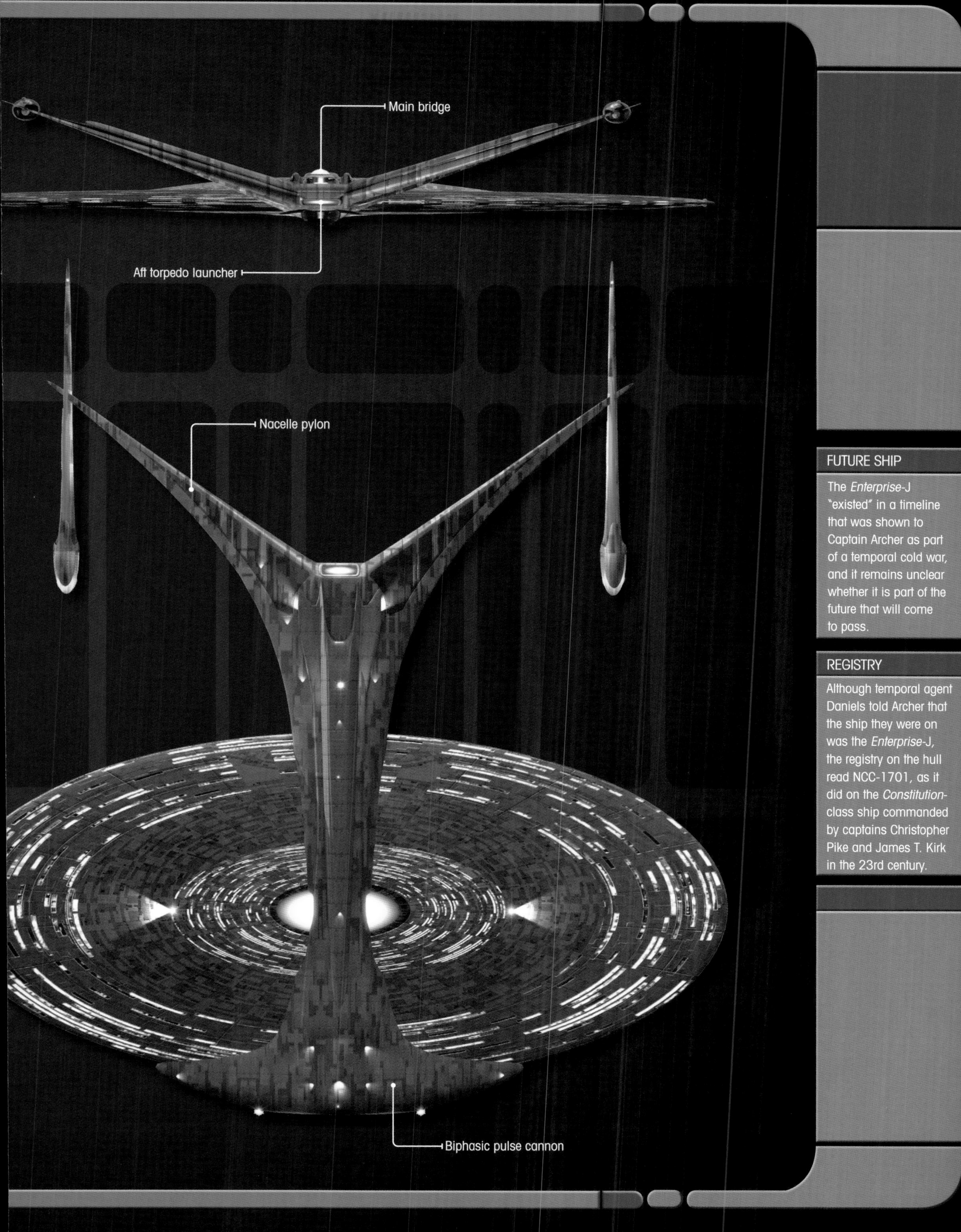

FUTURE SHIP

The *Enterprise*-J "existed" in a timeline that was shown to Captain Archer as part of a temporal cold war, and it remains unclear whether it is part of the future that will come to pass.

REGISTRY

Although temporal agent Daniels told Archer that the ship they were on was the *Enterprise*-J, the registry on the hull read NCC-1701, as it did on the *Constitution*-class ship commanded by captains Christopher Pike and James T. Kirk in the 23rd century.

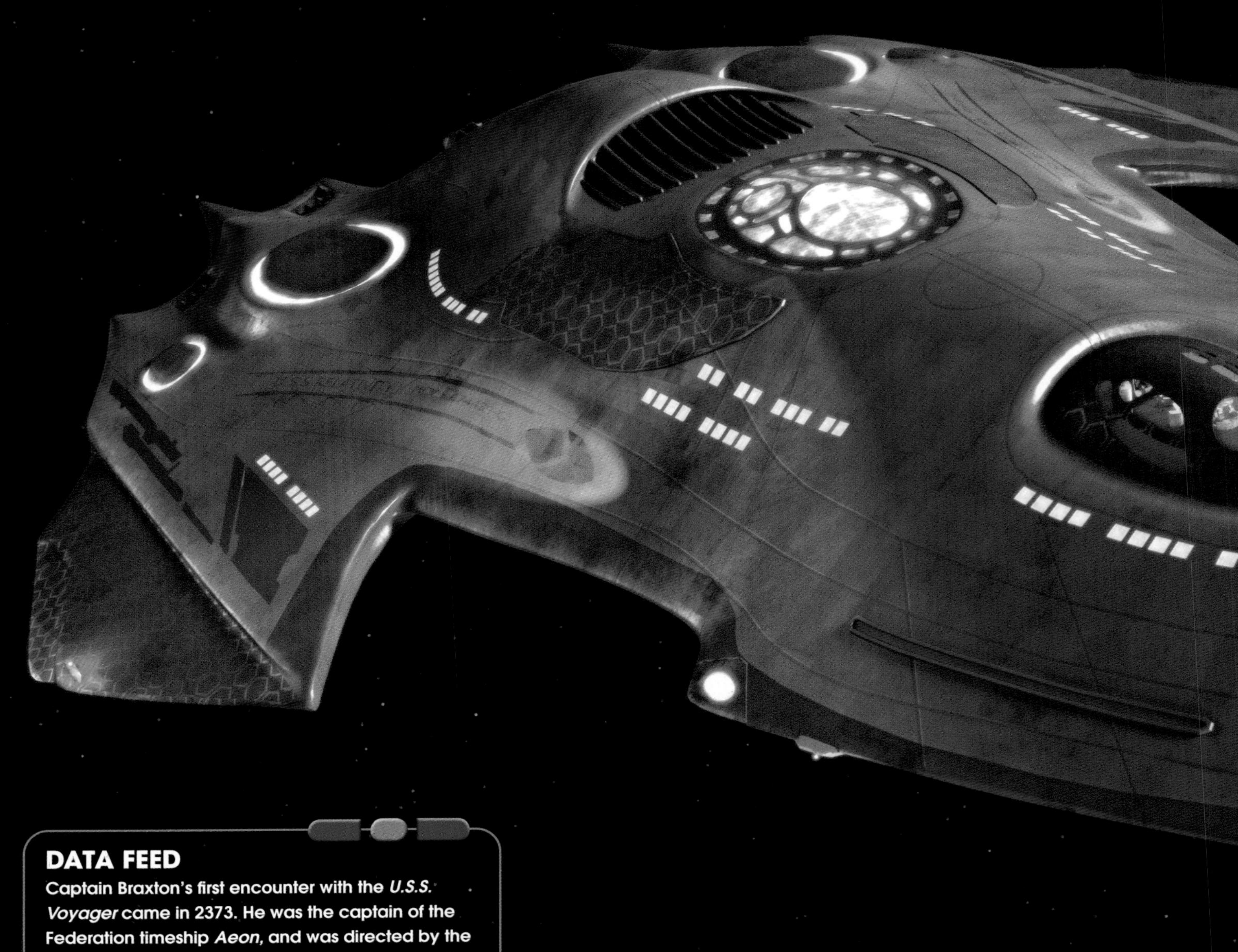

DATA FEED

Captain Braxton's first encounter with the *U.S.S. Voyager* came in 2373. He was the captain of the Federation timeship *Aeon,* and was directed by the Temporal Integrity Commission to travel back in time to destroy *Voyager*. It was believed that *Voyager* had been responsible for the destruction of the Sol system, but this proved not to be the case.

U.S.S. RELATIVITY NCV-474439-G

In the 29th century, the *U.S.S. Relativity* was dedicated to protecting the timeline from dangerous incursions.

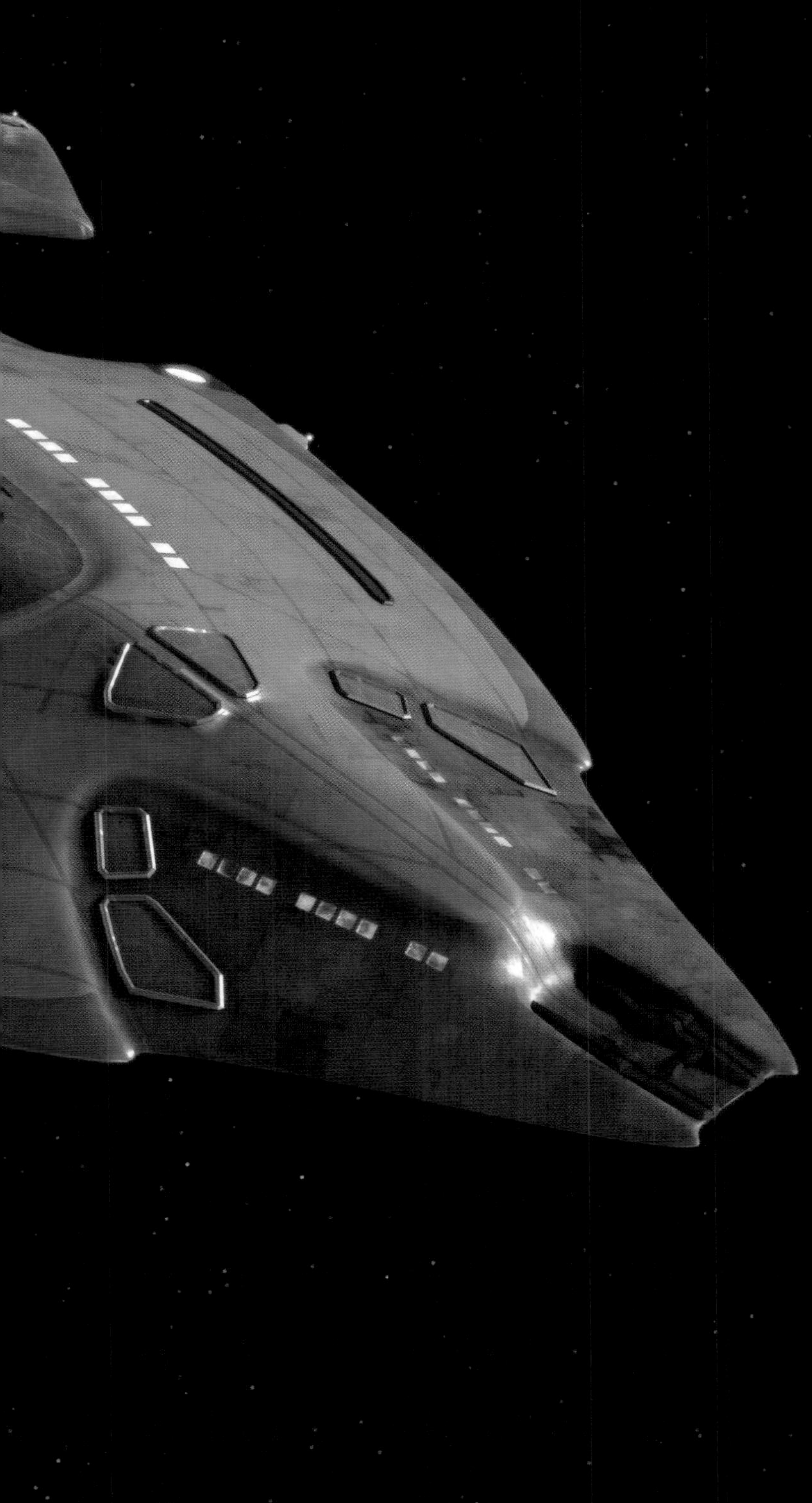

The *U.S.S. Relativity* was a *Wells*-class ship and the seventh vessel to bear the name. On behalf of the United Federation of Planets, its mission was to protect the timeline from disruptions and temporal anomalies caused by time travel. It was staffed by Starfleet officers under the direction of the Temporal Integrity Commission.

The *Relativity*'s systems were far in advance of anything available to Starfleet in the 24th century. The familiar LCARS terminals had been superseded by TCARS interfaces that were operated by touch or by simply moving a hand over them. Interestingly, this latter approach was favored by Starfleet designers in the 2250s.

To perform its duties, the *Relativity* was equipped with sophisticated sensors that could monitor the timestream. The majority of these sensors were concentrated in arrays around the front and sides of the ship. They were extremely powerful and could be used to monitor events hundreds of years in the past and thousands of light-years away from the *Relativity*'s position.

TEMPORAL WARP CORE

The *Relativity* was equipped with warp and impulse engines. Matter for the engines was brought in through a substantial intake on the top of the ship, set just behind the temporal warp core. This was the central element of the ship that allowed it to make journeys into the past.

The *Relativity* was designed to travel through time. However, the Temporal Integrity Commission appeared to favor making temporal transports, or sending smaller one-person vessels, such as the timeship *Aeon*, wherever possible.

▲ The *U.S.S. Relativity* was equipped with powerful sensors capable of scanning through space and time in order to protect the timeline against temporal incursions. If necessary, It could send in an undercover operative to restore the timeline.

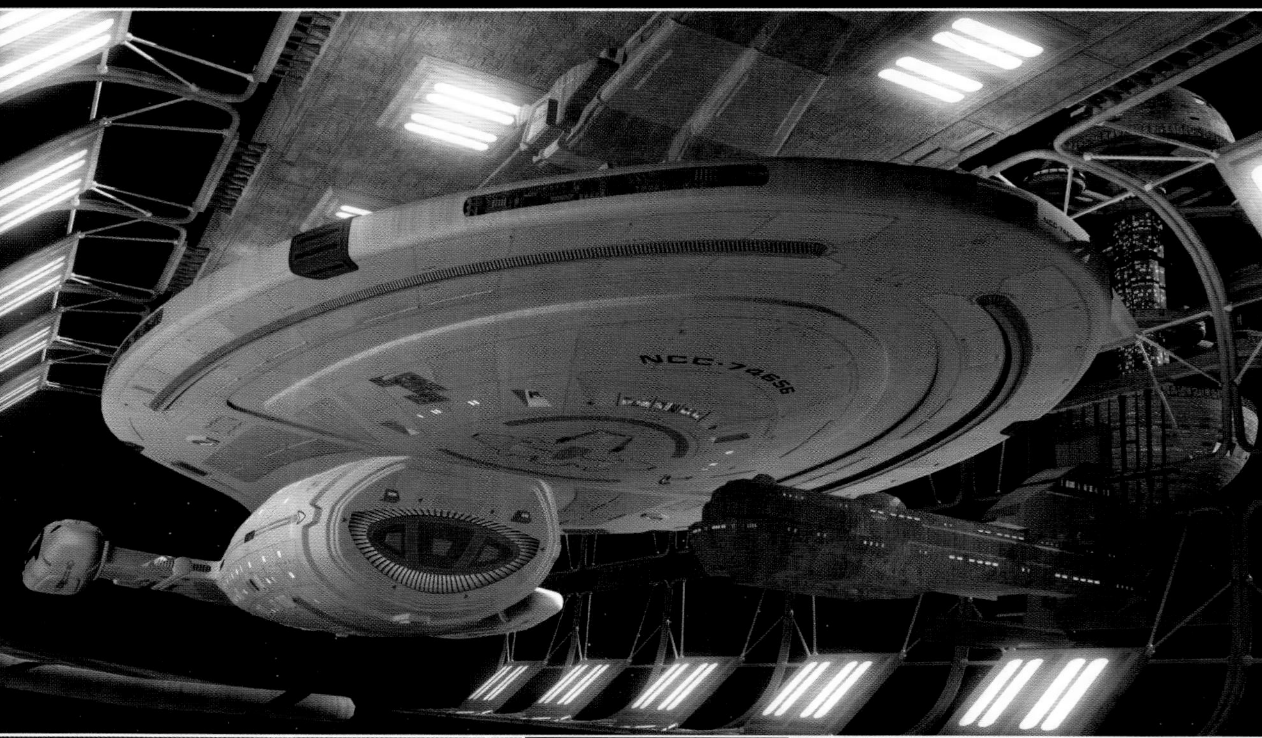

◀ The *Relativity* sent Seven of Nine back to when the *U.S.S. Voyager* NCC-74656 was undergoing its final phases of construction. Here, Seven was disguised as an ensign and managed to find the weapon that would blow apart the ship. She was not able to disarm it, however, and she had to be beamed out before her presence was revealed.

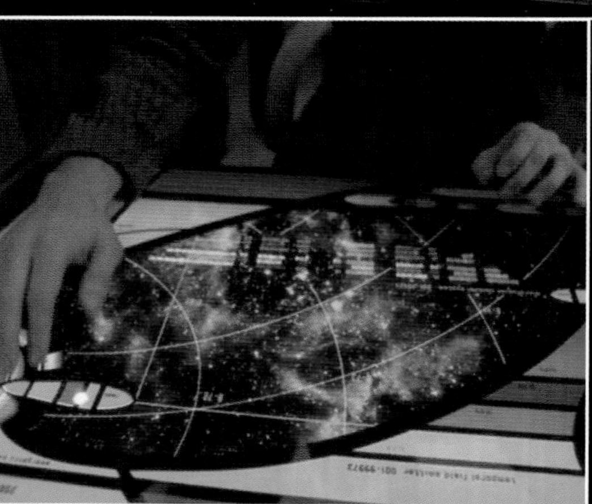

▶ The crew of the *Relativity* recruited Seven from 2375 to help find the device because her ocular implant was capable of detecting it. Seven was altered in order to look human, and sent to several time periods. Unfortunately, Seven died twice before discovering that Braxton was responsible.

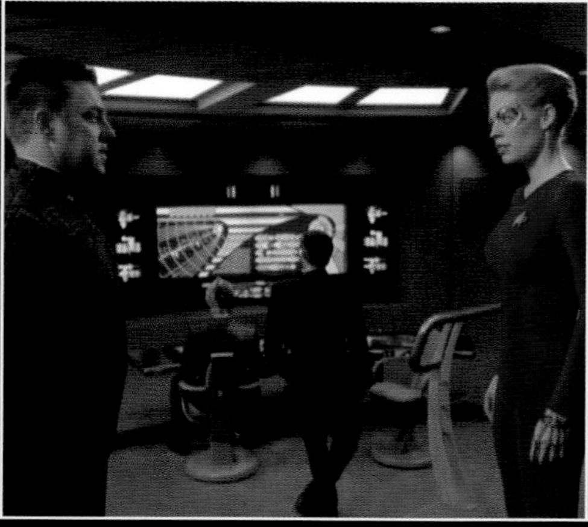

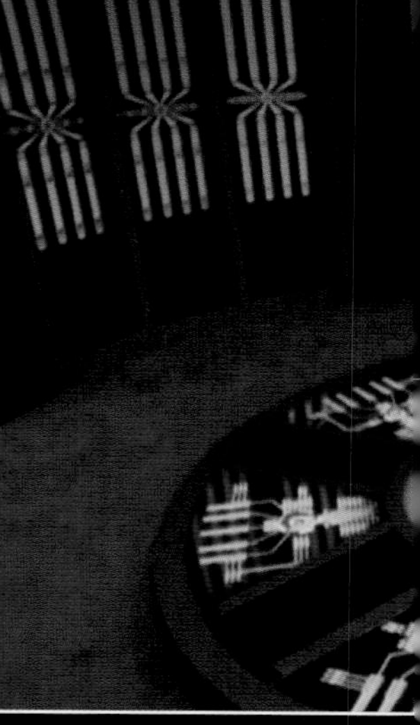

▲ The station at the front of the bridge was principally used to monitor the timestream and control the main viewer. This TCARS console could be activated by touch or by a slight hand movement over the controls.

The *Relativity*'s hull had been designed specifically for time travel, with carefully crafted temporal geometry contours. To make a journey through time, the ship had to generate a temporal field; its temporal matrix had to be carefully calibrated or the journey might have catastrophic consequences. For example, a smaller timeship arrived in the 29th century with an incorrectly calibrated matrix and created an explosion that destroyed the entire Sol system.

Although its mission was peaceful, the *Relativity* was armed and disruptors were positioned at various locations around the hull, with the powerful main disruptor in the ship's nose. The command center (or bridge) was positioned on top of the ship toward the front.

The *Relativity* was fitted with all the facilities familiar to Federation vessels, including a number of holomatrix rooms (the 29th-century equivalent of holodecks). The holomatrix rooms were often used to run simulations before operatives were sent into action, and to ensure that everything went to plan.

TEMPORAL TRANSPORTERS

The *Relativity* was also provided with temporal transporters that could beam individuals across time. A temporal transporter pad was located on the bridge. Before a transport was initiated, the crew raised the shields and targeted a specific time and location.

The temporal transporters were extremely advanced. They could pinpoint a specific location

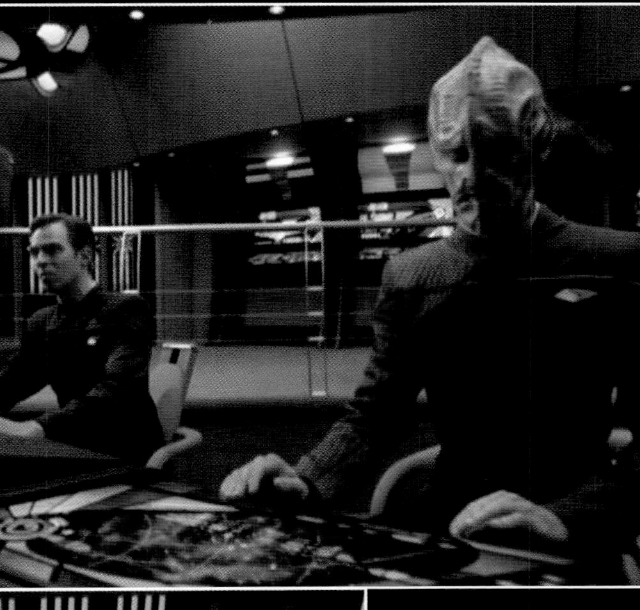

◀ Some of the *Relativity*'s crew were drawn from species that were discovered after the 24th century.

▶ Lieutenant Ducane was serving aboard the *Relativity* and took command after Captain Braxton was arrested.

▼ By the 29th century, Starfleet had abandoned the traditional two-hulled design. It still retained "wings" in the position once taken by the warp nacelles.

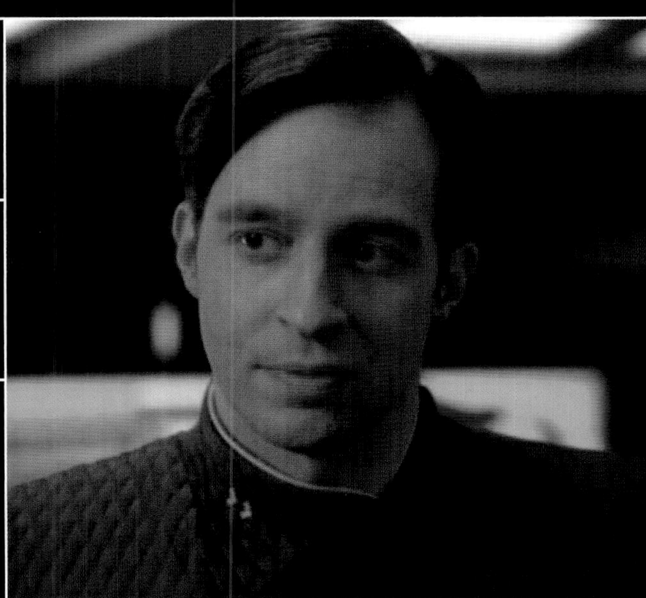

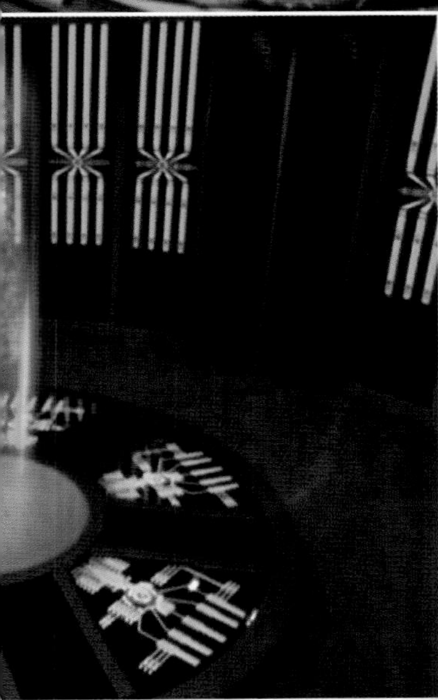

◀ The temporal transporter pad on the bridge was designed to send an individual back in time. This was much simpler than sending the *Relativity* itself back in time, where it might be discovered. If an individual was sent back to correct an incursion, it was much more likely that they could remain undercover. The crew could stay in contact with the operative through a temporal communicator.

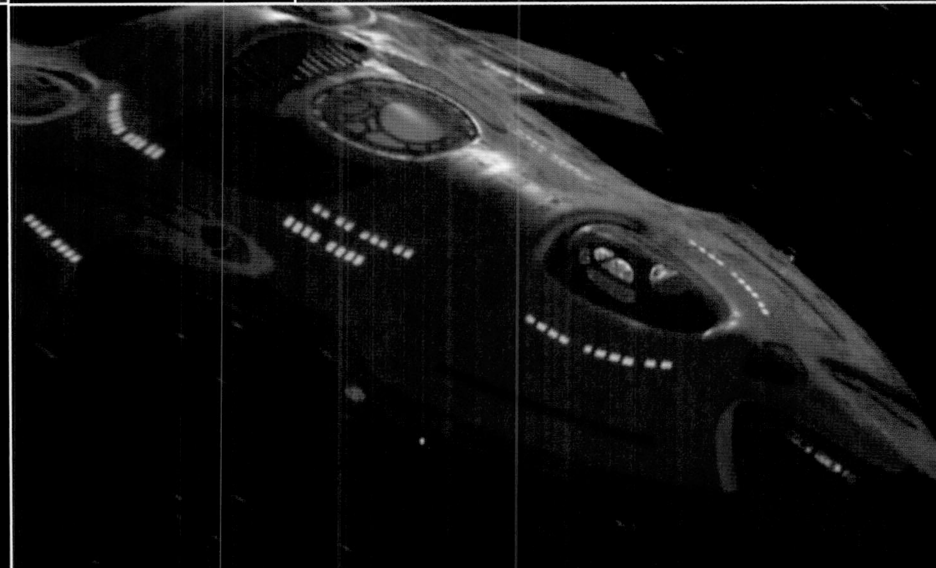

with ease, and were so accurate that they could be targeted to the microsecond.

Once an operative had been sent into the past, the *Relativity*'s crew could stay in contact via the ship's temporal communications system. Like the transporter, this could cross time with ease. Visual communication was not usually possible, so the crew had to rely on audio contact.

Normally, the inhabitants of the past had no memory of the *Relativity*'s involvement with their time, but on at least one occasion, it used operatives from the 24th century, and allowed them to retain their memories. As a consequence, two people from 2375 – Seven of Nine and Captain Janeway – remembered visiting the timeship and encountering its crew.

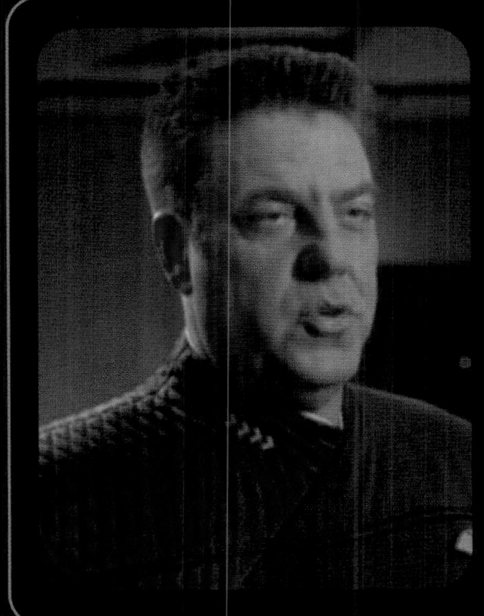

DATA FEED

The *Relativity* was involved in a mission to avert the destruction of the *U.S.S. Voyager*. Seven of Nine was recruited from that time period to apprehend the person responsible. It was eventually revealed that the saboteur was, in fact, a future version of Captain Braxton. He came to see that the *Voyager* crew were responsible for his eventual forced retirement, and that by obliterating it from the timeline, none of the events that caused his illness would have occurred.

MAIN BRIDGE

A rectangular viewscreen located at the front of the bridge displayed data about the timestream and the timeframe that the ship was monitoring. In front of the viewscreen was a large helm console, with seating for two officers. The captain's chair was situated on the port side of the upper level, while elsewhere on the bridge was a temporal transporter. This allowed a person to be beamed into the past, with the temporal sensors enabling the precise moment and location to be chosen.

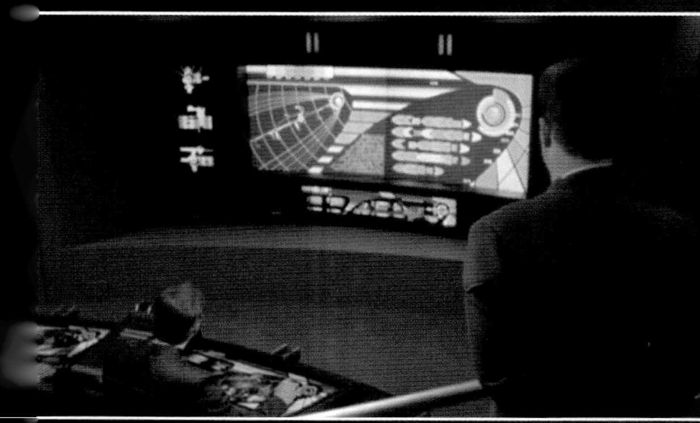

▲ From seating in front of the viewscreen, crewmembers could ocate past problems in the timeline, and find a way to put them right, vithout anyone from the past being aware that they were there.

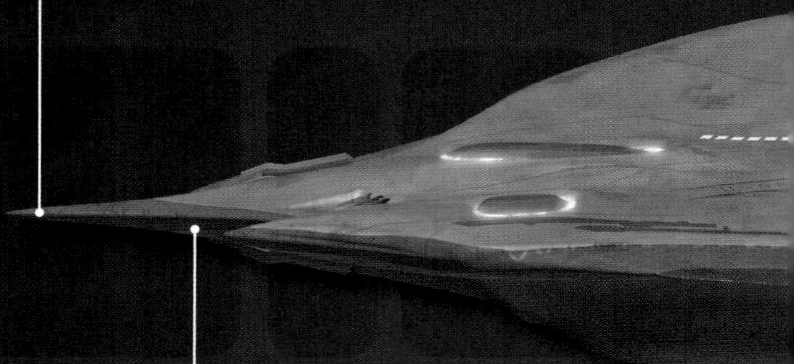

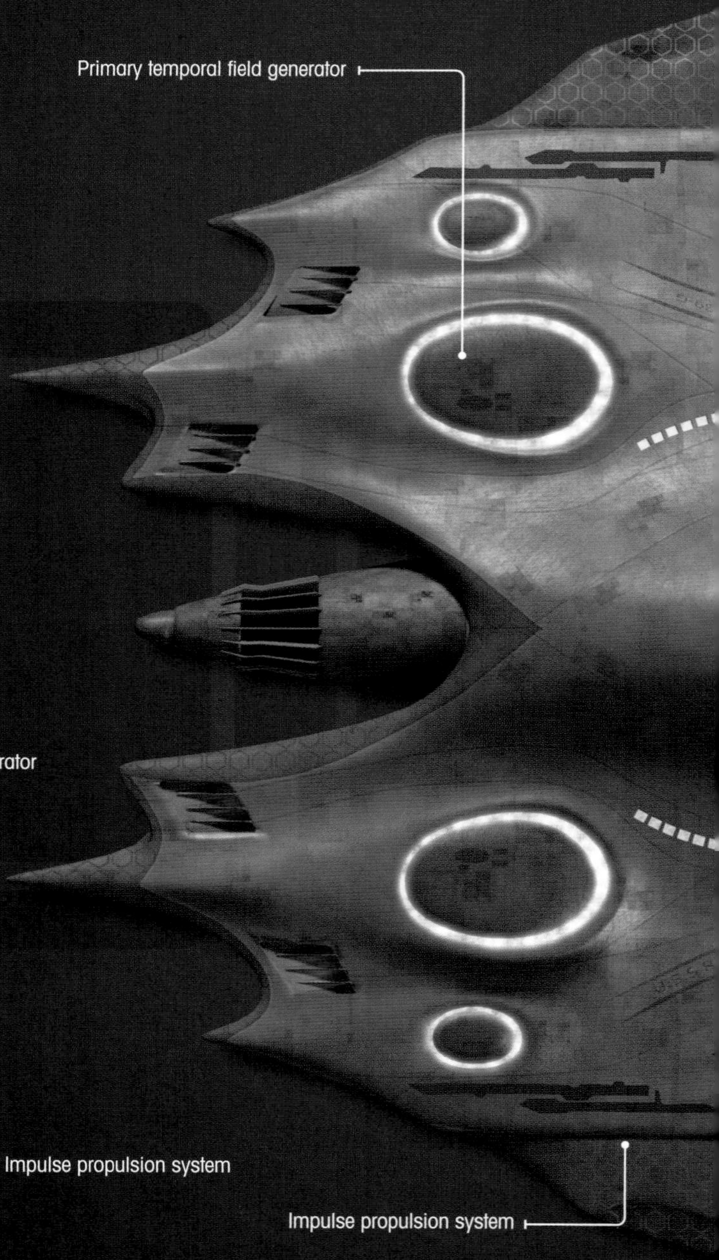

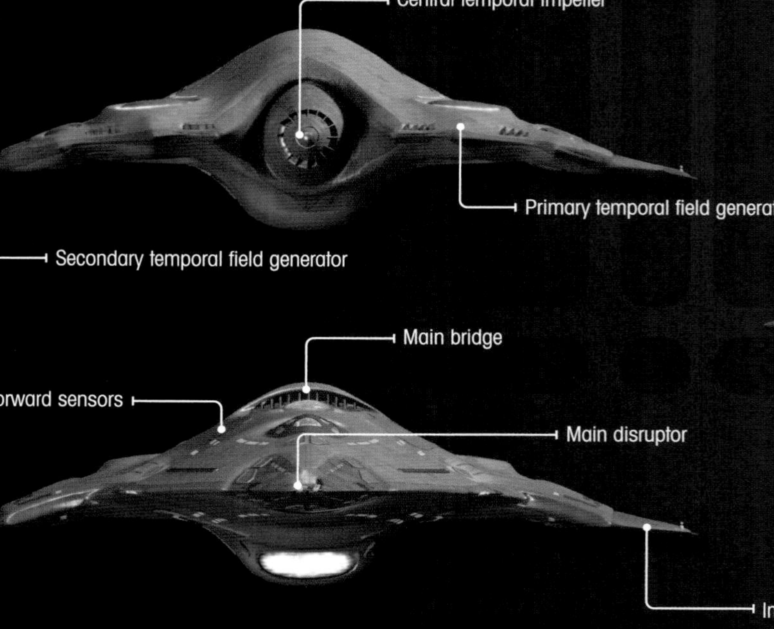

Central temporal impeller
Temporal geometry contours
Primary temporal field generator
Impulse propulsion system

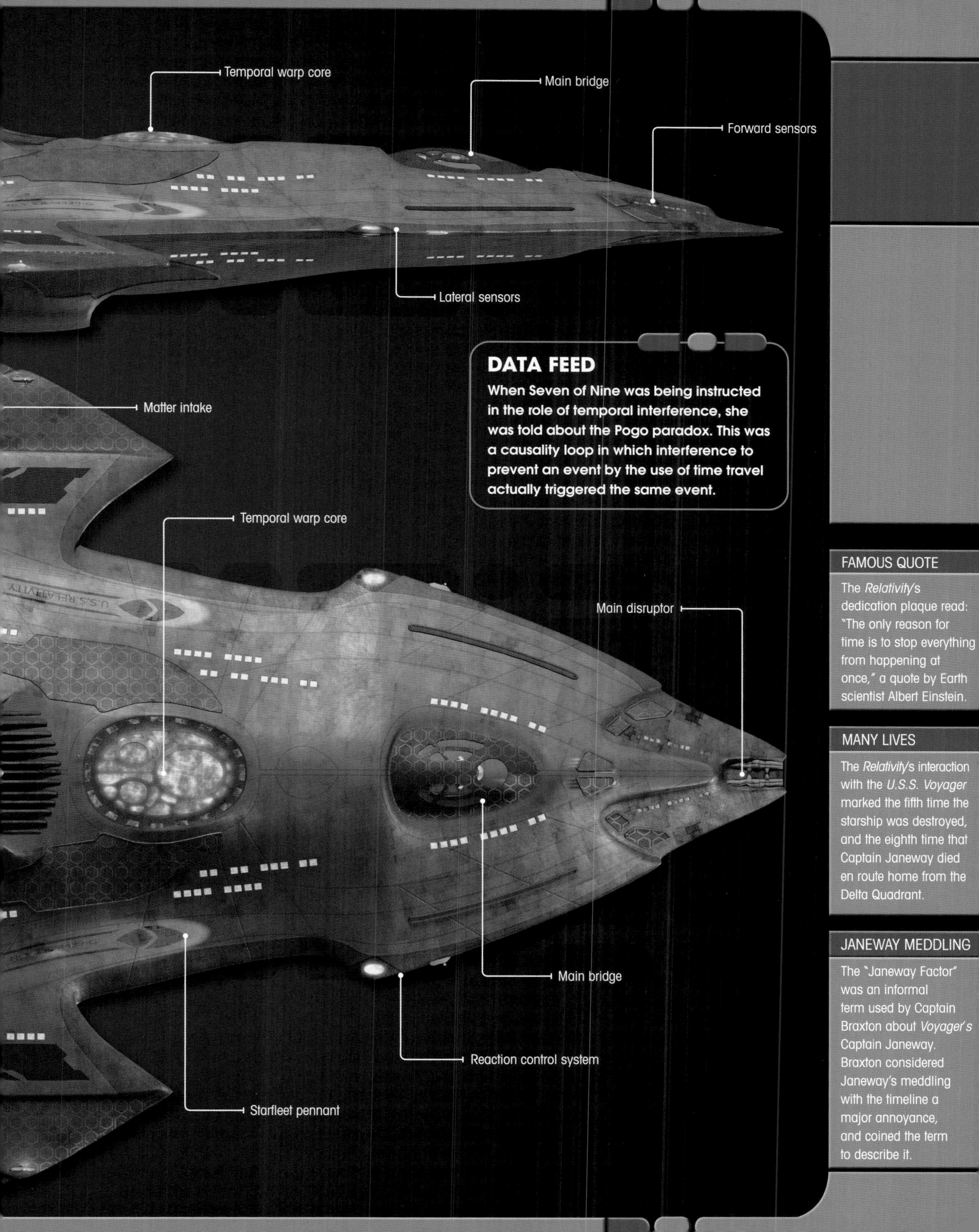

DATA FEED

When Seven of Nine was being instructed in the role of temporal interference, she was told about the Pogo paradox. This was a causality loop in which interference to prevent an event by the use of time travel actually triggered the same event.

FAMOUS QUOTE

The *Relativity*'s dedication plaque read: "The only reason for time is to stop everything from happening at once," a quote by Earth scientist Albert Einstein.

MANY LIVES

The *Relativity*'s interaction with the *U.S.S. Voyager* marked the fifth time the starship was destroyed, and the eighth time that Captain Janeway died en route home from the Delta Quadrant.

JANEWAY MEDDLING

The "Janeway Factor" was an informal term used by Captain Braxton about *Voyager's* Captain Janeway. Braxton considered Janeway's meddling with the timeline a major annoyance, and coined the term to describe it.

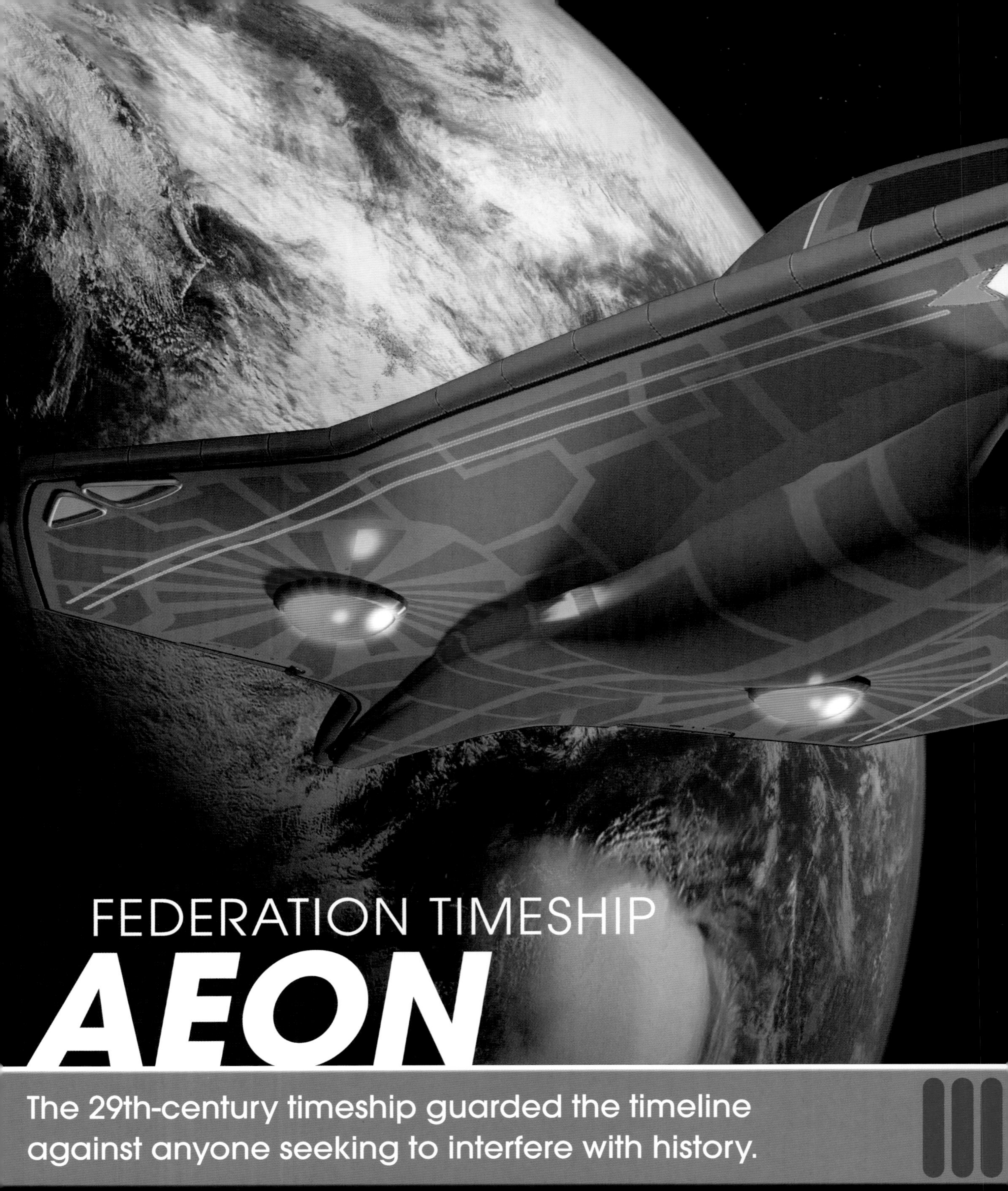

FEDERATION TIMESHIP

AEON

The 29th-century timeship guarded the timeline against anyone seeking to interfere with history.

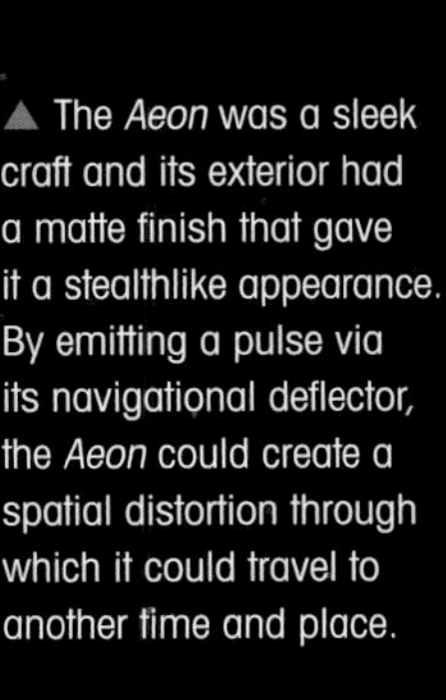

▲ The *Aeon* was a sleek craft and its exterior had a matte finish that gave it a stealthlike appearance. By emitting a pulse via its navigational deflector, the *Aeon* could create a spatial distortion through which it could travel to another time and place.

The single-seater *Aeon* was around six meters long and its cockpit had barely enough room for the pilot. However, its small size belied its key role for the Federation in protecting the timeline.

The *Aeon* was equipped with a hyper-impulse drive, but it was also capable of traveling to any time and place in the universe. By emitting a specialized kind of pulse through its navigational deflector beneath the nose of the ship, it could open an artificial spatial rift. This was a distortion in the space-time continuum – a kind of rip or tear in space – through which the craft could enter and emerge in a particular time and place that had been set by the pilot.

POLICING THE TIMELINE

The *Aeon* was part of the Temporal Integrity Commission, an agency set up by the Federation in the 29th century. Its purpose was to protect the timeline from any changes caused by time travel. This organization believed that the *U.S.S. Voyager* NCC-74656 was responsible for a monumental catastrophe in the 29th century, in which a temporal explosion destroyed Earth's entire solar system, taking billions of lives in the process.

To prevent this disaster from happening, Captain Braxton was ordered to take the *Aeon* and travel back in time to the Delta Quadrant to destroy *Voyager*. The *Aeon* emerged from a spatial rift in 2373 directly in front of *Voyager*. Then, without explanation, Braxton immediately charged his ship's subatomic disruptor and fired. Despite the *Aeon*'s size, its advanced weapon took out

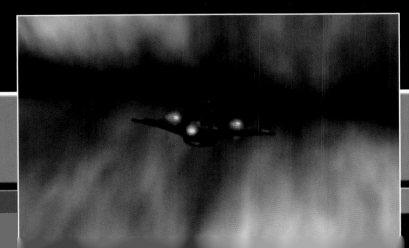

◀ In the aftermath of the destruction of the solar system in the 29th century, debris from the *U.S.S. Voyager*'s secondary hull was found in the wreckage. This led the people of that time to believe Captain Janeway's ship was responsible for the disaster, and the *Aeon* timeship was sent to 2373 in order to destroy *Voyager*.

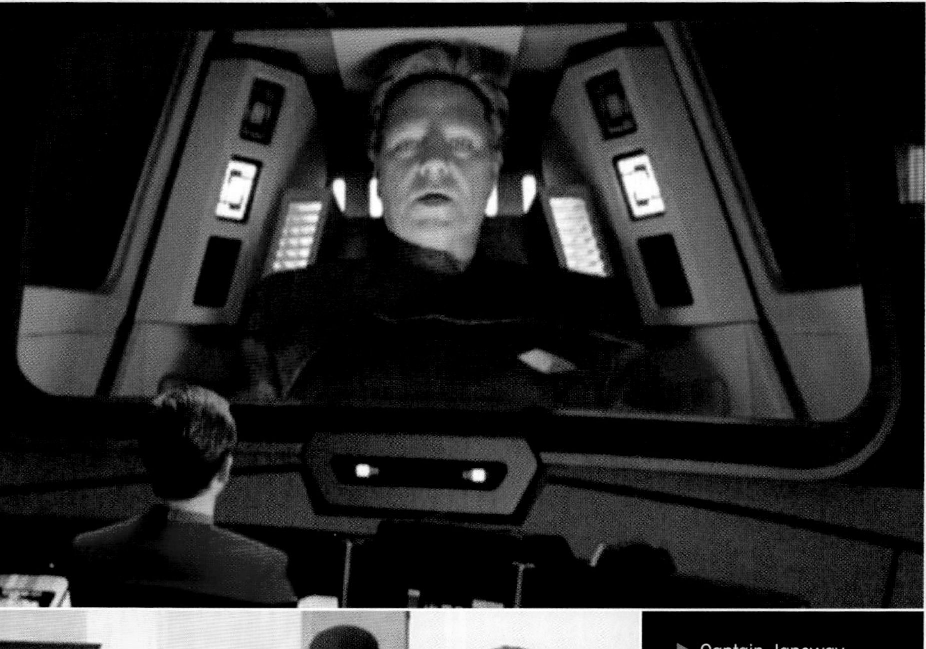

◀ Captain Braxton aboard the *Aeon* made contact with *Voyager* and told the crew that he had been sent from the 29th century to destroy them.

▶ After *Voyager* used its deflector beam to disrupt the *Aeon*'s weapon, the spatial distortion began to collapse and pulled both ships inside.

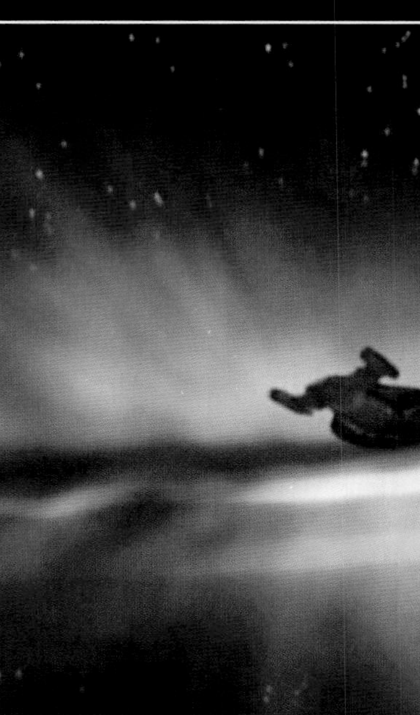

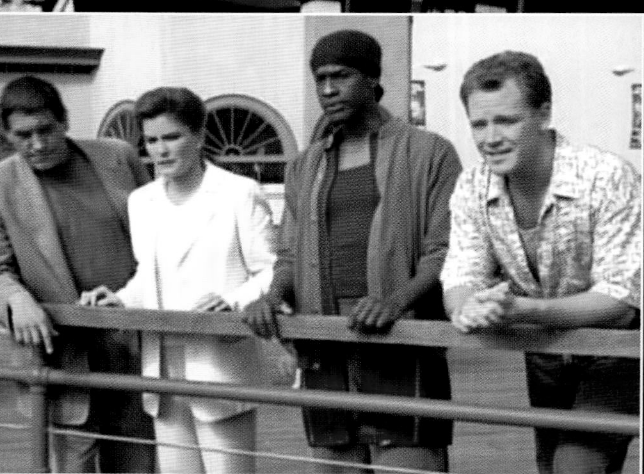

▶ Captain Janeway and her crew eventually tracked the *Aeon* to a secret room in Henry Starling's building. He had studied the ship's advanced technology and understood it enough to reverse engineer a whole host of computer hardware that was new to the 20th century.

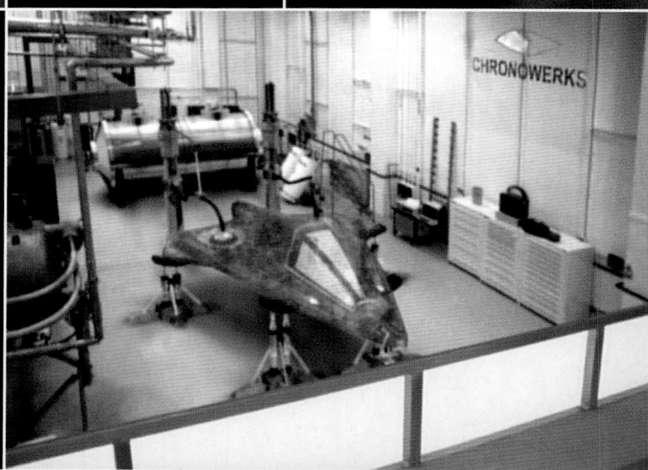

▲ Back in the 20th century, Janeway, Chakotay, Tuvok, and Paris donned appropriate clothing and beamed down to California to search for the *Aeon*. Their investigations revealed that although the *Aeon* had entered the rift just a few moments before *Voyager*, it had emerged in 1967, almost 30 years before them.

Voyager's shields and knocked them off-line with just one shot. *Voyager* tried returning fire with full phasers, but they had absolutely no effect on the *Aeon*'s 29th-century shields. *Voyager*'s molecular structure began to come apart under the attack, and Captain Janeway was forced to be more inventive in fighting back.

Desperately trying to save her ship, Janeway had *Voyager*'s deflector beam adjusted to match the frequency of the *Aeon*'s disruptor, which overloaded its emitter. The subspace rift began to destabilize, pulling both ships inside. In an instant, they emerged halfway across the Galaxy in orbit of Earth. It was not all good news, though. While they had finally reached home, the year was not 2373, but 1996. The *Voyager* crew later learned that although the *Aeon* had entered the rift just seconds before them, it emerged in 1967.

It transpired that Braxton had been forced to perform an emergency beam out before his ship crashed in a remote mountain range. Before he could get back to the *Aeon*, it was taken by a young man named Henry Starling. He went on to create a microcomputer revolution by cannibalizing the technology aboard the ship. In the ensuing years, he became one of the wealthiest and most influential people on the planet.

TERRIBLE REALIZATION

Meanwhile, Braxton realized that it was not *Voyager* that caused the huge catastrophe in the 29th century, but his own ship. He knew that if someone unfamiliar with the *Aeon*'s controls tried to fly it into the future without recalibrating the temporal matrix, it would cause a massive explosion that could destroy the solar system.

This was exactly what nearly happened. Starling planned to launch the *Aeon* and travel to the

▶ The *Aeon* had a large cockpit canopy that was opaque, while its wings had semi-spherical red orbs built into them at top and bottom. The ship's powerful subatomic disruptor was located in the nose.

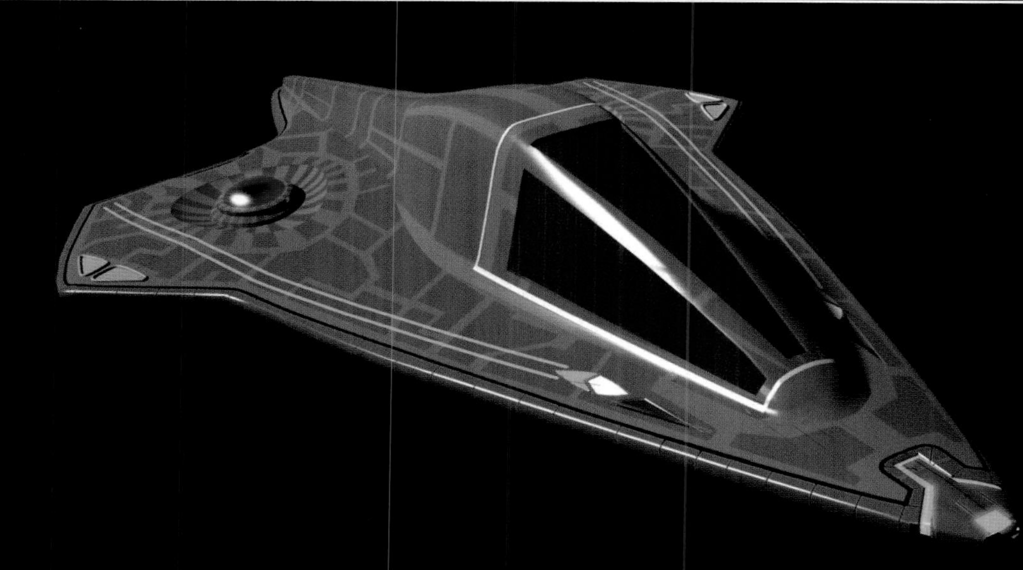

▼ The *Aeon* was launched through the roof of Starling's Chronowerx building. He planned to acquire more technology from the future, bring it back to the 20th century, and use it to make even more profit.

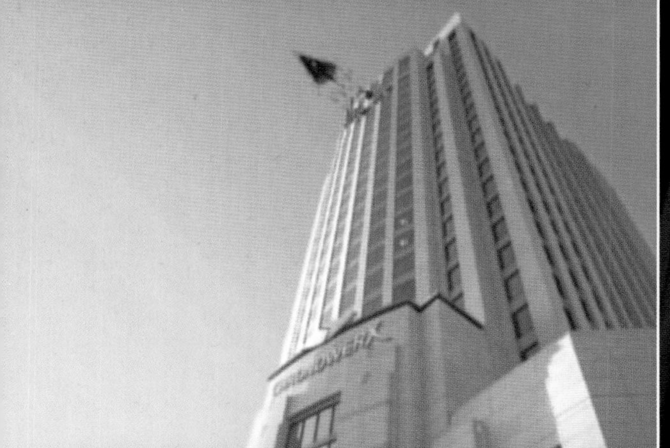

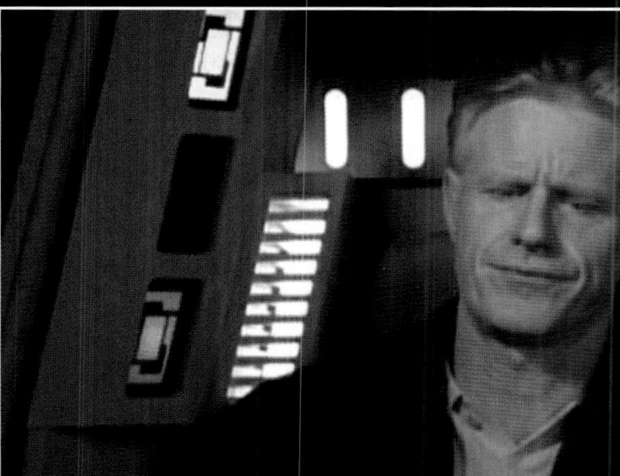

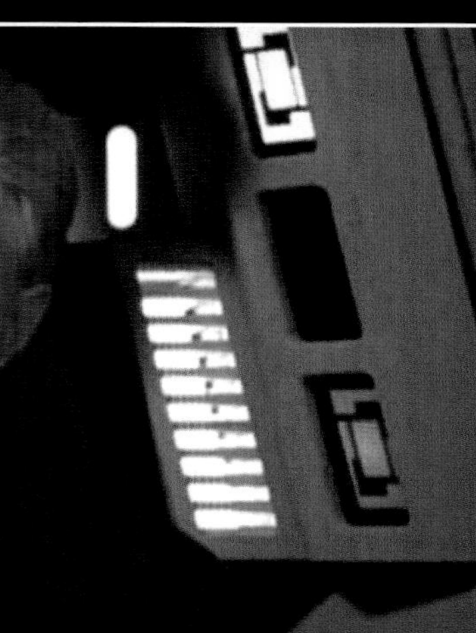

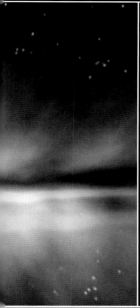

future where he could acquire more technology. He could then bring it back to his own time and exploit it to make more money.

Janeway and her crew tried to stop Starling, but he managed to elude them. Eventually, he activated the *Aeon*'s hyper-impulse drive and smashed through the top of a skyscraper where he kept the ship. Once in orbit, Starling jumped to warp 1 and initiated the *Aeon*'s temporal core. Just as he was about to enter the subspace rift, *Voyager* fired a photon torpedo that hit the *Aeon*, blowing it to pieces and closing the rift.

Seconds later, the rift reopened and the *Aeon* appeared. Captain Braxton opened communications with *Voyager*, but he had no knowledge of what had just happened. For him, the timeline in which he had traveled to the 20th century and Starling had been a computer mogul had not occurred. He was there because his ship's sensors had alerted him to *Voyager*'s presence in the 20th century and he had been sent to correct that anomaly. Janeway asked if Braxton could return them to Earth in the 24th century, but this was against the temporal prime directive. Instead, he opened a rift back to the precise time and location in the Delta Quadrant where *Voyager* had first encountered the *Aeon*.

▲ Starling would not believe Janeway's warning that he would cause a massive explosion in the 29th century if he tried to travel there. Fortunately, *Voyager* managed to destroy the *Aeon* before it could travel to the future.

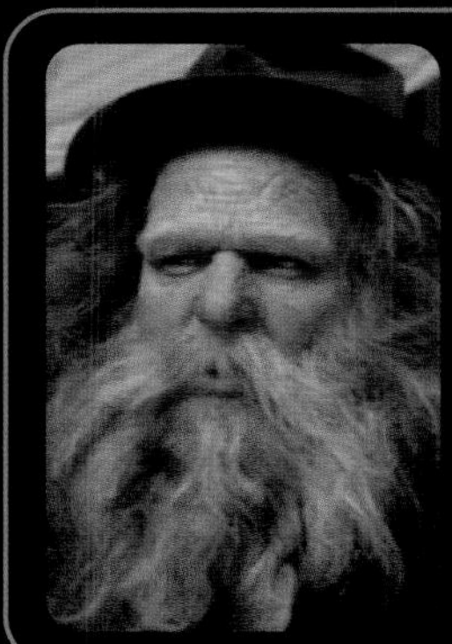

DATA FEED

When Captain Braxton first found himself in the 20th century, he tried to confront Henry Starling and get his ship back. Unused to the customs in late 20th-century California, Braxton was out of his depth. No one in authority listened to him and he was dismissed as a madman. Eventually, he was confined to a mental institution and pumped full of antipsychotics. By the time Captain Janeway found him, he was living on the streets and really had become mentally ill.

CHARMED LIFE

In 1967, Henry Starling was just a young man when he witnessed the extraordinary sight of a strange object crashing to the ground in the High Sierras of California. On investigation, he found the *Aeon*, largely intact.

Over the next 30 years, Starling used his primitive understanding of the *Aeon*'s technology to launch numerous computer innovations to the market. This made him a very wealthy man as he built up a corporate empire called Chronowerx Industries.

Like many of his time, Starling's greed knew no bounds and he wanted more wealth and more acclaim. He aimed to travel to the future in the *Aeon*, acquire more technology, return to his own time with it, and exploit it for yet more financial reward.

When Captain Janeway tracked the *Aeon* down to Starling's building, she tried to convince him that if he did not precisely calibrate the temporal matrix in the ship, it would cause a massive explosion when it emerged in the 29th century. Starling refused to believe her or just did not care, and would not give up the ship.

Eventually, Starling paid with his life as the crew of *Voyager* managed to blow up the *Aeon* seconds before it entered a spatial rift to the 29th century. This reset the timeline so that Starling never did discover the *Aeon*, nor did he become one of the most powerful magnates on the planet.

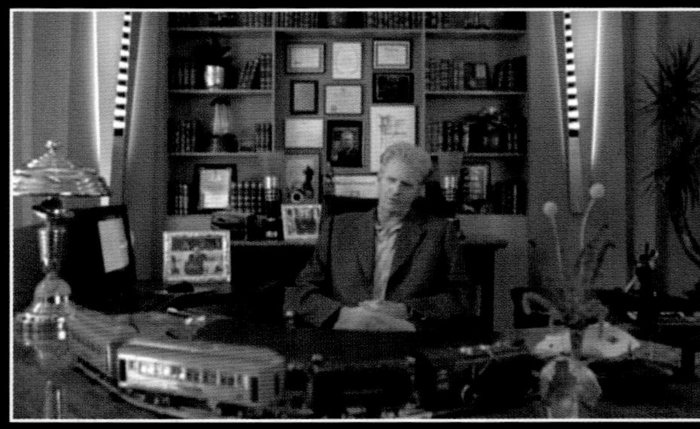

▲ Thanks to his discovery of the *Aeon*, Henry Starling was able to use its 29th-century technology to develop a number of computer innovations in the late 20th century that made him a wealthy man.

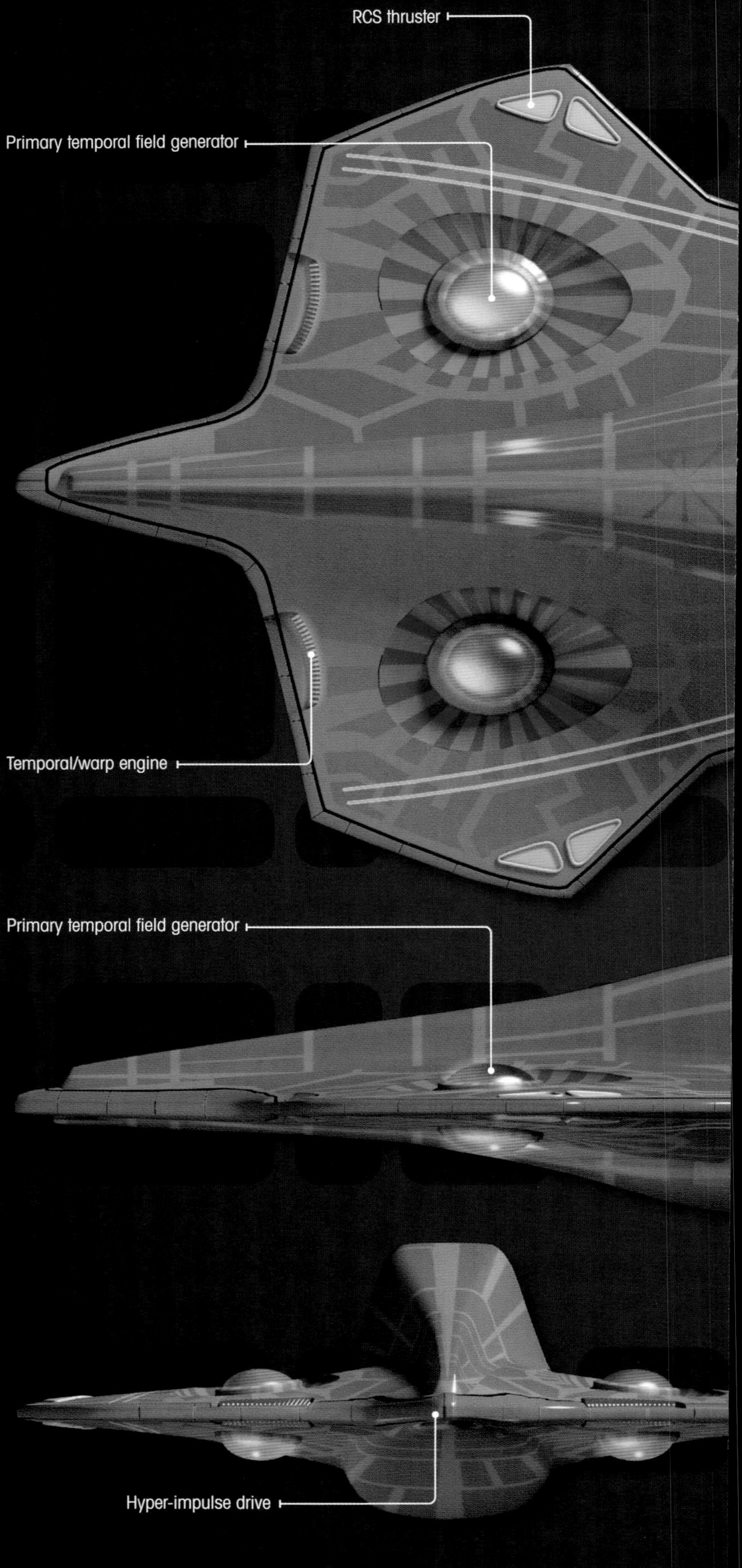

RCS thruster

Primary temporal field generator

Temporal/warp engine

Primary temporal field generator

Hyper-impulse drive

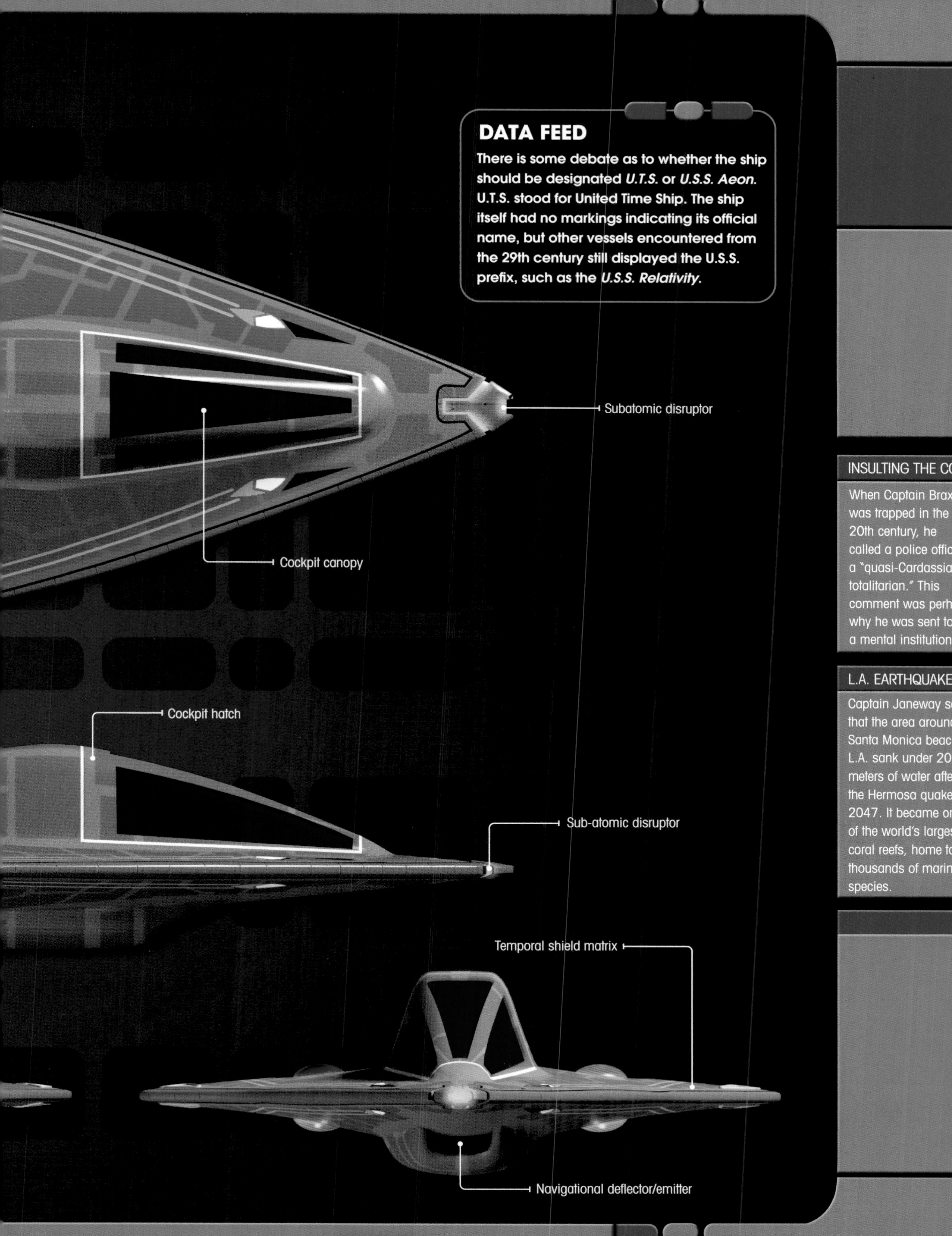

DATA FEED

There is some debate as to whether the ship should be designated *U.T.S.* or *U.S.S. Aeon*. U.T.S. stood for United Time Ship. The ship itself had no markings indicating its official name, but other vessels encountered from the 29th century still displayed the U.S.S. prefix, such as the *U.S.S. Relativity*.

INSULTING THE COPS

When Captain Braxton was trapped in the 20th century, he called a police officer a "quasi-Cardassian totalitarian." This comment was perhaps why he was sent to a mental institution.

L.A. EARTHQUAKE

Captain Janeway said that the area around Santa Monica beach in L.A. sank under 200 meters of water after the Hermosa quake of 2047. It became one of the world's largest coral reefs, home to thousands of marine species.

THE FUTURE
SIZE CHART

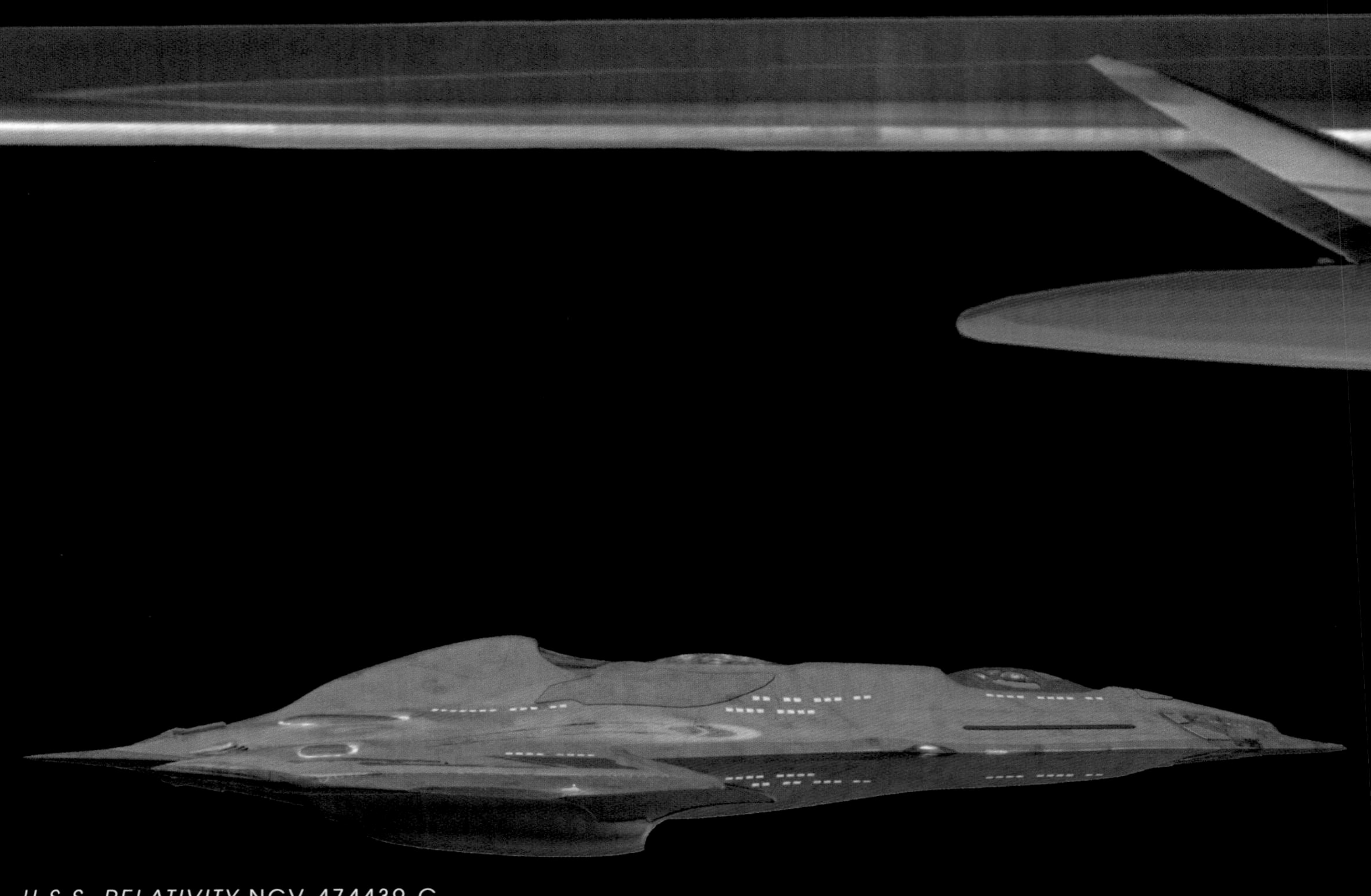

U.S.S. RELATIVITY NCV-474439-G

193m

FEDERATION TIMESHIP *AEON*

6m

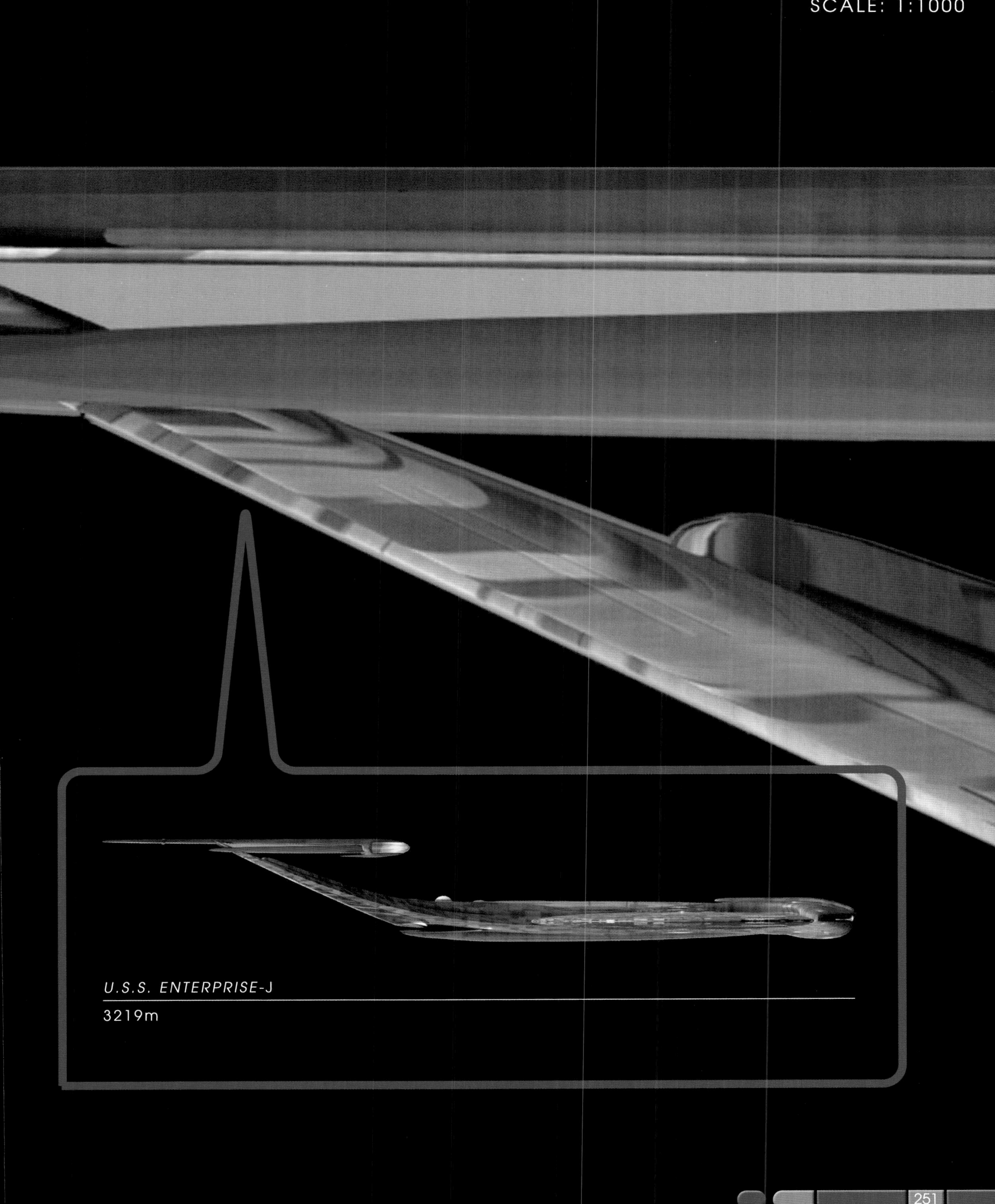
U.S.S. ENTERPRISE-J
3219m

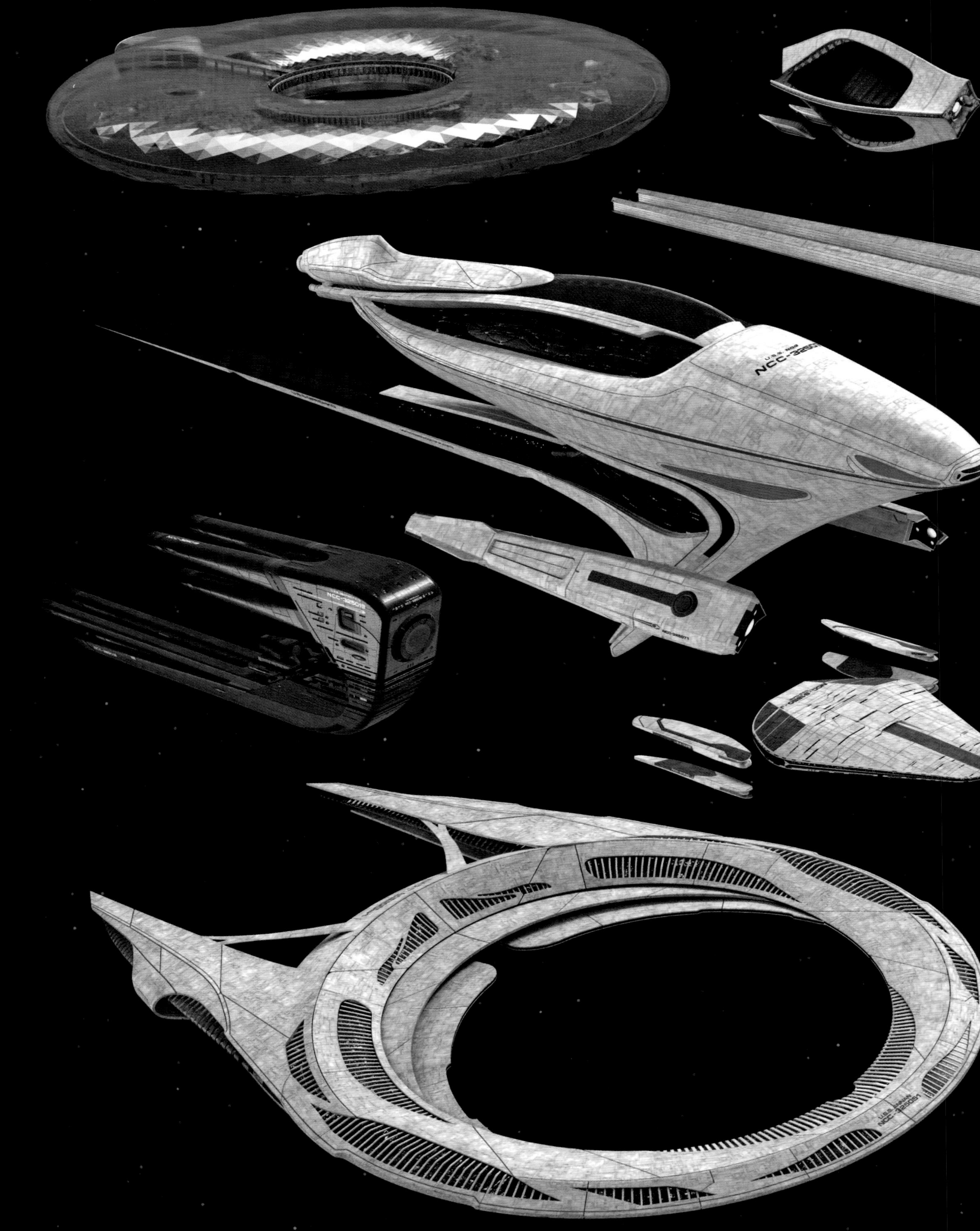

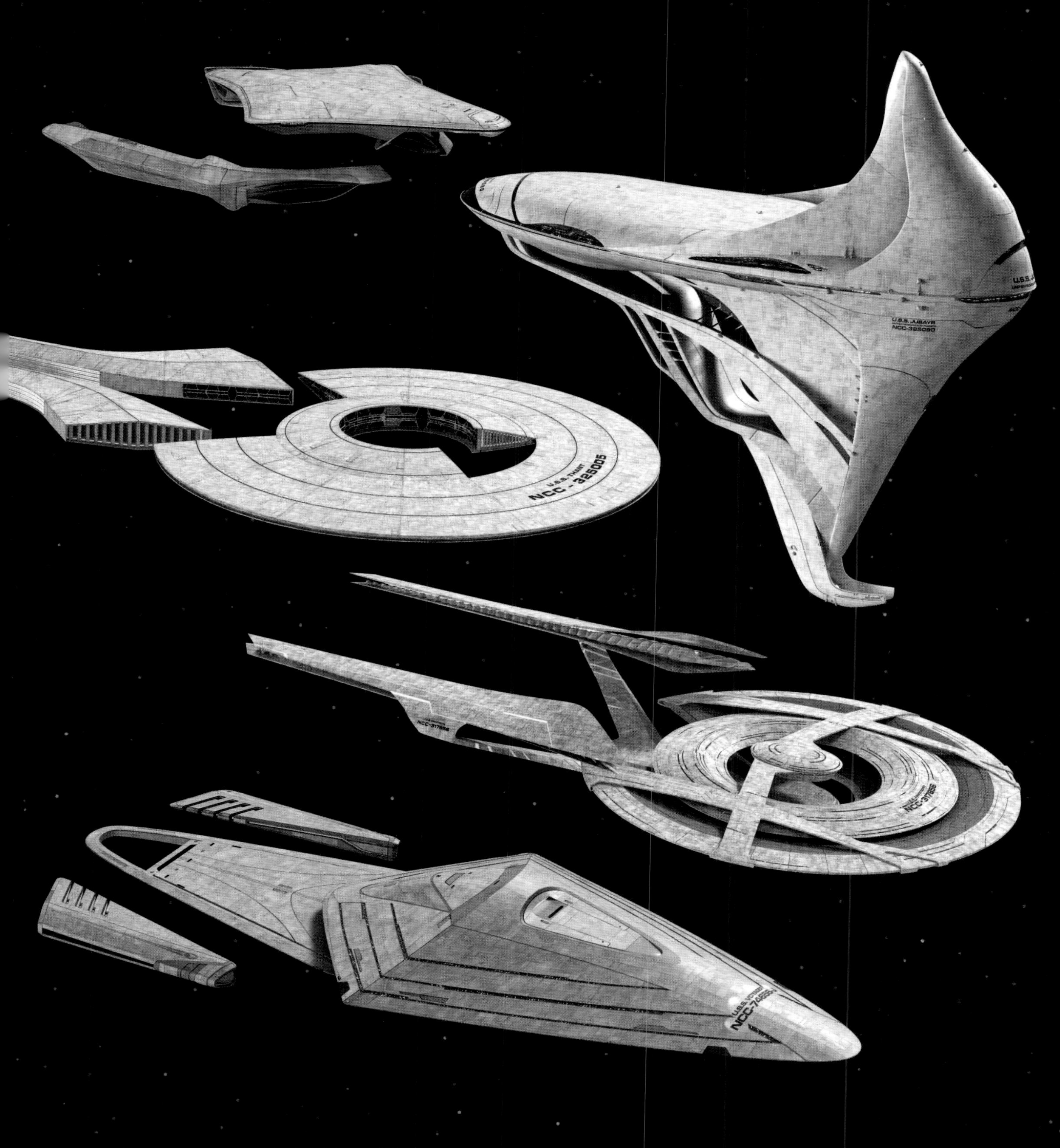

CHAPTER 5
32ND CENTURY

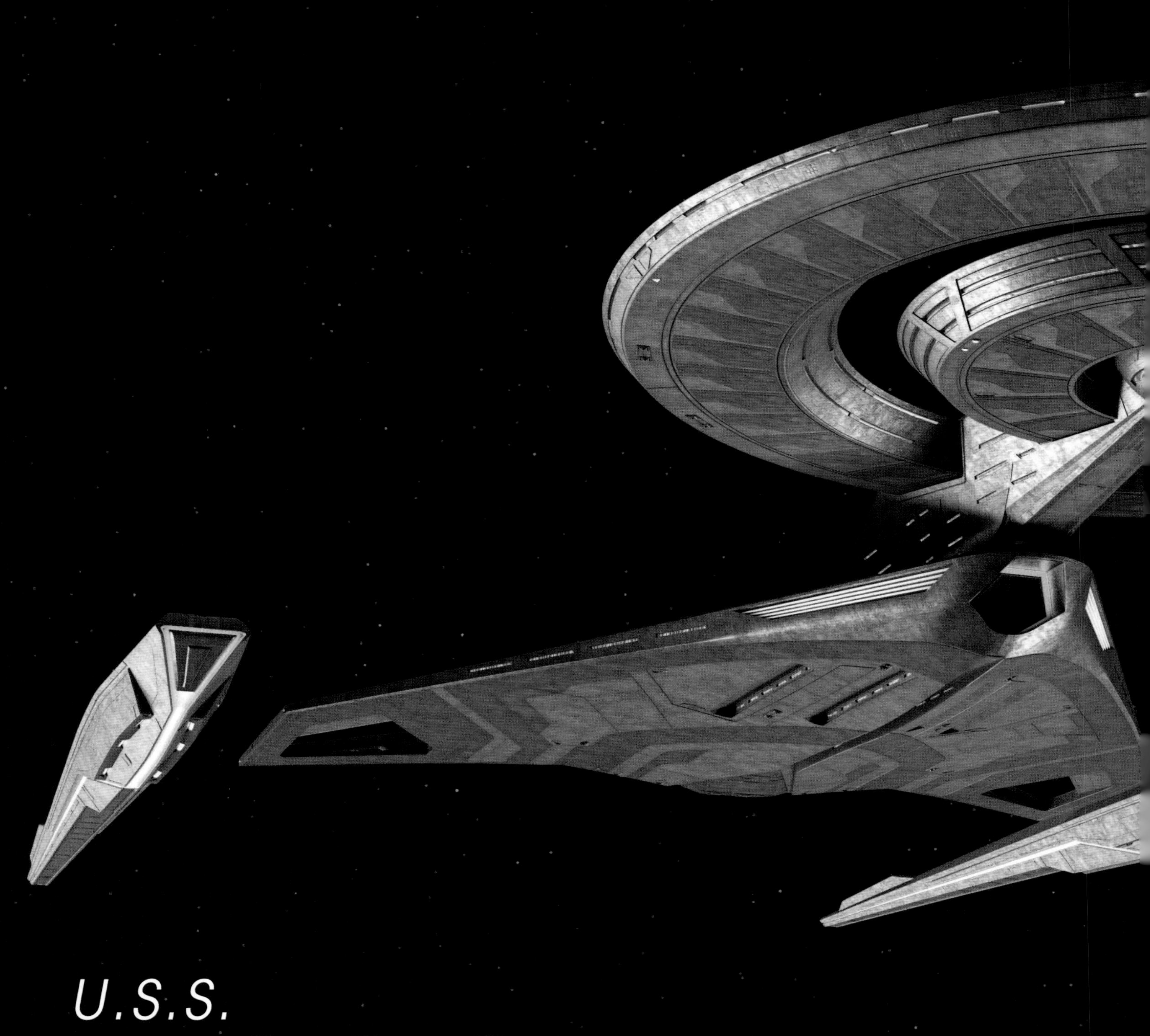

U.S.S. DISCOVERY-A

Along with an upgrade to personal crew technology, the *U.S.S. Discovery* underwent a 32nd-century refit.

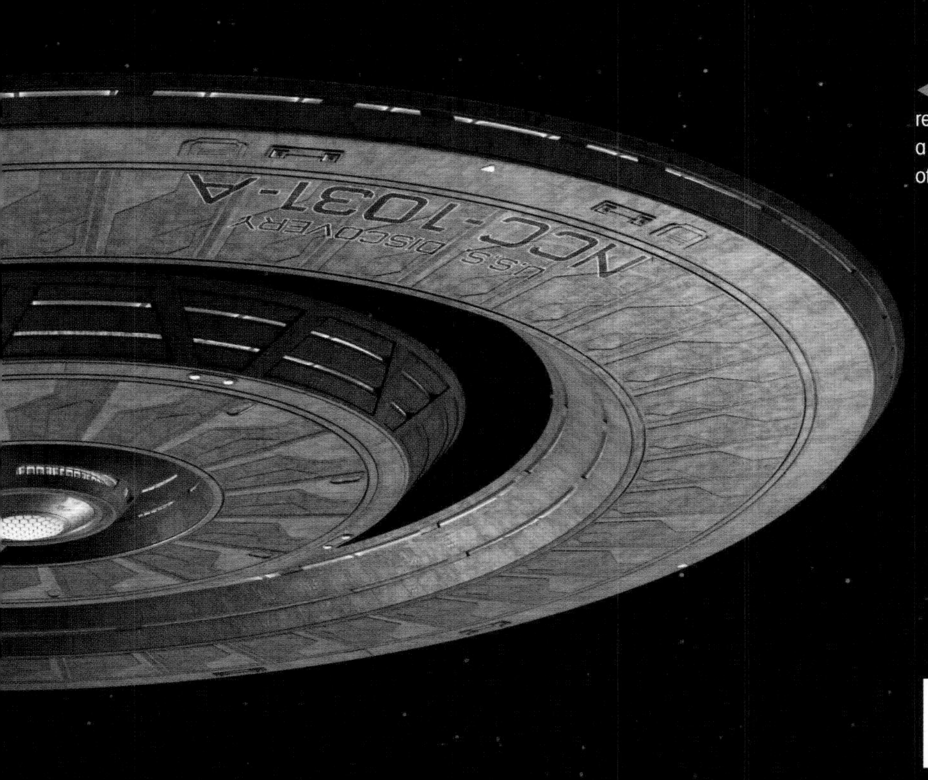

◀ The *U.S.S. Discovery*'s major refit in the 32nd century brought it a new registry and status as one of Starfleet's most important ships,

Following its temporal displacement to 3189, the 23rd-century *Crossfield*-class *U.S.S. Discovery* remained on active service with Starfleet. Due to the unique nature of its spore drive, *Discovery* was assigned to missions requiring rapid response. However, to function efficiently in the post-Burn era, the ship underwent a three-week refit and was recommissioned with the registry NCC-1031-A.

To bring *Discovery* in line with the technology of this era, the ship's warp engines received a major overhaul, with detached nacelles providing greater maneuverability and performance. Programmable matter was retrofitted into all workstations to enable a more efficient and individual control interface, while nanogel technology was also introduced into spore drive interfaces.

A final innovation that would be considered shocking to 23rd-century observers was the installation of a cloaking device. This enabled *Discovery* to function in the dangerous geopolitical scene of the 32nd century.

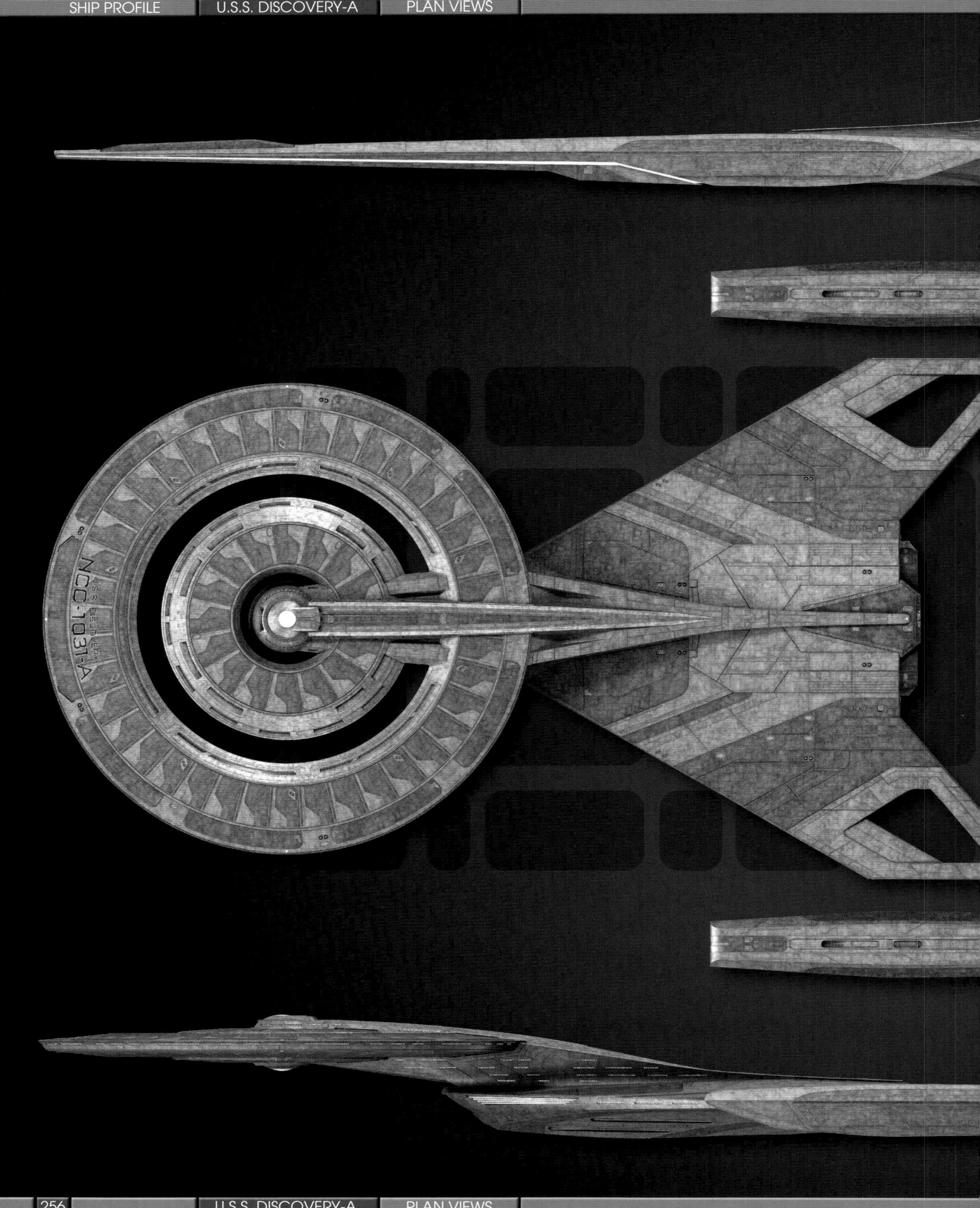
U.S.S. DISCOVERY
NCC-1031-A

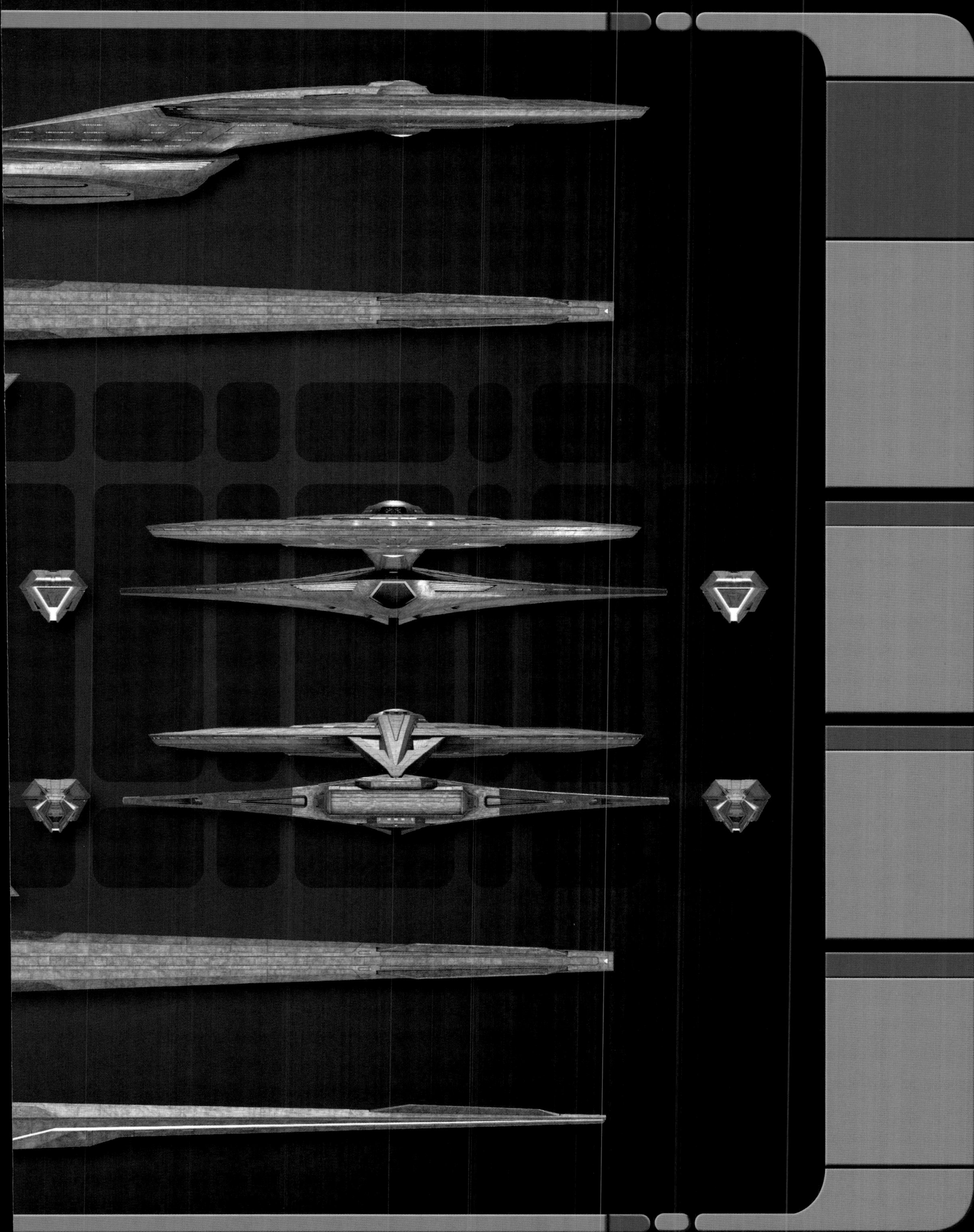

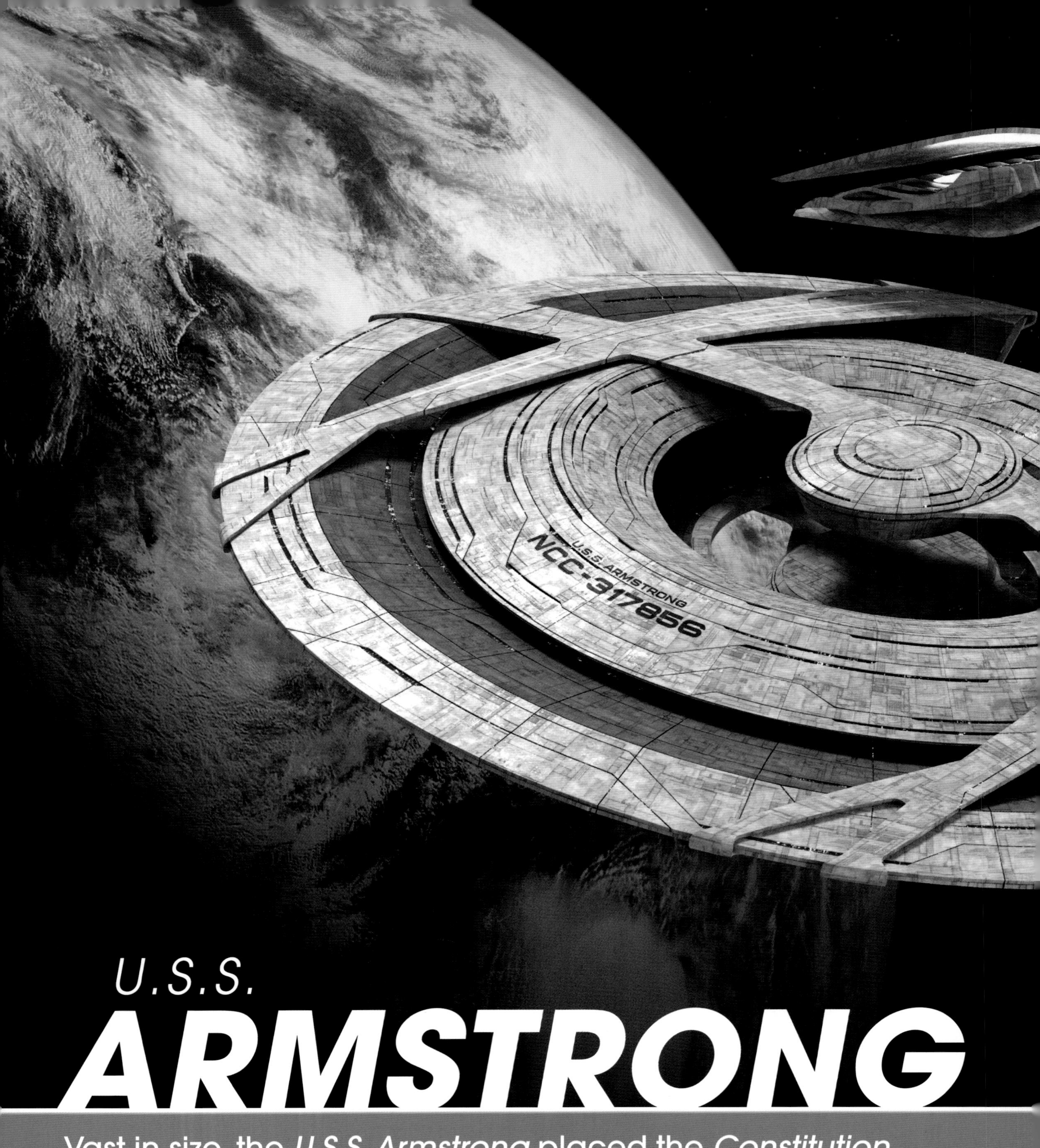

U.S.S. ARMSTRONG

Vast in size, the *U.S.S. Armstrong* placed the *Constitution* class at the forefront of 32nd-century Starfleet.

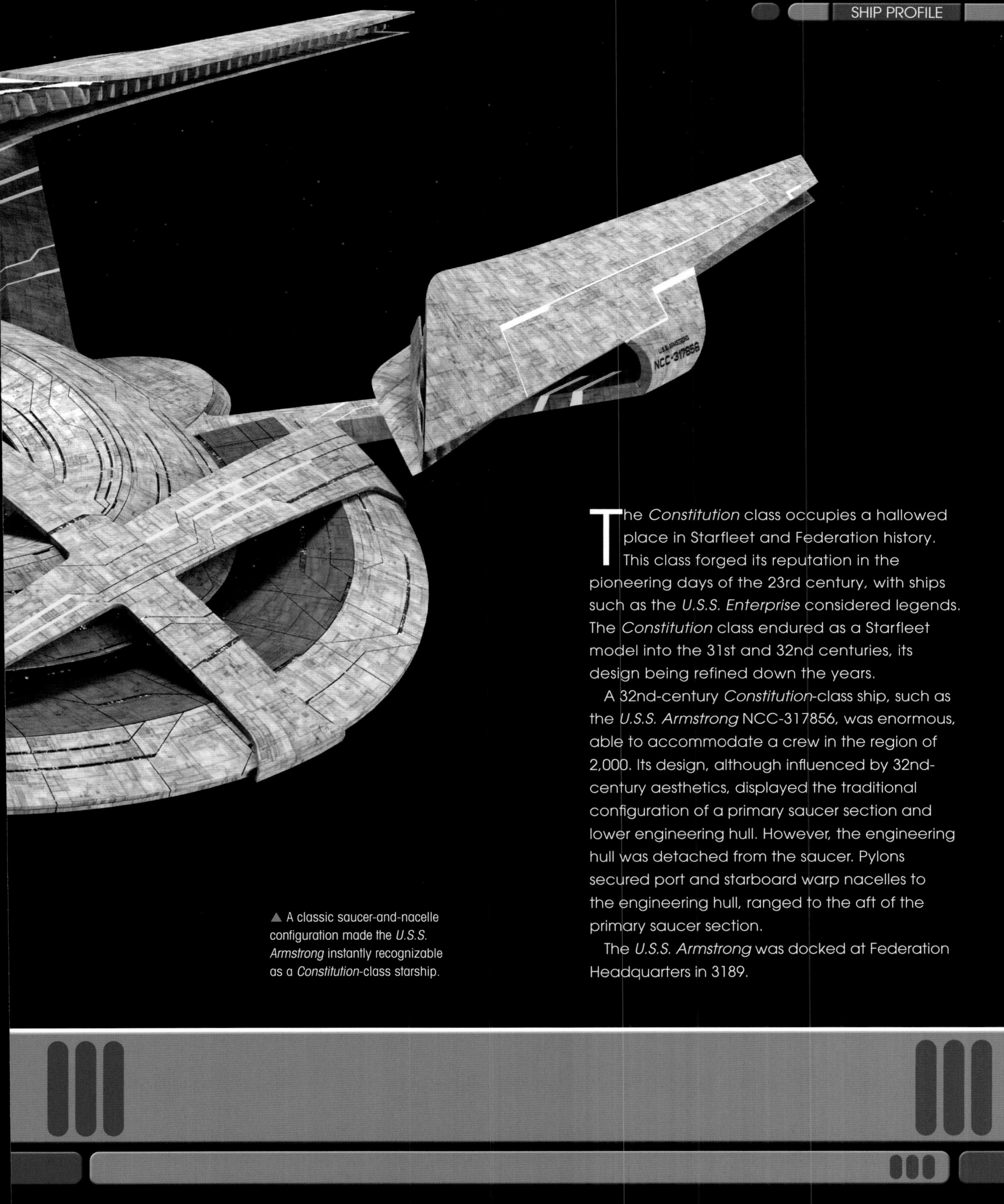

▲ A classic saucer-and-nacelle configuration made the *U.S.S. Armstrong* instantly recognizable as a *Constitution*-class starship.

The *Constitution* class occupies a hallowed place in Starfleet and Federation history. This class forged its reputation in the pioneering days of the 23rd century, with ships such as the *U.S.S. Enterprise* considered legends. The *Constitution* class endured as a Starfleet model into the 31st and 32nd centuries, its design being refined down the years.

A 32nd-century *Constitution*-class ship, such as the *U.S.S. Armstrong* NCC-317856, was enormous, able to accommodate a crew in the region of 2,000. Its design, although influenced by 32nd-century aesthetics, displayed the traditional configuration of a primary saucer section and lower engineering hull. However, the engineering hull was detached from the saucer. Pylons secured port and starboard warp nacelles to the engineering hull, ranged to the aft of the primary saucer section.

The *U.S.S. Armstrong* was docked at Federation Headquarters in 3189.

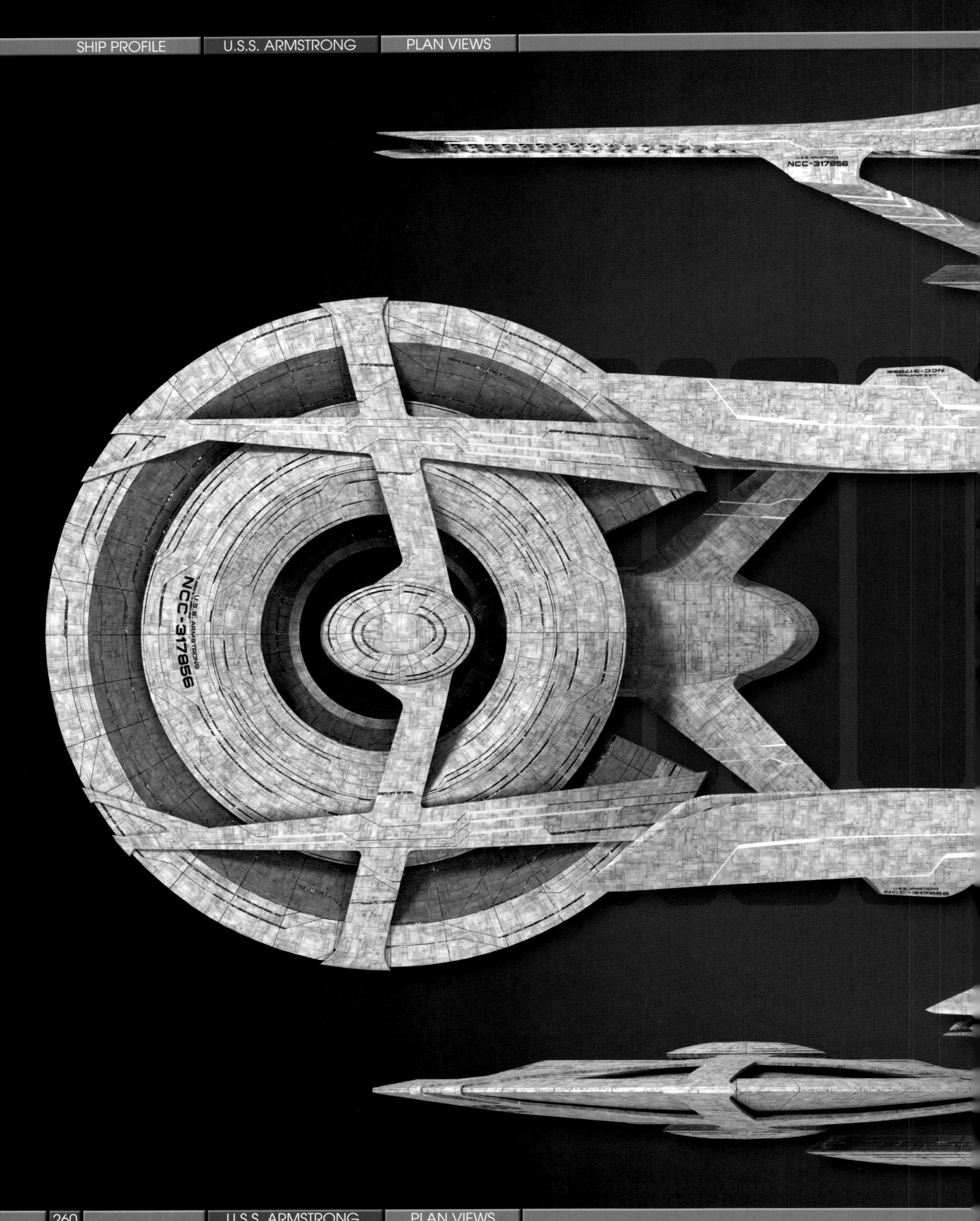
U.S.S. ARMSTRONG
NCC-317856
U.S.S. ARMSTRONG
NCC-317856
U.S.S. ARMSTRONG
NCC-317856

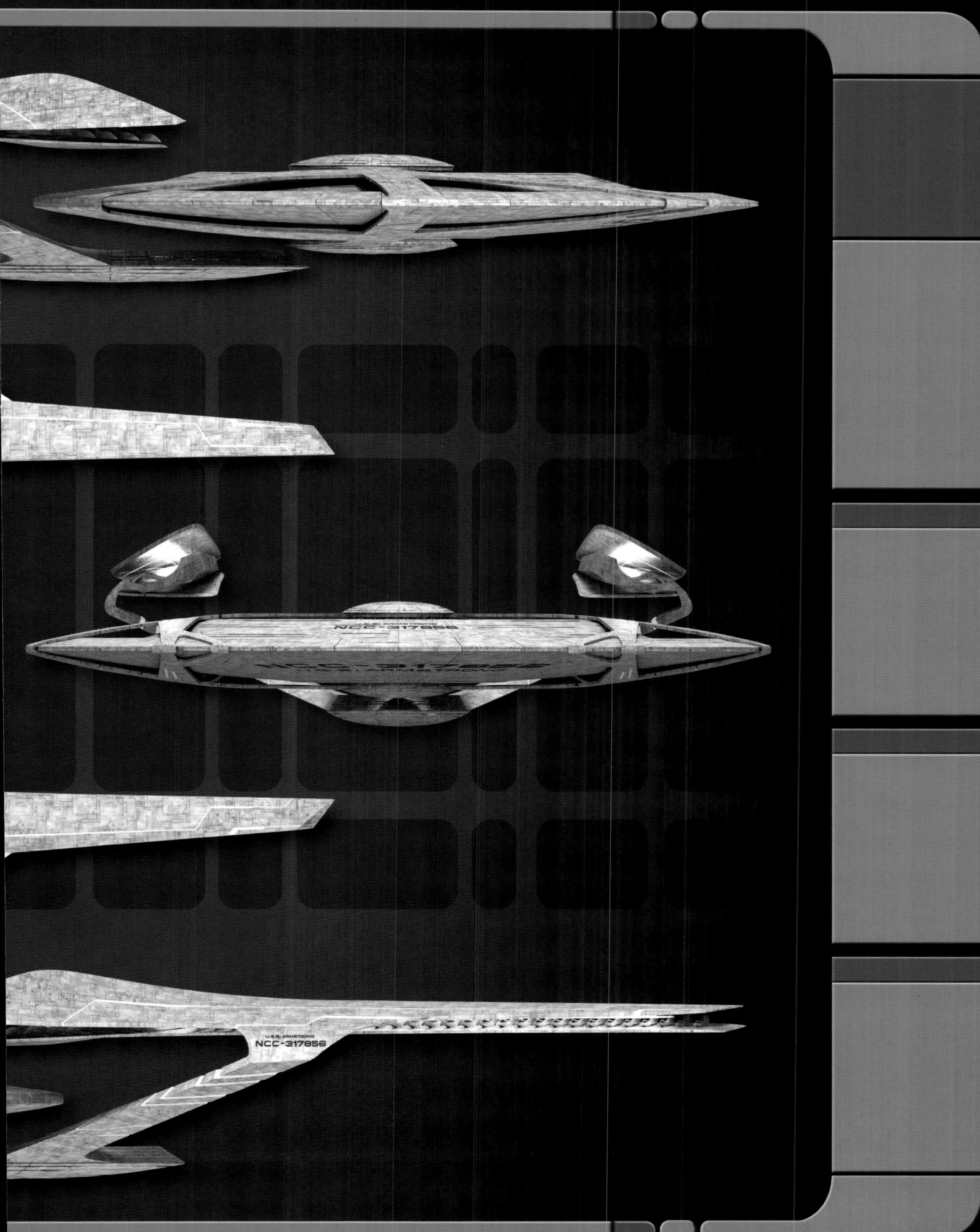

U.S.S. ARMSTRONG
NCC-317856
U.S.S. ARMSTRONG
NCC-317856

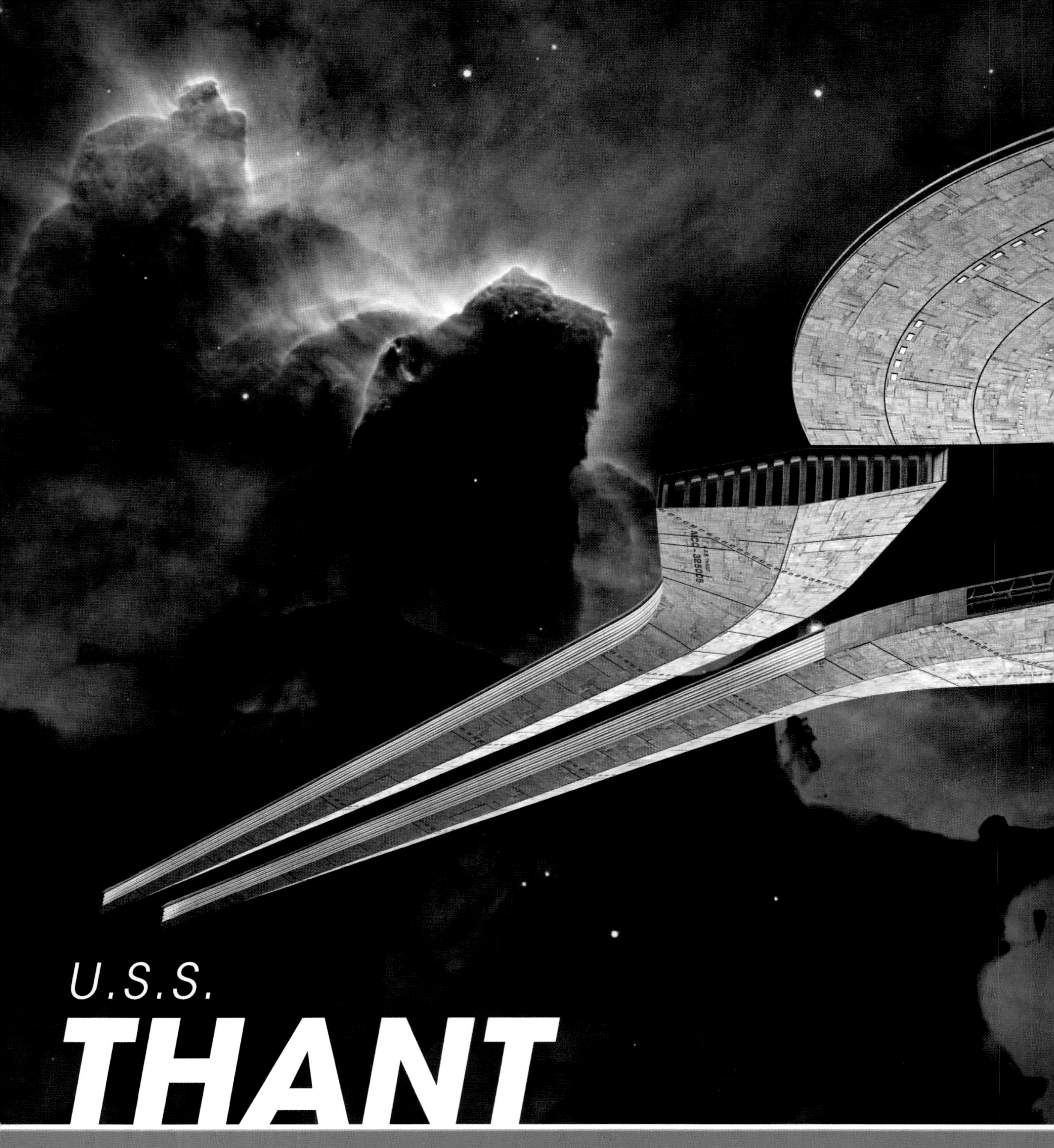

U.S.S. *THANT*

The keyhole shape of the *U.S.S. Thant* instantly marked it out from other 32nd-century ships.

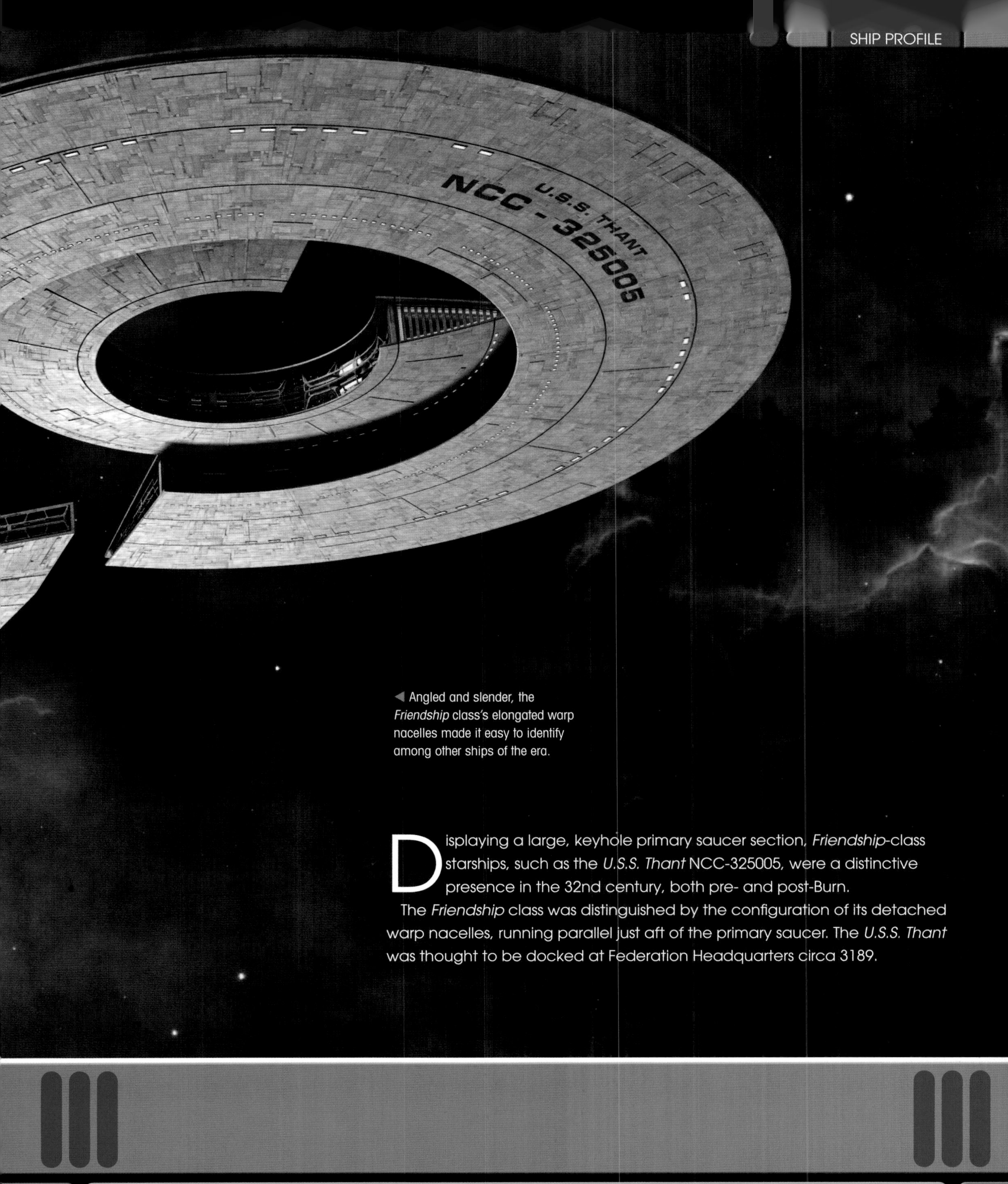

◀ Angled and slender, the *Friendship* class's elongated warp nacelles made it easy to identify among other ships of the era.

Displaying a large, keyhole primary saucer section, *Friendship*-class starships, such as the *U.S.S. Thant* NCC-325005, were a distinctive presence in the 32nd century, both pre- and post-Burn.

The *Friendship* class was distinguished by the configuration of its detached warp nacelles, running parallel just aft of the primary saucer. The *U.S.S. Thant* was thought to be docked at Federation Headquarters circa 3189.

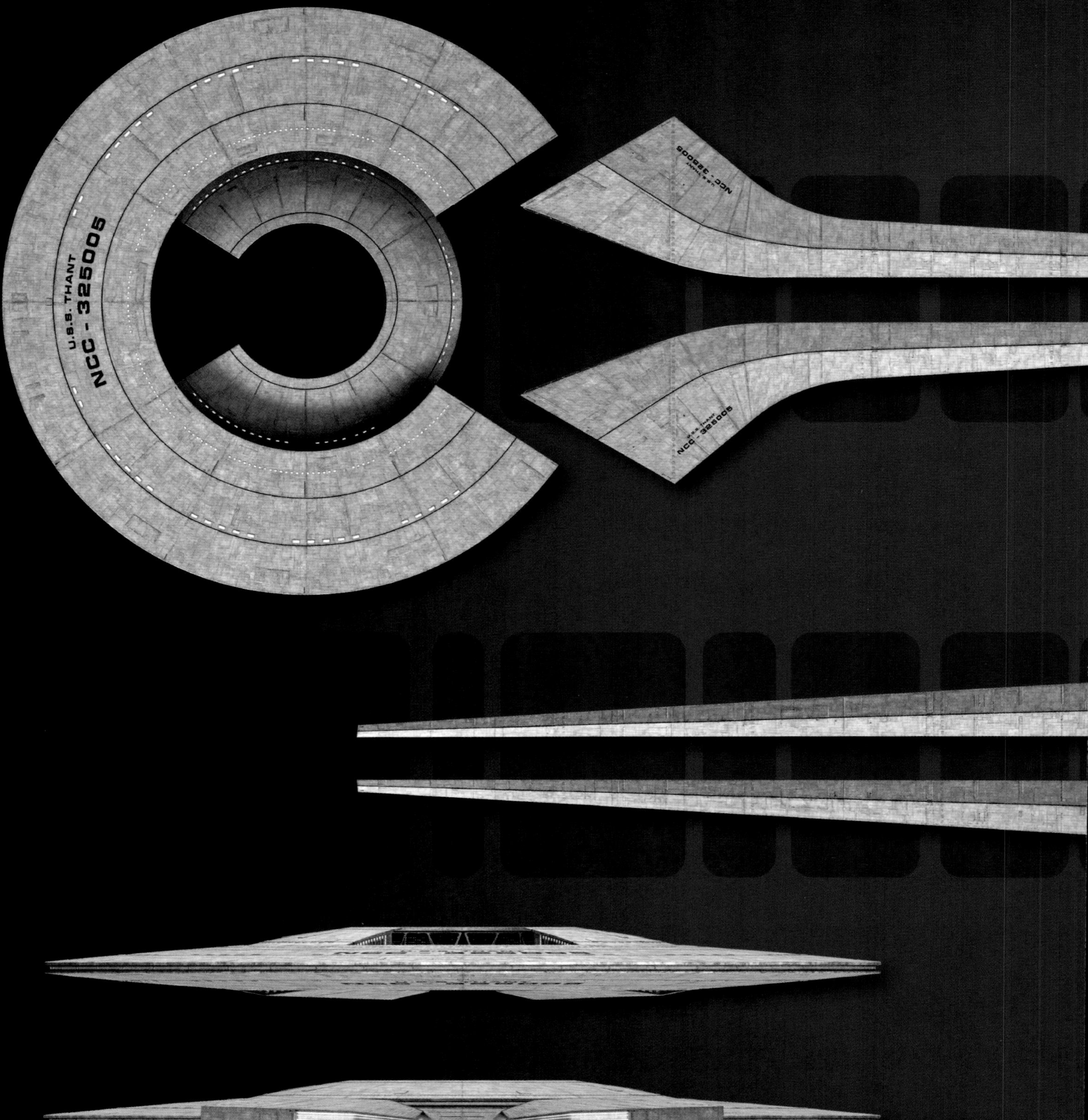

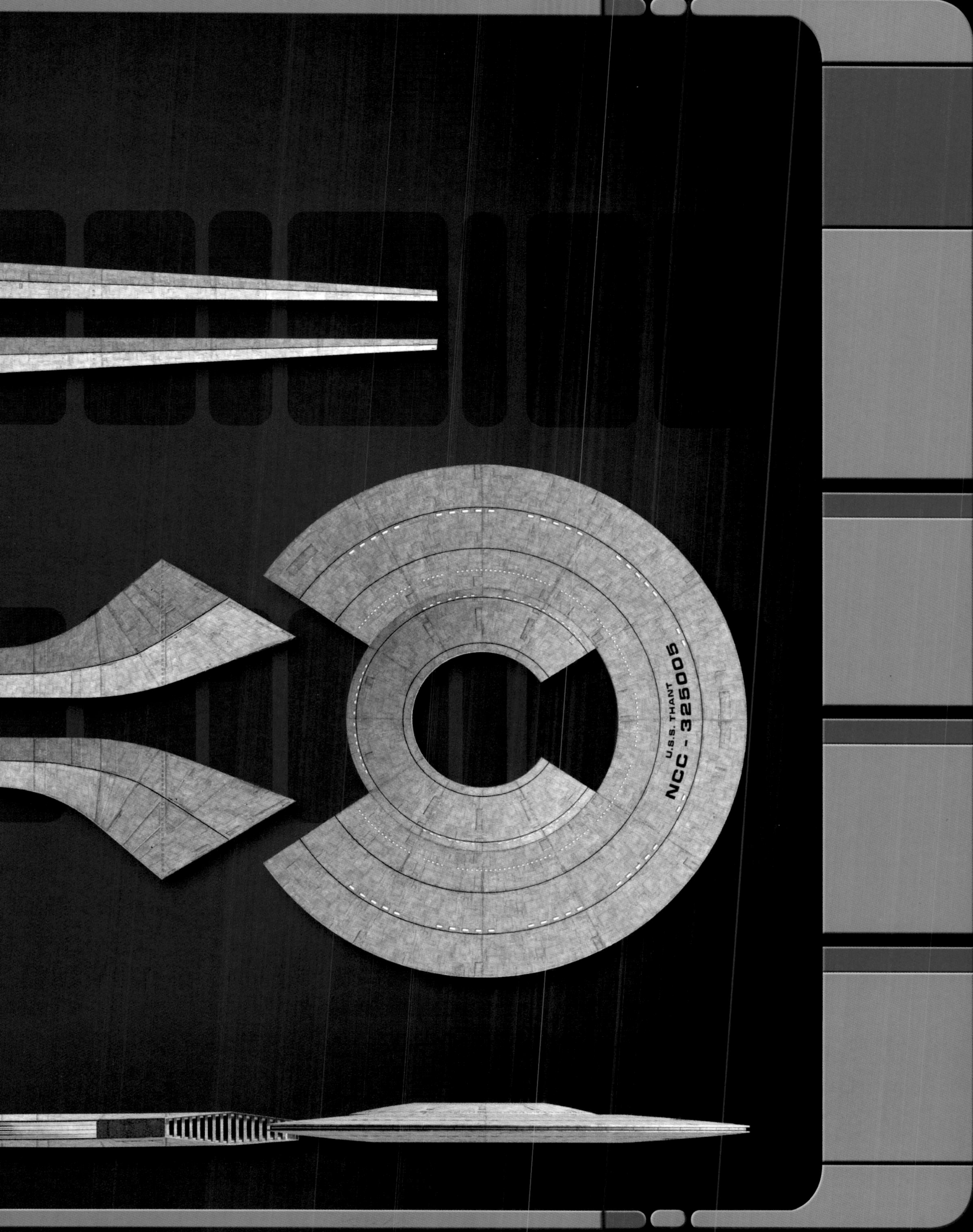

U.S.S. THANT
NCC - 3250005

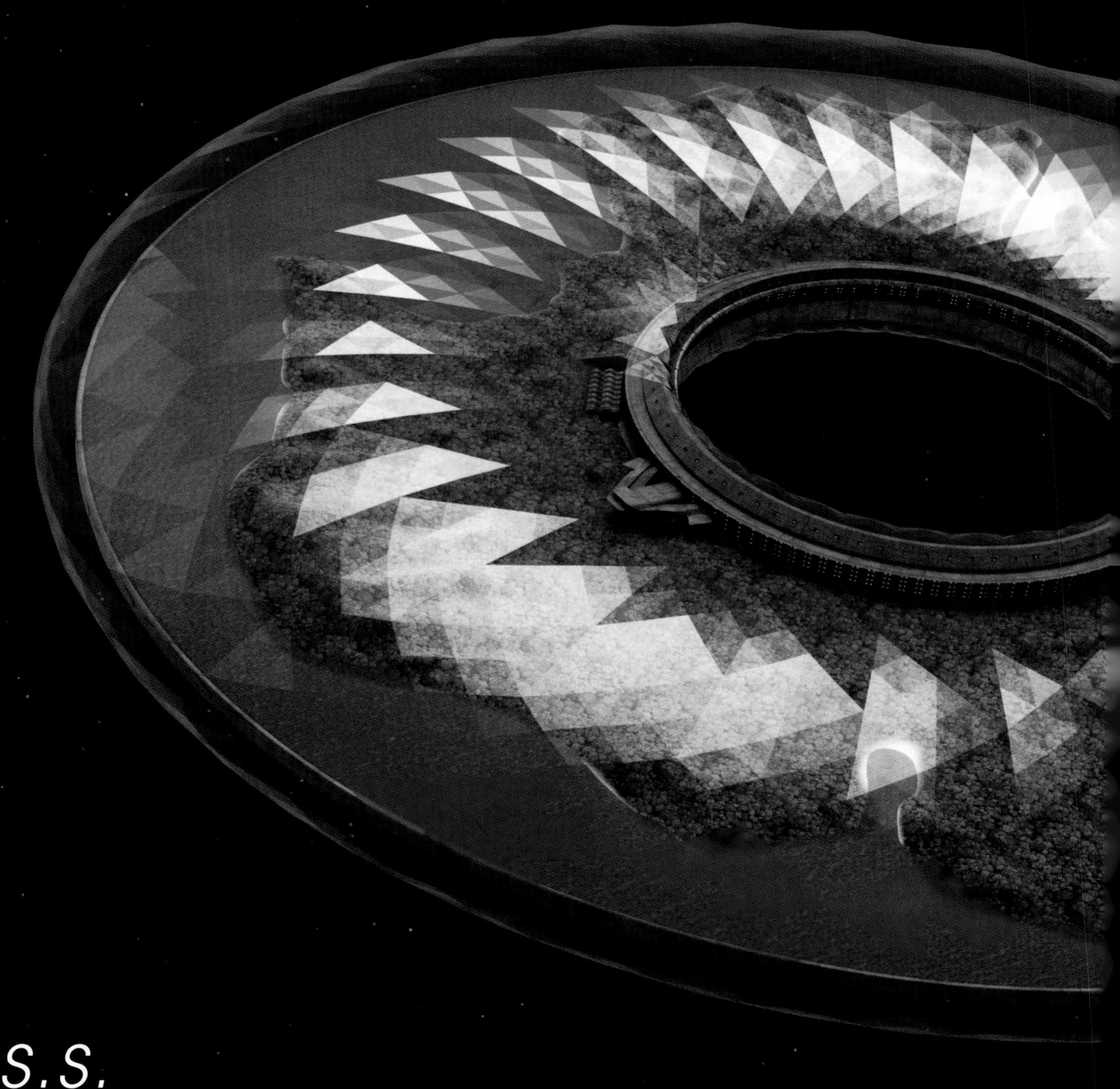

U.S.S.

MAATHAI

Angelou-class starships such as the *U.S.S. Maathai* provided the Federation with large rainforest habitats.

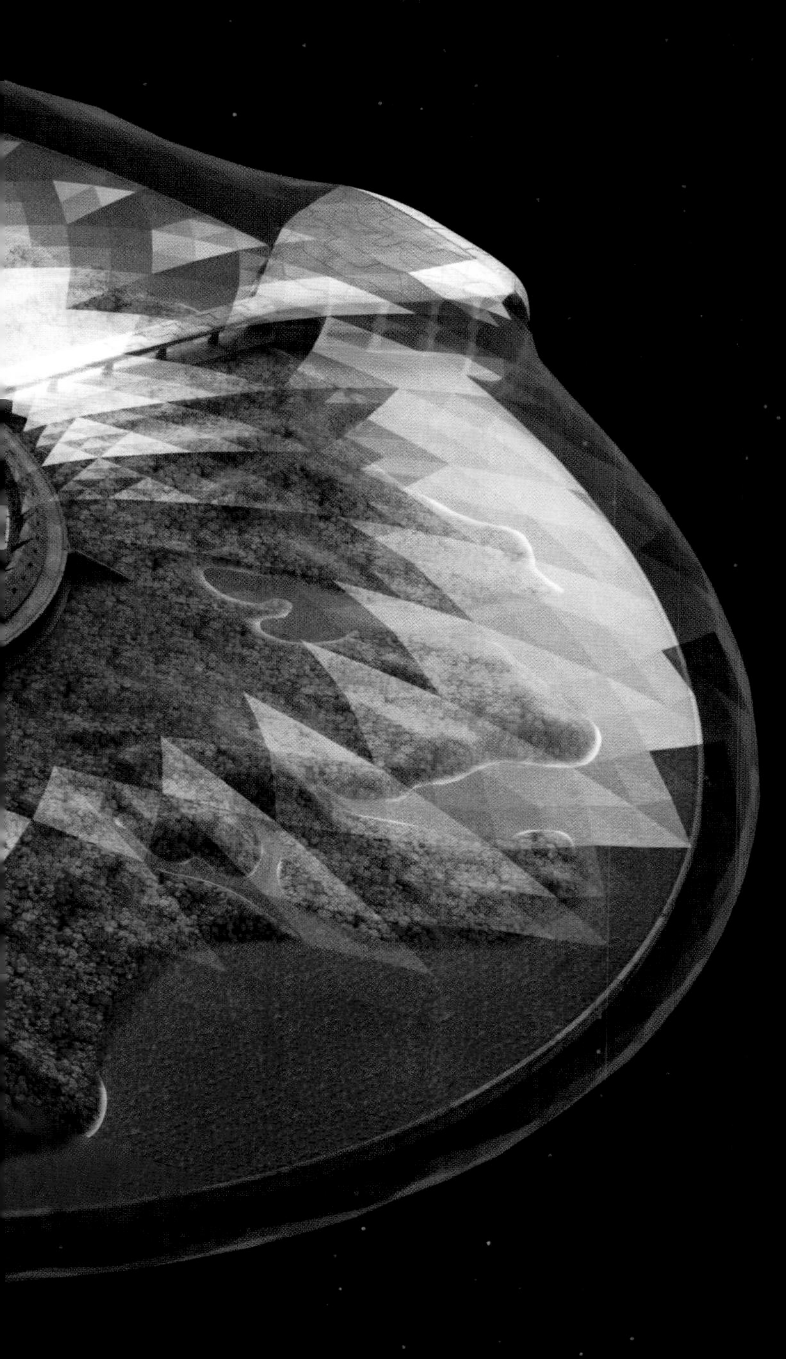

◀ The *Angelou* class was an impressive sight, the transparent, encircling hull revealing the extensive rainforest environment within.

In the pre- and post-Burn eras of the 31st and 32nd centuries, the large, torus-shaped vessels of the *Angelou* class acted as spaceborne ecosystems, giving the Federation the benefits of a considerable rainforest environment.

The rainforest ecosystems were contained beneath the ships' transparent hull plating, arranged around a ring at the center of the saucer. The ring was likely to accommodate crew areas away from the rainforest area. Propulsion systems were located on one edge of the saucer. An *Angelou*-class ship – possibly the *U.S.S. Maathai* NCC-325023 – was docked at Federation Headquarters on an unspecified stardate in 3189.

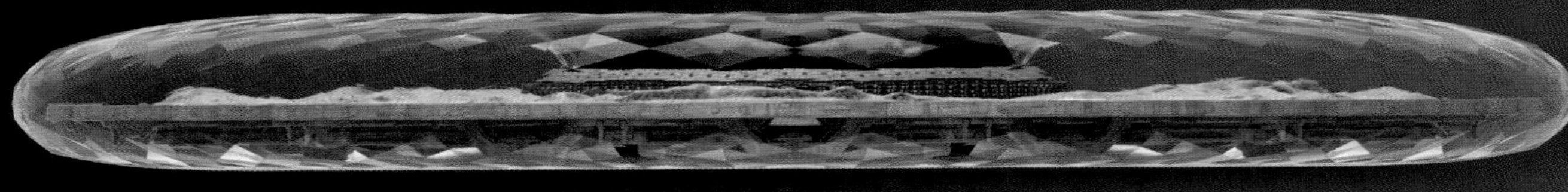

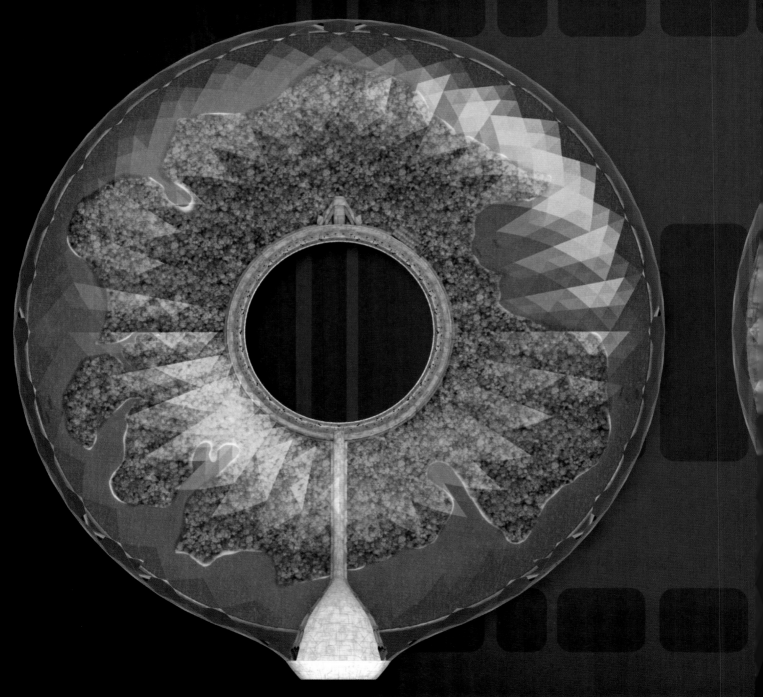

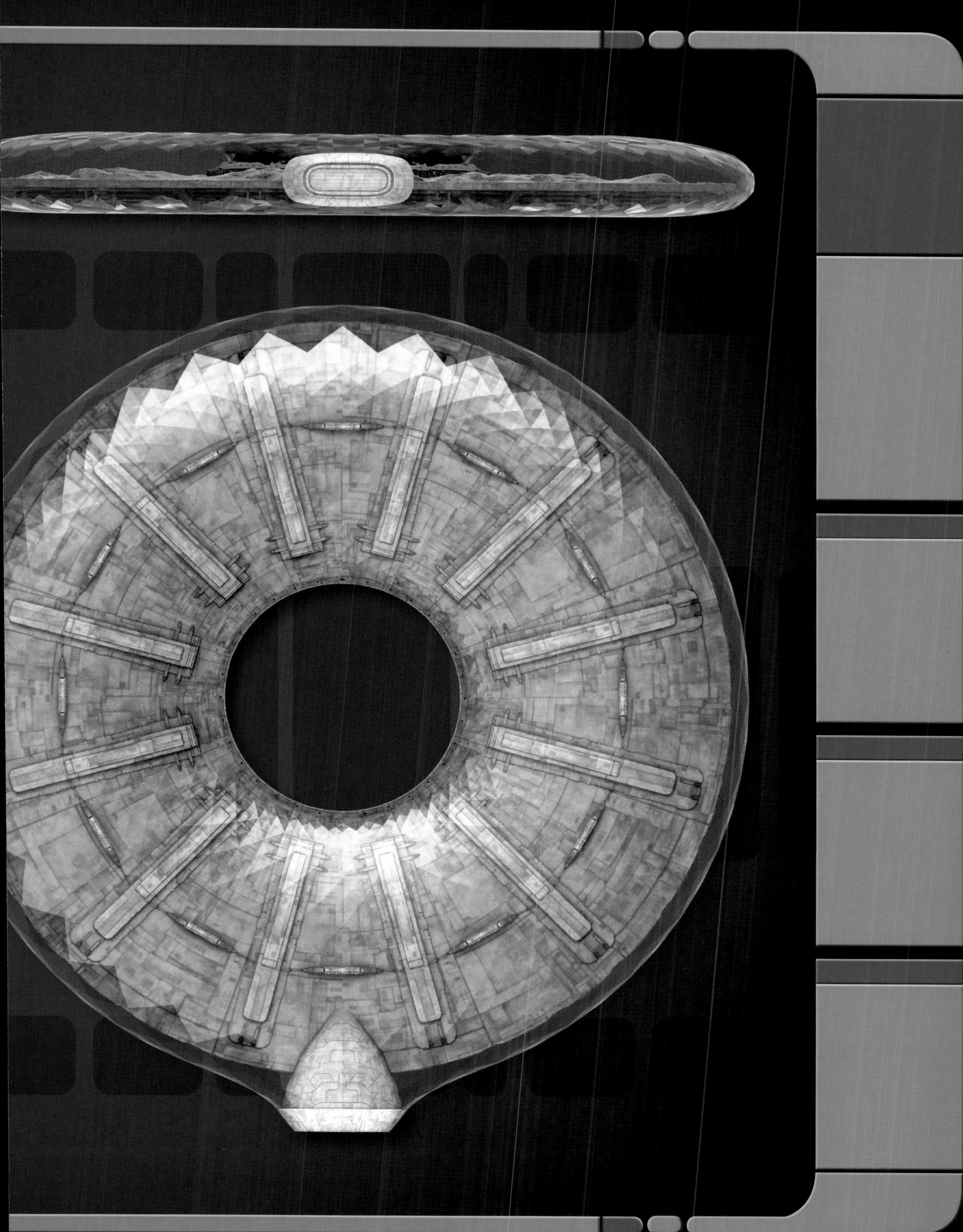

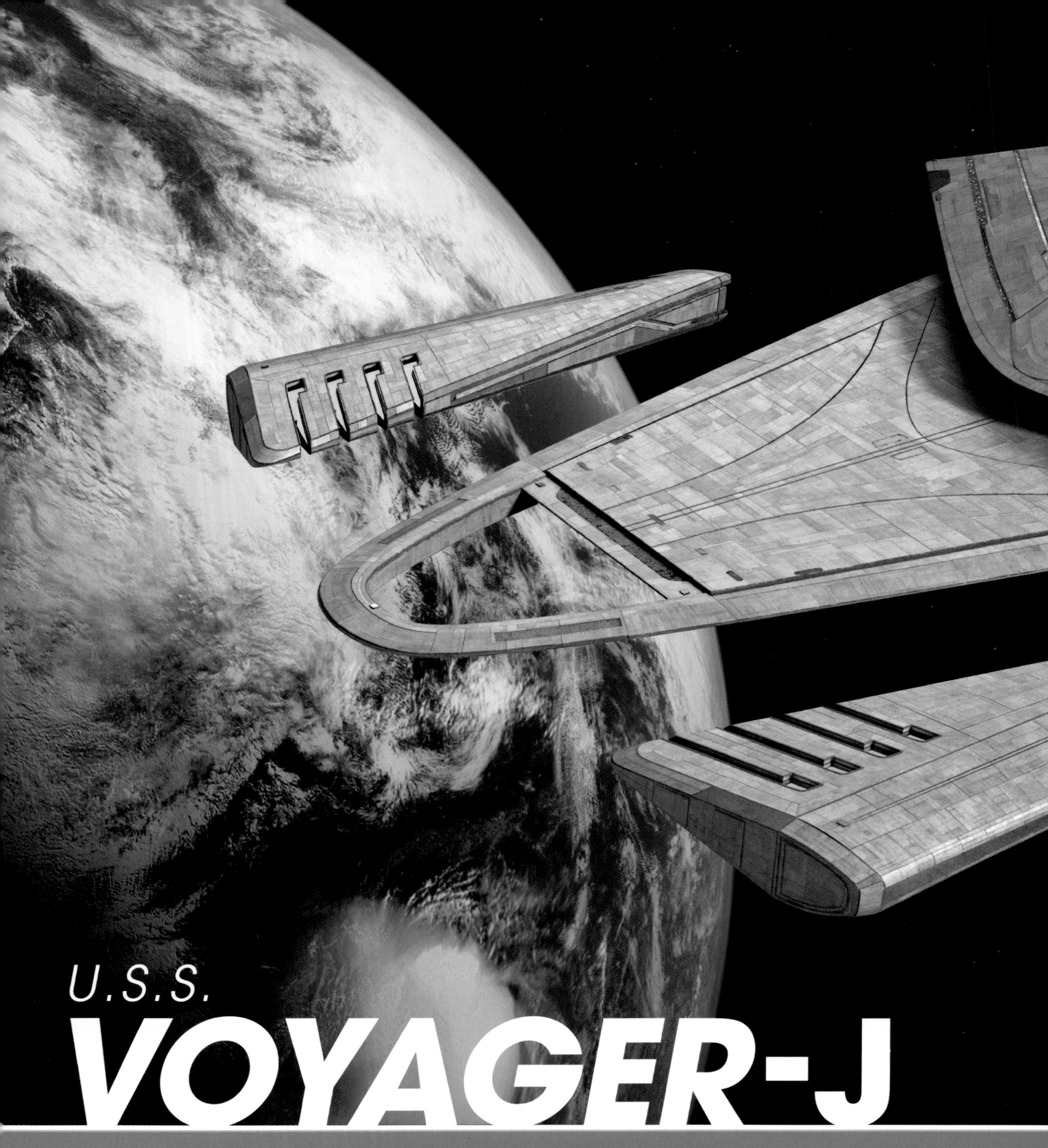

U.S.S. VOYAGER-J

The 32nd-century *U.S.S. Voyager* carried a Starfleet legend into the future, while honoring the great original.

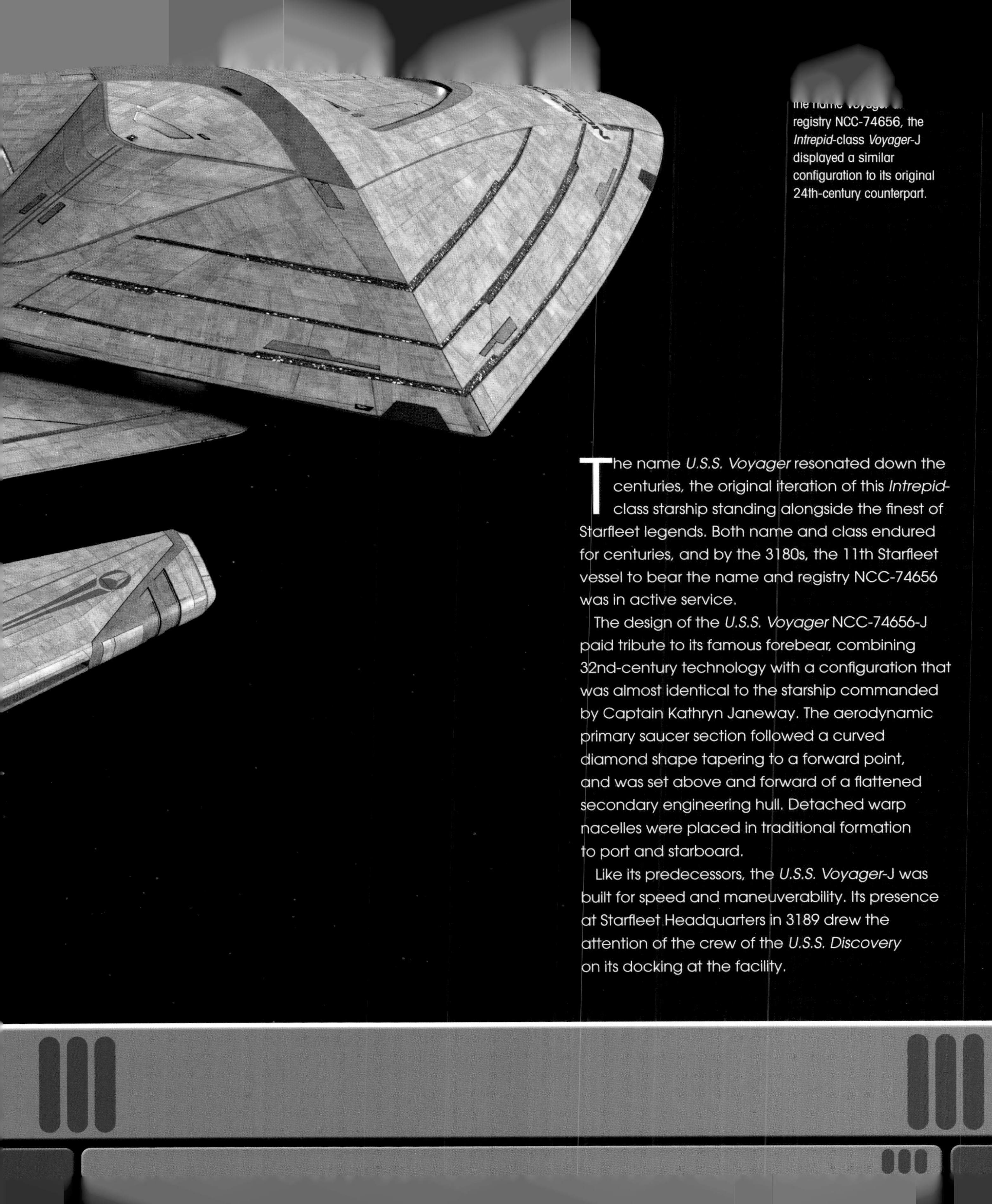

the name *Voyager* and registry NCC-74656, the *Intrepid*-class *Voyager*-J displayed a similar configuration to its original 24th-century counterpart.

The name *U.S.S. Voyager* resonated down the centuries, the original iteration of this *Intrepid*-class starship standing alongside the finest of Starfleet legends. Both name and class endured for centuries, and by the 3180s, the 11th Starfleet vessel to bear the name and registry NCC-74656 was in active service.

The design of the *U.S.S. Voyager* NCC-74656-J paid tribute to its famous forebear, combining 32nd-century technology with a configuration that was almost identical to the starship commanded by Captain Kathryn Janeway. The aerodynamic primary saucer section followed a curved diamond shape tapering to a forward point, and was set above and forward of a flattened secondary engineering hull. Detached warp nacelles were placed in traditional formation to port and starboard.

Like its predecessors, the *U.S.S. Voyager*-J was built for speed and maneuverability. Its presence at Starfleet Headquarters in 3189 drew the attention of the crew of the *U.S.S. Discovery* on its docking at the facility.

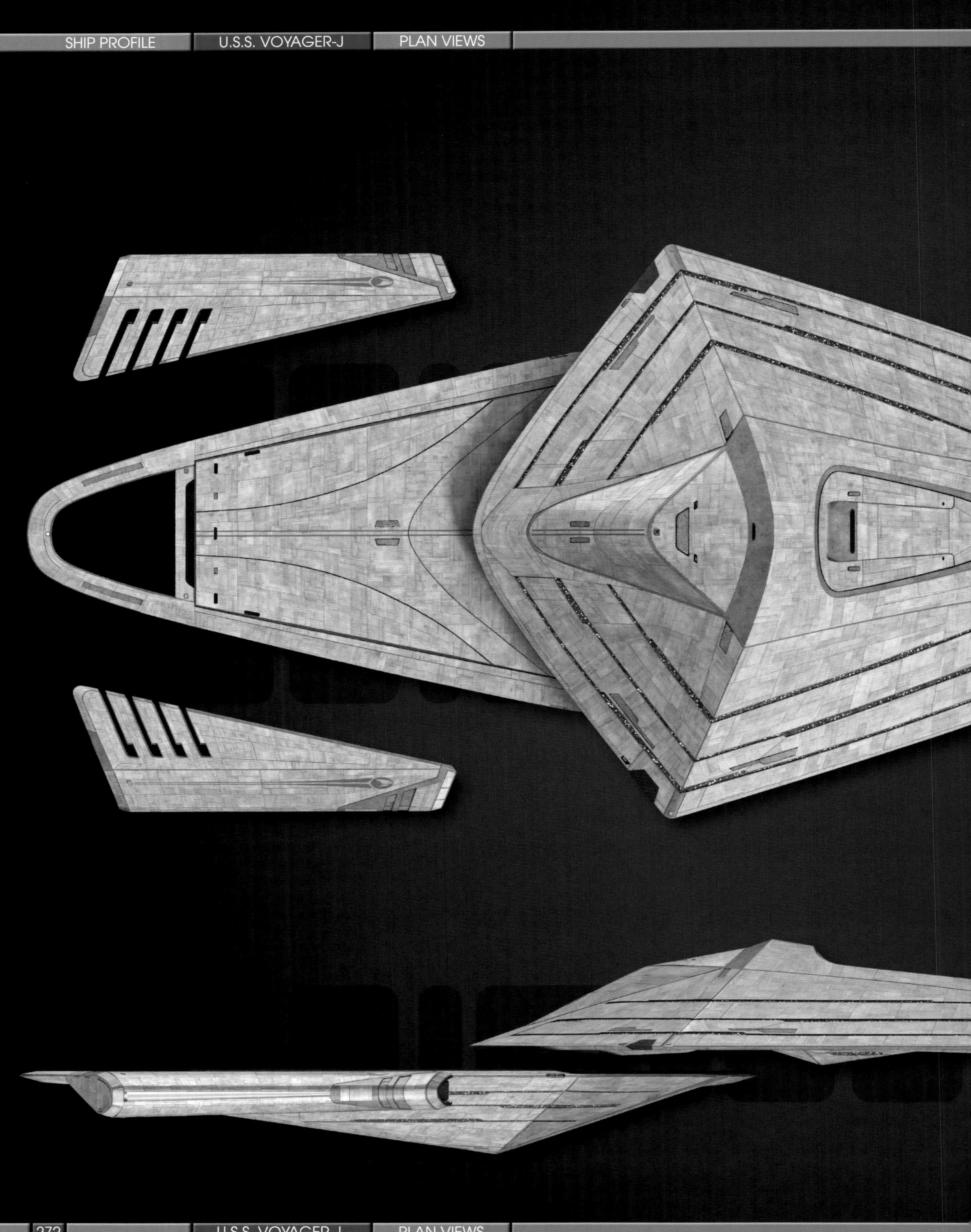

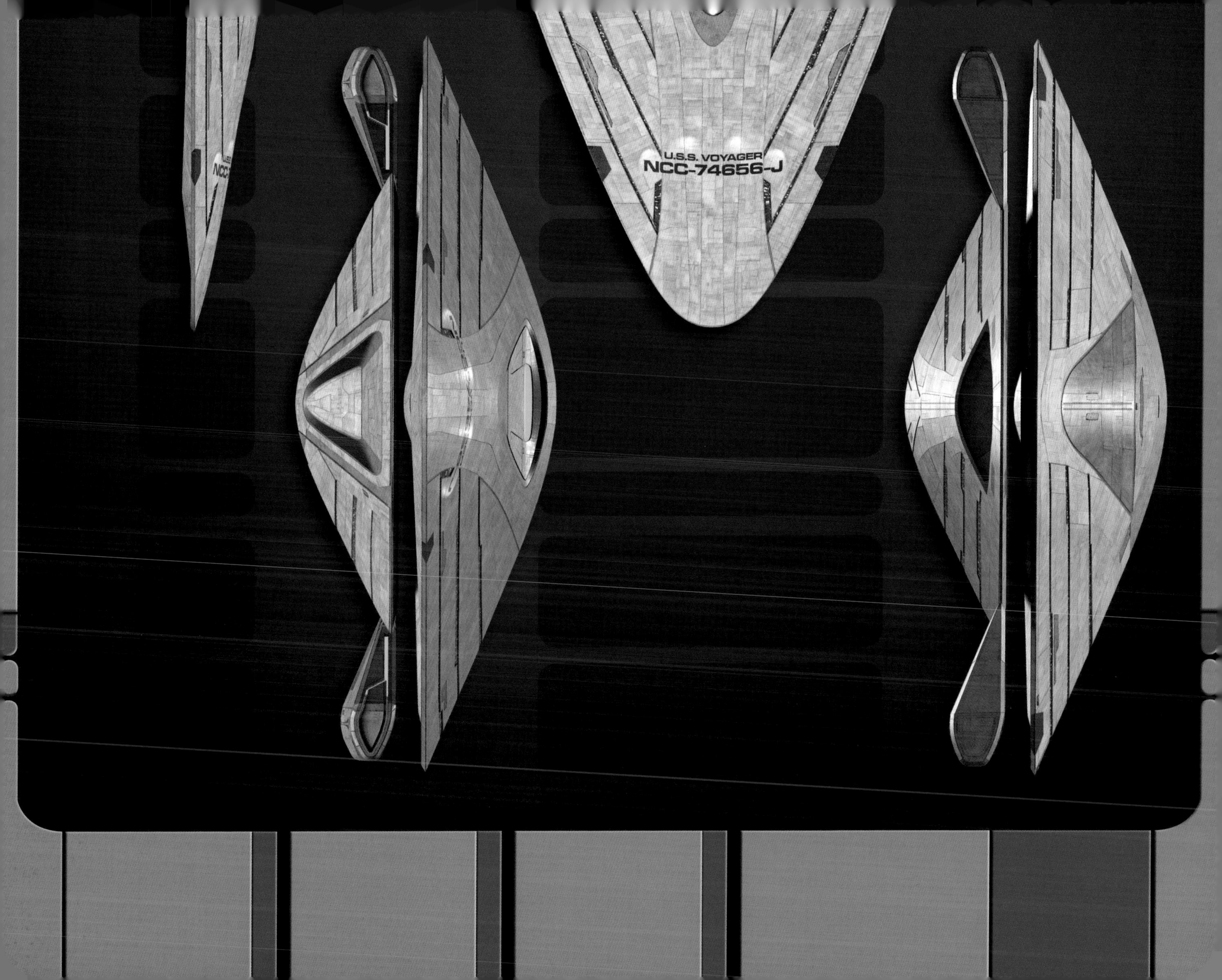
U.S.S. VOYAGER
NCC-74656-J

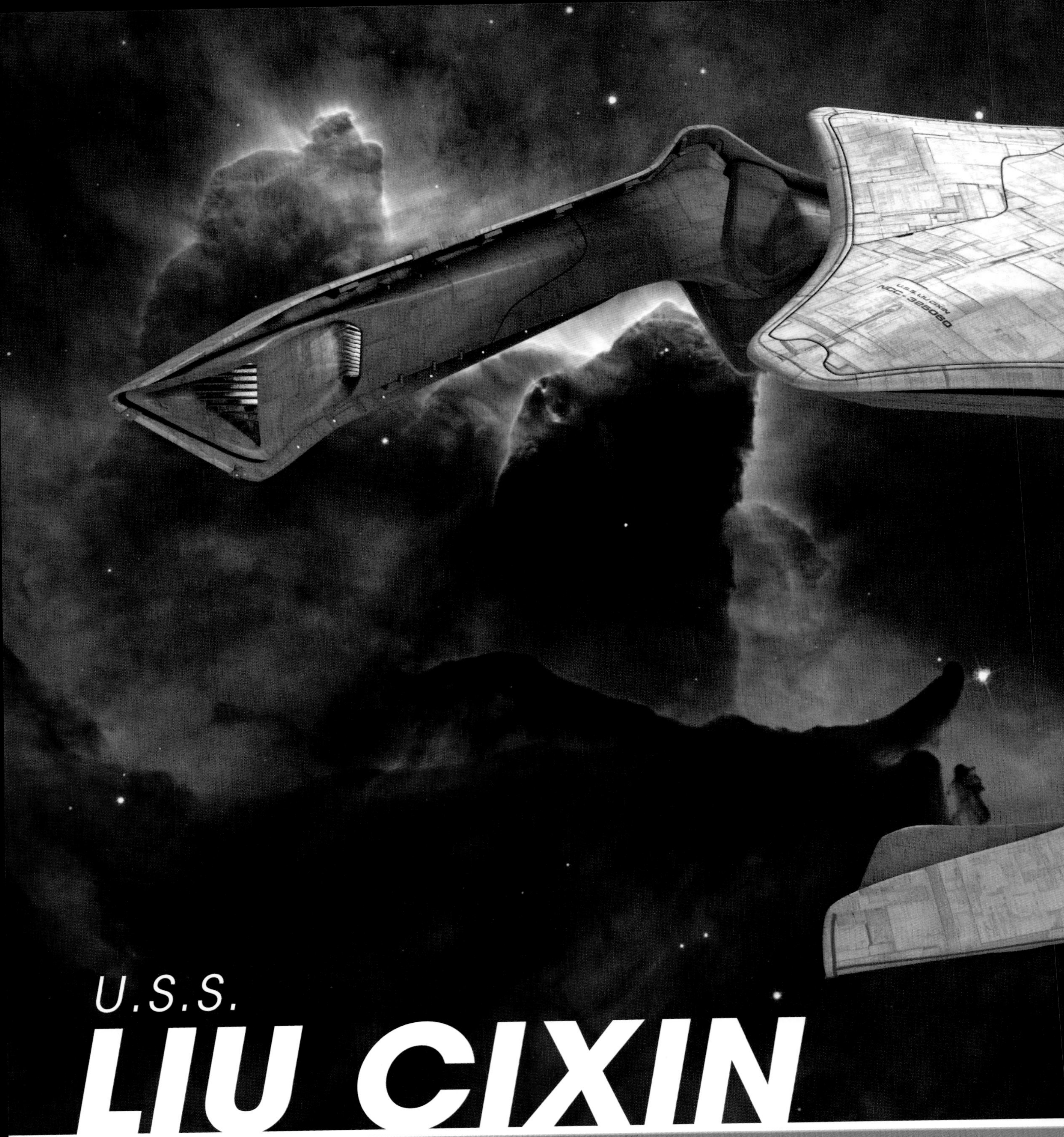

U.S.S. LIU CIXIN

Small but sleek, the *U.S.S. Liu Cixin* was a scout ship with a sharp, aerodynamic design.

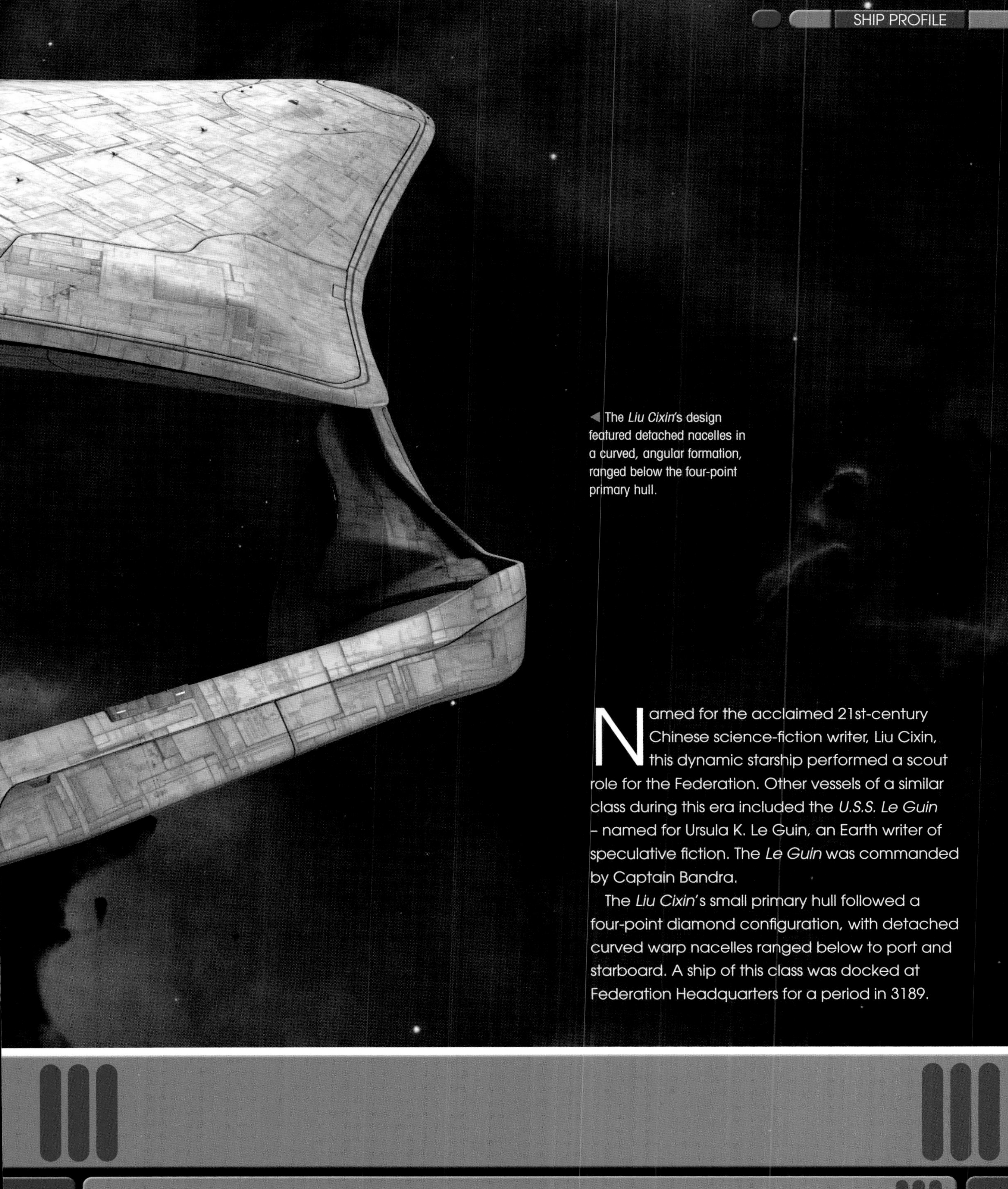

◀ The *Liu Cixin*'s design featured detached nacelles in a curved, angular formation, ranged below the four-point primary hull.

Named for the acclaimed 21st-century Chinese science-fiction writer, Liu Cixin, this dynamic starship performed a scout role for the Federation. Other vessels of a similar class during this era included the *U.S.S. Le Guin* – named for Ursula K. Le Guin, an Earth writer of speculative fiction. The *Le Guin* was commanded by Captain Bandra.

The *Liu Cixin*'s small primary hull followed a four-point diamond configuration, with detached curved warp nacelles ranged below to port and starboard. A ship of this class was docked at Federation Headquarters for a period in 3189.

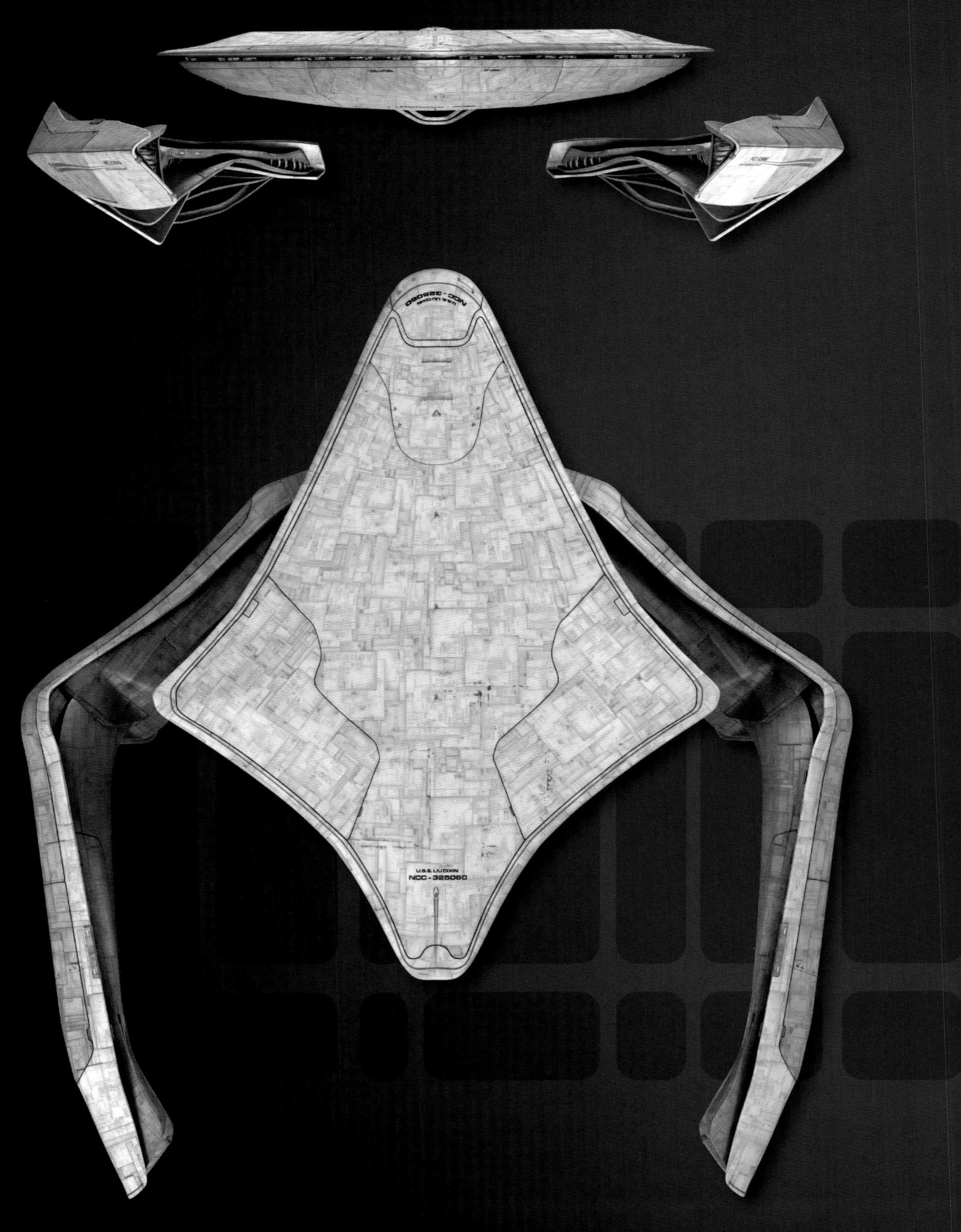
U.S.S. LIU CIXIN
NCC-325060
U.S.S. LIU CIXIN
NCC-325060

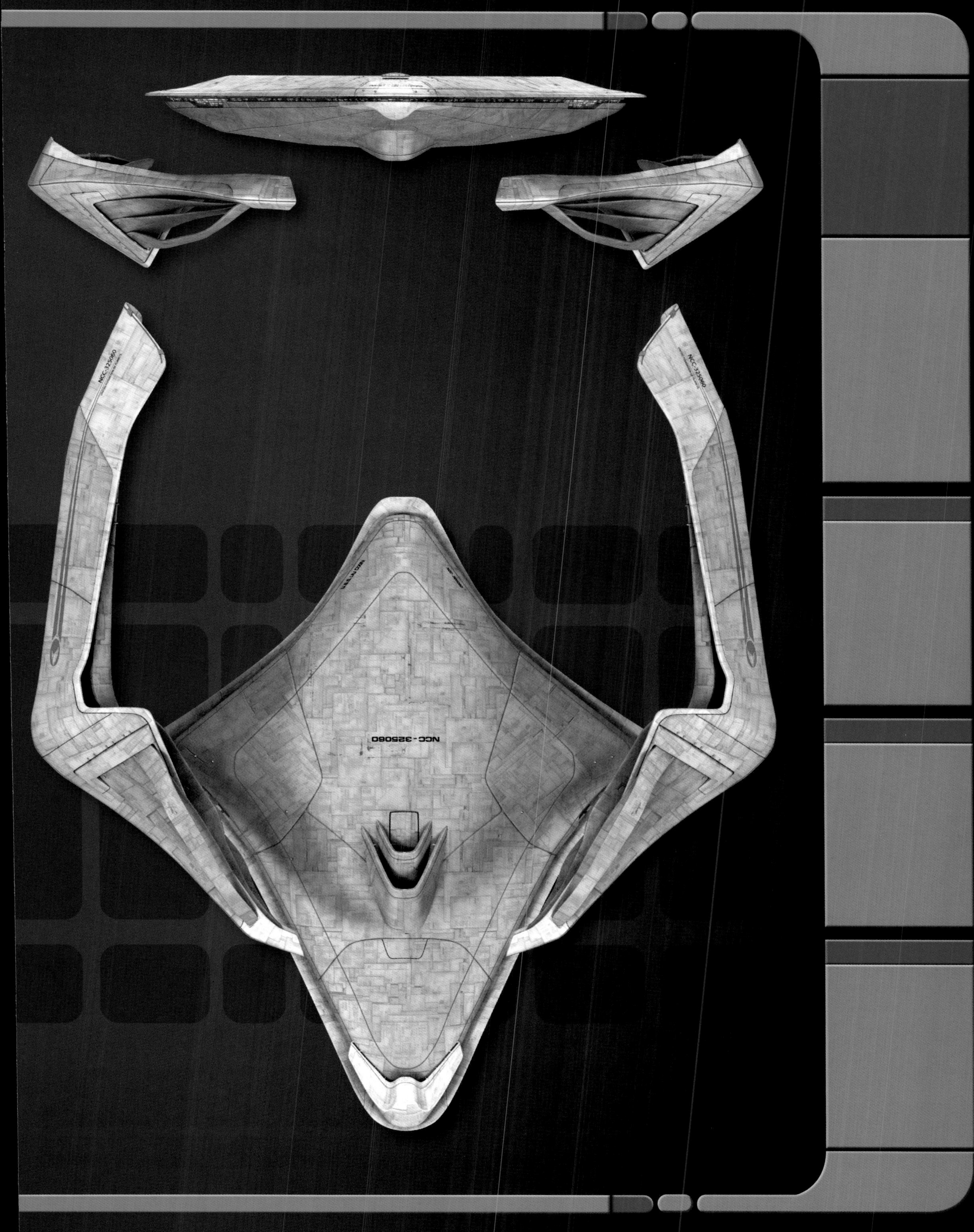
NCC-325060
NCC-325060
NCC-325060

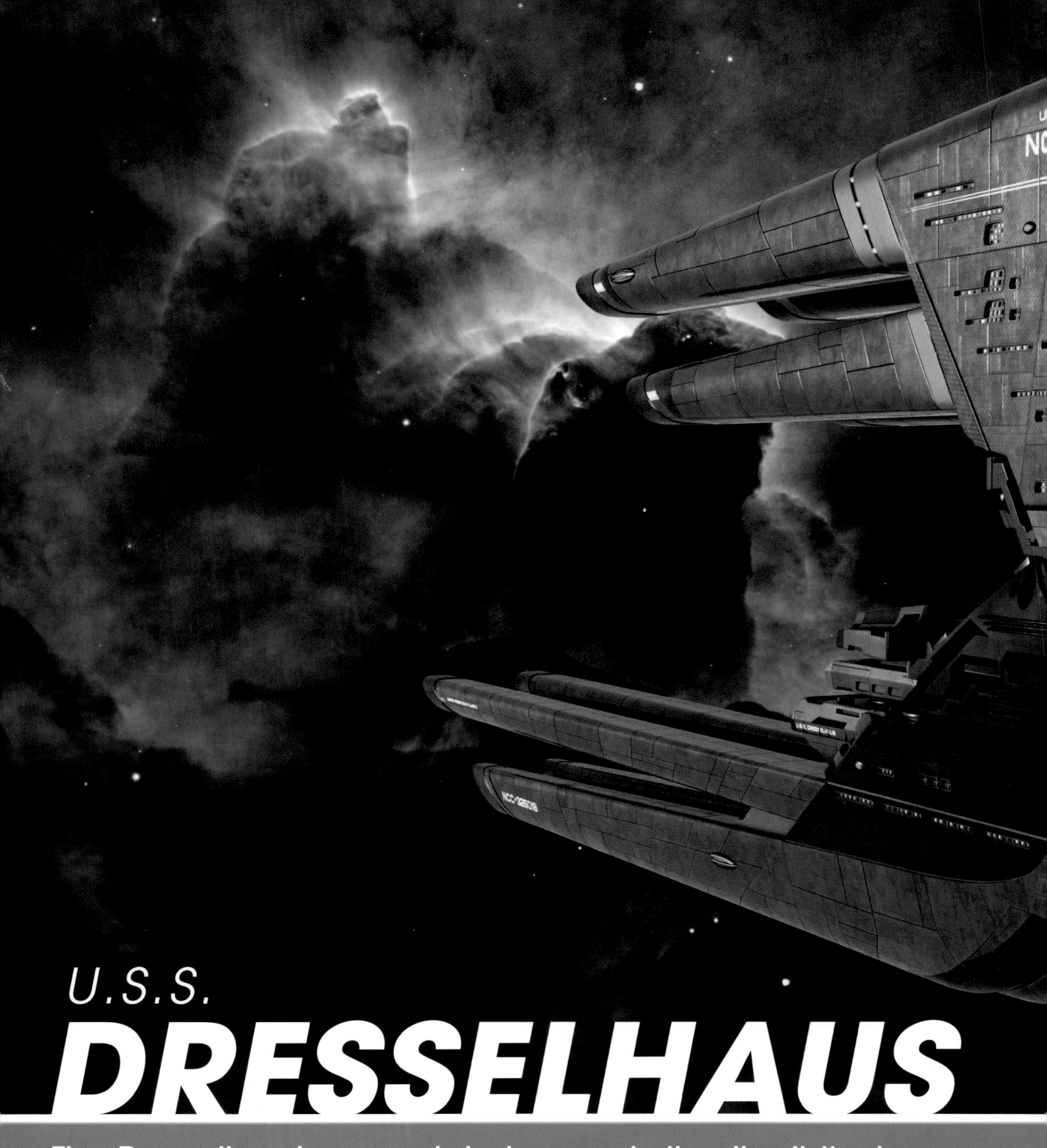

U.S.S.

DRESSELHAUS

The *Dresselhaus*'s rugged design made it quite distinct from contemporary starship engineering.

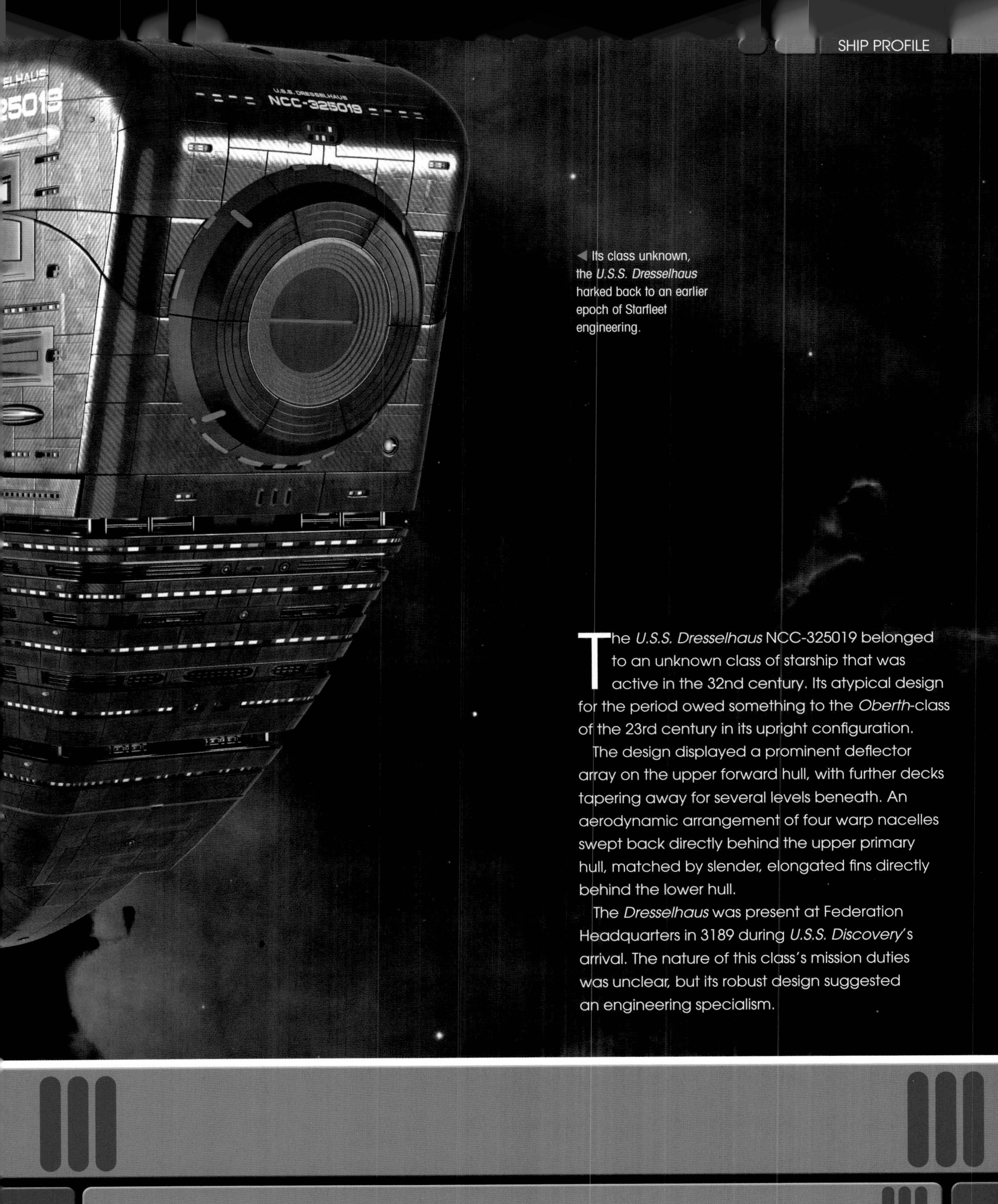

◀ Its class unknown, the *U.S.S. Dresselhaus* harked back to an earlier epoch of Starfleet engineering.

The *U.S.S. Dresselhaus* NCC-325019 belonged to an unknown class of starship that was active in the 32nd century. Its atypical design for the period owed something to the *Oberth*-class of the 23rd century in its upright configuration.

The design displayed a prominent deflector array on the upper forward hull, with further decks tapering away for several levels beneath. An aerodynamic arrangement of four warp nacelles swept back directly behind the upper primary hull, matched by slender, elongated fins directly behind the lower hull.

The *Dresselhaus* was present at Federation Headquarters in 3189 during *U.S.S. Discovery*'s arrival. The nature of this class's mission duties was unclear, but its robust design suggested an engineering specialism.

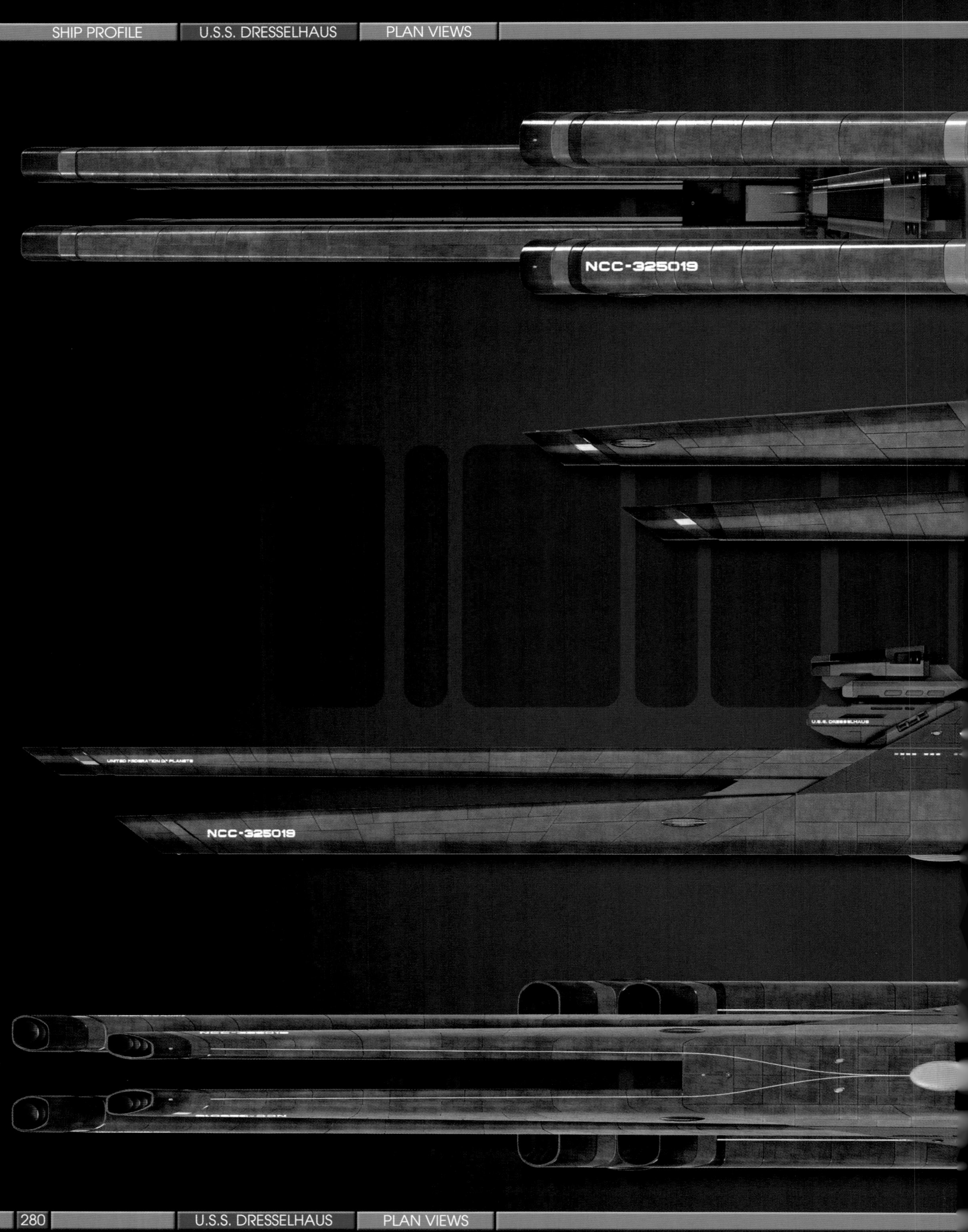
NCC-325019
U.S.S. DRESSELHAUS
NCC-325019

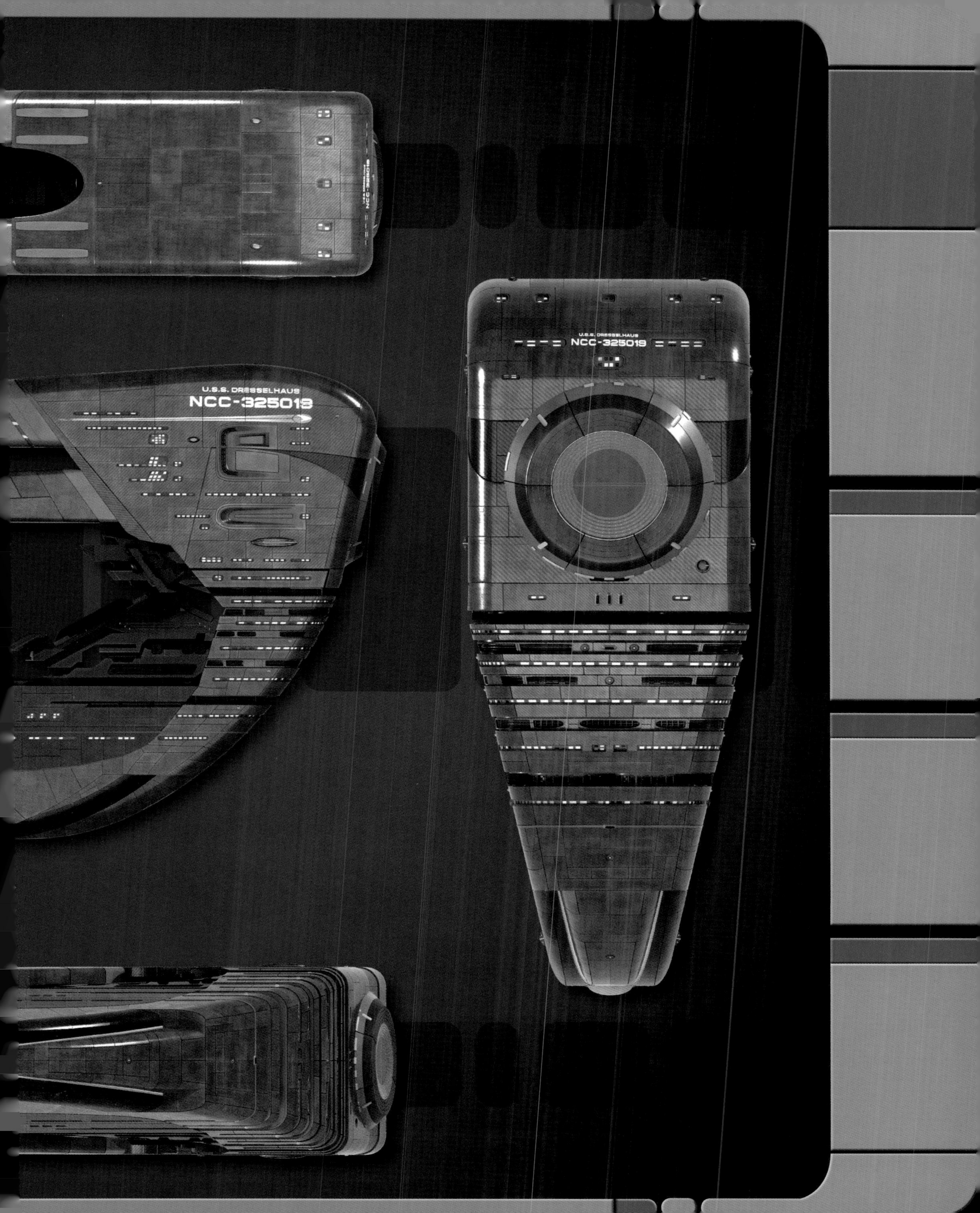
U.S.S. DRESSELHAUS
NCC-325019
U.S.S. DRESSELHAUS
NCC-325019

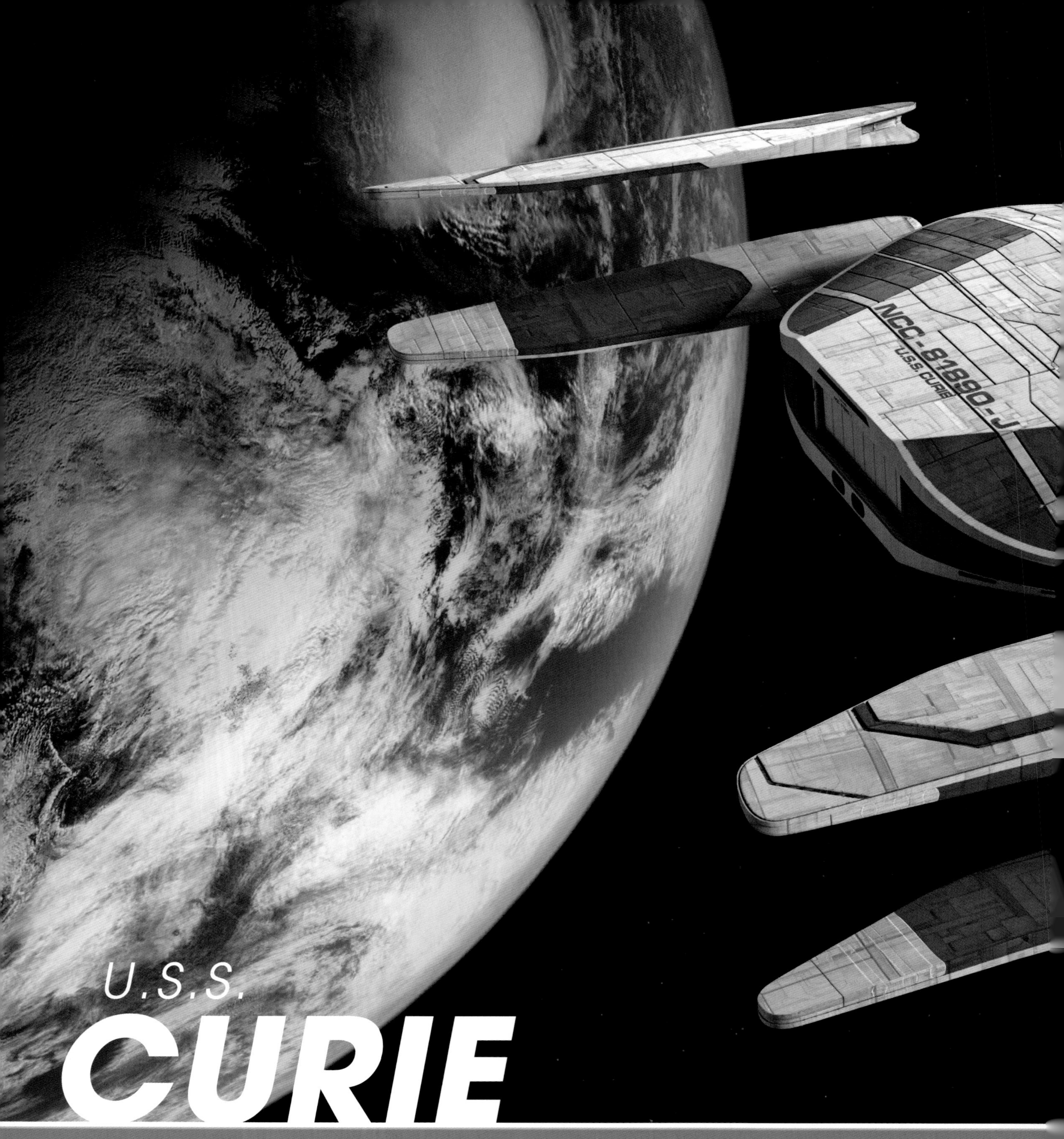

U.S.S. CURIE

With a distinctive quad configuration of nacelles, the *U.S.S. Curie* was the 11th iteration in a fine ship lineage.

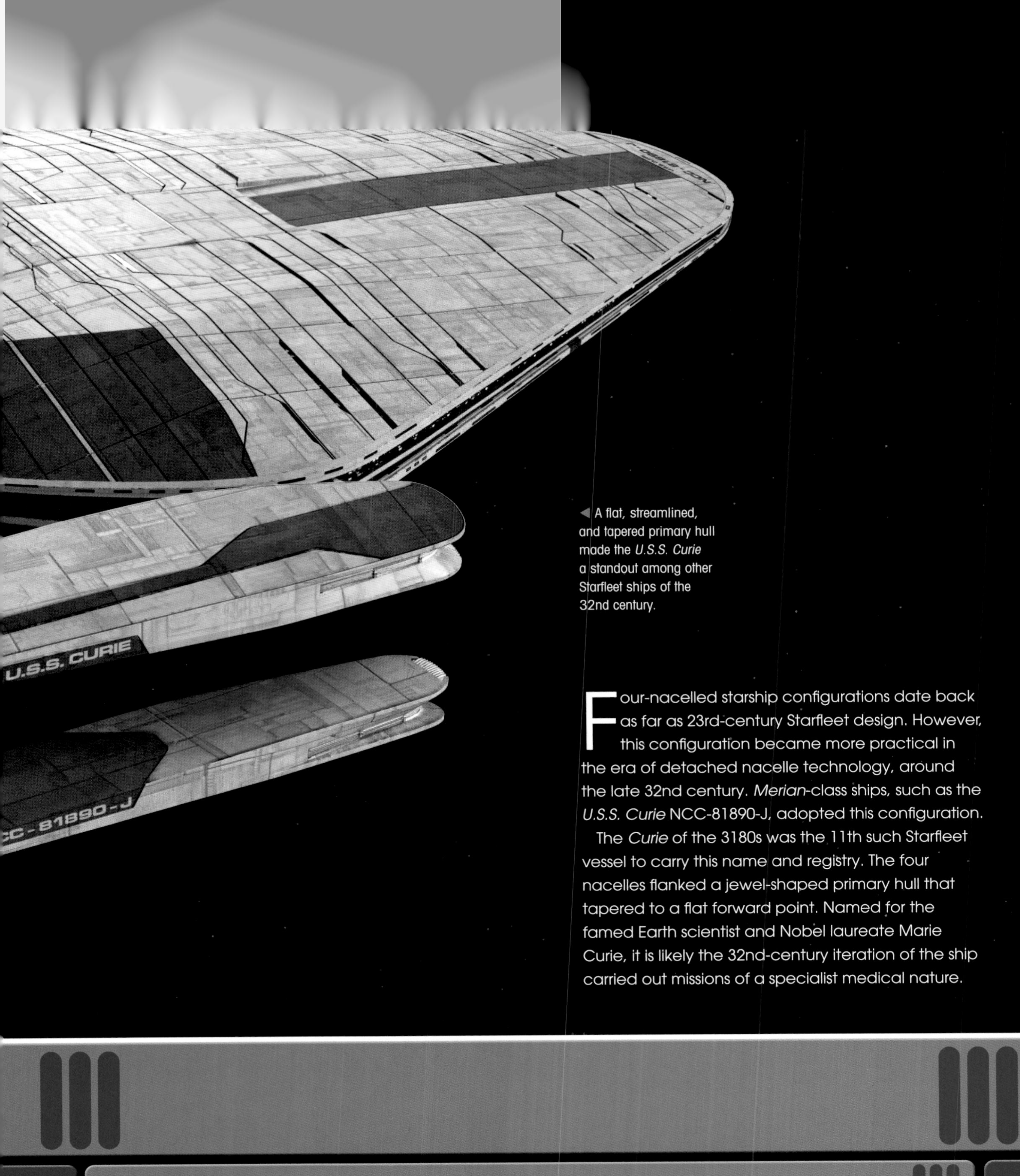

◀ A flat, streamlined, and tapered primary hull made the *U.S.S. Curie* a standout among other Starfleet ships of the 32nd century.

Four-nacelled starship configurations date back as far as 23rd-century Starfleet design. However, this configuration became more practical in the era of detached nacelle technology, around the late 32nd century. *Merian*-class ships, such as the *U.S.S. Curie* NCC-81890-J, adopted this configuration.

The *Curie* of the 3180s was the 11th such Starfleet vessel to carry this name and registry. The four nacelles flanked a jewel-shaped primary hull that tapered to a flat forward point. Named for the famed Earth scientist and Nobel laureate Marie Curie, it is likely the 32nd-century iteration of the ship carried out missions of a specialist medical nature.

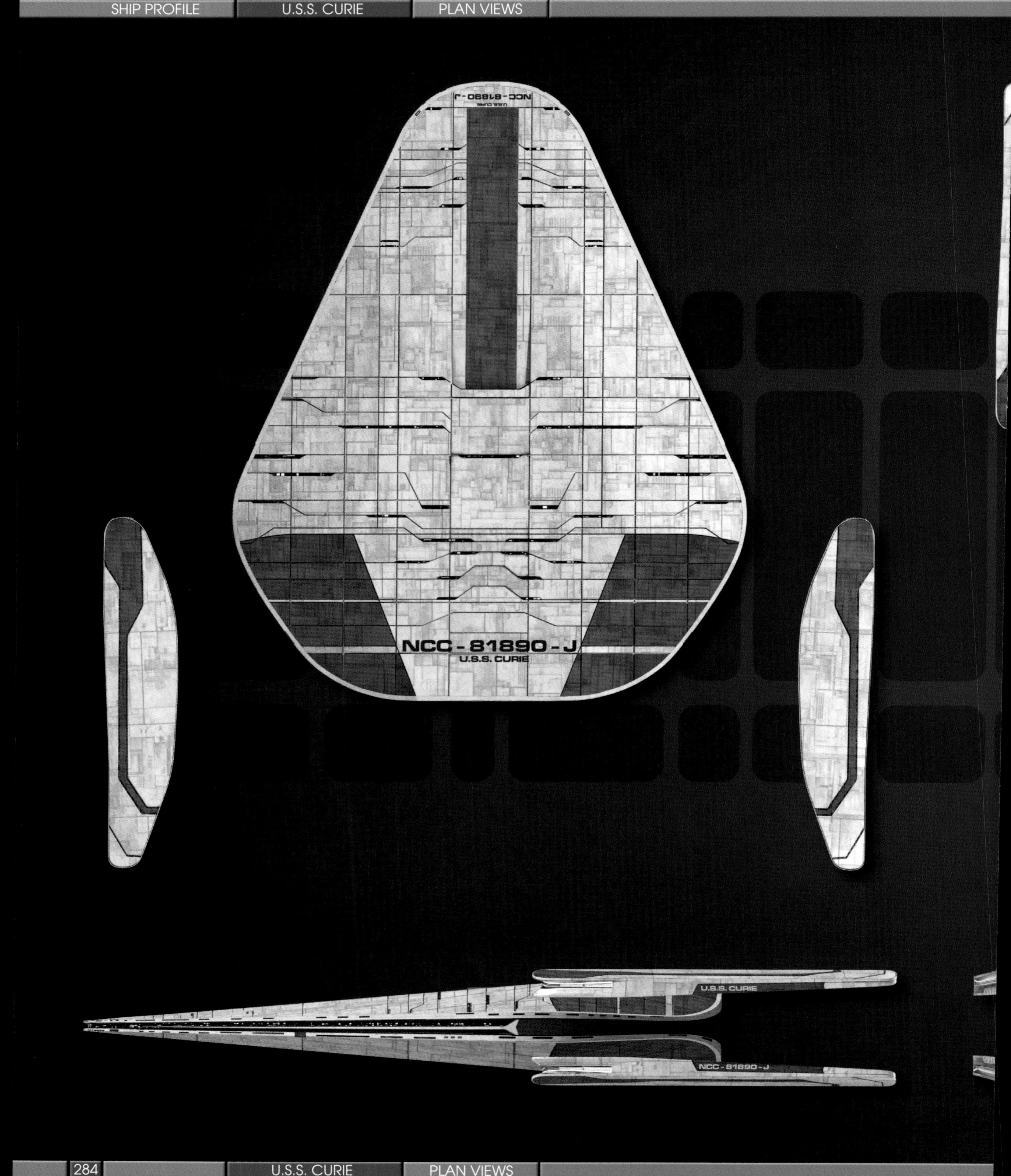
NCC-81890-J
U.S.S. CURIE
U.S.S. CURIE
NCC-81890-J

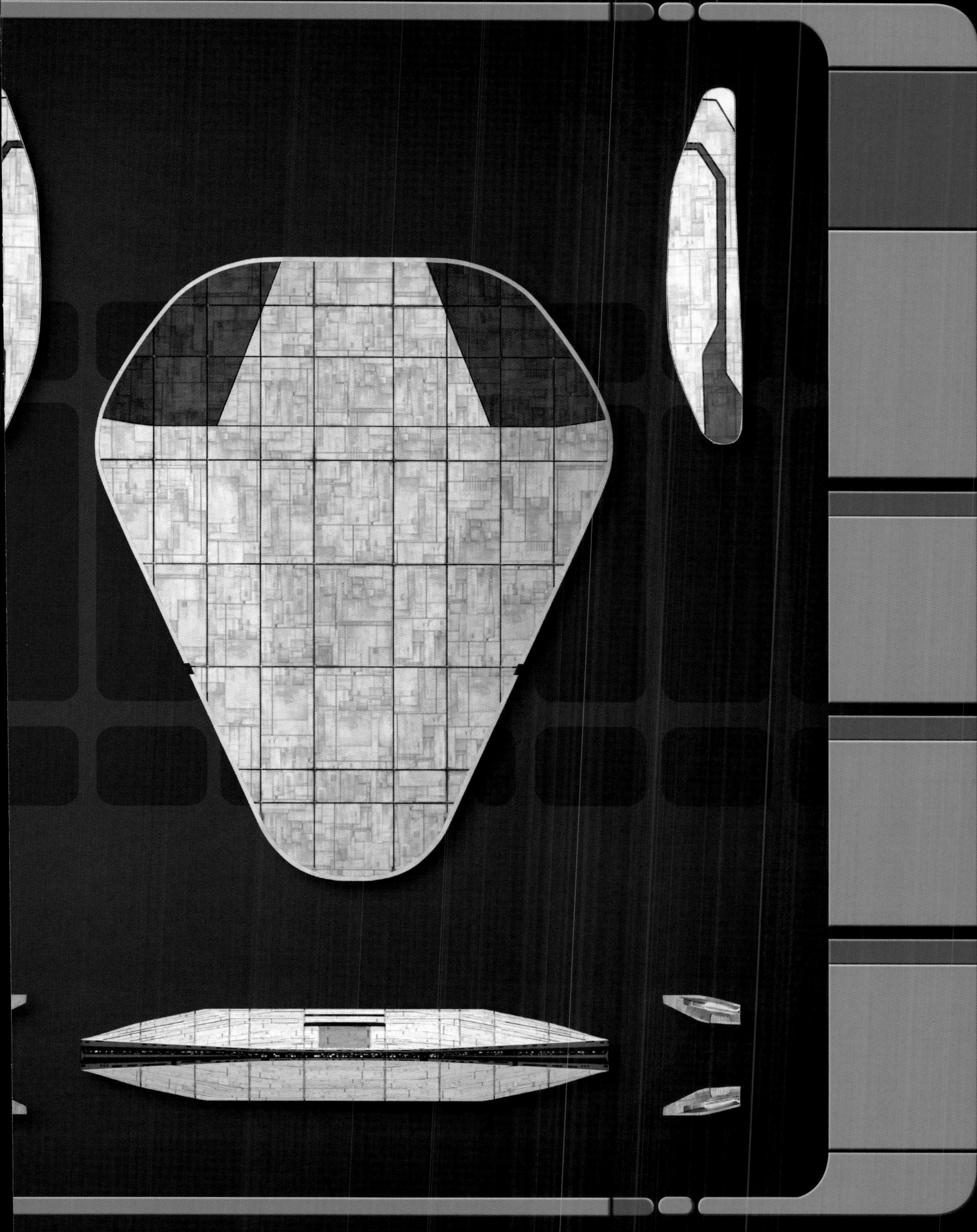

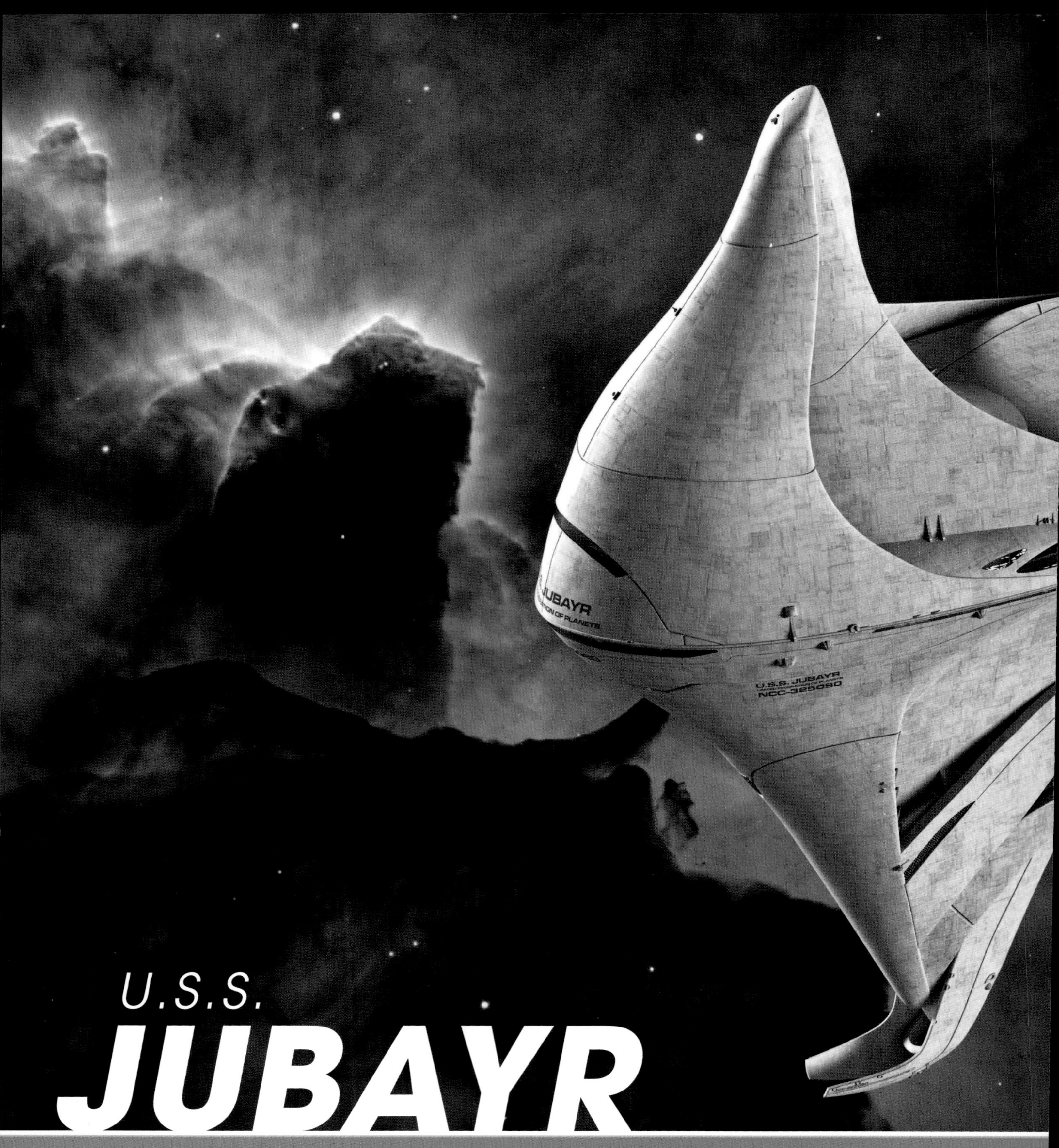

U.S.S. JUBAYR

In contrast to other 32nd-century designs, *U.S.S. Jubayr* referenced earlier, more traditional styling.

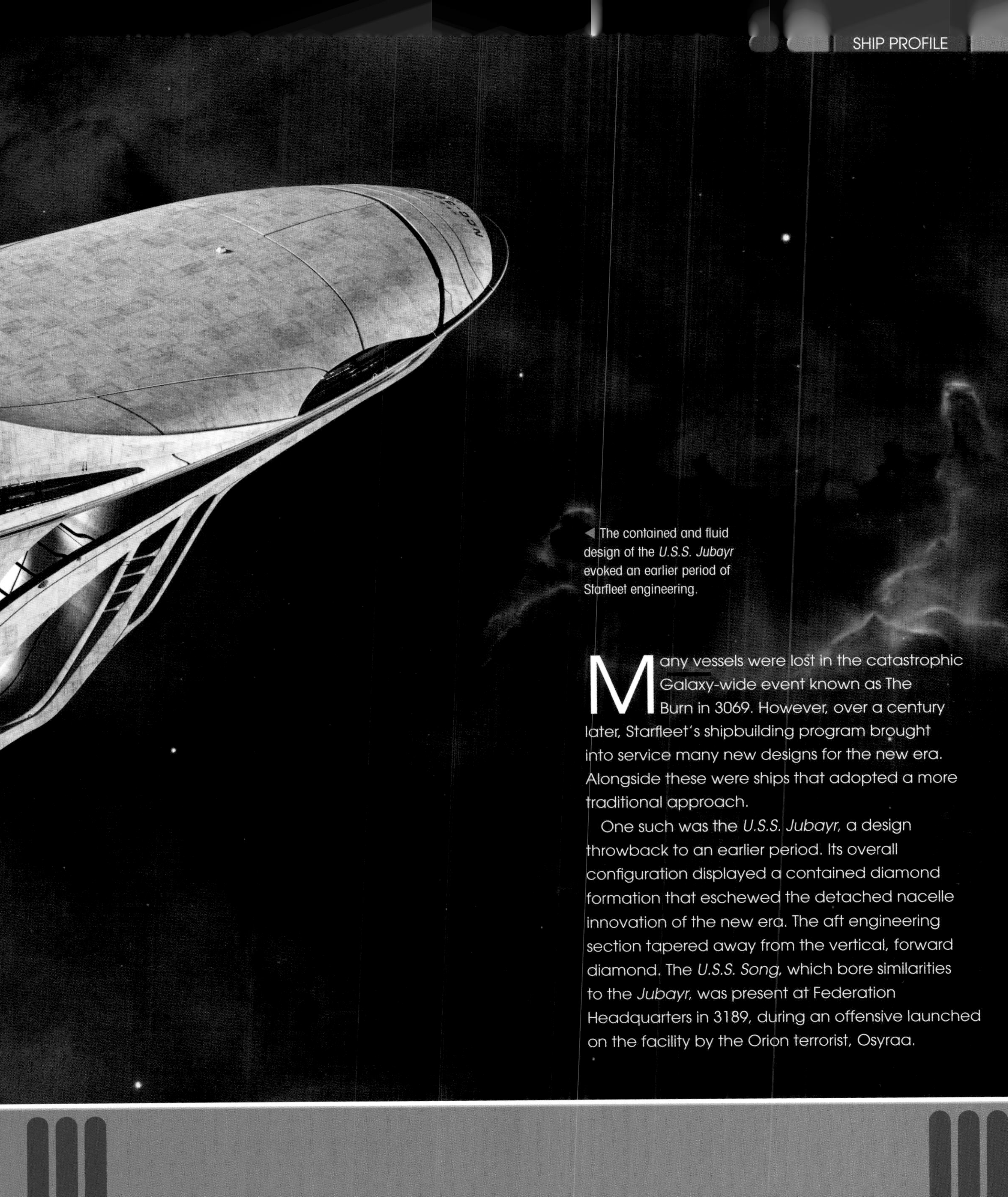

◀ The contained and fluid design of the *U.S.S. Jubayr* evoked an earlier period of Starfleet engineering.

Many vessels were lost in the catastrophic Galaxy-wide event known as The Burn in 3069. However, over a century later, Starfleet's shipbuilding program brought into service many new designs for the new era. Alongside these were ships that adopted a more traditional approach.

One such was the *U.S.S. Jubayr,* a design throwback to an earlier period. Its overall configuration displayed a contained diamond formation that eschewed the detached nacelle innovation of the new era. The aft engineering section tapered away from the vertical, forward diamond. The *U.S.S. Song,* which bore similarities to the *Jubayr,* was present at Federation Headquarters in 3189, during an offensive launched on the facility by the Orion terrorist, Osyraa.

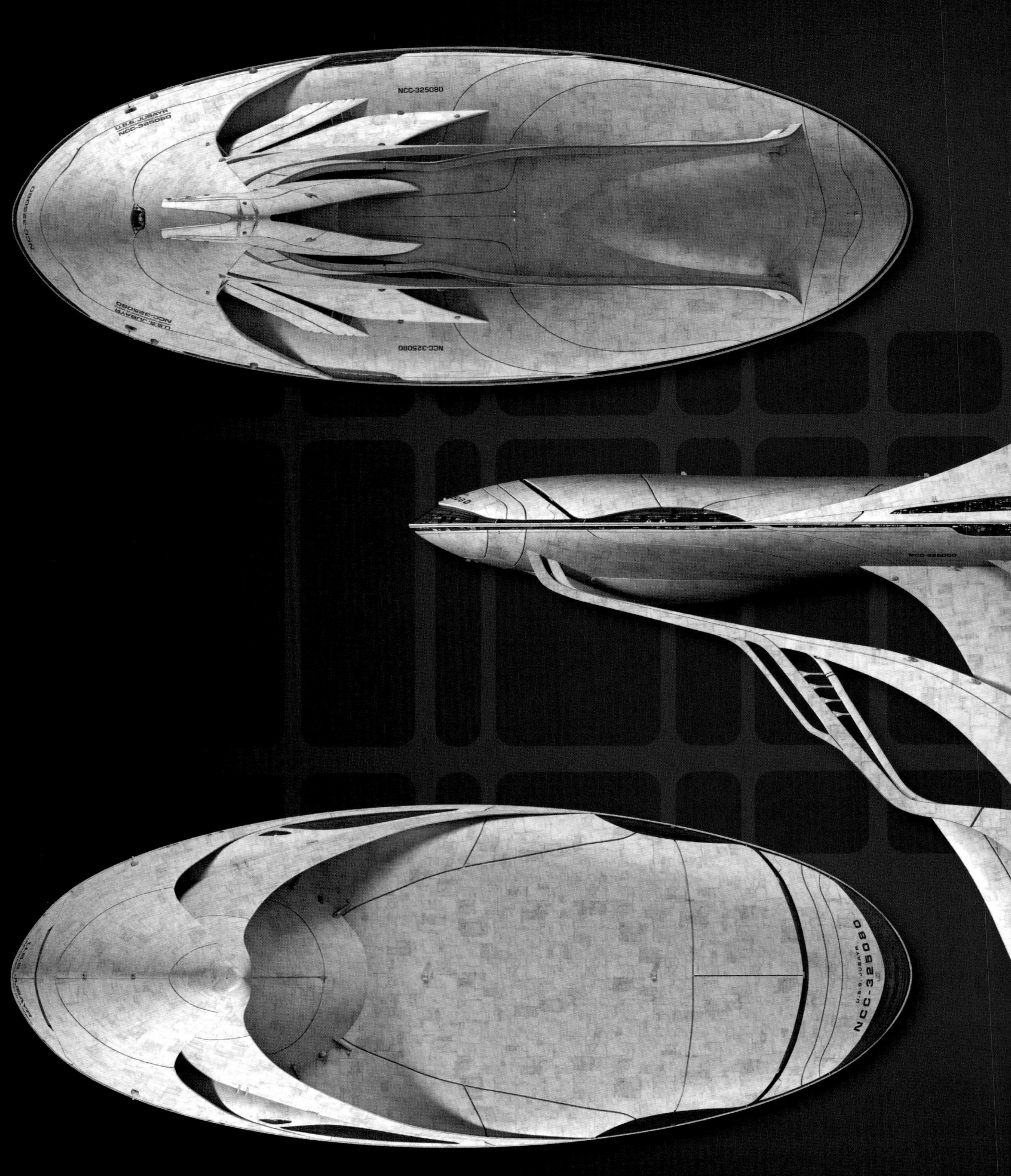
NCC-325080
U.S.S. JUBAYR
NCC-325080
NCC-325080
U.S.S. JUBAYR
NCC-325080
NCC-325080
NCC-325080
U.S.S. JUBAYR
NCC-325080

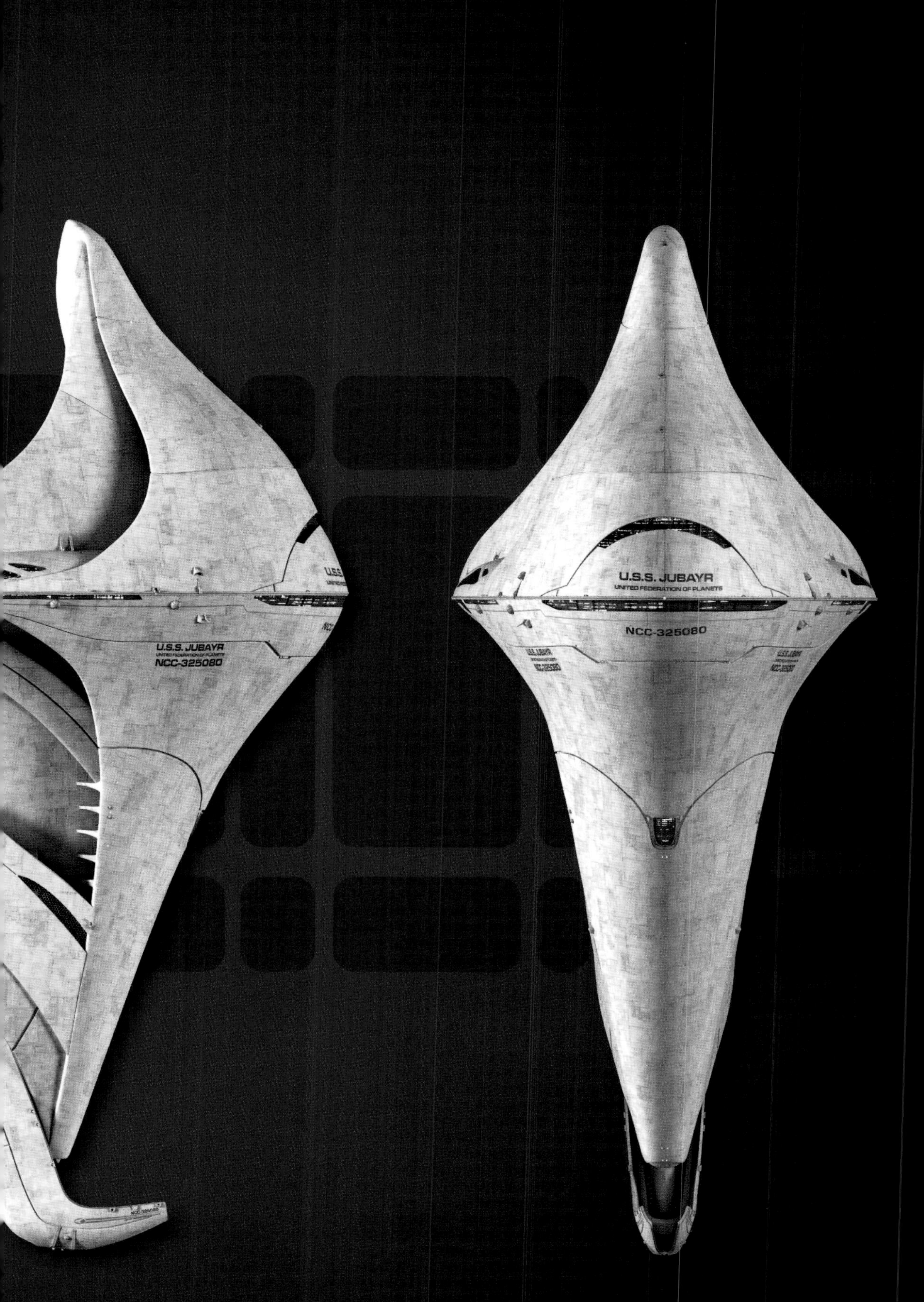
U.S.S. JUBAYR
UNITED FEDERATION OF PLANETS
NCC-325080
U.S.S. JUBAYR
UNITED FEDERATION OF PLANETS
NCC-325080

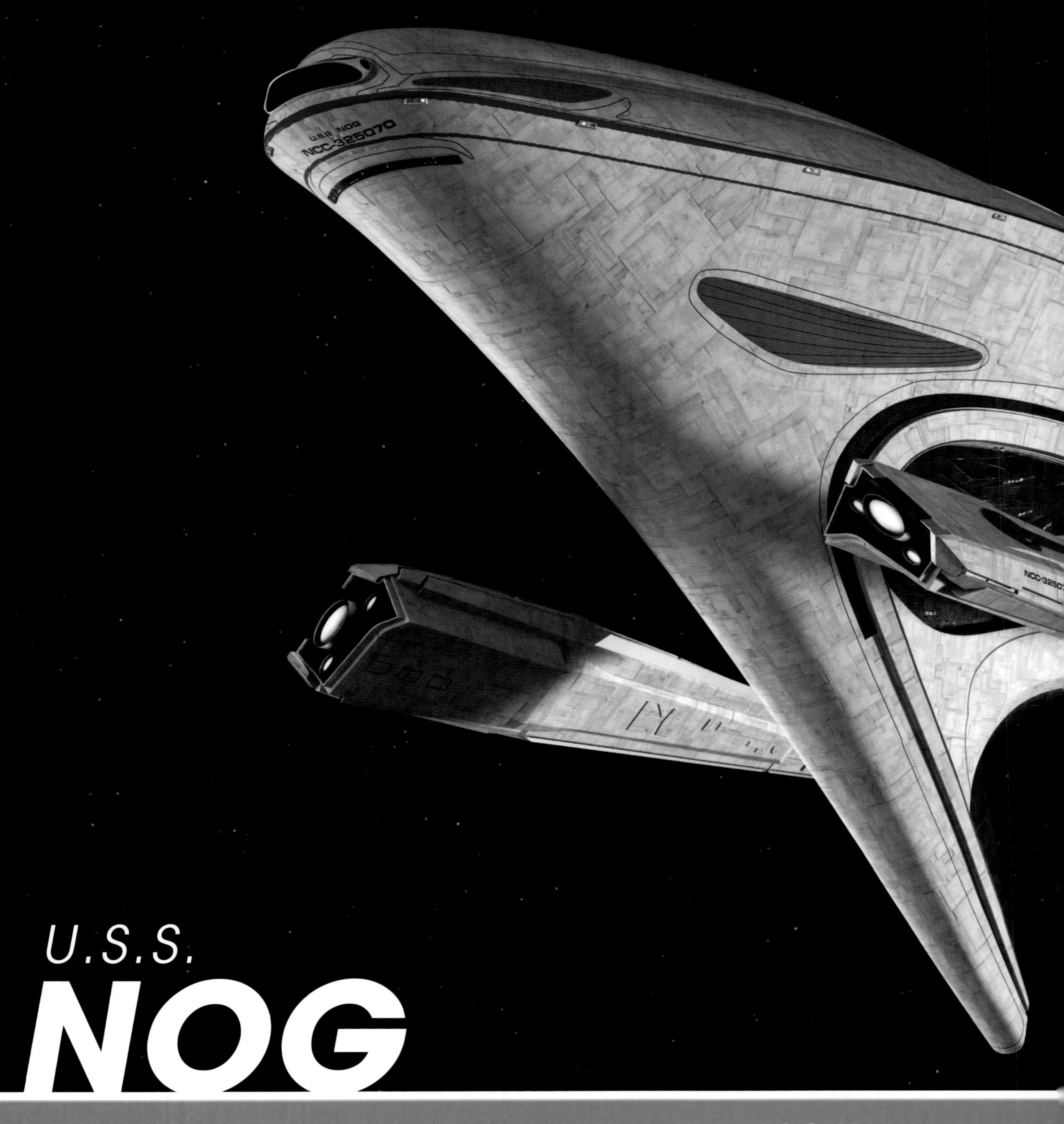

U.S.S. NOG

Named for a 24th-century Ferengi officer, the *U.S.S. Nog* took that Starfleet legend's name into the 32nd century.

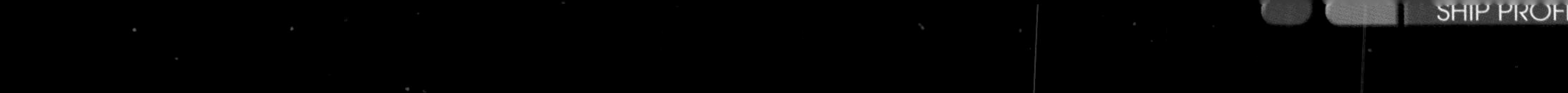

◀ The hallmark of the *Eisenberg* class was its upright, aerodynamic configuration.

The *U.S.S. Nog* NCC-325070 was an *Eisenberg*-class ship in service with Starfleet in the post-Burn era of the late 32nd century. The vessel was named to honor the first Ferengi officer to serve in Starfleet, in the 24th century.

The *Nog*'s configuration may have marked it out as a science vessel, its bulbous primary hull ranged above a tapered stem across several decks. A stabilizing secondary hull tapered below and aft of the primary hull, with detached warp nacelles located to port and starboard.

The *U.S.S. Nog* was docked at Federation Headquarters during the arrival of the *U.S.S. Discovery* in 3189.

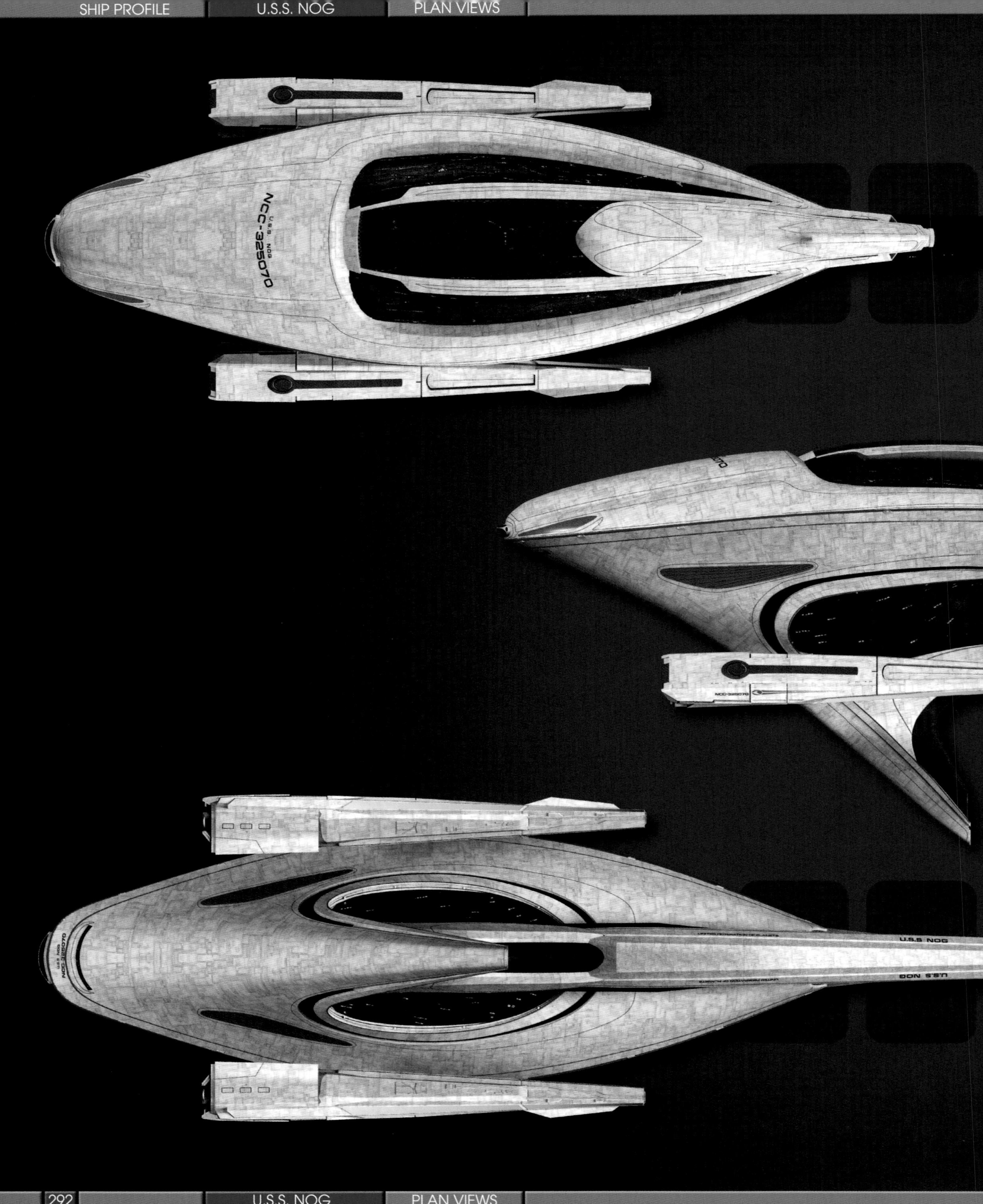
U.S.S. NOG
NCC-325070
U.S.S NOG
U.S.S NOG

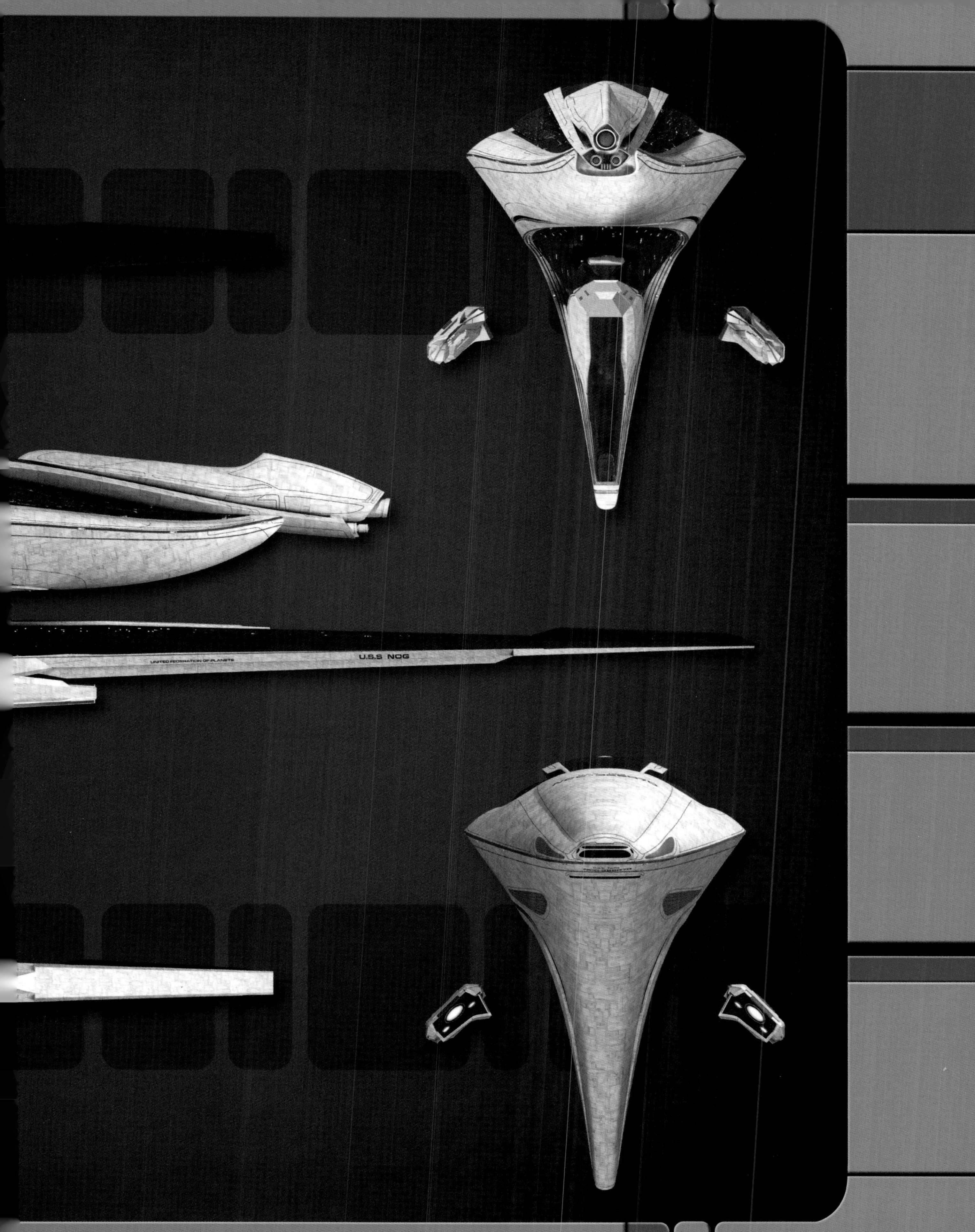
UNITED FEDERATION OF PLANETS
U.S.S NOG

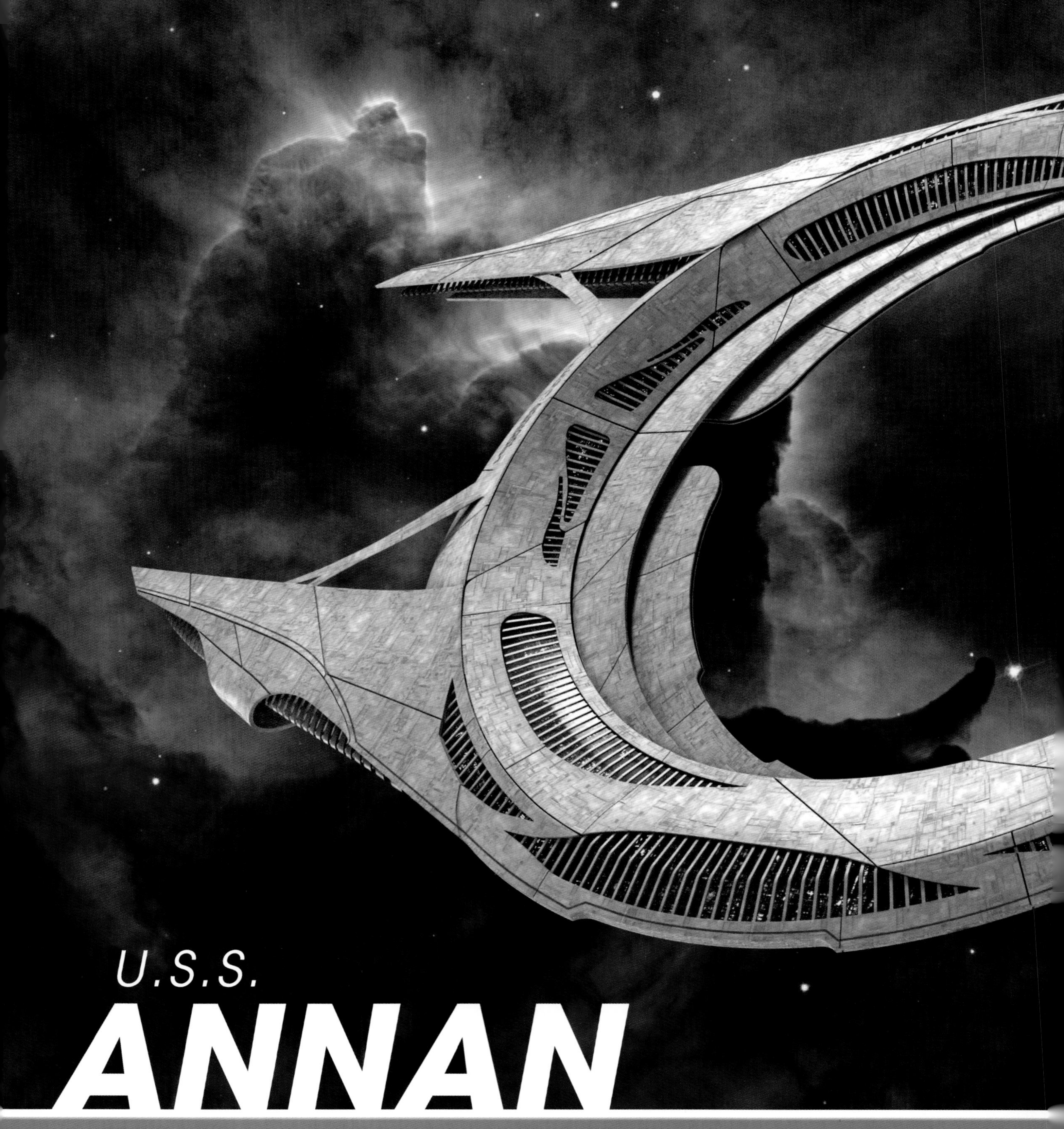

U.S.S. ANNAN

The *Annan* was one of the first 32nd-century Starfleet ships seen by *Discovery*'s crew at Federation HQ.

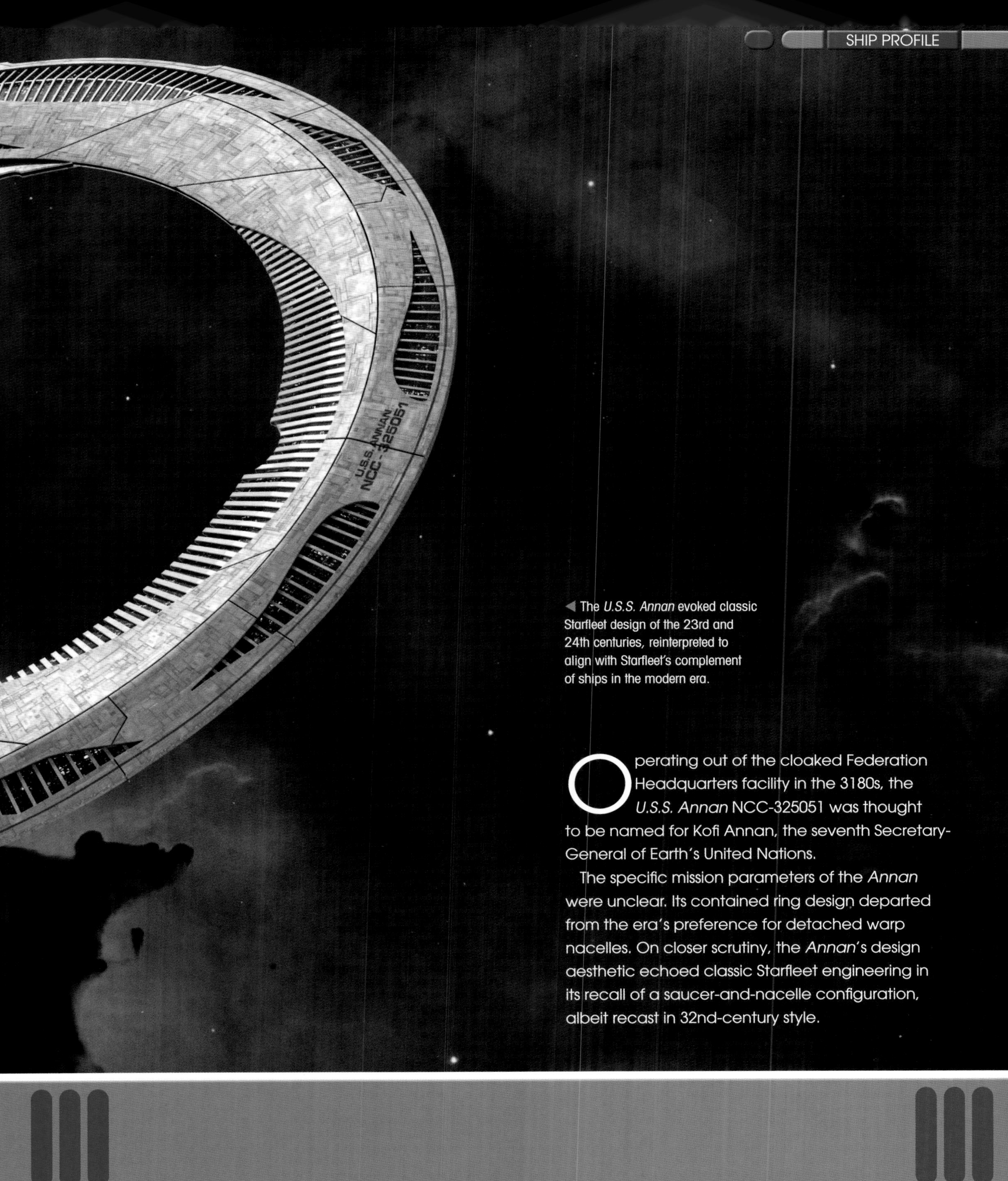

◀ The *U.S.S. Annan* evoked classic Starfleet design of the 23rd and 24th centuries, reinterpreted to align with Starfleet's complement of ships in the modern era.

Operating out of the cloaked Federation Headquarters facility in the 3180s, the *U.S.S. Annan* NCC-325051 was thought to be named for Kofi Annan, the seventh Secretary-General of Earth's United Nations.

The specific mission parameters of the *Annan* were unclear. Its contained ring design departed from the era's preference for detached warp nacelles. On closer scrutiny, the *Annan*'s design aesthetic echoed classic Starfleet engineering in its recall of a saucer-and-nacelle configuration, albeit recast in 32nd-century style.

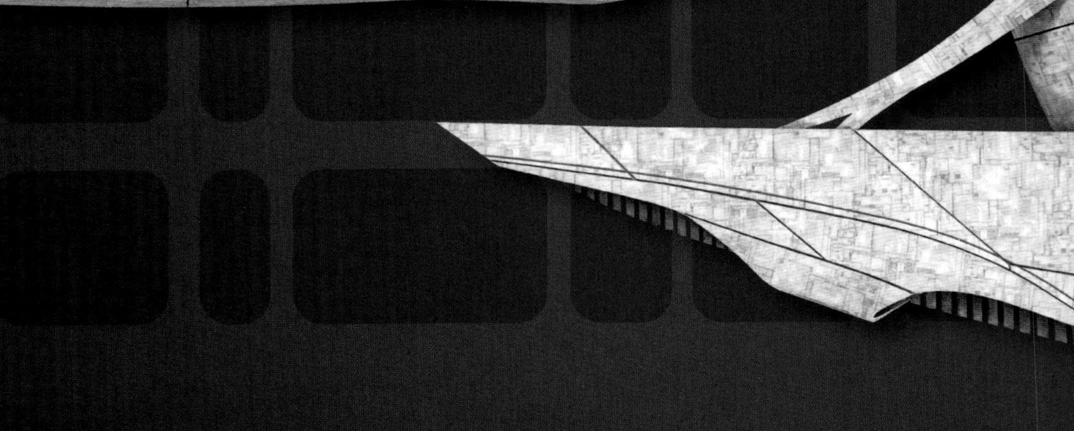
U.S.S. ANNAN
NCC - 325051

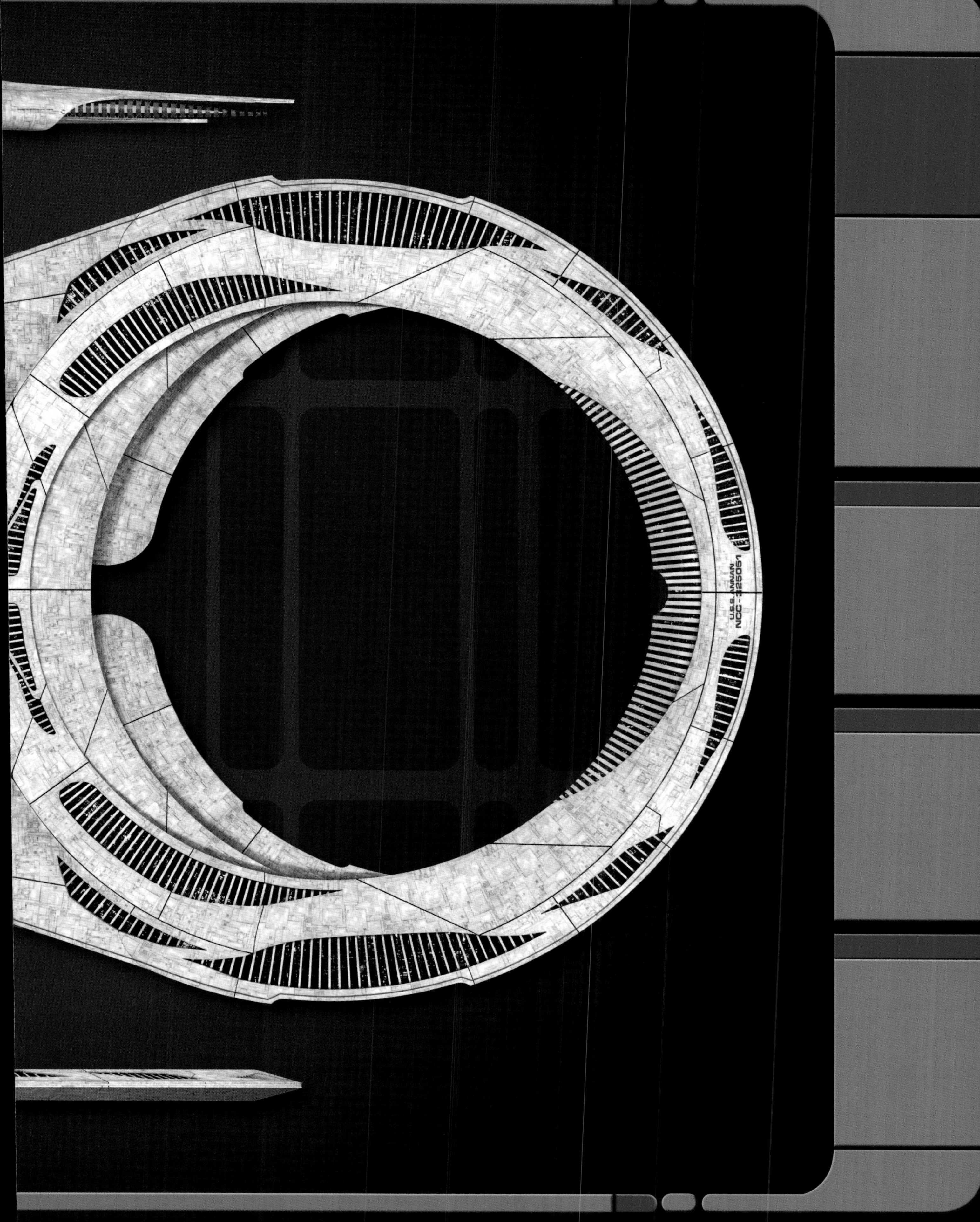
U.S.S. ANNAN
NCC-325051

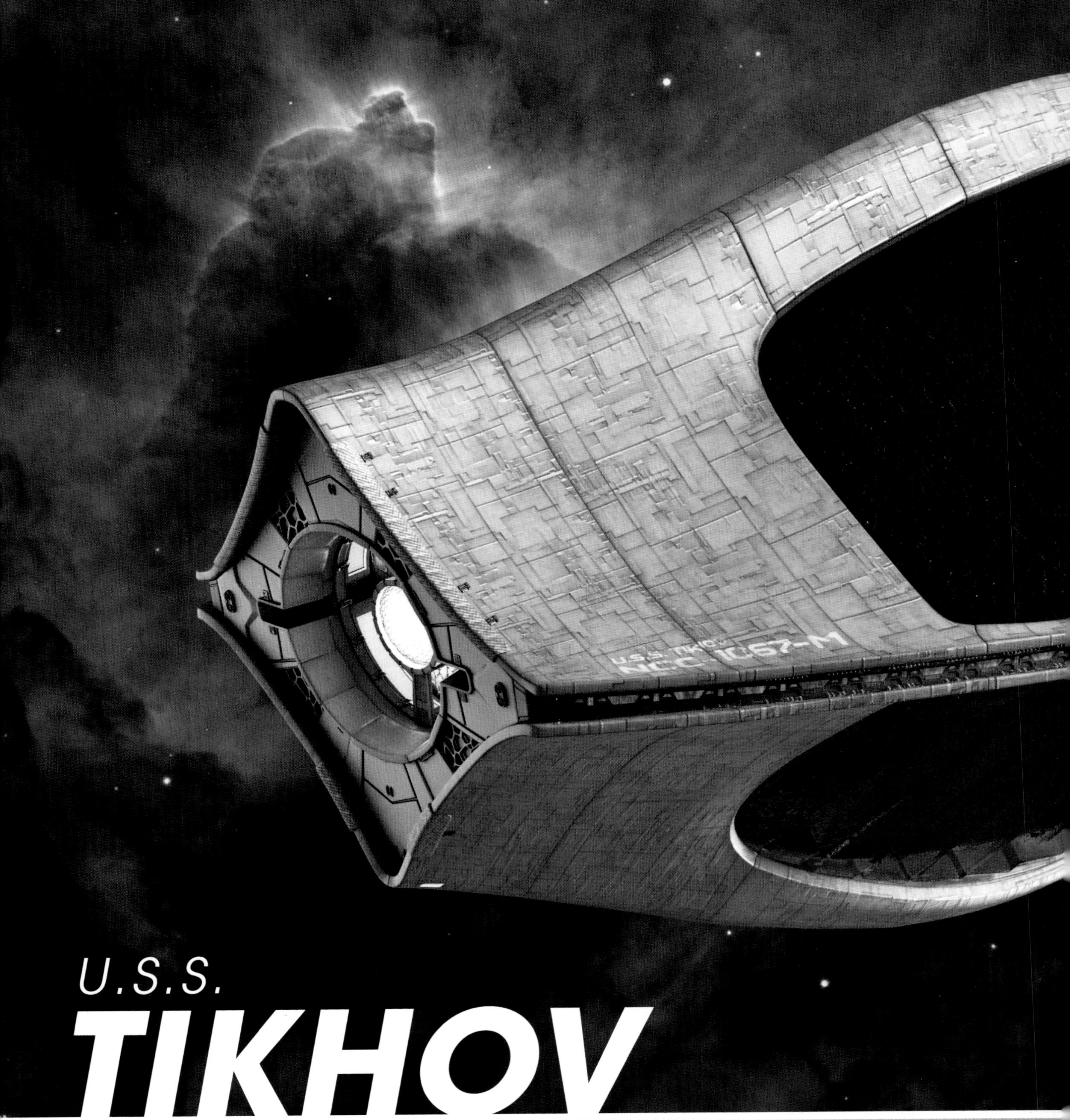

U.S.S. TIKHOV

The *U.S.S. Tikhov* continued the 23rd-century tradition of maintaining a centralized Federation seed vault ship.

◀ The *U.S.S. Tikhov* displayed a small, compact design, with a pleasing aesthetic reflecting its benign and vital role as a seed bank.

The *Tikhov*'s name dated back to the 23rd century when a *U.S.S. Tikhov* served as a seed vault vessel, holding a sample of every plant in the Galaxy. With the registry designation M, it was likely that the *Tikhov*'s 32nd-century iteration was part of the same lineage.

Since the 27th century, Federation worlds had rotated responsibility for stewardship of the *Tikhov* and its seed vault. The ship itself was not unlike a seed in outline, its primary hull taking in sweeping curves, flanked by small, detached warp nacelles.

In 3189, the *Tikhov* held the key to saving Kili refugees who had ingested mutated plants found on Urna. The *U.S.S. Discovery* was assigned the mission of locating the *Tikhov* to obtain uncontaminated samples. On arrival, the *Discovery* crew found the *Tikhov* stranded within an ion storm. Following its rescue from the ion storm, they found only one survivor of the family assigned to caretaking of the seed vault: the Barzan, Dr. Attis. After the required plant samples were successfully retrieved from the *Tikhov*, *Discovery*'s Barzan security officer, Commander Nhan, remained aboard to maintain watch over the seed vault on behalf of her world.

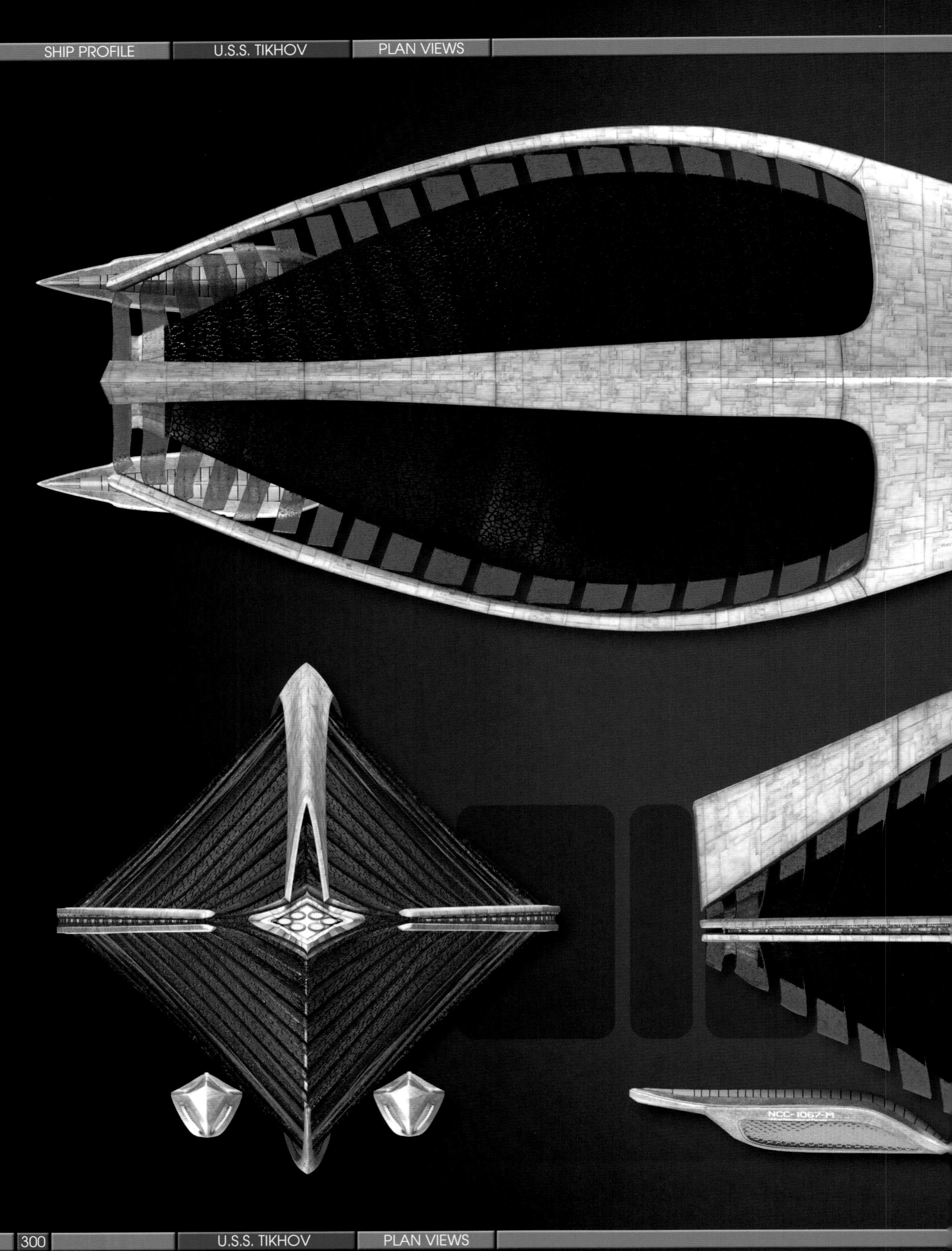
NCC-1067-M

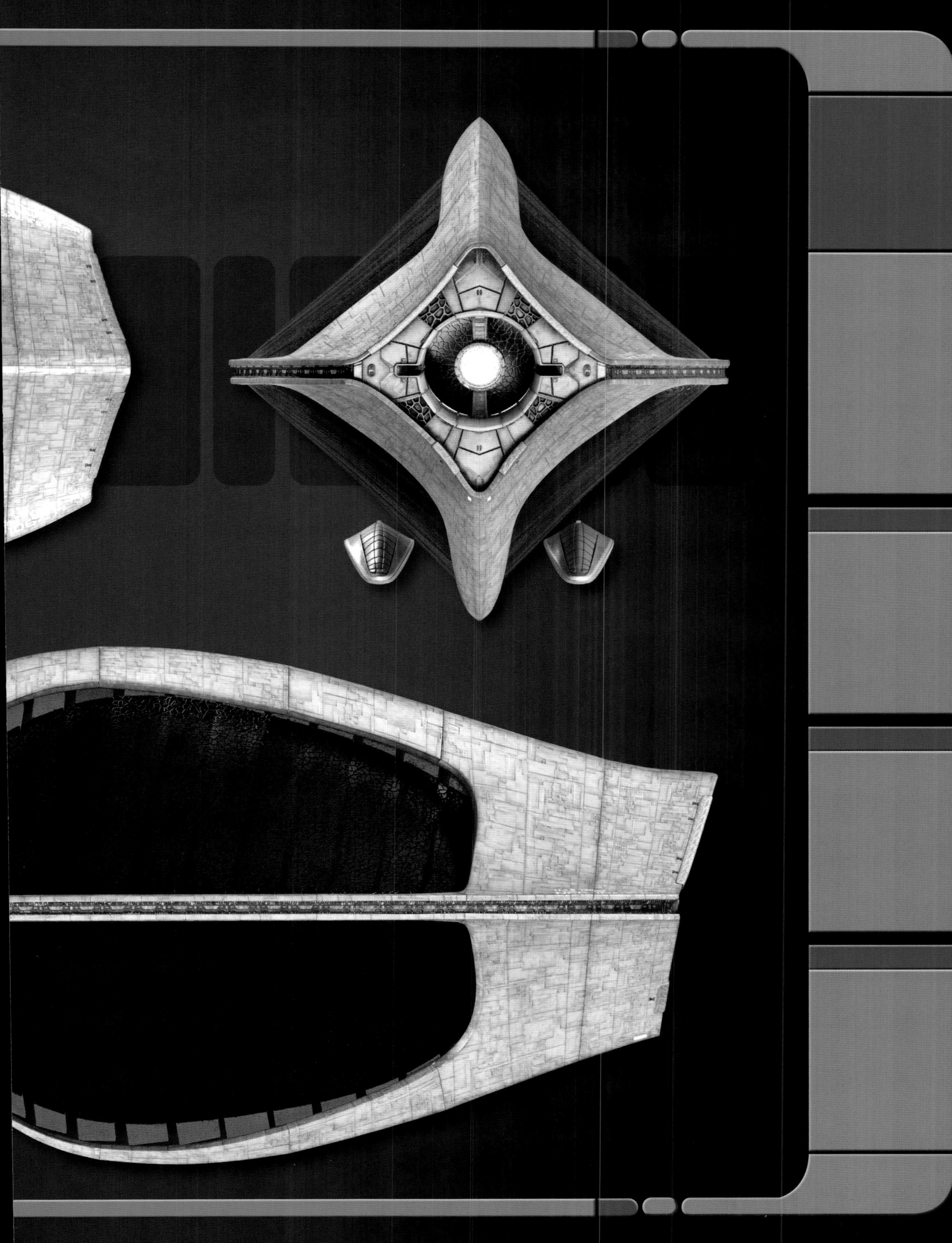

32ND CENTURY

SIZE CHART

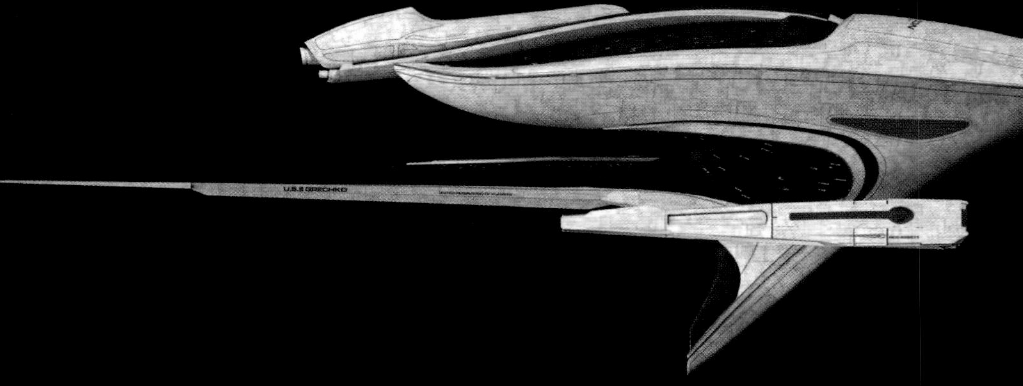

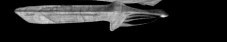

U.S.S. LIU CIXIN NCC-325060

415.4m

U.S.S. NOG NCC-325070

1212.1m

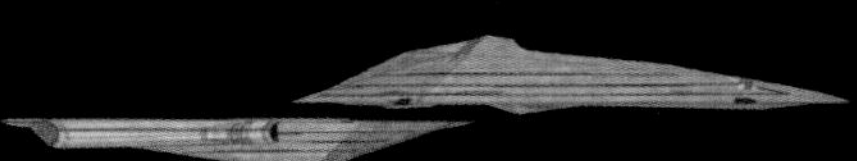

U.S.S. VOYAGER-J NCC-74656

452.95m

U.S.S. THANT NCC-325005

1188.72m

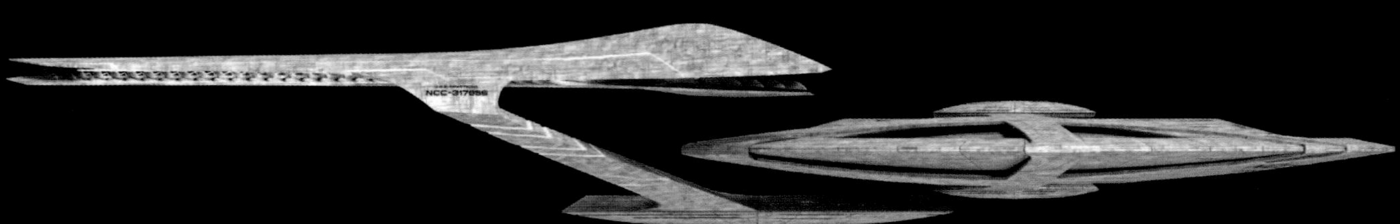

U.S.S. ARMSTRONG NCC-317856

1399.82m

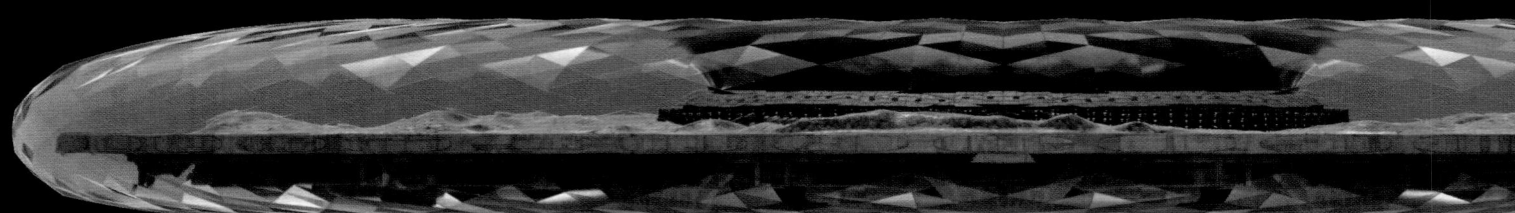

U.S.S. MAATHAI NCC-325023

2109.43m

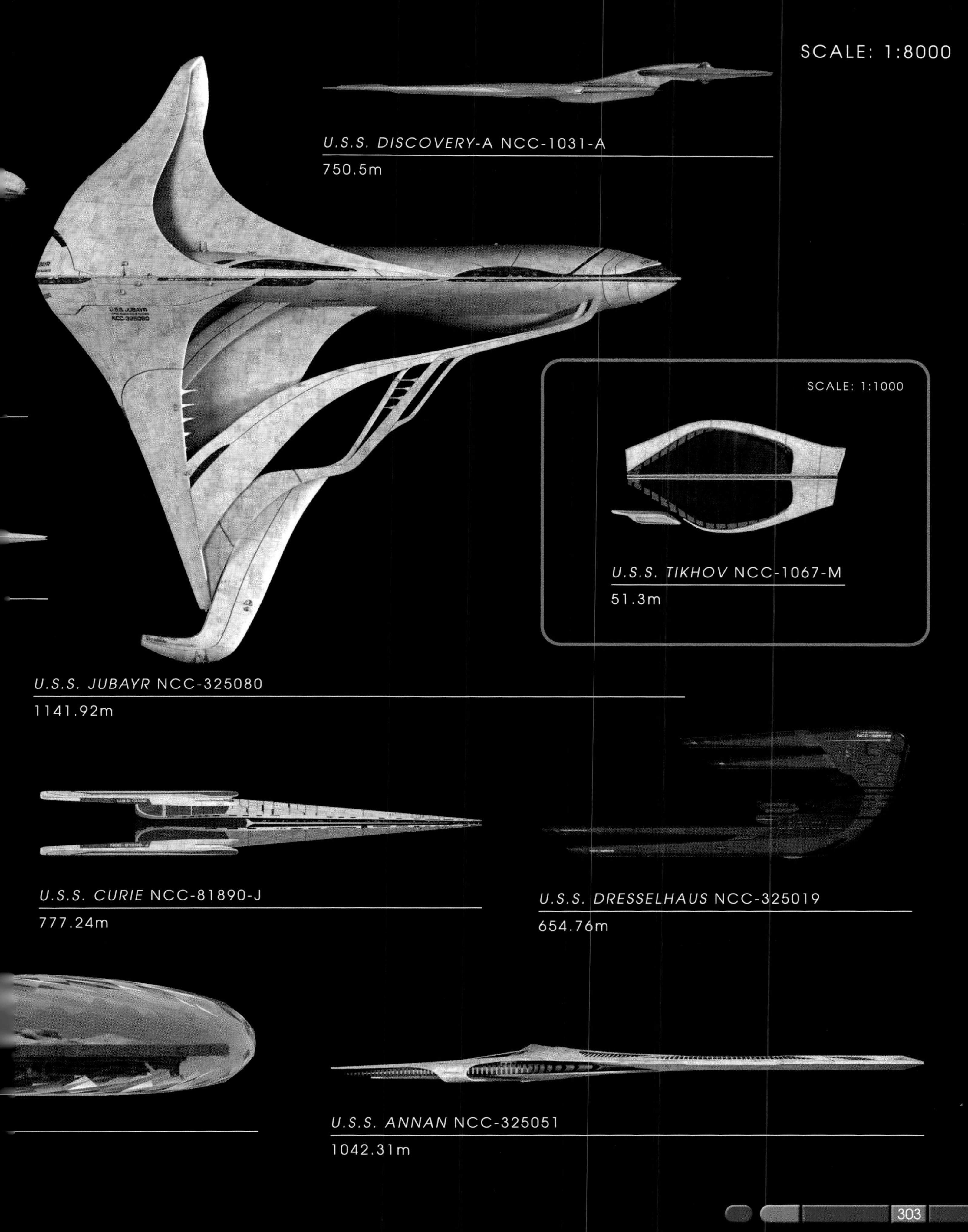

SCALE: 1:8000
U.S.S. DISCOVERY-A NCC-1031-A
750.5m
SCALE: 1:1000
U.S.S. TIKHOV NCC-1067-M
51.3m
U.S.S. JUBAYR NCC-325080
1141.92m
U.S.S. CURIE NCC-81890-J
777.24m
U.S.S. DRESSELHAUS NCC-325019
654.76m
U.S.S. ANNAN NCC-325051
1042.31m

CLASS LISTING

Raven type

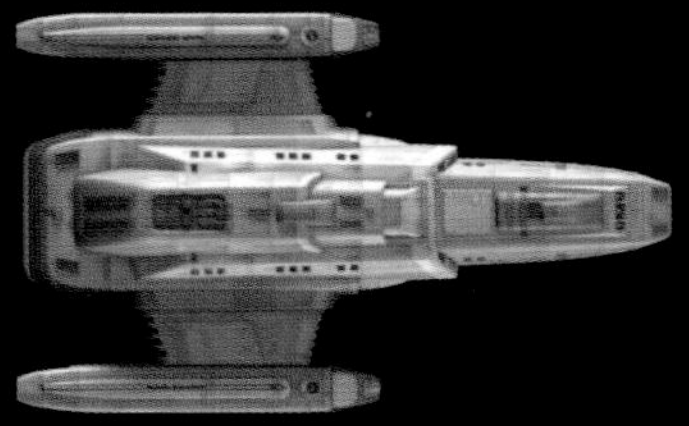

Danube class

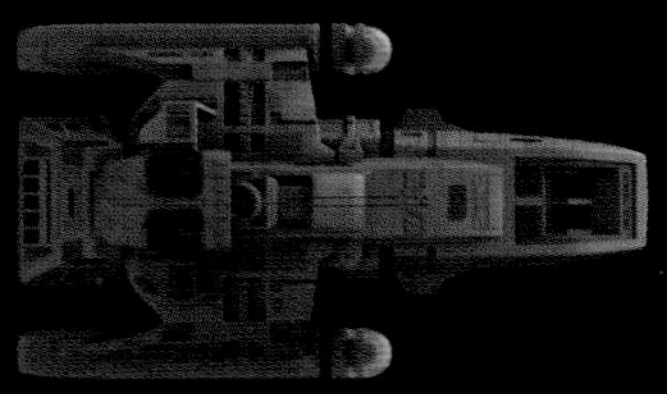

Other:
U.S.S. Gander NCC-72311
U.S.S. Ganges NCC-72454
U.S.S. Mekong NCC-72617
U.S.S. Orinoco NCC-72905
U.S.S. Rio Grande NCC-72452
U.S.S. Rubicon NCC-72936
U.S.S. Shenandoah NCC-73024
U.S.S. Volga NCC-73196
U.S.S. Yangtzee Kiang NCC-72453
U.S.S. Yukon NCC-74602

Delta Flyer type

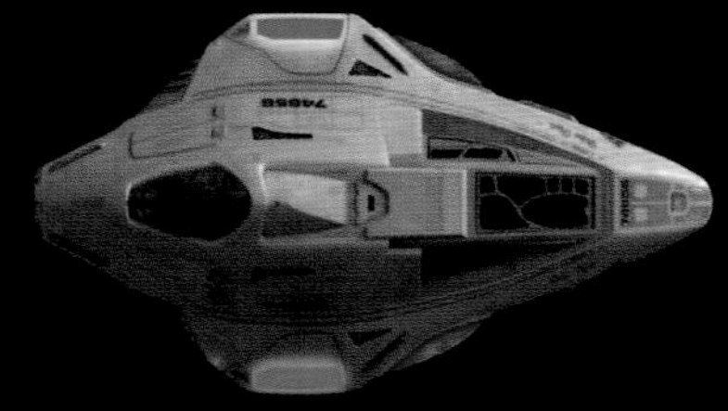

Other: *Delta Flyer* II

Constellation class

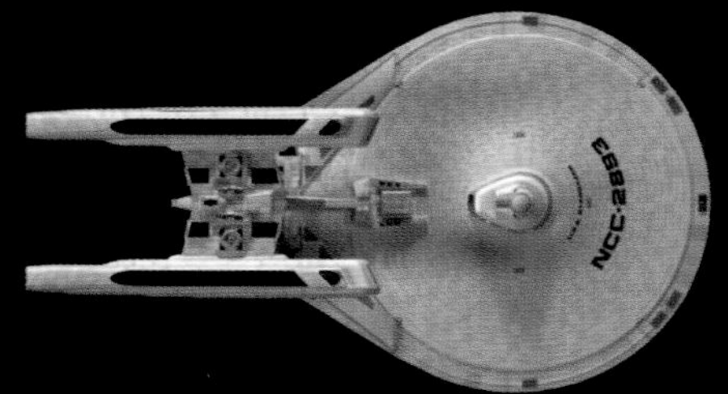

Other:
U.S.S. Constellation NX-1974
U.S.S. Hathaway NCC-2593
U.S.S. Victory NCC-9754

Ambassador class

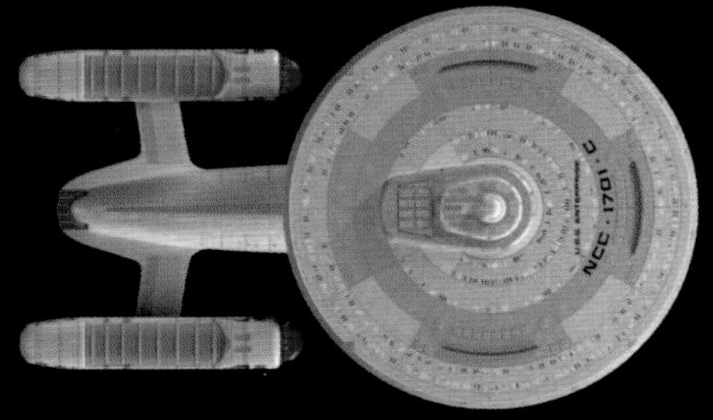

Other:
U.S.S. Excalibur NCC-26517
U.S.S. Horatio NCC-10532
U.S.S. Yamaguchi NCC-26510
U.S.S. Zhukov NCC-26136

Nebula class

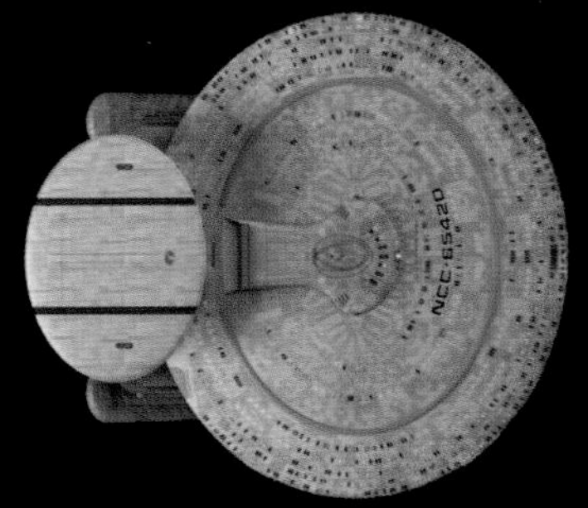

Other:
U.S.S. Bellerophon NCC-62048
U.S.S. Bonchune NCC-70915
U.S.S. Farragut NCC-60597
U.S.S. Honshu NCC-60205
U.S.S. Leeds NCC-70352
U.S.S. Lexington NCC-30405
U.S.S. Merrimac NCC-61827
U.S.S. Monitor NCC-61826
U.S.S. Prometheus NCC-71201
U.S.S. Sutherland NCC-72015
U.S.S. T'Kumbra NCC-62100

Galaxy class

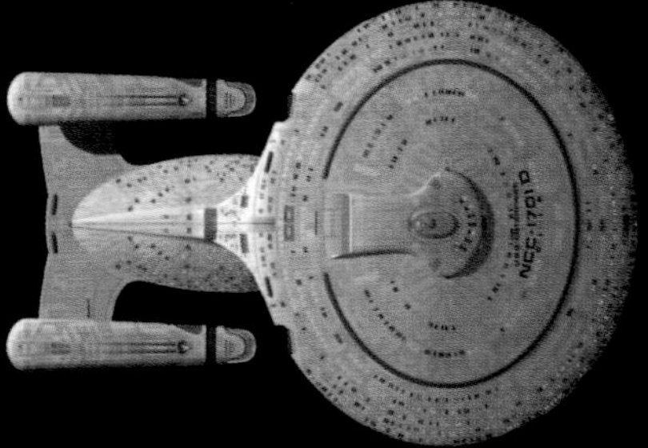

Other:
U.S.S. Challenger NCC-71099
U.S.S. Galaxy NCC-70637
U.S.S. Odyssey NCC-71832
U.S.S. Venture NCC-71854
U.S.S. Yamato NCC-71807

Miranda class

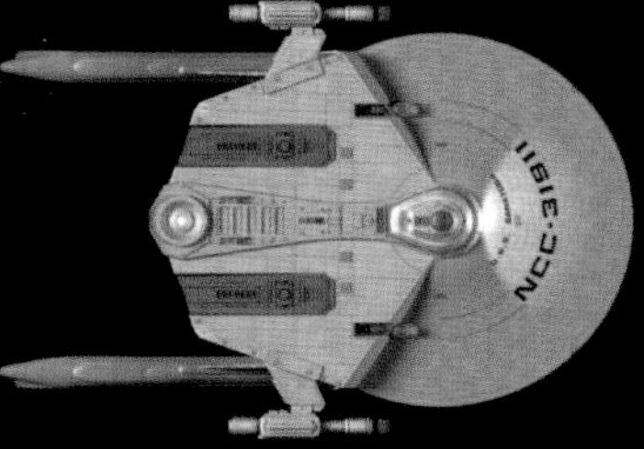

U.S.S. Saratoga NCC-31911 page 96

Other:

U.S.S. Antares NCC-9844
U.S.S. Brattain NCC-21166
U.S.S. Lantree NCC-1837
U.S.S. Majestic NCC-31060
U.S.S. Nautilus NCC-31910
U.S.S. Reliant NCC-1864
U.S.S. Saratoga NCC-1887
U.S.S. ShirKahr NCC-31905
U.S.S. Sitak NCC-32591
U.S.S. Tian An Men NCC-21382
U.S.S. Trial NCC-1948

Akira class

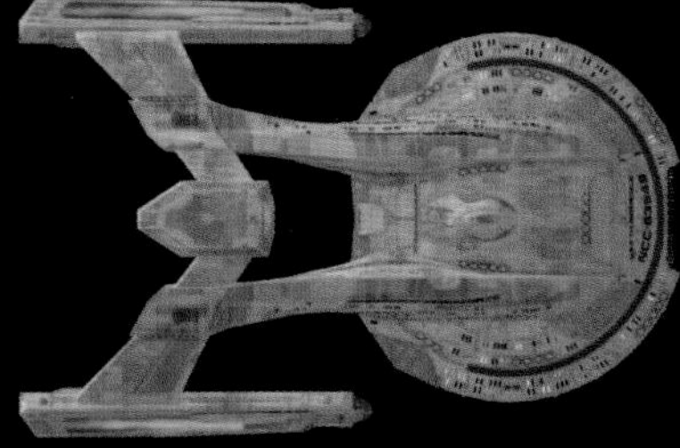

U.S.S. Thunderchild NCC-63549 page 102

Defiant class

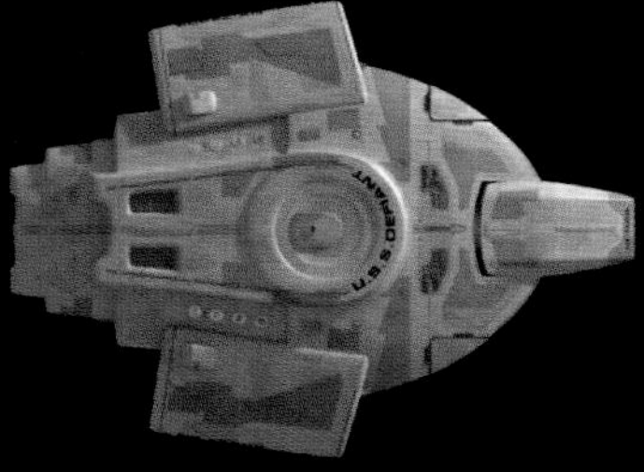

U.S.S. Defiant NX-74205 page 108

Other: *U.S.S. Valiant* NCC-74210

Cheyenne class

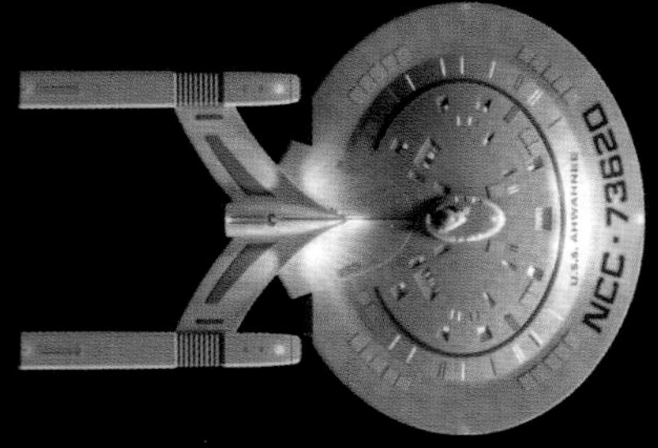

U.S.S. Ahwahnee NCC-71620 page 116

Springfield class

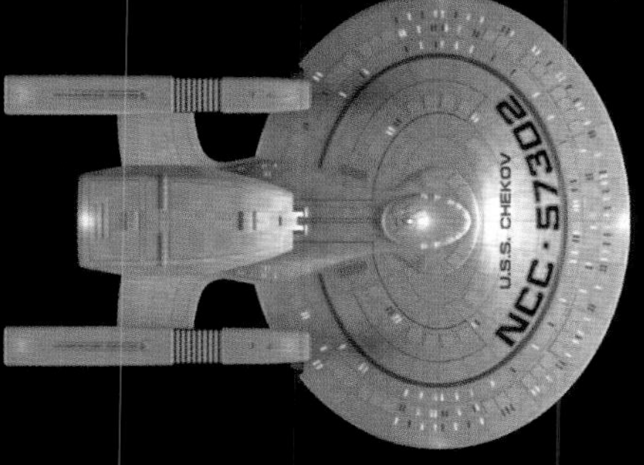

U.S.S. Chekov NCC-57302 page 120

Challenger class

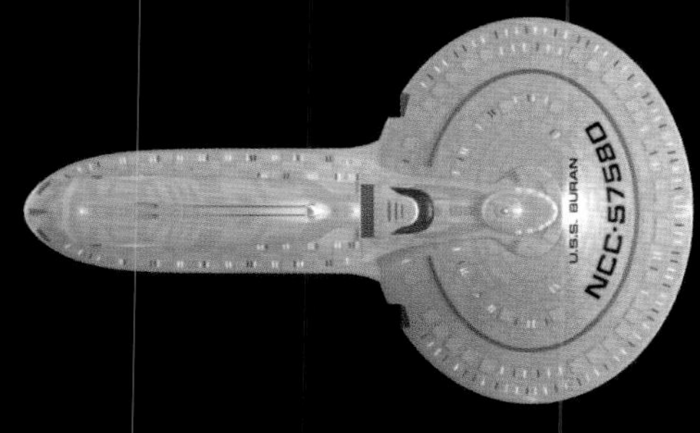

U.S.S. Buran NCC-57580 page 12

Freedom class

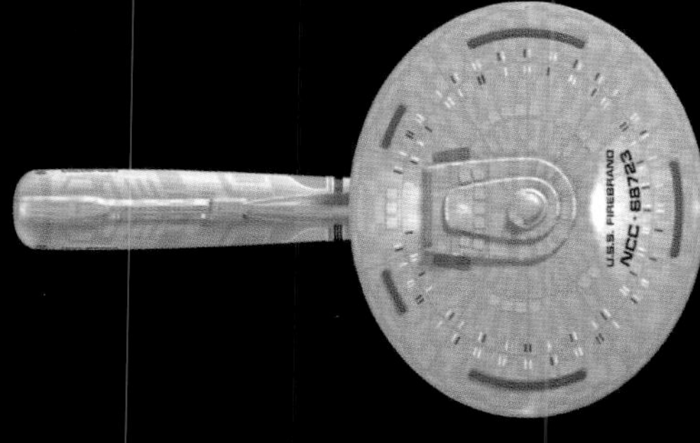

U.S.S. Firebrand NCC-68723 page 12

Other: *U.S.S. Franklin* NX-326

Niagara class

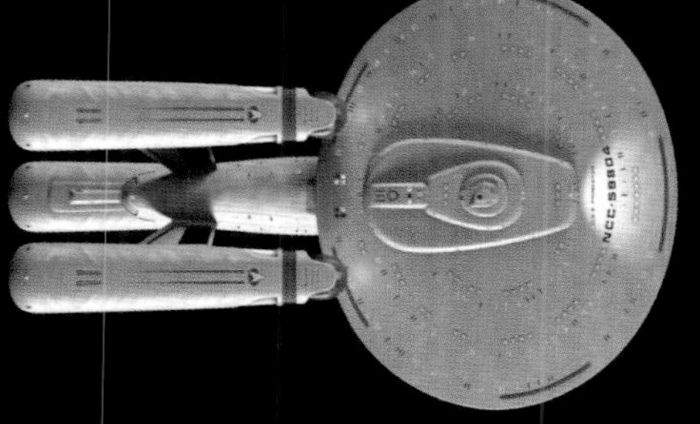

U.S.S. Princeton NCC-59804 page 13

Other: *U.S.S. Wellington* NCC-28473

New Orleans class

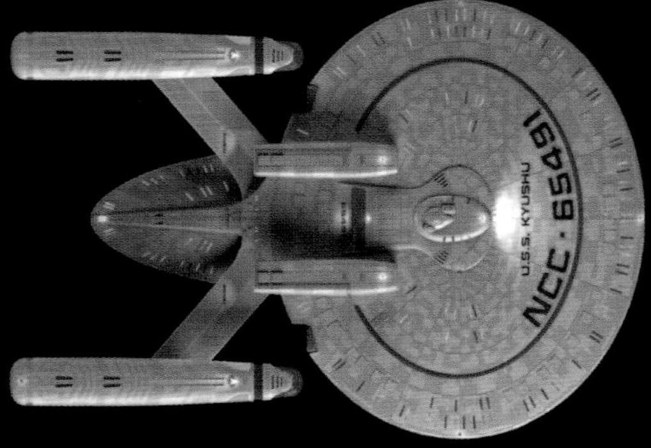

U.S.S. Kyushu NCC-65491 page 138

Other: *U.S.S. Thomas Paine* NCC-65530

Nova class

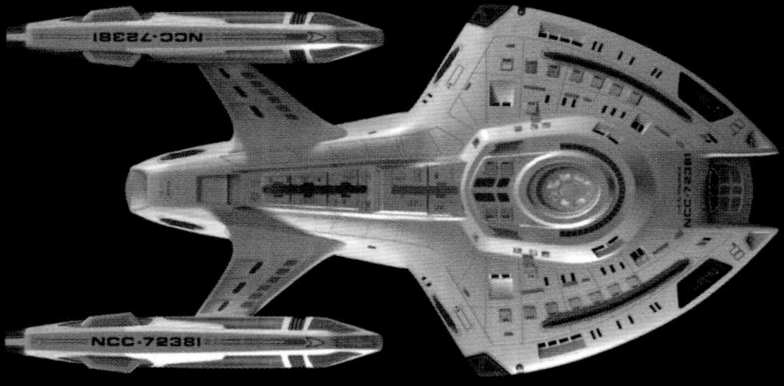

U.S.S. Equinox NCC-72381 page 144

Other: *U.S.S. Rhode Island* NCC-72701

Olympic class

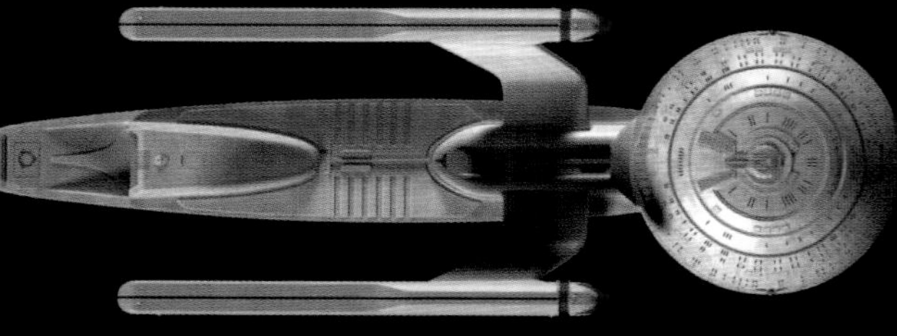

U.S.S. Pasteur NCC-58925 page 152

Intrepid class

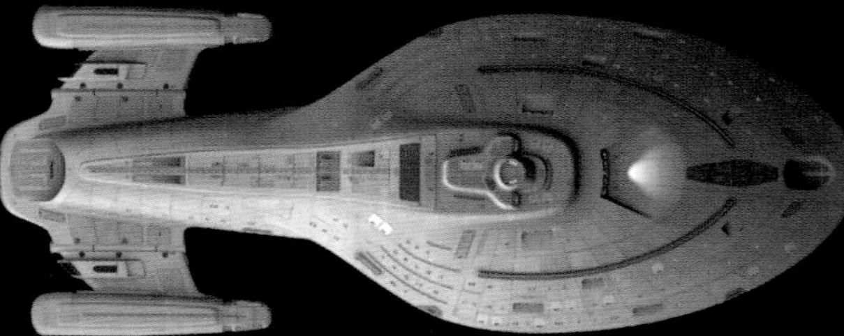

U.S.S. Voyager NCC-74656 page 162

Other: *U.S.S. Bellerophon* NCC-74705

Steamrunner class

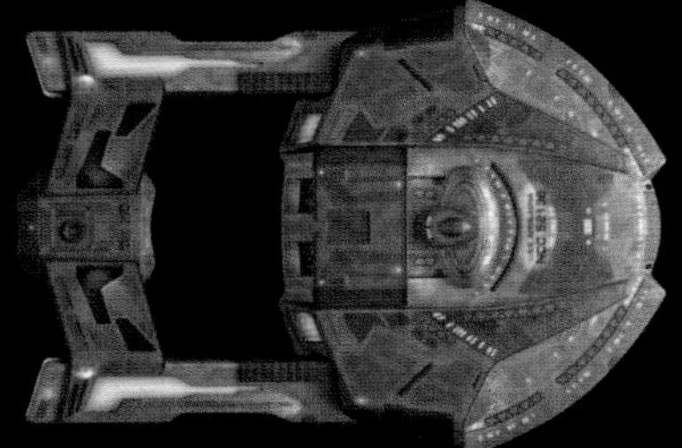

U.S.S. Kyushu NCC-65491 page 168

Other: *U.S.S. Appalachia* NCC-52136

Saber class

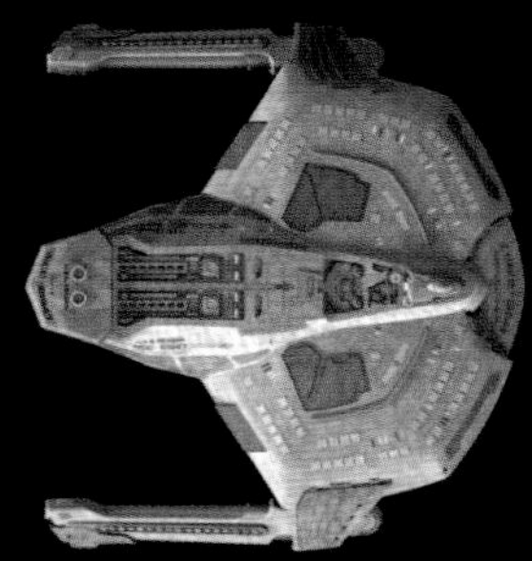

U.S.S. Yeager NCC-61947 page 174

Norway class

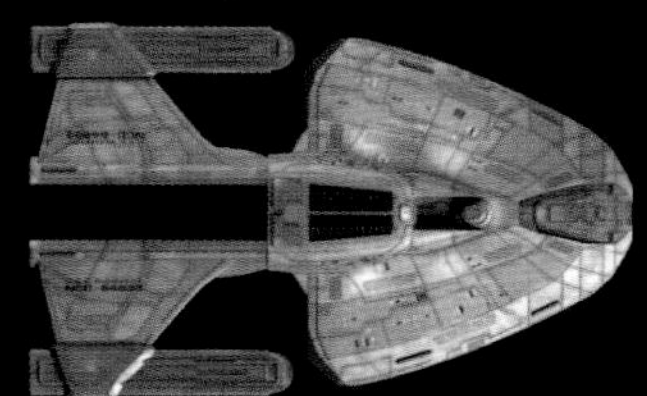

U.S.S.. Budapest NCC-64923

Centaur type

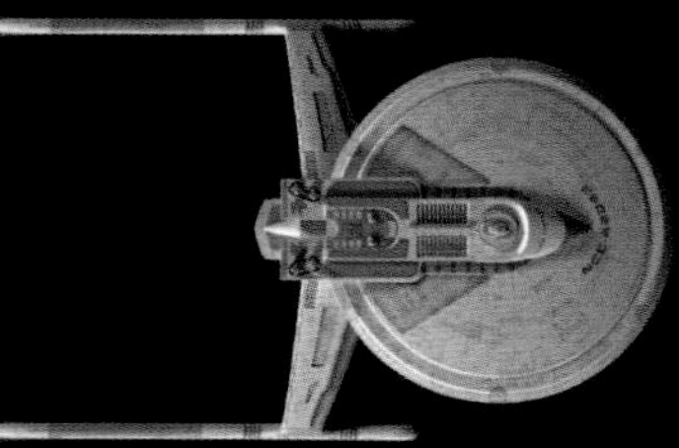

U.S.S. Centaur NCC-42043 page 194

Curry type

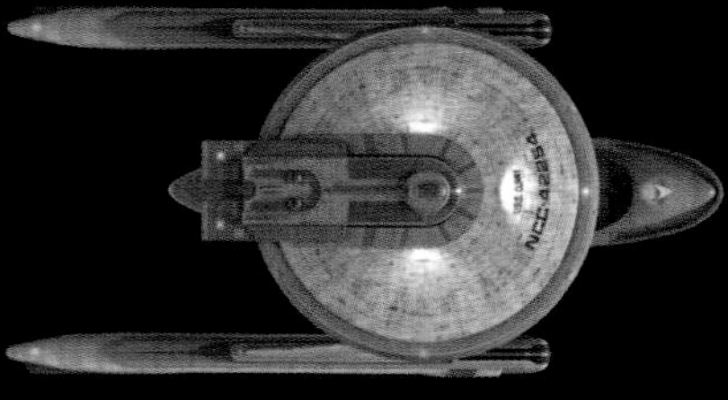

U.S.S. Curry NCC-42254 page 200

Sovereign class

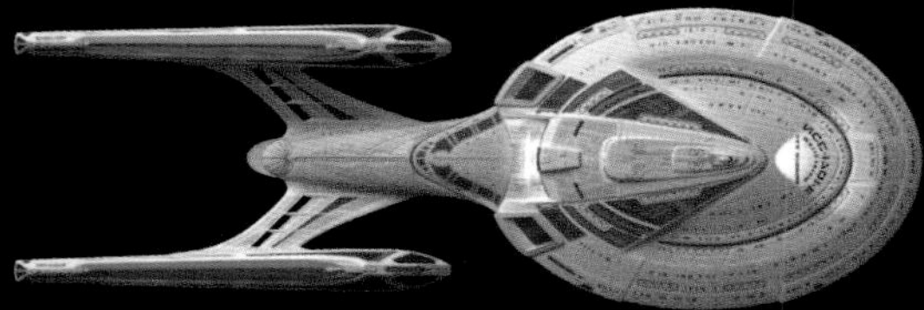

U.S.S. Enterprise NCC-1701-E page 206

Luna class

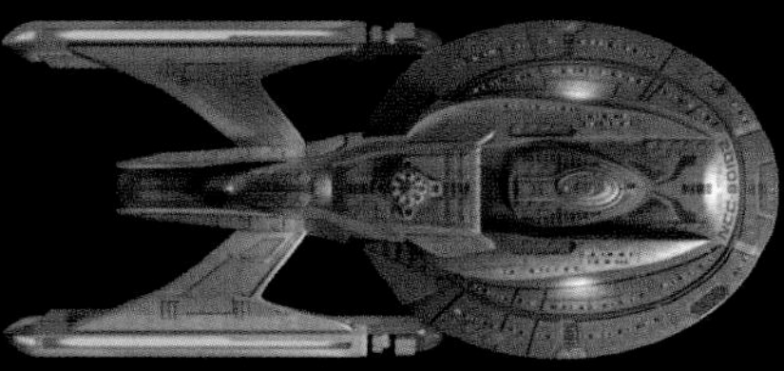

U.S.S. Titan NCC-80102 page 212

Parliament class

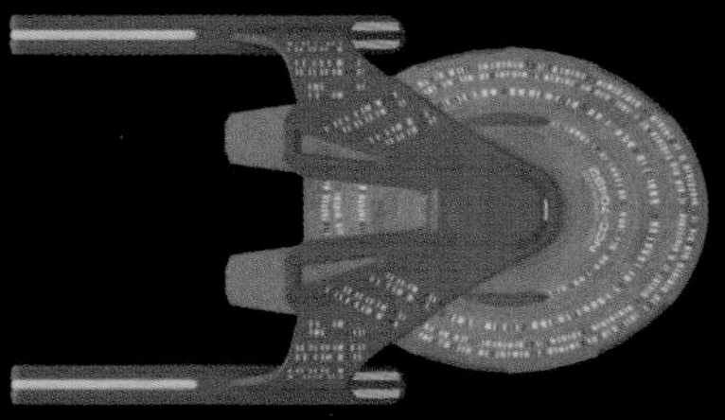

U.S.S. Vancouver NCC-70492 page 214

California class

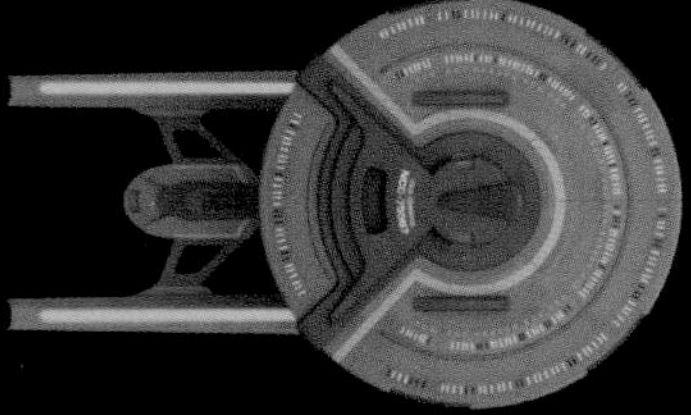

U.S.S. Cerritos NCC-75567 page 216

Other:

USS Alhambra
USS Mewrced NCC-87075
USS Rubidoux NCC-12109
USS San Clemente (uncertain)
USS Solvang NCC-12101

Wallenberg class

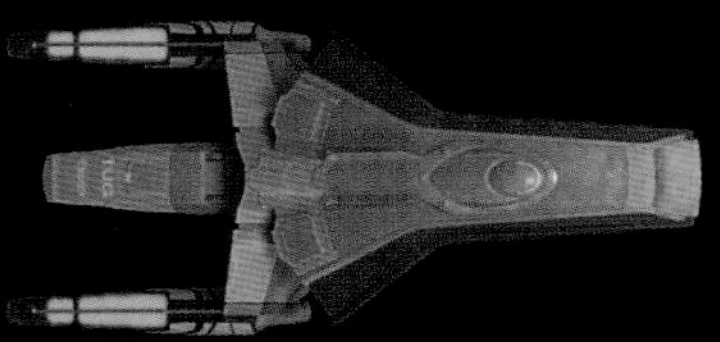

Tug (no formal registry) page 218

Inquiry class

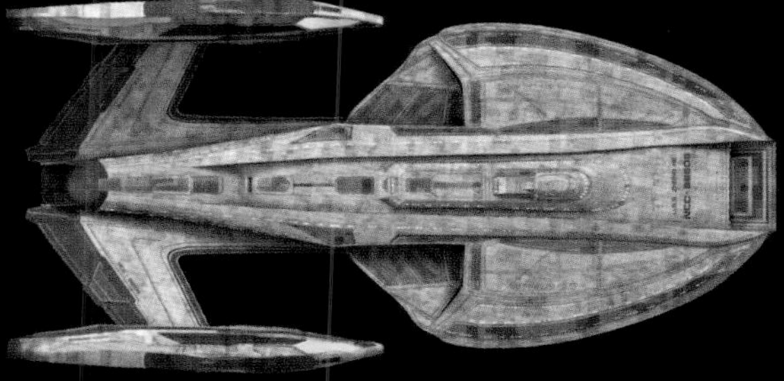

U.S.S. Zheng He NCC-86505 page 222

Other: USS Inquiry

Universe class

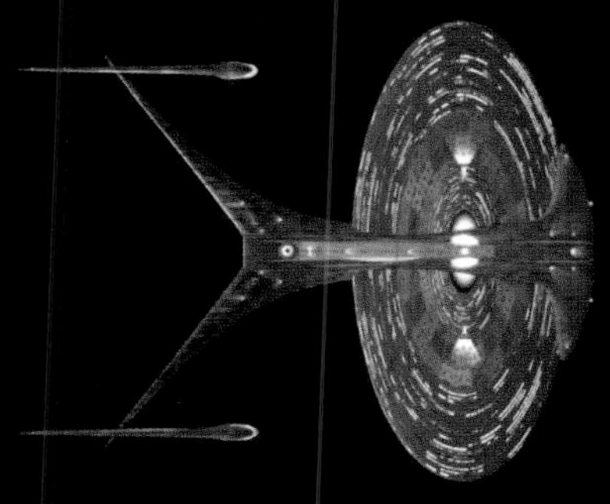

U.S.S. Enterprise NCC-1701-J page 234

Wells class

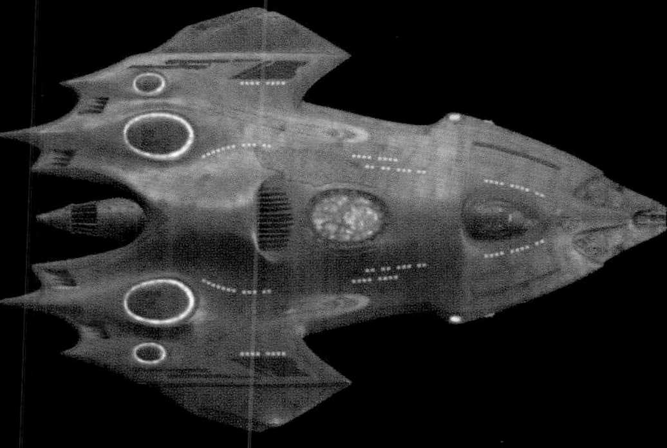

U.S.S. Relativity NCV-474439-G page 238

Epoch class

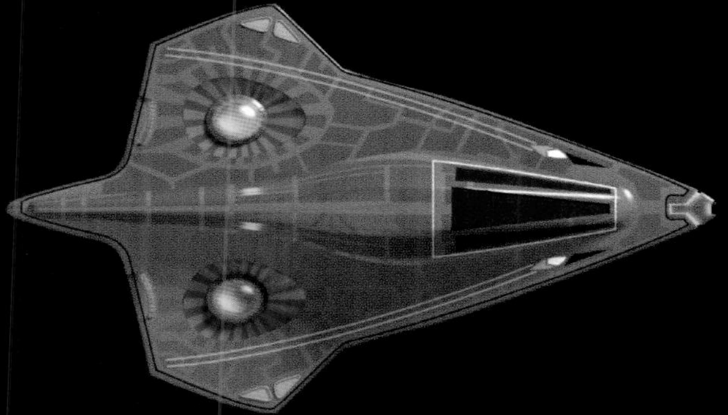

U.T.S. Aeon page 244

32ND CENTURY

Crossfield class

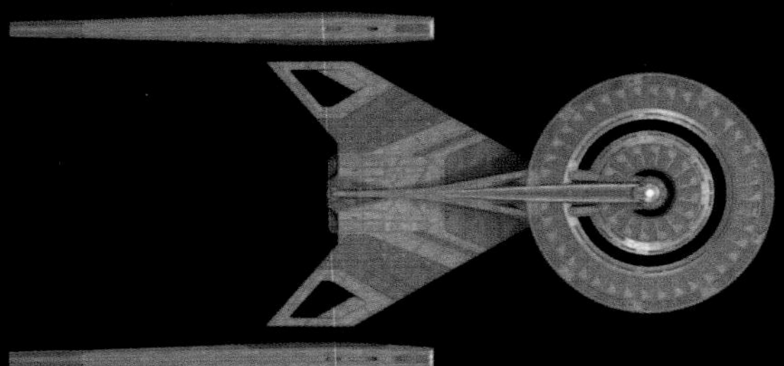

U.S.S. Discovery-A NCC-1031 page 254

Constitution class

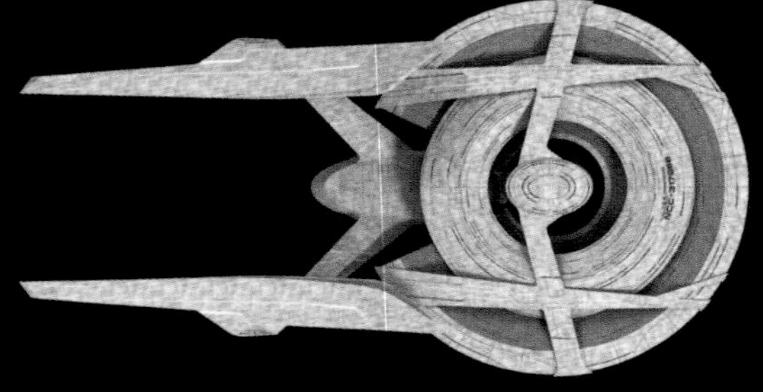

U.S.S. Armstrong NCC-317856 page 258

Other:

U.S.S. Excalibur NCC-1664-M *U.S.S. Noble NCC-325002*

Friendship class

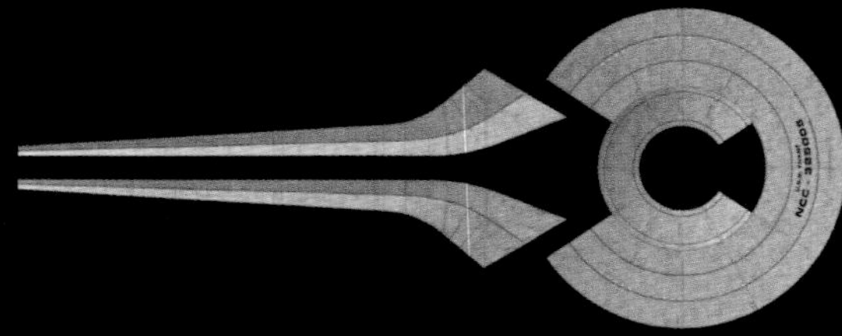

U.S.S Thant NCC-325005 page 262

Other:

U.S.S. Yang NCC-321616 *U.S.S. Yousafzai NCC-325010*

Angelou class

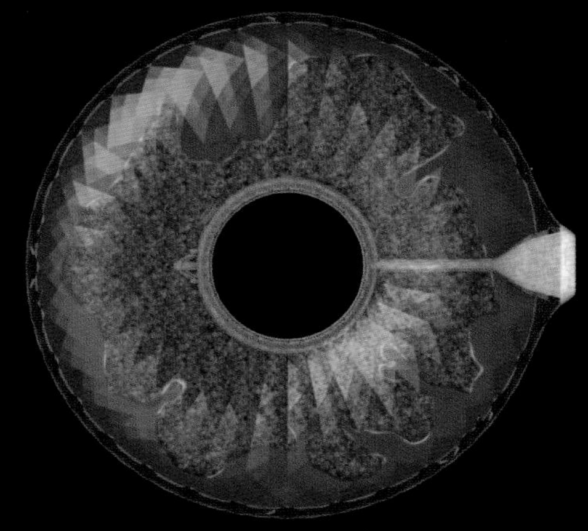

U.S.S. Maathai NCC-325023 page 266

Intrepid class

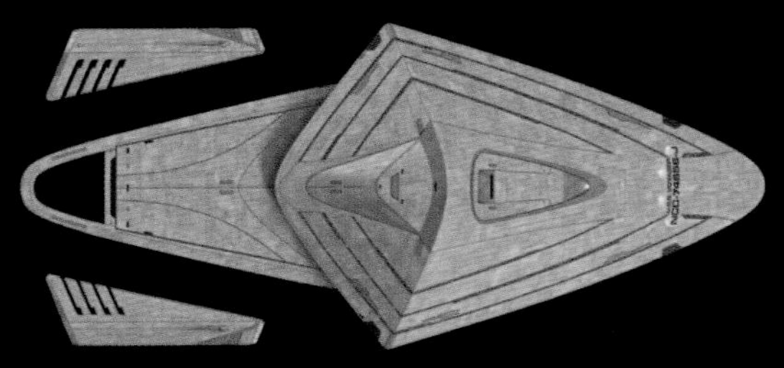

U.S.S. Voyager NCC-74656-J page 270

Class unknown

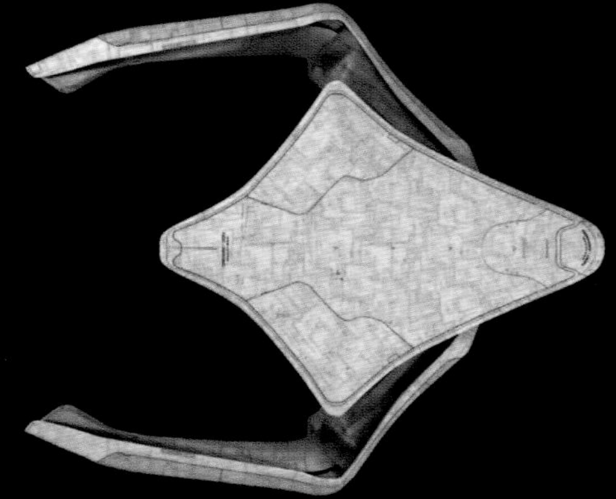

U.S.S Liu Cixin NCC-325060 page 274

Other:

U.S.S. Le Guin NCC-325059 *U.S.S.Zheng He* NCC-325057

Class unknown

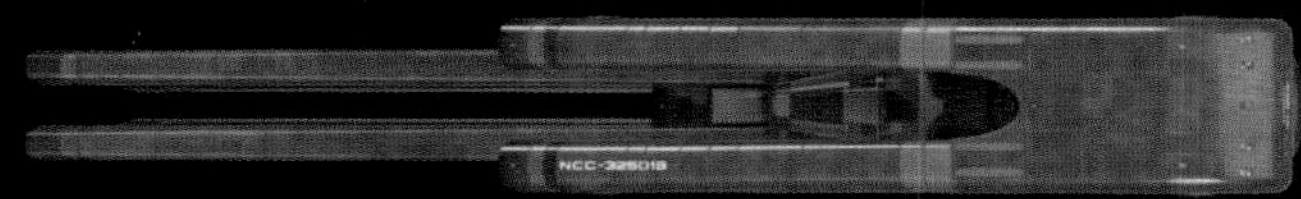

U.S.S. Dresselhaus NCC-325019 page 278

Other:
U.S.S LaMar NCC-325015 *U.S.S Pfau* NCC-3250174

Merian class

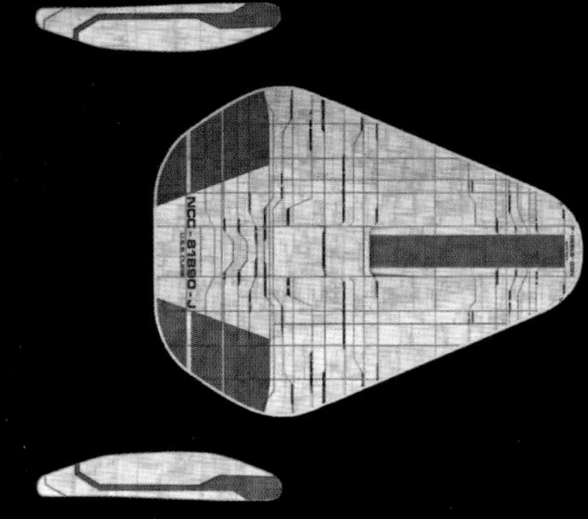

U.S.S Curie NCC-81890-J page 282

Other:
U.S.S. Le Guin NCC-325059 *U.S.S.Zheng He* NCC-325057

Class unknown

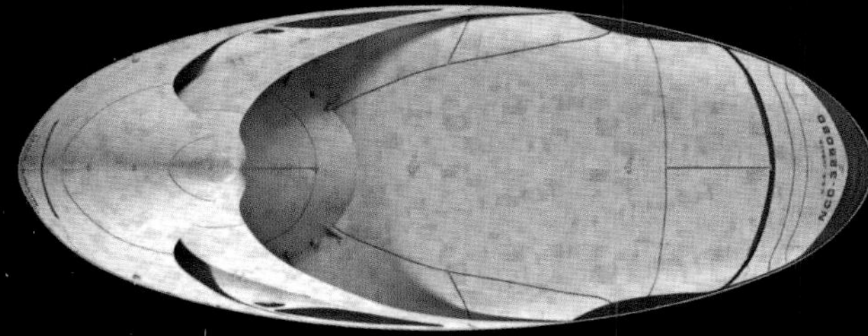

U.S.S. Jubayr NCC-325080 page 286

Other:
U.S.S. Shogun NCC-325082 *U.S.S. Song* NCC-325084

Eisenberg class

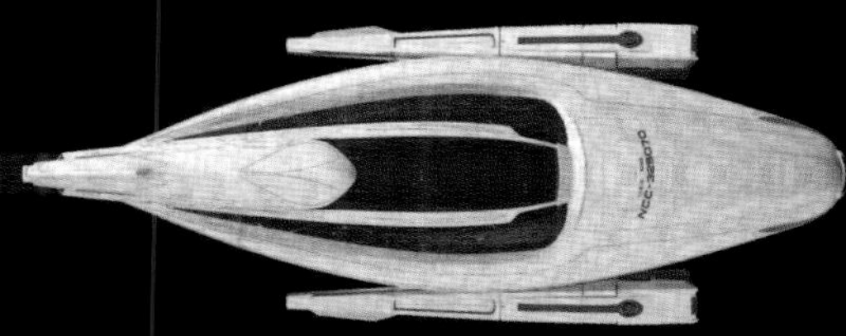

U.S.S. Nog NCC-325070 page 290

Other:
U.S.S. Grechko NCC-325071 U.S.S. Hansando NCC-325002
U.S.S. Cuyahoga NCC-325069

Class unknown page 294

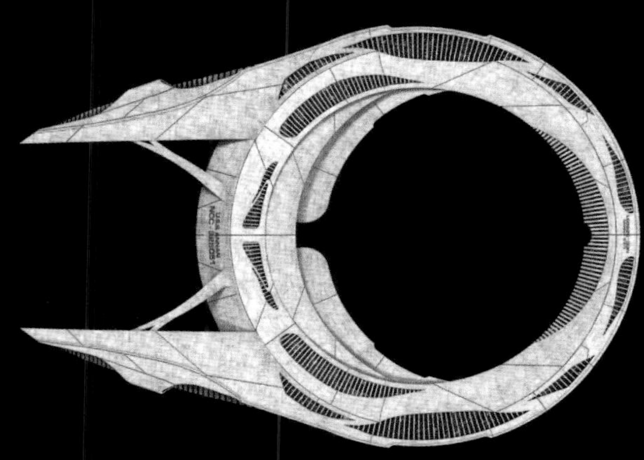

U.S.S Annan NCC-325051

Tikhov type page 298

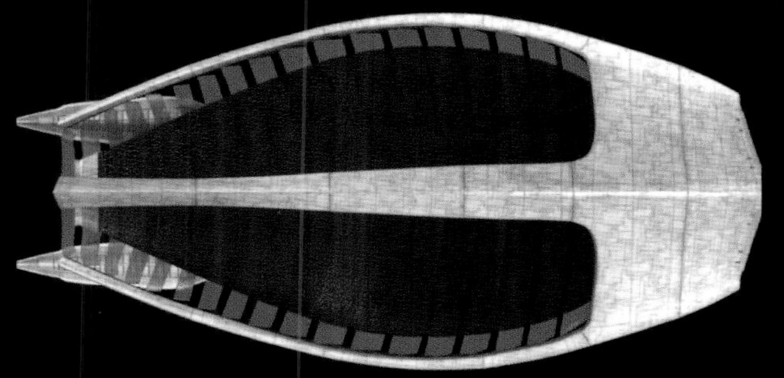

SHIPS

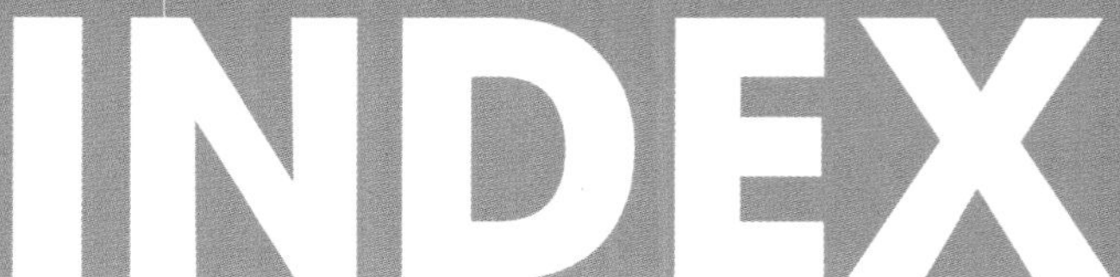

CLASS OR TYPE

COMMANDING OFFICERS

CREDITS

Editor: Ben Robinson

Project Manager: Jo Bourne

Writers: Ben Robinson, Marcus Riley, Mark Wright, and Matt McAllister

Sub Editor: Alice Peebles

Illustrators: Fabio Passaro, Ed Giddings, Adam 'Mojo' Lebowitz, and Robert Bonchune

Jacket Designer: Stephen Scanlan

Designers: Stephen Scanlan and Katy Everett

Additional research: Reka Turcsanyi and John Ainsworth

With thanks to the team at CBS: John Van Citters, Marian Cordry, and Risa Kessler

Published by **Hero Collector Books**, a division of Eaglemoss Ltd. 2021

Eaglemoss Ltd., Premier Place, 2 & A Half Devonshire Square, EC2M 4UJ, London, UK

Eaglemoss France, 144 Avenue Charles de Gaulle, 92200 Neuilly-Sur-Seine, France

Most of the contents of this book were originally published in *STAR TREK – The Official Starships Collection* and *STAR TREK DISCOVERY – The Official Starships Collection* by Eaglemoss Ltd. 2013-2021

ISBN ISBN 978-1-85875-999-9

Printed in China

www.herocollector.com